The Verbal Aspect Integral to the Perfect and Pluperfect Tense-Forms in the Pauline Corpus

"James Sedlacek's research offers a fresh way forward in understanding the Greek synthetic perfect tense-form based on his thorough investigation of both recent and older scholarship on the topic, on his own comprehensive analysis of the Pauline Corpus, and comparison between Paul and a diachronic Greek epistolary and moral literature corpus from 400 BCE to 400 CE. His work is both systematic and clear, complex and balanced, interdisciplinary and most innovative in arguing for the presence of both perfective and imperfective aspects in the Greek synthetic perfect."

—Revd. Svetlana Khobnya, Senior Lecturer in Biblical Studies and Languages, Nazarene Theological College, Manchester

"Sedlacek provides a coherent, well theorised, and carefully argued case for a complex aspect for the synthetic Greek perfect tense-form in the Pauline corpus and comparative sources from ca 400 BCE to 400 CE. His critique of previous scholarship on the topic identifies areas of misunderstanding in ways that will unsettle serious students of Hellenistic Greek and arouse their interest in Sedlacek's own constructive proposals."

—Todd Klutz, Senior Lecturer in Biblical Studies and Early Christian Literature, University of Manchester

"James Sedlacek's analysis of verbal aspect with respect to perfects in the Pauline writings brings to the table a multidisciplinary approach that invokes corpus linguistics in the pursuit of both semantic and pragmatic angles. He interacts with major published works on aspect, arguing that (plu-)perfect forms point to an imperfective state, a perfect action, or both, while noting that context-relevance cannot be discerned merely from the use of the form itself. Readers will appreciate the author's care in documenting his interactions via substantive citations of current scholarship as well as charting of the Pauline, classical and patristic Greek data that go to the argument. The discussion is engaging and quite informative in its pursuit of advancing our understanding of perfect 'tense' forms."

—Jonathan M. Watt, Professor of Biblical Studies, Chair of Department of Bible Christian Ministries and Philosophy, Geneva College, Beaver Falls, Pennsylvania

The Verbal Aspect Integral to the Perfect and Pluperfect Tense-Forms in the Pauline Corpus

Studies in Biblical Greek

D. A. Carson
General Editor

Vol. 22

The Studies in Biblical Greek series is part of the Peter Lang Humanities list.
Every volume is peer reviewed and meets
the highest quality standards for content and production.

PETER LANG
New York • Berlin • Brussels • Lausanne • Oxford

James E. Sedlacek

The Verbal Aspect Integral to the Perfect and Pluperfect Tense-Forms in the Pauline Corpus

A Semantic and Pragmatic Analysis

PETER LANG
New York • Berlin • Brussels • Lausanne • Oxford

Library of Congress Cataloging-in-Publication Control Number: 2022018956

Bibliographic information published by **Die Deutsche Nationalbibliothek**.
Die Deutsche Nationalbibliothek lists this publication in the "Deutsche
Nationalbibliografie"; detailed bibliographic data are available
on the Internet at http://dnb.d-nb.de/.

ISSN 0897-7828
ISBN 978-1-4331-9573-0 (hardcover)
ISBN 978-1-4331-9574-7 (ebook pdf)
ISBN 978-1-4331-9575-4 (epub)
DOI 10.3726/b19512

Peter Lang Publishing, Inc., New York
80 Broad Street, 5th floor, New York, NY 10004
www.peterlang.com

Contents

List of Figures   ix
Series Editor Preface   xi
Author's Preface   xiii

Introduction   1
1. Introductory Remarks   1
2. Linguistic Investigations into the Greek Language   2
3. Application of Linguistic Investigations to Exegesis   2
4. Thesis Statement   4
5. Chapter Organisation   6

Overview of Verbal Aspect Studies as Related to the Greek
    Perfect and Pluperfect Tense-Forms   9
1. Introductory Remarks   9
2. The Development of Verbal Aspect as a Term for
    Grammatical Analysis   11
3. Verbal Aspect as Related to the Greek Perfect and Pluperfect
    Tense-Forms   28
4. Conclusion   53

A Way Forward   57
1. Introductory Remarks   57
2. Consideration of Methods   59
3. Complexity of the Verbal Aspect for the Perfect Tense-Form   64
4. Implications for Complex Aspect   94
5. Conclusion   100

The Complex Aspect of the Perfect Tense-Form in the Pauline
   Corpus   103
1. The Verbal Data from the Pauline Corpus   103
2. Conclusion   165

Comparing the Pauline Corpus to a Diachronic Corpus of
   Epistolary and Moral Literature   167
1. Corpus-Based Approach   168
2. Defining the Limits of Both Corpora for Analysis   170
3. Purposes of the Greek Diachronic Epistolary and Moral
   Literature Corpus   172
4. Issues in the Greek Diachronic Epistolary and Moral
   Literature Corpus   173
5. Contents of the Greek Diachronic Epistolary and Moral
   Literature Corpus   175
6. Necessity for Corpus Approaches to Answer Certain
   Linguistic Questions   178
7. A Review of the Corpus Data   179
8. Conclusion   200

Conclusion   203
1. Summary and Restatement of the Thesis   203
2. Contribution to Knowledge   205
3. Limitations of the Research   206
4. Suggestions for Further Research   207

Bibliography   209

Appendix A: Rationale and Purpose of the Appendices   229
Appendix B: Chart of Morphemes   231
Appendix C: Chart of Stem Count   247

Appendix D: Chart of Stems by Frequency   259
Appendix E: Chart of Context   263
Appendix F: Chart of Adverbial Modification of Stative Perfects   281
Appendix G: Chart of Adverbial Modification of Eventive Perfects   295
Appendix H: Adverb Frequency Data   309
Appendix I: Key Adverbs   311
*Appendix J: Chart of Adverbial Modification of Perfects used in
Citational or Referential ways*   313
Appendix K: Chart of Pauline Corpus Examples with Perfects   327
Appendix L: Chart of Analysis Corpus Examples with Perfects   367
*Appendix M: Chart of Selected Verbs Found in the Perfect Tense-
Form within the Pauline Corpus Fully Conjugated*   381

Author Index   419
Text Reference Index   423
Subject Index   427

Figures

Figure 1:   Categories of linguistic elements   13
Figure 2:   Contrasting two aspects using a point-of-view   23
Figure 3:   Fanning's Aspectual System   30
Figure 4:   Olsen's Aspectual System   33
Figure 5:   Campbell's Aspectual System   38
Figure 6:   Porter's Aspectual System   40
Figure 7:   Different forms of the Greek Perfect   59
Figure 8:   Interruptibility of the previous clause   69
Figure 9:   Complex aspect   71
Figure 10: Stem comparison using four verb types   74
Figure 11: Reduplication syllable types on a cline   80
Figure 12: Reduplication effects situated along a cline   80
Figure 13: The two-fold path for lexemes developing into imperfectives   81
Figure 14: Complex aspect   84
Figure 15: Timeline of the synthetic Greek Perfect   85
Figure 16: The synthetic Greek Perfect in several time periods   86
Figure 17: The synthetic and periphrastic Perfects showing mirroring of
           components   88
Figure 18: Comparison between Ancient and Modern Perfects   89

Figure 19: Adverbs of Perfects in Perfect + Relative Clause Constructions 141

Figure 20: Adverbs of Perfects within Relative Clauses 141

Figure 21: Category A Lexemes 142

Figure 22: Category B Lexemes 143

Figure 23: Frequency of the Categories as a Ratio 144

Figure 24: Perfect forms of οἶδα 157

Figure 25: Inter-relatedness of "see" and "know" 161

Figure 26: Aorist forms of εἶδον 163

Figure 27: Bar Chart of the Number of Sources for the diachronic epistolary and moral literature corpus 176

Figure 28: Bar Chart of Wordcount by Century Divided by Genre 177

Figure 29: Bar Chart of the Total Wordcount by Century 177

Figure 30: Bar Chart of Total Wordcount by Genre 178

Figure 31: Comparison of the Perfect tenses in the subcorpora 180

Figure 32: Comparison of οἶδα usage in the subcorpora 181

Figure 33: Comparison of supplemental uses of Perfects across the subcorpora 181

Figure 34: Comparison of Category A Constructions 182

Figure 35: Comparison of Category B Constructions 183

Series Editor Preface

Successfully defended as a doctoral dissertation at the University of Manchester in 2020, this work breaks new ground in its understanding of the Greek synthetic Perfect tense-form (including the Pluperfect) distributed prominently in the Pauline corpus. While most theories argue that a single aspect is conveyed by the tense-form—usually the stative, the imperfective, or the perfective—Dr Sedlacek presents a detailed case for a complex aspect: the morphology of the synthetic Perfect tense-form, he asserts, contains both (1) a lexical core that points to perfectivity of the event (mirroring as it does the Aorist tense-form), and (2) a reduplicant grammaticalising imperfectivity that focuses on a state relevant to the event, and that relevance may be to the grammatical subject or to an object. Both of these aspects remain in tension in the Perfect tense-form. Neither aspect is ever entirely cancelled, but the complex model that Sedlacek advances allows scope for a variety of emphases. The author gains methodological control by comparing the Perfect and Pluperfect tense-forms in the Pauline corpus with uses in Greek letter writers from 400 BCE to CE 400. This work will become part of the "must read" list for scholars working on the Greek Perfect and, indeed, on aspect theory.

D. A. Carson
Trinity Evangelical Divinity School

Author's Preface

The idea for a project involving verbal aspect began years before when I was in my graduate program of study at Cincinnati Christian University, where I earned a Master of Divinity degree. The majority of my coursework there was in biblical languages and exegetical methods, and the role of Linguistics upon grammar was emphasised as a component of exegesis. William Baker introduced the works of Stanley Porter, Buist Fanning and Constantine Campbell to me in my Greek exegesis classes around 2007, and later asked me to review the *Basics of Verbal Aspect*, by Constantine Campbell when it was available from Zondervan in 2008. During my final year of my graduate program in 2009–2010, I had the opportunity to teach New Testament Greek at God's Bible School & College, where I had earned my undergraduate degree much earlier. Philip Brown, my immediate supervisor, engaged me frequently with discussions about issues raised in the works by Porter, Fanning and Campbell.

It was at that time I realised that the largest area of incompatibility between the three works lies in the application of verbal aspect to the Greek Perfect tenses. Additionally, I saw a different way forward to answer the problem of the Perfect. After graduating, I worked four years at Cincinnati Christian Schools teaching New Testament in High School. During this time, I reread the works by Porter, Fanning and Campbell and read much of the literature on verbal aspect and Perfect tenses in detail. After processing the relevant literature, I began to apply to PhD programs where I could develop my ideas more fully and put my research together. I participated in exegesis seminars for postgraduate researchers at Nazarene Theological College in preparation for a research programme. Once admitted into the PhD process, I received further development in Corpus Linguistics modules and seminars from both Lancaster University and the University of Birmingham, which together inform the method of this thesis. The courses from both of these institutions developed familiarity with current tools and practices in corpus linguistics along with a theory of corpus design.

Early drafts of most of the portions of the developing research were presented at Eastern Great Lakes Biblical Society, Stone-Campbell Journal Conference, Midwest Region Society of Biblical Literature Meeting, British New Testament Conference, and International Conference on Greek Linguistics. Two of these presentations are now published as peer-reviewed articles. In addition to the above conferences, I attended conference sessions on Linguistics or Pauline Literature at Society of Biblical Literature Annual Meeting, The Evangelical Theological Society, Tyndale Fellowship, The Chicago Linguistic Society, The Ehrhardt Seminars, and other seminars in the School of Arts, Languages, and Cultures at the University of Manchester.

This study identifies the verbal aspect for the Greek synthetic Perfect tense-form found in the Pauline epistles. The specific morphological components in the reduplicant and in the lexical core of the Perfect tense-form are used to construct a complex aspect relying upon Grammaticalisation. Diachronic considerations are maintained throughout the analysis. Criticism of the literature shows where either the nature of verbal aspect or the identity of the aspect for the Perfect tense-form is unclear. Several arguments point uniformly to a complex aspect for the Greek Perfect. Selected examples from the Pauline corpus are then analysed to test the complex aspect. A corpus-based study is defined and the use of the Perfect tense-form within the Pauline corpus is compared against a diachronic epistolary and moral literature corpus that results in the placement of the Greek synthetic Perfect tense-form on the respective grammaticalisation clines belonging to reduplicants and to perfectives equally. The comparison between Paul and Greek letter writers from 400 BCE to 400 CE shows that Paul uses the Perfect embedded within supplemental clauses more often than other writers. Paul also employs a greater variety of active lexemes in that role than other writers examined.

This study concludes that the verbal aspect for the Greek synthetic Perfect tense-form is complex, involving two verbal aspects, each related to a different part of the verbal complex. The reduplicant of the Perfect tense-form is imperfective, and places that aspect upon a state. This state may be relevant to the grammatical subject or to an object. The lexical core is perfective, and places that aspect upon an event relevant to the lexeme. The complex aspect argued in this work best explains the wide range of Perfect uses, and accounts for the diachronic history of this tense-form shifting its focus from present-like stative usages to past-like eventive usages.

Many people and entities mentioned next provided assistance toward the development of this project. First of all, I thank Stanley Porter, Buist Fanning, and Constantine Campbell for producing such engaging works on verbal aspect for the Greek language, which provided much thought for this project. I am indebted to their contributions for my own interest in the Greek Perfect, and to William Baker and A. Philip Brown, II, for emphasising to me the importance of their works. Secondly, I thank William Baker, Tom Thatcher, Kent Brower, Sarah Whittle, and Svetlana Khobnya for encouraging me to pursue a PhD in this area, and for placing value on this project. Thirdly, I thank the institutions that have shaped me for combining a linguistic approach with biblical exegesis. I thank God's Bible School & College and especially Robert England for generating in me an initial love for the Greek language. I thank Cincinnati Christian University and especially William Baker and Daniel Dyke for exposing to me the role for Greek language studies within the biblical exegesis process. I thank the Nazarene Theological College for providing a friendly and serious environment for conducting this research. I thank the University of Manchester for providing many helpful resources for this project. I thank the Corpus Linguistics department at Lancaster University for showing me the many ways corpora can be used to answer linguistic questions. I thank the Corpus Linguistics department at the University of Birmingham for the workshops toward analysing corpora data, and for the encouragement received toward analysing the Pauline letters as its own corpus. I thank the staff at Sketch Engine for hosting the corpora for this study and for helping me with technical difficulties. Fourthly, I thank the organisers of the conferences that allowed me to present papers related to this project, and fostered my own growth. These include the Eastern Great Lakes Biblical Society, the Stone-Campbell Journal Conference, The Midwest Region of the Society of Biblical Literature, The British New Testament Conference, the International Conference on Greek Linguistics, and the Post Graduate Research Seminars and One Day Theology Conferences at the Nazarene Theological College. Fifthly, I thank those who supervised this project and those who gave advice along the way. I thank Svetlana Khobnya for supervising this project and Dwight Swanson for co-supervising this project. I am indebted to their comments and critiques.

I thank David Lamb and Samuel Hildebrand for their critiques as well. I thank Geoffrey Horrocks for advice given on several occasions. Sixthly, I thank my thesis examiners, Todd Klutz and Dirk Jongkind, who found this project stimulating and compelling. I thank them for their questions, comments, and encouragement regarding publishing. Seventhly, I thank my wife, Aleyda Sedlacek for her support and encouragement throughout all phases of this project, including the years this was in development before the project was a reality. I am deeply indebted to her for being able to do this project. Eighthly, I thank friends and family who gave words of encouragement along the way. These include my two sons, James and Karl; my parents, Ron and Lois; my Pastor, Meredith Moser; my colleagues, Deborah Enos and Wayne Beaver; and great host of colleagues, friends, family members, and fellow students. Ninthly, I thank those who helped to build a friendship between the United States and the United Kingdom along with others maintaining that friendship, as this friendship between both countries provided me and countless others an opportunity to do research in the United Kingdom. Lastly and most importantly, I thank God for putting many events and people together which made all of these things possible.

Introduction

1. Introductory Remarks

The Greek synthetic Perfect tense-form[1] is used 345 times and the Pluperfect is used only once in the Pauline corpus. But what does Paul convey and what should the reader understand whenever the author chooses a Perfect tense? To make these concerns more difficult to answer, the meaning of the Perfect tense is debated among not only biblical scholars for the Greek of the New Testament, but among Indo-Europeanists as well. Some of the debate centres around theoretical issues related to the nature of verbal aspect and categorisation of linguistic data. Other debate involves the application of verbal aspect theory itself to the Perfect tense-form specifically and consequently relating the observed uses of the Perfect onto that aspect. This problem is not unique to Ancient Greek, since the Perfect tense-forms of most languages have proven to be difficult to categorise within the verbal aspect network of their respective verbal system.

Greek has a long literary history, where the Perfect tense-forms are abundant in Greek literature in both their synthetic and periphrastic varieties. The

---

1   A synthetic tense-form is a one-word form, where all the components of meaning are affixed onto the verb. This is opposed to analytic tense-forms that are comprised of two or more words.

synthetic form was highly productive in the Classical and Hellenistic Periods, and the periphrastic form is highly productive in the Modern Period.[2] This abundance of both types of Perfect tense-forms makes the Greek language an excellent place in general to study the development of the Perfect tense-form and determine its verbal aspect. The identification of this verbal aspect enables a better understanding of Paul's usage of the Perfect tense-form in his letters.

2. Linguistic Investigations into the Greek Language

A number of recent studies have emerged regarding the linguistic analysis of the Greek language. Several of these begin with the Greek textual data and then classify their findings in linguistic terms.[3] They often seek answers from linguistics to explain some of the findings.[4] Other studies begin with observable cross-linguistic phenomena and analyse the Greek text to see how that feature is exhibited in the Greek language, or whether it exists at all.[5] Mostly, the studies on Greek verbal aspect fall into the second category but seek rationale for their linguistic observations among the writings of Ancient grammarians of Greek.[6]

3. Application of Linguistic Investigations to Exegesis

The purpose of applying linguistics to the Greek language in this project is to enable a better understanding of the use of the Greek Perfect tense-form in the

---

2   Allen considers the Classical Period the point of high productivity for the synthetic Perfect due to the emergence of transitive lexemes in that period. Rutger J. Allen, "Tense and Aspect in Classical Greek: Two Historical Developments; Augment and Perfect," 81–121 in *The Greek Verb Revisited: A Fresh Approach for Biblical Exegesis*, edited by Runge and Fresch (Bellingham, WA: Lexham, 2016), 108; Horrocks shows the periphrastic perfect as the normal perfect in the Modern language. Geoffrey Horrocks, *Greek: A History of the Language and Its Speakers*, 2nd ed. (West Sussex: Blackwell, 2010), 300.

3   Porter, Fanning, and Campbell use this approach. Stanley E. Porter, *Verbal Aspect in the Greek of the New Testament, with Reference to Tense and Mood*. SBG:1, edited by D. A. Carson. (New York: Peter Lang, 1989, 1993); Buist M. Fanning, *Verbal Aspect in the Greek of the New Testament* (Oxford: Clarendon, 1990); Constantine R. Campbell, *Verbal Aspect, the Indicative Mood, and Narrative: Soundings in the Greek of the New Testament*. SBG: 13, edited by D. A. Carson (New York: Peter Lang, 2007).

4   Porter utilises Systemic Functional Linguistics, while Campbell uses Corpus Linguistics.

5   Dahl and Bybee, Perkins and Pagliuca use this approach. Östen Dahl, *Tense and Aspect Systems* (Oxford: Blackwell, 1985); Joan Bybee, Revere Perkins, and William Pagliuca, *Evolution of Grammar: Tense, Aspect, and Modality in the Languages of the World* (Chicago: University of Chicago Press, 1994).

6   Versteegh bases his analysis of the Greek language on the Stoic grammarians. C. H. M. Versteegh, "The Stoic Verbal System," *Hermes* 108:3 (1980): 338–357.

New Testament generally, and particularly in Paul's letters.[7] Exegetes, pastors and other biblical scholars are dependent upon a careful study of the Greek language to accurately portray the message of the New Testament.[8] The task of exegesis begins with the biblical text. Linguistics informs the linguistic interpretation of the text and is the background for a biblical interpretation of the text. Linguistics assists in understanding the previous Greek grammars and formation of new Greek grammars.[9] Those who seek to better understand the text of the New Testament keep one foot in the grammars and the other in linguistic methods.[10] Linguistic analyses of the Greek New Testament are a prerequisite to interpretation as they often provide more precision than the grammars. Linguistic analyses are independent of the grammars and working parallel to them, since they often inform in different ways than do grammars or lexica.

It is suggested that the scholar be critical of a number of factors regarding how linguistics relates to biblical studies. First, the scholar should be critical of how linguistics is informed as it relates to Greek. For example, linguistics should be informed by language data rather than by theory. Second, the scholar should be critical of how the grammars are informed for their structural categories and specific content.[11] For example, distinctions created in linguistics should be reflected

7   Connecting linguistics to the study of Greek is a helpful step for the analysis of any Greek text.
8   Fanning, Black and Campbell highlight the necessity of applying linguistics to the biblical text. Fanning, 422; David Alan Black, *Linguistics for Students of New Testament Greek: A Survey of Basic Concepts and Applications*, 3rd ed. (Grand Rapids, MI: Baker, 1995), 21; Constantine R. Campbell, *Advances in the Study of the Greek: New Insights for Reading the New Testament* (Grand Rapids, MI: Zondervan, 2015), 225. Porter points to its importance. Stanley E. Porter, "Introduction: Diglossia and Other Topics in New Testament Linguistics," 13–16 in *Diglossia and Other Topics in New Testament Linguistics*, JSNT Supp: 193, Studies in New Testament Greek: 6 (Sheffield: Sheffield, 2000), 16.
9   Campbell offers the idea that linguistics helps to explain grammar properly and enhances exegetical precision. Constantine R. Campbell, *Verbal Aspect, the Indicative Mood*, 123; Constantine R. Campbell, *Verbal Aspect and Non-Indicative Verbs: Further Soundings in the Greek of the New Testament*, SBG: 15, edited by D. A. Carson (New York: Peter Lang, 2008), 124.
10 Fanning mentions that linguistics informs exegesis. Fanning, 196. Cotterell and Turner view linguistics working in conjunction with other fields for exegesis. Peter Cotterell and Max Turner, *Linguistics and Biblical Interpretation* (Downers Grove, IL: Intervarsity, 1989), 32. Aubrey states that linguistics intersects with history and theology to interpret the text. Michael Aubrey, "The Value of Linguistically Informed Exegesis," 191–201 in *Linguistics and Biblical Exegesis*, edited by Douglas Mangum and Josh Westbury (Bellingham, WA: Lexham, 2017), 191. Porter emphasises that the type of linguistics accompanying theology and historical analysis should be modern. Stanley E. Porter, *Linguistic Analysis of the Greek New Testament: Studies in Tools, Methods, and Practice* (Grand Rapids, MI: Baker, 2015), 92. Caragounis emphasises that linguistics works alongside theological approach. He cautions that the exegete should keep all avenues open. Chrys Caragounis, *The Development of Greek and the New Testament: Morphology, Syntax, Phonology, and Textual Transmission* (Grand Rapids, MI: Baker, 2006), 233–234.
11 Porter and O'Donnell connect the refining of linguistic concepts to exegesis. Stanley E. Porter and Matthew Brook O'Donnell, "Semantics in Romans," 154–204 in *Diglossia and Other Topics in New*

in the grammars. Where grammars leave linguistic distinctions vague, conflated, or missing, adjustments to the grammars are necessary. Thirdly, the scholar needs to be critical of theologically informed grammars, lexica, or grammatical tools, because they may reveal more regarding the theological bias of their authors, than they do to reveal the Greek language. Without a healthy set of criticisms in place, the tendency is for one to follow one's favourite grammar or linguistic field to the exclusion of important evidence. Linguistics fits in the broader picture of exegesis as a component that precedes interpretation that is also independent from theological presuppositions.[12]

This thesis situates itself as a linguistic analysis of the Greek Perfect tense-form, while focusing upon the biblical text, and being informed by the historical usage of the Greek Perfect. This endeavour interacts with the biblical text to produce a linguistically informed understanding of Paul's usage of the Greek Perfect tense-forms. The scope of this study is to connect linguistic description with grammatical observations, and to provide terminology to show compatibility between the two wherever helpful. One of the goals of this study is to provide a linguistically sound understanding of the Greek Perfect. Another goal is to gain a better understanding of how the Pauline corpus uses the Greek Perfect, and then to situate the Pauline usage of the Perfect within the history of Greek literature. A subsidiary aim of this research is to propose a new understanding of Perfects of the Indo-European language family more generally based on linguistic principles.

4. Thesis Statement

The Greek Synthetic Perfect tense-form, the one seen in the Pauline corpus and predominantly seen from the Classical Period through the Hellenistic Period, is shown in this treatment to have two verbal aspects in a complex array, having

---

Testament Linguistics, JSNT Supp: 193, Studies in New Testament Greek: 6 (Sheffield: Sheffield, 2000), 189. Cotterell and Turner add that linguistics offers precision to older grammars. Cotterell and Turner, 27. In another work, Porter shows how verbal aspect enhances precision in lexical works. Stanley E. Porter, "Aspect Theory and Lexicography," 207–222 in *Biblical Greek Language and Lexicography: Essays in Honor of Frederick Danker*, edited by Bernard A. Taylor, John A. L. Lee, Peter R. Burton, and Richard E. Whitaker (Grand Rapids, MI: Eerdmans, 2004), 221. Black informs that linguistics relates the grammars to the interpretation. David Alan Black, *Linguistics for Students*, 3. Campbell states that linguistics corrects false assumptions in the grammars. Constantine R. Campbell, *Advances*, 120.

12 A larger treatment would include the nature of historical analysis and theological contributions, individual components of linguistics, philosophy, science, along with how all the pieces inter-relate.

perfective aspect related to the action of the lexical core and imperfective aspect related to any state, whether resultant or otherwise.[13] The Perfect tense-form can be used to emphasise either one of the two aspects, or both as the situation allows, depending upon whether the author has a state, event, or both in mind. This flexibility is shown to be in no violation of the uncancellability requirement.[14] This treatment builds its case based on grammaticalisation studies,[15] and supports its findings with diachronic analysis, morphology, theoretical linguistics, corpus methods, and cross-linguistic comparisons to ground its conclusions.[16] This study connects the diachronic development of the Perfect along with the morphological analysis of its stem to a perfective aspect when referring to events. After examining the process of grammaticalisation for the reduplicant,[17] this study connects the specific position of the Greek reduplicant along its grammaticalisation cline to an imperfective aspect that is then applied to states.[18] The set of pragmatic functions exhibited by both the Classical and Post-classical synthetic Perfect tense-forms and the Modern periphrastic Perfect tense-forms are parallel to each other illustrating the complex verbal aspect apparent in both types of Perfect tense-forms. This analysis of both types of Perfect tense-forms shows compatibility between them aspectually. Thus, the aspect complexity of the periphrastic Perfect is a model for understanding that of the synthetic Perfect.

---

13 The terms "perfective" and "imperfective" are described in the beginning of Chapter 2 and defined in detail in 2.5.1.

14 For any item related to meaning to be truly semantic, other elements in the context cannot be shown to cancel that meaning. The non-cancellability of a meaning is a requirement for it to be considered semantic rather than pragmatic. Since the Perfect is often shown to be related to a state in some contexts and to an event in others, this raises concern that either identified meaning for the Perfect might be cancellable, thus not semantic. This study will show that this flexibility does not violate this requirement.

15 Grammaticalisation is the study of how language changes over time. Although it is developed in more detail in the third chapter, it recognises the trends and known stages along the path for any item undergoing change.

16 Diachronic analysis takes the observed differences over time into consideration when assessing the core meaning of the Greek Perfect. Morphology simply looks at the shape of the Perfect tense-form in terms of its spelling and spelling differences from other tense-forms. Theoretical linguistics refers to critiquing abstract linguistic notions and grounding them into a theory. Corpus methods involves creating a corpus of literature to use as a tool for analysing the Perfect. The specific method used is defined in the fifth chapter. Cross-linguistic comparisons simply compare Greek data with that of other languages where the same phenomenon occurs. This is done for the sake of clarity regarding the Greek data.

17 A reduplicant is the syllable that is copied from part of the verb stem and added onto the front of the verb as a new syllable.

18 A cline refers to the trend in the direction of change and the specific pathway of change for language items that change in meaning over time. Different items move along different clines. For example, the clines observed for the development of perfectives is different from the one observed for the development of imperfectives.

5. Chapter Organisation

This study consists of six chapters. The second chapter critically reviews linguistic works on verbal aspect and grammatical works on the Perfect tense-forms from several fields. This chapter establishes the status of scholarship regarding the verbal aspect of the Greek Perfect tense-forms and concludes that much confusion exists among the descriptions of the verbal aspect for the Greek Perfect tense-form. The need for clarification is highlighted along with a fresh analysis for the verbal aspect of the Greek Perfect. The clarifications of definitions for verbal aspect as a linguistic category and the components under that category are outlined. Elements from the literature that are useful for constructing a way forward are contrasted with problematic elements. The chapter concludes that verbal aspect is subjective, non-temporal, and morphologically expressed.

The third chapter provides a way forward beginning with an explanation of grammaticalisation. Next, insights from theoretical linguistics, structural linguistics, cross-linguistic analysis, and morphology are used to support grammaticalisation in constructing a new model for the Greek Perfect. The nature of stativity as a verbal aspect from the literature is challenged based on how stativity functions differently than perfective and imperfective, and then judges this difference based on the criteria of semantics established in the previous chapter. The useful components from the literature are combined with some new observations to build a fresh understanding of the verbal aspect of the Perfect tense-form. A morphological comparison of tense-forms shows that the internal vowel spelling of the productive pattern for the Greek Perfect mirrors that of the Aorist. This idea is shown to be compatible with what is suggested by grammaticalisation. This chapter constructs the complex aspect model for understanding the verbal aspect of the Greek Perfect tense-form. The argument is established that the Greek Perfect tense-form contains within its morphology two aspects that remain in tension with each other, based on its morphology and diachronic development, and supported by analysis of adverb collocations. Reduplication studies support the claims made here.

The fourth chapter analyses the Pauline corpus. Various linguistic environments for the Perfect tense-forms of the Pauline corpus are included and analysed. This chapter examines stative contexts, eventive contexts, and contexts that have both components. The special case of οἶδα and the Perfect of communication lexemes found in citation and referential contexts are treated separately. Compatibility between the Pauline corpus and the complex aspect developed for the Perfect in the previous chapter is shown in the discussion of the verbal aspect of the Perfect tense-forms following the selected examples.

The fifth chapter introduces corpus linguistics as a tool to build data for analysis. The Pauline corpus and a larger diachronic epistolary and moral literature corpus spanning roughly eight centuries are both defined along with their uses. The Pauline corpus is the primary text analysed, while the diachronic corpus is a test corpus that is used to confirm the findings within the Pauline corpus, and provide balance to the general conclusions. The discussion of the data drawn from the two corpora shows that Paul's usage of the Greek Perfect is compatible aspectually with the other Greek letter writers and moralists. The unique usages of the Greek Perfect with the Pauline corpus are highlighted as well. The Pauline corpus contains more Perfect tense-forms inside supplemental clauses and employs a wider variety of eventive lexemes in this role than do the other writers examined. The compatibility between the complex aspect explained and supported in the third chapter and the observations in the Pauline corpus in the fourth chapter are highlighted in this chapter as well. The analysis corpus also shows examples of stative and eventive Perfect use, both long before and well after the New Testament period, further supporting the claim that the aspect of the Perfect is complex generally.

The sixth chapter draws the conclusion that the Perfect has a complex aspect, perfective for any action and imperfective for any state. Although these states primarily are states of the grammatical subject, whenever the state is relevant for the object, it will be imperfective also. This chapter articulates the contributions to linguistics, Greek grammatical discussions, and biblical studies. Next, the limitations of the size and scope of the test corpus are described. It closes by suggesting further research through expanding the test corpus and comparing all the tense-forms, and not only the Perfect tense-forms.

Overview of Verbal Aspect Studies as Related to the Greek Perfect and Pluperfect Tense-Forms

1. Introductory Remarks

The definition of verbal aspect as a linguistic category belonging to the larger category of semantics is of first importance, making sure that the definition fits the criteria derived from semantics. This is required before the verbal aspect of the Perfect tense-form can be analysed. Secondly, the members which make up the set of items called verbal aspects require definition, while ensuring that those members satisfy the criteria for verbal aspect and its larger category, semantics. The definitions of verbal aspect prominent in the literature include a view on an "internal temporal constituency" of a given situation,[1] and an author's "point-of-view" on a situation.[2] Both of these can be and sometimes have been misunderstood. When verbal aspect is understood as an internal temporal property, rather than a view on that property, this allows for confusion between aspect and temporal matters. The features relevant to time are better understood as the effect aspect has on time, rather than informing the definition for aspect. The view is

---

1 Bernard Comrie, *Aspect: An Introduction to the study of Verbal Aspect and Related Problems*. Cambridge Textbooks in Linguistics (Cambridge: Cambridge University Press, 1976), 3.
2 Fanning, 83.

primary. Understanding verbal aspect as a point-of-view from which an author views a situation leads problematically to seemingly endless possibilities for the points that can be described.[3] A view on a situation is primary rather than the point from which it is viewed. Further clarification is required in the definition of verbal aspect.

Not only does variety exist in the descriptions of verbal aspect as a semantic category, but in the descriptions of a specific verbal aspect for the Perfect tense-form as well. Some studies describe the semantics of the Perfect utilising verbal aspect, while others focus on some of the functions of the various tense-forms or on some of the practical applications of Perfect tense-forms more broadly.[4] Attempts to define the semantics of the Perfect range from being truly semantic to being somewhat temporal or functional.[5] One semantic description for the Perfect is "perfective," equating the aspect of the Perfect with that of the Aorist due to its actional component. Another semantic description is "imperfective," equating the Perfect with the Present and the Pluperfect with the Imperfect, due to the ongoing nature observed for the Present. A third type of aspect described in the literature is "stative," where the state of the grammatical subject is highlighted by the Perfect tense-form. Other descriptions combine features of tense

---

3   Fanning restricts his points-of-view to two, "inner" and "outer," but this restriction is based his understanding of aspect, and not on his definition. This limitation causes his handling of this definition to work well, in spite of the definition itself having some logical problems. Fanning, 36.

4   Primary examples of those which utilise verbal aspect are Stanley E. Porter *Verbal Aspect in the Greek of the New Testament*, SBG:1, ed. D. A. Carson (New York: Peter Lang, 1989, 1993, 2003, 2010); Fanning, *Verbal Aspect*; Kenneth L. McKay, *A New Syntax of the Verb in New Testament Greek: An Aspectual Approach*, SBG:5, edIted by D. A. Carson (New York: Peter Lang, 1994); and Campbell, *Verbal Aspect, the Indicative Mood*, SBG:13, edited by D. A. Carson (New York: Peter Lang, 2007). An example of one which emphasises functions is Kenneth L. McKay, "The Use of the Ancient Greek Perfect Down to the Second Century A.D.," *BICS* (1965): 1–21. Examples of those which focus on special application include C. M. J. Sicking, and P. Stork, *Two Studies in the Semantics of the Verb in Classical Greek*, Mnemosyne Supplements:160 (Leiden: Brill, 1996), especially where it treats aspect as two clauses come together, and Robert. Crellin, "The Greek Perfect Active System: 200 BC–AD 150" (PhD diss., Pembroke College: University of Cambridge, 2012), especially in its concern for transitivity and valency.

5   Examples of semantic studies include those mentioned before under verbal aspect along with those that examine the morphology, such as Sam Zukoff, "The Phonology of Verbal Reduplication in Ancient Greek: An Optimality Theory Approach" (MA diss., The University of Georgia, 2012); and Joan Bybee, *Morphology: A Study of the Relation Between Meaning and Form* (Amsterdam: John Benjamins, 1985). Temporal examples include Timothy Brookins, "Rethinking the Grammaticalization of Time in Greek Indicative Verbs," *JBL* 137:1 (Spring 2008): 147–168. Functional examples include Ernie Clarence Ricketts, "Discourse Function of Tense, Aspect, and Mood in Ancient Greek Hortatory Epistles" (PhD Diss., University of Texas at Arlington, 1999); and Ioannis Veloudis, "The Pragmatic Category 'Perfect,'" 129–136 in *Themes in Greek Linguistics*, CILT: 117, edited by Irene Philippaki-Warburton, Katarina Nicolaidas, and Maria Sifianou (Amsterdam: Benjamins, 1993).

or *Aktionsart* into their understanding of the Greek Perfect and mix functional or contextual material with the semantics.[6]

One problem in the above descriptions is that perfective and imperfective are opposites within the verbal aspect descriptions, raising the concern regarding how both could be possible. Since each aspect is selected for the whole tense-form by different scholars it is unclear how this decision is related to the morphology of the Perfect tense-form. Another problem is how stativity fits within a verbal aspect network, where complete (perfective) and incomplete (imperfective) views on the verb are items of the same set, while stativity seems to belong to a different linguistic category than do the perfective and imperfective. A third problem is how temporal descriptions relate to aspectual ones. A fourth problem is that for those whose definitions blend aspectual and pragmatic components, they obscure what verbal aspect is itself. Before these issues can be sorted out, it is helpful to review what verbal aspect is as a semantic category, and how this category fits into the overall meaning of verbs generally, and then to review more specifically what the verbal aspect is for the Perfect tense-form. Varieties in the descriptions of the Greek synthetic Perfect tense-form appear to be partly due to differences in how verbal aspect is understood.

2. The Development of Verbal Aspect as a Term for Grammatical Analysis

The analysis of verbal aspect as a category places boundaries on what items can be included as individual verbal aspects. Several scholars have distinguished verbal aspect as a category separate from tense, mood, lexical meaning, and *Aktionsart*. Concepts such as the subjectivity of aspect and uncancellability of semantics more generally emerge as components of this discussion, and are defined in this section. These definitions lead to refinements in the definition of the category of verbal aspect.

2.1. Situating Verbal Aspect within Linguistics

Before analysing verbal aspect as a verbal category, it is necessary to situate verbal aspect as a linguistic concept in its context. Verbal aspect is primarily a semantic category. Semantics involves the meaning of a particular form or lexeme before

---

6 Fanning combines aspect and *Aktionsart* to describe the Perfect. Fanning, *Verbal Aspect.*

it is contextualised. Semantics is divided into two portions. Formal semantics is related to meanings associated with forms of words, while lexical semantics is related to word definition. Since the present study is focused on verbal aspect, and thus formal semantics, the semantics of the form is most important, while lexical semantics will be mentioned only where helpful to avoid confusion. Porter defines "verbal aspect" as a component of semantics and related to the meaning of the verb form rather than to its function.[7]

Pragmatics is different from semantics in that it involves how a particular form or lexeme is used in certain contexts. Pragmatics also involves two components. First, the meaning of a particular word or form that arises because of a particular contextual setting is one element belonging to pragmatics. Olsen calls these "implicatures."[8] Second, pragmatics explains how a word might be used in one way or another to create a different effect. In this way, pragmatics includes functions of a word or a form. Each verb's relationship with various contexts produces the various pragmatic functions for that verb. A meaning associated with pragmatics is not durable apart from its context in contrast to one from semantics. As related to form, semantics refers to the core meaning of a grammatical form that is uncancellable by context, while pragmatics refers to the ways a grammatical form is used in context, and any meaning derived from this special use is cancellable by changing the context.[9] These pragmatic "meanings," "functions," or "uses" can be cancelled by changing the context, but in contrast to this, semantic "meanings" cannot be cancelled this way. This study avoids elements that rely on "use" or "function" to describe the verbal aspect of the Perfect because to do so would conflate semantics with pragmatics. The distinction between semantics and pragmatics will be maintained throughout this project. Figure 1 places the linguistic elements under their respective category.

This project is concerned with semantics as it analyses the verbal aspect of the Perfect. It is also concerned with the pragmatics of the Perfect where certain uses of the Perfect potentially confuse the research on aspect, and to show how its verbal aspect functions in these special circumstances. Keeping both elements separate is of importance along with developing and maintaining clear definitions of verbal aspect and *Aktionsart* as will be developed later.

---

7 Porter, "Defence," 30.
8 Mary Jean Broman Olsen, "A Semantic and Pragmatic Model of Lexical and Grammatical Aspect" (PhD diss., Northwestern University, 1994), 21.
9 Campbell, *Verbal Aspect, the Indicative Mood*, 24.

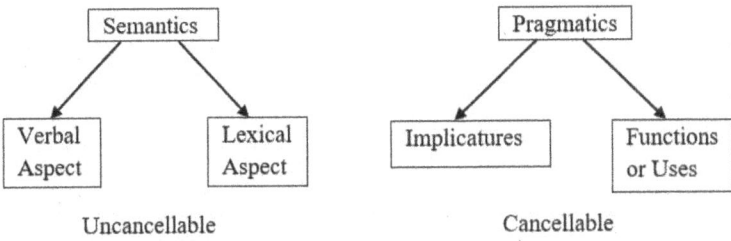

Figure 1: Categories of linguistic elements

Olsen provides some detail for when a semantic item is uncancellable. A semantic meaning cannot be cancelled without a contradiction occurring or reinforced without apparent redundancy.[10] When deciding whether or not a meaning is cancellable, it is helpful to apply a test to see whether a meaning is cancellable. Olsen provides a text for a lexical situation. For example, she supplies a basic sentence, "Elsie plodded down the walk." Since adding "slowly" or "not slowly" to the sentence runs into either contradiction or redundancy, slowly is a semantic meaning for the word "plodded." Also, since the concept of slowness cannot be cancelled for "plod," then the idea of "slowness" is semantic for the word "plod." On the other hand, adding the ideas of "tired" or "not tired" to the sentence produces sentences with meaning either way. Therefore, the idea of "tiredness" is a pragmatic implicature of the word "plod," rather than a semantic meaning for the word, because it is cancellable.[11] A person can be said to plod even if he or she is not tired. Although this is an example of "uncancellability" vs. "cancellability" within lexical semantics, when this same test is applied to semantics of a verbal form with similar results, the same division between semantics and pragmatics applies. The semantic components cannot be cancelled, while pragmatic ones can. Verbal aspect for the Perfect, if it is correctly identified, is likewise uncancellable by adding context. The goal in this study is to find a description for the verbal aspect of the Perfect tense-form that is not cancelled by context, so that it satisfies the semantic requirement for verbal aspect.

10 Olsen, 22.
11 Olsen, 22.

2.2. Related Semantic Concepts

Several semantic concepts directing the understanding of verbal aspect are developed over the next few sections. The subjectivity component distinguishes between elements that focus on the author's perspective, and those that focus objectively on the nature of the real situation. The subjectivity criterion is a test that must be met if something is considered a property of verbal aspect. The non-temporality of aspect is another important aspectual concept. It helps in keeping temporal ideas about the verb system separate from aspectual ideas. A tendency exists to conflate aspectual and temporal properties if one does not carefully separate them when discussing verbal aspect. Morphology of the Greek verb is a third important concept related to verbal aspect. The verb form encodes various meanings for the verb system in its morphemes; therefore, verbal aspect should be apparent in the morphology of the verb.

2.2.1. The Subjectivity Criterion

Within the realm of semantics, verbal aspect is defined as the authorial subjective viewpoint regarding a verb's action or state.[12] It is not the objective quality about any activity or situation.[13] The subjectivity criterion for verbal aspect was developed to oppose *Aktionsart*, which is an objective category. Lexical aspect, related to *Aktionsart* and often confused with verbal aspect, entails an objective portrayal of an action or state.[14] Phrases such as "this verb type refers to sudden activity" are an example of *Aktionsart*. Objective categories of language report on the actual situation referred to, including the type of action, while subjective categories report on how the speaker or author perceives the situation and portrays it, regardless of how the actual situation occurred.[15] Subjectivity also implies that the author has a choice in how to portray a situation. Aspect reports an action as either complete or incomplete in the perspective of the author, while *Aktionsart* reports on how the real situation unfolded, with a range of options available for describing different situations.[16] Another way of thinking how aspect relates to the action is that the author reports on the action as either whole or partial by using different verbal aspects.

---

12 Porter, Fanning, and Campbell have similar statements. Porter, *Verbal Aspect*, 36, 88; Fanning, 84. Campbell, *Verbal Aspect, the Indicative Mood*, 8.
13 Comrie, *Aspect*, 4.
14 Lexical aspect will be developed in the next section.
15 Porter, *Verbal Aspect*, 33, 37; Fanning, 31.
16 Porter, *Verbal Aspect*, 33.

Debate exists whether any of these categories is fully subjective or objective, but these categories still oppose each other and are distinct from each other in the matter of subjectivity and objectivity.[17] Although the debate is too large for a full treatment here, a few key points are necessary to establish the direction of this argument. Porter categorises aspect as fully subjective and *Aktionsart* as fully objective.[18] Fanning cautions against assigning too much subjectivity as the range of aspectual choices are often limited by context, and against assigning too much objectivity to *Aktionsart*, a lexical category, because the perspective of an author on an action does not always correspond to reality.[19] Another concern is that a speaker might not always have a choice of which aspect to use. This means that in some situations aspectual distinctiveness could be non-apparent. This choice may not be available or practical to the author or speaker for every situation, but in defining verbal aspect, this subjective choice stands in contrast to the objective nature of the situation itself. When a choice exists between aspectual forms, some effect will be noticed between the use of one tense-form or the other, and that difference in effect is related to aspect. The author chooses the tense-form based on how he or she wants to portray a situation that he or she reports to a reader. Fanning sees that the selection of any aspect may be limited for certain situations the author wishes to portray, but the speaker must choose one from the available choices.[20] This subjective authorial selection of a verb form is made sometimes to avoid implications of another aspect inherent in a different verb form of the same lexeme.[21]

The aspect that the author chooses is often the cause for a number of functional categories. One of these specialised functions belonging to pragmatics could also be a reason an author might choose one form over another. If the author were to choose a special function of a tense-form as the main reason for its selection, the author will use the aspect that is associated with that tense-form, and will not have as much freedom to select an aspect. Even taking Fanning's concerns into consideration, verbal aspect still has more subjectivity than *Aktionsart* in Fanning's own analysis. Campbell maintains that *Aktionsart* is primarily an objective category while aspect is primarily a subjective one.[22] Although various

---

17 Fanning, 34–35.

18 Porter, *Verbal Aspect*, 36.

19 Fanning's concern regarding a speaker using objective language to misrepresent the situation is unwarranted. This usage does not violate the principles of objectivity, because even if the speaker is intentionally misleading, the portrayal is still objective. Fanning, 34–35.

20 Fanning, 53.

21 Fanning, 53.

22 Campbell, *Verbal Aspect, the Indicative Mood*, 11.

scholars see different degrees of objectivity and subjectivity at work, the vast majority recognise this distinction and make allowances that neither element is either totally subjective or totally objective, but that aspect is more or less subjective and *Aktionsart* is more or less objective.

For the analysis of verbal aspect in this book, verbal aspect is considered a distinctively and generally subjective category when compared with *Aktionsart*. This distinction between subjective and objective components will be sufficient to filter items from the set of linguistic terms placed into the verbal aspect category. If an item is considered a verbal aspect, yet is not subjective, then that item is rejected from the category of verbal aspect in this study. However, it will not necessarily be automatically included in the category *Aktionsart*, if it is rejected from the category of verbal aspect. Not everything rejected as an aspect belongs in the *Aktionsart* category.

2.2.2. Non-Temporal Basis

Although a full treatment on tense is not developed in this thesis, a discussion about how aspect is related to time is necessary to sort out the conflation in the literature. Verbal aspect is a category distinct from tense, yet, somehow related to time.[23] Tense refers in some way to temporal reference, which can be of several types. Absolute temporal reference points to a specific time such as the past, the present, or the future.[24] Relative time works differently and places one item as belonging either before, at the same time as, or after another item, but both items could be in the past, in the present, or in the future.[25] Both items referred to under relative time might also belong to two different absolute reference times. When relative time is understood instead of absolute time, both items are related to each other instead of related to a present moment or a moment chosen by the speaker. The relationship of verbal aspect to time is different than either a reference to absolute time or to relative time. Aspect is somehow related to time yet does not refer to time itself, or any specific temporal location.[26] Fanning points out that verbal aspect produces temporal meanings, which are related to the internal action of the verb and not to deictic reference or tense.[27] From this it seems that for any temporal properties relevant to aspect, they are secondary to aspect and dependent upon it.

---

23 Comrie, *Aspect*, 3, 5.
24 Fanning, 109.
25 Porter, *Verbal Aspect*, 108.
26 Porter, *Verbal Aspect*, 107.
27 Fanning, 29.

Tense is more complex than just absolute time or relative time. Klein develops temporal properties further. Whenever a speaker speaks, he or she creates something called the topic time.[28] This topic time might be the present moment, or it could be any moment the speaker chooses. Usually if the speaker does not specify a topic time, then the present speech moment is understood to be that topic time. The topic time could be a point in time, but it does not have to be a point. It also could be a specified duration of time. Once the topic time is established by the speaker, the events mentioned by the speaker will be located in reference to that topic time.[29] Each event will be given its own event time. Deictic temporal references, such as past, present, and future, relate the event time of each event to the past, present, or future of that topic time. Olsen maintains that verbal aspect relates the event time to the reference time, while tense relates a reference time to a topic time which may be the speech time, or some other time indicated by the speaker.[30] Dahl develops nearly the same idea. Dahl defines aspect as "a type of relation between reference time and event time," and defines tense as "a type of relation between reference time and local evaluation time," or deictic centre.[31] He defines the perfective aspect as the event time being included in the reference time.[32] Basically, a perfective aspect has a reference time that includes all of the event time, while an imperfective aspect has a reference time that is less than the whole event time and places the reference time somewhere within the event time.[33] Another way to discuss this phenomena is to understand that the perfective views the endpoints of the action, while the imperfective does not. Sasse uses this approach after separating out a type of boundedness for aspect away from the types associated with *Aktionsarten*.[34] Typically "boundedness" refers to the *Aktionsart* value of telicity, but since Sasse defines three types of boundedness, his third definition works for aspect properties. Bary uses Formal Semantics to

---

28 Wolfgang Klein, *Time in Language*, Germanic Linguistics (London: Routledge, 1994), 3.

29 Olsen uses "deictic centre" to describe topic time but defines it the same as others do for topic time. Olsen, 7, 69, 138. Klein maintains the existence of three temporal elements as well using different terminology. Klein, 36. Smith also uses a three-way division of temporal components. Carlota Smith, *The Parameter of Aspect*, Studies in Linguistics and Philosophy: 43 (Dordrecht: Springer, 1997), 101.

30 Olsen, 7; See also, Klein, 140–141.

31 Dahl, *Time, Tense and Aspect*, 57. It seems he is depending partly on Smith (1997) and Grønn (2004).

32 Dahl, *Time, Tense and Aspect*, 76.

33 Klein, 118.

34 Hans-Jürgen Sasse, "Aspect and Aktionsart," *Encyclopedia of Languages and Linguistics*, ed. Keith Brown (Amsterdam: Elsevier, 2006), 535.

show how Klein's thesis, relating aspect to time, works for Greek Aorists and Imperfects.[35]

Dahl defines "aspect" as a "speaker's perspective on the internal temporal structure of a situation."[36] This is similar to Comrie's definition of verbal aspect, where the internal time of the action is in the speaker's view.[37] This means that each verbal aspect has a different view of the internal time of the action. This seems quite compatible with the ideas of Olsen and is similar to Fanning's statements regarding aspect.[38] A potential problem occurs whenever aspect is equated with the amount of time in view, thus conflating temporal properties with aspect. One way to keep them separate is to keep verbal aspect as the subjective perspective of the author, while leaving the internal temporal components as the objective components of what is in view when an author has a certain perspective. Using the endpoints explanation per Sasse, the perfective view on the activity is the verbal aspect, while the endpoints being in view is part of the objective character of the verb and more related to the internal time of the action. Although a strong relationship exists between the view on the internal time and the internal time itself, these need to remain separate in order to construct adequate tests for determining whether or not an item should be considered a member of the verbal aspect category.

2.2.3. Encoded by the Verb Form

The location of verbal aspect within the morphology of the verb is discussed next in order to connect verb forms to their respective aspects. The idea that verbal aspect is connected somehow to the morphology of the verb suggests that morphological concerns should shape the analysis of the Perfect. The viewpoint on the action or state described earlier, or the manner of viewing the action or state is morphologically expressed in the stem choice of the tense-form and is the primary meaning for that tense-form in all modes. The morphology of the verb contains the components for its verbal aspect. The connection between morphology and verbal aspect is sometimes ignored or left undeveloped by the theorists, but is a key component in this research. Aspects are not detected only through

---

35 Corien Bary, "Aspect in Ancient Greek: A Semantic Analysis of the Aorist and Imperfective" (PhD diss., Radboud Universiteit Nijmegen, 2009), 60. This work although helpful in its handing of verbal aspect, did not analyse the Greek Perfect.

36 Dahl, *Time, Tense and Aspect*, 30.

37 Comrie, Aspect, 3.

38 His ideas developed later on in the text are more closely related to those of Olsen rather than to those of Fanning.

contextual considerations,[39] but are denoted by certain elements in the stem of the verb.[40] Since the stem of the verb is the locus for verbal aspect, then the verbal aspect is not connected to the augment, or the primary and secondary endings, but something integral to the stem. This stem also cannot include the lexeme itself, since this provides the lexical aspect. The augment, endings, and lexical affixes need to be removed from the stem first in order to analyse this. The remaining difference between the tense-forms, once these morphemes are removed, is usually that of the internal stem vowel spelling, and this difference is most noticeable between the Present and the Aorist stems.[41] Therefore, this study is concerned with the differences in stem spellings where they are evident to determine aspectual affinities. Problematically, few studies in the available literature demonstrate how their respective decisions regarding verbal aspect are derived from the morphology of the Greek verb. This study will connect verbal aspect to explicit morphemes within the Greek Perfect tense-form.

2.3. Situation of Verbal Aspect among Other Elements Called "Aspect"

Several linguistic elements other than verbal aspect have been called "aspect," including lexical aspect, *Aktionsart*, and phasal aspect or aspectualisers. Early in the literature, these were often conflated with verbal aspect, but now have been defined as separate entities. These will be each described, followed by a statement of how this study will distinguish between their terminology and that for verbal aspect in light of the separation of these concepts.

Both verbal aspect and lexical aspect belong to the category of semantics which is related to the meaning of the words and forms themselves. Several items referred to by early grammars as individual verbal aspects, such as "punctual" or "durative," are now understood to belong to lexical aspect. Each verb has both a verbal and a lexical aspect. The difference between these two types of aspect is that verbal aspect is the meaning associated with the form of word, while lexical aspect is the meaning associated with the root word itself. Telicity refers to an

---

39 Aspect may be confirmed through contextual considerations, however.

40 Fanning, 15, 106–107; Campbell, *Verbal Aspect, the Indicative Mood*, 175, n. 53.

41 Dahl cites this particular difference as related to the process of grammaticalisation, where aspect grammaticalised onto the verb form. Östen Dahl, "The Tense-Aspect Systems of European Languages in a Typological Perspective," 3–25 in *Tense and Aspect in the Languages of Europe*, edited by Östen Dahl. Empirical Approaches to Language Typology: 20, EUROTYP: 6 (Berlin: Mouton de Gruyter, 2000), 10, 16.

action that reaches endpoint.[42] Iterativity refers to many actions repeated over and over. Semelfactive or punctual verbs refer to actions that have a short duration with almost no awareness that time transpires during the action.[43] These terms have often been used to describe the perfective aspect, but are now understood to be lexical instead. Durativity refers to actions without an end in view.[44] These actions also are seen as occurring over time, rather than a point in time. This term has often been used to describe imperfective aspect, but is now understood to be lexical as well. The main reason these elements are now analysed as types of lexical aspect is that they describe the objective situation of the verbal environment rather than the subjective portrayal by the author or speaker on that verbal environment. For example, when the author or speaker wishes to change perspective on the same situation, he or she will keep the same lexical aspect features while only changing the verbal aspect features.

Maintaining a distinction between verbal aspect as a semantic component related to the verb's form and lexical aspect as a semantic component of the word-level meaning throughout a study on verbal aspect is essential for clarity. The terms that describe an action or its manner reflect objectivity on the part of the speaker. Since these items are not part of the speaker's subjective portrayal, they are placed into lexical aspect and not considered a component of verbal aspect. Essentially the items in the lexical aspect set fail to meet the subjectivity criterion. Verbal aspect will be described by whether the situation is wholly or partially in view.

Aktionsart is a concept that is either derived from the lexical aspect directly or a combination of the lexical aspect and something else from the context. This term was mentioned briefly in 2.1 and 2.1.1, but needs a fuller treatment here. *Aktionsart* often appears in aspectual studies in lieu of the term "lexical aspect," due to its connection to the meaning of certain lexemes, but these two are distinct and require separate treatment.[45] *Aktionsart* is the "kind of action" that describes an objective reality belonging to the situation. The difference between lexical aspect and *Aktionsart* is that lexical aspect is the meaning associated with the root

---

42 Comrie, *Aspect*, 44; Smith, *Parameter of Aspect*, 16–24.
43 Comrie, *Aspect*, 42 and 44–51; Smith, *Parameter of Aspect*, 3.
44 Comrie, *Aspect*, 41–43; Smith, *Parameter of Aspect*, 19.
45 Porter keeps these concepts separate with *"Aktionsart"* and "lexis," where he defines lexis strictly and calls *Aktionsarten* abstractions based on lexis. Porter, *Verbal Aspect*, 35, 35 n. 15. Campbell keeps them separate in his diagrams on *Aktionsart* interactions. Constantine Campbell, *Basics of Verbal Aspect in Biblical Greek* (Grand Rapids, MI: Zondervan, 2008), 63 and following.

word, while *Aktionsart* is the meaning associated with a relationship between the root word and its greater context.

Recognising the distinction between aspect and *Aktionsart*, Fanning favours Bache over Comrie, because Bache keeps the aspect and *Aktionsart* separate regarding what information they each provide to the reader. Porter criticises Comrie for blending formal and functional definitions.[46] But he agrees with Bache that Comrie's definition of the Perfect tense is an *Aktionsart* definition and not an aspectual one.[47] The understanding Bache provides is an important distinction most studies now assume. Schmidt finds that the combined effort of Porter and Fanning has established for the scholarly community that aspect and *Aktionsart* are two separate elements distinct from each other.[48] Recent work by Moser still maintains that verbal aspect and *Aktionsart* are separate, but points out limitations in their total independence from each other.[49] They are related closely in certain circumstances. Following the research by Bache, Porter, Fanning, and Moser, this study will maintain the distinction between aspect and *Aktionsart*.

Phasal aspect is another type of aspect that needs eliminated from the verbal aspect discussion. This category includes items that point to a phase of activity. Terms that describe phasal aspect are often called aspectualisers.[50] An action can be understood to take place in stages or phases. Immanence refers to actions that are about to take place. Inception refers to the initial beginning of an action. Eventive focuses upon all elements during the whole of the action. The peak refers to the midpoint of an action. Culmination refers to the endpoint of an action. Stative focuses upon the aftermath of the event. Several of these terms have often been understood as components of verbal aspect, and later as *Aktionsart*. However, just like lexical aspect and *Aktionsart*, these items are more objective about the situation viewed, than they are subjective portrayals by the speaker. These terms also fail the subjectivity criterion, so they are not considered verbal aspects in this study. Stativity is understood by some as a verbal aspect, but as suggested above,

---

46 Porter, *Verbal Aspect*, 46.

47 Porter, *Verbal Aspect*, 46. Carl Bache, *Verbal Aspect: A General Theory and Its Application to Present-Day English*, Odense University Studies in English: 8 (Odense: Odense University Press, 1985), 20.

48 Daryl Schmidt, "Verbal Aspect in Greek: Two Approaches," 63–73 in *Biblical Greek Language and Linguistics: Open Questions in Current Research*, JSNTS 80, edited by Donald Carson and Stanley Porter (Sheffield: Sheffield Academic Press, 1993), 72.

49 Amalia Moser, "Aspect and Aktionsart: A Study on the Nature of Grammatical Categories," *Major Trends in Theoretical and Applied Linguistics: 1*. Eds. Nikolaos Lavidas, Thomai Alexiou and Areti-Maria Sougari (London: Versita, 2014), 114–117.

50 See Alice Freed, *The Semantics of English Aspectual Complementation* (Reidel: Dordrecht, 1979) and David Dowty, *Word Meaning and Montague Grammar* (Reidel: Dordrecht, 1979) for the foundations of this idea.

the concept of stativity appears more at home as a phase of an action rather than in either verbal aspect, lexical aspect, or in *Aktionsart* categories. Terms referring to some phase of activity will be excluded from the verbal aspect discussion, since they are generally objective.

2.4. Refining the Definition of Verbal Aspect

Within the definitions of verbal aspect itself, two prominent ideas emerge from the literature. First is the idea that verbal aspect is a point of view from which the author or speaker views the action or state. Secondly, the idea that the author or speaker views the action or state in a particular manner is assessed. These two definitions appear to be intertwined in the recent literature. After evaluating the strengths and the weaknesses of each idea some clarification is provided for definitions of verbal aspect.

2.4.1. Aspect as "Point of View"

The most common way to describe verbal aspect is to associate it with a point from which the action or state is viewed. Turner defines verbal aspect as "the tense stems indicate the point of view from which the action or state is regarded," thus providing clear wording for this understanding.[51] Fanning further adds that a relationship exists between the point of view and the action itself. He places perfective aspect outside the action and imperfective aspect inside the action relying on a point-of-view approach.[52] As Fanning describes viewpoint, only two possibilities exist for a point of view, either inside or outside the action. Smith also uses the term "viewpoint" to describe verbal aspect. Fanning sees himself as following both Bache and Smith in his developments.[53] In Figure 2, the dot represents the point of view from which an author or speaker views an action or state. The circle represents the situation the author or speaker is viewing. The placement of the dot implies that the author or speaker places himself or herself cognitively into a relationship with the situation so that he or she can talk about it.

In his list of definitional components of aspect, Fanning equates viewpoint with perspective, while describing it as a manner in which the action is viewed.[54] "Viewpoint" and "perspective" do not appear to be the same concept. In his summary, Fanning says aspect is that "focus or viewpoint," as if they are the same

---

51 Nigel Turner, *Syntax*, Grammar of NT Greek: 3 (Edinburgh: T & T Clark, 1963), 59.
52 Fanning, 26–27.
53 Fanning, 41.
54 Fanning, 79.

Perfective verbal aspect

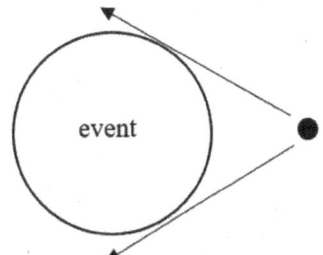

Imperfective Verbal Aspect

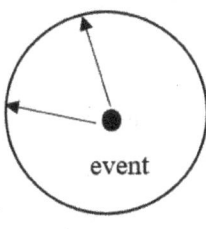

Figure 2: Contrasting two aspects using a point-of-view

thing.[55] While both ideas seem to hold for aspect in general, one has to be primary and the other derived from that primary one or one is an effect of the other. Repeatedly, his explanations of aspect favour the focus, perspective, or "way of viewing" idea over the idea of the point from which the view is taken, but he uses both terms interchangeably.[56] Looking back at Figure 2, the idea of viewpoint belongs to the "dot," while the ideas of the type of view or focus belong to the relationship between the two "arrows" and the "event."

Fanning's understanding of verbal aspect, a semantic category, along the lines of "point-of-view" is similar to pragmatic discussions that involve remoteness and proximity. The terms "inside" and "outside" suggest proximity and remoteness. To further emphasise this, he later adds "near" view and "distant" view as equivalents. The viewpoint from which an action is viewed has more to do with the pragmatic discussion of proximity or remoteness than it does with the semantic discussion of verbal aspect. One is either "close" to the action or "far" from the action. A relationship may exist between perfectivity and remoteness, and between imperfectivity and proximity, but remoteness and proximity are effects belonging to pragmatics and should not be used to define verbal aspect. Campbell defines aspect as "viewpoint," borrowing from Evans and Bache.[57] While understanding verbal aspect as a viewpoint may indicate a subjective choice by the speaker to view a situation either from nearby or from afar, it does not say much

---

55 Fanning, 84.
56 His definitions say one thing, while his descriptions provide for a different definition.
57 Campbell, *Verbal Aspect, the Indicative Mood*, 8; T. V. Evans. *Verbal Syntax in the Greek Pentateuch: Natural Greek Usage and Hebrew Interference* (Oxford: Oxford University Press, 2001), 18; Carl Bache, "Aspect and *Aktionsart*: Towards a Semantic Distinction," *Journal of Linguistics* 18 (1982): 57–72, 64.

about how the situation is viewed. More clarity regarding the nature of verbal aspect follows from definitions that identify the type of view that is taken, rather than from definitions which describe the viewpoint from which the situation is viewed. Terminology that emphasises the type of view is preferred because these will say more about how the situation is viewed, rather than from where it is viewed.

2.4.2. Aspect as "Perspective on a Situation"

Moorhouse's definition provides clarity regarding the idea of verbal aspect as a perspective. "Aspect represents the manner in which the action etc. is envisaged as occurring by the speaker. This 'way of looking at the action' is itself basically temporal, showing not when, but how the action occurs in relation to time."[58] While his inclusion of temporality is problematic, his wording of "way of looking," is better than "point-of-view." After defining the event time structure as a combination of nucleus and coda, Olsen then defines grammatical aspect as different "ways of viewing" the event time structure. Olsen's understanding of aspect includes the idea that it represents how an event takes place over time, rather than linking an event to a specific time.[59] In her model, the nucleus includes the entire time of the action, and coda begins at the endpoint of the action and includes any time after the action that is contextually relevant. Although her model is different from Moorhouse's, her temporal connections to aspect are similar. She is more precise than either Turner or Fanning regarding the definition of aspect as she does not conflate the "way of viewing" idea together with the "point-of-view" idea. She maintains that verbal aspect is a way of viewing and not a point-of-view. Olsen understands both tense and aspect to be concerned with time, but from complimentary perspectives. She distinguishes between tense and aspect in that tense locates situations in a relationship to a reference time, while aspect looks at the internal time of the situation.[60] Not all scholars involve temporality when explaining aspect as a way of viewing. McKay defines aspect as a category "by which the author shows how he views each event."[61] Porter defines verbal aspect as "a synthetic semantic category (realized in the forms of verbs) used of meaningful oppositions in a network of tense systems to grammaticalize the author's

---

58 His general description is conflated with temporal elements, but this portion is clearly defining verbal aspect. A. C. Moorhouse, *The Syntax of Sophocles*, Mnemosyne Supp: 75 (Leiden: Brill, 1982), 181.

59 Olsen, 6.

60 Olsen, 7. See also, Comrie, *Aspect*, 3.

61 Porter, *Verbal Aspect*, 49.

reasoned subjective choice of a conception of a process."[62] Porter's definition adds an emphasis on the form and subjectivity to the basic idea that verbal aspect is a way to view a situation. Neither McKay's nor Porter's view includes temporal matters. In spite of their differences in models and relation to temporal matters, all of these scholars show that verbal aspect is a manner of seeing an action or a kind of viewing of the action rather than a viewpoint from which the action is viewed.

The "point-of-view" idea mentioned earlier can work with some adaptation if two points-of-view are defined and the set of aspect members are limited to two items, but does not work if multiple points-of-view are defined. Many of the defined points from which an author views a situation are not aspectual but temporal. For example, viewing a situation from the point-of-view after the event is a temporal idea rather than an aspectual idea, although some describe this as an aspectual idea.[63] Maintaining verbal aspect as a way of viewing the situation is necessary to avoid potential conflation between temporal and aspectual properties. Although treated as identical in Fanning's approach, the "way of looking at the action" is a bit different than "a point of view from which an action is viewed."[64] The "way of looking at the action" says more about the speaker or author choosing to view a situation in a particular way, while the "point-of-view" idea portrays either a spatial or temporal location from which the speaker or author must view the situation, and is less subjective than perspective. The point-of-view idea seems closer to the discussion regarding tense or the pragmatic element of remoteness, than it does to verbal aspect. The approach in this section defines aspect so that non-aspectual items do not enter the set. This "manner-of-viewing" definition limits the options available, so that false items do not confuse the nature of verbal aspect. Point-of-view allows too many non-aspectual ideas, including objective ones, to enter into the set, while manner-of-viewing restricts the set better.

2.4.3. Summary of Definition

The manner of viewing the situation is seen as primary over the "point-of-view" approach for explaining verbal aspect. The manner of viewing the situation best answers the subjectivity requirement, and best avoids conflation with temporal matters. This approach also fits semantics better since using it limits the options

---

62 Porter, *Verbal Aspect*, 88.
63 Those who describe the Perfect as an "anterior," use this explanation.
64 Fanning, 84.

for verbal aspect to those that are semantic rather than pragmatic. Verbal aspect is the subjective manner in which an author views a situation, separate from tense and mood, and this choice is reflected in the form of the verb itself.

2.5. Elements of the Verbal Aspect Category Set

The literature for verbal aspect contains two items that describe opposite individual aspects. Both the perfective and the imperfective can be defined as ways that a speaker or author views a situation. The definitions of both members of the verbal aspect set will show how they fit the semantic category of verbal aspect defined above.

Dahl discusses perfectivity as representing situations that are completed, and imperfectivity as representing those that are in progress.[65] Narrative literature shows the functional difference between these two aspects the best.[66] Since both of these individual aspects are easily applied to the Aorist and Present tense-forms, these tenses will be discussed briefly before analysing the aspects in relation to the Perfect. It is necessary to visit the definitions of perfective and imperfective using the Present and Aorist, because it is less clear from the literature how to apply these aspects correctly to the Perfect tense-forms.

McKay describes perfectivity clearly by reference to the Aorist tense-form. The Aorist describes a situation simply and in an undefined manner, and is the normal aspect for expressing totality of the situation.[67] This description is compatible with the definition established earlier for the category of verbal aspect as a "way of viewing" a situation, in that McKay understands this aspect to represent viewing the situation as simple, undefined, and total.[68] By using language associated with the manner of viewing, McKay's definition provides security that perfectivity belongs to the verbal aspect category.

Several adjustments to the perfective as simple, whole action appear in the literature. Olsen proposes that the perfective aspect presents a coda view of the situation, and the reference time intersects the event time structure at the coda.[69] Here she combines the manner of viewing with its target, the temporal constituency in view. Olsen calls perfective "complete action," and the imperfective,

---

65 Dahl, *Time, Tense and Aspect*, 12. He might have said "complete" rather than "completed," and "incomplete," rather than "in progress." This distinction is developed in the next section.
66 Dahl, *Time, Tense and Aspect*, 12.
67 Summarised from McKay, *A New Syntax*, 30.
68 The word "simply," a manner adverb provides a manner of viewing.
69 For Olsen, the Nucleus of the situation includes all the activity of the verbal lexeme, and the Coda includes anything that results from stopping the action or that is a result of the action. Olsen, 69, 72.

"incomplete action."[70] By using precise terms she avoids the problems associated with connecting the perfective to "completed action." Her definition accounts for why a perfective appears to place the speaker outside of the event, and accounts for the past temporal reference typically associated with the perfective. Because her model of the perfective has the reference time intersecting with the event time structure of the situation at its coda, a stative interpretation might result.[71] This is an important consideration because it provides a way to potentially link perfective verbs to stative readings.

According to McKay, the imperfective aspect refers to a process without including the completion of an action.[72] This aspect is seen primarily in the Greek Present and Imperfect tense-forms. His definition of the imperfective also accounts for the way a speaker views a situation. Using a different framework, Olsen proposes that imperfective aspect presents the nucleus view of the situation, and the reference time intersects the event time structure somewhere within the nucleus. Her definition accounts for the ongoing effects of imperfective verb usage, and for the temporal reference.

2.6. Summary

The definition for verbal aspect as a semantic category involving the author's subjective portrayal of a verbal situation is a better definition than others due to its omission of either temporal or objective elements. Since the verbal aspect category is encoded within the morphology of the verb, a morphological approach is included in the method for the next chapter. The subjectivity criterion was useful to shape the accepted definition for verbal aspect as a linguistic category in this section, and to determine what items belonged in its set. Two members of the verbal aspect category, perfective and imperfective, are identified as belonging to its set. Perfective aspect encodes the speaker viewing the verbal situation in its entirety, while imperfective aspect encodes an incomplete view of the verbal situation. Some implications of this are that the perfective includes the whole process of the action including the starting point and end point. The imperfective on the other hand will neither view the whole activity, nor include both the starting point and the ending point of the action. The next section will review

70 Olsen, 74.
71 Olsen, 111.
72 McKay, *A New Syntax*, 29.

how the verbal aspect category and its members relate to the Perfect tense-form specifically.

3. Verbal Aspect as Related to the Greek Perfect and Pluperfect Tense-Forms

The Perfect and Pluperfect are described in a greater variety of ways in the literature than are the Aorist, Present and Imperfect tense-forms. The division between formal and functional approaches divides scholars on how to approach the Greek verb system, affecting both methods employed and conclusions reached. Differences in preferred terminology affect how their works are received by critics, and differences in how to conceptualise verbal aspect as a category affect how the specific aspect is selected for the Greek Perfect.

3.1. History of Development

Several concepts of the Perfect have developed over time. Many of these are not compatible with each other, and the set of definitions provided next show the state of confusion in the literature. This section assesses a number of definitions of the Perfect that are either aspectual or have aspectual components. After the assessment, suggestions are offered regarding how to proceed.

3.1.1. The Perfect Tense-Form Defined as a Perfective

Several scholars recognise that the Greek Perfect and Pluperfect tense-forms consist of perfective verbal aspect. This section describes their understanding of verbal aspect as it pertains to the Perfect and Pluperfect tense-forms, and critiques each one. Perfective verbal aspect is the aspect that summarises the situation or presents it in summary form. It also views the situation as a whole without regard for its internal make-up. Generally speaking, those who find perfective aspect in the Perfect and Pluperfect tense-forms use two aspects instead of three to describe the Greek verbal system as a whole. Usually, scholars who use two aspects see either tense or *Aktionsart* as the element other than aspect which provides oppositions in the verbal decision tree.

Fanning defines the Perfect as having perfective verbal aspect, anterior tense, and stative *Aktionsart.*[73] Fanning theorises two options for the Perfect as it refers

---

73 Fanning, 119–120.

to the prior event. Either the Perfect is like the Aorist and views the event in summary fashion and is perfective or else it is neutral, not placing an aspect upon the event which caused the state. He decides the perfective option works best, since both the Perfect and Aorist yield an ingressive sense on stative lexemes. Also, the Perfect summarises the action much the same way as an Aorist.[74] Fanning sees the primary aspectual opposition among the tenses to be that between the Aorist and the Present, with the Perfect being a secondary opposition to both the Present and the Aorist in the area of stativity, an item he places into the *Aktionsart* category. The Perfect shares the aspect of the Aorist.[75] The Perfect tense-forms are similar to the Aorist tense-forms with activities, since they summarise the action and are external to the action itself.[76] The Perfect is similar to the Aorist in verbs of accomplishment in that both indicate the completion of the action.[77] In both activities and accomplishments the Perfect adds the consequence of the action.[78] Fanning keeps aspect and *Aktionsart* separate at the definitional level, but in places his description of verbal aspect for particular forms resembles discussion over *Aktionsart* thus conflating the two. He views the verbal system as having two aspects, perfective and imperfective. Using this paradigm, he concludes that the Perfect and Pluperfect tense-forms are primarily resultant states from prior actions, are past-referring and have perfective aspect.[79]

Fanning connects verbal aspect to morphology in general, but does not provide details. Fanning's decision that Perfect and Aorist have the same aspect but different *Aktionsart* goes against the idea that verbal aspect is morphologically driven since both of these forms as whole forms contain morphological differences, which are not discussed in his work. Since he concludes that the difference between the Aorist and Perfect is one of *Aktionsart*, then the morphological features of the Perfect and Pluperfect tense-forms should point to this *Aktionsart* in some way, but it is unclear how. His work is also unclear as to why the Perfect tense-form has a consistent *Aktionsart*, while other tense-forms do not. This is concerning because *Aktionsart* is related to lexical meaning and context, and not to tense-forms. Fanning's decision tree for aspect within the verbal system might be diagrammed as in Figure 3. For the boxes with two tense-forms, the decision

---

74 Fanning, 118–119.
75 Fanning, 122.
76 Fanning, 147.
77 Fanning, 147.
78 Fanning, 147, 153.
79 "Past referring" is best understood to refer to the action component only for Perfect, but might include both the action and the resultant state for the Pluperfect.

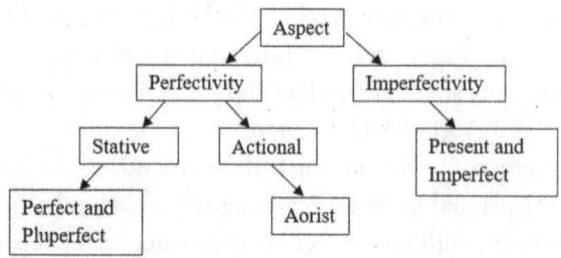

Figure 3: Fanning's Aspectual System

yet to be made is one of temporal reference. Past and non-past will further sep-arate these.

Because of the apparent placement of the division between actional and sta-tivity within a system that is marked for each division, one would expect that stative or both stative and actional are marked somehow. Once this marking is identified, then an explanation for why both Perfects and Aorists can refer to states is required. The division between action and state is more basic than the morphological system. This calls into question both the placement of stativity as something added to a perfective, and whether or not this added component is the main difference between an Aorist and Perfect. Once Fanning's ideas are diagrammed, a second concern emerges that, if stativity is a subdivision of the perfective aspect, why does the imperfective aspect not require a similar subdivi-sion among tense-forms to portray states? In the imperfective both tense-forms can interchangeably represent either states or actions.

Fanning next says that aspect is so intertwined with its context that it is affected by it. This means that not only is the implication or meaning affected, but the actual verbal aspect is affected as well. While his point that the interac-tion between verbal aspect and other features needs to be investigated is valid, his statement that verbal aspect itself is affected runs counter to what most linguists say who connect verbal aspect to semantics. This is because semantics should not be changed by context.

To many critics, his work conflates verbal aspect, a verb form category, with *Aktionsart*, a lexical aspect category which interacts with a specific context. Carson sees Fanning's work as seriously flawed, due to its conflation of aspect and *Aktionsart*.[80] Porter's critique of Fanning's work is that it falls short because it

---

80 Donald A. Carson, "An Introduction to the Perfect Debate," 18–25 in *Biblical Greek Language and Linguistics: Open Questions in Current Research*, JSNT Supp: 80, edited by Stanley E. Porter and D. A. Carson (Sheffield: JSOT, 1993), 25.

attempted to harmonise the new with the old.[81] The result of such harmonisation is that grammatical and lexical semantics are conflated.[82] Porter views Fanning's definition of the Perfect as traditional, in that he sees it denoting a "state or condition resulting from a completed action."[83] Porter finds that Fanning's definition of the Perfect fails on his own definitions of *Aktionsart* and aspect.[84] Schmidt critiques Fanning's lack of connecting aspect to morphology.[85] He also states that Fanning accepted traditional categories of tense usage without evaluating them.[86] Evans finds Fanning's approach flawed and agrees with Porter's criticism of Fanning's conflation of aspect and *Aktionsart*.[87] Olsen criticises Fanning and Smith by extension for not making clear distinctions between semantics and pragmatics.[88]

Olsen describes the verb for all tense-forms as having a nucleus and a coda.[89] The nucleus contains the action of the verb, and the coda contains any aftermath or resulting state from that verb's action, if either might become important in the context. She also defines aspect in a temporal manner, where the perfective views the time of the situation in summary, and the imperfective views the time of the situation in detail. The combination of a bipartite view of the verb with the temporal definitions for verbal aspect guides Olsen toward the understanding that a Perfect tense-form is perfective because it looks at the coda of the verb and not the nucleus. Instead of being a property of how an author views the situation, Olsen's description is more about the temporal target that is in view. Olsen does not approach her research from the framework of any one particular theory on verbal aspect, but rather she examines how grammatical aspect contributes to the "aspectual interpretation" through its view on the event time structure represented by its lexical aspect features.[90] Thus, she combines lexical aspect and verbal aspect to provide a comprehensive aspectual interpretation. Olsen's description of the verb itself as consisting of both a nuclear event and a coda is helpful in

---

81 Stanley E. Porter, "In Defence of Verbal Aspect," 26–45 in *Biblical Greek Language and Linguistics: Open Questions in Current Research*, JSNT Supp: 80, edited by Stanley E. Porter and D. A. Carson (Sheffield: JSOT, 1993), 36.
82 Porter, "In Defence," 37.
83 Porter, "In Defence," 38.
84 Porter, "In Defence," 38.
85 His comment is due to the lack of details in Fanning's work. Schmidt, 65.
86 Schmidt, 67.
87 Evans, *Verbal Syntax*, 29.
88 Fanning depends upon Smith in a number of places. Olsen, 21.
89 Olsen, 69, 72.
90 Olsen, 71.

separating some verbal components and her inclusion of both verbal aspect and lexical aspect allows discussion of how each produces certain effects.

When analysing the Perfect tense-form, Olsen connects perfective grammatical aspect with a tense operator, and eliminates the need for a separate aspect to explain the perfect tense-form.[91] She understands each form to have both tense and aspect. For her the perfective aspect normally provides the continuing relevance that seems to occur with a perfect tense-form.[92] In this way she links a stative interpretation to the perfective aspect. She points out that two different temporal frames of reference are possible for the perfect tense-form, because the reference time is present, while the event time is prior to that reference point.[93] Olsen analyses the Perfect tense-form as perfective in its aspect, because the situation has reached its coda by the reference time.[94] Olsen defines the Perfect tense-form as having both perfective aspect and present tense to account for its features which oppose it to the Aorist, which has perfective aspect and past tense. She understands them opposing in tense only and not in aspect. It is unclear how a form viewing a situation from its coda can be said to be stative, and then not describe how that state is viewed. Her description includes only how the action is viewed.

Her definition of the aspect of the Perfect tense-form preserves her definitions of tense and aspect, in that tense is deictic locating the timeframe of the reference time to a deictic centre, while aspect is non-deictic and explains how the event time is viewed.[95] The advantage of Olsen's understanding is that she maintains aspect as a way of viewing rather than the target of such a view. She agrees with both Fanning and Binnick that the Perfect and Pluperfect tense-forms are also perfective along with the Aorist.[96] Olsen's understanding of the verbal aspect network might be diagrammed in Figure 4.

Olsen's analysis focuses upon tense and whether or not a verbal form marks the intersection of the reference time with the event or with the event coda. This intersection of reference time with the nucleus of the event is equivalent to imperfective aspect and the intersection of reference time at the coda reflects the perfective aspect.

---

91 Olsen, 169.
92 Olsen, 174.
93 Olsen, 175.
94 Olsen, 297.
95 Olsen, 181.
96 Olsen, 321.

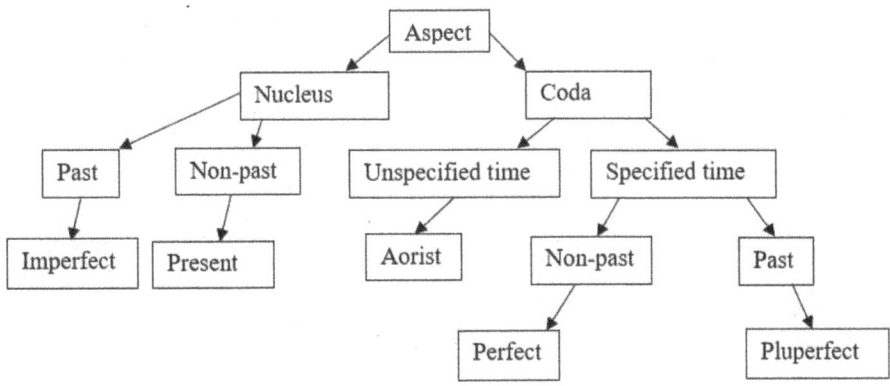

Figure 4: Olsen's Aspectual System

Caragounis is known for addressing the meaning of the Perfect while keeping in mind the whole history of the Greek language. He demonstrates how the Perfect began to be used instead of the Aorist in Greek. This occurred only rarely before the New Testament, but increased in frequency by the time of the New Testament, and appears commonly in later Greek.[97] The Perfect is used in place of a Present tense at times as well.[98] The Perfect tense-form is the most complex of the Greek verbal system, because it relates the past to the present, and the focus can shift from the event to the state.[99] His general definition connects the past to the event and the present to a state.[100] He further relates the Perfect to the Aorist while focusing on events, and the Perfect to the Present while focusing on states.[101]

He relates the intensive uses of the Perfect to recently accomplished past actions.[102] The Perfect as stative is usually intransitive.[103] When Perfects combine with transitive verbs, the effect is more like that of the Aorist, but when they combine with intransitive states, they are more like the Present tense.[104] When referring to the concept that the Perfect transitions from the meaning of a state

---

97 Caragounis, *The Development*, 110.

98 Caragounis, *The Development*, 155.

99 Chrys Caragounis, *New Testament Language and Exegesis: A Diachronic Approach*, WUNT: 323, edited by Jörg Frey (Tübingen: Mohr Siebeck, 2014), 140–141.

100 Caragounis, *New Testament Language*, 141.

101 He calls these states "conditions." Caragounis, *New Testament Language*, 142–143.

102 Caragounis, *New Testament Language*, 144.

103 Caragounis, *New Testament Language*, 144–145.

104 Caragounis, *New Testament Language*, 145.

based on a prior action in the Classical Period to its eventual use as a narrative past tense like the Aorist, Caragounis establishes that this past tense use began even in Classical times and slowly increased in frequency until the Byzantine times, where the past tense use was its main use.[105] Relevant to this research, Caragounis finds ἐσκήκα in 2 Cor 2:13 as one of the examples of the Perfect used like an Aorist in the New Testament.[106] Also, in 2 Cor 11:25, πεποίκα is Aoristic.[107] He bases these decisions on the idea that the event is in view and not a state. Additionally, the Perfect is imbedded in a series of Aorists in a narrative summary.

Collectively the scholars in this section define the Perfect as a perfective, where the verbal situation is viewed in its entirety. All of them understand an event as the situation being viewed. This connection between the event and perfective aspect is retained for the analysis in the next chapter. These scholars also see tense as one of the main differences between the Aorist and Perfect, although Caragounis illustrates that the Perfect can share tense with Aorist as well. The next chapter will decide where to place the present temporal reference of many Perfects.

3.1.2. The Perfect Tense-Form Defined as an Imperfective

Several scholars consider the Greek Perfect and Pluperfect tense-forms as imperfectives. Imperfective verbal aspect is the one that expands the situation or presents it in an ongoing way. It also views the internal make-up of the situation without regard for its whole. Generally speaking, those who find imperfective aspect in the Perfect and Pluperfect tense-forms use two aspects instead of three to describe the Greek verbal system as a whole, although they understand that something other than aspect has been inserted into the Greek tense-form system.

Evans concludes that the Perfect tense-form is an imperfective expressing a state.[108] Evans defines the Perfect as having stative force, imperfective aspect, and non-past temporal reference. He decides that lexical semantics produces the effect where a prior action might be implied, but does not develop how this is produced lexically.[109] He also does not explain where this stative force comes from. In a later analysis section, Evans states that the selection of a Perfect instead of an Aorist is difficult to understand unless as an imperfective; the Perfect simply

---

105 Caragounis, *New Testament Language*, 153.
106 Caragounis, *New Testament Language*, 164.
107 Caragounis, *New Testament Language*, 165.
108 Evans, *Verbal Syntax*, 32.
109 Evans, *Verbal Syntax*, 32.

establishes the relationship between two clauses as one idea, whereas an Aorist would make them separate ideas.[110]

Campbell places the Perfect and Pluperfect tense-forms into the imperfective category along with the Present and Imperfect. Campbell looks at narrative functions and then seeks the semantic values of the verb that best explain those functions.[111] He uses only two aspects, but decides the Perfect and Pluperfect are "heightened" in their proximity or remoteness from their respective imperfective counterparts, the Present and Imperfect tense-forms. He does not explain how the morphological features of the Perfect or Pluperfect connect to this "heightening." If verbal aspect is to be understood as morphologically expressed, then it is difficult to understand how the Perfect and the Present share the same verbal aspect while having different stems, as well as the Pluperfect and Imperfect.

As a system, Campbell's paradigm is helpful in that it allows for aspectual differences between the Aorist and the Perfect and Pluperfect, and allows for aspectual similarities between the Present and Perfect, and between the Imperfect and Pluperfect. Campbell's employment of "heightened" proximity or remoteness language belongs more to the pragmatic discussion of narrative function, or perhaps discourse function of the verb, than it does to semantics. His view does not explain why most of the verbal systems encode semantic information while the Perfect encodes pragmatic information. Campbell's paradigm is unhelpful in that it conflates pragmatics terminology with semantics terminology, and that it connects pragmatic implicatures of "heightened-ness" to the aspect of the Perfect form. While his view appears better on morphological grounds by grouping the Aorist and Future together, the opposite effect is created when he places the Perfect and Present, two morphologically dissimilar forms, into the same category, and likewise the Pluperfect and Imperfect into the same category.

He defines the main aspectual opposition as perfective and imperfective, where perfective sees the whole situation from outside it and the imperfective sees the developing situation from the inside of it.[112] Aspect is a semantic category, which means it is grammaticalised in the verbal morphology, and a necessary part of that verb.[113] This is technically an assumption, but one that is becoming standardised.[114] Aspect is reserved for grammatically expressed viewpoint features

---

110 Evans, *Verbal Syntax*, 152-153.
111 Campbell, *Verbal Aspect, the Indicative Mood*, 4.
112 Campbell, *Verbal Aspect, the Indicative Mood*, 8.
113 Campbell, *Verbal Aspect, the Indicative Mood*, 9.
114 Campbell, *Verbal Aspect, the Indicative Mood*, 9.

while *Aktionsart* is used for procedural characteristics, often expressed lexically.[115] This is how Campbell introduces "lexical aspect." Campbell rejects "completed action" or "in-progress action" as categories for aspect, since they are objective and describe how the action has occurred or is occurring, and thus they belong to *Aktionsart*.[116] The placement of "completed" into the *Aktionsart* category is not necessarily valid, since completed-ness does not describe how the action occurred, only that it did occur. Campbell sees that perfective aspect connects to completed action and imperfective aspect connects to action in progress, but completed actions and actions-in-progress are implications of aspect rather than aspectual descriptions themselves.[117] Here he carefully avoids conflation between verbal aspect and objective components. Aspect is a semantic category and subjective while *Aktionsart* is an objective one, although these two may be inter-related, where aspect affects the perceived *Aktionsart*.[118]

Because Campbell approaches his study from the standpoint that no native speakers exist for the language he is investigating, he adopts a functional approach. He decides that generative approaches are insufficient since the minds of the Ancient Greek speakers cannot be analysed.[119] A way to counter this idea would be to analyse the Neohellenic Greek speaker as a relevant competent mind for understanding Ancient Greek. A critique against Campbell's rationale for his method is that if no native speakers exist, then the social pragmatic layers of the language are also non-existent, and this hampers the systemic functional approach as equally as a lack of native speakers would be for the generative approach. Campbell chooses to be as inductive as possible to prevent the situation where the aspectual value is assumed and then read into the texts.[120]

For Campbell the Perfect tense-form as primarily a discourse form, and thus aligns it with the Present.[121] However, he does not develop either how the Perfect opposes the Present in discourse nor why it shares the same aspect as the Present. He assumes that the Perfect and Present have the same aspect since they co-occur in discourse contexts. The "drawing-in" of the reader creates a proximate context in discourse, where proximity is located with imperfectivity in discourse.[122]

---

115 Campbell, *Verbal Aspect, the Indicative Mood*, 10, borrowed largely from Evans, *Verbal Syntax*, 17.
116 Campbell, *Verbal Aspect, the Indicative Mood*, 11.
117 Campbell, *Verbal Aspect, the Indicative Mood*, 11.
118 Campbell, *Verbal Aspect, the Indicative Mood*, 12.
119 Campbell, *Verbal Aspect, the Indicative Mood*, 19. For a fuller comparison, see John Lyons, *Language and Linguistics: An Introduction* (Cambridge: Cambridge University Press, 1981), 224-235.
120 Campbell, *Verbal Aspect, the Indicative Mood*, 184.
121 Campbell, *Verbal Aspect, the Indicative Mood*, 184.
122 Campbell, *Verbal Aspect, the Indicative Mood*, 185.

Campbell then states that the "striking overlap of the Perfect indicative with the Present in discourse contexts strongly suggests that it shares the same aspect as the latter tense-form."[123] Discourse is cited as having a generally imperfective context, because it is "unfolded before the reader."[124]

If collocation of tense-forms in certain text types should indicate that they share the same verbal aspect, then it should be possible to find this trait in other text types as well. In narrative contexts the Aorist and Imperfect are in opposition, and these do not share the same aspect, yet they are distributed heavily in the same text type. This observation counters Campbell's idea that shared distribution in a text type suggests similar aspect. It seems more likely that tense-forms existing in discourse would be in opposition to each other as they are in narrative. An alternative solution is to see the Present and Perfect sharing temporal reference, or perhaps proximity, in discourse contexts rather than sharing identical verbal aspect, but Campbell does not address this possibility. This is also mirrored in the narrative context where the Aorist and Imperfect share temporal reference, while having opposite verbal aspect. Campbell could have viewed discourse as a proximate context, rather than an imperfective context, opposing narrative as a remote context. Then, it would be clear that the Perfect and Present shared a pragmatic property of proximity rather than an aspectual property of imperfectivity. He emphasises the use of the Perfect in discourse contexts partly to counter the conclusion by Wackernagel and Chantraine, that the Perfect gradually assumed roles of the Aorist, and lost its distinctiveness, and then became obsolete.[125] This discourse context establishes a clear role for the Perfect not shared with the Aorist, thus it appears to remain distinct from the Aorist. Wackernagel and Chantraine's claim has merit though since the Perfect eventually was used like the Aorist. Cross-linguistic information supports the claim made by Wackernagel and Chantraine in that the Perfect and Aorist came to overlap each other's roles. For example, Latin dismissed the Aorist once this occurred and made the Perfect tense-form into a simple preterite.[126] Campbell does not treat verbal stems here or the formal properties of the verbs. Campbell's understanding might be diagrammed as in Figure 5.

While Campbell's system places the aspect division as the primary one, his apparent placement of remoteness/proximity division as next in the order of

---

123 Campbell, *Verbal Aspect, the Indicative Mood*, 185.
124 Campbell, *Verbal Aspect, the Indicative Mood*, 185.
125 Campbell, *Verbal Aspect, the Indicative Mood*, 184.
126 Caragounis, *New Testament Language*, 152.

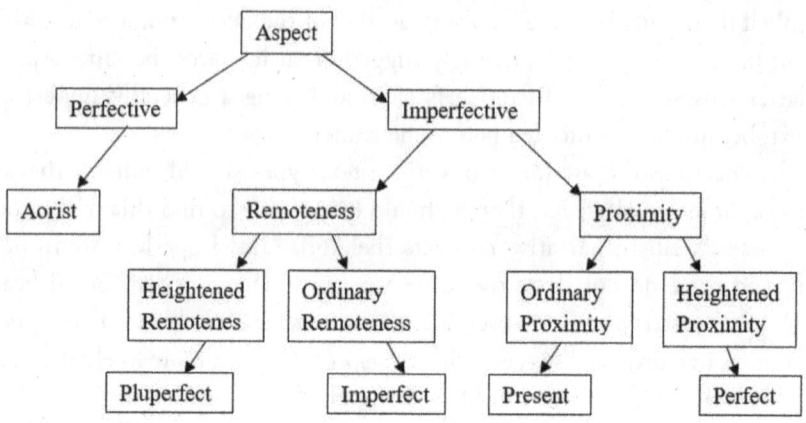

Figure 5: Campbell's Aspectual System

divisions seems misplaced as remoteness appears to be based on the augment in his model. The "heightening" comes last and seems connected to the reduplicant. The reduplicant is closer to the stem generally, so this division should come before one based on the augment.

Evans connects the imperfective aspect of the Perfect to a state. Campbell suggests this connection earlier, but later applies the imperfective aspect of Perfect tense-forms to ongoing action. It seems that at some level both scholars see a connection between imperfectivity and states. This connection between imperfective aspect and a stative situation is retained for the analysis in the next chapter.

3.1.3. The Perfect Tense-Form Defined as a Stative

Several scholars recognise that the Greek Perfect and Pluperfect tense-forms consist of stative verbal aspect. Stative verbal aspect is the one that describes a state of the subject having performed an action. It also does not view the action which causes this state, but focuses instead on the status of the subject of the sentence. Generally speaking, those who find stative aspect in the Perfect and Pluperfect tense-forms use three or more aspects instead of two to describe the Greek verbal system as a whole, although they usually define verbal aspect as a linguistic category more precisely than scholars discussed previously.

McKay states that "the perfect tense expresses the state or condition of the subject of the verb."[127] He qualifies this further, "The perfect aspect expresses the

---

127 McKay, *A New Syntax*, 45.

state or condition of the subject of the verb, as a result of an action (logically a prior action)."[128] Retention of the "logically prior action" is one way that McKay's explanation is different from that of Porter. McKay retains the "logically prior action" as a necessary component, while at the same time he carefully avoids definite temporal reference for this component. He later adds a qualification to his definition, "The ancient Greek perfect expresses the state or condition of the subject of the verb, as the result of a prior action, but most often with comparatively little reference to the action itself."[129] For McKay the subject of a Perfect tense-form is usually responsible for the event that caused this state.[130] He lists a few verbs in Greek that usually seem only stative in the Perfect tense. He names οἶδα as the most common of these.[131] The event which produces the state in a Perfect tense may remain part of the context enough to become modified by an adverbial phrase that normally modifies an Aorist.[132] This ability of the Perfect to have the same adverb type that modifies Aorist tense-forms will be analysed later to determine that many of these same Perfects are eventive rather than stative. McKay is also convinced that an Aorist verb might have been used instead of the Perfect where the Perfect denotes a past action.[133] McKay's analysis allows for two interpretations for the Perfect, a present state and a past action, but does not delineate when each will be evident, or why both are available.

Porter introduces a "rigorous and thorough application of systemic linguistics" to the Greek verb system.[134] He analyses the Greek verb system, including his treatment of verbal aspect from the perspective of Halliday's work on Systemic Functional Linguistics.[135] Porter relates the study of linguistics to the

---

128 McKay, *A New Syntax*, 31.

129 Kenneth L. McKay, "On the Perfect and Other Aspects in New Testament Greek," *NovT* 23:4 (1981): 296.

130 McKay suggests that one effect of the Perfect has over the Aorist, is to highlight responsibility of the subject. McKay, "The Use of the Perfect," 40; McKay, *A New Syntax*, 32. Also see Chantraine, *Histoire du Parfait*, 176.

131 McKay, *A New Syntax*, 31. The necessity of this conclusion for οἶδα as present-only is countered in Chapter 4 by illustrating that this verb is really a Perfect in all respects having both a reference to prior complete action and present relevance of a continuing state from that completed action.

132 McKay, *A New Syntax*, 32. McKay mentions two other places where he deals with this idea; Kenneth L. McKay, "On the Perfect and Other Aspects in New Testament Greek," *NovT* 23:4 (1981): 314–322; and Kenneth L. McKay, "Style and Significance in the Language of John 21:15-17," *NovT* 27:4 (1985): 326-327.

133 McKay uses 1 Cor 15:4 as an example. This passage is treated in greater depth in Chapter 4.

134 Porter, *Verbal Aspect*, 1.

135 Carson and Silva both point out that Porter's analysis is not dependent on his model, Systemic Functional Linguistics. Carson, "Porter/Fanning Debate," 24. Moisés Silva, "A Response to Fanning and Porter on Verbal Aspect," *Biblical Greek Language and Linguistics: Open Questions in Current Research*, JSNT Supp. 80, edited by Stanley E. Porter and D. A. Carson (Sheffield: JSOT, 1993), 77.

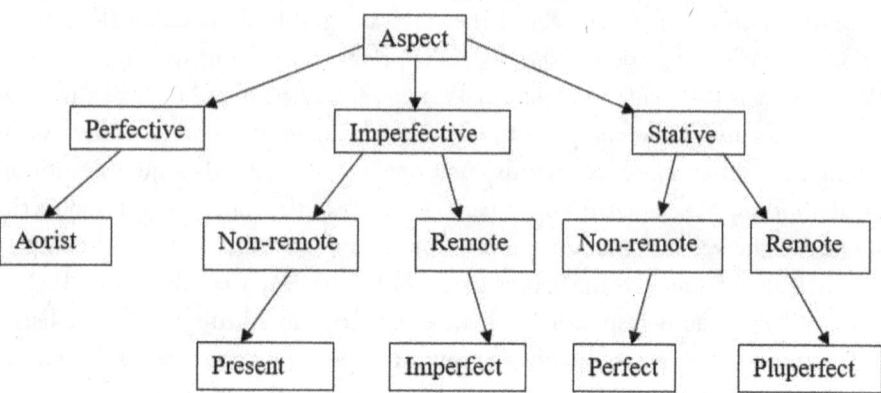

Figure 6: Porter's Aspectual System

hermeneutical task of interpreting what an author meant.[136] Porter prefers a functional approach over a formal since he views Greek as a dead language.[137] In doing so, Porter equates "formal" with psychological approaches, in a way that suggests that he opposes cognitive models as well.[138]

Porter uses three aspects to explain the Greek verbal system instead of two aspects preferred by most theorists.[139] He calls the third aspect "stativity" and places the Perfect and Pluperfect tense-forms into the third aspect. Using this paradigm, Porter decides that stativity is the uncancellable aspect for the Perfect and Pluperfect and that tense along with *Aktionsart* are determined from the context. He defines the stative element in stativity as the "state of the subject" of the verb.[140] Porter's model might be diagrammed as in Figure 6.

Positively, Porter's view on how verbal aspect connects to the various verb forms carefully groups morphologically similar forms into the same aspectual category. The main difference between Porter and many others is that he understands that three aspects exist in the Greek verbs system, rather than two for the others. The aspect division is primary in his model while remoteness is last. This makes better sense of the order of morphemes, than do Fanning's or Campbell's. His model is the cleanest one of the models analysed in the literature review.

---

136 Porter, *Verbal Aspect*, 3.
137 Porter, *Verbal Aspect*, 7.
138 Porter, *Verbal Aspect*, 7.
139 Porter, *Verbal Aspect*, 89.
140 Porter, *Verbal Aspect*, 259.

The first set of criticisms against stativity as a proper aspect for the Perfect tense-form, counters the idea that this state belongs to the grammatical subject in every case. Campbell criticises the understanding that a Perfect is a state of the subject, because this description fails to explain what occurs with transitive lexemes.[141] Transitive lexemes apply that relevant state more with the object rather than with the subject. Campbell, for example, challenges McKay's interpretation of John 7:22. Here, McKay states, Moses is the responsible party for giving the people circumcision because of the Perfect tense, but Campbell states that the Patriarchs are the responsible party, reminding that the text itself says that it is not Moses. Campbell's point regarding who is actually responsible seems a bit forced here as Moses is still responsible for writing down the words of the Patriarchs and transmitting the circumcision tradition to the Israelites through the act of writing the Torah. The point of John 7:22 is that it, first, addresses the common perception of the people that Moses is responsible for circumcision and then moves to a more precise agent, namely Patriarchs. As it is evident, a Perfect might portray the responsibility of the subject for the action. This possibility will be retained in this study as a pragmatic implicature. Even though Campbell's criticism of McKay's responsibility of the subject appears to be forced, his critique of stativity for transitive verbs seems valid, as an event is more in view here rather than a state.

The next set of criticisms against stativity for the Perfect involves the idea that the Perfect is not the only tense-form that displays a state. Fanning recalls that the lexical component of verbs often denotes the resultant values for the verb, and for these, a stative idea is apparent for both Perfects and Preterits.[142] This means an Aorist can be stative as well. Evans states that stative verbs exist in both Present and Aorist tense-forms, and not only Perfect tense-forms.[143] The voice of the verb makes a difference in the stative force of both the Perfect and the Aorist, where passive prefers a state and the active prefers an event.[144] Even though this is true, the Perfect allows for a stronger sense of state than does the Aorist in Greek, and this difference does not seem to be a lexical property.[145]

---

141 He is critiquing McKay's wording, although Porter's idea is similar. Campbell, *Verbal Aspect, the Indicative Mood*, 166.

142 Fanning, 115. Robert William McCoard, *The English Perfect: Tense-Choice and Pragmatic Inferences* (Amsterdam: North Holland, 1978), 44-45, 56-60.

143 Evans, *Verbal Syntax*, 30.

144 Fanning, 115.

145 Fanning, 116; McKay, "On the Perfect and Other Aspects," 316-322.

The third set of criticisms involves whether or not "stativity" belongs in a category called, "verbal aspect. " Porter's paradigm is helpful in that it allows for aspectual differences between the Aorist and the Perfect and Pluperfect, but appears to make the error of conflating *Aktionsart* with aspect by using the term "stativity" to refer to the aspect of the Perfect, since this is defined as a state of the subject and a state is usually understood as a lexical property. Comrie draws attention to the idea that the opposite of stativity is dynamicity, another lexical property.[146] This makes sense, because pairs of opposites like stativity and dynamicity belong in the same set. Typically, dynamicity and stativity are placed in the *Aktionsart* category. It as though one must either keep both of these as lexical properties, or somehow not see them as opposites if they are members of different sets. Fanning criticises Porter's portrayal of the Perfect's aspect as stative, due to "stative" belonging to the *Aktionsart* category. Although Fanning champions the idea of stativity as belonging to the Perfect, he categorises this component as an *Aktionsart* rather than an aspect.[147] Whether this term is properly belonging to the *Aktionsart* category or not, it is apparent that it is not a viewpoint from which a speaker views a situation, neither is it a manner for a speaker to perceive a situation.

Several scholars voice concern over moving stativity from an *Aktionsart* category to the aspect category. For example, Schmidt connects Porter's approach to the Greek Perfect with *Aktionsart* approaches, since "stative" is the term he chose.[148] Evans decides that stativity for the Perfect is an *Aktionsart* that became grammaticalised into that form.[149] This assumes that stativity is a lexical property that was added to the Perfect tense form, and that it is independent from the form. For Olsen stativity is not a semantic feature because the pragmatic context and the particular verb form used provide variation between stative readings and dynamic readings.[150] She categorises stativity as a pragmatic interpretation. Olsen decides that the state-like properties that the Perfect tense-forms exhibit occur due to perfective aspect combining with dynamic lexical aspect.[151] Campbell suggests that in general, stativity is regarded as an *Aktionsart* rather than an aspect.[152] Porter's definition of aspect for the Perfect still says more about the status of the

146 Comrie, *Aspect*, 48, 50.
147 Fanning, 117.
148 Schmidt, "Two Approaches," 71.
149 Evans, *Verbal Syntax*, 22.
150 Olsen, 268.
151 Olsen, 324.
152 Campbell, *Verbal Aspect, the Indicative Mood*, 171.

subject than it does about the author's perspective on the situation. This makes the state of the subject an objective situation in view, rather than a subjective portrayal by the speaker or author.

While Fanning's claim that stativity is not a verbal aspect is seemly valid, his placement of "stativity" in the *Aktionsart* category is still problematic. He criticises Porter for the same reason Porter criticises him. Each says that the other is not rigorous in maintaining the distinction between aspect and *Aktionsart* in theory. Citing McKay for support, Fanning describes that for situations that are apparently stative, the perfective focuses on an entrance to that state, while the imperfective focuses on the ongoing state.[153] This is helpful in that it distinguishes between how the Aorist and Present handle stative lexemes; and this distinction will prove useful for examining the state associated with the Perfect.

Both of the scholars who connect stative aspect to the Perfect also connect this state with subject of the sentence. After the critics interact with both views, it is increasingly unclear how to categorise states and stativity. Is a state a lexical property? Or is it an *Aktionsart*? Or is it an aspect? Clear criteria are needed to separate issues here. Due to "state of the subject" being a potential aspect for the Perfect, the connection of stativity to verbal aspect as a subjective category will be analysed further in the next chapter.

3.1.4. The Perfect Tense-Form Defined Temporally

Tense and temporal reference are two related categories variously thought to relate either to the form of the verb, to a particular morpheme in the verb, or to the contextual temporal markers around the verb. The idea that the Perfect tense-form had a temporal reference is ancient. Porter cites Dionysius Thrax as categorising the Aorist, Imperfect, Perfect, and Pluperfect as past tense forms.[154] Porter follows Robins in his critique of Dionysius.[155] The Stoics, on the other hand, placed the Perfect into the present reference category rather than the past.[156]

Mourelatos sees the Perfect as denoting the phase of time reference rather than an aspect. This is understood as a phase after the action has occurred. This specifically marks the action as prior to and relevant to a reference point, or

---

153 Fanning, 139.
154 Porter, *Verbal Aspect*, 19.
155 Porter, *Verbal Aspect*, 20. R. H. Robins, "Dionysius Thrax and the Western Grammatical Tradition," *Transactions of the Philological Society* (1957): 67-106; R. H. Robins, *A Short History of Linguistics* (London: Longmans, 1979), 36.
156 Porter, *Verbal Aspect*, 21.

state.[157] This puts the differences between the Perfect and others in a tense category rather than an aspect category. It is not clear if the Perfect marks the action as prior to the state and places it in the past. For example, any action that causes a state to exist must be logically prior to that state. This priority is a necessary property of all actions relative to their resultant states, and true whether a Perfect tense-form or a different tense-form is used to portray the situation.

Citing McCoard, Fanning reminds that both "he has died" (Perfect) and "he died" (Preterite) have the same present relevance that the person is dead, thus posing problems for the Greek Perfect being uniquely stative.[158] In other words, one does not require a Perfect tense-form to see the connection between a prior event and a consequent state. This further supports the idea that the connection between event and state is not based on either the Perfect tense or upon aspect, but upon something intrinsic to logic. Fanning understands the relationship between the event and state in the Perfect as temporal, although he admits that a logical relationship is possible.[159]

When discussing tense, Olsen distinguishes between event time, reference time, speech time, and a deictic centre.[160] Using the concept of the deictic centre, Olsen analyses the Pluperfect as providing past time reference relevant to this deictic centre. This is largely due to combining past time reference and perfective aspect.[161] Olsen discusses the Perfect tense-form as combining present time reference with perfective aspect. She decides that the Perfect is the perfective form for the present time since the Present needs a perfective to fill the paradigm. This combination explains why the Perfect tense-form exhibits a present reference.[162] This explanation contrasts this tense-form with the Aorist tense-form, in that while both are perfective, the Perfect tense-form has present tense while the Aorist tense-form has none. Her analysis does not address how the Perfect uses its aspectual or temporal framework to refer to past events.

Caragounis says that the Greek verb forms express aspect and time equally.[163] For Caragounis, the Perfect tense-form expresses Perfective aspect along with past temporal reference.[164] In a similar vein, Crellin defines the Perfect aspect

---

157 Fanning, 107. A. P. D. Mourelatos, "Events, Processes, and States," *Linguistics and Philosophy* 2 (1978): 415-434.

158 Fanning, 111; McCoard, 44-45, 56-60.

159 Fanning, 112.

160 Olsen, 6.

161 Olsen, 294.

162 Olsen, 296.

163 Caragounis, *The Development of Greek*, 317.

164 Caragounis, *The Development of Greek*, 318.

as "placing a reference point from which an event is viewed as having previously taken place."[165] This reference point can occur at the time of speaking, or at some other relevant point in time. However, the Greek Perfect does not consistently select a timeframe, behaving sometimes like a simple Present or Imperfect tense.[166]

The relationship between the Perfect tense-form and its temporal reference is more complicated than simply having a specific reference or having none would imply. To specify some of this complexity, Crellin lists situations where the Perfect will express past time reference:

- If the verb does not describe an atelic state that the subject participates in.
- If the verb describes a causative change-of-state and it has a specialised non-reducing stem.
- If the verb describes a causative change-of-state and has a labile stem that can be used in a non-reducing way.

For situations where past reference is optional:

- If the verb is a non-causative change-of-state verb.
- If the verb describes a causative change-of-state and it has a specialised non-reducing stem.
- If the verb describes a change-of-state that both a subject and an object participate in.

For situations where past reference is not found:

- The subject was inanimate and fixed.
- The resultant state was referenced immediately.
- The Perfect active was used in a control construction, expressed a command, or expressed a wish.
- The adverb ετι was collocated with the verb.

For situations where past reference was found:

- Direct reference was made to the period prior to the reference time, perhaps by an adverb.

---

165 Crellin, "The Greek Perfect," 49.
166 Crellin, "The Greek Perfect," 50.

- The resultant state came about in an adjunct phrase.[167]

The first set involves lexical semantics, the second involves valency, and the third and fourth involve close contextual considerations. Crellin sees the problem complicated by the issue of transitivity and in particular the verbs which exhibit labile transitivity.[168] This type of transitivity is for causative change-of-state verbs where the agent who caused the action is not in the context and the patient that received the action is in the subject position.[169] Crellin's work establishes the complexity of the relationship between the Perfect tense-form and temporal reference, and in doing so, accounts for when the Perfect can be either past-referring or present-referring. His work also provides clues as to why the Perfect tense-form can do both.

Tense or temporal properties are subsumed under remoteness/proximity division in some systems. Remoteness is the broader concept including remote time, logical remoteness, and narrative remoteness.[170] For Campbell remoteness is primarily a spatial category, and subsumes the other three types of remoteness under that one.[171] This placement of "spatial remoteness" might be better placed under a logical remoteness category, because it is a cleaner paradigm to have all of the remoteness categories as deriving from logical remoteness.[172] His description of remoteness later in the paragraph seems to fit the idea of logical remoteness being primary. "The 'distance' evoked by remoteness is thus not physical or literal, but is rather figurative and abstract—used in order to achieve linguistic purposes."[173] Campbell concludes that the Perfect tense contains present temporal reference.

Deciding that a Perfect tense-form is strictly a tense, such as the "Extended Now" theory does, presents an understanding that does not consistently work for Greek Perfects because Perfect tense-forms can take adverbs of a time different than the reference time, just like the Aorist can take adverbs of the present time.[174] Although according to Porter, both Dionysius and the Stoics made an error by "overemphasizing tense," and that they incorrectly identified what aspect

---

167 Crellin, "The Greek Perfect," 252, 253.
168 Crellin, "The Greek Perfect," 70.
169 Crellin, "The Greek Perfect," 64.
170 Campbell, *Verbal Aspect, the Indicative Mood*, 15. Campbell's understanding is largely borrowed from Rodney J. Decker, *Temporal Deixis of the Greek Verb in the Gospel of Mark with Reference to Verbal Aspect*, SBG: 10 (New York: Peter Lang, 2001), 41.
171 Campbell, *Verbal Aspect, the Indicative Mood*, 15.
172 His conclusion is consistent with Grammaticalisation theory where spatial items lead to more grammatical categories, and from concrete to abstract.
173 Campbell, *Verbal Aspect, the Indicative Mood*, 15.
174 Fanning, 109.

was, it seems apparent that native speakers of Greek in close temporal proximity to our NT writings understood the Greek verb to contain temporal reference.[175] If the ancient grammarians analysed the Perfect to have temporal properties, then writers contemporary with the ancient grammarians would have selected the Perfect based on this understanding. It seems best to understand the Perfect as having some associations with temporal reference, but not go to the extreme of assigning it an absolute temporal reference time.

Temporal reference is carried out by deixis, such as the words, νῦν, which indicates present time, along with ἄρτι, ἤδη, πάλιν, ὡς, τότε, πάντως, ἕως, μέχρι, ὅταν, and πρίν.[176] Porter explains that temporal reference is associated with verbal forms due to implicature, but this is not part of the aspect for that verbal form.[177] An implicature can be cancelled by the presence of another feature in context while aspect cannot.[178] The relationship between tense-form usage and temporal reference is a convention.[179] McKay is parallel to Porter in the understanding that temporal reference is not primary to the tense-form. McKay suggests that the Perfect tense appears mostly in present time contexts and timeless contexts.[180] For Porter indicative and non-indicative are the two sets of inflectional forms for Greek, but he does not discuss Injunctive forms anywhere in his work, other than to dismiss their relevance.[181] These Injunctive forms may be the source for tenseless, aspect-only verbal ideas.

The debate regarding temporal reference moves outside the scope of this project and will not be developed further here. Although temporal reference is an important consideration, discussion of temporal properties has little to do with aspect. The main reason to address tense at this point is to rule out the idea that temporal reference has the same connection to the morphology of the Perfect as does verbal aspect. Those who connect the tense of the Perfect with the past, usually mention an event and those who connect it to the Present usually mention a state.

---

175 Porter, *Verbal Aspect*, 22.
176 Porter, *Verbal Aspect*, 101.
177 Porter, *Verbal Aspect*, 103.
178 Porter, *Verbal Aspect*, 104.
179 Porter, *Verbal Aspect*, 104.
180 McKay, *A New Syntax*, 45.
181 Porter, *Verbal Aspect*, 164.

3.1.5. The Perfect Tense-Form Defined as an Anterior

The Perfect tense is regarded by some scholars as an anterior. This means that it is a Present looking back on the past. This idea of the anterior often combines temporal elements with aspectual ones, which makes it difficult to separate what is aspectual from what is temporal. Because of this blending, the anterior needs treated in a separation section. It relies on a view of aspect similar to the "point-of-view" from which the author views a situation, rather than a "way of viewing" preferred in this study. Most scholars analyse "anterior" as a temporal category, rather than aspectual, so it is treated here.[182]

Dahl's application of formal linguistics to Vedic Sanskrit deserves special attention at this point. Vedic Sanskrit is from the same Indo-European language family as Greek. The Vedic Perfect exhibits the same features of reduplication as the Greek Perfect, and it eventually becomes a narrative past tense in later Sanskrit much like the Perfect did in Greek. Dahl examines Vedic Sanskrit from two perspectives, "formally oriented theoretical semantics" and "linguistic typology."[183] His method includes gaining "precise ideas about the semantic motivation behind a given set of discourse functions in the sense that the cluster of readings associated with a given morphological category provides important heuristic clues for determining its semantic properties."[184] He begins with pragmatics to arrive at semantics. In his overall methodology he is similar to Campbell. He analyses the whole set of functions to see what common thing motivates them. He identifies two sets of problems which he calls intra-paradigmatic coherence and inter-paradigmatic contrasts. In other words, all the verbs of a given tense-form need to have something in common, and each tense-form needs to have something that consistently contrasts it with the remaining tense-forms.[185] Here he calls remoteness both temporal and subjective.[186] This is contra Campbell who calls it spatial and aspectual remoteness.

---

182 This is regarded as a member of the "tense" category, rather than the "aspect" category. Reichenbach develops the pieces to construct anteriority. Hans Reichenbach. *The Elements of Symbolic Logic* (London: Collier-MacMillan, 1947), 287-298. Klein develops this in relation to the Perfect. Klein, 29. Johnson applies this to the verbal aspect discussion. Marion R. Johnson, "Unified Temporal Theory," *Tense and Aspect*, Syntax and Semantics: 14, edited by Philip J. Tedeschi and Annie Zaenen (New York: Academic Press, 1981), 152. McCoard develops "extended-now" theory. McCoard, 123. Von Stechow provides further development of these ideas. Arnim von Stechow, "Eine erweiterte Extended-Now Theorie für Perfekt und Futur," *LiLi* 113 (March 1999): 88.

183 Eystein Dahl, *Time, Tense and Aspect in Early Vedic Grammar: Exploring Inflectional Semantics in the Rigveda*, Brill's Studies in Indo-European Languages & Linguistics: 5 (Leiden: Brill, 2010), 1.

184 Dahl, *Time, Tense and Aspect*, 3.

185 Dahl, *Time, Tense and Aspect*, 5.

186 Dahl, *Time, Tense and Aspect*, 7.

Dahl defines the Present as having the speech time, event time, and reference time coexisting. The reference time coexists with the event time for the Past tenses, but both occur before the speech time. The Perfect tenses have the speech time consistent with the reference time, but occurring after the event time.[187] Dahl leaves out the key component of a deictic centre from which all the reference times matter in context. His claims about speech time are valid for deictic centre but less likely of the speech time consistently, which could be removed in time from the event time, reference time and deictic centre. He later introduces the deictic centre as "perspective time," or "local evaluation time."[188]

Dahl states that the perfective aspect across languages generally possesses as its most salient reading a sequential progression of verbs within a narrative.[189] This is consistent for the Aorist in both Vedic and Greek. He articulates that iterative readings are more likely to appear with the perfective and habitual readings with the imperfective.[190] Also, the perfective is compatible with a multi-event reading when the cardinality is finite; otherwise, the imperfective will be used.[191] He relates the perfective to the necessity of keeping the event time within the boundaries of the reference time.[192] This appears to provide a temporal boundary for a situation viewed in the perfective.[193] This provides interesting support for a temporal definition of aspect. In this matter Dahl is closer to Comrie rather than to Bache. This is also similar to how Sasse constructs the effects of verbal aspect.[194]

Dahl defines the aspect of the Perfect as "anterior aspect," calling it a "partial precedence relation between event time and reference time, such that the event time partially precedes or is co-extensive with reference time."[195] He seems to combine the two foci of the Perfect to arrive at this definition. The event must be prior to the reference time, and something must extend to the reference time and perhaps beyond. Anterior aspect is a way of handling the aspect of the Perfect as a whole without distinguishing between components of its internal makeup. The fact that a Perfect can take an adverb of durativity, shows that it can coextend the event time to the reference time.[196] This is his way of accounting for how the

---

187 Dahl, *Time, Tense and Aspect*, 49.
188 Dahl, *Time, Tense and Aspect*, 56.
189 Dahl, *Time, Tense and Aspect*, 78.
190 Dahl, *Time, Tense and Aspect*, 80.
191 Dahl, *Time, Tense and Aspect*, 80.
192 Dahl, *Time, Tense and Aspect*, 80.
193 Dahl, *Time, Tense and Aspect*, 80. He is reading Corien Bary (2007, 2009) on Ancient Greek here.
194 Sasse, 535.
195 Dahl, *Time, Tense and Aspect*, 82.
196 Dahl, *Time, Tense and Aspect*, 84.

addition of an adverb of "for ten years" can extend the verbal idea to the reference moment. However, he states that it extends the event time, which shows he has not separated the verbal components. It is better to say that it extends the relevance of the event to the reference time since the event is long ago completed. His examples show that the event was finished much earlier. It may be even better to say that the consequences of the completed event extend to the reference time.

Dahl has elaborated how the Perfect overlaps the Aorist partially but not fully in usage, as well as shows one area where it does not overlap the Present fully. He has already established a general Present emphasis for the Perfect tense and sees that it much overlaps the Present tense-form usage. A Perfect does not denote a situation which is located immediately after the time of speech, while the Present often does.[197] He establishes that the Perfect is restricted to the boundary of the speech time, while the Present may move past it a bit.[198] This provides a strong argument that the Perfect indicative and Present indicative do not fully overlap in temporal reference.[199] He concludes that the Perfect is a present that is retrospective only while the Present is both retrospective and prospective.[200]

On the whole, Dahl establishes that the Perfect tense-form is temporally vague, locating temporal reference anywhere from the event occurring before the reference time up to the event occurring at the same time as the reference time. He does this to establish anterior aspect, but to get that done, his examples definitely alternate between a perfective action and an imperfective state. What he does not establish is that it is always one or the other in his data, and if an action is in view, the perfective aspect works, and if a state is in view, then the imperfective aspect works equally well. The same dichotomy between uses is observed for Greek.

3.1.6. The Perfect Tense-Form Defined Using Its Pragmatic Functions

A number of descriptions of the Greek Perfect tense-forms do not attempt to define a Perfect aspectually, but instead describe it functionally. In other words, they describe the situations that languages might use a Perfect, rather than define its semantics.

Fanning identifies that the grammars have a remarkable consistency in their treatment of the Perfect tense-form.[201] Basically different grammars and scholars

---

197 Dahl, *Time, Tense and Aspect*, 351.
198 Dahl, *Time, Tense and Aspect*, 351.
199 Dahl, *Time, Tense and Aspect*, 351.
200 Dahl, *Time, Tense and Aspect*, 352.
201 Fanning, 103.

define the Perfect as having both a past action causing the condition or state in reference, and a condition or state following that action.[202] The difference between the grammars is usually a matter of emphasis, where some will emphasise the former action and others will emphasise the state or condition.[203] Fanning cites many others as well that argue this situation for the Indo-European Perfect generally.[204] Fanning provides the consensus among scholars that a prior action leading to a state is a linguistic feature separate from perfective and imperfective.[205] This idea suggests that the shift from state to action is somehow categorically different than verbal aspect.

Dahl groups the different readings of the Perfect into two categories. He defines "extended now" to refer to the interval that extends from some earlier point to the present moment of speech or writing. The first category has the event time located prior to the reference time, and the extended-now interval denotes a state holding true after the termination or completion of the event. The second one has the event time interval as coextensive with the reference time and the extended-now interval is interpreted as a continuous state.[206] The grouping of these ideas are roughly compatible with the ideas of the Perfect having either a perfective active event or an imperfective stative situation interpretation.

Since the idea of increased transitivity is often suggested as the reason for the Perfect tense-form to change from a stative present to an eventive past, it is necessary to resolve the issues of how objects and subjects relate to verbs. Crellin provides a study on Perfect tense-forms where he shows how valency, and thus argument structure is affected once a lexeme is placed into a Perfect tense.

Crellin notices a connection between the root stem and the ability of the Perfect to show valency reduction.[207] He establishes later that the Perfect shows valency reduction more often than non-perfect tense-forms, along with the observation that all of the verbs that do this belong to a class of verbs he calls causative change-of-state verbs.[208] Next he analyses lemma which show non-reduction. In the verbs which showed non-reduction, they had a κ attached to the stem.[209] The non-reducing stems are more frequent than the valency reducing ones in a ratio

---

202 Fanning, 104.
203 Fanning, 104.
204 Fanning, 105.
205 Fanning, 106.
206 Dahl, *Time, Tense and Aspect*, 363.
207 Crellin, "The Greek Perfect," 103.
208 Crellin, "The Greek Perfect," 114.
209 Crellin, "The Greek Perfect," 116, 117, 118, 119.

of 10:3.[210] After analysing the corpus statistics, Crellin concludes that for verbs with two stems, one with a kappa and other without a kappa, the kappatic form is used in non-reducing situations while the root stem is used for valency reduction, although verbs that have only one stem, use it for either situation.[211]

Next, Crellin concludes from his analysis that the core semantics of the Perfect must predict that the Perfect active stem of causative change-of-state verbs tends more often to be valency reducing than not.[212] While this articulation still is specific lexically, and might refer more to lexical semantics of causative change-of-state verbs than it does to Perfect semantics, it is equally apparent that the Perfect prefers to view the state following an action, and likewise the state following the change-of-state verbs rather than the event portion which caused those states. This means that the Perfect's connection to stative readings is parallel to this valency reduction phenomenon. Crellin's work is most helpful to the present discussion to rule out the κ within the kappatic Perfects from consideration as a morpheme for verbal aspect. It is related instead to the verbal argument structure. Also, Crellin's work suggests that stativity of the Perfect has a strong connection to its valency reducing stems, thus posing a challenge for stativity belonging to the Perfect tense-form itself.

3.2. Refining the Problem

As it is evident, most scholars separate verbal aspect from tense and *Aktionsart*. They together illustrate how verbal aspect works for a number of Greek tense-forms, especially for the Present and Aorist. They are divided over how to categorise and semantically describe the Perfect. Fanning regards the aspect for the Perfect as perfective, but this is not explained from morphology, nor does the connection to perfective fully explain stative Perfect uses. Stativity is regarded an *Aktionsart*, but it is unclear how this works as context does not appear to shape stativity of the Perfect in the same way that it shapes lexical matters. Campbell regards the Perfect as imperfective, but this neither explains eventive Perfects that are past-referring, nor does it treat stative Perfects well. Relegating stativity to lexis is as unhelpful as placing it into *Aktionsart*. It can explain stative lexemes, but does not explain why the Perfect will be stative while other tense-forms of the same lexeme will be eventive. Porter regards the aspect of the Perfect as

---

210 Crellin, "The Greek Perfect," 117.
211 Crellin, "The Greek Perfect," 126.
212 Crellin, "The Greek Perfect," 160.

stative, but it is unclear how perfective, imperfective, and stative all belong to the same set. It is also unclear how to explain past-referring, event-oriented Perfects. Likewise, it is unclear how stativity is subjective, since it is a state belonging to the subject or perhaps an object that is in view, rather than a manner in which the speaker views a situation. While a greater clarity emerged in verbal aspect studies regarding the Present, Imperfect, and Aorist tense-forms, the same level of clarity has not emerged for the Perfect tense-form.

These three scholars generally are able to keep verbal aspect as a separate category in their definitions.[213] However, all their efforts together do not fully explain the semantic features for the Perfect tense-form seen over time. The changing focus of the Perfect from state to event is unexplained by all three models. Due to this observation, the verbal aspect for the Perfect tense-form remains an unresolved area. The disagreement between the scholars is due in part to the specific element each scholar focused upon leading to the definition of the verbal aspect of the Perfect tense-form, in part to their respective decisions as to what belongs to *Aktionsart* categories, and in part to decisions regarding temporal reference.

The problem is that the Perfect exhibits temporal properties similar to a past tense and to a present tense at the same time. The Perfect also appears to view events in a summary manner, while viewing states in an ongoing manner. Additionally, the Perfect seems to portray present-like states early in a language and then transition over time to mark past-like events. Not only does the Perfect change its focus from state to event and its temporal reference from present to past, but these transitions are substantial, while the Aorist and Present change very little compared to the Perfect. The goal is to locate a semantic for the Perfect that explains all of these behaviours.

4. Conclusion

This chapter has illustrated several different approaches to analysing the Perfect tense-form, with a variety of conclusions involving a single aspect and several clues that suggest the way forward for research. Several areas are yet unresolved; however, a growing consensus is emerging concerning several elements relevant to verbal aspect studies in general and to the different behaviours of the Perfect tense-form.

---

213 Their handling of verbal aspect later in their works produces some problems as they discuss verbal aspect and relate specific aspects within this category to the tense-forms.

A consensus exists regarding the need to separate the verbal aspect from *Aktionsart*. Verbal aspect is related to the stem of the verb and is more subjective than *Aktionsart*, which is more objective and related to the lexical meaning of the word.[214] Therefore, special attention will be given to definitions of verbal aspect that remain subjective. Also, a consensus exists regarding the distinction that must be maintained between semantic and pragmatic components. Pragmatic components can be cancelled by context, while semantic ones cannot. Verbal aspect is both subjective and semantic.

Disagreement exists in the literature regarding temporal reference of the Greek verbs, except for one area. The tense-forms do not point to absolute time. In other words, a one-to-one correspondence between a tense-form and an absolute objective time reference is not observed. However, debate exists whether or not relative time or subjective time is in view. This debate over the verb system in general affects the understanding of the temporal reference for the Perfect. The Perfect is variably understood to be past, present, or non-temporal. The discussion on tense is beyond the scope of this project, but those who understand a past temporal reference usually focus on the event, and those who understand a present temporal reference usually focus on the state. The relationship between these two paired sets is informative.

A consensus exists regarding the nature of perfectivity and its contrasting aspect, imperfectivity. Perfective aspect is related to a complete view of a situation, while imperfective aspect is related to an incomplete view of a situation. Scholars mostly agree that the Greek Aorist has perfective aspect, while the Present and Imperfect have imperfective aspect. However, little agreement exists regarding the Perfect. Fanning concludes that the verbal aspect of the Perfect is perfective, treating its action much like the Aorist.[215] He also understands the Perfect tense-form to have anterior temporal reference and stative *Aktionsart*. Campbell's view is that the Perfect is imperfective, treating its action like the Present.[216] The decision that the Perfect and Present both had imperfectivity is due to the high frequency that the Perfect tense-form occurs in contexts dominated by the Present tense-form. The Perfect has a higher sense of proximity than the Present in Campbell's view.[217] Rather than to opt for either perfective or imperfective,

---

214 Many theorists present verbal aspect and *Aktionsart* as absolutely subjective and absolutely objective respectively. The wording presented here is an attempt to soften the absoluteness a bit to allow for scalable possibilities, while maintaining their general character of subjective and objective as they oppose each other.

215 Fanning, 112, 119-120.

216 Campbell, *Verbal Aspect, the Indicative Mood*, 184, 199.

217 Conversely, the Pluperfect had a higher sense of remoteness over the Imperfect in his view.

Porter defines a third aspect called "stativity," which grammaticalises "the state or condition of the subject as conceived by the speaker."[218] In spite of the disagreement over the Perfect, the purpose for defining the Perfect and one item of methodology are largely agreed upon. The general goal among the scholars is to find the simplest definition for the verbal aspect of the Perfect that adequately explains the most data. This goal also serves to measure the quality of each definition of the Perfect. The analysis of the Perfect as connected to all the tense-forms in a system is considered a better method over analysing the Perfect in isolation from the other tense-forms.

Strengths of the literature reviewed here include a number of careful definitions which avoid both vagueness and conflation. Terminology is established in the literature that enables a discussion of semantic components that allows analysis of each feature separately. Many of the works reviewed articulate the improvements Bache provides over Comrie's definitions, which help to maintain a separation between aspect and *Aktionsart*. Avoidance of temporally laden terms is helpful when keeping elements of verbal aspect as a separate category from tense.

Several unresolved issues remain. The definition of verbal aspect in general is either defined as a "viewpoint" or a "kind-of-view." These are not the same and one's choice here affects both the number and type of potential verbal aspects understood for a language. Defining aspect with temporal terms is either promoted by some scholars or avoided by others. Remoteness is either defined in spatial terms, temporal terms, or logical terms. Attempting to relate Perfects that emphasise a contextually prior action to those that emphasise a contextually current state, while at the same time using a single definition for the verbal aspect of the Perfect produces the most varied element in the approaches and conclusions reached. Thus, the identity of the verbal aspect for the Perfect remains unresolved. Also, since the aspect of the Perfect is variously understood, the manner in which the Perfect opposes the Present or Aorist is unresolved. The way to categorise stativity is unresolved because it is variously understood as a phase of activity, an *Aktionsart*, or as a verbal aspect. This raises another problem regarding whether οἶδα is stative because it is lexically stative, or because it is in Perfect form. The method to analyse the Perfect is debated since valid arguments are articulated for avoiding either diachronic or synchronic approaches. Both approaches base

---

218 Porter, *Verbal Aspect*, 259.

the need to avoid researcher bias as the primary reason for avoiding the other, yet both entail some bias either way.

Several elements from the literature are useful for a foundation to build upon in the next chapter. Understanding verbal aspect as the way a speaker views a situation is primary. Excluding a temporal or objective understanding of verbal aspect prevents conflation of semantic categories. Connecting the verbal aspect of the Perfect to its morphemes is essential to answer why this tense-form behaves like the Aorist sometimes and like the Present at other times, and why the Perfect changes so much over time compared to the other tense-forms. The diachronic analysis includes comparing a Pauline synchronic corpus with a diachronic corpus along with analysing modern periphrastic Perfects compared to ancient synthetic Perfects.

A Way Forward

1. Introductory Remarks

Several salient themes from the literature are important for further development. First, a strict definition of verbal aspect as a category separate from tense and *Aktionsart* is required, and the individual aspects that each tense-form portrays must be members of the same set under that strict category definition. Second, the specific verbal aspect for the Perfect must relate to the diachronic shift in meaning that is apparent for that tense-form, remembering that this form is the one with the greatest shift among all the other tense-forms. Third, the uses that are recognised for the Greek Perfect tense-form must flow naturally from the verbal aspect chosen for the Perfect tense-form. Fourth, the morphology of the Greek Perfect must be compared especially to the Present and Aorist. This stem comparison is performed in order to relate the verbal aspect discussion to the morphemes in the tense-forms. Fifth, the synthetic Greek Perfect should be compared to the periphrastic Greek Perfect because both ways of forming Perfects overlap in their uses, and potentially have a similar aspectual framework. Sixth, the Perfect tense-form overlaps the usage of the Present and Aorist, so much so that the set of functions for the Perfect appears to be dependent upon semantic components similar to the imperfectivity of the Present in some situations and to the perfectivity of the Aorist in others. Seventh, the adverbs that modify Perfect tense-forms suggest what sort of aspect is integral to the Perfect tense-form. A corpus examination of the collocated adverbs provides a fruitful analysis for determining whether a Perfect tense-form highlights an event or a state. These concerns are developed into arguments for a complex aspect in this chapter.[1] While any one of these arguments might not be convincing alone, the combination of these seven elements as a set will both refine the verbal aspect discussion for the Greek language, and more precisely identify the verbal aspect for the Perfect tense-form.

As these seven components are developed in this chapter, it is important to keep in mind the variety of Greek Perfect tense-forms available for analysis. Figure 7 lists a number of Greek Perfect tense-forms for comparison. These represent the different types of Perfects based on morphology. Since morphology is related to aspect and a key component for the argument in this work, all these types are considered in order to counter arguments against a connection between aspect and morphology since different verbs have different spellings. If the verbal aspect established for the Greek Perfect is to be coherent, and also grounded in the morphology, then all of these types need to be considered. It will be shown through the sections of this chapter that all of these morphological types share some common aspectual features that set them apart from the rest of the tense system. This allows researchers to identify the verbal aspect for these as a set, and base that decision on the morphology.

The first four forms are observed throughout the Classical, Post-Classical and Early Byzantine Periods. These are the ones found in the Pauline corpus. The main difference between the four older forms has to do with their reduplication type and particular phonological processes of their reduplication. They are similar in that they are all synthetic forms and have the same uses. The last two forms are representative of the types in Modern Greek, or Neohellenic. The main difference between the two modern forms is that the first one refers to resultant states that accept a direct object and the second one refers to general states of the subject that do not have a direct object. They are similar in composition in that they have one Present and one Aorist form. Aspectually, they are comprised of an imperfective plus a perfective. These are provided in order to analyse verbal aspect of the Perfect diachronically, and because they shed light on how the Perfects are formed more generally.

---

1 This complex aspect is defined in 3.2.1.

Classical and Post-Classical Greek		
Example	Type	Explanation
οἶδα	reduplication	Laryngeal doubling producing vowel diphthong
γέγραπται	reduplication	Consonant plus standardised vowel, or "Ce" type
ἠγαπημένοι	reduplication	Vowel lengthening
ἀκηκόασιν	reduplication	Attic Reduplication
Modern Greek		
ἔχω λύσει	auxiliation	Present + Aorist infinitive
εἶμαι δεμένος	auxiliation	Present + Aorist participle

Figure 7: Different forms of the Greek Perfect. This analysis of the first form was developed in an earlier paper, James E. Sedlacek, "Reimagining οἶδα, Indo-European Etymology, Morphology, and Semantics Point to Its Aspect" *Conversations with the Biblical World* (2016) 206–220, and appears later in this chapter. Haspelmath labels the last form as a new resultative to oppose the other anterior periphrastic "have" perfect. Martin Haspelmath, "From Resultative to Perfect in Ancient Greek," 187–224 in *Nuevos estudios sobre construcciones resultativos. Funcion* 11–12, edited by José Luis Iturrioz Leza (Universidad de Guadalajara: Centro de Investigación de Lenguas Indígenas, 1992), 219.

2. Consideration of Methods

The issue of the linguistic method is a matter of debate when researching questions of meaning. Various concerns involve researcher bias, the need for objectivity in order to be able to test results, and for congruency between the method and the kind of answer it produces. This section will detail one of the issues around objectivity, select a method, and show how the selected method helps answer the research question, "What is the verbal aspect of the Greek Perfect tense-form?"

2.1. Defence of the Eclectic Approach

Both Porter and Campbell prefer functional approaches to linguistics over formal approaches due to the extinction of the language.[2] Campbell further describes

---

2 Porter, *Verbal Aspect*, 7; Campbell, *Verbal Aspect, the Indicative Mood*, 19. They cite John Lyons in support of this idea.

systemic functional approaches as inductive (vs deductive).[3] Although both Porter and Campbell contrast their preferred method, "functional linguistics," over against "formal linguistics," they seem opposed to generative linguistics that depend on cognitive linguistics for its framework, rather than oppose all forms of formal linguistics.[4] Cognitive linguistics of this type analyses how the ancient speaker must have conceived his or her language to work, and then make deductions from this. The problem with a cognitive approach, according to Porter and Campbell, is that today's researchers cannot obtain confirmation from the ancient speaker regarding how they understood their language to work a certain way before the researcher makes any deductions. To a certain extent, scholars using cognitive approaches are subjective regarding how they perceive that the ancient speaker understood the language to work before they make deductions about language that are more objective. This subjectivity by the researcher is considered a weakness because it introduces bias into the analysis before objective decisions are made.

Dahl, like Porter and Campbell, admits that native speakers are unavailable for interpreting ancient languages[5] and that no theoretical approach will make up for the lack of native speakers[6] but he further provides a critique of the single-method approach, and especially a functional one. He then champions the eclectic method. He selects Formal Semantics and Typology as his framework for analysing Vedic.[7] This approach provides the ability for testing hypotheses related to the meaning of grammatical categories.[8] The deductive method avoids subjective judgments when analysing the language. Its opposite, the inductive approach, relies too much on the researcher's reading skill of the language.[9] Functional linguists who rely on inductive approaches have a subjective bias also. The researchers believe that they already fully understand the word string they are researching and then draw conclusions based on how well they read the language. Even though they avoid the subjectivity involved in analysing the unavailable

---

3 Campbell, *Verbal Aspect, the Indicative Mood*, 8, 17, 29-30.

4 This is evidenced by the use of the terms "psychological," "mental patterns," "non-mentalist." Porter, *Verbal Aspect*, 7, 104; Campbell, *Verbal Aspect, the Indicative Mood*, 17. Neither one appears to be countering the type of formal linguistics that uses mathematical approaches.

5 The assumption is that none exist for the purpose of their methods. Dahl, even though he shares Porter and Campbell's concerns regarding not having native speakers, uses nearly an opposite approach for many of the same reasons they cite for their approaches.

6 Dahl, *Time, Tense, and Aspect*, 29.

7 Dahl, *Time, Tense, and Aspect*, ix.

8 Dahl, *Time, Tense, and Aspect*, ix.

9 Dahl, *Time, Tense, and Aspect*, 29.

ancient mind, they introduce another form of subjectivity in the assumption of their reading ability. Just as the cognitive linguist does not have confirmation, neither does the inductive functionalist. Dahl's statement serves as a precaution for scholars that approach languages inductively without consulting native speakers for verification of their hypotheses.[10] In light of this observation, it may be impossible to approach a text without some subjective component. Dahl's concern has legitimacy for the examination of the Greek text. Caragounis confirms Dahl's concern with an example of this kind of flaw in linguistic approaches to Greek " . . . more seriously, misinterpretations of Greek text abound," when referencing researchers doing inductive approaches without a confirmation.[11]

In addition to Dahl's usage of Typology and Formal Semantics, he incorporates cross-linguistic parallels throughout his work, mostly from Indo-European languages. He also uses comparative and historical linguistics to determine the Vedic tense/aspect system.[12] In summary, he employs a collection of methods to produce results. His eclectic approach produces results that can be tested and either passed or failed by the scientific method. Overall, the method in the current study adopts a bias toward the deductive approach utilising multiple methods for analysis showing where they point to the same answer. Rather than cobble a method from pieces of different methods, where the results depend upon the exact arrangement of the pieces, the method in this work argues from one method and then uses other methods to show that they illustrate the same principle. Instead of a cobbled method, it is a group of methods in parallel pointing to the same answer. This study depends on concepts developed in Grammaticalisation Theory for understanding the changes that take place over time within a language. Additionally, this study utilises elements of historical linguistics, morphology, and corpus linguistics where they support the same conclusion. The methods selected for support are typical of many analyses for language change and have proven to be useful for understanding language.

10 In this case, Ancient Greek speakers.
11 His statement is about Porter's work on verbal aspect, but his section applies to several verbal aspect theorists who analyse Ancient Greek from an "Anglo" perspective. Caragounis, *The Development of Greek*, 320. He provides numerous examples in 320-336. Caragounis suggests that English-speaking researchers would do well to consult native Modern Greek speakers to provide some of this confirmation.
12 Eystein Dahl, "Tense and Aspect in Indo-Iranian Part 1: Present and Aorist," *Language and Linguistics Compass* 5:5 (2011): 265-281; "Tense and Aspect in Indo-Iranian Part 2: The Perfect, Futurate, Participial and Periphrastic Categories," *Language and Linguistics Compass* 5:5 (2011): 282-296.

2.2. Definition of Grammaticalisation

Grammaticalisation is explained by Lehmann as a process that changes a lexical item into a grammatical one, or changes an item from less grammatical to more grammatical.[13] This process is characterised by gradual change, where various language items have different degrees of grammaticalisation within the given language.[14] This process often begins with a lexical item, that gets placed into a new syntactic construction. At this point the lexeme takes on a grammatical role. The syntactic construction then reduces to a synthetic one, where the grammaticalised lexeme becomes an affix onto the other word in the construction. Eventually phonological changes occur within the word allowing inflexions to attach.[15] Hopper and Traugott add further important characteristics to Grammaticalisation as the study of language change where a lexical item comes into certain linguistic contexts and then serves grammatical functions.[16] They define a "cline" as the typical direction many items take that have the same kind of changes in the same order.[17] The typical cline is that a lexeme moves from a content item, to a grammatical word, to a clitic, and then to an inflexion.[18] Four parameters mark the level of grammaticalisation. "Extension" is where the lexeme is used in a new context. "Desemanticisation" is where the lexeme loses some of its lexical properties. For example, it might lose its lexical meaning and become a state. "Decategoricalisation," is where the lexeme loses its original semantic category. Here it might lose the category "lexical verb" and becomes a particle toward some grammatical purpose. "Erosion" is where it loses phonological substance.[19] This happens when the lexical syllable gets reduced to a few phonemes. These parameters are typical features for grammaticalised items.

13 Christian Lehmann, *Thoughts on Grammaticalization*, 3rd ed., Classics in Linguistics: 1 (Berlin: Language Science, 2015), 13.

14 Lehmann, *Thoughts*, 15.

15 Lehmann, *Thoughts*, 16.

16 Paul J Hopper and Elizabeth Closs Traugott, *Grammaticalization*, 2nd ed., Cambridge Textbooks in Linguistics (Cambridge: Cambridge University Press, 2003), 1.

17 Hopper and Traugott, *Grammaticalization*, 6.

18 Hopper and Traugott, *Grammaticalization*, 7. A clitic occurs when a lexeme reduces phonologically and attaches itself to another word much like a prefix or suffix.

19 Bernd Heine and Tania Kuteva, *The Changing Languages of Europe*, Oxford Linguistics (Oxford: Oxford University Press, 2006), 43-44.

2.3. Applying Grammaticalisation to Perfect Tense-Forms

Grammaticalisation applies to Perfect tenses in two ways. The reduplicant is the portion of the synthetic Perfect tense-form that is considered grammaticalised. It is understood to be a copy of the original lexeme, but once added before the verb, it has a new context, and begins its grammaticalisation process. The meaning of multiple actions or iterative actions is likely early in the grammaticalisation process, but this changes over time. The first copy of the verb lexeme begins to lose some of its lexical meaning once the verb acquires new contexts that do not mean two or more occurrences of the same action. It also loses some of its morphological bulk as the first syllable erodes. The first copy of the lexeme is reduced to a helping verb at this point and is not a main verb. Later the reduplicant attaches onto the second verb becoming a clitic, and erodes even more once it is attached. A more detailed analysis of reduplication is provided in 3.2.2.2.

The lexical verb "have" or "be" is located before a perfective lexeme to form periphrastic Perfects in Modern languages. The verb "have" or "be" becomes an auxiliary by the same process of grammaticalisation stated earlier for the reduplicant. The verb "have," originally a verb of possession, when it acquires a new context in front of a verb through extension instead of a in front of a noun, desemanticises. Here it loses the meaning of "possess." It now includes a stative meaning. It loses its category of lexical verb in this context and becomes an auxiliary. Once in front of a lexical verb, this stative component adds grammatical information to the main verb. In both English and Greek, the auxiliary verb has not yet lost morphological bulk and is not yet a clitic as it still remains unattached to the following verb. This only means that it has not grammaticalised to the same extent as had the synthetic Greek Perfect by the time of Homer.

Although these two methods of forming Perfects are different, both develop in a parallel fashion, and grammaticalisation explains their meaning. In both formation types, the first component is the grammaticalised component, and the second component is a lexical verb. Both processes of reduplication and auxiliation follow similar pathways, creating states out of either the reduplicant or the auxiliary verb. It will be important to consider this parallel in the analysis of the Greek Perfect.

3. Complexity of the Verbal Aspect for the Perfect Tense-Form

This section will first counter the idea that stativity is a third aspect along with perfective and imperfective by illustrating that it is more objective than the other members. Then, the section will show how the Perfect has two aspects, each connected to a different part of its morphology, and each logically connected to a different part of the verbal process. Seven complementary arguments are presented and their combined force points toward the understanding of complex verbal aspect for the Perfect.

3.1. Challenging the Concept of "Stativity" with the Subjectivity Criterion

Defining verbal aspect as the subjective way in which the author or speaker views and consequently portrays the verbal activity or state that he or she is referencing emerges from the literature. It is the view of an author or speaker on that situation and not something objective about the situation in view. Since an author or speaker can view the same situation as either an incomplete process or a complete situation, this reveals the priority of the author or speaker having a subjective choice.

Under the umbrella category of verbal aspect, several definitions have been explained and defended for the specific verbal aspects of the various Greek tense-forms. "Perfective" is associated with the Aorist tense-form, and "imperfective" is associated with the Present and Imperfect tense-forms. "Perfective" is the aspect speakers use when viewing the situation in its entirety. "Imperfective" is the aspect speakers use when viewing the situation partially. At first glance, it appears that neither of these two explain the aspect of the Perfect tense-forms, yet the existence of these two as defined above also appear to exclude the existence of any third aspect. For example, if the speaker either views the situation completely or incompletely, this does not leave room for something in between the two that shares the same category. Introduction of a third aspect would have to be something quite unlike these two, and would thus raise suspicion that it does not belong to the same category as the first two.

This leaves several possibilities for the aspect of the Perfect: perfective, imperfective, or something quite different. Several scholars have tried to understand the Perfect as either one or the other of these possibilities, yet with the difficulties established in the previous chapter. Fanning prefers perfective,[20] Campbell prefers imperfective,[21] Porter prefers something else, such as "stativity,"[22] The concept of "stativity" does not seem to belong to the same set, where "perfective" and "imperfective" are members. "Perfective" and "imperfective" by definition relate to the speaker or author's subjective perspective on a situation, and are unrelated to the grammatical subject or verb lexemes in the sentence. "Stativity" is related to the state of the grammatical subject in the sentence, so it points to something more objective in character rather than to something subjective. It is not a way the speaker or author is able to view the situation but a new situation related to the grammatical subject that is viewed instead.

In order to assess the concept that stativity is not subjective, it is necessary to examine a few sentence examples in English, as the implicatures of each word string will be familiar to readers. Also, the Pauline corpus does not contain examples of the Aorist, Present, and Perfect tense-forms having the same immediate context. Selecting an English example allows the analyst to alter only the verbal lexeme. A Greek example or two that performs similarly to each English example will be included.

First, this analysis will assume stativity can be a verbal aspect and attempt to understand it as a subjective element related to the author. Second, it will construct a theoretical model for the verbal aspect of the Perfect. Take the following examples where the speaker views the verb "walk," in a situation where Jack walks to the store.

A.	I view "walk" completely	= Jack <u>walked</u> to the store.
B.	I view "walk" incompletely	= Jack <u>was walking</u> to the store when . . .
C.	I view "walk" statively	= Jack <u>has walked</u> to the store. (Jack is in the state of being a person who walked to the store at least once.)

In A, "completely" provides the speaker's manner of viewing Jack's walking situation. In B, "incompletely" provides the speaker's manner of viewing Jack's walking. This is the same action viewed in different ways by the speaker, only by changing the aspect form. In C, regardless of how "statively" is defined, "stative" doesn't provide the speaker's view, but provides an objective reality related to the

---

20 Fanning, 112, 119-120.
21 Campbell, *Verbal Aspect, the Indicative Mood*, 184, 199.
22 Porter, *Verbal Aspect*, 259.

subject, Jack. Jack's status is the "thing" that is in view, but his status is not the way the speaker views the situation. At this point it is increasingly difficult to consider "stativity" as belonging to the category of verbal aspect where its members are authorial subjective portrayals of a situation. The state of the subject is the situation that is portrayed by the author in some manner not yet defined by "stativity."

While a Perfect originally and usually lends itself to stative readings, this state is viewed by the author in a similar way as to how imperfective actions are viewed. The difference is that the objective component in view has changed, while the manner of viewing remains the same. Perfect verbs view states imperfectively in the same manner as imperfective verbs view actions.

After adding a second clause to the previous examples, it is easy to see how the aspect of the verbs of both clauses construct the two situations either as overlapping them or separating them. For example, when two perfective clauses are joined by "when," the actions are understood to be separate, and sequential, without the second one interrupting the first. The non-interruptibility of two perfective clauses is attested more often in the narrative genre.

A. Jack <u>walked</u> to the store, when Sally found him.

In A, the action of Sally finding Jack typically follows the action of Jack walking, so that typically Jack arrives to the store before Sally finds him, and certainly not during the event of Sally finding him. The typical implication is that Sally found Jack at the store. If the sentence was understood to mean that Jack began his walk after Sally found him, then an optional implication is that Jack walked to the store as a consequence of Sally finding him. A similar Greek example occurs in 1 Cor 16:3.[23]

1.) ὅταν δὲ παραγένωμαι, οὓς ἐὰν δοκιμάσητε, δι' ἐπιστολῶν τούτους πέμψω ἀπενεγκεῖν τὴν χάριν ὑμῶν εἰς Ἰερουσαλήμ· (1 Cor. 16:3)

Then, when I arrive, I will send those whom you approve with letters of explanation to carry your gift to Jerusalem. (NET)

---

23 Examples like these were numerous in narrative literature, yet difficult to find in the Pauline corpus. Some did exist in the Pauline corpus and are provided here, but more frequent examples exist in the Gospels and Hebrews. Searches were performed using "when" inside English text and ἐπεί or ὅτε in Greek text.

[παραγένωμαι, Aorist subjunctive middle indicative; πέμψω Future active indicative]

In example 1, Paul's action of coming to Corinth is complete before he sends out the approved persons. Typically, the employment of the Aorist keeps actions separate. Although the second verb is a Future, this separateness would be the same if Paul used two Aorists as well. This separateness of the actions is not aspect itself but one of the implications of aspect when joining two clauses. The action of the sending the chosen does not interrupt the action of coming to Corinth. The inclusion of the word "when" in most English translations helps force this implication in English, but this particle is not needed in the Greek for the actions to be separate.[24] The use of ὅταν in this passage may be included to indicate uncertainty in the arrival time, and might have been translated "whenever."

In a similar construction to that in A, but with the first clause having an imperfective verb, the second clause in B interrupts the action of the first clause.

B. Jack <u>was walking</u> to the store, when Sally found him.

In B, the action of Sally finding Jack interrupts the action of Jack walking, so that Sally finds him while Jack is still enroute to the store. The implication is that Sally found Jack before he arrived at the store. A similar example is in Gal 2:12.

2.) πρὸ τοῦ γὰρ ἐλθεῖν τινας ἀπὸ Ἰακώβου μετὰ τῶν ἐθνῶν συνήσθιεν· ὅτε δὲ ἦλθον, ὑπέστελλεν καὶ ἀφώριζεν ἑαυτὸν φοβούμενος τοὺς ἐκ περιτομῆς. (Gal. 2:12)

For, until some people came from James, he used to eat with the Gentiles; but when they came, he began to draw back and separated himself, because he was afraid of the circumcised. (NAB)

[ἦλθον, Aorist active indicative; ὑπέστελλεν and ἀφώριζεν, Imperfect active indicative]

In example 2, Peter's action of withdrawing and separating are given with an imperfective aspect while the arrival of people from James is given in perfective aspect. It seems implied that the arrival of the Jerusalem party interrupts Peter's withdrawal and separation attempt, but not the other way around. It is almost

---

24 The ESV, KJV, NAB, NASB, NET, NIV, NLT, RSV and CSB all include "when." The adverb "after" also works here, but the translations do not have it. None of the translations use "while," which definitely marks simultaneity.

as if when the people from James arrived, Peter was in the middle of the act and continued to carry it out in their presence.[25]

If a perfect tense-form points to a state as a property of the subject, then this state is just as interruptible as the imperfective action in B.

C. Jack <u>has walked</u> to the store, by the time that Sally found him.

In C, the action of Sally finding Jack occurs once his status as a person who has been to the store is established. The possible implications are that Sally found Jack once he achieved the status as a person who walked to a store at some point in the distant past or near past. Sally's action is not related to Jack's action per se, but to his status. His status began before Sally found him, and continues after Sally found him in much the same way as his walking preceded Sally finding him, in example B, and continued after Sally finds him. The whole duration of Jack's status is not in view by the speaker, as only a portion of it is in view when Sally finds him. It seems best here to understand that a Perfect tense-form has a property of imperfectivity whenever a state of the subject is primarily the situation in view. Imperfective is the manner in which a speaker or author views this state of the grammatical subject. 2 Cor 2:3 has an example like this.

3.) καὶ ἔγραψα τοῦτο αὐτό, ἵνα μὴ ἐλθὼν λύπην σχῶ ἀφ' ὧν ἔδει με χαίρειν, πεποιθὼς ἐπὶ πάντας ὑμᾶς ὅτι ἡ ἐμὴ χαρὰ πάντων ὑμῶν ἐστιν. (2 Cor. 2:3)

And I wrote this very thing to you, so that when I came I would not have sadness from those who ought to make me rejoice, since I am confident in you all that my joy would be yours. (NET)

[ἔγραψα, Aorist active indicative; πεποιθὼς, Perfect active participle]

The main verbs to observe in example 3 are the Aorist of the first clause and the Perfect of the last clause. The intervening clauses are rationale for the first clause, rather than part of the mainline. The clause syntax is "I wrote X, because I am persuaded that Y is true." The aspect of "wrote" is perfective, but the Perfect "persuaded/am confident" is imperfective because this state was both preceding the writing action and following it. One does not write because of confidence or

---

25 The translations all have difficulty bringing out this nuance. Most (ESV, KJV, RSV, NET, and CSB) translate as though all the verbs were Aorist. Several (NIV, NAB) have "began to withdraw," for the Imperfect verbs. All of these avoid the nuance that Peter was caught in the act, but the Greek verb tenses suggest it is possible and the context of Paul reprimanding Peter supports this understanding.

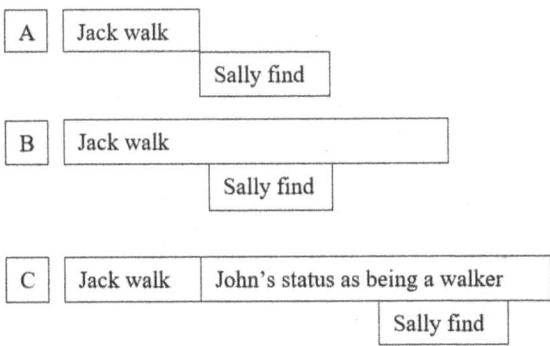

Figure 8: Interruptibility of the previous clause

persuasion unless the state is in effect before writing. Also, this status holds true at least until the letter is delivered and read, and likely much further. Most likely Paul's confidence remained in place indefinitely. Paul uses the Perfect to view and portray his status in an incomplete or imperfective way.

These effects can be mapped out with temporal diagrams using the understanding that aspect views either a portion or the whole of the situation time. Figure 8 shows how the clause, "when Sally found him," intervenes during the imperfective verbal action in B in much the same manner as it does the imperfective stative situation in C.[26]

However, not all examples of Perfect tense-forms can be shown to point to a state. Sometimes a Perfect tense-form points to the actional component of the verbal lexeme instead of pointing to the status of the subject. In these cases, the action is viewed more like the perfective verbal action.

D. Jack <u>has given</u> Sally the book on Monday.
E. Jack <u>has given</u> Sally the book for a week.

In D, the adverbial phrase, "on Monday," indicates a temporal element that modifies the action of giving and not the status of Jack as a giver. His status as a giver of books clearly extends past Monday, so Monday doesn't modify his status.

---

26 Rijksbaron asserts that the action of the Present can be interrupted, while the action of the Aorist cannot. This corresponds to the perfective belonging to a whole action, the imperfective belongs to an action that is only partially in view. Albert Rijksbaron, *The Syntax and Semantics of the Verb in Classical Greek*, 3rd ed. (Amsterdam: Gieben, 2002), 2 n.2. This is parallel to the observation by Sicking, that the imperfective-headed clause has the ability to be interrupted by other clauses and the perfective-headed clause does not have that ability. *Sicking and Stork*, 103-104.

While his status may be relevant to the context elsewhere, the completeness of his action of giving is modified by the adverbial phrase, "on Monday." In E, the adverb phrase, "for a week," indicates a temporal element that modifies the state of Jack as a giver, and not the action of Jack giving. Jack does not take a week to finish the process of giving the book. If Sally keeps the book more than a week, Jack's status will undergo a change, as he moves from "giver" to something more like "reclaimer." This adverbial phrase modifies the duration of that state. It seems better here to understand the Perfect tense-form as having a property of perfectivity when the lexical action of the verb is the situation in view. Perfective is the manner a speaker or author views the lexical action of a Perfect. Likewise, whenever the state of the subject is in view, imperfective is the manner in which that state is viewed. Similar examples exist in the Pauline corpus.

> 4.) καὶ ὅτι ἐτάφη καὶ ὅτι ἐγήγερται τῇ ἡμέρᾳ τῇ τρίτῃ κατὰ τὰς γραφὰς (1 Cor 15:4)

And that he was buried, and that he has been raised on the third day according to the scriptures.

[ἐγήγερται, Perfect middle indicative]

> 5.) καὶ φωτίσαι [πάντας] τίς ἡ οἰκονομία τοῦ μυστηρίου τοῦ ἀποκεκρυμμένου ἀπὸ τῶν αἰώνων ἐν τῷ θεῷ τῷ τὰ πάντα κτίσαντι, (Eph 3:9)

And to enlighten everyone what [is] the plan of the mystery, the one that has been hidden from the ages in God, the one who created all things.

[ἀποκεκρυμμένου, Perfect middle participle]

Both examples 4 and 5 show a Perfect tense-form modified temporally, but with the same observations as with D and E. The first locates the time of a perfective action and the second marks the duration of an imperfective state. Both of these examples are discussed extensively in Chapter 4.

The data from A-E and examples 1–5 leads to a possible formulation of Perfect of a state = imperfective, and Perfect of the action = perfective. The key is to determine when an action is in view and when a state is in view, and provide an answer to the question whether or not both can be in view for the same occurrence of the verb. As shown in examples D and E, the adverb is often an indicator of whether the action or state is in view. Likewise, the type of adverb indicates the type of aspect in the verb that is modified by the adverb. The idea that the Perfect

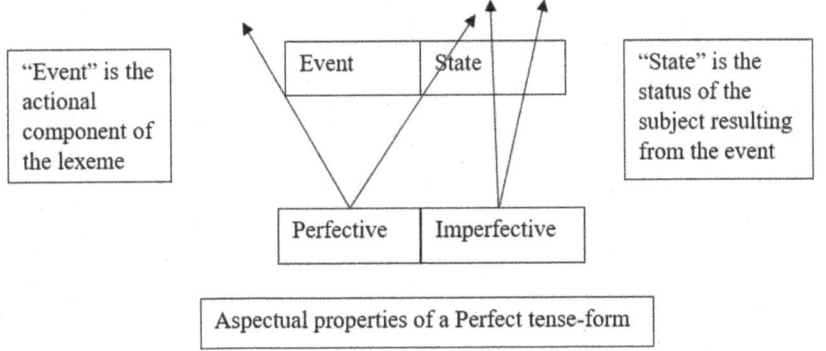

Figure 9: Complex aspect

exhibits both of the aspects seen as individual aspects on other tense-forms leads to the idea that its aspect is complex, where perfectivity is applied to any actional component of the event and imperfectivity is applied to any state that is apparent logically after the event. This state can include the status of the subject, or the status of the object.

In Figure 9, whenever the eventive component of the lexeme is the situation in view, then it is viewed perfectively as a whole action, but if the status of the subject is in view, it is viewed imperfectively and may be interrupted by new situations. The breadth of the arrows indicates whether the situation is fully or partially in view. The event is fully in view with the perfective aspect, and the state is partially in view with the imperfective aspect.

In this section the concept of stativity as a verbal aspect was assessed and found to be more objective than subjective. This is due to the possibility of viewing this state as an objective property of the subject, while at the same time stativity is not clearly a way to view this state as way the author views the situation. Since the state in view is only partly in view, and tends to exceed the reference time, it is better to understand the manner an author views this state as imperfective. The Perfect also appears to have a different aspect when a state is in view than it does for events, pointing to a complex aspect.

3.2. Two Aspects for the Perfect Tense-Form Based on Its Distinctive Morphology

The morphology of the Perfect has two components that require analysis.[27] First, the vowel and consonant spelling of the stem of the Perfect tense-form is compared to the stems of the Present and Aorist tense-forms.[28] Second, the morphology of the attached reduplicant in front of the lexical stem is analysed from cross-linguistic comparisons. The "κ" found just after the lexical stem and just before the endings is closely connected to valency based on Crellin's study.[29] Therefore, the "κ" is not analysed as belonging to verbal aspect in this project, contra the decision by Buth and Ellis.[30] This κ morpheme arrives later in the development of Perfect tense-forms in the Greek language historically, and is therefore an unlikely candidate for the locus of verbal aspect in the morphology of the Greek synthetic Perfect.[31]

3.2.1. Perfectivity Determined by Stem Morphology and Diachronic Shift

The Perfect tense-form points to a perfective action in at least two ways. First of all, the lexical core of the Perfect mirrors the perfective Aorist in its stem spelling whenever the Aorist stem is different from the Present stem. Secondly, the diachronic shift for Perfect tenses cross-linguistically involves movement from true Perfects to simple perfectives over time. This section will argue that perfectivity is related to the action denoted by the verbal lexeme for the Perfect tense-form by means of both of these observations.

---

27 A revision of a conference presentation on part of this subsection was published in a conference proceedings publication. James E. Sedlacek, "A Diachronic Analysis of the Form of the Greek Perfect and Its Associated Uses: Arguing for a Complex Verbal Aspect," *Proceedings of the 13th International Conference on Greek Linguistics (7-9/9/2017, London): Selected Papers* (London: University of Westminster, 2019; online at http://icgl13.westminster.ac.uk/) 235-247. The conference presentation was revised further and expanded for this chapter.

28 Fanning mentions the idea that aspect is located in the stem of the verb. Fanning, 15, 31-32; Dahl asserts that the stem as the likely locus of aspect, and places this type of aspect representation in the advanced stage of grammaticalisation. Dahl, *Tense and Aspect*, 10, 16.

29 Crellin, 116-119.

30 Randall Buth, "Perfect Greek Morphology and Pedagogy," 416-429 in *The Greek Verb Revisited: A Fresh Approach for Biblical Exegesis*, edited by Steven R. Runge and Christopher J. Fresch (Bellingham, WA: Lexham, 2016), 422; Nicolas J. Ellis, "Aspect-Prominence, Morpho-Syntax, and a Cognitive Linguistic Framework for the Greek Verb," 122-160 in *The Greek Verb Revisited: A Fresh Approach for Biblical Exegesis*, edited by Steven R. Runge and Christopher J. Fresch (Bellingham, WA: Lexham, 2016), 134. Ellis appears to base his decision on typology, noticing how close the κ morpheme is to the stem. These scholars connect the κ to perfectivity, however the data Crellin analysed on valency shows a stronger connection between the κ and transitivity and valency, than to verbal aspect.

31 Mary Niepokuj, *The Development of Verbal Reduplication in Indo-Eurpopean*. JIES Monograph: 24 (Washington, D. C.: Institute for the Study of Man, 1997), 132.

3.2.1.1.The Perfect Stem Morphology Mirrors That of the Perfectives In order to understand how the Perfect is similar to the Aorist, several Perfect tense-forms are displayed next to the Aorist and Present tense-forms that match them in their respective position in their paradigms. These lexemes were selected from each variety of stem-types from within the Pauline corpus, to illustrate how different stem-types compare. The stem formation type is outlined in detail later in this section. Four lexemes are chosen to represent the stem formation variety, while at the same time lexemes are avoided that were either defective or those that have phonological reduction processes that have hidden their morphological differences. The same paradigm positions are represented for each lexeme for clarity.[32] These lexemes are displayed in Figure 10.

The procedure in Figure 10 is to first account for each morpheme in each example and eliminate from consideration the morphemes that are not associated with verbal aspect, so that the aspectual morphemes remain for ease of comparison. I next compare and contrast the aspectual morphology of the tense-forms. Any preceding part of the verb not underlined belongs either to reduplication or augmentation, and the following parts not underlined belong to the endings. This underlined portion will not include infixes thought to belong to lexical matters or to valency.[33] The result is to show how the Perfect stem is closely related to the Aorist stem through its mirroring of its stem vowel, and not closely related to the Present stem due to a different stem vowel.

At first glance, the main difference to be observed is that the Present stem has a different pattern in its vowel or consonant spelling than the Aorist stem. This difference between the Present and Aorist is commonly presented as the main aspectual division.[34] The point of Figure 10 is to show that the Perfect consistently mirrors the Aorist stem spellings, while at the same time consistently opposing the Present even throughout a range of mode and the formation type variety.

In the first set from Figure 10, the Present tense-form is spelled with ου diphthong, where the contract vowel ο is visible before the υ vowel.[35] The ου is a diphthong due to the assimilation of the contract vowel ο and the first vowel of the verbal ending. The Perfect and the Aorist mirror each other by providing an ω vowel in both forms. In the second set, the middle stem vowel of Present tense-form

---

32 This refers to maintaining the same position in the paradigm for each verb.

33 This includes the "κ" as this morpheme points to valency rather than aspect.

34 Lars Johanson, "Viewpoint Operators in European Languages," 26-187 in *Tense and Aspect in the Languages of Europe*, edited by Östen Dahl. Empirical Approaches to Language Typology: 20, EUROTYP: 6 (Berlin: Mouton de Gruyter, 2000), 42.

35 The Imperfect is not displayed here, but it mirrors the Present each time.

φανερο- (reveal)	Present	Aorist	Perfect
2pl Active Indicative	φανερουτε	εφανερωσατε	πεφανερωκατε
Active Infinitive	φανερουν	φανερωσαι	πεφανερωκεναι
Masc Gen S Act Ptcp	φανερουντος	φανερωσαντος	πεφανερωκοτος

εὑρισκ- (find)	Present	Aorist	Perfect
2pl Active Indicative	εὑρισκετε	εὑρησατε	ἡυρηκατε
Active Infinitive	εὑρισκειν	εὑρησαι	ἡυρηκεναι
Masc Gen S Act Ptcp	εὑρισκοντος	εὑρησαντος	ἡυρηκοτος

ἱστ- (stand)	Present	Aorist	Perfect
2pl Active Indicative	ἱστατε	εστησατε	ἑστηκατε
Active Infinitive	ἱσταναι	στησαι	ἑστηκεναι
Masc Gen S Act Ptcp	ἱσταντος	στησαντος	ἑστηκοτος

τασσ- (arrange/order)	Present	Aorist	Perfect
2pl Active Indicative	τάσσετε	ετάξατε	τέταχατε
Active Infinitive	τάσσειν	τάξαι	τεταχέναι
Masc Gen S Act Ptcp	τάσσοντος	τάξαντος	τεταχότος

Figure 10: Stem comparison using four verb types.. This chart compares a few forms belonging to a few lexemes. A fuller chart containing more stems is in Appendix M, and a weblink is included there to a much larger one that compares all the Perfects in the Pauline corpus with all possible verbs for those lexemes.

is spelled with an ι. The Perfect and Aorist mirror each other by providing an η vowel in both forms, opposing the ι in the Present.[36] In the third set, the Present tense-form stem is spelled with an α vowel before the endings. Again, the Perfect and Aorist mirror each other by spelling the stem with an η vowel. In the fourth set, the stem has a consonantal spelling change instead of a vowel spelling change. Here,

---

36 The -σκ- morpheme is an added infix to the Present only, and is thought to provide lexical information to the stem, so the fact that the Aorist and Perfect do not share this morpheme is unrelated to aspect and therefore not analysed here.

the double -σσ- is opposed by a guttural, -χ- consonant. Again, the Perfect mirrors the Aorist and opposes the Present, but the spelling is disguised in the Aorist since the -χσ- combines into the letter -ξ- due to phonological processes. The Perfect stem mirrors the Aorist consistently across the examples given in Figure 10.[37]

Although many forms could be included in Figure 10, these four sets of examples illustrate several varieties within the Greek verb system. First, an indicative verb is chosen, the 2nd person, plural active indicative, along with the active infinitive and the masculine genitive singular active participle. The point of this set is to demonstrate consistency of the Perfect mirroring the Aorist and opposing the Present across the various moods. Secondly, several verbs are included that reveal a variety of formation types for the Perfect tense-form. The first set contains a verb with a contract vowel, the second set contains a verb with a vowel in the initial position and an -σκ- morpheme in the Present, and the third set contains a verb with a reduplicated Present. The fourth set contains a verb that has several of its features more regular in its structure, but has a consonantal spelling change, rather than a vowel change. The purpose of these four sets is to display the consistency of Perfect still mirroring the Aorist, while opposing the Present across the various types of lexical formation for the Greek Perfect.

In pre-Greek Indo-European, the Perfect used to be formed with an o vowel opposing a e vowel in the Present and an absent vowel in the Aorist.[38] Remnants of this old system exist in some of the fossilised forms of many Indo-European languages.[39] This three-vowel alternation system is called *Ablaut*[40] and seems to pre-exist the endings associated with the tense-forms.[41] These are respectively referred to as the e-grade, o-grade, and zero-grade.[42] It is easier to understand the

---

37 Examples exist where all three forms have the same vowels, thus opposition with the Present is difficult to show, but mirroring still exists between Perfect and Aorist. An example of this is πλήρ-, where the perfect vowel is the same as all three forms, the Present, πληρῶ; Perfect, πεπλήρωκα; and Aorist, ἐπλήρωσα. Cases also exist where none of the three forms mirror each other in a clear way, but for these forms the Perfects and Aorists are provided from different stems, such as 1st Aorist coupled with 2nd Perfect or vice versa. An example of this is πειθ-, where the Perfect πέποιθα is different from both the Aorist ἔπεισα and Present, πείθω, but this is due to the language retaining the strong Perfect and weak Aorist. An older Perfect, πέπεικα, fell out use. It is sufficient to recognise that the Perfect and Aorist, although not identical in spelling, form themselves according patterns that mirrored a different form of the Perfect or Aorist, and thus contain the same aspect.

38 Robert S. P. Beekes, *Comparative Indo-European Linguistics: An Introduction*, 2nd ed. (Amsterdam: Benjamins, 2011), 176, 263.

39 Oswald J. L. Szemerényi, *Introduction to Indo-European Linguistics* (Oxford: Clarendon, 1996), 83.

40 Other terms include "gradation", "alternation," and "apophony." Szemerényi, 83.

41 Kenneth Shields, *A History of Indo-European Verb Morphology*, CILT: 88 (Amsterdam: Benjamins, 1992), 13.

42 James Clackson, *Indo-European Linguistics: An Introduction*, Cambridge Textbooks in Linguistics (Cambridge: Cambridge University Press, 2007), 54.

Perfect as not sharing an aspect with the Aorist, when the languages of Europe had three vowels dividing the tense-forms, and more likely to understand it sharing an aspect with the Aorist whenever they have the same vowel. Some Greek verbs retained this three-vowel alternation, but most Greek Perfects were formed from reduplicant plus zero-grade vowel spelling, mirrored to the Aorist. Several examples retaining the three-vowel system are presented below:

e	o	0/
λείπω (ε+ι)	λέ-λοιπα (o+ι)	ἔλιπον (0/+ι)
ἐλεύσομαι (ε+υ)	εἰλήλουθα (o+υ)	ἤλυθον (0/+υ)[43]

The e-vowel and o-vowel drop out of the Aorist. The other vowels of the stem remain, such as ι and υ. The o-grade may have been dropped from some later Perfects due to making the forms uniform with the productive pattern.[44] The full-grade (e-grade) of the stem is connected with imperfectivity across Indo-European languages, and the zero-grade is connected with perfectivity.[45] The fact that the productive pattern for Greek Perfects reveals primarily a zero-grade indicates that a perfective aspect belongs to the lexical verb in the Perfect. Interestingly, the reduplicant retains a e-grade even though it is otherwise fully reduced onto the stem, suggesting a parallel between the reduplicant and imperfective verbs.

Since verbal aspect is thought to be marked by the stem formation of each verb, rather than by the verbal endings or other morphemes in the word, this observation suggests that the verbal aspect for any lexeme in the Aorist should be different from the aspect of that same lexeme in the Present since they have different internal vowels. Consequently, the Aorist should have the same as the aspect as the Perfect, since it shares the same internal stem phonemes. The observation that the Perfect shares the aspect of the Aorist in its lexical core from Figure 10 accounts for the situations where the Perfect tense-form is used for a past action much like the Aorist is used. This mirroring alone does not account for why the Perfect tense-form often is used to indicate a present-like state, although an Aorist, another perfective, can be used to indicate such a state.[46] The fact that so

---

43   Several sources provide this verb. This set is from Szemerényi. I add the symbols to his list, and show how the vowels combine in the brackets. Szemerényi, 84.

44   Michael Meier-Brügger, *Indo-European Linguistics* (Berlin: De Gruyter, 2003), 206.

45   Lehmann provides different terminology, but essentially he means the same thing. Winfred P. Lehmann, *Theoretical Bases of Indo-European Linguistics* (London: Routledge, 1993), 179.

46   Fanning, 115-116.

many Perfects are used to point to a state may be a reason why the morphological connection to the Aorist has often been overlooked or perhaps even downplayed. This connection between the lexical core of both the Perfect and Aorist simply reflects that the action referred to by the Perfect mirrors that of the Aorist in that they both view the action perfectively.

Aspectually, the action in both the Perfect and Aorist is understood to be whole, entire, or complete.[47] This is the main idea of the perfective, which opposes the imperfective or incomplete situation. This is no surprise that aspect belonging to the lexical core should be the same for both the Perfect and Aorist, since whenever the Perfect is used for an event, it typically represents a complete action.

3.2.1.2.The Diachronic Trend of the Tense-Form Follows the Development of Perfectives
Haspelmath indicates that the oldest meaning associated with the Greek Perfect in the Homeric Period is a state.[48] Drinka confirms that many older perfects were stative and intransitive.[49] Drinka states that across the Indo-European language family, "resultatives" and "completives" can both move toward anterior over time and eventually become past perfectives. This indicates a diachronic trend for Perfects of multiple languages to change over time into a simple perfective.[50] Drinka even adds old statives as a new category to the list of items that become anteriors.[51] The meaning for the Perfect shifted from the state to the event in Classical Greek as the Perfect Active began to take on agent-oriented roles, opposing the Perfect Middle.[52] The Greek synthetic Perfect in the Byzantine Period finally becomes a perfective, and the Periphrastic form later takes on the role of the Perfect.[53] In the Modern Period, Greek has two Perfect items, εχω + aorist infinitive, and the copula (form of ειμι) + aorist passive participle.[54] In both cases the modern Greek periphrastic Perfect is comprised of an imperfective stative auxiliary verb and a perfective lexical verb, thus highlighting two aspects working in conjunction.

---

47 Fanning, 97, 113, 118-120.
48 Haspelmath, "From Resultative to Perfect," 193.
49 Bridget Drinka, "The Evolution of Grammar: Evidence from the Indo-European Perfects," 117-133 in *Historical Linguistics 1997, Current Issues in Linguistic Theory:* 164, edited by Monika S. Schmid, Jennifer R. Austin, and Dieter Stein (Amsterdam: John Benjamins, 1998), 119.
50 Drinka, "The Evolution of Grammar," 119.
51 Drinka, "The Evolution of Grammar," 129.
52 Haspelmath, "From Resultative to Perfect," 214.
53 Haspelmath, "From Resultative to Perfect," 218.
54 Haspelmath, "From Resultative to Perfect," 219.

This shift occurred cross-linguistically among the languages that make up the Indo-European family of languages. It is important to observe that this shift of the Perfect from stative, to resultative, to simple perfective is a change that is only observed for the Perfect. Other forms shift in meaning as well, but nothing as dramatic as that of the Perfect, where it changes from present to past and from state to event, resulting in a seemly opposite meaning. The simple perfectives and simple imperfectives suffer relatively few shifts across the diachronic spectrum. It seems that something more complex must be true of the aspect of the Perfect for it to have such a shift not observed for the other tense-forms.

As the Greek synthetic Perfect changes from a seemingly purely stative role during the Homeric Period of the Greek language to an eventive past tense role in the Byzantine Period, another change takes place parallel to it. A greater number and type of lexemes are found using a Perfect tense-form in later periods. In the Homeric Period, the lexemes used are largely statives, or at least intransitives. Later in the Classical Period more transitive lexemes appear in the Perfect tense-form.[55] It seems apparent that the lexical variety, or the shift in lexical class observed in the Perfect tense-forms, may be partly responsible for some degrees of the changing semantic force shown by the Greek synthetic Perfect tense-form. If the changing lexeme variety is linked to certain changes in the meaning of the Perfect, then the collection of these changes in meaning are effects of the Perfect on that lexeme, rather than being identical to its verbal aspect. Therefore, it is difficult to see "stativity" or "intensity" as belonging to the aspect integral to the Perfect, when transitive verbs provide a different sense. It seems better to understand both stativity and intensity to be effects that the aspect of the Perfect has upon these situations, or effects of aspect upon specific lexemes, rather than view stativity or intensity as examples of verbal aspect. The need to identify where in the verb the present-like state comes from leads the analysis to the reduplicant attached in front of the verbal stem.

3.2.2. Imperfectivity Determined by Grammaticalisation of the Reduplicant

Reduplication refers to the copying of the initial portions of the verb creating a syllable, called the reduplicant, which is then added back onto the stem.[56] Reduplication is observed across languages and corresponds with a variety of lexical or grammatical meanings. Scholars who study these effects over time,

---

55 Wackernagel, "Perfektum," 4.

56 Phonological "copying" is the term preferred for this process, although see Sharon Inkelas and Cheryl Zoll, *Reduplication: Doubling in Morphology, Cambridge Studies in Linguistics* (Cambridge: Cambridge University Press, 2005) for an alternate theory based on morphological processes.

and cross-linguistically have revealed a relationship between the type of reduplication and its likely meaning.[57] Reduplication occurs in a variety of patterns.
The first of these is total reduplication where the full lexical stem of the word is
copied, producing the complete verbal stem two times. This type is the source
for all other types under discussion.[58] Next is "CVC" reduplication where the
first syllable of the stem is copied and then added to the original stem. Next is
"CV" reduplication, where only the first consonant and vowel are copied and
then added to the original stem. Next is "Ce" reduplication where only the first
consonant is copied from the stem, and a vowel standardised for the tense-form
is added to that consonant, and then the combination is added to the original
stem.[59] The difference between "CV" and "Ce" reduplication is that under "CV"
reduplication, the vowel will be different for each lexeme based on its unique
vowel after the first consonant, and that under "Ce" reduplication, the vowel is
the same for every verb of that follows the pattern. Finally, "C" reduplication is
observed, where only the first consonant is added to the stem without an intervening vowel. The process of erosion is one of the elements of grammaticalisation
that occurs when a lexeme grammaticalises into an aspectual entity. These steps
are posited along a cline, where the lexical meaning declines as the reduplicant
material decreases, and the grammaticalised meaning increases generally according to the degree of fusion of the reduplicant onto the stem.[60] This loss of lexical
meaning is desemanticisation and results in a lexical verb or syllable becoming
a state. Once the reduplicant loses its identity as a lexical verb, and becomes
aspectual, it has become decategoricalised. Figure 11 illustrates the reduplicant
erosion cline.

This cline for the meaning of verbs with reduplication includes verbs with
continuative, frequentive, intensive, iterative, habitual, stative, and imperfective
meanings. This cline has a particular order where verbs that exhibit greater material in the reduplicant favour interpretations that duplicate the lexical meaning,
and verbs that exhibit less material in the reduplicant favour interpretations closer
to the general grammatical category of imperfectivity. Frequentive verbs typically
occur at the beginning of this cline using total reduplication.[61] Total reduplication
can include intensive, frequentive, continuative, and iterative meanings for the

---

57 These scholars include Joan Bybee, John Frampton, Ryan Sandell, and Sam Zukoff.

58 Bybee, Perkins, and Pagliuca, *Evolution of Grammar*, 167.

59 This vowel may represent some properties belonging to the original vowel grade of an aspect form, such
    as the e-grade with the imperfective aspect.

60 Bybee emphasises this relationship. Joan Bybee. *Morphology*, 36.

61 Bybee, Perkins, and Pagliuca, 166.

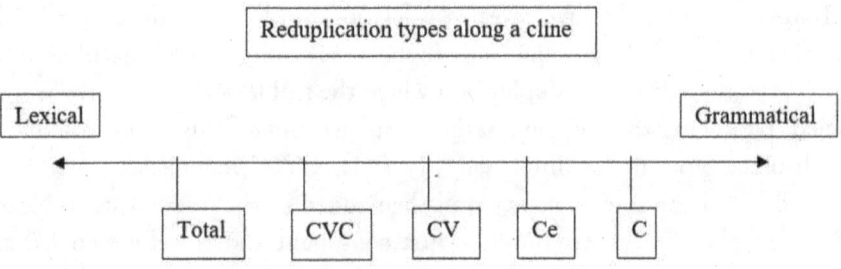

Figure 11: Reduplication syllable types on a cline

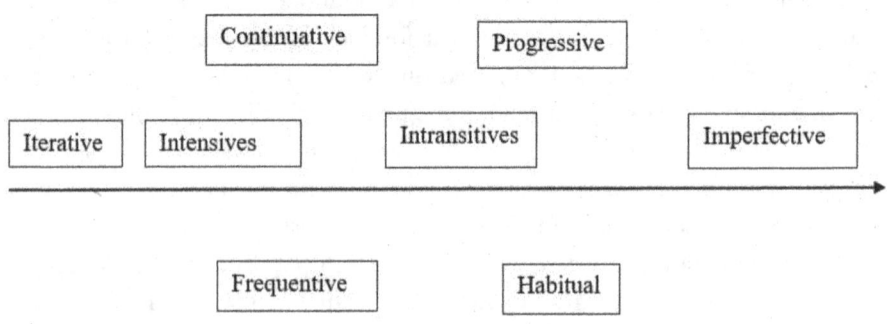

Figure 12: Reduplication effects situated along a cline

verbs.[62] Verbs exhibiting partial reduplication typically lend themselves to intransitive interpretations.[63] The endpoint of this cline is imperfectivity.[64] Figure 12 situates the range of meanings from the literature along the cline described.

This development of reduplication from iteratives to imperfectives mirrors the development of imperfectives from lexical items discussed more generally.[65] Their clines are parallel. This mirroring occurs both in the direction of the two clines and in the details along the two clines. Bybee, Perkins, and Pagliuca show how the grammatical category of imperfective develops from certain lexical

---

62 John Frampton includes iteratives. John Frampton, *Distributed Reduplication*, Linguistic Inquiry Monographs (Cambridge, MA: Massachusetts Institute of Technology Press, 2009), 42. Bybee, Perkins, and Pagliuca include the frequentive, continuative, and iterative lexemes, Bybee, Perkins, and Pagliuca, *Evolution of Grammar*, 167.

63 Bybee, Perkins, and Pagliuca, *Evolution of Grammar*, 171.

64 Bybee, Perkins, and Pagliuca, *Evolution of Grammar*, 171.

65 Drinka shares a similar flowchart that has "intransitives" and "imperfectives" in opposite order. Also, her chart contains 2 paths, where mine has a separating line. Drinka, 126.

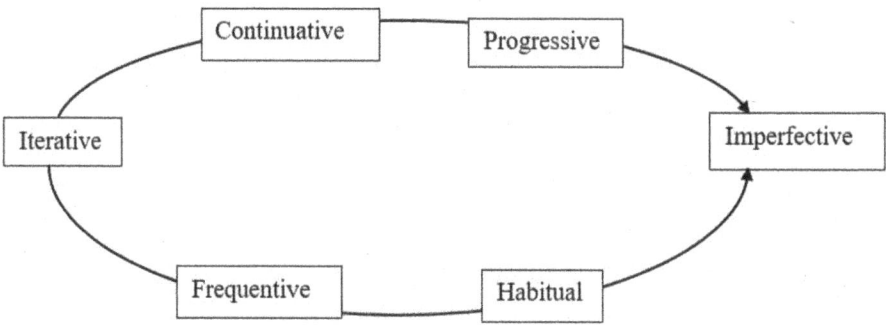

Figure 13: The two-fold path for lexemes developing into imperfectives

items. In that analysis, they indicate that the cross-linguistic data shows two paths moving from iterativity to imperfectivity.[66] These two paths are predicted by lexical selection. Figure 13 illustrates the two paths, where the upper involves processes and the lower involves countable actions.

For the Greek synthetic Perfect, the most productive method of reduplication copies the first phoneme of the stem and repeats that sound while inserting the ε vowel between the reduplicating consonant and the stem. For example, if the stem is λυ-, then the reduplicant plus stem is λελυ-. The vowel is always the same for the Perfect regardless of the stem vowel. For example, the reduplicant plus stem is not *λυλυ-. Other forms of Greek reduplication involve vowel initial stems where the vowel is simply lengthened, and a few examples "VC" reduplication where the initial vowel and its first consonant is copied and then added to the original stem. Zukoff provides an analysis of "VC" reduplication that combines the effect of laryngeals to "Ce" reduplication that explains the phenomenon of "VC" reduplication.[67] Basically "VC" reduplication is a result of "Ce" reduplication when "C" is a laryngeal or is preceded by one. Greek Perfect reduplication is located on the cline of reduplication near the end of the process of the reduplicant reducing onto the stem. This suggests that the reduplicant of the Perfect contains a highly grammaticalised meaning rather than a lexical meaning.

---

66   Bybee, Perkins, and Pagliuca, *Evolution of Grammar*, 139-142, 165-166.
67   Sam Zukoff. "On the Origins of Attic Reduplication," 257-278 in *Proceedings of the 25ᵗʰ Annual UCLA Indo-European Conference*, edited by Stephanie W. Jamison, H. Craig Melchert, and Brent Vine (Bremen: Hampen, 2014), 266-275.

Among the salient meanings argued for the Perfect, stative, intransitive, and intensive occur early in the history of the reduplicated Perfect.[68] This suggests that this is the starting point in the cline for "Ce" reduplication of the Greek Perfect. As it moves from intransitive or intensive, it is expected to move toward general imperfectivity. Since reduplication as a process mirrors imperfectivity as a process, I suggest that this is where the reduplicant for the vast majority of reduplicated Perfects belongs.[69] The reduplicant of the Classical, Hellenistic, and New Testament Greek Perfect is imperfective with stative force. Reduplication points towards a different aspect for the Greek Perfect than does its verbal stem. After comparing the Greek reduplication type with the cross-linguistic data, the Greek reduplication is right near the end of the cline observed for reduplication. From that alone, one should expect the reduplicant to refer to some kind of state in an imperfective manner. This accounts for the vast majority of the stative usages of the Greek Perfect tense-form.

Any given language will not have all the stages of development of reduplication evident in the language at any point in time. Written languages tend to have one dominant form or method codified, and lose the earlier forms during an earlier period of the language history. Spoken varieties of the language and colloquial dialects of the main language often preserve some of the remnants of earlier reduplication considered linguistic fossils. It is necessary to base our understanding of the reduplicant on languages broadly that have recent reduplication in their lower register of language to observe how this trend occurs. Greek is compared with the cross-linguistic trend, because its forms are static with one form type and very late meanings associated with the reduplicant.

3.2.3. Summary

The combination of both the morphological similarity of the Perfect tense-form's lexical core with the Aorist's, and the grammaticalisation of reduplication cross-linguistically, suggests that the Perfect tense-form has both perfective and imperfective verbal aspect integral to the form in its morphology. Some may criticise this suggestion on the basis that two incompatible aspects are argued for the

---

68 For a treatment on Stative Perfects, see Stanley E. Porter, *Verbal Aspect*, 245-290. For a treatment on early intensives, see Georg Curtius. *The Greek Verb: Its Structure and Development*, translated by Augustus S. Wilkins and Edwin B. England (London: John Murray, 1880), 375. For a treatment on intransitivity through valency reduction, see Crellin, 2012.

69 Bybee, Perkins, and Pagliuca do not link reduplication with imperfectivity, but provide the framework that shows reduplication mirroring the development of imperfectives. Bybee, Perkins, and Pagliuca, *Evolution of Grammar*, 139-142, 165-166, 171.

Greek Perfect. For example, one cannot view a situation both completely and incompletely at the same time. This is not the case however. It is possible to view the event and its resulting state in different ways. Both grammaticalisation and morphology support the case that the Perfect tense-form contains both aspects, where these two aspects each rest on a different portion of the verbal process. The reduplicant is imperfective and applies that aspect onto the state belonging to the Perfect, whether the contextually relevant state is that of the subject, or of the subject and object. The lexical core is perfective, and applies that aspect onto the action which leads to the state.[70] This means that the Greek synthetic Perfect tense-form contains two aspects specifically related to two different parts of the verbal process. The complex aspect of the Perfect opposes the Aorist in that the Aorist views both events and states the same way, as perfective, but the Perfect allows the state to be viewed as imperfective. This complex aspect of the Perfect likewise opposes the Present in that the Present views both events and states alike, imperfectively, while the Perfect allows the event to viewed perfectively. This complex aspect also accounts for the similarity of the Perfect to the Aorist when referencing complete events in the later periods of the Greek language, and the similarity of the Perfect to the Present when referencing states in earlier periods.

The aspect for the Perfect tense-form is a "complex aspect," because not only do both aspects come together in the Perfect tense-form, but they each point to a different part of the verbal process, one to the event and the other to the state. The diagram below illustrates the aspect for the Greek Perfect tense-form.

In Figure 14, the perfective lexical core points to the event and has a complete perspective on it, so that the whole event is referenced. The imperfective reduplicant provides a partial view of the resulting state, so that the state can be viewed as enduring through time following the event. The endpoints of the state are not in view using the imperfective aspect.

3.3. Two Aspects for the Greek Synthetic Perfect Tense-Form Based on the Stative and Eventive Usage

The uses for the Greek synthetic Perfect appear to undergo transition over time. Some of these uses were highly apparent during specific periods of the Greek language, while other uses were observed occurring over several periods of the language. The meaning of a simple state without reference to an action is proposed

---

70 This is consistent with the lexeme being an action lexeme.

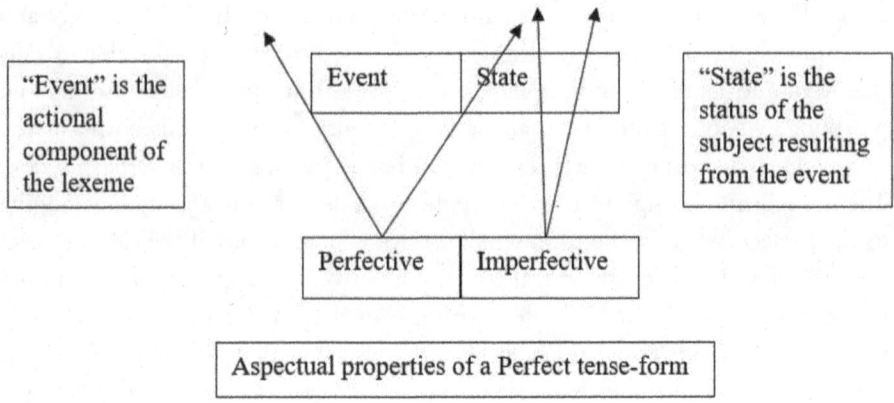

Figure 14: Complex aspect

for the earliest Greek Perfect.[71] Perfects of this type contain stativity, but also this state has contextual effects that appear ongoing; thus, the state is viewed imperfectivity here as well. "Resultative" Perfects come later.[72] This is where a state is the focus, but a prior action is implied. For these Perfects stativity is apparent, but actional properties are evoked as the reason for that state. These actional properties are usually seen as past completed events, so perfectivity relates to those actional properties. The meaning of "anterior" is given to some Perfects that focus on an event while implying a continued state.[73] This is where a complete action is the focus, but a following state is implied. For these Perfects stativity is still apparent, but a greater focus is on the event that caused that state. Lastly, some Perfects are simple past tenses.[74] Here the focus is not on a state, but on the actional properties alone. These actional properties are seen as complete, so perfectivity is the aspect. These changes are gradual so that the usage commonly

71 This includes pre-Greek examples through to Homer's usage. McKay begins his understanding here. Kenneth McKay, "The Use of the Ancient Greek Perfect," 6. Friedrich supports this placement. Paul Friedrich, "On Aspect Theory and Homeric Aspect," *International Journal of American Linguistics* 40:4, part 2 (October 1974): S 1-S 44, S 16. Allen rejects this, and begins his order with the next stage. Allen, "Tense and Aspect," 102-103; Haspelmath, 193.

72 Allen, "Tense and Aspect," 103. Paul Freidrich, "On Aspect Theory and Homeric Aspect," *International Journal of American Linguistics* 40:4, part 2 (October 1974): S 1-S 44, S 16.

73 This stage emerges largely due to the inclusion of transitive lexemes in the Perfect tense-form. Allen, "Tense and Aspect," 108-109. See Friedrich as well. Friedrich, "On Aspect Theory," S 19.

74 This is apparent from constant collocation with Aorists in summary narrative passages. Amalia Moser, "Tense and Aspect after the New Testament," 539-562 in *The Greek Verb Revisited: A Fresh Approach for Biblical Exegesis*, edited by Steven R. Runge and Christopher J. Fresch (Bellingham, WA: Lexham, 2016), 553; Caragounis, *The Development of Greek*, 110; Allen, "Tense and Aspect," 112.

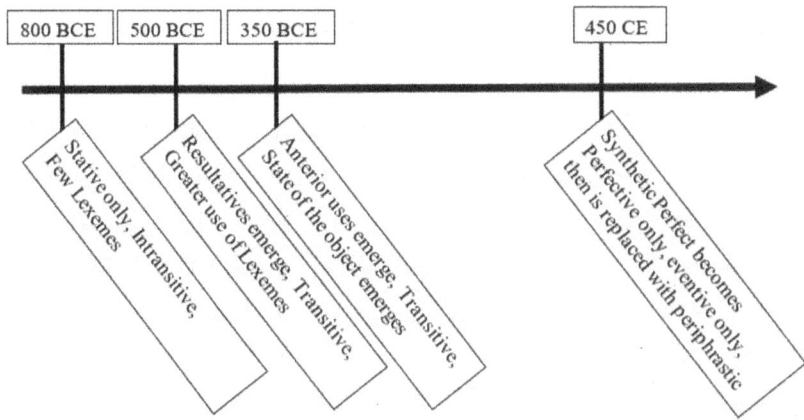

Figure 15: Timeline of the synthetic Greek Perfect. The dates on the timeline correspond roughly to those suggested by Caragounis for the phases of the Greek language. The first is the one Caragounis calls Epic, from 800–500 BCE. The next one Caragounis calls Classical, but refers to it with an "A," since Attic is primary. This goes from 500–300 BCE in his data, but I chose 350 because it seems prudent for this date to occur after Alexander the Great. The next and longest period, Caragounis calls Hellenistic, and in his data runs until 300 CE. He has a section called proto-Byzantine running from 300 to 600 CE between the Hellenistic and Byzantine Periods. Since this marks a transitional period from Hellenistic to Byzantine, I decided to select the midpoint of this period, 450 CE as the dividing point between Hellenistic and Byzantine. This date also corresponds roughly with the end of the early church fathers' writings, and more precisely the end of the Epistolary corpus constructed later in this study.

found in later times was still seen in the earliest layers, although rarely.[75] What is seen by viewing the Perfect diachronically is that the possibilities for meaning include state, imperfective, action, and perfective.

The timeline in Figure 15 places these uses roughly into chronological perspective.

Next, the aspect-target pairs are mapped out and connected to the time period of their most prevalent uses. What is seen by viewing the Perfect uses this way is that the possibilities include imperfective state, imperfective state in focus

---

75 Caragounis, *The Development of Greek*, 154; Caragounis provides a list of ancient examples using the Perfect tense-form as a simple past tense referring to the event. Caragounis, *New Testament Language*, 153-157.

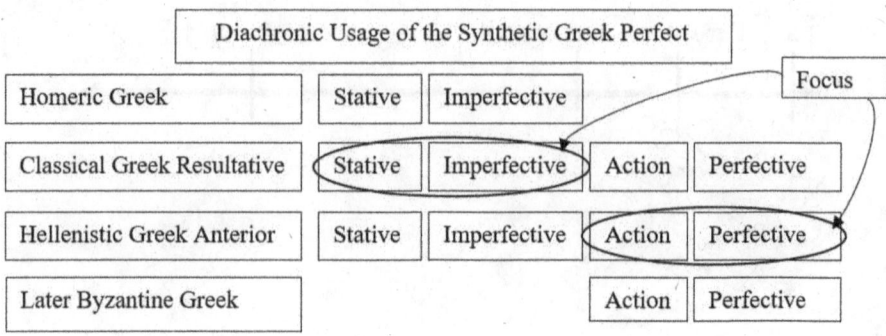

Figure 16: The synthetic Greek Perfect in several time periods

implying a perfective action, a perfective action in focus implying an imperfective state, and a simple perfective action often called a preterite.

Once this collection of properties is mapped out as shown in Figure 16, it seems apparent that the usage that has the potential to explain the usages for all the periods is the one for either the Classical or Hellenistic Greek Periods, which incorporates both perfectivity and imperfectivity.[76] The logic is that when a form has the components that allow both a stative and an eventive reading, then it can provide either one of those two readings alone in different settings. Two examples are presented next showing how the Perfect can be read either as a state or an event.

The first example shows a Perfect pointing to a state belonging to the subject. The Perfect in the example is a middle participle.

> καὶ μὴ ἀσθενήσας τῇ πίστει κατενόησεν τὸ ἑαυτοῦ σῶμα [ἤδη] <u>νενεκρωμένον</u>, ἑκατονταετής που ὑπάρχων, καὶ τὴν νέκρωσιν τῆς μήτρας Σάρρας· (Rom 4:19)

> And he did not weaken in faith when he understood his body already <u>having been decayed</u>, because he was about one hundred years old, and the deadness of the womb of Sara;

The verb νενεκρωμένον, "having died," displays the status of Abraam as unable to produce children. His sterility along with Sara's is the matter under discussion

---

76 This chart represents the trend, and does not cover all the examples contrary to each period. Examples, though rare, of all three usages can be found in the earlier periods. Caragounis provides several examples of Perfects behaving like the third type in the Classical Period. Caragounis, *New Testament Language*, 151-154.

in this context. The event of losing the ability to procreate is not in focus here, but the status of this inability. This is the context that makes the miracle of Isaac so amazing later. This status is viewed as an enduring problem, so imperfectivity best describes the author's way of viewing this state.

The second example shows a Perfect pointing to an event. This Perfect is an active infinitive.

Τί οὖν ἐροῦμεν <u>εὑρηκέναι</u> Ἀβραὰμ τὸν προπάτορα ἡμῶν κατὰ σάρκα; (Rom 4:1)

Then, what will we say Abraham <u>has found</u>, our forefather according to flesh?

The verb εὑρηκέναι, or "has found" manifests the action of Abraam finding justification by faith prior to its relevance being discussed. It is clear from the fact Abraam is long dead that his action of finding justification occurred before Paul analyses that it came about by faith to the Roman church. Paul's portrayal of Abraam's finding action is as a complete event, whole, and does not elaborate on the process. This event is viewed perfectively because it is entire. This pair of examples illustrate the importance for a verbal aspect definition for the Perfect that can account for imperfectivity for states and perfectivity for events.

3.4. Two Aspects for the Synthetic Perfect Tense-Form Verified by the Modern Periphrastic Perfect Replacement for the Synthetic Perfect

Eventually the Greek synthetic Perfect disappeared from use and was replaced with periphrastic constructions. The periphrastic Perfects of Greek and other Indo-European languages have two words to perform the uses of what the reduplicant-plus-stem combination was doing for the synthetic Perfect. The modern languages mirror the aspect of synthetic Perfects in their periphrastic Perfects. The Indo-European family of languages show the trend of moving from reduplicated synthetic Perfects to periphrastic Perfects comprised either of "be" + a perfective or "have" + a perfective.[77] In both cases the auxiliary verb is an imperfective immediately followed by a perfective lexical verb. This cross-linguistic trend mirrors what happened in the Greek language. The fact that a

---

77 English forms Perfects this way. For a treatment on this shift in Romance languages, see Michaela Cennamo, "The Rise and Development of Analytic Perfects in Italo-Romance," *Grammatical Change and Linguistic Theory: The Rosendal Papers*, LA: 113, edited by Thórhallur Eythórsson (Amsterdam: John Benjamins, 2008), 115-142.

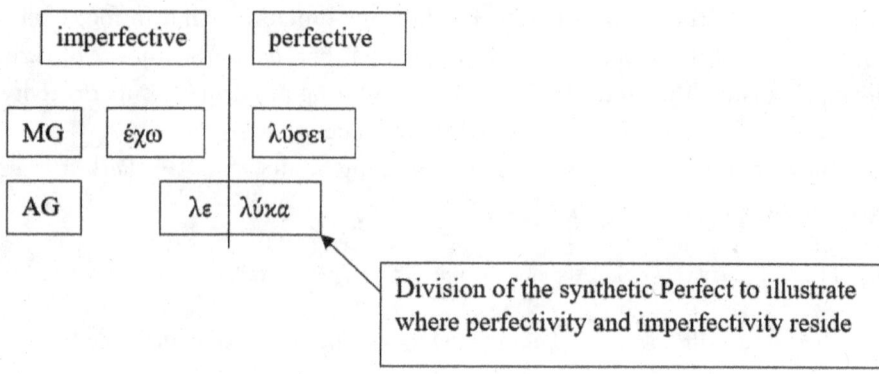

Figure 17: The synthetic and periphrastic Perfects showing mirroring of components

similar process occurred in so many languages in a parallel fashion suggests that similar forces are at work to bring about this change. As the periphrastic Perfects replaced the synthetic ones, the new form took on the roles of the old form, with the result that the old synthetic form either dropped out of use, became a simple perfective, or was retained only in some nouns or adjectives that had been formed from a Perfect.[78]

The idea that a periphrastic Perfect comprised of verbs with two different verbal aspects could somehow replace a synthetic Perfect is difficult to explain unless the two methods of forming a Perfect have a similar verbal aspect structure. It seems best here to suggest that the synthetic Perfect tense-form also had both aspects that are seen in the periphrastic Perfect, and that both worked in much the same way, where imperfectivity focused on the state, while the perfectivity focused on the action.

Figure 17 shows how the synthetic Perfect is comprised of both aspects where the reduplication carries the imperfective stative information and the core lexeme carries the perfective actional information. The relationship between both types of forms is their complex aspect.

Once Greek moved to the periphrastic Perfect after the Byzantine Period, the auxiliary verb occupied the place where the reduplication of the synthetic Perfect

---

78   Rubino adds that several Greek nouns formed this way as well. Carl Rubino, "Reduplication: Form, Function and Distribution," *Studies on Reduplication*. EALT: 28, edited by Bernard Hurch (Berlin: Mouton de Gruyter, 2005), 22. Caragounis states that the Neohellenic Perfect expresses an action like the Aorist along with Present results. This suggests that the modern periphrastic Perfect corresponds to the synthetic Perfect with Anterior force of the Classical Period. Caragounis, 160.

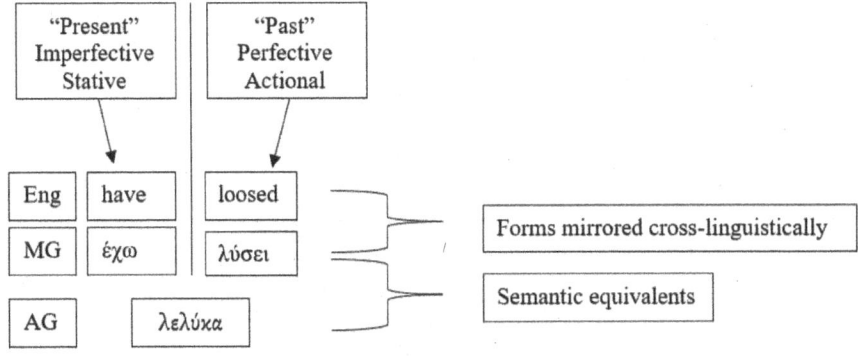

Figure 18: Comparison between Ancient and Modern Perfects

had been, and the lexical core was provided by the Aorist tense. The Modern Greek Perfect is comprised of an imperfective modal verb followed by an Aorist participle or infinitive. Figure 18 illustrates the relationship between the Greek synthetic Perfect and periphrastic Perfect, and relates them both to the English Perfect.

The English periphrastic Perfect is placed over the Modern Greek periphrastic Perfect to illustrate their structural similarity. Both the English and Greek forms have an auxiliary verb at the front, formed from a Present tense, that marks an imperfective view on a stative situation. Likewise, both forms have a lexical verb that marks a perfective action formed from a past tense. Next the older Greek synthetic Perfect is placed below the pair illustrating how its components correspond with the above verbal components.

Although auxiliation is a different process than reduplication, both are parallel to each other in that the first lexeme is usually a state that is seen as enduring over time, and both are collocated with perfective lexemes to form Perfects. Likewise, both reduplication and auxiliation are grammaticalisation processes. Both begin as a lexical verb with unique semantic content, but move toward a general stative meaning, and then acquire grammatical categories in order for them to form Perfect tenses.

The auxiliary verb + Aorist construction of Modern Greek has fully replaced the reduplicated Perfect of Ancient Greek. The Neohellenic periphrastic Perfect tense-form is most commonly used to refer to a complete action where the results of this action are more in focus than is the prior action.[79] This means that it

---

79 Holton, Mackridge, and Philippaki-Warburton, *Greek: A Comprehensive Grammar*, 300-301.

mirrors the usage of the synthetic Perfect tense-form during the Classical Greek period. This usage further suggests that the two types of Perfects share similar semantics. The complex aspect understanding for the Greek Synthetic Perfect best explains why a periphrastic expression with two verbs, each having a different aspect, can replace the synthetic form and share semantic properties. A single aspect understanding for the synthetic Perfect cannot explain why both form types are equivalent.

3.5. The Role of Adverb Collocation Data

When discussing tests to separate classes of stative verbs, Rothmayr states that manner adverbs do not collocate with strict states and must correlate with an event of some kind.[80] She further illustrates how certain locative adverbs also locate the event and not a state.[81] Katz writing around the same time, also discusses the incompatibility of manner adverbs with stative verbs.[82] Katz traces the notion of this incompatibility back to Harris and Jackendoff.[83] Both Rothmayr and Katz include some seemingly stative verbs that do collocate with manner adverbs as exceptions to that general statement of incompatibility. Their respective lists of stative verbs that collocate with manner adverbs contain mostly cognitive verbs and posture verbs.[84] These verbs are known to have both eventive and stative readings at the same time across many languages.[85] Due to the special nature of stative readings of both of these classes of verbs, the study will avoid them while analysing the adverb collocations. The reason is that their stative readings may have more to do with their verb class and less to do with the Perfect tense-form. Since stative verbs of only this class are seen with manner adverbs, as long as they are avoided in the study, the remaining verbs should follow the

---

80 Antonia Rothmayr, *The Structure of Stative Verbs*, Linguistik Aktuell: 145 (Amsterdam: John Benjamins, 2009), 31. Rothmayr is writing on stative verbs while analysing their argument structure.

81 Rothmayr, 32.

82 Graham Katz, "Manner Modification of State Verbs," 220-248 in *Adjectives and Adverbs: Syntax, Semantics, and Discourse*, Oxford Studies in Theoretical Linguistics, edited by Louise McNally and Christopher Kennedy (Oxford: Oxford University Press, 2008), 221.

83 Harris develops this by illustrating the incompatibility of "is" with "slowly." Zellig Harris, *The Mathematical Structure of Language*, Interscience Tracts in Pure and Applied Mathematics: 21 (London: Wiley, 1968), 66. Jackendoff separates S-adverbs from VP-adverbs, where S-adverbs are subject-oriented and can collocate with states, and VP-adverbs are predicate-oriented and must collocate with an action verb. Ray Jackendoff, *Semantic Interpretation in Generative Grammar*, Current Studies in Linguistics (Cambridge, MA: MIT Press, 1972), 47-105.

84 Rothmayr, *Structure of Stative Verbs*, 29-32; Katz, "Manner Modification," 223.

85 For a treatment on how Indo-European posture verbs grammaticalize from actions to states while retaining both meanings in the language, see Tania Kuteva, "On 'sit'/'stand'/'lie' auxiliation," *Linguistics* 27-2 (1999): 191-213.

dictum that stative verbs do not collocate with manner adverbs. Perfect tenses that are from neither the cognitive class nor the posture class that also have manner adverbs cannot be stative.

Stative verbs generally tend to attract temporal modifiers of a duration of time as opposed to a specific point in time. Another way to tell if the verb is eventive rather than stative is find verbs modified by an agent who performed the action.

The idea that a Perfect tense-form is "stative" emerged as one of the definitions for its verbal aspect within the debate over the meaning of the Perfect.[86] Since certain manner adverbs are observed as collocating with only eventive verb situations, a search was performed of the Perfect tense-forms within the Pauline corpus to see if any of these manner adverbs collocated with Perfects. The idea is that if Perfect tense-forms are modified by certain manner adverbs, this collocation will show that the Perfect tense-form can refer to the event and not only to a state and provide further evidence that a Perfect can be either stative or eventive, and in some situations be both stative and eventive. A search of these Perfect tense-forms was also performed for durative adverbs and expressions of agency.[87] The reason such adverbs are valuable to this research is that adverbs simply modify what is already inherent in the properties of the verb. If the adverb modifies an event, then the event is what the verb is about. If the adverb modifies a state, then the verb is stative. Thus, the adverb illustrates the aspect already in the verb and provides more information to the verb.

For Greek, some of these adverbs are single-word units and others are prepositional phrases.[88] Several significant single-word adverbs appear in this corpus,

---

86 Stativity of the Perfect is primarily defended by Porter. Porter, *Verbal Aspect*, 259.

87 All the adverbs and adverbial expressions were collected in Appendix I to see which ones could reliably predict either an event or a state, and these three were the most significant, with durative time adverbs predicting states, and agency expressions and manner adverbs predicting events.

88 The connection between prepositions and adverbs is addressed in Greek grammars and focused treatments on prepositions. Wallace connects these two and exhibits some exceptions. Daniel Wallace, *Greek Grammar Beyond the Basics: An Exegetical Syntax of the New Testament* (Grand Rapids, MI: Zondervan, 1996), 356. Harris connects adverbs and prepositions in Greek parallel to what was happening in Indo-European more generally. Murray Harris, *Prepositions and Theology in the Greek New Testament: An Essential Reference Resource for Exegesis* (Grand Rapids, MI: Zondervan, 2012), 27. Bortone traces the development from locative expressions through to adverb and prepositional expressions. He reminds that Aristotle had grouped both adverbs and prepositions together. Peitro Bortone, *Greek Prepositions: From Antiquity to the Present* (Oxford: Oxford University Press, 2010), 27. Luraghi discusses the connection between adverbs and prepositions as well and provides examples for a number of complexities. She also connects prepositions to an original spatial meaning. Silvia Luraghi, *On the Meaning of Prepositions and Cases: The Expression of Semantic Roles in Ancient Greek*, SLCS: 67 (Amsterdam: John Benjamins, 2003), 75, 315.

such as εἰκῇ, Gal. 4:11; καλῶς, 1 Tim. 5:17; and νυνὶ, 1 Cor. 15:20.[89] In addition to single-word adverbs, Greek uses prepositional phrases adverbially. Several significant types of these were observed in this corpus, such as ἐν + dative, ἀπό + genitive, κατά + accusative, διά + genitive, ὑπό + genitive, and ἐπί + accusative.[90] These phrases included expressions of manner, agency, and durative time.

A few salient examples will suffice to illustrate both eventive and stative Perfects in the Pauline corpus. The first example contains an adverb of manner collocated with a Perfect tense-form. The idea is to see whether it modifies an action or a state.

φοβοῦμαι ὑμᾶς μή πως <u>εἰκῇ</u> κεκοπίακα εἰς ὑμᾶς. (Gal 4:11)

I fear for you, that perhaps I have laboured toward you <u>in vain.</u>

The adverb can be understood as a dative "in vain," or an adverb "vainly." Parallel translations provide the same meaning.

I fear for you, that perhaps I have laboured toward you <u>in vain</u> (Gal 4:11)[91]

I fear for you, that perhaps I have <u>vainly</u> laboured toward you.

The question is whether the Perfect tense-form κεκοπίακα (I have laboured) refers to a subject-oriented state, or a previous action. The adverb εἰκῇ (vainly) will either modify the action of Paul labouring for the Galatians, or it will modify Paul's state after having done so. The subject's state does not appear to continue vainly. It appears that the original action was suggested as being performed vainly, and any state of the subject is unmodified by this adverb in this context. The following translation would imply that εἰκῇ (vainly) modifies a state.

*I fear for you, that perhaps I am <u>vainly</u> in some state due to having laboured toward you. [92]

This interpretation is awkward at best.

The next example will contain a Perfect tense-form modified by an agent. The point is to see whether the agent is that of the original action or is somehow connected with continuing the state.

---

89 Others of less significance are displayed in Appendices F, G, and J.

90 A fuller list is in Appendix I.

91 These translations are mine, providing alternate ways to translate the prepositional phrase. The English translations largely read like the first example, unless they alter the verbal structure making the adverb into a verb and the verb into a noun, "I have wasted my efforts . . . ".

92 The use of "*" marks an awkward construction generally, in this case an awkward translation to show the difficulty of understanding a stative Perfect force here.

Πᾶσα ψυχὴ ἐξουσίαις ὑπερεχούσαις ὑποτασσέσθω. οὐ γὰρ ἔστιν ἐξουσία εἰ μὴ ὑπὸ θεοῦ, αἱ δὲ οὖσαι <u>ὑπὸ θεοῦ</u> τεταγμέναι εἰσίν. (Rom. 13:1)

Let every soul be subordinated to those who are being held above with author-ity. For authority does not exist except by God, and the ones existing are those which have been organized <u>by God</u>.

The question here is whether God is an agent for the organising action related to the authorities, or somehow an agent for their continued existence. While the first instance of ὑπὸ θεοῦ (by God) might be best said to relate to continued exis-tence, due the verb ἔστιν, the latter instance expects that the agent ὑπὸ θεοῦ (by God) is related to τεταγμέναι (have been organised) and not to εἰσίν (they are). The following translation might be apparent if the agent did not relate to the action of organising.

*Let every soul be subordinated to those who are being held above with author-ity. For authority does not exist except by God, and the ones existing are those which are <u>by God</u> [and] have been organised [by an unnamed entity].

This is also an awkward use of the agentive phrase ὑπὸ θεοῦ (by God), and it is best to understand the agent as modifying the action of organising. Supplying an agent or a manner adverb does not add the eventive character to the Perfect, it simply modifies the existing event already in the verb.

The next example contains a durative time element collocated with a Perfect tense-form. The point is to show the relationship of this type of modification with stative readings of the Perfect.

καὶ φωτίσαι [πάντας] τίς ἡ οἰκονομία τοῦ μυστηρίου τοῦ ἀποκεκρυμμένου <u>ἀπὸ τῶν αἰώνων</u> ἐν τῷ θεῷ τῷ τὰ πάντα κτίσαντι, (Eph 3:9)

And to enlighten everyone what is the stewardship of the mystery, the one that has been hidden <u>from the ages</u> in God, the one who created all things.

The question here is whether ἀπὸ τῶν αἰώνων (from the ages) modifies the hiding event or specifies the duration of the state of hiddenness. If the ages were an entity from which something was hidden, such as "I hid the ball from John," then the phrase might suggest more an action and not some state of the subject. Hiddenness is the state of the mystery in this passage, and "ages" functions as an expression of durative time, since the point Paul makes here is that this mystery had been hidden from the beginning up until this time. God did not have to keep hiding this mystery away from each moment in time, it simply was hidden once, and kept hidden until the point in time Paul was referencing. This means the durative time element refers to the whole period of hiddenness, and not to the moment of hiding the mystery. The Perfect tense-form is stative in this example.

The first two examples have a Perfect tense-form pointing to an event, shown by the manner adverb and the agency expression, and the last example has a Perfect tense-form pointing to an enduring state, shown by the durative temporal adverb. Perfect tenses can be used both ways, and whenever the event is in view, the action is viewed perfectively. In contrast, whenever the state is in view, it is viewed imperfectively to bring out its duration. These observations fit nicely with the arguments formulated in an earlier section and provide more support for the Perfect containing a complex verbal aspect. This aspect is observed whenever one Perfect tense-form may be modified as though it were a perfective event, and another as though it were an imperfective state. It appears that the author chooses whether to use the Perfect as a state or as an event and modifies it accordingly in context. The adverbial modifiers are what lets the reader know which way the Perfect is used in a specific context. Not all Perfect tense-forms are modified by adverbs, so for these contexts it is less clear how to decide whether the Perfect has stative or eventive focus. However, for the Perfects that are modified by adverbs, the Pauline corpus data shows both eventive and stative uses of the Perfect.[93]

4. Implications for Complex Aspect

The existence of complex aspect for the Perfect tense-form implies several things for this research. First, if this view is correct, then support for complex verbal aspect can be garnered from the grammars of the Greek language. Second, diachronic corpora will provide significant support for the existence of both aspects if complex aspect is correct for the Perfect. Therefore, an analysis of such a corpus is discussed in Chapter 5. Third, the Pauline use of the synthetic Greek Perfect can be situated within the cline of development observed for the Perfect. The situation within the Pauline corpus is described in the latter half of the fifth chapter.

---

93 See Appendices F, G, H and I.

4.1. The Historical Understanding of the Greek Perfect

Comparing the grammars shows compatibility between the idea of the Perfect having a complex aspect and the historical description of the Greek Perfect. This section includes the major grammars, especially those with a historic approach to the language. This section attempts to be chronological in reference to the publication of the ideas in the grammars, but keeps multiple volumes of the same grammar together, even when they are separated in time.

Matthiae places the Perfect with the past tenses but labels the Perfect as a past form relative to something else, while Aorist is simple past.[94] By calling this a "relative past," he accounts for the action of the Perfect being relevant to a non-past state. He further provides that the connection to the present may be in either the consequences of the action or its circumstances.[95] This condition which results from a barely emphasised action continues on and remains in place at the reference time.[96] His definition is not aspectual, but focuses on the eventive and temporal properties of the Perfect. Helpfully he connects past time to the event and present time to the state.

Buttmann states that the Perfect connects a past event with the present time.[97] This is similar to how the Aorist verb denotes the past action in narrative, but an added Imperfect can point to the state resulting from that action described by the Aorist in narrative contexts.[98] Although his description is temporal and pragmatic rather than aspectual, it is interesting that he compares the Perfect to the situation where an Aorist (a perfective) plus an Imperfect (an imperfective) are jointly used to indicate a state arising from an action. The idea that two aspects on separate lexemes can link an action to a state is parallel with the idea emerging in this chapter where the Perfect tense-form contains both aspects to accomplish this. His son later contrasts the Perfect with the Aorist as a tense containing present relevance opposing the narrative sense (past) belonging to the Aorist, but later adds that some Perfects are used the same way as an Aorist with no distinction between the tenses.[99] His description is not aspectual, but begins with temporal properties and then moves to functional uses. He highlights the diachronic shift

---

94 Augustus Matthiae, *A Copius Greek Grammar*, 5th ed., Vol. 1 (London: Murray, 1832), 254.

95 Augustus Matthiae, *A Copius Greek Grammar*, 5th ed., Vol. 2 (London: Murray, 1832), 832.

96 Matthiae, *A Copius Greek Grammar*, Vol. 2, 840-841.

97 Philip Buttmann, *Intermediate or Larger Greek Grammar* (London: Black, Young and Young, 1833), 350.

98 P. Buttmann, 351.

99 Alexander Buttmann, *A Grammar of the New Testament Greek* (Andover: Draper, 1873), 196.

of the Perfect to a simple past form, and suggests this change began before the time of the NT.[100] This last component provides validation for the concerns of grammaticalisation developed earlier.

Jannaris states that "the Perfect denotes an action as already accomplished for the present time."[101] This makes it the best past tense for discourse, but it can have present-only force as well.[102] Here he links the Perfect to its pragmatic use in discourse, and he connects the Perfect to its temporal uses. The pragmatic function in discourse connects well with how Paul uses most of the Perfects in his letters.

Curtius describes the Perfect as a Present tense and stative, owing this to its reduplication.[103] Later he describes Perfects that focus on completed action. Here it seems these are limited to certain lexemes, but some of the lexemes in this category are used both ways, either as a present state in one instance or as a past action in another.[104] This flexibility provides some confirmation for the complex aspect developed in this project. Although his description is temporal rather than aspectual, he is careful to apply action and state to the effects of the Perfect on its context rather than on lexeme or the Perfect tense-form, itself.

Burton describes the Perfect as "an action as standing at the time of speaking complete."[105] His wording is more careful than might be first assumed. He avoids saying the action is past, and the reference time is present. This avoids an overly temporal understanding. The fact he mentions the action is complete rather than completed, is closer to an aspectual understanding than most of the grammars. He does add that a past action is implied, but is careful to label it an implication.[106] His understanding regarding the Perfects which only exhibit present states, is that the former action has dropped from the mind of the users.[107] This is congruent with the idea that the speaker can choose the way the Perfect gets expressed. The stative-only use is restricted to certain lexemes.[108] He also includes the use of the Perfect as a simple past tense.[109]

---

100 A. Buttmannn, *A Grammar of New Testament Greek*, 196-197.

101 Antonius N. Jannaris, *An Historical Greek Grammar* (London: Macmillan, 1897), 438.

102 Jannaris, 438-439.

103 Georg Curtius, 377-378.

104 Curtius' examples all come from Homer, belonging to the earliest phase of the Greek language mentioned in this project. Curtius, 380.

105 Ernest DeWitt Burton, *Syntax of the Moods and Tenses in New Testament Greek* (Chicago: University of Chicago Press, 1898), 37.

106 Burton, 37.

107 Burton, 37-38.

108 Burton, 38.

109 Burton, 39-44.

Moulton observes that the Perfect generally connects a prior action to a later state. He includes examples both before and after the NT, where some Perfects were used to point to a past action and others to only a present state.[110] Turner later in the series adds that the original Perfect did not refer to the action, but to a present state of the subject and only occurred in intransitive situations.[111] Between the two scholars, the details of a form changing its focus through time is apparent.

Robertson describes the Perfect as "continuance of a perfected or completed action."[112] He further reminds that originally the tense-forms were timeless, meaning without temporal properties.[113] However, he does not replace temporal relations with aspect in his description, but focuses instead on a "kind of action" for each tense-form, called *Aktionsart*.[114] He is aware of the terminology for aspect, as he mentions "others use perfective," but seems as though he views it an alternative term for *Aktionsart*.[115] Robertson makes clear that the earliest Perfects were present states.[116] Under the category of "extensive perfect," he says that "the perfect is both punctiliar and durative."[117] It is interesting here that he provides terminology very close to that of having two aspects. He prefers the two *Aktionsarten* over the aspectual words, perfective and imperfective, although he considers them alternative terms. Additionally, he understands this dual nature to allow for the presence of only one of these parts of the Perfect to appear on one context and the other to appear in another.[118] This is roughly congruent with the hypothesis of this project, where the Perfect has two aspects, one on a state and the other on an action. Some contexts use both, but others may use either one or the other. Although using different terminology, his dual nature concept is congruent with complex aspect.

Blass and Debrunner describe the Perfect as combining "in itself . . . the present and the aorist in that it denotes the *continuance* of *completed action*."[119] Blass

110 James Hope Moulton, *A Grammar of New Testament Greek*, Vol. 1, Prolegomena, 3rd ed. (Edinburgh: T & T Clark, 1908), 140-145.

111 Turner, *Syntax*, 81-83.

112 Archibald T. Robertson, *A Grammar of the Greek New Testament in the Light of Historical Research* (New York: Hodder and Stoughton, 1914), 823.

113 Robertson, 824.

114 Robertson, 824.

115 Robertson, 823.

116 Robertson, 892.

117 Robertson, 893.

118 Robertson, 893.

119 Italics are original. Friedrich Blass and Albert Debrunner, *A Greek Grammar of the New Testament and Other Early Christian Literature*, translated and revised by Robert W. Funk (Chicago: University of Chicago Press, 1961), 175.

and Debrunner state that some Perfects only denote a state during the present.[120] They also provide that later in time, Perfects were used in the place of Aorists as past tenses, with a few of these uses in the New Testament.[121] The combination of Aorist plus Present, seems to accommodate the aspectual package observed in this study.

Wallace begins his section on the tenses with the statement that the Greek tenses encode both aspect and time. It appears he is aware that a distinction between aspect and *Aktionsart* is needed, but his summary statement of aspect as a "kind of action," seems as though he views them synonymously.[122] He later separates aspect and *Aktionsart* as locating aspect in the form itself and *Aktionsart* as an effect the verb has with its context.[123] He understands the Perfect tense-form combines both perfective and imperfective aspect, where the state is imperfective and the action is perfective.[124] He cites both McKay and Fanning for support, but neither of them state this view. It seems he has combined both of their prior discussions to create this understanding. His statement is congruent with the findings of this study.

The new Cambridge reference grammar discusses verbal aspect in its description of the Greek verb tense-forms.[125] Verbal aspect is described as having two aspects, both complete and incomplete.[126] Verbs with the Present stem have incomplete aspect, and those with the Aorist stem have complete aspect. The grammar departs from using aspectual terminology when verbs using a Perfect stem are then described. The Perfect is explained as involving a state resulting from a preceding completed action.[127] This description is a pragmatic one rather than an aspectual one.

The main thing the grammars supply is a temporal and pragmatic definition of the Greek Perfect. Additionally, many clearly state that the Greek Perfect can be used of an action or a state. When referring to a state, the tense-form behaves as a present tense, and when referring to an action, it behaves as a past tense. While the terms "present" and "past" might not be the best terms to describe

---

120 Blass and Debrunner, 176.
121 Blass and Debrunner, 177.
122 Wallace, 496, 499.
123 Wallace, 499-500.
124 He supplies "portrayed externally" and "portrayed internally" to refer to these two aspects, depending on Fanning's division of internal and external view. Wallace, *Beyond the Basics*, 501, 573.
125 Evert van Emde Boas, Albert Rijksbaron, Luuk Huitink, and Mattieu de Bakker, *Cambridge Grammar of Classical Greek* (Cambridge: Cambridge University Press, 2019).
126 These correspond with perfective and imperfective respectively. van Emde Boas, et al., 405.
127 van Emde Boas, et al., 406.

the location of either the state or the action, temporal terminology was the best the earlier grammars had available. Once the discussion of *Aktionsart* and aspect began, the grammars tend to avoid the temporal descriptions since the tense-forms could be used in ways different from what their "tense" suggested. As the grammars dropped temporal terminology, they replaced it with first *Aktionsart* terminology (such as punctiliar and durative) and then aspect terminology (such as perfective and imperfective). Once the Perfect is understood as having both aspects as developed in this project, it is easy to comprehend how both past and present reference would attach by implication to both aspects of the tense-form, where present reference is implied by the imperfective, and past reference by the perfective.

As far as the older grammarians are concerned, they are essentially correct in describing the Perfect, but in the effects of its aspect on time, rather than providing a definition of aspect for the Perfect. So, where the older grammarians describe the Perfect as a present state, or a past action, I suggest revising the wording somewhat. The Perfect describes an imperfective state, or a perfective action respectively. The grammars as a whole do not provide anything that contradicts the view set forth in this project, but instead support the idea that a Perfect contains a complex aspect. Furthermore, the complex aspect developed in this project best explains the history of Greek grammars on the subject of the Perfect Tense.

4.2. Implications of the Complex Aspect for the Method and Analysis

Since the verbal aspect of the Perfect tense-form is understood to be complex, having a perfective aspect on the lexical core, referring to events, and an imperfective aspect on the reduplicant, referring to states, the difficulty will be to understand when a Perfect emphasises each aspect and what the linguistic environments are for each instance. Both the Pauline corpus and the diachronic epistolary and moral literature corpus will be investigated to find the possible linguistic environments and discover when a Perfect will be eventive and when it will be stative, based on the nature of complex aspect described in this chapter.

5. Conclusion

This chapter has argued from morphology that the stem vowel and consonant spellings of the lexical core and the reduplicant of the Greek synthetic Perfect each point to different verbal aspects. The stem of the Perfect mirrors the Aorist in its vowel or consonantal spelling, and the reduplicant belongs to the formation of imperfectives. The fact that the Perfect mirrors the Aorist in its stem spelling and its reduplicant is associated with imperfectives together suggest that both perfectivity and imperfectivity are viable aspectual components for the Greek synthetic Perfect. Utilising Grammaticalisation Theory, this chapter connects the Greek synthetic Perfect to two separate clines noticed in grammaticalisation, that of the development of perfectives, and that of reduplication as it mirrors the cline of development of imperfectives. The extension of the Perfect to active contexts is consistent with a late position in its grammaticalisation cline. The erosion of the morphological bulk of reduplicant combined with its desemanticisation suggests that it is a stative morpheme with imperfective properties. The form of the Greek synthetic Perfect is located near the end of both clines. For the developments of perfectives, this is evidenced by its disuse as a form without further development and for imperfectives this is evidenced by its reduplicant type, which is Ce, showing a nearly full reduction onto the stem. This location on both clines suggests that both perfectivity and imperfectivity are highly grammaticalised components for the Greek synthetic Perfect. The cross-linguistic mirroring of these two aspects in the Modern language periphrastic perfects along with a mirroring of their uses suggests that this complex aspect was also the situation for the earlier synthetic Perfects. This analysis of the Greek synthetic Perfect tense-form further suggests that an analysis of the Perfect tense-forms cross-linguistically might demonstrate a complex aspect for the Perfects of other languages.

The set of arguments taken together in this chapter all suggest complex aspect for the Greek Perfect. First, they point to an imperfectivity regarding any state produced by the Perfect. Secondly, they point to a perfectivity when action is implied or focused upon. Thirdly, they suggest that the mere presence of the Perfect tense-form is not enough to decide whether that Perfect is using one or both of these aspects, but contextual development is required to illustrate which one or ones of these might be in view. Just because one or the other aspect may not be contextually relevant does not mean it was cancelled. Adding context does not cancel either aspect; it merely emphasises either the perfective event or the imperfective state. This uncancellability satisfies the semantic concerns in Chapter 2.

One item in this section that more clearly points to the presence of a state or an action than others is the adverb. For this reason, analysing the adverb modifying the Perfect will be of importance to the rest of this research. Alexiadou provides some criteria for adverb attraction, where durative adverbs combine with the imperfective, and count adverbs, cardinal adverbs and point adverbs combine with the perfective.[128] Psaltou-Joycey includes prepositional phrases and syntactical considerations when analysing when adverb phrase indicate temporality in Perfects.[129] In summary, the Perfect will be understood as pointing to an imperfective state, a perfective action, or both, with the understanding that the form does both, but both might not be contextually relevant.

128 Artemis Alexiadou. "On Aspectual and Temporal Adverbs," *Themes in Greek Linguistics*. CILT: 117, edited by Irene Philippaki-Warburton, Katarina Nicolaidas, and Maria Sifianou (Amsterdam: John Benjamins, 1993), 147.

129 Angeliki Psaltou-Joycey, "Specification of Temporal Intervals and Situations in the Perfect," *Themes in Greek Linguistics*. CILT: 117, edited by Irene Philippaki-Warburton, Katarina Nicolaidas, and Maria Sifianou (Amsterdam: John Benjamins, 1993), 154.

The Complex Aspect of the Perfect Tense-Form in the Pauline Corpus

This chapter first presents examples drawn from the Pauline corpus and analyses their context. Second, the chapter relates the morphology and context of each Perfect tense-form to its verbal aspect. Discussion from the various commentaries is included when relevant to the meaning of the Perfect tense, and then evaluated. The verbal aspect for each instance selected from the corpus is analysed in light of the complex aspect developed earlier. Also, aspect-focused language will be suggested for describing the semantics of the Perfect tense within the commentaries regarding each instance where it is absent. Finally, the findings of this chapter are shown to support the complex aspect developed in Chapter 3.

1. The Verbal Data from the Pauline Corpus

The verb examples discussed in this section are divided into five categories. The first three are those which point to a state, to an action, or to both a state and an action. The decision whether a state or an action is in focus is based on broad contextual consideration from Appendix E, and specifically on adverb type from Appendices F and G. Both Appendices F and G are synthesised and statistically reported in Appendix H. Examples within the appendices, which are categorised in the same way on all the appendices in which they appear, are selected for discussion in this chapter.[1] The fourth category of verbs have a special pragmatic function. The fifth section deals with a verb where its lexical meaning is debated, supplying historical analysis that it is considered a linguistic fossil in the literature. Each subsection will contain an example, followed by an analysis of its morphology, context, and verbal aspect.

1.1. Verbs Which Have a Stative Component

This section will analyse the morphology of Perfect tense-forms within the Pauline corpus that appear to be stative in meaning, along with the surrounding context. These examples are chosen because the linguistic environments around the Perfect tense-form do not contain modifiers for an action nor references to an action. The section on morphology will analyse the lexical form of each Perfect tense-form, track the changes to the stem of the form in its formation to the Perfect tense, and account for the various morphemes that comprise the tense-forms. The section on context will account for any temporal modifiers, note especially the function of any adverbs, and indicate the pragmatic function that arises from the verb in its context.

> 6.) Παῦλος δοῦλος Χριστοῦ Ἰησοῦ, κλητὸς ἀπόστολος <u>ἀφωρισμένος</u> εἰς εὐαγγέλιον θεοῦ, (Rom 1.1)
>
> Paul, a servant of Christ Jesus, called an apostle <u>having been set apart</u> for the Gospel of God.[2]

[ἀφωρισμένος, participle]

This participle has several issues that affect its morphology. First of all, it does not have reduplication of the first consonant of the stem as is typical for the synthetic Greek Perfect. Secondly it does not have the trademark -κ- of the synthetic Greek Perfect tense-form due to being a middle form. Thirdly, the addition

---

1 These appendices account for factors that determine whether a Perfect is stative or eventive in each context in the Pauline corpus. Since each appendix categorises the Perfects using different criteria, it is deemed best to use only the Perfects that are categorised similarly in both. Broad context considerations determine the category in Appendix E, and specific adverb type determines the category in Appendix H and Appendix I. It is possible that the two methods might not always produce the same result for every Perfect. Examples that are strongly categorised the same way through both methods are provided in order to prove the case for complex aspect.

2 Translation is mine.

of a preposition affects the shape of its initial phonemes. This Perfect tense-form from Rom 1:1 appears stative in its setting.[3] The participle is ἀφωρισμένος, which means "having been set apart" for some purpose.[4] The lexical form of this participle is ἀφορίζω, and it is a combination of the prefix ἀπό, containing the idea of "from" with the main verb ὁρίζω, containing the idea of "to make boundaries," or "to divide." When this preposition and verb occur together, the sense of separating items from each other emerges as the main idea. Often the translation for this compound verb is "to separate from," where one item is separated from the others.[5] When the verb ἀφορίζω is formed into the Perfect participle ἀφωρισμένος, it undergoes a slight change in the stem of the verb. The initial present stem of this verb is ὁριζ-. The -ζ- changes to a -σ-, then adds the middle/passive participle morpheme -μεν- and the nominative singular -ος. This same stem change, from -ζ- to -σ-, is observed whenever any verb ending in -ιζω becomes either an Aorist or a Perfect. This tendency of both forms to alter this stem in the same way suggests that something exists in common between the Aorist and the Perfect tense morphologically. No -κ- exists within this Perfect tense-form, since the -κ- does not appear in the Perfect middle forms. The initial -ο- vowel becomes -ω-, since the morpheme in the reduplicant is simply a lengthened vowel, rather than using a Ce reduplication. The rough breathing mark from the beginning of this stem ὁριζ- is combined with the -π- of the preposition ἀπό and changes the preposition's form to ἀφ-.

In this context, it is Paul that has been separated from a larger group of people for a purpose. Whoever or whatever it is that Paul has been separated from is unclear in the immediate context, but this group might be the Pharisees, Christians in general, or the apostles as a group, or if a purpose is in view, this purpose might be the purpose of any of these groups. If it is the Pharisees or their purpose that Paul was separated from, then this refers back to his conversion experience on the road to Damascus. Dunn suggests that this separation relates to the conversion experience, but equates the conversion with the commissioning of Paul for his special mission.[6] If it is the Christians in general or their purpose that this group refers to, then this refers back to his having become an apostle.

---

3 This is the only occurrence of this stem in the Perfect tense-form in the Pauline corpus. The other instances of this verbal stem are either Aorist or Imperfect.

4 The meaning reported for all words and particles initially in this study is gleaned from the most basic meanings provided in LSJ. Derived meanings are shown as combinations of particles or the word interacting with its context.

5 See the KJV translating this lexeme in Luke 6:22; ESV and RSV in 2 Cor 6:17; KJV, NAB, NASB, NET, and NIV in Gal 1:15; and NIV in Gal 2:12.

6 James D. G. Dunn, *Romans 1–8*, WBC: 38A (Dallas, TX: Word, 1998), 9.

Fitzmeyer suggests that this separation was that from other Christians, making a comparison to the Levites being set apart from the Israelites for the special purpose of religious service.[7] Cranfield sees this separation as toward a "special ministry within the Christian community," due to the phrase being parallel with κλητὸς ἀπόστολος.[8] If it is the apostles as a group, or their purpose that Paul has been separated from, then this refers to his mission to the Gentiles specifically. Schreiner suggests that the use of καλεῖν and ἀφορίζειν together in Gal 1:15 referring to Gentile evangelism relates their usage in Romans 1:1 to Paul's specific selection to Gentile ministry.[9] Since the only clue in the context of Romans 1:1 is the modifying phrase, εἰς εὐαγγέλιον θεοῦ, it is better to connect the use of ἀφωρισμένος to Paul's selection for apostleship.

If this participle had been followed by a genitive word or phrase, then that word or phrase would have been the element that Paul was separated from.[10] Instead, this word is followed by another prepositional phrase beginning with the word εἰς. This following phrase indicates the element Paul is called toward, rather than the element he has been separated from. Jewett states that this preposition indicates the goal for Paul's separation in the context.[11] Dunn relates it to the reversal of a separation from Gentiles in the Torah, to a separation toward the Gentiles.[12] In this context, Paul has been separated from some unnamed group, and toward the purpose of the gospel. Moo suggests that this participle both indicates Paul's special function and further describes his calling.[13] Lenski understands contra Moo, that this phrase should be related in apposition to Παῦλος, rather than to κλητὸς ἀπόστολος.[14] Cranfield agrees with Lenski.[15] As an apposition, this participle indicates that Paul is the one who has been separated or set apart for the purpose of the gospel. There are no adverbs or temporal modifiers for this participle. The pragmatic function of this participle is to be both adjectival

7 Joseph A. Fitzmyer S. J., *Romans: A New Translation with Introduction and Commentary*, AB: 33 (New Haven: CT: Yale University Press, 2008), 232.

8 C. E. B. Cranfield, *A Critical and Exegetical Commentary on the Epistle to the Romans*, ICC (London: T&T Clark, 2004), 54.

9 Thomas R. Schreiner, *Romans*, BECNT: 6 (Grand Rapids, MI: Baker, 1998), 33.

10 For examples of this verbal stem in the Aorist having prepositional phrases beginning with ἐκ indicating the item the subject was separated from, see 1 Cor 6;17 and Gal 2:12.

11 Robert Jewett and Roy David Kotansky, *Romans: A Commentary*, Hermeneia—A Critical and Historical Commentary on the Bible, edited by Eldon Jay Epp (Minneapolis, MN: Fortress, 2006), 102.

12 Dunn, 9.

13 Douglas J. Moo, *The Epistle to the Romans*, The New International Commentary on the New Testament (Grand Rapids, MI: Eerdmans, 1996), 42.

14 R. C. H. Lenski, *The Interpretation of St. Paul's Epistle to the Romans* (Columbus, OH: Lutheran Book Concern, 1936), 29.

15 Cranfield, 53.

and an indicator of the status of the author as one who has been set apart. It is this status that is contextually relevant and marks this Perfect participle as providing a state rather than an event.

This verb indicates the state of Paul having been set apart by God from some group or purpose toward the purpose of the Gospel. This state is presented with a view toward its "ongoing"-ness. Lenski relates this participle to the present-ness of Paul's condition.[16] Mounce discusses the Perfect tense-form here pointing to the "ongoing effects."[17] Thus, this state of being set apart is viewed imperfectively since it is the background for Paul to write this letter and the platform for authority from which he speaks. Although an event surely marked the entrance into this state, it is not referenced in this context. Had it been referenced, it would likely have been viewed as a complete past event, so perfectivity would work for that event.

7.) ὃν προέθετο ὁ θεὸς ἱλαστήριον διὰ [τῆς] πίστεως ἐν τῷ αὐτοῦ αἵματι εἰς ἔνδειξιν τῆς δικαιοσύνης αὐτοῦ διὰ τὴν πάρεσιν τῶν <u>προγεγονότων</u> ἁμαρτημάτων (Rom 3.25)

Whom God put forth [as] a propitiation through faith in his blood toward a sign of his righteousness on account of the passing over of the sins that <u>have come into existence before</u>.

[προγεγονότων, participle]

This participle has some issues that affect its morphology as well. First of all, this participle does not form its Perfect according to the Greek productive formation. It is an inherited form from a late stage in Indo-European.[18] It is reduplicated in the normal way, however. This participle also has a preposition at the beginning, but this time it does not affect the initial phonemes.[19] This verb from Rom 3:25 is stative in its setting. Some categorise προγεγονότων as a stative verb

---

16 Lenski, 29.

17 Robert H. Mounce, *Romans*, NAC: 27 (Nashville, TN: Broadman & Holman, 1995), 60 n.3.

18 Beekes and van Beek connect the ablaut spelling of the Perfect in Greek to that of Sanskrit, Gothic, and Latin. Robert S. P. Beekes and Lucian van Beek, *Etymological Dictionary of Greek*, vol. 1 (Leiden: Brill, 2010), 272-273. Rix connects the same to the ablaut spelling in Sanskrit and Old Irish. Helmut Rix, *Lexicon der IndoGermanischen Verben* (Weisbaden: Reichert, 2001), 163-165.

19 This verbal stem occurs 19 times in the Perfect tense-form in the Pauline corpus. Only this occurrence has the preposition πρό attached. Other prepositions that appear on this stem include μετά, with the sense of "come to exist later," or "to migrate," and παρά, with the sense of "to come beside," or "to arrive."

due to its lexeme, γίνομαι, being stative, but its morphological features are consistent with other Perfect tense-forms that yield a stative meaning.[20] This participle begins with γίνομαι, meaning "become" or "come to exist," as its lexeme, and then adds the preposition προ- to the beginning adding a temporal sense of "before." When the verb γίνομαι is formed into the Perfect participle προγεγονότων, it undergoes a slight change in the stem of the verb. The initial present stem of this verb is γίγν-. This is because it is a reduplicated present tense-form. The second -γ- fell out of use after the Classical Period, changing the stem spelling to γίν-. This obscures what is going on with the stem change, so it is necessary to recreate the Classical stem to understand what occurs inside the form. Starting with γίγν-, the present reduplicant γί- must be removed, yielding γν-. This is the perfective stem, normally associated with the Aorist. In the Indo-European ablaut system, the Present normally had an -ε- vowel between the consonants, while the Perfect had -ο- vowel, and the Aorist had none. The absent vowel changes to a -ο-, due to the Indo-European ablaut, then adds the active participle morpheme -οντ- and the genitive plural -ων. The participle morpheme amalgamates dropping out the -ν-. This same stem change, from -ε-, or a null vowel in the case of a reduplicated Present, to -ο-, is observed whenever any Perfect tense-form from Indo-European was retained in the Greek language. The reduplication, participle morphemes, and endings will be consistent with typical Greek verbs indicating that the Greeks applied their system of endings and reduplication to all stems regardless of origin. No -κ- exists within this Perfect tense-form, since the -κ- does not appear in the Perfect tense-forms that are derived by ablaut formations from Indo-European. The initial γε- reduplicant is expected since it has a Ce reduplication, and is the typical method for Greek Perfect tense-forms to be reduplicated.

In this context, this participle describes the noun ἁμαρτημάτων, or "sins." This participle is modified by the preposition attached to the beginning, προ-. This preposition functions temporally to indicate that these sins are the ones that had come to exist already, or "before." The participle itself functions as an adjective to the noun, indicating what kind of sins were in view as having been passed over. The combination is that the "passing over" occurred relevant to the sins that had come to exist before some point that is not determined directly from the immediate phrase. This point-in-time is either the time before Christ was offered as a sacrifice, if the sins are referring to the sins of all humanity;[21] or

---

20 Wallace discusses the stative behaviour of this verb when followed by a predicate nominative. Wallace, *Beyond the Basics*, 40.

21 Lange takes this view, because individual sins of the future time are not in view. John Peter Lange, et al., *A Commentary on the Holy Scriptures: Romans* (Bellingham, WA: Lexham, 2008), 134. Cottrell takes

the time before one accepts the application of that sacrifice, if the sins are referring to everyone's individual sins. Whichever period of time the "before" refers to, the Perfect participle describes the noun by indicating the status of the sins being passed over as committed sins. This status is the main point of this verb and a stative reading is preferred for this participle. Morris understands both the event existing before the reference time due to the preposition, and the continuing status of these sins enduring at least until the time of the crucifixion as being relevant for this "unusual verb."[22] The preposition is more related to the event than to the state as no need exists to include the preposition if only the status of committed sins is relevant. The inclusion of the preposition means that certain sins committed earlier are in view as opposed to later or future commissions of sin. This means the participle is also eventive, but without a stated event in the context. However, the lack of a stated event might be due to each person having a different event of committing sin, and the author wants to reference all of those events generally.

This verb indicates the state of sins having come to exist at some prior point being passed over by God. This state of prior existence is presented with a view toward its "ongoing"-ness. This state of prior existence is viewed imperfectively since it is the background for the action of sins being passed over by God. Although an event surely marks the entrance of sin, this is not referenced in this context, although its time is alluded to by the preposition. Had an event been referenced, it would likely have been viewed as a complete past event, so perfectivity would work for this event. Likewise, if a series of related events were in view, each of them would be viewed perfectively.

8.) Πᾶσα ψυχὴ ἐξουσίαις ὑπερεχούσαις ὑποτασσέσθω. οὐ γὰρ ἔστιν ἐξουσία εἰ μὴ ὑπὸ θεοῦ, αἱ δὲ οὖσαι ὑπὸ θεοῦ <u>τεταγμέναι</u> εἰσίν. (Rom 13:1)

Let every soul be submitted to authorities who are arranged over them. For no authority exists except by God, now those who are existing—they are the ones who <u>have been instituted</u> by God.

[τεταγμέναι, participle]

---

this view as well, based on the crucifixion satisfying God's just-ness. Jack Cottrell, *Romans*, The College Press NIV Commentary (Joplin, MO: College Press, 1996), 150.

22   Leon Morris, *The Epistle to the Romans*, PNTC (Grand Rapids, MI: Eerdmans, 1988), 183.

This participle is formed more closely to the productive pattern in Greek than the first two participles, but has one issue that affects its morphology. First of all, this participle has an internal stem change from its lexical form. It is reduplicated in the normal way, however. This verb from Rom 13:1 is stative in its setting.[23] This participle comes from the lexeme τάσσω, meaning "order" or "organize." It is often connected to various prepositional prefixes, but occurs without them in this instance. When the verb τάσσω changes into the Perfect participle τεταγμέναι, it undergoes a slight change in the stem of the verb. The initial Present stem of this verb is τασσ-. The -σσ- changes to a -γ- in the case of a middle, or a -χ- in the case of an active form. Then, since it is middle here, adds the middle/passive participle morpheme -μεν- and finally the nominative plural -αι. The stems of the Aorist and Perfect mirror each other in this stem change from the Present. This mirroring suggests that something exists in common between the Aorist and the Perfect tense morphologically. No -κ- exists within this Perfect tense-form, since the verbs with a final hard stop simply aspirate for the active, and have a hard stop, or unaspirated final consonant in the middle or middle/passive. The aspirated consonant occurs whenever the -κ- might occur for the typical Greek Perfect. Since this participle does not have the aspirated consonant, this is the same thing as other Perfects that do not have the -κ-. The initial τε- reduplicant is expected since this verb follows a Ce reduplication, which is the typical method for Greek Perfect tense-forms to be reduplicated.

In this context, this participle follows the plural article αἱ that has the noun ἐξουσία, or "authorities," from the previous clause for its referent. This participle is modified by the prepositional phrase, ὑπὸ θεοῦ, or "by God," occurring just before it. This prepositional phrase functions to provide the agent who organised the existence of the authorities. The participle itself functions as a substantive, but describes the noun ἐξουσία, or "authorities," indicating that the authorities in existence did not cause themselves, or provide themselves with power, but their power is derived from God ordering them into power. Since the ongoing status of these authorities as having been ordered by God is the main consideration for this participle, a stative reading is preferred for this participle. Cranfield understands that the Roman Emperor and civil officials are the authorities Paul has in mind here.[24] None of the commentaries consulted discussed either the Perfect

---

23 This is the only Perfect tense-form of τάσσω without an attached preposition in the Pauline corpus. Another example of this verbal stem without a preposition attached exists in 1 Cor 15:16 in the Aorist tense-form. Most often this verbal stem has a preposition attached in front, such as ἀντί, σύν, or ὑπό.

24 Cranfield, 663.

form, or any possible stative or eventive properties associated with its use in this context.[25]

This verb indicates the state of authorities having been ordered or organised by God. This state is presented with a view toward its "ongoing"-ness. This state is viewed imperfectively since it is the background for the authorities to exist and practice their limited power derived from God's eternal power. No event is suggested as the entrance into this state, but if one had been included, it would have been presented as complete, and prior to the state. Thus, it would have perfectivity. This event is likely to be either the beginnings of human government, or a series of events as God causes governments to rise and fall.

9.) θύρα γάρ μοι <u>ἀνέῳγεν</u> μεγάλη καὶ ἐνεργής, καὶ ἀντικείμενοι πολλοί. (1 Cor 16:9)

Because a great and energetic door has opened to me, and many [are] lying against [it or me].

[ἀνέῳγεν, indicative]

This indicative Perfect tense-form has several issues that affect its morphology. First of all, this indicative verb has its reduplication formed by apparently lengthening the initial vowel of the stem. This verb never uses the -κ-, as it follows the theme of aspirating the final consonant. This verb from 1 Cor 16:9 is stative in its setting.[26] This participle comes from the lexeme οἴγω, meaning "open." In this case, a preposition ἀνά, meaning "up" or "up to," is compounded on the front of the verb, yielding the idea of "to open up." When the verb οἴγω changes into the Perfect indicative ἀνέῳγεν, it undergoes a slight change in the stem of the verb. The initial present stem of this verb is οἴγ-. The -γ- changes to a -ξ- in the case of a middle, or -χ- in the case of an active form, then adds the Perfect 3rd singular ending, -εν. The stems of the Aorist and Perfect mirror each other in this stem change from the Present. This mirroring suggests that something exists in common between the Aorist and the Perfect tense morphologically. No -κ- exists within this Perfect tense-form, since the verbs with a final hard stop simply

---

25 Most were concerned either with the specifics of human government, or the question of submission and rebellion.

26 This verb occurs twice more in the Pauline corpus in the Perfect tense-form, 2 Cor 2:12, and 2 Cor 6:11, along with one more in the Aorist in Col 4:3. All of the Perfect tense-forms have the same issue in the context of the state of the door being open as the focus. The Aorist subjunctive in Col 4:3 is praying for the same thing, but a state of openness is desired and not yet come to reality. Therefore, the Aorist is still anticipating God's action, while the Perfects are enjoying the status of an open door in the context.

aspirate for the active, and have a hard stop, or unaspirated final consonant in the middle or middle/passive. The aspirated consonant occurs whenever the -κ- might otherwise occur for the typical Greek Perfect. The initial εω- reduplicant is due to the initial consonant being the digamma, ϝ, which later disappeared from use. Once the digamma reduplicates, it yields ϝεϝοιγ-, and later when the digamma fell out of use, this was εοιγ-, which reduced to εωγ-.[27]

In this context, this indicative verb describes the state of being for the great and effective door that had been opened up. Paul is choosing to remain in Ephesus on the basis of the open status of this door of opportunity. This verb is modified by the dative personal pronoun, μοι, or "to me," or "for me," occurring just before it. This dative pronoun functions to provide the indirect object who has benefitted from the door being opened up. The indicative verb itself functions as the main verb of the clause, indicating the status of the door. Since the ongoing status of this door as having been opened up for Paul is the main consideration for this verb, a stative reading is preferred for this tense-form.[28]

Paul does not provide a hint at what action opened this door, or who the agent was that opened it, although we can safely assume that he understood God as the ultimate agent in any case. Oster asserts that two verses earlier, Paul's use of the phrase, "if God permits," indicates that he understands God as the agent for this door.[29] Conzelmann relates Paul's use of this figure of speech to 2 Cor 2:12, where "in Christ" modifies the same verb in the expression and is either a location of realm for the opening or hints at Christ being the agent.[30] If Christ is understood to be the realm of the opened door, then God is still the agent who opened it. Thiselton states this verb is intransitive here,[31] although this is not the most precise way to describe a passive verb where "door," the subject of the sentence, is the item that received the action of the verb. The door which received the opening action is in context. It is better to call this verb "passive" and "agentless"

---

27 For a similar analysis with digamma, see 1.5 for the verb οἶδα.

28 Many commentators translate "a door is standing open," emphasising the stative sense. See Archibald T. Robertson and Alfred Plummer, *A Critical and Exegetical Commentary on the First Epistle of St. Paul to the Corinthians*, ICC (New York: T&T Clark, 1911), 390; Anthony C. Thiselton, *The First Epistle to the Corinthians: A Commentary on the Greek Text*, NIGTC (Grand Rapids, MI: Eerdmans, 2000), 1330; Charles J. Ellicott, *St. Paul's First Epistle to the Corinthians: With a Critical and Grammatical Commentary* (London: Longmans, 1887), 335.

29 Richard Oster, *1 Corinthians*, The College Press NIV Commentary (Joplin, MO: College Press, 1995), 1 Cor 16:9.

30 Hans Conzelmann, *1 Corinthians: A Commentary on the First Epistle to the Corinthians*, Hermeneia—A Critical and Historical Commentary on the Bible (Philadelphia, PA: Fortress, 1975), 297.

31 In spite of my quibble over terms, he does handle the verb correctly as reporting on the status of the door. Thiselton, 1330.

rather than "intransitive." This Perfect indicative verb portrays the state of door having been opened up for Paul. This state is presented with a view toward its "ongoing"-ness. This state is viewed imperfectively since it is the background for Paul to remain in Ephesus and resist those who are opposing the Gospel.

10.) ἡμεῖς δὲ πάντες <u>ἀνακεκαλυμμένῳ</u> προσώπῳ τὴν δόξαν κυρίου κατοπτριζόμενοι τὴν αὐτὴν εἰκόνα μεταμορφούμεθα ἀπὸ δόξης εἰς δόξαν καθάπερ ἀπὸ κυρίου πνεύματος. (2 Cor 3:18)

Now we all in a face <u>having been unveiled</u> are reflecting the glory of the Lord being transformed into the same image from glory into glory exactly as from the Lord, the spirit.

[ἀνακεκαλυμμένῳ, participle]

This participle has several issues that affect its morphology. First of all, this participle has its reduplication formed in the normal productive Greek pattern. This participle does undergo a stem change from its lexical form. This lexeme never uses the -κ-, and this seems to be related to the fact it forms its Perfect by aspirating the last consonant of the verbal stem. Also, this participle has a preposition added to the beginning modifying the lexical input slightly. This participle from 2 Cor 3:18 is stative in its setting.[32] This verb comes from the lexical form ἀνακαλύπτω, meaning "to unveil" or "to reveal." This lexical entry is comprised of the ἀνά preposition, containing the idea "up," and the root verb καλύπτω, which means "to cover," or "to veil." The compound verb often has the idea of uncovering an item, as the addition of the preposition offers the opposite meaning of the lexeme. When the verb ἀνακαλύπτω changes into the Perfect participle ἀνακεκαλυμμένῳ, it undergoes a stem change where the -π- of the stem is aspirated to -φ-. The Present stem is καλυπτ-, and this is changed to καλυφ-. Apparently, whenever the participle morpheme -μεν- is added, the aspirated letter amalgamates to this morpheme producing καλυμμεν-. The stems of the Aorist and Perfect mirror each other in both this stem change from the Present, and in the amalgamation of the aspirated letter to the participle morpheme. This mirroring suggests that something exists in common between the Aorist and the Perfect tense morphologically. The initial κε- reduplicant is expected since it constructs a Ce reduplication, and is the typical method for Greek Perfect tense-forms to

---

32   The occurrence in 2 Cor 3:14 is not different.

be reduplicated. Also, the participle morpheme and dative singular endings are added to the stem after its stem change.

In this context, this participle describes the state of the face as unveiled as one beholds himself or herself in a mirror. The verb is not modified by any adverbs or prepositional phrases. This unveiled face is changed in stages as the image of Christ is transforming it into his image. This unveiled status is necessary to view the face as it transforms. The participle functions adjectivally to describe the face. The status of the face is important contextually for the transformation to be observed. Since the ongoing status of the face as being unveiled is contextually relevant to believer viewing his or her face, then it is the main consideration for this verb, and a stative reading is preferred for this tense-form.

This participle indicates the state of the face being unveiled for the viewing event like that of being in front of a mirror. This state is presented with a view toward its "ongoing"-ness to the extent that while this state of unveiled-ness occurs, the face can be viewed. The Perfect participle does not carry with it the force that this state is permanent or irreversible as Harris suggests, but allows for such a state, or for a temporary state that holds true until at least the reference time chosen by the author.[33] This state is viewed imperfectively since it is the background for believers to view their face, and then see the transformation. While an event of unveiling the face could be implied, it is not mentioned in context, nor is it emphasised. Had one been included, it is expected that the unveiling event would be portrayed as a complete past event, so perfectivity would be its aspect.

11.) Τὸ στόμα ἡμῶν ἀνέῳγεν πρὸς ὑμᾶς, Κορίνθιοι, ἡ καρδία ἡμῶν <u>πεπλάτυνται</u>· (2 Cor 6:11)

Our mouth has been opened up toward you, Corinthians, our heart <u>has been opened wide.</u>

[πεπλάτυνται, indicative]

This indicative Perfect tense-form has several issues that affect its morphology. First of all, this indicative verb has its reduplication formed in the normal productive Greek pattern. This verb never uses the -κ-, and this seems to be related to the fact that it ends in a liquid letter, -ν. This verb from 2 Cor 6:11 is

---

33 Harris' concern probably is due to theological concerns here rather than Perfect tense semantics. Murray J. Harris, *The Second Epistle to the Corinthians: A Commentary on the Greek Text*, NIGTC (Grand Rapids, MI: Eerdmans, 2005), 313.

stative in its setting.[34] This verb comes from the lexeme πλάτυνω, meaning "to widen" or "be wide." When the verb πλάτυνω changes into the Perfect indicative πεπλάτυνται, it does not undergo a stem change. It simply adds the reduplicant and the normal Perfect endings. Although both tense-forms of this lexeme are rare, having only one occurrence in the NT for each, the stems of the Aorist and Perfect mirror each other in having no stem change from the Present. While in these cases, this mirroring shows parallel between the morphology of the Perfect and Aorist, it is not certain to contrast the Present here due to all the tense-forms existing in parallel, with no stem change. No -κ- exists within this Perfect tense-form, but many features of the Perfect are not present here due to no stem change occurring from the Present to the Aorist and Perfect. The initial πε- reduplicant is expected since it constructs a typical Ce reduplication. Also, the middle/passive ending -ται is added to the unchanged stem.

In this context, this indicative verb describes the state of Paul's heart. This widened heart is in parallel with the open mouth in the preceding clause. Paul is using this verb in a metaphorical way, referring to his love for the Corinthian Christians. This status of Paul's heart is the backdrop for Paul to make his appeal to the Corinthians to receive God's salvation. Since the ongoing status of Paul's heart as having been widened for the Corinthians is the main consideration for this verb, a stative reading is preferred for this tense-form. Although this verb can be translated as a passive, Martin suggests middle is best, since it highlights the subject's involvement in opening his heart.[35]

This state of Paul's heart is presented with a view toward its "ongoing"-ness. It is viewed imperfectively since it is the background for Paul to make his appeal to the Corinthians to receive the Gospel. Paul does not address the event related to this state. Harris mentions the Perfect tense implies a previous action, but the state is still the focus here.[36] Furnish comments that "the verb is perfect in tense but present in meaning."[37] His concern seems to be that typically the opening event is finished while the emphasis is on the state which has present relevance. Lenski makes clear the idea that the state of a widened heart is in effect through

---

34   This is the only Perfect tense-form for this stem in the Pauline corpus. The Aorist imperative in 2 Cor 6:13 is a command for the Corinthian church to reciprocate the state that Paul has initiated. The state is not yet a reality and the action of widening their hearts is still anticipated. Therefore, the Perfect is stative while the Aorist is eventive.

35   Ralph P. Martin, *2 Corinthians*, WBC: 40 (Dallas, TX: Word, 1998), 185.

36   Harris, 488.

37   Victor Paul Furnish, *II Corinthians: Translated with Introduction, Notes, and Commentary*, AB: 32A (New Haven, CT: Yale University Press, 2008), 360.

to the time of the writing of the letter.[38] This is in accordance with the state of the Perfect holding true to the reference time.

12.) ἀλλ᾽ ὁ μὲν ἐκ τῆς παιδίσκης κατὰ σάρκα <u>γεγέννηται</u>, ὁ δὲ ἐκ τῆς ἐλευθέρας δι᾽ ἐπαγγελίας. (Gal 4:23)

Now, the son of the servant girl has been born according to the flesh, but the son of the free woman through a promise.

[γεγέννηται, indicative]

This indicative Perfect tense-form has several issues that affect its morphology. First of all, this indicative verb has its reduplication formed in the normal productive Greek pattern. This verb does undergo a stem change from its lexical form. This verb never uses the -κ-, and this seems to be related to the fact that its stem ends in a vowel -α. This verb from Gal 4:23 is stative in its setting.[39] This verb comes from the lexeme γεννάω, meaning "to be born" or "to give birth to." When the verb γεννάω changes into the Perfect indicative γεγέννηται, it undergoes a stem change where the last vowel of the stem is lengthened. The Present stem is γεννα-, and this is changed to γεννη-. The stems of the Aorist and Perfect mirror each other in this stem change from the Present. This mirroring suggests that something exists in common between the Aorist and the Perfect tense morphologically. No -κ- exists within this Perfect tense-form, because the middle voice does not take a -κ-, while the active often does. The initial γε- reduplicant is expected since it constructs a typical Ce reduplication. Also, the middle/passive ending -ται is added to the stem after its stem change.

In this context, this indicative verb describes the state of birth of the child in the story about Abraham and Hagar. The verb is modified by the prepositional phrase, κατὰ σάρκα, meaning "according to flesh." This phrase is often understood as an adverb of manner. Lenski understands it as a manner adverb when he translates, "has been born in (mere) flesh fashion."[40] Arichea and Nida translate similarly, with "Ishmael is described as *born in the usual way*."[41] Hansen also sees this phrase as an adverb of manner in the translation he analyses, "it

---

38 R. C. H. Lenski, *The Interpretation of St. Paul's First and Second Epistle to the Corinthians* (Minneapolis, MN: Augsburg, 1963), 1074.

39 This is the only occurrence of this stem in the Pauline corpus.

40 Lenski, 234.

41 Daniel C. Arichea and Eugene Albert Nida, *A Handbook on Paul's Letter to the Galatians*, UBS Handbook Series (New York: United Bible Societies, 1976), 111.

happened *in the ordinary way*,"[42] This child, Ishmael, has been born according to the flesh. Bruce argues that "according to flesh" here refers to "the ordinary course of nature," without the moral negativity typically associated with "flesh."[43] This manner of birth is then contrasted against Isaac having been born according to the promise. However, the grammars do not generally consider this preposition to mark an adverb of manner. In this usage it functions more like a comparative or a referential. Wallace groups this use under "standard," supplying a translation "in accordance with."[44] Harris sees this context in particular as defining κατὰ opposing it with "though the spirit" as an opposite means.[45] At this point it is not necessary to understand this as an adverb of manner, thus allowing for a stative reading. Both the "standard" and "means" understandings derive from the "down from" idea. The status of Ishmael is an important contextual element, as he did not historically receive an inheritance due to his status and his mother's status. This negative status along with Isaac's positive status is the backdrop for Paul to create an allegory involving earthly Jerusalem and the "above" Jerusalem. Since the ongoing status of Ishmael as being unable to inherit is contextually relevant to Paul's argument, then it is the main consideration for this verb, and a stative reading is preferred for this tense-form.

This verb indicates the state of Ishmael's birth. Burton remarks that "the perfect γεγέννηται is provided in preference to the Aorist ἐγενήθη, because the writer is thinking not simply of the historical fact but of the existing result of that fact."[46] This is his way of saying the verb is stative here. This state is presented with a view toward its "ongoing"-ness to the extent that he could not inherit from Abraham. This state is viewed imperfectively since it is the background for Paul to create his allegory of the two sorts of Jerusalem. Paul does not reference the birth event itself directly, although one can be implied if the adverb, κατὰ σάρκα, employed here, is interpreted as an adverb of manner. If the implication of event is accepted, then the event of Ishmael's birth would be viewed perfectively. The verb here is primarily stative.

---

42 He is analysing the NIV. G. Walter Hansen, *Galatians*, The IVP New Testament Commentary Series (Downers Grove, IL: InterVarsity, 1994), Ga 4:22.

43 F. F. Bruce, *The Epistle to the Galatians: A Commentary on the Greek Text*, NIGTC (Grand Rapids, MI: Eerdmans, 1982), 217.

44 Wallace, 377.

45 Harris, 151-152.

46 Ernest DeWitt Burton, *A Critical and Exegetical Commentary on the Epistle to the Galatians*, ICC (New York: Scribner's, 1920), 253.

13.) καὶ φωτίσαι [πάντας] τίς ἡ οἰκονομία τοῦ μυστηρίου τοῦ <u>ἀποκεκρυμμένου</u> ἀπὸ τῶν αἰώνων ἐν τῷ θεῷ τῷ τὰ πάντα κτίσαντι, (Eph 3:9)

And to enlighten everyone what [is] the plan of the mystery, the one that <u>has been hidden</u> from the ages in God, the one who created all things.

[ἀποκεκρυμμένου, participle]

This participle has several issues that affect its morphology. First of all, this participle has its reduplication formed in the normal productive Greek pattern. This participle does undergo a stem change from its lexical form. This participle never uses the -κ-, and this seems to be related to the fact it forms its Perfect by aspirating the last consonant of the verbal stem. This participle from Eph 3:9 is stative in its setting.[47] This verb comes from the lexical form ἀποκρύπτω, meaning "to cover" or "to conceal." This lexical entry is comprised of the ἀπό preposition, containing the idea "from," and the root verb κρύπτω, which means "to hide," "to cover," or "to conceal." The compound verb often has the idea of keeping one thing hidden from another entity. When the verb ἀποκρύπτω changes into the Perfect participle ἀποκεκρυμμένου, it undergoes a stem change where the -π- of the stem is aspirated to the -φ- consonant. The Present stem is κρυπτ-, and this is changed to κρυφ-. Apparently, whenever the participle morpheme -μεν- is added the aspirated letter amalgamates to this morpheme producing κρυμμεν-. The stems of the Aorist and Perfect mirror each other in both this stem change from the Present, and in the amalgamation of the aspirated letter to the participle morpheme. This mirroring suggests that something exists in common between the Aorist and the Perfect tense morphologically. No -κ- exists within this Perfect tense-form, because this lexeme forms its Perfect through aspiration rather than adding a -κ-. The initial κε- reduplicant is expected since it constructs a Ce reduplication, and is the typical method for Greek Perfect tense-forms to be reduplicated. Also, the participle morpheme and genitive singular endings are added to the stem after its stem change.

In this context, this participle describes the state of the mystery for the specified duration "the ages," which may refer either to eternity or to the preceding ages of time. Anders understands that this time of hiddenness began at creation, and runs through until the revelation of Gentile inclusion after the crucifixion.[48] The

---

47 The occurrences in 1 Cor 2:7 and Col 1:26 have the same features as this verb. The topic is the same in all three.

48 Max Anders, *Galatians-Colossians*, HNTC: 8 (Nashville, TN: Broadman & Holman, 1999), 129.

verb is modified by two prepositional phrases. The first phrase is ἀπὸ τῶν αἰώνων, meaning "from the ages." Lincoln discloses that αἰώνων should be understood temporally, since the entities from whom the mystery was hidden are generations of humanity, due to the parallel in Col 1:26.[49] Barth states that "the preposition *apo* can denote only duration."[50] This phrase is an adverb of time duration that provides the length of time the state was apparent. This kind of temporal phrase does not modify an action. The second phrase is ἐν τῷ θεῷ, meaning "in God." This phrase is either the location where the mystery was hidden or possibly it indicates the person who is responsible for the concealment. Lincoln prefers the locative sense that the mystery was hidden inside God.[51] Bratcher and Nida reveal that Col 3:3 uses the same phrase in a locative manner.[52] Barth suggests the dative following a passive verb often marks the agent.[53] This mystery has been hidden from the preceding generations of humanity. The participle functions adjectivally to describe the mystery. The status of the mystery is important contextually, since this status was in place for a long time and recently was revealed. Since the ongoing status of the mystery as being hidden is contextually relevant to Paul's urging the Ephesians to know its revelation, then it is the main consideration for this verb, and a stative reading is preferred for this tense-form.

This participle indicates the state of the mystery being hidden for many ages of time only to be revealed recently relative to the time of the writing. This state is presented with a view toward its "ongoing"-ness to the extent that a long duration of time is explicit in context, "from the ages." This state is viewed imperfectively since it is the background for Paul to urge the Ephesian readers to become aware of the new revelation regarding this old mystery. The act which causes the mystery to become hidden is not mentioned.

The absence of the -κ- is observed for all the occurrences of Perfect tense-forms where a stative meaning is the main contextually relevant meaning. They show consistent reduplication either through Ce reduplication or initial vowel

---

49 Andrew T. Lincoln, *Ephesians*, WBC: 42 (Dallas: Word, 1990), 184.

50 He discusses one other possibility for αἰώνων, where it might refer to "demons" instead of "ages," but understands the preposition to be durative either way. Markus Barth, *Ephesians: Introduction, Translation, and Commentary on Chapters 1–3*, AB: 34 (New Haven, CT: Yale University Press, 2008), 343. Best discusses both "from ages" and "from demons," and decides they could be related answers. Ernest Best, *A Critical and Exegetical Commentary on Ephesians*, ICC (Edinburgh: T&T Clark, 1998), 320.

51 Lincoln, 185.

52 Robert G. Bratcher and Eugene Albert Nida, *A Handbook on Paul's Letter to the Ephesians*, UBS Handbook Series (New York: United Bible Societies, 1993), 78.

53 Barth, 344.

reduplication leading to a lengthened vowel. The form is typically either a Perfect middle indicative or middle participle. The verbs that are most likely to have a stative meaning do not appear commonly in the active form. The two forms that possess an active form do not form their active forms using a -κ- between the verbal stem and its endings. The majority of these verb forms are participles that function adjectivally.

The contexts around these verbs have few modifiers, but those with modifiers have durative temporal adverbs. The commentators that focus on verbal properties mention present states, and ongoing features for these verbs, while most discuss other matters unrelated to verbal meaning. Whether or not these Perfects refer to states is not seriously contested. Since the state that the author emphasises is viewed as ongoing, either continuing from some distant point in the past, or extending indefinitely into the future beyond the reference time, an imperfective aspect works best to explain the Perfect in these examples. The portrayal of this state in an imperfective way also allows for new events and situations to intervene during the reality of that state.

1.2. Verbs Which Have an Actional Component

This section will analyse the morphology of Perfect tense-forms along with the context surrounding each tense-form within the Pauline corpus that appear to be actional in meaning. The actional properties of several Perfect tense-forms are determined by the presence of certain adverbial expressions, which modifies the verb by including a medium through which the action is taken, an agent for the action, a party for whose interests the action is taken, or a cause for the action. All instances of each lexeme are analysed in this chapter for any lexeme that attracts at least one of these modifiers.

The morphology, context, and contribution to verbal aspect are discussed in this section for each verb. The section on morphology will analyse the lexical form of each Perfect tense-form, track the changes to the stem of the form in its formation to the Perfect tense, and account for the various morphemes that comprise the tense-forms. The section on context will account for any temporal modifiers, analyse the function of any adverbs, and explain the pragmatic function that arises from the verb in its context. These adverbs may be single-word adverbs or prepositional phrases. The section concerning contribution to verbal aspect will summarise the findings for each verb, and then evaluate what each verb contributes to the complex aspect understanding of Perfect tense-form. This helps to establish how the two aspects affect the various linguistic contexts for each verb.

14.) ἡ δὲ ἐλπὶς οὐ καταισχύνει, ὅτι ἡ ἀγάπη τοῦ θεοῦ <u>ἐκκέχυται</u> ἐν ταῖς καρδίαις ἡμῶν διὰ πνεύματος ἁγίου τοῦ δοθέντος ἡμῖν. (Rom 5:5)

But hope does not dishonour, because the love of God <u>has poured out itself</u> in our hearts through the Holy Spirit, the one who was given to us.[54]

[ἐκκέχυται, middle indicative verb]

This verb has several issues that affect its morphology. First of all, it has reduplication of the first consonant as is typical for the synthetic Greek Perfect. Secondly it does not have the trademark -κ- of the synthetic Greek Perfect tense-form due to being a middle, rather than an active. Thirdly, the addition of a preposition εκ- adds to the bulk of this tense-form. This Perfect tense-form from Rom 5:5 appears actional in its setting.[55] The Perfect indicative middle is ἐκκέχυται, which means "having been poured out" usually for some purpose. The lexical form of this verb is χέω, and it is a combination of the prefix ἐκ, containing the idea of "out" with the main verb χέω, containing the idea of "to pour," or "to shed."[56] When this preposition and verb occur together, the sense of completely pouring one item out of another or pouring out enough of one item from another to affect some result emerges as the main idea. Often the translation for this compound verb is "to pour out," or "to shed," where one item is affectively applied to another. In this context, it is the love of God that God has poured out onto a group of people so that they are fully affected. This verb is followed by two prepositional adverb phrases, one a dative locative phrase which either points to the location of action or the location of the state following the action, and the other a genitive means or agency phrase that points to either the means or agent of the action.[57] When the verb χέω changes into the Perfect middle indicative verb ἐκκέχυται, it undergoes a slight change in the stem of the verb. The initial present stem of this verb is χε-. The -ε- changes to a -υ-, then adds the middle endings participle morpheme -ται to the end of the changed stem. This same stem change, from -ε- to -υ-, is observed whenever any verb in this class becomes either an Aorist or a Perfect.[58] This suggests that something exists in common between

---

54 Translation is mine.
55 This is the only occurrence of this stem in the Perfect tense-form in the Pauline corpus. The other instances of this stem are Aorist.
56 For the use of ἐκ, see Harris. *Prepositions and Theology*, 103–107.
57 This is the non-temporal use of the preposition διά. It marks the medium through which an action affects another entity. This medium can either be the means or the intermediate agent, and sometimes the ultimate agent.
58 See Appendix B for examples of verbs in this class.

the Aorist and the Perfect tense morphologically. No -κ- exists within this Perfect tense-form, since the -κ- does not appear in the Perfect middle forms. This verb does have the -κ- in its Perfect active forms. This verb occurs with normal Cε reduplication for its Perfect tense-form.[59]

This middle Perfect verb appears in a supplemental information section of the NT letter to the Romans. Throughout Rom 5:1–4, a conclusion is drawn from the information at the end of chapter 4, and Rom 5:5, the current verse, is a supplemental clause explaining the word "hope" at the end of 5:4. The supplemental clause continues through the end of Rom 5:5, where the conclusion from 5:1–4 resumes in 5:6. Another supplemental clause occurs in 5:7 as well. The pragmatic function of this verb in 5:5b is to indicate the reason that "hope" does not shame the believer in 5:5a. This verb is further modified by two prepositional phrases that provide first, the location and second, either the medium or intermediate agent for the Perfect tense-form.[60] The locative phrase might supply the location for either the action or realm for the state of that action having been performed, while the phrase providing the medium must supply information related to the action of the verb and not related to its state.[61] As a medium, the Holy Spirit is then also the cause for the love of God in the believer.[62] It is this prepositional phrase which hints that the verb is more than merely stative, since its context modifies its action.

This verb indicates the action of God through the Holy Spirit pouring out his love on the believers. The first prepositional phrase supplies the location for either the action or its state, but the second prepositional phrase clearly modifies its action by including a medium for that action. If the first prepositional phrase

59 This late-stage reduplication indicates a highly grammaticalised meaning as argued in chapter 3.

60 Fitzmyer calls the Holy Spirit a medium specifically. Joseph A. Fitzmyer S. J., *Romans: A New Translation with Introduction and Commentary*, AB 33 (New Haven, CT: Yale University Press, 2008), 398. Osborne also describes the Holy Spirit in this passage as the medium for love. Grant R. Osborne, *Romans*, The IVP New Testament Commentary Series (Downers Grove, IL: InterVarsity, 2004), 131. Cottrell along with Jewett and Kotansky discuss the Holy Spirit as agent. Jack Cottrell, *Romans*, vol. 1, The College Press NIV Commentary (Joplin, MO: College Press Pub. Co., 1996), 182; Robert Jewett and Roy David Kotansky, *Romans: A Commentary*, Hermeneia—A Critical and Historical Commentary on the Bible, ed. Eldon Jay Epp (Minneapolis, MN: Fortress, 2006), 357.

61 Fitzmyer discusses the resulting state. Fitzmeyer, 398. Schreiner, Moo and Dunn discuss both the prior nature of the action and the current nature of the state. Thomas R. Schreiner, *Romans*, BECNT: 6 (Grand Rapids, MI: Baker, 1998), 257; Douglas J. Moo, *The Epistle to the Romans*, NICNT (Grand Rapids, MI: Eerdmans, 1996), 305; James D. G. Dunn, *Romans 1–8*, WBC 38a (Dallas: Word, 1998), 253. Morris also includes the action of the Holy Spirit. Leon Morris, *The Epistle to the Romans*, PNTC (Grand Rapids, MI: Eerdmans, 1988), 221.

62 Lange makes this connection. John Peter Lange, et al., *A Commentary on the Holy Scriptures: Romans* (Bellingham, WA: Lexham, 2008), 163.

indicates that the verb is a state, then that state must be viewed imperfectively, but if the first phrase indicates an action, then that action must be viewed as perfective. Definitely the second prepositional phrase points to an event, and further implies the event must be viewed perfectively. Toews discusses that this Perfect tense-from "suggests an ongoing state that is the result of a once-for-all event."[63] In saying this he views both aspects here. It is not clear that the first phrase definitely points to a state, so it is better to analyse this instance as emphasising the event, rather than as a proof of both aspects. Little is added to the meaning of this clause if the verb had been Aorist rather than Perfect.

15.) ᾧ δέ τι χαρίζεσθε, κἀγώ· καὶ γὰρ ἐγὼ ὃ <u>κεχάρισμαι</u>, εἴ τι <u>κεχάρισμαι</u>, δι' ὑμᾶς ἐν προσώπῳ Χριστοῦ, (2 Cor 2:10)

but to whom you are forgiving a thing, I also; for also the person whom <u>I have forgiven</u>, if <u>I have forgiven</u> anything, [I have forgiven] on account of you before Christ,

16.) εἰ γὰρ ἐκ νόμου ἡ κληρονομία, οὐκέτι ἐξ ἐπαγγελίας· τῷ δὲ Ἀβραὰμ δι' ἐπαγγελίας <u>κεχάρισται</u> ὁ θεός. (Gal 3:18)

For if the inheritance [be] from law, then [it is] no longer from promise; but God <u>has freely given</u> [it] to Abraham through a promise.

[κεχάρισμαι, κεχάρισται, middle indicative verb]

This verb has several issues that affect its morphology. First of all, it has reduplication of the first consonant and the intervening vowel ε as is typical for the synthetic Greek Perfect. For this verb the reduplicant is not identical in form to the initial stem consonant. The reduplicant takes a non-aspirated form of the initial stem consonant, so χ- becomes κ-. Secondly, it does not have the trademark -κ- after the stem typical of the synthetic Greek Perfect tense-form due to being a middle. Thirdly, the last consonant of the stem -ζ changed to an -σ before adding the endings. This verb from 2 Cor 2:10 and Gal 3:18 is actional in both of its settings. These verb forms are derived from the lexeme, χαρίζομαι, which means "to give freely," or in some contexts, "to forgive," and other contexts, "to

63   John E. Toews, *Romans*, Believers Church Bible Commentary (Scottdale, PA: Herald Press, 2004), 138.

show oneself gracious."[64] The gracious idea seems primary as the first two ideas are ways to accomplish showing grace or being gracious. The gracious idea also best explains why this verb prefers the middle form, and is consistent with the meaning of the cognate noun, χάρις, or "grace." This verb occurs in the Aorist, Present and Future within the corpus, but no occurrences of the Perfect participle exist. When the verb χαρίζομαι is formed into the Perfect middle κεχάρισμαι, it undergoes a slight change in the stem of the verb. The Present stem of this verb is χάριζ-. The -ζ- changes to a -σ-, then the middle endings -σαι, -ται are added to the end of the changed stem. This same stem change, from -ζ- to -σ-, is observed whenever any verb in the -ιζω class becomes either an Aorist or a Perfect.[65] This suggests that something exists in common between the Aorist and the Perfect tense morphologically. No -κ- exists within this Perfect tense-form, since the -κ- does not appear in the Perfect middle forms. This verb does not occur with active forms where the -κ- might be expected. This verb occurs with normal Cε reduplication for its Perfect tense-form.

In the context of 2 Cor 2:10, this verb describes the act of one person forgiving another.[66] Both of the verb forms are within a conditional clause pair that provides supplemental information to the first clause in this verse. The καὶ γαρ construction begins the supplement, which then continues through the end of the verse. The first occurrence of the verb is modified by two prepositional phrases. The first is introduced by διὰ and provides the cause or reason for Paul to co-forgive another person along with the Corinthian believers. The second is introduced by εν and indicates the authority before whom this action is taken. Barnett relates Christ as witness to the custom of ensuring "two or three witnesses" for such an action.[67] Harris and Furnish believe that this interpretation of the prepositional phrase is most likely due to Paul using a Greek equivalent to the Hebrew expression "*lipnē*," or "in the presence of."[68] Thrall prefers this interpretation due to the fact that Paul typically is aware that God or Christ witness his

---

64 Harris expresses that when the context of graciousness and favour includes remission of sins, then κεχάρισμαι takes on the meaning of "forgive." Murray J. Harris, *The Second Epistle to the Corinthians: A Commentary on the Greek Text*, NIGTC (Grand Rapids, MI: Eerdmans, 2005), 231-232.

65 See Appendix B for examples of verbs in this class.

66 Harris, Barnett and Burton describe this verb as actional in this setting. Harris, 231-232; Paul Barnett, *The Second Epistle to the Corinthians*, NICNT (Grand Rapids, MI: Eerdmans, 1997), 130; Ernest DeWitt Burton, *A Critical and Exegetical Commentary on the Epistle to the Galatians* (ICC; New York: Scribner's, 1920), 186.

67 Barnett, 130.

68 Harris, 232–233; Victor Paul Furnish, *II Corinthians: Translated with Introduction, Notes, and Commentary* (AB: 32A; New Haven, CT: Yale University Press, 2008), 157.

activity.[69] The second occurrence of the verb is collocated with the direct object τι, indicating the object which receives the action of forgiveness.

In the context of Gal 3:18, this verb describes the idea of one person freely giving something to another. Here God freely gave inheritance to Abraham through a promise. This verse is an explanation providing rationale for the ideas in the previous verse. This verb is modified by a genitive prepositional phrase beginning with διά that provides the medium through which the action of the verb occurred. The collection of these occurrences highlights the actional properties of the verbs through the choices of prepositional phrases employed by the author. The idea of a continuing state beyond the initial action is also likely for these verbs, but is not indicated by the prepositional phrases conclusively.[70] Bruce understands a continuing state exists along with the action to Abraham, but bases the state on the continued blessing upon Abraham's descendants.[71] This continuance would still be relevant if an Aorist was used, so it cannot be used to prove the Perfect is stative here.

This verb in 2 Cor 2:10 indicates the action of Paul forgiving another man for the sake of the Corinthian believers who already had forgiven the man. The first prepositional phrase supplies the cause or reason for the action, while the second prepositional phrase modifies either its action or its state by indicating the location. Locational phrases can be argued to modify verbal actions or states equally. Even though the locational phrase could indicate either action or state for the verb, the first prepositional phrase clearly marks an action whether it is understood as a cause of or a reason for that action. Martin understands this verb to be an action.[72] While a state possibly indicated by the second phrase might be viewed imperfectively, the action indicated by the first phrase must be viewed perfectively. Baker understands that this action of forgiving is complete in this context.[73] Although an Aorist here would make the same sense of the

---

69 Thrall lists Rom 2:17, 4:2, 5:11, and 8:21 in support of this idea. Margaret E. Thrall, *A Critical and Exegetical Commentary on the Second Epistle of the Corinthians* (ICC; London: T&T Clark, 2004), 180–181.

70 Bruce, Longenecker and Burton give contextual reasons for understanding a continuing state beyond the initial action. F. F. Bruce, The Epistle to the *Galatians: A Commentary on the Greek Text* (NIGTC; Grand Rapids, MI: Eerdmans, 1982), 174; Richard N. Longenecker, *Galatians*, WBC: 41 (Dallas, TX: Word, 1998), 134; Burton, 186.

71 F. F. Bruce, *The Epistle to the Galatians: A Commentary on the Greek Text* (NIGTC; Grand Rapids, MI: Eerdmans, 1982), 174.

72 Ralph P. Martin, *2 Corinthians* (WBC: 40; Dallas: Word, Incorporated, 1998), 39.

73 His statement that the action is complete because Paul used the Perfect tense, does not rule out Paul using an Aorist for the complete action also, but whenever an event is in view and a Perfect is used, then that event will be complete. William R. Baker, *2 Corinthians*, The College Press NIV Commentary (Joplin, MO: College Press, 1999), 110.

sentence that the Perfect brings, the author chose a Perfect possibly to highlight his responsibility in performing the action. Plummer takes this approach due to the emphatic ἐγώ in front of the first occurrence of the Perfect verb.[74]

In Gal 3:18, the verb indicates the action of God freely giving an inheritance to Abraham through a promise. The prepositional phrase supplies the medium for that action and does not modify a state. This action must be viewed perfectively in this instance. In both cases, little is added to the meaning of either clause if the verb had been Aorist rather than Perfect. The absence of the -κ- morpheme shows that the -κ- is not a firm indicator of perfectivity, since this Perfect is perfective without it. Most of the English translations treat this Perfect as though it were an Aorist.[75]

> 17.) ὅτι εἴ τι αὐτῷ ὑπὲρ ὑμῶν <u>κεκαύχημαι</u>, οὐ κατησχύνθην, ἀλλ᾽ ὡς πάντα ἐν ἀληθείᾳ ἐλαλήσαμεν ὑμῖν, οὕτως καὶ ἡ καύχησις ἡμῶν ἡ ἐπὶ Τίτου ἀλήθεια ἐγενήθη. (2 Cor 7:14)

that if in a certain thing to him about you <u>I have boasted</u>, I am not put to shame, but as we spoke all things in truth to you, even so our boasting of you before Titus is become truth.

[κεκαύχημαι middle indicative verb]

This verb from 2 Cor 7:14 is eventive in its setting. This verb form is derived from the lexeme, καυχάομαι, which means "to boast," or in some contexts, "to speak loudly." This verb occurs in the Aorist, Present and Future within the Pauline corpus.[76] When the verb καυχάομαι is formed into the Perfect middle κεκαύχημαι, it undergoes a slight change in the stem of the verb. The initial Present stem of this verb is καύχα-. The final -α- changes to a -η-, and then the middle ending -μαι is added to the end of the changed stem. This same stem change, from -α- to -ω-, is observed whenever any verb in the -αω class becomes either an Aorist or a Perfect.[77] This pattern is true of all the contract vowel verbs, and the short vowel becomes lengthened for the perfective stem. This suggests

---

74 Alfred Plummer, *A Critical and Exegetical Commentary on the Second Epistle of St. Paul to the Corinthians* (ICC; New York: T&T Clark, 1915), 62.

75 Consider, the KJV, RSV, NRSV, NCV, ESV, NIV, NLT, LEB, and NET have "gave," and the HCSB has "granted." The YLT has "did grant." Only the ASV and NASB have an English Perfect.

76 A search on the lemma in BibleWorks 10 yields 8 Aorist, 6 Future, 1 Perfect, and 20 Present tense-forms of this lexeme.

77 See Appendix B for examples of verbs in this class.

that something exists in common between the Aorist and the Perfect tense morphologically. No -κ- exists within this Perfect tense-form, since the -κ- does not appear in the Perfect middle forms. This verb does not occur in active forms where the -κ- might be expected. This verb occurs with normal Cε reduplication for its Perfect tense-form.

In the context of 2 Cor 7:14, this verb describes the act of one person boasting about another group of people to a third party. This verb form is within a clause that provides the rationale for the comfort in the preceding verse. The ὅτι construction begins the rationale, which then continues through 7:15. The verb is modified by a prepositional phrase beginning with ὑπέρ. This prepositional phrase contains the party Paul is boasting about to Titus. Paul boasted on behalf of the Corinthian believers.[78] This prepositional phrase modifies the action of the verb by including the beneficiary of the action performed by the subject.

This verb in 2 Cor 7:14 indicates the action of Paul boasting to Titus on behalf of the Corinthian believers. The implication is that Paul is boasting about them to Titus. The prepositional phrase "about you" supplies the party that is being highlighted or helped by the boasting. The action modified by this prepositional phrase must be viewed perfectively. This phrase also represents the content of speech between Paul and Titus. This verb has 3 arguments: 1. The person speaking, Paul, 2. The content, "about you." and 3. The recipient of the words, Titus. This verb should be understood to have an action component due to the fact it has the verbal content along with an indirect object. Harris does not rule out the event in either of the options he considers, either an aoristic perfect, or one that includes the action and the state.[79] Except for possibly highlighting the responsibility of the subject in the action, the author might have used an Aorist here instead of the Perfect.

18.) καὶ ὄντας ἡμᾶς νεκροὺς τοῖς παραπτώμασιν συνεζωοποίησεν τῷ Χριστῷ,- χάριτί ἐστε σεσῳσμένοι (Eph 2:5)

---

78 Even though Harris, Thrall and Martin emphasise the past-ness of the action for this context, they point to a condition or state persistent since that action. Harris, 549; Margaret E. Thrall, *A Critical and Exegetical Commentary on the Second Epistle of the Corinthians*, ICC (London: T&T Clark, 2004), 489; Ralph P. Martin, 2 Corinthians, WBC: 40 (Dallas: Word, 1998), 241-242. Their view is preferable to that of Lenski, who sees a continuing action rather than a state following that initial action. R. C. H. Lenski, *The Interpretation of St. Paul's First and Second Epistle to the Corinthians* (Minneapolis, MN: Augsburg, 1963), 1118.

79 He does not consider a "stative only" option here. Harris, 550.

even while we were dead in sins, he made us alive together in Christ, -by grace you are <u>ones having been saved</u>-

19.) Τῇ γὰρ χάριτί ἐστε <u>σεσῳσμένοι</u> διὰ πίστεως· καὶ τοῦτο οὐκ ἐξ ὑμῶν, θεοῦ τὸ δῶρον· (Eph 2:8)

For by grace, you are <u>ones having been saved</u> through faith; and this not from yourselves, [it is] the gift of God;[80]

[σεσῳσμένοι, middle participle]

This participle has several issues that affect its morphology. First of all, it has reduplication of the first consonant and the intervening vowel ε as is typical for the synthetic Greek Perfect. Secondly, it does not have the trademark -κ- of the synthetic Greek Perfect tense-form due to being a middle. Thirdly, the final -ζ- of the stem changes to a -σ-. One is not able to determine whether the participle from Eph 2:5 is actional or stative in its setting, but the participle is Eph 2:8 is actional in its setting.[81] This verb form is derived from the lexeme, σῴζω, which means "to save," "to rescue," or in some contexts, "to bring salvation." This lexeme occurs in the Aorist, Present and Future within the corpus, but most often as a Future or Aorist subjunctive.[82] When the verb σῴζω is formed into the Perfect middle participle, σεσῳσμένοι, it undergoes a slight change in the stem of the verb. The Present stem of this participle is σωζ-. The -ζ- changes to a -σ-, then the middle participle morpheme, -μεν-, is added and then the endings associated with the noun are added to the end of the changed stem. This same stem change, from -ζ- to -σ-, is observed whenever any verb in the -ιζω class becomes either an Aorist or a Perfect.[83] This suggests that something exists in common between the Aorist and the Perfect tense morphologically. No -κ- exists within this Perfect tense-form, since the -κ- does not appear in the Perfect middle forms. This participle does not occur in the corpus with Perfect active forms where the -κ- might be expected. This participle occurs with normal Cε reduplication for its Perfect tense-form.

---

80 Translation is mine.
81 Both instances are included for thoroughness, but only the one instance is clearly determined.
82 Barth sees the Perfect tense-form of this lexeme as a simple replacement for the Present, Future and Aorist occurrences elsewhere in the Pauline corpus. Marcus Barth, *Ephesians: Introduction, Translation, and Commentary on Chapters 1-3*, AB: 34 (New Haven, CT: Yale, 2008), 221.
83 See Appendix B for examples of verbs in this class.

In the context of Eph 2:5, this participle describes persons who have been saved by grace. It is a periphrastic construction where ἐστε is combined with the participle. The whole phrase is a parenthetical statement.[84] Boles understands it as an interruption.[85] The dative word χάριτί modifies either the participle or the periphrastic construction as a whole by indicating either means or location for either the action of becoming saved or the state of being saved.[86] The emphasis on grace as the means suggests an action has occurred, but this suggestion alone is not enough to be determinative whether this participle indicates a state or an action. Lincoln sees a complete action is in view here, but bases this decision on equating "saving" with "justifying," due to the collocated χάριτί, or "by grace." Paul normally uses this collocate with justifying and not saving.[87] The context of Eph 2:8 is more clearly pointing to an action than Eph 2:5. The participle in this context contains only one additional modifier, a prepositional phrase of medium or intermediate agency. Here, διὰ πίστεως includes the medium for the action of saving the persons mentioned by the verse.[88] Abbott understands this to be the medium.[89] Lange prefers to understand the phrase as indicating the means.[90] The presence of this medium implies that the participle is actional. Both participial forms are within clauses that provide the rationale. The first participle provides the rationale for God's action of loving in 2:4, and the participle in 2:7 provides rationale for God's action of showing his mercy. The rationale provided in 2:5 is an interruption of the main flow of thought, and in 2:8, this rationale is in a structured clause introduced by γὰρ.

---

84 Abbott recognises this material is not part of the mainline. Thomas Kingsmill Abbott, *A Critical and Exegetical Commentary on the Epistles to the Ephesians and to the Colossians*, ICC (New York: Scribner's, 1909), 49.

85 Kenneth L. Boles, *Galatians & Ephesians*, The College Press NIV Commentary (Joplin, MO: College Press, 1993), Eph 2:5.

86 Best and Abbott emphasise a stative reading here, while Lincoln and O'Brien emphasise both the action causing the state and the resultant state. Ernest Best, *A Critical and Exegetical Commentary on Ephesians*, ICC (Edinburgh: T&T Clark, 1998), 217; Abbott, *A Critical and Exegetical*, 49; Lincoln, *Ephesians*, 102; Peter Thomas O'Brien, *The Letter to the Ephesians*, PNTC (Grand Rapids, MI: Eerdmans, 1999), 169.

87 He notices that this Perfect is embedded within a series of Aorists. Lincoln, *Ephesians*, 104.

88 This exegesis might be seen to depend on understanding the "faith" to be that of the individual believer. The main alternate view, that the "faith" is the faithfulness of Jesus on the Cross to do God's will, is also permissible here, but it does not change the fact that faith is a medium for the saving action. It merely alters whose faith is the medium, Christ's or the believer's. Therefore, the participle is actional either way "faith" might be understood.

89 Abbott, *A Critical and Exegetical*, 51.

90 He also understands "by grace" to be the motive, rather than means. John Peter Lange, et al., *A Commentary on the Holy Scriptures* (Bellingham, WA: Lexham, 2008), 80.

This Perfect participle in Eph 2:5, 8 indicates the action of God saving the believers at Ephesus by his grace, and in Eph 2:8, through the medium of their faith.[91] In the case of Eph 2:8, the preposition supplies the medium for the action. The action modified by this prepositional phrase must be viewed perfectively. In this case, little is added to the meaning of the clause if the verb had been Aorist rather than Perfect. Boles conveys that this verb form highlights the "finished reality of salvation."[92] In this way, he highlights the eventive nature of the Perfect in this context. Barth recognises that the Perfect form on this lexeme is rare for Paul, because Paul usually presents salvation in either the Present, Future, or Aorist tense-form, with Future being the most frequent, rather than the Perfect.[93] One may agree with Ellicott though that the Perfect serves to highlight the believer's present state, where the Aorist might not.[94]

20.) ὅτι ἦτε τῷ καιρῷ ἐκείνῳ χωρὶς Χριστοῦ, <u>ἀπηλλοτριωμένοι</u> τῆς πολιτείας τοῦ Ἰσραὴλ καὶ ξένοι τῶν διαθηκῶν τῆς ἐπαγγελίας, ἐλπίδα μὴ ἔχοντες καὶ ἄθεοι ἐν τῷ κόσμῳ. (Eph 2:12)

that at that time you were apart from Christ, <u>ones having been alienated</u> from the citizenship of Israel and strangers from the covenant of promise, not having hope and godless in the world.

21.) ἐσκοτωμένοι τῇ διανοίᾳ ὄντες, <u>ἀπηλλοτριωμένοι</u> τῆς ζωῆς τοῦ θεοῦ διὰ τὴν ἄγνοιαν τὴν οὖσαν ἐν αὐτοῖς, διὰ τὴν πώρωσιν τῆς καρδίας αὐτῶν, (Eph 4:18)

Ones having been darkened in the understanding, <u>having been alienated</u> from the life of God through the ignorance, the one that is in them, through the hardness of their hearts.

22.) Καὶ ὑμᾶς ποτε ὄντας <u>ἀπηλλοτριωμένους</u> καὶ ἐχθροὺς τῇ διανοίᾳ ἐν τοῖς ἔργοις τοῖς πονηροῖς, (Col 1:21)

---

91 Whether this is their active faith or Christ's faithfulness will not change its status as a medium through which an action took place.

92 Boles, Eph 2:8.

93 Markus Barth, *Ephesians: Introduction, Translation, and Commentary on Chapters 1–3*, AB: 34 (New Haven: Yale University Press, 2008), 221. Best calls it unusual. Best, *A Critical and Exegetical*, 217.

94 He states that the Perfect connects the past and the present, but this wording belies a misconception, as other means can provide this connection. What the Perfect does allow is for an action in the past and a state in the present to be viewed with different aspects and all of this by one verb. Charles J. Ellicott, *St. Paul's Epistle to the Ephesians: With a Critical and Grammatical Commentary, and a Revised Translation* (London: Longmans, 1884), 40.

And you formerly were <u>ones having been alienated</u> and enemies in the understanding with the evil deeds.

[ἀπηλλοτριωμένοι, middle participle]

This participle has several issues that affect its morphology. First of all, it has a formation of the Perfect where the initial vowel is lengthened, rather than having typical Perfect reduplication. Secondly, it does not have the trademark -κ- of the synthetic Greek Perfect tense-form due to being a middle. Thirdly, the final -ο- of the stem changes to a -ω-. In this setting the participle also has a preposition ἀπό attached at the head of the form, shortened to ἀπ-. This participle in both Eph 2:12 and Col 1:21 is undetermined in those settings, but is actional in Eph 4:18. This verb form is derived from the lexeme, ἀλλοτριόω, which means "to alienate," "to estrange," or in some contexts, "to become a stranger." This lexeme occurs only as a Perfect passive participle within the corpus. When the verb ἀλλοτριόω is formed into the Perfect middle participle, ἀπηλλοτριωμένοι, it undergoes a slight change in the stem of the verb. The Present stem of this participle is ἀλλοτριο-. The -ο- changes to a -ω-, then the middle participle morpheme, -μεν-, is added and then the endings associated with the noun are added to the end of the changed stem. The shortened preposition is also attached to the beginning of the form. This same stem change, from -ο- to -ω-, is observed whenever any verb in the -οω class becomes either an Aorist or a Perfect.[95] This is consistent with all the contract vowel verbs having a final vowel lengthening process to mark the perfective. This suggests that something exists in common between the Aorist and the Perfect tense morphologically. No -κ- exists within this Perfect tense-form, since the -κ- does not appear in the Perfect middle forms. This participle does not occur in the corpus with Perfect active forms where the -κ- might be expected. Instead of reduplication, this participle occurs with initial vowel lengthening for its Perfect tense-form.

All of the references for this lexeme are in supplemental clauses to the main development. These supplements provide explanation for the terms, "apart from Christ," "darkened in understanding," and "you." In the context of Eph 2:12, this participle describes person who has been separated from citizenship of Israel. The genitive construction supplies the item from which the subject of the participle has been separated from. Since the genitive phrase modifies the participle by providing the item that the subject has been separated from, it might suggest

---

95 For examples of verbs in this class, see Appendix B.

that the action of separating has occurred, but this suggestion is not enough alone to be determinative whether this participle indicates a state of separation or an action of separating.[96] The context of Eph 4:18 is more clearly pointing to an action. The participle in this context is modified by a genitive phrase indicating that the subject implied by the participle is separated from the life of God. This participle is further modified by two prepositional phrases providing a cause for the separation. The first instance of the διὰ preposition introduces the medium, "ignorance," through which the subject has been separated from the life of God.[97] The second instance of the διὰ preposition indicates the cause or reason, "hardness of heart," for the separation. Grammatically, either or both of these prepositions might be either causal or provide a medium, but the solution given above works best when both prepositional phrases modify the same verb. The presence of this medium implies that the participle is actional as it is inconceivable for a state to remain due to the medium.[98] The participle in Col 1:12 describes persons alienated from God in the realm of their minds, and in their actions. This participle is modified by two dative phrases of location, where one is the bare dative and the other is introduced by the ἐν preposition. Although one may argue for a "dative of means" for either of these phrases, the locative idea for the dative case works well here, and the choice between the two is inconclusive as to whether the participle is actional or stative.[99]

This participle in Eph 2:12, 4:18, and Col 1:21 indicates the action by an unnamed party as alienating the plural subject from a divine benefit because of their wickedness and through their ignorance. Although Eph 2:12 and Col 1:21 are inconclusive, the Eph 4:18 reference is decidedly actional. The prepositional phrase supplies the medium through which the alienation action occurred. The action modified by this prepositional phrase must be viewed perfectively. In this

---

96 Lincoln emphasises a stative reading for this participle, but Abbott reminds that this verb "to estrange" is always actional due to the inclusion of "estrange from." Lincoln, 137; Abbott, 57.

97 Lincoln and Best see this prepositional phrase functioning causally as well as the following one. Lincoln, 278; Best, 420. Lenski sees both phrases as causal also, but has the second prepositional phrase indicate the cause for the first one. Lenski, 555-556.

98 Contra what is discussed here, O'Brien emphasises a stative reading for this participle. O'Brien, 188-189, 321.

99 Lohse and Abbott emphasise a stative reading for this participle. Edward Lohse, *Colossians and Philemon: A Commentary on the Epistles to the Colossians and to Philemon*, Hermeneia—A Critical and Historical Commentary on the Bible (Philadelphia, PA: Fortress, 1971), 62-63; Abbott, 225. On the other hand, Dunn, Barth, Blanke, Beck and Lenski emphasise that this state had an initial action. Dunn, 105, f.n. 3; Marcus Barth, Helmut Blanke, and Astrid B. Beck, *Colossians: A New Translation with Introduction and Commentary*, AB: 34A (New Haven, CT: Yale University Press, 2005), 219; R. C. H. Lenski, *The Interpretation of St. Paul's Epistles to the Colossians, to the Thessalonians, to Timothy, to Titus and to Philemon* (Columbus, OH: Lutheran Book Concern, 1937), 68-69.

case, little is added to the meaning of the clause if the verb had been Aorist rather than Perfect.

23.) διὰ τοῦτο παρακεκλήμεθα. Ἐπὶ δὲ τῇ παρακλήσει ἡμῶν περισσοτέρως μᾶλλον ἐχάρημεν ἐπὶ τῇ χαρᾷ Τίτου, ὅτι <u>ἀναπέπαυται</u> τὸ πνεῦμα αὐτοῦ ἀπὸ πάντων ὑμῶν· (2 Cor 7:13)

For this [reason] we have been comforted. And upon our comfort, we are abundantly overjoyed upon the joy of Titus, because his spirit <u>has been refreshed</u> by all of you.

24.) χαρὰν γὰρ πολλὴν ἔσχον καὶ παράκλησιν ἐπὶ τῇ ἀγάπῃ σου, ὅτι τὰ σπλάγχνα τῶν ἁγίων <u>ἀναπέπαυται</u> διὰ σοῦ, ἀδελφέ. (Phlm 1:7)

For I have great joy and comfort upon your love, because the bowels of the saints <u>have been refreshed</u> through you, brother.

[ἀναπέπαυται, middle indicative verb]

This verb has several issues that affect its morphology. First of all, it has reduplication of the first consonant as is typical for the synthetic Greek Perfect. Secondly, it does not have the trademark -κ- of the synthetic Greek Perfect tense-form due to being a middle. Thirdly, the addition of a preposition ἀνα- adds to the bulk of this tense-form. This Perfect tense-form from Phlm 1:7 appears actional in its setting.[100] The Perfect indicative middle is ἀναπέπαυται, which means "having been refreshed," or "having taken rest." The lexical form of this verb is παύω, and it is a combination of the prefix ἀνα, containing the idea of "up" with the main verb παύω, containing the idea of "to rest," or "to be refreshed." When this preposition and verb occur together, the sense of completely resting up or resting enough from one workload or stress to be ready for another emerges as the main idea. Often the translation for this compound verb is "to be refreshed," or "to rest," where one item is affectively recuperated from some kind of labour. In both of these contexts, a body of saints or an individual saint is said to be refreshed by the efforts in Christ of the addressee. In 2 Cor 7:13, the verb is modified by one prepositional adverb phrase that provides the agent who supplied the refreshment. In Phlm 1:7, the verb is modified by a prepositional phrase that supplies the medium through which the refreshment occurred. When the verb παύω changes

---

100   The other instances of this verbal stem are Aorist.

into the Perfect middle indicative verb ἀναπέπαυται, it does not undergo a change in the stem of the verb. The initial Present stem of this verb is παυ-. The stem adds the middle endings -ται to the end of the unchanged stem. This lack of stem change occurs in several verbs.[101] No -κ- exists within this Perfect tense-form, since the -κ- does not appear in the Perfect middle forms. This verb does have the -κ- in its Perfect active forms, but no examples occur in this corpus. This verb occurs with normal Cε reduplication for its Perfect tense-form.

This middle Perfect verb appears in a supplemental information section of both letters. The clauses both verbs are in are explanations for the preceding material. Both contexts have an expression of joy and comfort, and these Perfect tense-forms help supply the explanation for that joy and comfort. The supplemental information in both cases involves the last half of the verse. The pragmatic function of this verb in both cases is to present supplemental information for those who needed a fuller explanation. This verb in 2 Cor 7:13 is modified by a prepositional phrase that provides the agent for the refreshing action or state, or perhaps a cause for the refreshing.[102] This context is not determinative for whether the verb is actional or stative.[103] The same verb in Phil 1:7 is clearly eventive. It is further modified by a prepositional phrase that provides the medium through which the action of refreshing occurred.[104] It is this prepositional phrase which implies that the verb is more than merely stative, since its context modifies its action though supplying a medium for action.[105]

This verb in Phlm 1:7 indicates the action of Philemon refreshing the saints by his example in following Christ. The prepositional phrase supplies the medium for the action of refreshing and that medium is Philemon. The action indicated by the verb must be viewed perfectively. Little is added to the meaning of this clause if the verb had been Aorist rather than Perfect.

All of the Perfect tense-forms analysed in this section belong to contexts where their respective clauses provide supplemental information to the main development in the letter. The majority of the verbs that refer to an event were

---

101 These verbs are presented in Appendix B.

102 Furnish calls this the source rather than an agent. Furnish, *II Corinthians*, 390.

103 Harris and Lenski emphasise both an initial action and resulting state for this verb. Harris, 548; Lenski, 1118. Furnish cites 1 Cor 16:18 in support of the idea that one's "refreshment" usually has an agent, and that agent performs an action that causes the subject's refreshment. Furnish, 397.

104 Bruce concludes that Philemon is the medium for their refreshing. Both Bruce and Mellick emphasise the action Philemon took which produced the refreshment for the Colossians. Bruce, 210; Richard R. Melick, *Philippians, Colossians, Philemon*, NAC: 32 (Nashville, TN: Broadman & Holman, 1991), 356.

105 Lenski connects the action of Philemon refreshing the Colossian church to a resultant state of them remaining refreshed. Lenski, 958.

middle indicative forms found inside clauses that provided supplemental material. Several were substantival middle or passive participles. None of the verbs, either indicative forms or participles possessed an active form. The absence of the adjectival uses of the participle was observed for all the occurrences of Perfect tense-forms where an actional meaning was determined as the main contextually relevant meaning. Had an adjectival participle been observed, a stative reading of the participle would have been expected.

Since the middle voice has an affinity for stative interpretations, the presence of modifiers might have forced an eventive reading for an otherwise stative tendency. Many of these Perfects were modified with adverbs that suggest the verb pointed to an event rather than a state. Commentators debate whether these Perfects emphasise events or states. This is in contrast to the commentary on the Perfects in the previous section, where no debate exists. This debate observed may be due to the implied states that were apparent to some commentators and not to others.

This eventive meaning in these examples is viewed perfectively since the whole action was in focus, rather than a portion of the action. Since the completeness of the action was in focus, this fits best with a perfective view that additionally does not allow for intervening actions during the reality of that action. All new clauses and verb forms generally interrupt states following actions rather than the action which is viewed as complete. Therefore, states are imperfective and actions are perfective when belonging to a Perfect tense-form. The connection of imperfectivity to states and perfectivity to actions supports the claims made in Chapter 3 regarding the existence of complex aspect for the Perfect tense-form.

1.3. Verbs Which Have Either an Actional or Stative Component

The previous two sections illustrate verbs that are either stative or eventive. In this section, at least one verb in the Pauline corpus fits the criteria to qualify as both. It takes contextual modifiers that can modify it either way. The ability of the Perfect tense-form to describe both an event and a state provides further proof for its complex aspect.

25.) καὶ ὅτι ἐτάφη καὶ ὅτι ἐγήγερται τῇ ἡμέρᾳ τῇ τρίτῃ κατὰ τὰς γραφὰς (1 Cor 15:4)

And that he was buried, and that <u>he has been raised</u> on the third day according to the scriptures.

[ἐγήγερται, middle indicative verb]

In order to better illustrate the problems of approaching the semantics of the Greek Perfect with a single verbal aspect, this text is selected to demonstrate that the Perfect can have both perfectivity and imperfectivity for the same lexeme. The verbal aspect involved for the Perfect does not depend on lexeme type, since both aspects are apparent for the same lexeme. The perfect tense-form in this verse is imbedded in a section summarising the theology about Christ, where one would expect Aorist tense-forms, and most of the other verbs are Aorist. The only other non-Aorist verb is a Present tense-form in v. 6, which is a rhetorical diversion from the summary, and thus not part of it. The Perfect tense-form is example 25 is not a diversion from the summary, but is part of that summary. As such, it is a Perfect tense-form placed into a context where one would expect only Aorists.

Normally the Aorist is the summary tense in narrative literature, and here Paul is narrating the events of Christ in a summary fashion, but the stream of Aorists includes a Perfect verb, ἐγήγερται, here in this example.[106] Most translations translate this verb similar to an Aorist Passive and few like an Aorist Active.

"that he was buried, that <u>he was raised</u> on the third day in accordance with the Scriptures," (ESV)

"And that he was buried, and that <u>he rose again</u> the third day according to the scriptures:" (KJV)

"and that He was buried, and that <u>He was raised</u> on the third day according to the Scriptures," (NASB)

The vast majority of English Bibles have a reading much like that of the NASB or ESV, and the second largest group has a reading like the KJV. Another valid way to translate this verb is "he has been raised," per the provided translation earlier, but no English version has this reading. Other translations that are different from either reading described are usually more free translations, rather than literal, and do not preserve the structure of the Greek text; thus, they do not provide more options for translating the Perfect.

The majority of the English translations handles the Perfect tense-form no differently than they do the simple Aorist Perfectives, most likely due to the fact that this passage places the Perfect tense-form into a parallel structure with

---

106 This string begins in 15:3 with ἀπέθανεν, and includes ἐτάφη of 15:4, and ὤφθη of 15:6, 7, and 8.

Aorist passive tense-forms. While this parallelism might suggest that perfectivity is expressed by all these verbs, one is reminded that out of all these actions in this Christological summary, the only one that has a state with continued relevance at the time of writing the letter is the verb, ἐγήγερται. The author chose the Perfect tense-form to highlight the fact that the state of Jesus being still raised from the dead is still relevant, while the states of Jesus being dead and buried no longer are. Immediately those who analyse this verb as a "stative" see the application of McKay's and Porter's ideas here. The fact that this very form is used later in 1 Cor 15:12–29 to develop theology on the continued relevance of the resurrection of Jesus strongly suggests a stative reading.

The Perfect form is more complex than simply a state, however. With the parallelism with Aorist passives suggesting a common perfective aspect and both the greater and immediate context suggesting the continued relevance of the state, one must look to other data to help solve the issue.

Often overlooked in the grammatical analysis of verbs are the words or phrases which modify the verb in its own clause. These include adverbs, prepositional phrases, and in some cases dative or genitive phrases. In the immediate context of the verb, ἐγήγερται, a dative phrase, τῇ ἡμέρᾳ τῇ τρίτῃ, appears to modify it. Robertson and Plummer find this phrase odd with a Perfect, but this is because it does not modify the state.[107] While some may decide that this dative phrase helps to locate the moment of the raising in time, and thus conclude this phrase modifies the verb temporally, this is not the only effect it has. An argument could be made that this temporal phrase modifies a temporal component of the verb, and through that conclude that the verb has some inherent temporal property. Alternatively, the dative phrase might be argued to be supplying that temporal information to an otherwise non-temporal verb. It is difficult to argue the temporal relationship either way, but in either of these arguments, the dative phrase has to modify something in the verb, and it is clearly the moment of the raising that it modifies, and thus modifies the perfective prior action and not the imperfective state relevant at the present. It locates that moment in time in which Jesus was raised from the dead. This dative phrase cannot be modifying the state of continued relevance, since that state's relevance is continued beyond the third day, and its present relevance to the author as a state is important as seen in his developments further in this chapter. In modifying that moment, it must modify

---

107 Robertson and Plummer, *A Critical and Exegetical*, 334.

the action of the Perfect tense-form which caused the relevant state of Christ being risen.[108] Johnson notices that the author makes claims for the historicity of all the items in the list, death, burial, and resurrection, mainly using Aorists. Using the Perfect ἐγήγερται does not alter the claim, as the historical claim still exists while using the Perfect form.[109] Establishing the action of the resurrection of Jesus in history fosters the use of its subsequent state as a relevant state to the present moment later in 1 Cor 15.

The prepositional phrase, κατὰ τὰς γραφὰς, "according to the scriptures," also modifies this Perfect tense-form. With this phrase, Paul emphasises that Jesus being raised on the third day is either predicted by the scriptures, or models itself after scripture. Fee understands this phrase to emphasise that Jesus' resurrection modelled itself by arriving on the third day as did so many salvific events in the OT.[110] This phrase alludes to a presumably OT text where Jesus can be said to have fulfilled that passage by being raised on the third day. Hos 6:1–3 has a moment of raising on the third day, after which Israel will live. Even though the parallel is somewhat forced, since it is the Israelites that are raised in Hos 6:1–3, Paul's statement might be in reference to this passage in the form of analogy. Another way to understand this is that many scriptural things are accomplished on the third day, and since Jesus is raised on the third day, much like other things in scripture are accomplished on the third day, then his being raised in that time-frame can be said to be "according to the scriptures."[111] Typically, Greek prepositions along with their phrases modify verbs rather than other dative phrases or verbs plus a dative phrase, so it is better to understand the raising event to be all that the "according to scripture" phrase refers to and the reference to the third day as simply locating the raising event. To understand the "according to scripture" to modify a raising event on the third day forces it to modify more than the verb. In any case, the phrase, κατὰ τὰς γραφὰς, modifies the perfective action of being raised, or the moment of that action,[112] and it does not modify the consequent state. Earlier in the passage, the same prepositional phrase, κατὰ τὰς

---

108 This phrase might arguably be modifying the moment of entrance into that state. Although an action which caused the entrance into the state and a moment of entering that state are seemingly different analyses, they both suggest that the endpoint of the action is in view either way.

109 Alan F. Johnson, *1 Corinthians*, The IVP New Testament Commentary Series: 7 (Downers Grove, IL: InterVarsity, 2004), 285.

110 Gordon D. Fee, *The First Epistle to the Corinthians*, NICNT (Grand Rapids, MI: Eerdmans, 1987), 727–728.

111 Conzelmann, *1 Corinthians*, 257.

112 Perhaps the entrance into a state, but not the imperfective state in its duration.

γραφὰς, modifies an Aorist passive tense-form in much the same way with all the same difficulties, and clearly not modifying a state.[113]

The combination of the modifiers and the parallelism point to perfectivity for the Perfect tense-form. The further development of the relevance of a state of Christ being risen in 1 Cor 15:12–29 points to a state for the perfect tense-form, where Paul develops theology based on that state. Thus, in close context, both the resulting state of this action and the prior moment of this action are emphasised. Orr and Walther suggest that the reason for a Perfect in example 25 is to include "the continued effect of the action" along with dating the action.[114] It should be immediately clear that the perfective action component of the Perfect must be temporally prior to the continuing state of the Perfect. This passage shows the Perfect being used in a way consistent with the description of complex aspect developed in the third chapter. Complex aspect for the Perfect tense-form has properties of both perfectivity for the action and imperfectivity for a state that exhibits a pragmatic durativity.

In 1 Cor 15:4, perfectivity is suggested as the verbal aspect for the perfect tense-form in reference to its action component. This is supported in part by the dative phrase which modifies the action rather than the state, and further supported by the prepositional phrase also modifying that action. This much is broadly similar to the view defended by Fanning and Olsen. The following state resulting from the action is defined as imperfective, which is broadly similar to the view defended partially by Porter and Campbell.[115] The state belonging to this verb is recognised seriously, especially since it is contextually relevant further down in the chapter. Stativity is best viewed in an imperfective way so that present relevance at the speech time might be established or relevance established as coexisting with some other reference time in the context. If a verb is seen to be both an action and a following state, then the Perfect tense-form can be said to view the action as a whole through perfective aspect and view the state using

---

113 ὅτι χριστὸς ἀπέθανεν ὑπὲρ τῶν ἁμαρτιῶν ἡμῶν κατὰ τὰς γραφάς· (1 Cor 15:3) Here, the prepositional phrase modifies ἀπέθανεν, "died," which is a perfective. The fact that the same prepositional phrases modify the Perfect tense-form in 15:4 and the Aorist in 15:3 in the same manner is further evidence that the Perfect tense-form is to be understood in parallel with Aorist perfectives.

114 William F. Orr and James Arthur Walther, *I Corinthians: A New Translation, Introduction, with a Study of the Life of Paul, Notes, and Commentary*, AB: 32 (New Haven, CT: Yale University Press, 2008), 317.

115 Porter's explanation includes stativity, although he would not see this state necessarily as a result of the action, and Campbell would explain it as imperfective, although he has a tendency to relate the imperfectivity to the action rather than the state.

an imperfective aspect to allow other activities to interrupt that state or to signal present relevance of that state.

This example supports the idea that the Greek Perfect possesses two aspects, perfective and imperfective, and these two aspects point respectively one to the event and the other to the state. The collocation of this Perfect with Aorists in the summary narrative passage, and the presence of the temporal locative adverb both point to a perfective event. The fact that Christ's risen status is important several verses later, viewed as ongoing, points to an imperfective state. Most Perfects tend to be found as showing either a perfective event or an imperfective state, but not both. This example shows both aspects using the same lexeme. This example highlights the complex aspect developed in Chapter 3. This complex aspect helps explain why the same Perfect can point to a perfective event in one context and to an imperfective state in a different context, while being modified differently.

1.4. Verbs Which Are Used to Provide Citations

Several of the lexemes within the Pauline corpus were noticeably occurring frequently in the same structural contexts. The situation where a Perfect tense-form of a lexeme related to writing, speaking, or cognition preceded a relative clause which then provided the content for the written material, speech, or thought, appeared too often to be random. This was then labelled "Perfect + Relative Clause" construction for the purpose of categorising this usage in the charts in this section. Once this construction type was observed, all occurrences of the same type were then analysed to see what varieties existed, and whether or not a pattern emerged. All of the lexemes, which were in Perfect tense-forms in the various constructions that satisfied the type, were then tabulated from the corpus to see what the other tense-forms were doing relative to the Perfect tense-form. This was performed also to establish the frequency that the Perfect tense-form appeared in this construction type as opposed to the same lexeme outside this construction type.

Several constructions were observed that fit the "Perfect + Relative Clause" type. These are then grouped into categories "A" and "B" according to syntax. Category A involves some form of the Perfect outside a relative clause. Several varieties exist of this syntax, and are listed with their respective frequency in the chart in Figure 19.

Category B involves some form of the Perfect inside a relative clause, where the Perfect was the head verb. Several varieties exist of this syntax as well,

	Syntax	Occurrence count
1	Pf + ὅτι + clause	75
2	καθὼς + Pf + clause (without relative pronoun)	19
3	καθὼς + Pf + ὅτι + clause	2
4	καθὼς + Pf + ὥσπερ + clause	1
5	clause + καθὼς + Pf (without relative pronoun, content clause preceding the Pf)	1
6	Pf + ὥς + clause	1
7	καθὼς + ὥσπερ + Pf + clause	1
8	καθάπερ + Pf + ὥς + clause	1
9	καθάπερ + Pf + clause (without relative pronoun)	1

Figure 19: Adverbs of Perfects in Perfect + Relative Clause Constructions. These examples were compiled by performing a complex search in Logos 8, where collocations of the Perfect and the conjunction were tallied. Only the ones where the Perfect was outside of the subordinate clause are included here.

	Syntax	Occurrence count
1	ἵνα + clause headed by a Pf	11
2	ὅτι + clause headed by a Pf	9
3	ὥστε + clause headed by a Pf	6
4	ὅτι + clause headed by a Pf + καθὼς + clause	2
5	ὅτι + clause + clause headed by a Pf	1

Figure 20: Adverbs of Perfects within Relative Clauses. The same type of search was performed for this table as was the previous, except that only the examples with the Perfect inside the subordinate clause are included here.

although fewer in number, and less frequently occurring as well. These are listed in Figure 20.

The position of the Perfect tense-from relative to its clause is what syntactically distinguishes them, but some of the relative clause markers themselves might also mark this distinction.[116] Only ὅτι is observed in both charts, but with

---

116 It might be apparent later that these categories are reducible into fewer functional categories, but they are all provided here as syntactical varieties that are observed.

	Lexeme	Occurrence count	% of the Pf of this lexeme in this construction category	% of this lexeme appearing in Pf tense-form
1	οἶδα	64	62.13	78.03
2	γράφω	36	76.47	66.67
3	πείθω	12	63.16	86.36
4	προείρηκεν	4	100.00	100.00
5	ἐλπίζω	1	40.00	29.41
6	δοκιμάζω	1	100.00	8.33
7	πιστεύω	1	25.00	13.33
	Totals	119		
	Averages	17	66.68	54.59

Figure 21: Category A Lexemes. Οἶδα occurs so rarely in the Present tense-form, and not once in the Pauline corpus, that the percentage for the Perfect are higher than they might otherwise be.

a different word order in each. Both of these categories of constructions involve conjunctive words that are classified as adverbial in function and are related to subordinate clauses.[117]

The lexemes are listed next that occur in Perfect tense-form in this construction type, along with the raw count of their respective occurrences.[118] They are ranked according to occurrence count, and for those with the same number of occurrences, they are presented in the order they appear in the corpus. While the lexeme count within the corpus provides a rough measuring device that shows certain verbs occur more frequently than others in the corpus, for precision it is necessary to include percentages of tense-form distribution and context types. The lexical count is shown along with percentages of the lexeme occurring in these constructions as opposed to outside of these constructions. Likewise, these counts are shown with percentages of the Perfect tense-form occurrence as opposed to other tense-forms of the same lexeme. These percentages are calculated in order to perceive actual frequency. This provides a more precise way of measuring frequency than a simple lexeme count. Each lexeme is listed again with its frequency within the construction category. The lexemes appearing in Category A constructions are listed in Figure 21. The lexemes appearing in category B constructions are likewise listed in Figure 22.

---

117 Wallace classifies them this way. Wallace, *Beyond the Basics*, 674-677.
118 The lexemes are recorded in Present tense-form unless the lexeme is considered defective or suppletive, where in those cases it is recorded in Perfect tense-form.

	Lexeme	Occurrence count	% of the Pf of this lexeme in this construction category	% of this lexeme appearing in Pf tense-form
1	γίνομαι	4	11.11	13.95
2	οἶδα	4	3.88	78.03
3	ἀνθίστημι	2	66.67	42.86
4	ἀναπαύω	2	100.00	50.00
5	πληρόω	2	22.22	47.37
6	πιστεύω	2	50.00	13.33
7	ἐπαγγέλλομαι	1	50.00	50.00
8	ἐκχέω	1	100.00	33.33
9	τίθημι	1	100.00	8.33
10	ἐκπίπτω	1	100.00	50.00
11	μιμνήσκομαι	1	50.00	100.00
12	δίδωμι	1	100.00	1.45
13	ἵστημι	1	16.67	54.54
14	καυχάομαι	1	100.00	4.76
15	ἀσθενέω	1	100.00	8.33
16	καταγινώσκω	1	100.00	100.00
17	ἀπαλλοτριόω	1	33.33	100.00
18	ἐλήλυθεν	1	100.00	1.82
19	τελειόω	1	100.00	100.00
20	ἁγιάζω	1	25.00	62.25
21	καταρτίζω	1	50.00	50.00
22	πείθω	1	5.26	86.36
23	παρασκευάζω	1	33.33	100.00
24	προεπαγγέλλομαι	1	100.00	50.00
25	πληροφορέω	1	100.00	25.00
26	ἐξαρτίζω	1	100.00	100.00
27	ἵστημι	1	14.29	53.85
	Totals	37		
	Averages	1.37	64.14	51.32

Figure 22: Category B Lexemes

	Total Category construction occurrences	Total lexemes	Average occurrences for each lexeme within category
Category A	119	7	17.00
Category B	37	27	1.37
Ratios A:B	3.2:1	.25:1	12.4:1

Figure 23: Frequency of the Categories as a Ratio

The choice for lexeme in the category A constructions appears restricted, and the lexemes selected are repeated often throughout the corpus, while the lexemes in category B constructions do not appear to be so restricted, and are mostly one-time occurring, or occurring far less frequently in these constructions than those in category A constructions. For the few lexemes that occurred in both category A and category B constructions, these lexemes generally occurred much more frequently in the category A constructions than they did in the category B constructions.[119]

At the same time, not all of the data collected above is relevant to the issue or immediately usable. Some lexemes appeared in their respective constructions only once, and skewed their respective percentage too highly. A larger corpus would show fewer lexemes with only one occurrence, and the data set for a larger corpus would less frequently report 100% for any percentage category. In spite of these shortcomings, a trend is observable in the data set above, and it shows that for category A constructions, a few lexemes occur many times, and for category B constructions, many lexemes occur once or a few times each. For the lexemes observed in category B constructions, that also occur rarely in Perfect tense-form, the data set shows that this construction category accounts for the majority of the perfect tense usage for this lexeme.

The difficulty lies in just exactly how to measure the data set. One potential solution is to look for the averages using the data sets as a whole. This allows us to mathematically analyse the observed data without allowing the one-time occurring lexemes to skew the statistics.

A lexeme appearing in any of those constructions of category A is 12.4 times more likely to reappear throughout category A constructions, than the lexemes appearing in category B constructions are to reappear there. This gives us a measure of the difference in frequency between lexemes in categories A and B. This suggests at a minimum that constructions of category A are attracting specific

---

119 πιστεύω is the exception as it occurred one time only in each category of construction.

lexemes more so than are those of category B. This also implies some sort of specialisation of this category of constructions. More analysis is needed at this point to determine what is motivating this attraction of specific lexemes.

At this point, category B constructions are seen as the "normal" set due to attracting a variety of lexemes as opposed to category A, which selects lexemes for a specialised cognitive or communication function explained further in the analysis section. The focus of this chapter will now shift to category A constructions to understand better what motivates their use. The statistics for occurrences in the category B constructions are far less remarkable than for the category A constructions, but a few noteworthy examples will be included after the category A constructions are analysed.

The section will first analyse the lexemes and their context from the table in Figure 21 in one section, and show how they are related to the pragmatic concern of citing or referencing older material. Next, the lexemes and their context from the table in Figure 22 will be analysed, and shown to supply information where the lexical selection is unrestricted. Lastly, the results are related to the complex verbal aspect described in the third chapter.

Category A Data:

An example of each of the nine constructions from the corpus for the category A type is provided next along with discussion. These examples are representative of how this type is functioning in the corpus. In each example in this section, the structural elements that define the construction are underlined with a single straight line, the Perfect tense-form is underlined with a double straight line, and the content clause is underlined with a wavy line. This is done in both the Greek example and the English translation provided.

26.) <u>οἴδαμεν</u> δὲ <u>ὅτι</u> τὸ κρίμα τοῦ θεοῦ ἐστιν κατὰ ἀλήθειαν ἐπὶ τοὺς τὰ τοιαῦτα πράσσοντας. (Rom 2:2)

But <u>we have perceived</u> (<u>we know</u>) <u>that</u> the judgment of God is according to truth upon those that practice these things.

In example 26, the Perfect tense-form precedes the conjunction ὅτι, which in turn introduces the content for what was already perceived by the author and at least some of his readers. Jewett and Kotansky see the "οἴδαμεν ... ὅτι" construction as a "formula to introduce a well-known fact that is generally accepted."[120] Cranfield

---

120 Jewett and Kotansky, *Romans*, 198. Dunn concurs. Dunn, 80.

suggests that the exact construction with the particle, οἴδαμεν δὲ ὅτι, also carries the idea that the author expects the readers to accept the idea that they know this item.[121] Paul uses the clause containing the Perfect tense-form to provide a rationale for why we are judged if we judge others from the previous verse. This rationale places this verse in a supporting role for the main clause in the previous verse. In the current verse, Paul invites his readers to remember the knowledge they have acquired at some earlier point in time. This time of prior acquisition of knowledge is undetermined in the context. For the readers who may be new acquaintances of Paul or newly aware of his teaching, instead of Paul evoking knowledge they already perceived, they are instead invited to participate with others who did, and share in this knowledge.[122] Morris understands that Paul likes to "enlist the intelligent cooperation of his readers."[123] The prior event referred to by the Perfect is relevant only to those who did perceive this truth before. This construction is the most frequent one in category A and most commonly occurs with the lexemes οἶδα and γράφω. It occurs 75 times throughout the Pauline corpus. The pragmatic function of this lexeme in the Perfect in this construction is referential, where the author refers to material the readers are supposed to know in order to develop impact with the readers.

27.) δικαιοσύνη γὰρ θεοῦ ἐν αὐτῷ ἀποκαλύπτεται ἐκ πίστεως εἰς πίστιν, καθὼς γέγραπται· ὁ δὲ δίκαιος ἐκ πίστεως ζήσεται. (Rom 1:17)

For the righteousness of God has been hidden in him out of faith toward faith, just as it has been written: *The righteous will live out of faith.*

In example 27, the main clause is in 1:17a, and the supporting clause begins with the conjunction καθὼς, which precedes the Perfect tense-form. The clause containing what was written follows immediately after the Perfect. The formula "γέγραπται + citation" here is used to present a quotation from Hab 2:4b that Paul employs to enhance his argument. The reading of the quotation in Romans differs from the LXX.[124] The citation itself is the content for the writing action that occurred in the undetermined past. The clause providing the formula to

---

121 Cranfield, *A Critical and Exegetical*, 143.
122 This special understanding regarding the people who do not have a prior acquisition of the knowledge is the rhetorical effect of "we," and not an effect of the Perfect tense-form.
123 Morris, *Romans*, 110.
124 The exact version of the LXX Paul seems to quote is MS 763, which is likely a harmonisation of the original LXX with the Palestinian text. It differs from the MT, but the Pesher, 1QpHab 7:5–8:3 contains the concepts. Joseph A. Fitzmyer S. J., *Romans: A New Translation with Introduction and Commentary*, vol. 33, Anchor Yale Bible (New Haven, CT; London: Yale University Press, 2008), 265.

introduce the citation is a supporting clause bringing evidence to bear on the argument in the main clause. Thus, the Perfect provides supplemental information and is not part of the mainline. Hab 2:4b was written at an earlier point in time. This is a real event in the past evoked by γέγραπται. The readers are invited to acquaint themselves with the source text as they assess Paul's argument. This type of construction where γέγραπται appears followed by an OT citation appears frequently throughout the corpus. Jewett and Kotansky call this construction a traditional one.[125] Dunn states that this is a consistent way to document evidence for arguments.[126] The pragmatic function of this lexeme in this construction is usually to cite other written material in order to develop arguments.

> 28.) <u>καθὼς γέγραπται ὅτι</u> οὐκ ἔστιν δίκαιος οὐδὲ εἷς, (Rom 3:10)

> <u>Just as it has been written that</u> *there is not a righteous one, not [even] one,*

In example 28, the main clause is in the prior verse. The current verse contains a supporting clause that has the conjunction καθὼς preceding the Perfect tense-form to introduce a citation. Just like the previous example, the cited material was written earlier, and Paul enhances his argument that no one is righteous in the previous verse with the citation. The readers of Paul's letter are invited to acquaint themselves with the source text as they assess Paul's argument. The main difference between this construction and several others is that it has both conjunctions καθὼς and ὅτι where most of the occurrences use only one or the other. This construction occurs only twice in the corpus, and might be considered a mixture of the first two constructions.[127]

> 29.) μὴ γένοιτο· γινέσθω δὲ ὁ θεὸς ἀληθής, πᾶς δὲ ἄνθρωπος ψεύστης, <u>καθὼς γέγραπται· ὅπως</u> ἂν δικαιωθῇς ἐν τοῖς λόγοις σου καὶ νικήσεις ἐν τῷ κρίνεσθαί σε. (Rom 3:4)

> May it never be: rather let God be true, and every man a liar, <u>just as it has been written:</u> <u>That</u> *you might be justified in your words and prevail as you judge.*

In example 29, the main clause is in the first part of the verse. The supplemental clause begins with the conjunction καθὼς preceding the Perfect tense-form which in turn introduces a citation. Just like the previous examples, the written

---

125 Jewett and Kotansky, 144.
126 Dunn, 44.
127 The other instance occurs at Rom 4:17.

material was written much earlier, and Paul uses it to enhance his argument that human actions can cause God's word to seem untrue. The readers of Paul's letter are invited to acquaint themselves with the source text as they assess Paul's argument. The main difference between this construction and one immediately preceding is that it has the conjunction ὅπως where the previous one had ὅτι. This construction and all of the following constructions in category A occur one time only.

30.) μηδὲ εἰδωλολάτραι γίνεσθε <u>καθώς</u> τινες αὐτῶν, <u>ὥσπερ γέγραπται</u>· ἐκάθισεν ὁ λαὸς φαγεῖν καὶ πεῖν καὶ ἀνέστησαν παίζειν. (1 Cor 10:7)

Neither become idolaters <u>just as</u> some of them, <u>as it has been written</u>: *The people sat to eat and to drink and stood up to play.*

In example 30, the main clause is in the first part of the verse. The supplemental clause begins with the conjunction ὥσπερ preceding the Perfect tense-form to introduce a citation. Just like the previous examples, the written material was written much earlier, and Paul uses it to illustrate the potentiality of his followers going astray and falling under similar judgment. The readers of Paul's letter are invited to acquaint themselves with the consequences of the early Israelites within the source text as they assess their spiritual journey. The main difference between this construction and ones immediately preceding is that it uses the conjunction ὥσπερ where the previous one used καθὼς. The conjunction καθὼς is in the prior clause, but performing a comparative role rather than introducing a supporting clause. The clause with the Perfect tense-form is in a supplemental role to introduce a citation.

31.) οὐκ ἀπώσατο ὁ θεὸς τὸν λαὸν αὐτοῦ ὃν προέγνω. ἢ <u>οὐκ οἴδατε</u> ἐν Ἠλίᾳ τί λέγει ἡ γραφή, <u>ὡς</u> ἐντυγχάνει τῷ θεῷ κατὰ τοῦ Ἰσραήλ; (Rom 11:2)

God did not reject his people which he recognized before. Or, <u>have you not perceived</u> about Elijah where the writing is saying, <u>how</u> he interceded to God on behalf of Israel?

In example 31, the main clause is in the first part of the verse. The supplemental clause begins with the conjunction ἢ preceding the Perfect tense-form which in turn introduces the content of what was supposed to have been perceived. Much like the first example, Paul expects his readers to have already perceived the truth regarding Elijah prior to the time of writing the letter. Whether or not Paul's readers understood the truth concerning Elijah, they are invited to interpret the source text in the way that Paul did. Some might question that a "real" event of perceiving did not occur prior to this state knowing since the audience might not have perceived this truth about Elijah before reading the letter, and on the basis of this, they might question the necessity of an event logically preceding the state for a Perfect tense. In this context, however, it is not necessary for any of the readers to have already perceived the truth concerning Elijah, since the point of the passage is that Paul expected that they had already perceived this. The main difference between this construction and the first example is that it uses the conjunction ὡς where the first one used ὅτι. Another difference is that even though Paul is citing an OT reference, he does not use γέγραπται. This is because he was not using this text to prove a point, but challenging the readers' concept of the text. The pragmatic purpose of this construction is referential.

32.) τὸ γὰρ ὄνομα τοῦ θεοῦ δι' ὑμᾶς βλασφημεῖται ἐν τοῖς ἔθνεσιν, <u>καθὼς γέγραπται</u>. (Rom 2:24)

For *the name of God through you is being blasphemed among the nations,* <u>just as it has been written</u>.

Example 32 is similar to other citation examples examined earlier, but the content clause precedes the conjunction καθὼς and Perfect tense-form. This verse functions as a supplemental clause to the previous 3 verses, which contain the main point in the form of five questions. This verse responds to the answer "yes," if that answer were to be provided by the minds of the readers to the five questions in the previous verses.[128]

33.) <u>καθάπερ οἴδατε</u>, ὡς ἕνα ἕκαστον ὑμῶν ὡς πατὴρ τέκνα ἑαυτοῦ (1 Thess 2:11)

<u>Just as you have perceived,</u> as [we conducted ourselves] with each one of you as a father with his children

Example 33 is similar to examples 28 and 29 earlier, but the conjunction καθάπερ is used instead of καθὼς, and the conjunction ὡς is used instead of ὅτι or ὅπως.[129] This construction does not introduce a citation, because the lexeme is οἶδα instead of γράφω, but introduces something Paul's readers have already perceived. They had observed Paul's manner of interacting with them as a spiritual father, so Paul evokes that memory to support the main idea in the previous verse that his

---

128 Paul expects that the readers will answer "yes" to his earlier questions. Paul's response to this "yes" answer through using this verse supports the provided conclusion.

129 The word καθάπερ appears only in the Pauline corpus, Hebrews and Attic Greek. Blass and Debrunner, §453, 236.

conduct among the Thessalonians was blameless. Just like earlier examples of this lexeme, it is not necessary for all of the readers to have already observed this, but only a few. Others who were not previously aware of this perception are invited to become acquainted with Paul's conduct through communion with the ones who were aware of this. The prior event is relevant for the ones who had made this observation before the time of writing of this letter.

34.) μὴ ἐν πάθει ἐπιθυμίας <u>καθάπερ</u> καὶ τὰ ἔθνη τὰ <u>μὴ εἰδότα</u> τὸν θεόν, (1 Thess 4:5)

Not in the passion of desire <u>just as</u> also the nations which <u>have not perceived</u> God,

Example 34 is a bit different from the other examples in two ways. The conjunction καθάπερ introduces a clause providing an example of those who did not control their flesh. The conjunction is not related to the Perfect tense-form in the same way as the prior examples. The conjunction καθάπερ performs a comparative role comparing Paul's readers with the godless nations. The Perfect participle functions as an adjective modifying "the nations." However, similar to a verb, the participle does take a direct object, θεόν, specifying the content of the perception. This lexeme of perception functions like the earlier instances of the lexeme οἶδα, where those instances were followed by a content clause. The Perfect tense-form introduces the content of perception, and functions in a referential way, rather than in a citational way. The lack of a proper concept of God is related to the Gentiles' lack of self-control.

Within category A the first two constructions have some lexical variety for the Perfect tense-form, as the other constructions are observed with either only οἶδα or γράφω. Only seven lexemes are observed for the first two constructions, and the set of lexemes appears to be restricted to verbs of writing, speaking, and cognition. In the instances where writing and speaking lexemes are found, such as γράφω and προείρηκεν, the author evokes a memory for his readers. Either this is their memory recalled for supporting an argument in his letter or it is his own memory that he is sharing with his readers. Where verbs of cognitive activity are encountered, such as οἶδα, πείθω, ἐλπίζω, δεδοκιμάσμεθα, and πιστεύω, the author evokes the memory of at least some of his readers in most contexts.[130] This set of lexemes in the Perfect tense-form relate to the complex aspect established earlier for the Perfect. The thing remembered is a perfective action, where the lexical

---

130 In negated or irrealis contexts, the author might expect that his readers should have this memory when they do not.

core specifies the nature of the action as a cognitive process, speech, or writing. The memory as shared with someone else is a state that has endured since the time of cognition, speech, or writing, and it is relevant to something the author wishes to say or cause his readers to do. This state is imperfective, meaning that it is presented as incomplete or without endpoints in view.

This next section will now illustrate two examples from category B, to compare and contrast category B constructions with those of category A. Both of these examples provide some sort of supplemental information to the main clause or some item in the main clause. However, the verbs for these examples will belong properly to the subordinate clause introduced by a conjunction, rather than sit outside the clause. The Perfect tense-forms in these constructions do not take an object of informational content like those in category A, but are part of the informational content introduced by the conjunction.

35.) Οὐ γὰρ θέλω ὑμᾶς ἀγνοεῖν, ἀδελφοί, τὸ μυστήριον τοῦτο, ἵνα μὴ ἦτε [παρ'] ἑαυτοῖς φρόνιμοι, <u>ὅτι</u> πώρωσις ἀπὸ μέρους τῷ Ἰσραὴλ <u>γέγονεν</u> ἄχρι οὗ τὸ πλήρωμα τῶν ἐθνῶν εἰσέλθῃ (Rom 11:25)

For I do not wish for you to not recognise, brothers, this mystery, so that you might not be conceited: <u>that</u> a hardening of parts <u>has come to exist</u> for Israel until which time the fulness of Gentiles has entered.

In example 35, the subordinate clause introduced by the conjunction ὅτι provides supplemental information that defines or explains the word μυστήριον or "mystery" in the main clause. Here the content in the subordinate clause supplements the noun rather than supplements a Perfect tense-form as the examples in Category A did. This is due to the placement of the Perfect tense-form inside the clause. The clause still functions as providing supplemental information using a Perfect tense-form to accomplish this.

36.) εἰς τὸ εἶναί με λειτουργὸν Χριστοῦ Ἰησοῦ εἰς τὰ ἔθνη, ἱερουργοῦντα τὸ εὐαγγέλιον τοῦ θεοῦ, <u>ἵνα</u> γένηται ἡ προσφορὰ τῶν ἐθνῶν εὐπρόσδεκτος, <u>ἡγιασμένη</u> ἐν πνεύματι ἁγίῳ. (Rom 15:16)

In order for me to be a minister of Jesus Christ toward the Gentiles, ministering the gospel of God, <u>so that</u> the offering of the Gentiles [be] acceptable, <u>having been sanctified</u> in the Holy Spirit.

In example 36, the subordinate clause is introduced by the conjunction ἵνα, and it provides supplemental information that explains the result for Paul being appointed to minister to the Gentiles. The result is that the Gentiles will be offering something acceptable to God. The Perfect participle ἡγιασμένη introduces an apposition further defining what εὐπρόσδεκτος, or "acceptable" means.

In both of these examples, the subordinate clauses containing the Perfect tense-forms provide a definition for a term in the main clause. These definitions include material that provides the logical basis for term in the main clause. The "hardening of parts" provides a basis for a mystery that Paul has to explain, and "having been sanctified" provides a basis for being "acceptable." Both of these statements of basis are logically prior to the present state Paul refers to. In example 35, the "hardening of parts" is logically prior to any mystery needing to be explained and in example 36, an offering "having been sanctified" is logically prior to its being accepted. Even though Paul refers to a futurity of Gentile acceptance, the sanctification of the offering is still prior to that acceptance. Both of these examples relate to the complex aspect described for the Perfect in that their lexeme points to a complete action perfectively, while states enduring from those actions are contextually relevant and seen imperfectively.

In both category A and category B, the Perfect tense-form is related to supplying additional information to the main clauses. The difference is that for category A, the Perfect tense-form introduces a content element that supplements an argument, but in category B, the Perfect tense-form is part of the content and is part of the supplemental clause. The syntactical difference of the Perfect tense-form being outside the clause allows it to announce the content clause, and being inside the content clause allows it to be part of the content clause. Another striking difference is that category A lends itself to citation of previous material, while category B lends itself to definition and description of current material, although these definitions may be based upon prior events. While any lexeme might be used in category B, those in category A are lexically restricted to verbs of cognition and communication. While these lexemes in these contexts are usually seen as stative, the author uses these supplemental clauses to evoke a memory of a prior event or to establish a prior basis for something in the main clause. In both cases it is possible to understand a prior event and a present state having a role in the author's usage of these Perfect tense-forms. This provides further support for the complex aspect of the Perfect, where the action of the Perfect is viewed perfectively, and the state is viewed imperfectively.

The use of category A constructions with lexemes of cognition or communication serves the pragmatic purpose of evoking a memory or recognition of a prior event, in order to support an argument in the main clause. The author or speaker wishes either to evoke some content out of the audience's or reader's memory with the Perfect tense-form of cognitive lexemes, or to bring it to initial awareness from someone else's writing or speech with communication lexemes. It is pragmatics that dictates the lexical selection and the construction types used for category A. Perfect tense-forms used in this way are not "front-grounded,"[131] but are used to provide background[132] information for the foregrounded arguments of the main clause. Collectively, this set of Perfect tense-forms serves to introduce content clauses, where the content is either an idea that the reader has in his or her mind due to a previous experience he or she has had and the author evokes that memory, or an idea a reader introduces to his or her mind as a result of another person's efforts, and the author evokes his or her own memory regarding the previous experience of that other person, such as another author or speaker. In the latter case, the author's awareness is being shared with a new audience.

The verbal aspect of the Perfect tense-form appears to hold two different aspects on two different parts of the verbal process. The lexical core follows the pattern of perfectives in its internal spelling, suggesting that the actional component related to the verb is complete. The reduplicant on the front of the tense-form belongs to the development of imperfectives, and points to a resulting state from that prior action imperfectively.[133] This is a complex aspect compared to that of the Aorist or Present, and accounts for why most languages today prefer two separate words to express a Perfect.[134] The lexical aspect of verbs of cognition and communication expect some sort of mental concept or idea to be introduced. The Perfect naturally fits the situation where this concept or idea is being remembered.[135] The usage of the Perfect tense-form naturally fits the citation formula where the content is currently relevant although it was generated earlier.

The corpus for the research in this chapter was limited to Pauline epistles to see how a single New Testament author or editor uses Perfect tense-forms in

---

131 Porter emphasises that Perfect tense-forms are front-grounded. The evidence he provides seems to be primarily from narrative contexts. Stanley E. Porter, *Idioms of the Greek New Testament.* Biblical Languages: Greek: 2. 2nd ed. (Sheffield: Sheffield Academic Press, 1999), 23; Porter, *Verbal Aspect*, 92-93.

132 Runge emphasises the supporting role of the Perfect tense-form in nonnarrative contexts. Steven E. Runge, "The Contribution of Verb Forms, Connectives, and Dependency to Grounding Status in Nonnarrative Discourse," 221-272 in *The Greek Verb Revisited: A Fresh Approach for Biblical Exegesis*, edited by Steven E. Runge and Christopher J. Fresch (Bellingham, WA: Lexham, 2016), 236.

133 This understanding of the morphology of the Greek synthetic Perfect tense-form was developed in an earlier paper, "Connecting the Morphology of the Greek Perfect to Its Aspectual Properties," presented on April 7, at the 2017 annual *Stone-Campbell Journal* Conference, at Johnson University in Knoxville, TN.

134 Modern Greek uses a periphrastic perfect today.

135 This provides a natural fit for the construction where a "subject has said before that X . . . ," "subject has perceived (knows) that X . . . ," or "subject has written that X . . . "

nonnarrative literature.[136] The findings support the idea that in nonnarrative literature, the Perfect often provides supporting material or backgrounded material to the mainline. The supplemental constructions observed in this section account for 38% of all Perfect tense-forms in the Pauline corpus. For the lexemes counted in these constructions, 93% of the Perfect tense-form occurrences for that lexeme were used in situations supporting the mainline. This implies that the supplemental usage observed here is a significant role for the Perfect tense-form. Broader research needs to be performed on other nonnarrative genres, authors, and eras to confirm this usage. As this is performed, the statistics reported here will be refined, especially to the extent that it allows for more refined lexical study on the various lexemes found in these constructions.

The Perfect tense-form has in view, both a state relevant to the present moment in the immediate context and an event prior to that state. For the verbs in the constructions discussed in category A, the state is the idea that exists or should exist in the mind, while the event is related to the prior acquisition of that knowledge for cognitive lexemes, or the original action of the idea creator for communication lexemes. The Perfect tense-form allows for both the prior event and the state to be relevant in the context. The lexical core of the Perfect tense-form points to the perfective action that has already been completed, while the reduplicant on the front of the Perfect tense-form points to the currently relevant state. This complex aspect helps explain how a Perfect tense-form of a verb of cognition or communication can evoke currently relevant content from information created through a prior event. The pragmatic need for citing sources, statements, or ideas while making arguments led to both the lexical selection and syntax for the instances observed in category A. The fact that the synthetic Perfect tense-form is largely attracted to these situations suggests that its aspect is more complex than other tense-forms, allowing for two separates parts of the verbal process to be viewed in two different ways.

1.5. Οἶδα[137]

One lexeme has caused the theorists some particular difficulties both in its classification lexically and in its aspectual properties in the Perfect tense-form. The

---

136 The focus upon one author and one genre avoids problems surrounding author style, and including others requires a larger treatment.

137 A version of this subsection was previously published after being presented at Eastern Great Lakes Biblical Society and revised. James E. Sedlacek, "Reimagining Οἶδα: Indo-European Etymology, Morphology and Semantics Point to its Aspect," *Conversations with the Biblical World* 36 (2016): 143-163. This version is revised further since that article was published.

unique problems related to this lexeme have caused some to connect its apparent stativity to its Perfect tense-form, while others connect this stativity to this lexeme as a lexical property apart from the Perfect tense-form. This lexeme also has some rare morphology not seen in most of the Greek Perfects. For those reasons, it deserves a separate treatment. This section shows that this lexeme behaves as other Perfects described earlier in this study.

In Greek verbal aspect studies, opposing parties in the debate over the Perfect tense-form have portrayed the aspect of the verb οἶδα in differing ways, either to support their own position or to undermine that of their opponent. McKay denies that οἶδα implies a prior action which caused its state. "As a perfect, οἶδα is remarkable in that although it is one of the most commonly used perfects it rarely, if ever, conveys any clear implication of the action by which its state (of knowledge) was established."[138] McKay makes his case that the Perfect tense-form is generally stative, and emphasises the stativity of this verb deriving from being a Perfect. Porter emphasises stativity through the presence of the Perfect tense-form as well. Porter states that οἶδα does not "offer a paradigmatic choice of forms."[139] Consequently, he emphasizes that this verb is aspectually vague. Campbell counters the connection between the Perfect tense-form and stativity by appealing to lexical aspect. "The important point, however, is that οἶδα is *already* stative simply because of its lexical meaning, and irrespective of its expression as a perfect indicative."[140] Among those debating the verbal aspect of the Greek Perfect tense-forms, this verb is either a stative because it is a Perfect tense-form, or it is stative because of its lexeme, and the Perfect tense-form is immaterial to its stativity.

This next section will provide a morphological analysis for οἶδα. It will first assess the lexical meaning along with the morphology of the lexical stem. This is a lengthier discussion as this lexeme has been debated as a stative in recent literature. It will next explain the Perfect morphology of οἶδα, and show how it is a normal reduplicated Perfect.

One of the most recurring Perfect tense-forms in Pauline literature is οἶδα in various forms. This verb is often translated with the gloss, "I know," and in many Biblical Greek grammars, this verb is categorised as a verb of knowledge.[141]

---

138 McKay. "On the Perfect," 299.

139 Porter, *Verbal Aspect*, 283-284.

140 Campbell, *Verbal Aspect, the Indicative Mood*, 188.

141 William D. Mounce. *Basics of Biblical Greek: Grammar*, 3rd ed. (Grand Rapids, MI: Zondervan, 2009), 407. David Alan Black, *Learn to Read New Testament Greek*. Expanded Edition (Nashville, TN: Broadman & Holman, 1994), 71. Black also erroneously states that this verb only occurs in Perfect and Pluperfect forms. Machen provides only the gloss, "I know," and shows only the Perfect

While this tense-form of the verb is typically used this way since at least the time of Homer, this gloss is a practical solution to aid in translation, but it does not adequately explain the meaning of the verb or the existence of other tense-forms of this verb with meanings different than "I know."[142] The Aorist tense-forms, such as εἶδον, are often placed into a chart under a different verb, ὁράω, "I see," in first-year NT Greek grammars, and lexically grouped with other verbs about seeing.[143] It appears that the various forms of this verb are categorised according to function rather than form. In other words, one tense-form is presented as one lexical item, while the other as a different lexical item. Classical Greek grammars handle this verb slightly better than do the Biblical Greek grammars, in that they often place both together or mention the existence of the other relevant form(s).[144] However, this falls short of an explanation. Some of the intermediate grammars and reference grammars include more data, but still fall short of defining this verb, and short of explaining how two very different meanings are associated with this lexeme.[145] The diagram in Figure 24 below shows all the occurrences of every Perfect tense-form of this lexeme within the Pauline Corpus.[146] Each form is listed with its occurrence count below it.

and Pluperfect forms in his verb chart. J. Gresham Machen, *New Testament Greek for Beginners* (New York: Macmillan, 1923), 251, 218, 263. In a footnote, Porter provides a link to the proper origin of this word, εἴδω, which is also labelled, "obsolete." Stanley E. Porter, Jeffrey T. Reed, and Matthew Brook O'Donnell, *Fundamentals of New Testament Greek* (Grand Rapids, MI: Eerdmans, 2010), 321.

142 A. T. Murray translates οἶσθα, as, "you know." Homer, *Il.*, 1.365. A. T. Murray, *Homer: The Iliad with an English translation*, Vol. 1. Loeb Classical Library, Edited by G. P. Goold (Cambridge, MA: Cambridge University Press, 1978), Examples within Homer's works are too numerous to catalogue here in detail.

143 Black, 227. Mounce, 408. Machen, 259. H. E. Dana and Julius R. Mantey, *A Manual Grammar of the Greek New Testament* (New York: Macmillan, 1955), 327.

144 Morwood calls the Perfect tense-form of this verb a Present and he calls the Pluperfect tense-form of this verb an Imperfect, even though it is placed in the chart as an Aorist. Like the grammars mentioned earlier, he places the Aorist of this verb under ὁράω, "I see." James Morwood, *Oxford Grammar of Classical Greek* (Oxford: Oxford University Press, 2001), 104-105. *LSJ* points to εἴδω, but does not clear up the confusion caused by the grammars. *LSJ* "εἴδω" 483. Smyth groups the forms together, yet provides the same glosses without explanation. Herbert Weir Smyth, *Greek Grammar for Colleges* (New York: American Book Company, 1920), 21-218, § 794.

145 Blass and Debrunner connect οἶδα, the Perfect to εἴδω, the Present tense-form, but still places εἶδον, the Aorist, under ὁράω, "I see," without mentioning the connection between these verbs. Blass and Debrunner, *A Greek Grammar*, 50-51, §99, 101. Wallace does not discuss the meaning of the verb, so while his work does not repeat the error of separating the forms of this verb into two lexical entries, one does not become more informed regarding the connection of these forms. Wallace, *Beyond the Basics*.

146 I use a lemma search in *BibleWorks 10*, and rely on the morphological tagging provided by this software for the Nestlé-Aland text, 27th edition.

Indicative Mood		
	1st person active	2nd person active	3rd person active

	1st person active	2nd person active	3rd person active
Singular	οἶδα	οἶδας	οἶδε(ν)
	15	4	8
Plural	οἴδαμεν	οἴδατε	οἴδασι
	11	26	0

Subjunctive Mood		

	1st person active	2nd person active	3rd person active
Singular	εἰδῶ	εἰδῇς	εἰδῇ
	2	1	0
Plural	εἰδῶμεν	εἰδῆτε	εἰδῶσι
	1	1	0

Imperative Mood		

	1st person active	2nd person active	3rd person active
Singular	---	ἴσθι	ἴστω
	---	0	0
Plural	---	ἴστε	ἴστωσαν
	---	1	0

Participle		

	Nom masc active	Nom fem active	Nom neut active
Singular	εἰδὼς	εἰδυῖα	εἰδόν
	5	0	0
Plural	εἰδότες	εἰδυῖαι	εἰδότες
	24	0	0
	Acc masc active	Acc fem active	Acc neut active
Singular	εἰδότα	εἰδυῖαν	εἰδότα
	0	0	1
Plural	εἰδότας	εἰδυίας	εἰδότας
	0	0	0
	Dat masc active	Dat fem active	Dat neut active
Singular	εἰδότι	εἰδυίᾳ	εἰδότι
	0	0	0
Plural	εἰδῶσι(ν)	εἰδυίαις	εἰδῶσι(ν)
	1	0	0

Infinitive		

	active	passive	---
	εἰδέναι		---
	8		---

Figure 24: Perfect forms of οἶδα

While this verb occurs throughout the corpus, it is sufficient to examine one example to reference the connection between this verb and its primary gloss within a context. The first Pauline occurrence of this verb is in Rom 2:2.[147]

37.) οἴδαμεν δὲ ὅτι τὸ κρίμα τοῦ θεοῦ ἐστιν κατὰ ἀλήθειαν ἐπὶ τοὺς τὰ τοιαῦτα πράσσοντας. (Rom 2:2)

but we know that the judgment of God is according to truth upon those who practice these things (unrighteous things).

This is a Perfect active first-person plural form. It is one of 11 occurrences of this exact form, and one of 64 occurrences of the Perfect indicative of this verb in the Pauline corpus.[148] And as the grammarians suggest, the English translations generally provide, "I know," for this verb.[149] The most common word following this verb in the corpus is ὅτι. This is because usually this verb is formulaic in that it introduces some idea that the subject desires to call to attention to his or her readers.[150] The usual translation is "I know that . . . ," so in this case, "we know that . . . ," introduces the idea the author wished to call to attention, which is "the judgment of God is according to truth upon those who practice these things."

Campbell and Evans analyse this verb as stative due to having a stative lexeme, while Porter analyses this verb as being stative due to having a Perfect tense-form. Logically then, either this verb is always stative, or it incurs stativity through having the Perfect tense-form. The verbal idea of "knowing" appears to be a fairly stative idea across languages and knowing something does not generally imply activity. Translations consistently provide a stative gloss. Those who classify this verb as stative due to having a stative lexeme, usually do not prefer to have this verb included in a list of verbs being analysed for verbal aspect, where the Perfect

---

147 In canonical order, not historical order.

148 All thirteen books attributed to Paul in the canon are included in this corpus. Regardless of which position scholars might take regarding authorship of individual letters, the Early Church's understanding that these thirteen letters belonged together and, in some way, reflected Paul's teaching, led to them being collected as a set. As such, this body of letters provides a consistent genre of epistolary literature for the Hellenistic Period, and deserves to be analysed as a genre corpus whether written by one author or several.

149 In this instance, the ESV, NASB 1977, NASB 1995, HCSB, NIV 1984, NAB 1991, NAB 2011, TNIV, RSV, NRSV, NLT, NKJV, NIV 2011, NIV (UK), NIRV, GNV 1599, ERV, DARBY, CEB, and ASV all have "We know." The TYN, BISHOP's, and KJV all have "We are sure," while the NJB has "We are aware."

150 This occurs as early as in Homer's writings as well, but more rarely. Only three instances of this verb followed by the relative clause containing the content of what was to be known exist in the *Iliad*. Homer, *Il.*, 11.408, 13.674-675, 20.433-434.

tense-form is said to produce the stativity. Often this verb is called a "fossil," and this is put forth as a reason to dismiss it from examination.[151] Those who analyse the stativity arising from this verb as that being due to the Perfect tense-form claim that this verb shows no hint of a prior action which causes the state; thus, it makes a good example for the Perfect tense-form being stative in aspect.

First, this verb needs to be examined using some principles from Historical Linguistics. The verb οἶδα originally did not have "I know" as its central meaning, and was a verb with true eventive properties, rather than only stative properties. Wackernagel connects this verb to the Indo-European root ϝειδ-.[152] The letter "ϝ" is an archaic letter where the early Greek alphabets retained a letter much like the Hebrew "wau," or ו.[153] Its pronunciation was much like the Latin vocalic "u" or consonantal "v." It is usually rendered in Indo-European dictionaries today by a "w." This letter fell out of use as the Greeks modified their alphabet, adding vowels and relocating some consonants. Its presence is often signified by Greek vowel diphthongs where a small "w" sound can be heard. For example, the "oi" in οἶδα has a fairly pronounced "w" between the ο and ι. This allowed the Classical Philologists to deduce a ϝειδ- root behind this word. Wackernagel suggests some sort of state for this verb, but one derived from a completed process, much like other Perfects.[154] He explains this as, "Through seeing I have reached the state of knowing," and links the Perfect οἶδα to the Aorist, εἶδον, which is found frequently in the NT, and the Latin uidi-, from which English derives the words, "vision," and "video."[155] It is worth observing that his explanation includes both seeing and knowing together. Chantraine likewise connects these two verb forms as one verb, and they are still connected in the most recent etymological works attributed to him.[156] Beekes connects εἶδον to the Sanskrit, *ávidat*, a verb of seeing, after providing an Indo-European root, h₁é-uid-et.[157] Later, using the

---

151 See Evans, *Verbal Aspect*, 42, for an example of dismissal of Stanley Porter's examples due to fossilisation. Fossilisation basically means that this word follows older rules for words carrying its form, and not the rules of word formation used at that time, so functions are assigned to it by the current language users.

152 Wackernagel decided the form οἶδα did not have reduplication, but this was before Laryngeal theory was developed. David Langslow, editor. *Jacob Wackernagel "Lectures on Syntax," with Special Reference to Greek, Latin, and Germanic* (Oxford: Oxford University Press, 2009), 217. This work is a translation of Wackernagel's lecture notes, and is the only form of them published.

153 This letter was called a digamma.

154 Langslow, 218.

155 Langslow, 218.

156 Pierre Chantraine, *Dictionaire Étymologique de la Langue Grecque: Histoire des Mots*. Sous la direction de Alain Blanc, Charles de Lamberterie, Jean-Louis Perpillon (Paris: Klincksiek, 1999), 779-780.

157 Beekes, 235. The "h" along with a subscripted number (such as h₁, or h₂) represents the presence of a laryngeal. The subscripted numbers each represent different laryngeals. Laryngeals are basically a

Indo-European root, uoid-h₂e, he connects οἶδα with the Sanskrit *véda*, and Latin *vīdī*.[158] In a different work, Beekes along with Beek connect these two verbs, οἶδα and εἶδον, to a common root, *ueid-.[159] Beekes makes a further connection of this Greek verb to the noun εἰδώς, or "witness," and the infinitive, ἰδεῖν, "to note," or "to observe." Soon after the first Historical Linguists explained this verb, Laryngeal Theory was developed to explain some phonological processes not yet understood. Applying principles of Laryngeal Theory, Lehmann explains the reduplication for οἶδα as the form having lost both the initial digamma and a laryngeal, after adding the reduplicant.[160] This explains why this verb does not have an apparent Ce pattern observed in most Greek Perfects.[161] It used to have it, but lost some of its features. Mallory and Adams connect both of these verbs together noting that οἶδα is the Greek Perfect for *woide-, meaning "I have seen," and οἶδα has a connection to the root *weid-, from which the verbs of seeing are derived.[162]

At this point, one might assume that the abstract idea of "knowing" evolved from the concrete expression of "seeing." Verbs of knowing are commonly connected to verbs of experience, such as verbs involving one of the five senses.[163] In a section about knowledge and epistemology within his larger work on philosophical being, Kahn counters the argument that the abstract idea of "knowing" was derived from the concrete idea of "seeing," by illustrating that both uses of this root are equally ancient.[164] He also shows the parallel between concrete and abstract uses in both Greek and Vedic literature. Whether abstract uses of the

---

sound not written in the alphabets of most languages that explains the current existence of long vowels at the end of a syllable and consonantal sounds at the beginning of a vowel-initial syllable. This idea also helps explain some derivational differences between languages that have a common "parent" language, where the descendant languages made different decisions.

158 Beekes, 238.

159 Beekes and van Beek, *Etymological Dictionary of Greek*.

160 Winfred P. Lehmann, *Proto-Indo European Phonology* (Austin: University of Texas Press, 1952), 76.

161 This symbol, Ce (sometimes written as CeC), refers to the Greek Perfect pattern where the first consonant of the reduplicant copies the first stem consonant, and an ε vowel is inserted between them. This pattern is different from CVC patterns where the vowel can be different or be copying the first vowel. In the verb under analysis the vowel is shaped by the combination of the losses of initial digamma and laryngeal as the reduplication syllable is added.

162 J. P. Mallory and D. Q. Adams, *The Oxford Introduction to Proto Indo-European and the Proto Indo-European World* (Oxford: Oxford University Press, 2006, 2007, 2008).

163 For example, the Spanish verb *saber*, "to know," is derived from the Latin *savor*, "to taste." Interestingly, the English language has both meanings in its words derived from this Latin word. Consider the English "savor," "savory," "savant," and the slang "savvy." While these might be seen as lexicalisations, it remains clear that a connection exists between verbs of the five senses and verbs of knowing in the mind.

164 Charles H. Kahn, *The Verb "Be" in Ancient Greek* (Indianapolis, IN: Hackett, 2003).

Seeing	Both	Knowing
Vision (verb and noun)	Visionary	Wisdom
Visible	View (does not always	Wise
Video	refer to viewing with the	Unwise
Visual	eyes)	Advise
Witness	Viewpoint	Advice
Visual	Advisor	Visualize
Visor	Ideal	Wit
Invisible		Witty
		Idea
		Ideation
		Envision

Figure 25: Inter-relatedness of "see" and "know"

word derive from the concrete uses or not, it remains clear that a strong connection exists between verbs expressing one of the functions of the five senses and verbs of knowing.

Even in English, the words derived from this same Indo-European root involve both lexical domains of seeing and knowing.[165] Figure 25 lists a number of related occurrences of the same lexeme in English overlapping both lexical domains.

This dual lexical domain evidence from English permits a further investigation into the Greek verb οἶδα through examining the Aorist tense-forms of εἶδον in the Pauline corpus. Both verbs are derived from the same root. The survey below is tabulated partly to show that both Perfect and Aorist tense-forms are found in roughly the same frequency within the corpus. The other reason for the survey is to assert that all of these occurrences were translated as forms of "seeing," and were eventive rather than stative. The following chart in Figure 26 illustrates the findings of that survey.[166]

1 Cor 2:9 provides an example of the Aorist of this verb. The typical gloss for the Aorist is "to see."

---

165 Many of these selections are from Alois Walde. *Vergleichendes Worterbuch der Indogermanischen Sprachen.* Herausgegeben und Bearbeitet von Julius Pokorny. 3 Banden. Originally published in 1930, 1927, and 1932 (Berlin und Leipzig: Walter De Gruyter, 1973). The ṳied-2 entry is in Band II, 236-239. The rest are deduced from association through prefixes, like "unwise" is to "wise." Greek has νῆις and νήῐδος for unknowing, showing the connection to the root, -ιδ, "νῆϊς," *LSJ*, 1173. Notice especially how "wit" and "witness" fall into opposite sides of this chart.

166 Even though the strong Aorist Subjunctive appears to be identical to the strong Perfect Subjunctive in the chart, the form found in the text was not augmented, thus aiding the determination that it was Aorist and not Perfect.

38.) ἀλλὰ καθὼς γέγραπται· ἃ ὀφθαλμὸς οὐκ εἶδεν καὶ οὖς οὐκ ἤκουσεν καὶ ἐπὶ καρδίαν ἀνθρώπου οὐκ ἀνέβη, ἃ ἡτοίμασεν ὁ θεὸς τοῖς ἀγαπῶσιν αὐτόν. (1 Cor 2:9)

But just as it is written; what eye <u>did not see</u>, and what ear did not hear, and did not ascend upon the heart of man, what God has prepared for those who love him.

The lexical analysis is necessary in order to analyse οἶδα as a true Perfect. Once both the Aorist forms and Perfect forms of this verb are viewed as the same verb, then the verb can be understood to have actional and stative readings. The Perfect tense-form οἶδα may now be seen as an active verb, which means "having seen." The rise of the idea of "knowing" from this verb is a logical consequence of having seen, having viewed, or having perceived an idea. This verb comes about as a reduplication of the digamma, "ϝ," which dropped out of use in the Greek alphabet. The basic idea is that the root is ϝειδω, pronounced either "uido" or "wido." The Present, Perfect, and Aorist roots are formed according to the Indo-European ablaut. The Present stem retains the vowel ε, while the Perfect changes the ε to ο due to ablaut, and the Aorist drops the root vowel ε altogether. This leaves ϝειδ-, ϝοιδ-, and ϝιδ- as the Present, Perfect, and Aorist stems, respectively. This was then reduplicated normally as ϝεϝοιδ-, and its Aorist in the indicative augmented as εϝιδ- . As the digamma falls out, this leaves behind ειδ-, οιδ-, and ιδ- as the stems where the second and third stems ultimately form οἶδα and εἶδον, respectively.

As far as meaning goes, the Perfect form of οἶδα retains the idea of a state brought about by some action. Since the Present form means "I see," and the Aorist form means, "I saw," then the Perfect form means "I have seen." Knowing is the logical consequence of having seen.[167] Once the Perfect of this lexeme is glossed, "I know," this gloss lexicalises only the state, whereas the gloss, "I have seen," preserves that action which caused the state. Another way to gloss this verb is "have perceived," as demonstrated below. This gloss is preferred when analysing the connection between the tense-forms, as it fits nicely into both semantic domains of seeing and knowing. The meanings of these glosses are provided to show that a particular gloss or translation can obscure the reason why this verb is a Perfect tense-form. When a different gloss for οἶδα is supplied in the translation of the verses cited earlier, an eventive sense comes to the forefront rather than a stative sense, or is included rather than the stative standing alone.

---

167 Knowledge might be said to be the logical consequence of actions by any of the five senses.

Aorist Indicative		
	1st person active	2nd person active	3rd person active
Singular	εἶδον	εἶδες	εἶδε(ν)
	2	0	2
Plural	εἴδομεν	εἴδετε	εἶδον
	0	1	0

Aorist Subjunctive		
	1st person active	2nd person active	3rd person active
Singular	εἴδω	εἴδῃς	εἴδῃ (ἴδῃ)
	0	0	1
Plural	εἴδωμεν	εἴδητε	εἴδωσι
	0	0	0

Aorist Imperative (Epic)		
	1st person active	2nd person active	3rd person active
Singular	---	ἴδε	ἰδέτω
	---	2	0
Plural	---	ἴδετε	ἰδέτωσαν
	---	1	0
	1st person middle	2nd person middle	3rd person middle
Singular	---	ἰδοῦ (usually labelled a particle)	ἴδεσθε
	---	9	0
Plural	---	ἰδέσθω	ἰδέσθωσαν
	---	0	0

Aorist Participle		
	Nom masc active	Nom fem active	Nom neut active
Singular	εἰδών (spelled ἰδών)	εἰδοῦσα	εἰδόν
	1	0	0
Plural	εἰδόντες	εἰδοῦσαι	εἰδόντα
	2	0	0
	Acc masc active	Acc fem active	Acc neut active
Singular	εἰδόντα	εἰδοῦσαν	εἰδόν
	0	0	0
Plural	εἰδόντας	εἰδούσᾱς	εἰδόντα
	0	0	0
	Dat masc active	Dat fem active	Dat neut active
Singular	εἰδόντι	εἰδούσῃ	εἰδόντι
	0	0	0
Plural	εἰδοῦσι(ν)	εἰδούσαῖς	εἰδοῦσι(ν)
	0	0	0

Aorist Infinitive

Figure 26: Aorist forms of εἶδον

39.) <u>οἴδαμεν</u> δὲ ὅτι τὸ κρίμα τοῦ θεοῦ ἐστιν κατὰ ἀλήθειαν ἐπὶ τοὺς τὰ τοιαῦτα πράσσοντας. (Rom 2:2)

but <u>we have perceived</u> that the judgment of God is according to truth upon those who practice these things. (unrighteous things)[168]

ἀλλὰ καθὼς γέγραπται· ἃ ὀφθαλμὸς οὐκ <u>εἶδεν</u> καὶ οὓς οὐκ ἤκουσεν καὶ ἐπὶ καρδίαν ἀνθρώπου οὐκ ἀνέβη, ἃ ἡτοίμασεν ὁ θεὸς τοῖς ἀγαπῶσιν αὐτόν. (1 Cor 2:9)

But just as it is written; what eye <u>did not perceive</u>, and what ear did not hear, and did not ascend upon the heart of man, what God has prepared for those who love him.

Once this gloss is appropriated, the connection between the Perfect and the Aorist is clearer. Likewise, the prior action is more evident with the Perfect, than it is with the gloss "we know," and the cognitive sense is more apparent in the Aorist than it is with "see" verb forms.

This change of gloss shows that the typical gloss chosen for translating οἶδα is the reason why the Perfect tense-form of οἶδα has been analysed as showing no hint of the action that caused the state.[169] This verb is stative because it is a Perfect tense-form. The Perfect tense-form allowed for a stative reading for perceiving, which was roughly equivalent to the expression of knowing.[170] The idea of knowing is a functional equivalent, and is the main way the verb οἶδα was used in Classical and Hellenistic Periods of the Greek language. Functionally, it is necessary to analyse it as stative, but it is not due to its lexeme being stative, it is due to it being a Perfect tense-form. When it is examined according to its form, and once the whole verb including the Aorist is analysed yielding a central semantic lexical domain of mental perception, then it can be seen as a true Perfect, quite like other Perfects in the Greek language. If the aspect of the Greek Perfect is analysed to be stativity, then this verb further supports that claim, and arguments ruling out this verb from the analysis are without foundation. If the aspect of the Greek Perfect is analysed as a combination of two aspects, where the actional component is perfective and the stative component is imperfective, then his verb

---

168 Translation is mine, and is provisional. This translation shows both the idea of seeing and knowing.

169 It seems that the gloss is chosen due to pragmatic concerns, rather than semantic ones, and serves to obscure how the Perfect tense-form affects this verb.

170 To say that "knowing" derived from "seeing," pushes the evidence too far, since they might have been simultaneous, but at least the Perfect tense-form of seeing or perceiving is roughly equivalent to that of knowing.

provides material for that investigation as well, since the lexical domain suggested in this paper provides for both a logically prior complete action of perceiving which can be understood as perfective, and a logically deduced state of knowing which can be understood as imperfective.

2. Conclusion

The several sections of this chapter each support the idea of complex aspect for the Greek synthetic Perfect tense-form. The first section on stative verbs showed the aspect for that state as imperfective, due to only a portion of that state being in view. The second section on eventive verbs showed the aspect to be perfective, since the whole event was in view. Also, the actions referred to by those Perfects were not interrupted by another action. This is a feature of perfectives. The third section on verbs having both actions and states showed that different contexts for the same lexeme could have opposite effects, as its perfectivity could be highlighted when the tense-form has an event role, or its imperfectivity could be highlighted when the same lexeme serves in a stative role. The fourth section on verbs selected for the pragmatic function of citation and reference show these two aspects together. The citation or referential lexemes evoke a memory of the prior moment of writing, speaking, or thinking, and then present the memory as a state for consideration with other current ideas. The prior action is viewed perfectively, while the item in mind is presented imperfectively. The fifth section is a lexical analysis of οἶδα. Due to its etymology, it involves a prior action of perception as well as presents the stative idea of knowing. This provides clarity regarding whether or not this lexeme is strictly stative. It is both eventive and stative, depending upon which tense-form is used. The usage of this verb in the Perfect is consistent with that of other Perfects where it refers to an action of cognition and to a state of knowing. The moment of cognition is perfective and the continued state of knowing is imperfective. All of the sections of this chapter provide examples that further substantiate the complex aspect for the Perfect, where the event is perfective and the state is imperfective. Also, the Perfect may be used for either the state, or event, or both.

Comparing the Pauline Corpus to a Diachronic Corpus of Epistolary and Moral Literature

The science of linguistics has been making various inroads into our interpretation of the GNT ever since James Barr critiqued the study of biblical languages.[1] Stanley E. Porter, Jeffery T. Reed, Stephen H. Levinsohn, and Steven E. Runge, have all impacted the study of the GNT through various disciplines of linguistics. This chapter continues in the vein of importing linguistic analysis to biblical studies, by clarifying issues with and providing solutions for building a diachronic corpus for the grammatical analysis of Greek epistles. Next, this chapter compares the Perfect across the whole diachronic analysis corpus to determine whether or not a complex aspect is viable for understanding the Pauline usage of the Greek synthetic Perfect tense-form. This chapter also assesses the Pauline usage of the Greek Perfect and places Paul's usage within the cline observed for grammaticalisation.

---

1 James Albert Barr, *The Semantics of Biblical Language* (Oxford: Oxford University Press, 1961).

1. Corpus-Based Approach

One of the ways to address the placement of the Pauline perfect usage within Greek literature at large is to compare its use against a diachronically balanced corpus of similar written material. This comparison has the benefit of analysing large data sets in order to provide validation for observations within a smaller piece of literature. Corpus Linguistics as a method for biblical studies has been championed by Matthew Brook O'Donnell working in conjunction with OpenText. org.[2] Various corpora of the Greek language have been constructed to study the language, and have value for studying the GNT.[3] The method in this chapter is a corpus-based approach, and not a corpus-driven approach. The diachronic epistolary and moral literature corpus is constructed to understand the development of the Perfect tense-form over time.[4] This study seeks to examine the period that the synthetic form was most productive, from 400 BCE to 400 CE, because this will shed light on Paul's usage. The diachronic approach helps to understand the meaning of the Greek Perfect tense-form by seeing how it is changing over a long period of time, while keeping track of key developments or changes in its usage. This helps to understand both the development of the Perfect tense-form and the placement of Paul's usage in that diachronic timeline.

The purpose for the analysis corpus is to see whether Perfect tense-forms in various time periods are used in the same way as they are within the Pauline corpus, or differently. The contexts for various examples of the Perfect tense-form in the analysis corpus are analysed to see if the complex aspect of the Perfect tense-form is evident before and after the Pauline corpus. If examples are found demonstrating that the Perfect tense-form contains both perfective and imperfective verbal aspect across the diachronic span of the corpus, then the collected data provides further substantiation for the complex aspect idea developed in this project, by showing that Paul's usage is typical among the Greek letter writers and moralists.

---

2 Matthew Brook O'Donnell, *Corpus Linguistics & the Greek of the New Testament*. New Testament Monographs:6 (Sheffield: Sheffield Phoenix, 2005).

3 These include the BibleWorks and LOGOS systems that centre upon the NT, using the latest critical GNT editions, and includes text archives, like the *Perseus Digital Library* and the *Thesaurus Linguae Graecae* that have certain older critical GNT editions.

4 This development of the Perfect is addressed in grammaticalisation studies cross-linguistically. Joan Bybee and Östen Dahl, "Creation of Tense and Aspect Systems in the Languages of the World," *Studies in Language* 13-1 (1989): 67-77; see also Heine and Kuteva, 36-42, 140-152.

1.1. Rationale for the Corpus Linguistic Method

Corpus Linguistics is usually a method of doing linguistics, rather than strictly being a branch of linguistics.[5] It is an empirical approach to studying language as opposed to a rationalist approach.[6] It uses large data sets and allows the researcher to study patterns emerging from that dataset. This method is sub-divided into corpus-driven approaches and corpus-based approaches, where the former uses the data to create the questions, and the latter begins with outside questions that the data must answer.[7] Corpus-driven approaches use corpus linguistics as a branch of linguistics, while corpus-based approaches use corpus linguistics as a method to answer questions for another branch of linguistics.[8] A potential flaw for corpus-based approaches is that they may not select the data that does not fit the theoretical framework that formed the question, even if that data could help answer the question.[9] The Greek diachronic epistolary and moral literature corpus in this study uses a corpus-based approach, since its purpose is to answer questions asked in the fields of theoretical linguistics, historical linguistics, grammaticalisation, and literary criticism. This corpus-based approach will be concerned that it does not miss seeing the contradictory data suggested above. Noam Chomsky, a rationalist, gave corpus linguistics its most serious critiques. He questions the validity of corpus methods for answering why certain constructions are permissible in a language.

> "You can take as many texts as you like, you can take tape recordings, but you'll never get the answer. One reason you'll never get the answer is that the texts don't show it. You'd have to look for complicated data which shows you where the things were before they were raised. Well, you're not going to get that from a corpus."[10]

---

5   Paul Baker, "Corpus Methods in Linguistics," 93-113 in *Research Methods in Linguistics*, edited by Lia Litosseliti (London: Continuum, 2010), 93.
6   Baker, "Corpus Methods," 94.
7   Tony McEnery, and Andrew Hardie, *Corpus Linguistics: Method, Theory, and Practice*, Cambridge Textbooks in Linguistics (Cambridge: Cambridge University Press, 2012), 6.
8   McEnery, and Hardie, 6.
9   Baker, "Corpus Methods," 95.
10   Taken from an interview between Bas Aarts and Noam Chomsky. Bas Aarts, "Corpus Linguistics, Chomsky, and Fuzzy Tree Fragments," 5-13 in *Corpus Linguistics and Linguistic Theory: Papers from the Twentieth International Conference on English Language Research on Computerized Corpora (ICAME 20) Freiburg im Breisgau 1999*, Language and Computers: 33, edited by Christian Mair, and Marianna Hundt (Leiden: Belgium, 2000), 6.

Chomsky argues that corpora will include statements that are not grammatically correct or ill-formed by the initial speaker or writer, and these will skew the results.[11] He does not believe that analysing corpora could produce reliable results valuable for the linguist. "Any natural corpus will be skewed. Some sentences won't occur because they are obvious, others because they are false, still others because they are impolite. The corpus if natural, will be so wildly skewed that the description would be no more than a mere list."[12]

Certain phrases will be more frequent in the corpus due to the specific speakers or writers being more populous than the others, and a researcher will only see the frequency, and not the reason for the frequency.[13] Chomsky also adds that a native speaker of any language can quickly answer why a construction is used without doing a corpus study.[14] To counter some of Chomsky's concerns, the corpus-based approach in this study is anchored in grammaticalisation and supported by historical linguistics. These fields will ask the questions and predict contradictory data to look for. Also, since the Ancient Greek language is the focus, this minimises some of the concerns regarding needing native speaker intuition.[15]

2. Defining the Limits of Both Corpora for Analysis

Before launching into the problems of corpus design and corrective measures, it is helpful to define the Pauline corpus and indicate its limits. Next the same is conducted for the diachronic epistolary and moral literature corpus.

---

11 Noam Chomsky, *Aspects of the Theory of Syntax* (Cambridge, MA: Massachusetts Institute of Technology Press, 1965), 4; Noam Chomsky, *Syntax Structures*, 2nd ed. (Berlin: Mouton De Gruyter, 2002), 15. Also see Desagulier for a recent example from a live interview. Guillaume Desagulier, "Noam Chomsky's Colorless Green Idea: « Corpus Linguistics Doesn't Mean Anything »," in *Around the word*, 05/12/2017, online, available from https://corpling.hypotheses.org/252.

12 This comment was made during the session discussion after he presented his paper, "A Transformational Approach to Syntax." Hill recorded the discussion verbatim following each paper. Hill, A. A., editor, *The Proceedings of The Third Texas Conference on Problems of Linguistic Analysis in English, May 9-12, 1958* (Austin: University of Texas Press, 1962), 159.

13 Tony McEnery, and Andrew Wilson, *Corpus Linguistics: An Introduction*, Edinburgh Textbooks in Empirical Linguistics (Edinburgh: Edinburgh University Press, 2001), 10.

14 This was during a discussion between Noam Chomsky of MIT and Anna Granville Hatcher of John Hopkins University during a panel discussion on linguistics that took place during the second session of the conference. A. A. Hill, editor, *The Proceedings of The Third Texas Conference on Problems of Linguistic Analysis in English, May 9-12, 1958* (Austin: University of Texas Press, 1962), 29.

15 This does not disregard the intuition of current native speakers of the Neohellenic language, a concern often raised by Chrys Caragounis. The intuition of native Neohellenic speakers is encouraged.

The Pauline corpus is analysed here as a complete literary collection. This does not mean that this approach is insensitive to authorial issues. It means that because this collection entered the manuscript tradition early as a collection, it is likely edited by the same hand even if a second author is determined for the Pastoral letters or others within the collection. One might see a single author corpus in this collection, or a collection of a few authors edited by later scribes with the authority to do so into a single collection, sometime early in the Christian tradition. Either way, it is appropriate to study this collection as a corpus of its own, and not subdivide it into possible authors or redactors. All thirteen of the letters associated with Paul are included in this corpus. The conclusions attained in this study do not depend on Paul specifically authoring every text within Pauline corpus, and thus cannot be disqualified on the basis of pseudonymous authorship or other theory of authorship. The point is for hypotheses to be passed or failed on the merits of their linguistic acumen.

The theory of corpus design and corpus methods informs the development of a diachronic epistolary and moral literature analysis corpus. The analysis corpus is limited to the timeframe from 400 BCE until 400 CE. A number of concerns include overall size, breadth of genre, and balance both in diachrony and in text type. An analysis corpus needs to be large enough to provide frequency data for the researcher. Breadth allows the results to apply toward better understanding of Greek. Balance prevents the skewing of the results.

While bigger is generally better, the size of the corpus needs to be larger for corpus-driven approaches than it does for corpus-based approaches. When examining features across a wide variety of genres, more text is required in the corpus than it is for single genre or narrow genre selection. Monitor corpora usually number over 100,000,000 words. A monitor corpus of all available texts is too large for this type of study, and since the documents are historical items, with relatively little chance of new items being included in the future, a monitor corpus is necessarily unbalanced. A smaller corpus is more suitable for studying ancient texts.[16] A specialised corpus of one genre or a narrow selection of genres can be much smaller, closer to 500,000 words.[17] A general agreement exists that any corpus should be at least 250,000 words.[18] The issue of size also includes the wordcount for each subdivision within the corpus.[19] From this it is necessary to

---

16 O'Donnell, *Corpus Linguistics*, 108.

17 Baker, "Corpus Methods," 95, 99.

18 Almut Koester, "Building Small Specialised Corpora," 66-79 in *The Routledge Handbook of Corpus Linguistics*, edited by Anne O'Keeffe and Michael McCarthy (London: Routledge, 2010), 67.

19 Douglas Biber, Susan Conrad, and Randi Reppen, *Corpus Linguistics: Investigating Language Structure and Use*, Cambridge Approaches to Linguistics (Cambridge: Cambridge University Press, 1998), 249.

provide enough words in each subdivision of the corpus in order to compare one subdivision with the other.

While different goals necessitate different sizes for the corpus, some sort of breadth is expected if instances within the corpus are meaningful towards an understanding of the language as a whole.[20] A corpus that is meant for study should represent the language as well as possible.[21] When a corpus is spread over a diachronic timespan, or across multiple genres, each time period needs to have similar quantities of data, so that one time-period does not skew the results. Likewise, each genre needs to have an equal number of words to keep one category from skewing the results. These categories of genre also need to be marked, so that the results can be tabulated by date or by genre. The questions about the nature of the Ancient Greek language will also arise, so the corpus needs to have texts that are representative of what is available in that language in order to avoid skewing the results.

3. Purposes of the Greek Diachronic Epistolary and Moral Literature Corpus

The Greek diachronic epistolary and moral literature corpus was designed to provide a diachronic and a varied genre tool[22] to analyse the grammar and style of the Pauline corpus. The genres include letters and moral treatises. The diachronic balancing satisfies the main purpose of this study, since the diachronic considerations are primary, and the genre considerations are secondary. This corpus cannot answer every question,[23] but it is balanced as much as it can be for diachronicity. This means that the answers regarding diachronic usage suggested by the data will be easier to defend, while answers regarding genre differences will have to be nuanced carefully.

The diachronic epistolary and moral literature corpus will address a number of questions: "Does the Pauline corpus use Perfect tense-forms in ways that are different from other letters or writings on moral or ethical matters?" "If differences are discovered, how are they to be described or categorised?" "Are any of the

---

20 Representativeness depends on balance. Tony McEnery, Richard Xiao, and Yukio Tono, *Corpus-Based Language Studies: An Advanced Resource Book*, Routledge Applied Linguistics (London: Routledge, 2006), 16.
21 Baker, "Corpus Methods," 99.
22 The genres are strictly those used to convey ethical discourse.
23 Some of the problems are highlighted in Section 5.1.

differences observed specific for a certain genre?" "Does the Perfect in the Pauline corpus combine with new adverbs, or typical ones?" The analysis corpus needs to have several features built into it in order for it to be able to address questions such as these.

4. Issues in the Greek Diachronic Epistolary and Moral Literature Corpus

Several difficulties were encountered while building the corpus. First, the corpus was built from texts that were digitally available from either the *Perseus* package available in *Logos*, or from other website versions of the text that did not involve copyright and use restrictions. Once the data was collected, the texts were dated according to the schema in *Thesuarus Linguae Graecae*. After the dating was performed, these texts were placed into *SketchEngine*, an online tool for corpus data analysis. Several problems are observed and solutions are postulated next.

4.1. Problems Observed in the Analysis Corpus Creation

After creating the initial corpus, several problems were apparent for the functionality of this corpus. Generally, the more data that is placed into a corpus, the more the results obtained accurately reflect the actual language. However, including all of the available extant Greek letters into the corpus produced problems of imbalance, which resulted in some centuries being over-represented due to having many letters and other centuries being under-represented. Secondly, as these letters were collected, it was observed that many of the extant letters were too short to contain a variety of syntactic constructions and clause structures. Also, many letters were historically recorded after removing typical "letter style" components such as the "greeting" or the "farewell."[24] The fuller letter was lost

---

24 Ceccarelli discusses the Early Greek letter as having three parts, Greeting, Body, and Farewell. Paola Ceccarelli, *Ancient Greek Letter Writing: A Cultural History* (600-150 BC) (Oxford: Oxford University Press, 2013), 35. Some letters never had these components. Ceccarelli, *Ancient Greek Letter*, 99. Scholarship regarding the Pauline letter format is divided with some scholars such as White understanding three formal components, while others such as Porter understand five formal elements, including a Thanksgiving section and Paraenesis. John L. White, "Ancient Greek Letters," 85-105 in *Greco-Roman Literature and the New Testament*, SBL Sources for Biblical Study: 21, edited by David E. Aune (Atlanta, GA: Scholars, 1988), 97. Stanley E. Porter, *The Apostle Paul, His Life, Thought, and Letters* (Grand Rapids, MI: Eerdmans, 2016). The difference between these views is that under a three-part analysis the Thanksgiving section is considered part of the Opening, and the Paraenesis is considered part of the Body.

to history. The letter form is not the only way ethical matters were handled, but the moral treatise was also used historically as well. Since Paul's letters handle ethical matters, it is important to compare them with ethical treatises in addition to comparing them with letters. One difficulty of adding more data to certain centuries with less data is that many of the available letters that purport to be from those centuries were pseudonymously written during the 1st Century CE, which already contains enough data.

4.2. Solutions for the Problems Observed

Leaving out some of the bulk of letters available for the centuries with ample letters allows for the corpus to be somewhat diachronically balanced. Since many letters were available that contained multiple pages of material, and most of the larger letters are complete with traditional letter style components, the researcher decided that the larger letters should be in the corpus rather than the smallest ones for centuries with plentiful data. The larger letters are preferred since they are complete. Some centuries had only short letters. In this case they were included simply to have some representative data for that century. For example, the letters of Aristotle are far shorter than any NT letter, but are the only ones available for that century. When small letters were the only available documents for a given century, they were included as long as they were not truncated or missing portions of the letter.

Since the Pauline letters deal with moral and ethical topics, it was important for the corpus to include letters that deal with moral or ethical concerns, along with an equivalent number of letters that do not. The letters that do not contain moral or ethical concerns were largely those of rulers or philosophers. Moral treatises are included alongside the epistolary corpus in order to see if differences are observed between letters and other genres when handling similar topics. The inclusion of the moral treatises helped to balance the inequality in the corpus by providing more data for the centuries that had very little letter data. Also, since similar concerns are conveyed by moral epistles and moral treatises, this shared concern makes it logical that both of these would have similar constructions involving the Perfect tense-form. This similarity legitimises the inclusion of moral treatises for studying the function of the Perfect tense in moral letters. For the pseudonymous letters, the fact they often imitate the older style helps offset the concern that they are difficult to date. Solutions reached for the corpus design should be seen as tentative at this point, although they provide a way to balance the centuries with fewer letters.

4.3. Summary

After implementing the solutions from the previous section, the analysis corpus for this research contains letters with moral or ethical content, letters without a focus on moral or ethical matters, and treatises that have a moral or ethical content. The distinctions between categories within the corpus are marked so that the data will lead to conclusions regarding special uses of various constructions.

To satisfy the diachronic requirement, the analysis corpus is comprised of letters spanning from 400 BCE–400 CE, a period of roughly 800 years. These letters are written mostly at both ends of the time period, and during the 1st century CE. Mostly, the frequency of available letters corresponds to periods of social and political stability in the Greco-Roman world.

5. Contents of the Greek Diachronic Epistolary and Moral Literature Corpus

The moral letter corpus contains letters of the NT, and from the church fathers. For the 1st century CE, the NT dominates the selection. From the NT, this corpus includes the thirteen letters of Paul, three letters from John, and two letters from Peter, along with one letter each from Jude and James. Two letters of Clement appear as well. For the 2nd century CE, seven letters of Ignatius are included, along with one letter each from Polycarp, Barnabas, and Diognetus. From the 4th century CE, seven letters of Basil of Caesarea are included. This division of the corpus contains over 89,000 words.

The letters corpus contains letters mainly from philosophers or grammarians. For the 4th century BCE, five letters from Aristotle are included, along with the thirteen pseudonymous letters of Plato. From the 3rd century BCE, two letters of Anacharsis are included along with three letters of Epicurus. From the 1st century CE, two letters of Aeschines, one letter each of Crates, Xenophon, and Aristippus are included, along with four letters of Diogenes, three letters of Heraclitus, and eight letters of Isocrates. Fourteen letters of the Cynic philosophers are included in this century as well. For the 4th century CE, five letters from the Emperor Julian are included. This corpus contains over 55,000 words.

The moral discourse corpus contains larger argumentative pieces that were written to address ethics in the Polis. From the 4th century BCE, four ethical works of Aristotle are included. From the 1st century CE, two works of Dionysius of Halicarnassus as are included, from the 2nd century CE, twelve ethical works

Corpus Composition Information, by Quantity of Sources

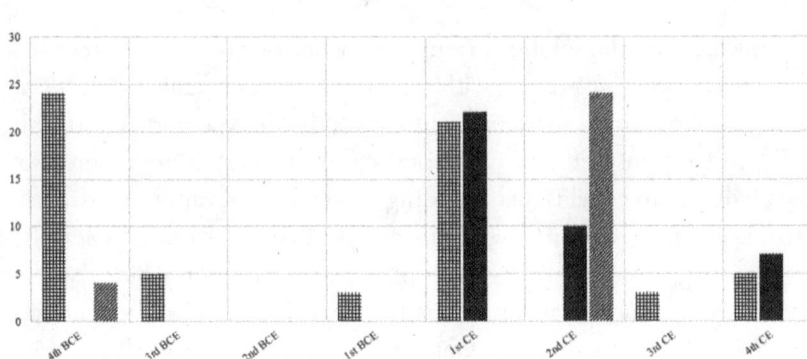

Figure 27: Bar Chart of the Number of Sources for the diachronic epistolary and moral literature corpus

of Plutarch are included, along with six ethical works of Epictetus. This division, although containing the fewest sources, is the largest within the corpus, containing over 158,000 words.

Several gaps appear in the timeline as little or nothing was observed for the 1st and 2nd centuries BCE, and the 3rd century CE. Besides having centuries without data, each subsection of the corpus is under-represented in several of the centuries where data exists. Letters were more frequent at both ends and the middle of the timeline. Philosophical discourses were more frequent at the height of either Greek or Roman rule. Moral letters were absent before the 1st century, and then highly frequent during the 1st century CE, with some decline afterwards. A bar chart showing the sources by genre and century is presented in Figure 27, and another showing the wordcount by genre and century in Figure 28.

These divisions were balanced for the centuries spanned within the corpus. That being said, more letters survive history from the 4th Century BCE, 1st Century CE, and 4th Century CE, than from other centuries. It appears these centuries were either the peak periods of literary production or at least the peak periods with retention of epistles, and the corpus necessarily reflects that. Finally, a wordcount is established for the whole corpus by date, and then by genre. Bar charts of both are presented next.

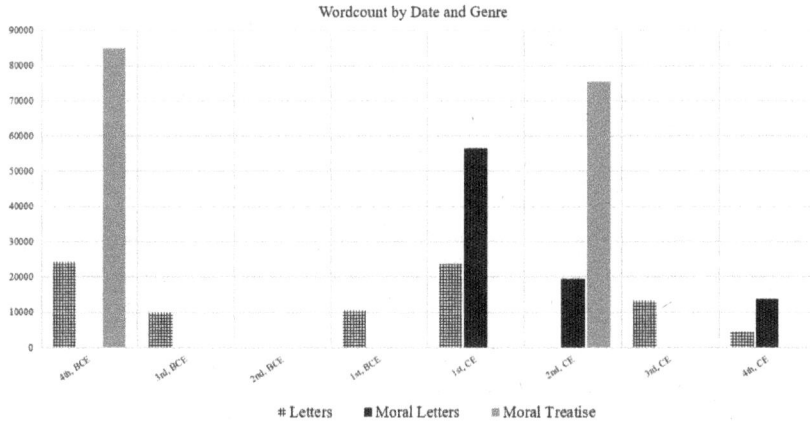

Figure 28: Bar Chart of Wordcount by Century Divided by Genre .

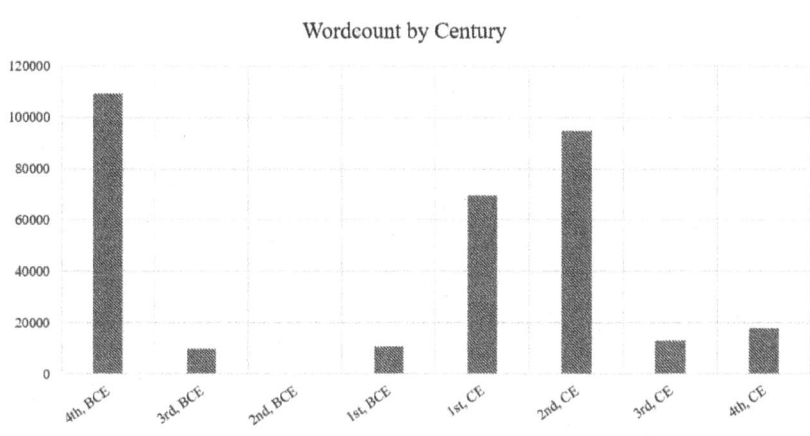

Figure 29: Bar Chart of the Total Wordcount by Century

Figure 29 shows a fairly even spread of data between three of the centuries examined.[25] Three of the centuries have no available data, and two of these centuries have sparse data.[26] Since a fairly even balance is provided by the corpus

---

25 The dating for the individual letters is provided by *Thesauarus Linugae Graecae*. http://stephanus.tlg.
   uci.edu/Iris/indiv/csearch.jsp#doc=tlg&aid=&wid=&q=epistula&dt=timeline&cs_sort=1_sortn
   ame_asc&st=author_text&aw=&verndipl=0&per=50&c=3&acp=&editid=.
26 Some electronically available texts for the missing centuries do exist at *Thesauarus Linugae Graecae*, but
   they are protected and restricted from being placed in a corpus due to copyright laws.

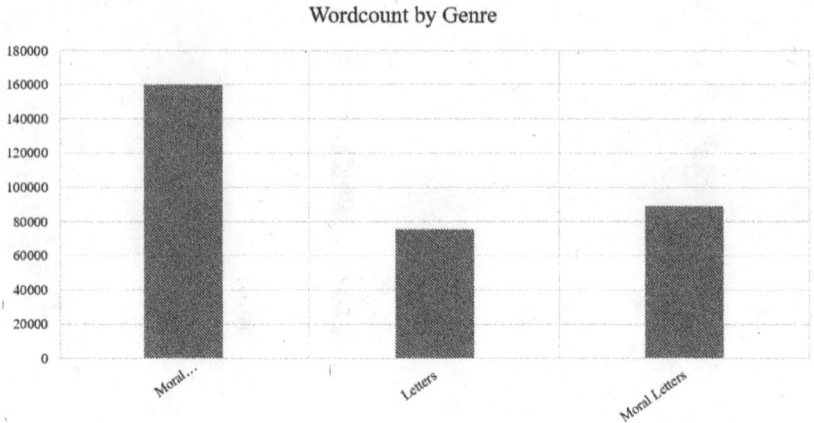

Figure 30: Bar Chart of Total Wordcount by Genre

for the three most represented centuries, this shows that the corpus is capable of examining some features diachronically. The total wordcount for the corpus is 213,887 words.

Figure 30 shows that the moral treatises outweigh both the letters and moral letters combined. This shows some imbalance in the corpus to answer some questions related to the differences between moral letters and treatises. But if the moral treatises were compared to the letters and moral letters combined, this imbalance is overcome. Also, it is impossible to add to the letters corpus to make the letters division more strongly represented, because it will place too much weight on the 1st century CE, and make diachronic comparison difficult to defend.

6. Necessity for Corpus Approaches to Answer Certain Linguistic Questions

Not all questions require a corpus approach, but to answer certain questions in relation to grammaticalisation, a diachronically balanced corpus is necessary. Language change happens gradually over a long period of time, and usually a given period of the language has the new and old forms or meanings side-by-side. The new form or meaning does not completely eliminate the older one, but the frequency of the two side-by-side will change and be noticeable in diachronic

studies.[27] A diachronically balanced corpus-based approach can see those changing ratios and predict when the language has entered known points along a
grammaticalisation cline. Often the type of adverbs attracted to verbs will be an
indicator of changing stages in grammaticalisation,[28] so a corpus-based approach
is helpful to find these collocations and discuss their frequency relative to a timeline. Changing frequency distributions is the main way these stages of grammaticalisation can be visualised.

7. A Review of the Corpus Data

The next section compares the Pauline corpus with a Greek analysis corpus that
has epistles and moral discourse from an 800-year timespan. First, it reminds
the reader what was discovered in the Pauline corpus. Second, it announces
the findings from the analysis corpus. Third, it compares and contrasts both
corpora. Fourth, it establishes how Paul fits into the broader diachronic stream
regarding Greek Perfect tense-form usage. Several examples will be selected from
the Pauline corpus to represent each type of linguistic environment observed in
that corpus. Similar examples will be located in the diachronic epistolary and
moral literature corpus and their similarity to those found in the Pauline corpus
discussed.

    The relative frequency of each environment will be analysed for a selection of
the subcorpora throughout the diachronic epistolary and moral literature corpus.
As only some texts exist currently tagged, the whole corpus cannot yet be analysed in this way. Aristotle's Nicomachean Ethics, from 330 BCE and seven of
Basil of Caesarea's letters from 370 CE will be compared to the Pauline corpus.
These are on opposite ends of the timeline supplied in this study. These documents are also large document collections that are from the centuries with the
most data in the corpus. Thus, this subsample is sufficient to draw some important conclusions. A trend will be established from this data. The Pauline examples
will then be situated along the observed trend.

27 Frantisek Lichtenberk, "On the Gradualness of Grammaticalization," 37-80 in *Approaches to Grammaticalization: Focus on Theoretical and Methodological Issues*, 19:1, edited by Elizabeth Closs Traugott and Bernd Heine (Amsterdam: John Benjamins, 1991), 37.
28 George J. Xydopoulos, "Tense and Temporal Adverbs in Greek," 263- 276 in *Studies in Greek Syntax*, edited by Artemis Alexiadou, Geoffrey Horrocks, and Melita Stavrou, Studies in Natural Language and Linguistic Theory: 43 (New York: Springer, 1999), 269.

Subcorpus Section	Subcorpus Wordcount	Total Number of Perfects	Percentage of PF in the Subcorpus	PPM
Pauline Corpus	34574	345	1.00%	9978.60
Aristotle *Nicomachean Ethics*	56624	660	1.17%	11655.83
Basil's Letters (7 selected letters)	13583	1907	14.04%	140396.08

Figure 31: Comparison of the Perfect tenses in the subcorpora

The first thing observable from examining the subcorpora is that Paul is slightly less likely in general to use a Perfect tense than Aristotle, who is 400 years earlier than Paul, although the number is close. Paul is much less likely to use a Perfect tense than Basil of Caesarea, who is over 300 years after Paul. Basil is fourteen times more likely to use a Perfect than Paul. Figure 31 shows the total count of Perfects in each subcorpus and reports the relative frequency within that subcorpus reported as a percentage and as parts-per-million. The parts-per-million number allows subcorpora of differing sizes to be compared fairly.

Because the verb οἶδα occurs frequently in a number of Pauline construc-tions, this verb was also counted in the subcorpora under comparison. The sec-ond item apparent from the data, is that Paul uses οἶδα nearly three times more often than Aristotle and nearly twice as often as Basil of Caesarea, when they use a Perfect. However, Basil uses this word ten times more frequently in general than does Paul, but due to the fact he uses a much higher number of perfects generally, it is still a relatively small percentage of those Perfects. Figure 32 illustrates the frequency of οἶδα in each subcorpus.

Because the use of the Perfect either introducing or residing in supplemental clauses was important for this study, these were compared across the subcorpora. Paul uses the Perfect for these roles roughly seven times more often than does Aristotle, and even more often when compared to Basil of Caesarea. Basil's per-centage of perfects used this way out of his total Perfect usage is quite low, but this low frequency is perhaps skewed due to his much higher use of the Perfect in main clauses than other writers. When the parts-per-million words is examined,

Subcorpus Section	Number of oida Occurrences in the Subcorpus	Percentage of the total PF in the Subcorpus	PPM
Pauline Corpus	98	28.41%	2834.50
Aristotle *Nicomachean Ethics*	75	11.36%	1324.53
Basil's Letters (7 selected letters)	299	15.68%	22012.81

Figure 32: Comparison of οἶδα usage in the subcorpora

Basil is still fairly close to the frequency of Aristotle for this usage. Figure 33 shows the percentage and relevant frequency for supplemental Perfects.

Another place where Paul is different from the other writers is how he uses the Perfect tenses in supplemental clauses. Aristotle and Paul use about the same percentage of their Perfects introducing supplemental clauses, while Basil uses them much less often. Aristotle and Paul use only communicative or cognitive lexemes in the Perfect when introducing supplemental information. The main way this is done is "you know that . . . ," "you heard that . . . ," "they said that . . . ." Paul employs a variety of lexemes here, including "know" and "write," while Aristotle uses mostly "say" lexemes. Basil uses this construction type only twice, once with a communication lexeme "know" and once with a stative "it seems that

Subcorpus Section	Number of Supplemental PF in the Subcorpus	Percentage of the total PF in the Subcorpus	PPM
Pauline Corpus	131	37.97%	3788.97
Aristotle *Nicomachean Ethics*	38	5.76%	671.09
Basil's Letters (7 selected letters)	8	0.42%	588.97

Figure 33: Comparison of supplemental uses of Perfects across the subcorpora

Subcorpus Section	Category A Constructions in the subcorpus	Percentage of the total PF in the Subcorpus	Stative Lexemes	Communication Lexemes	Active Lexemes
Pauline Corpus	102	77.85%		118	
Aristotle *Nicomachean Ethics*	30	78.95%		30	
Basil's Letters (7 selected letters)	2	25.00%	1	1	

Figure 34: Comparison of Category A Constructions

. . . ." Figure 34 reports the frequency of the construction type and the count of the lexeme type in the Perfect tense. Other than the specific lexeme chosen, Paul is quite similar in his usage of Category A constructions to Aristotle and not at all similar to Basil of Caesarea. Cognitive and Communicative lexemes are kept separate from other active lexemes in these tallies because of their debated status and their specialised function described earlier in the fourth chapter.

In the category B constructions, Paul shows a departure from being similar to Aristotle. Although his percentage of supplemental Perfects in category B constructions is nearly the same as Aristotle's, and very different from Basil's, his lexeme type is quite different from the ancient period. Aristotle is more likely to use a stative lexeme or communicative lexeme in these constructions, but Paul is far more likely to use a verb of activity unrelated to cognition or communication.[29] Even Basil later on is very similar to Paul in this regard. Figure 35 shows the relevant percentages and lexeme type count.

What one deduces from the rather crude statistics performed on this small sample from the corpus is that as the Greek language moves through its development, the Perfect tense is found more and more frequently inside supplemental clauses, where the Perfect is part of the clause, and employs a greater variety of lexeme type. The active lexemes are more frequent in these constructions in later Greek, than in earlier Greek. This trend is consistent with the idea that

---

29 Paul's lexical distribution is reported in Figure 22 and Figure 22, in Section 1.4 of Chapter 4.

Subcorpus Section	Category B Constructions in the subcorpus	Percentage of the total PF in the Subcorpus	Stative Lexemes	Communication Lexemes	Active Lexemes
Pauline Corpus	29	22.14%	5	9	22
Aristotle *Nicomachean Ethics*	8	21.05%	3	3	1
Basil's Letters (7 selected letters)	6	75.00%	2		4

Figure 35: Comparison of Category B Constructions

the Perfect increases the frequency of its usage in an event-oriented way as it grammaticalises.

7.1. The Verbal Data from the Pauline Corpus

The verbal data from the Pauline corpus shows a high frequency of Perfect tenses used statively, and many describing an event. Paul uses a number of Perfects to make citations. He uses οἶδα in its stative sense in the Perfect form for this purpose frequently. A preference is shown for the middle forms to be more frequently stative than the active forms,[30] but this is not rigidly held,[31] leading to the conclusion that the -κ- morpheme is neither perfective, nor de-stativising, but possibly more related to transitivity, valency, and object affectedness. The Perfect middle participle was frequently found using a stative sense where it described another entity in the clause or in the head clause.[32]

---

30 Compare one active form with seven middle forms in chapter 4, section 1.1.

31 Consider that the next section, 1.2, on eventive Perfects, had a number of middle forms as well.

32 Of the eight forms discussed in chapter 4, section 1.1, five were middle participles, and these all were adjectival, modifying either a noun or if with an article, then used as a substantive still providing more information for another noun. In the next section, 1.2, on eventive Perfects, the participles were not adding description to another component.

7.2. The Verbal Data from the Diachronic Epistolary and Moral Literature Corpus

While a full statistical study is not possible at this time as the whole corpus is not morphologically tagged, a manual search throughout these letters produced examples from various time periods that are similar to the ways Paul used the Perfect tense-form in his day. Most of the types of uses discussed in the fourth chapter were found in the analysis corpus throughout the diachronic timespan of the corpus.

7.2.1. Stative Examples

The first section of verbs discussed in the Pauline corpus included those that had a stative reading. Just like the stative perfects in the Pauline corpus, the examples discussed in this section are mostly middle participles which describe nouns, or other substantives in the clause. This section will go through several stative examples selected from the analysis corpus in chronological order.

> 40.) Τούτων δὴ <u>γεγονότων</u> καὶ ἐχόντων οὕτω, σχεδὸν κατὰ τὴν ἐμὴν δόξαν εὑρήκαμεν ὃ σὺ ἐπέστειλας, ὅπως δεῖ πρὸς ἀλλήλους ἡμᾶς ἔχειν.[33]

So now that this <u>has occurred</u>, and things are in this state, we have pretty well found an answer, as I think, to the question how we ought to behave towards each other.[34]

In example 40, Plato is responding to Dionysius in a lengthy attempt to resolve their shattered relationship by sending a letter. The Perfect, γεγονότων, focuses more on the status of the predicament Plato and Dionysius are in, than it does on any event that led to it. The Perfect participle is stative and simply describes Τούτων, "these things," by categorically qualifying them as "things that happen."[35] The participle is unmodified by adverbs, prepositional phrases, dative phrases, or genitive phrases.

> 41) διὸ χαλεπὸν ἀποτρίψασθαι τοῦτο τὸ πάθος <u>ἐγκεχρωσμένον</u> τῷ βίῳ.[36]

---

33 Pl., *L.* 313c; Plato, *Platonis Opera*, edited by John Burnet (Medford, MA: Oxford University Press, 1903), 3:313.

34 Plato, *Timaeus, Critias, Cleitophon, Menexenus, Epistles: English Text*, translated by R. G. Bury, LCL: 234, edited by G. P. Goold (Cambridge, MA; London, England: Harvard University Press, 1929), 413.

35 Another Perfect in this example, εὑρήκαμεν, will be discussed later.

36 Aristot., *Nic. Eth.* 2.3.8; Aristotle, *The Nicomachean Ethics: Greek Text*, edited by Jeffrey Henderson, LCL (Cambridge, MA: Harvard University Press, 1934), 82.

Hence this feeling is hard to eradicate, <u>being engrained</u> in the fabric of our lives.[37]

In example 41, Aristotle uses a Perfect middle participle, ἐγκεχρωσμένον, to describe πάθος, or "feeling." The case endings on both words show that the participle is related to that noun. Rackham might have translated the participle as "having been planted," emphasising the action, but due to the stative sense implied in this context where the participle is clearly adjectival modifying the previous noun, he translates it as a present state. The prefix ἐν on the front of the participle suggests a location for the feeling, which corresponds with the dative phrase following it. The dative phrase provides the location in much the same way as a prepositional phrase ἐν τῷ βίῳ would. Just like the majority of stative Perfects in the Pauline corpus discussed in Chapter 4, both of these examples use the participle form.

42.) νόμος τε γὰρ παριτητέος ἐς φύσιν καὶ φύσις ἐς νόμον καὶ καλοῦμεν αὐτοῖν τὸ μὲν ἀρχήν, τὸ δ' ἑπόμενον, <u>κεκληρώσθω</u> δὲ ἀρχὴν μὲν φύσις, νόμος δὲ τὸ ἕπεσθαι, οὔτε γὰρ ἂν νόμος ἐτειχοποίησεν ἢ ὑπὲρ τείχους ὥπλισεν,[38]

And therefore, the law must be set forth in nature and nature in law, and we call of them both on one hand the thing which is old, on the other the thing which follows, and <u>having chosen</u> on the one hand nature as old, and on the other law as to follow, and therefore neither could the law make walls nor make ready on behalf of walls,[39]

In example 42, Philostratus uses the Perfect middle imperative form to establish a basis for why the law is derived from nature rather than the other way around. Although this example is arguably eventive, nothing modifies the Perfect form, and no event is hinted at in the context, as this phrase is simply a logical basis for the next phrase. It is the state of nature being logically prior to laws based on nature that defines the limitations and extent of derived laws.

---

37 Aristotle, *The Nicomachean Ethics*, translated by H. Rackham, LCL: 29, Revised edition, edited by Jeffrey Henderson (Cambridge, MA; London: Harvard University Press, 1934), 83.

38 Philostr., *L.* 2.2; Carl Ludwig Kayser, *Flavii Philostrati Opera*, Vol. 2, Philostratus the Athenian (Leipzig: Teubner, 1871), 260.

39 Translation is mine. "Original" might also be used instead of "old."

43.) Αἰσχύλος μὲν γὰρ Ἰσθμοῖ θεώμενος ἀγῶνα πυκτῶν, ἐπεὶ πληγέντος τοῦ ἑτέρου τὸ θέατρον ἐξέκραγε, νύξας Ἴωνα τὸν Χῖον 'ὁρᾷς ' ἔφη 'οἷον ἡ ἄσκησίς ἐστιν; ὁ <u>πεπληγὼς</u> σιωπᾷ, οἱ δὲ θεώμενοι βοῶσιν'[40]

Aeschylus at the Isthmian games was watching a boxing-match, and when one of the men was hit the crowd in the theatre burst into a roar. Aeschylus nudged Ion of Chios, and said, "You see what a thing training is; the man <u>who is hit</u> says nothing; it is the spectators who shout."[41]

In example 43, Plutarch uses a Perfect active participle to describe the state of the boxer as a person being hit. The translation provided emphasises the stative force through using a present copula "is" along with the verb. The verb σιωπᾷ is the verb in this clause, meaning "is silent." This Perfect participle together with its article functions as the subject for that verb. Within the article + participle construction the participle describes the entity referred to by the article. This means the participle can be analysed as an adjective modifying the article. The participle itself is unmodified and describes the state of the subject, which is in contrast to the action of the spectators, who make great noise even though they are not involved in the match.

44.) ἀλλ' ὅταν τὰ <u>κεκρυμμένα</u> ζητοῦντες ἐν ἀλλοτρίοις σκεύεσι καὶ φορτίοις ἀναστρέφωνται.[42]

but when in the search for <u>concealed</u> goods they pry into baggage and merchandize which are another's property.[43]

Plutarch uses another Perfect in a stative way in example 44. Here the Perfect is another participle and this time it is a middle form. It functions as a substantive with the article τὰ, so as to construct "the concealed things." The translator supplied "goods," rather than the generic "things," since the context was about customs at a border or port. The participle is unmodified itself and simply describes the sort of things that were being searched for. This type of Perfect is the type most

---

40 Plut., *De prof. in virt.*, 8; Plutarch, *Moralia*, edited by Gregorius N. Bernardakis, vol. 1 (Medford, MA: Teubner, 1888), 192.

41 Plutarch, *Moralia*, edited by Frank Cole Babbitt, vol. 1 (Medford, MA: Harvard University Press, 1927), 425.

42 Plut., *De cur.*, 7; Plutarch, *Moralia*, edited by Gregorius N. Bernardakis, vol. 3 (Medford, MA: Teubner, 1891), 343.

43 Plutarch, *Moralia*, edited by W. C. Helmbold, vol. 6 (Medford, MA: Harvard University Press, 1939), 491.

frequently found in stative situations, where the participle is middle, unmodified, and behaves in a way similar to an adjective, and in this case it behaves as a substantive which provides further detail on the otherwise generic "things."

45.) οὕτω δεῖ καὶ τὸν ἐσπουδακότα ἑαυτὸν πᾶσι τοῖς μέρεσι τῆς ἀρετῆς ἀπεργάσασθαι τέλειον, οἱονεὶ πρὸς ἀγάλματά τινα κινούμενα καὶ ἔμπρακτα, τοὺς βίους τῶν ἁγίων ἀποβλέπειν καὶ τὸ ἐκείνων ἀγαθὸν οἰκεῖον ποιεῖσθαι διὰ μιμήσεως.[44]

so too he who is <u>anxious</u> to make himself perfect in all the kinds of virtue must gaze upon the lives of the saints as upon statues, so to speak, that move and act, and must make their excellence his own by imitation.[45]

In example 45, Basil writes to Gregory using a Perfect active Participle to describe the man who wishes to achieve perfection. The participle is unmodified and is a substantive due to the article. The translator emphasises the stative force by using the copula + adjective construction to translate it much the same way a predicate adjective would function. The state of anxiety is what is meant by the Perfect Participle and no action necessarily precedes it. Although one can theorise an entrance into this state as eventive, it is not part of this context.

These stative examples come from roughly 400 years before Paul's time through to 400 years after. All of these examples are quite similar in the way they use Perfects to convey states. Typically, they are unmodified, although they could have durative temporal modifiers without disrupting their stative sense. Perhaps more variety of examples being obtained once the analysis corpus is tagged for morphological and construction searches would yield some examples with durative temporal modifiers. The manual search did not produce any. As the corpus presently exists, it is still able to show that Paul's usage of Perfects to convey states is typical for the Greek language, and well-represented diachronically.

7.2.2. Eventive Examples

The second section of verbs discussed in the Pauline corpus included those that had an eventive context. Just like the eventive perfects in the Pauline corpus, the examples discussed in this section are contain active forms and indicative forms,

---

44 Basil. *L.*, 2.6; Basil of Caesarea, *Saint Basil: The Letters: Greek*, edited by E. Capps et al., LCL: 1 (Cambridge, MA: Harvard University Press, 1926–1934), 16.

45 Basil of Caesarea, *Saint Basil: The Letters*, translated by. Roy J. Deferrari and Martin R. P. McGuire, LCL: 1, edited by E. Capps et al. (Cambridge, MA: Harvard University Press, 1926–1934), 17.

although some middle participles are found as well. More examples of the -κ-Perfects are in the eventive section. This section will go through several eventive examples selected from the analysis corpus in chronological order. Many of these are modified by prepositional phrases or adverbs that do not permit a stative reading. Of the ones that do not have these adverbs, the context was clearly disallowing a stative-only reading.

46.) καὶ ταῦτα λέγω ὡς οὐχ ὑγιές τι Κρατιστόλου καὶ Πολυξένου πρὸς σὲ εἰρηκότων,[46]

However, I do not say this as though what Cratistolus and Polyxenus <u>have told</u> you is to be trusted;[47]

In example 46, Plato is responding to accusations from Dionysius that he has been running a slander campaign against him. Here, the Perfect Participle εἰρηκότων refers more to the event of speech rather than to its continued complications. The malicious content of the speech is more the matter of concern to both author and recipient. The author may have used the Perfect tense-form here rather than the Aorist to highlight the responsibility of both speakers for the social effects of their speech, and to eliminate himself from taking blame for the words of others.[48] This event of speech is viewed as perfective in summary by the author, and points back to the historical event generated by the malicious speakers. The resulting status of disharmony between Plato and Dionysius is the occasion for this letter. This status might be viewed as imperfective, or ongoing causing the need for Plato to write back to Dionysius. However, this status is not in view in the immediate vicinity of the verb, so the Perfect is mostly eventive here as it recounts a historical event.

47.) τοῦτο οὖν ἡμῖν ἔτι σὺν θεῷ εἰπεῖν ἔξεστιν, εἴ τι ἄρα μὴ καλῶς <u>πέπρακται</u> κατὰ τὴν ἔμπροσθεν συνουσίαν, ἐπανορθώσασθαι καὶ ἔργῳ καὶ λόγῳ.[49]

46 Pl., *L.* 310c; Plato, *Timaeus, Critias, Cleitophon, Menexenus, Epistles: Greek Text*, LCL, edited by G. P. Goold (Cambridge, MA: Harvard University Press, 1929), 442.

47 Plato, *Timaeus, Critias, Cleitophon, Menexenus, Epistles: English Text*, translated by R. G. Bury, LCL: 234, edited by G. P. Goold (Cambridge, MA: Harvard University Press, 1929), 403.

48 McKay suggests that one effect of the Perfect is to highlight responsibility of the subject. McKay, "The Use of the Perfect," 40; McKay, *A New Syntax*, 32. Also see Chantraine, *Histoire du Parfait*, 176.

49 Pl., *L.* 311d; Plato, *Timaeus, Critias, Cleitophon, Menexenus, Epistles: Greek Text*, LCL, edited by G. P. Goold (Cambridge, MA: Harvard University Press, 1929), 406.

In our case, then—if God so grant—it still remains possible to put right whatever <u>has been</u> amiss in word or deed during our intercourse in the past.[50]

In example 47, Plato is concluding that the discord between himself and Dionysius is solvable. The Perfect middle Indicative πέπρακται is modified by two items. First, the prepositional phrase, κατὰ τὴν ἔμπροσθεν συνουσίαν, or "during our prior interaction," marks durative time. While this kind of temporal adverb is typical for states, this one instead marks a series of actions spread out over time. The plural event allows durative temporal adverbs to be used. The adverb also connects this action to the past. This Perfect is also modified by μὴ καλῶς, indicating that some of the actions were not good. This adverb describes the manner of actions, and does not describe the state resulting from those actions. This Perfect tense-form is modified twice by adverbs that point to the event and not to the state. This example is from around 400 years before Paul.

48.) ἐπεὶ δ' ὁ παράνομος ἄδικος ἦν ὁ δὲ νόμιμος δίκαιος, δῆλον ὅτι πάντα τὰ νόμιμά ἐστι πως δίκαια· τά τε γὰρ <u>ὡρισμένα</u> ὑπὸ τῆς νομοθετικῆς νόμιμά ἐστι, καὶ ἕκαστον τούτων δίκαιον εἶναι φαμέν.[51]

It is therefore clear that all lawful things are just in one sense of the word, for what is lawful <u>is decided</u> by legislature, and the several decisions of the legislature we call rules of justice.[52]

In example 48, Aristotle is defining the relationship between a lawful thing and justice, by describing the law-making process. In the explanation, Aristotle uses a Perfect middle participle, ὡρισμένα, modified by a prepositional phrase, ὑπὸ τῆς νομοθετικῆς, providing the agent for the action. The translator chose to emphasise the present state using "is decided" above, however the presence of the agent implies a more eventive understanding. The translator might have used "has been decided by the legislature" instead. Either way it is translated, the preposition modifies an event and not a state. The preposition ὑπὸ + the genitive is a frequent way to mark the agent for actions, especially for middle or passive verbs where the subject is not an agent. The inclusion of an agent means the action is important contextually.

50 Plato, *Timaeus, Critias, Cleitophon, Menexenus, Epistles: English Text*, translated by R. G. Bury, LCL: 234, edited by G. P. Goold (Cambridge, MA: Harvard University Press, 1929), 407.

51 Aristot., *Nic. Eth.* 5.1.12; Aristotle, *The Nicomachean Ethics: Greek Text*, LCL, edited by Jeffrey Henderson (Cambridge, MA: Harvard University Press, 1934), 256–258.

52 Aristotle, *The Nicomachean Ethics*, translated by H. Rackham, LCL: 29, revised edition, edited by Jeffrey Henderson (Cambridge, MA: Harvard University Press, 1934), 257–259.

49.) Ὁ Μένανδρος ἡμῶν ἐπὶ τὴν τῶν Ἰσθμίων θέαν εἰς τὴν Κόρινθον ἐλθεῖν <u>βεβούληται</u>.[53]

Our Menandros <u>has decided</u> to go to Corinth for the Isthmian games;[54]

In example 49, Glykera is writing to Bakchis for him to protect her lover and his friend Menandros while he is in Corinth. She uses the Perfect middle Indicative βεβούληται to highlight that Menandros was desiring this trip before going. At the time of the letter, he has already arrived in Corinth, and Glykera is asking for his protection. His desire was expressed to her prior to going, and the Perfect here represents that earlier action. The infinitive phrase simply provides the content of Menandros' decision, so nothing modifies the Perfect directly. Both of the prepositional phrases modify the infinitive. The fact that his wish precedes him going is simply logical, so the eventive property must be deduced from that logical necessity. He could certainly still be wishing for this trip while already there, but this nuance is unlikely from the text. At any rate, the infinitive "to go" implies the action of travel is after the deciding action, and the further context of the letter shows he is already there. The Perfect indicates the action perfectively and points to Menander's responsibility for the action of deciding. The reason that Glykera would highlight Menander's responsibility in his decision is due to the fact that she did not think his travel was a good idea.[55] If properly assigning responsibility was not important here, Glykera might have used an Aorist rather than the Perfect.

50.) ἀλλ' ἐγὼ μὲν οὐχ ὅτι τῆς τυραννίδος <u>ἀφήρησαι</u> ἄχθομαι, ὦ Διονύσιε, ἀλλ' ὅτι ἐλευθεριάζεις ἐν τῇ Ἑλλάδι τὰ νῦν,[56]

But I am not upset because you <u>have been deprived</u> of absolute power, Dionysius, but because you now live as a free man in Greece[57]

In example 50, Diogenes recounts a conversation he had with Dionysius in a letter to Eugnesius. In that conversation he uses a Perfect tense to remind

---

53 Alciph., *Ep.*, 4.2.1; Patrick Granholm, *Alciphron: Letters of the Courtesans, Edited with Introduction, Translation and Commentary* (Uppsala: University of Uppsala, 2012), 66.

54 Granholm, 67.

55 See McKay, "The Use of the Perfect," 40; McKay, *A New Syntax*, 32; and Chantraine, *Histoire du Parfait*, 176.

56 Diog. Sin., *Ep. ad Eug.*, 8.2.6; Abraham Malherbe, *The Cynic Epistles*, SBL Sources for Biblical Study: 12 (Missoula, MT: Scholars, 1977), 100.

57 Malherbe, 101. "Greece" does not have punctuation after it in the translation.

Dionysius of his recent fall from power as dictator. Diogenes was not upset that the dictator had been removed from power, but that Dionysius suffered no punitive consequences for the actions he had taken while he had been dictator. The Perfect middle Indicative ἀφήρησαι is modified by the genitive phrase, τῆς τυραννίδος, indicating what Dionysius had been deprived of. The agent is unnamed, but implied. This deposition of the tyrant was a recent past event and Diogenes uses the Perfect to refer that historical event. Diogenes contrasts the past event of Dionysius being deposed, which could cause someone to be potentially upset, with the present reality of Dionysius not being executed for his crimes, which is the reason for Diogenes' distress. This contrast of past event to present situation is reinforced by the insertion of contrastive conjunction ἀλλά between both clauses followed by νῦν combined with a Present tense marking a deictic shift between former event and present state.

51.) περὶ δὲ φιλοκοσμίας σὺ μέν, ὦ Εὐρυδίκη, τὰ πρὸς Ἀρίστυλλαν ὑπὸ Τιμοξένας <u>γεγραμμένα</u> ἀναγνοῦσα πειρῶ διαμνημονεύειν[58]

In regard to love of finery, I beg, Eurydice, that you will read and try to remember what <u>was written</u> to Aristylla by Timoxena;[59]

In example 51, Plutarch writes to Eurydice and mentions another piece of writing. Plutarch uses the Perfect middle Participle γεγραμμένα to refer this other piece. Typically, in the examples discussed earlier, Perfect middle Participles refer to states rather than events, but this one is modified by both the agent and indirect object. The prepositional phrase, πρὸς Ἀρίστυλλαν, indicates who Timoxena was writing to, and ὑπὸ Τιμοξένας names Timoxena the agent. Agency phrases point to the agent for the action, thus this Perfect is eventive rather than stative. The action of Timoxena writing is viewed perfectively by Plutarch as he is more concerned with the matters he addresses in his own writing, and he uses this other written piece as a reference. The writing in this context is a reference to a historical event with current benefit for the reader.

---

58 Plut., *Con. praec.*, 48; Plutarch, *Moralia*, edited by Gregorius N. Bernardakis, vol. 1 (Leipzig: Teubner, 1888), 354.

59 Plutarch, *Moralia*, edited by Frank Cole Babbitt, vol. 2 (Medford, MA: Harvard University Press, 1928), 337.

52.) ἀφορῶν εἰς τὴν φύσιν τῆς ἀντικειμένης δυνάμεως, ἥτις ὡς ἀστραπὴ <u>πέπτωκεν</u> ἀπὸ τοῦ οὐρανοῦ, καὶ ἐξέπεσε τῆς ὄντως ζωῆς διὰ τὸ ἐπίκτητον ἐσχηκέναι τὴν ἁγιότητα καὶ ἐπηκολουθηκέναι τῇ κακῇ βουλῇ τὴν ἀλλοίωσιν. [60]

if you will consider the nature of the opposing power, which like a flash of lightning <u>fell</u> from heaven,[61] and fell out of the true life, all because its holiness was an acquired attribute and its change a consequence of its evil desire. [62]

In example 52 Basil of Caesarea uses the Perfect active Indicative πέπτωκεν to refer to Satan's fall. This Perfect is modified twice. The prepositional phrase, ἀπὸ τοῦ οὐρανοῦ, supplies the origination point of the falling action. It does not modify a status. The adverb ὡς ἀστραπὴ is an adverb of manner, and thus implies an action rather than a state. The author used this Perfect to focus so much on the event that the translator used "fell" rather than "has fallen," which translates this verb the same way as one might the Aorist. Basil uses another verb ἐξέπεσε, an Aorist, in parallel to the Perfect πέπτωκεν, where both verbs reference the same action. If a Perfect tense-form was rigidly used to refer to a state, then the Aorist in this example is a more likely place to use a Perfect, since the state of Satan's fall still remains. Since the Perfect here is modified by both a phrase and an adverb that point to the action, and is parallel to the Aorist in the next clause, it seems that Basil uses the Perfect perfectively to view the event of Satan falling.

These examples together show similarity with the way in which Paul uses the Perfect tenses when focusing on the event perfectively, rather than the state. Although Chapter 4 contained a section involving a Pauline example where the same lexeme was found to be modified both ways, imperfective and perfective, no more of these were discovered in the analysis corpus, so a section on them will not be apparent here. Some of these may yet be discovered once the analysis corpus is tagged for this kind of search. Just because no others were found, does not mean that Paul's usage is incorrect, only that it is rare.

7.2.3. Citational and Referential Examples

The fourth section of verbs in the Pauline corpus contained examples that were used either in citational, referential, or supplemental situations, and certain

---

60 Basil. *L.*, 8.21; Basil of Caesarea, *Saint Basil: The Letters: Greek*, edited by E. Capps et al., LCL: 1 (Cambridge, MA: Harvard University Press, 1926–1934), 80–82.
61 Basil references Luke 10:18 here.
62 Basil of Caesarea, *Saint Basil: The Letters*, translated by. Roy J. Deferrari and Martin R. P. McGuire, LCL: 1, edited by E. Capps et al. (Cambridge, MA: Harvard University Press, 1926–1934), 81–83.

syntax was observed dividing the Pauline examples into two categories. The first of these was category A, where the Perfect was outside the clause and the clause was often the object of the Perfect. This category was lexically restricted to verbs of communication. The second was category B, where the Perfect was the main verb inside the subordinate clause. This category involved a much wider range of active verbs, and was not lexically restricted as observed. Several examples of citational, referential, or supplemental Perfects were discovered in the analysis corpus and are reported below.

53.) καὶ <u>γέγραφας</u>, ὡς φασί, χαῖρε καὶ ἡδόμενον βίοτον διάσωζε τυράννου.[63]

and <u>wrote</u>,[64] as they say, this verse—I wish thee joy! And may'st thou always keep the tyrant's life a life of pleasantness.[65]

In example 53, Plato is reminding Dionysius of a greeting that he had written down earlier, after saying it to spectators. Plato is recounting a historical event where Dionysius said these words to the crowd and then had them written. Dionysius said these words to Greek deity at Delphi. The force of the Perfect is eventive in that it recalls an event from the past, but stative also as the written status of these words is evoked for Dionysius' memory. The syntax is much like the category A examples from Chapter 4, where the Perfect of a communication lexeme precedes a citation clause. One main difference is that no ὅτι or other clause marker exists just before the citation as part of the clause. The ὡς φασί clause is an interposed unit, thus supplemental, and ὡς is not part of the citation clause, but only the reference to the crowd making a report on Dionysius' behaviour.

54.) πῶς πρακτέον αὐτάς· αὗται γάρ εἰσι κύριαι καὶ τοῦ ποιὰς γενέσθαι τὰς ἕξεις, <u>καθάπερ εἰρήκαμεν</u>. [66]

since our actions, <u>as we have said</u>, determine the quality of our dispositions.[67]

63 Pl., *L*. 315b; Plato, *Timaeus, Critias, Cleitophon, Menexenus, Epistles: Greek Text*, LCL, edited by G. P. Goold (Cambridge, MA: Harvard University Press, 1929), 424.

64 Dionysius is the writer. "You wrote," is the force of the 2ⁿᵈ singular ending.

65 Plato, *Timaeus, Critias, Cleitophon, Menexenus, Epistles: English Text*, translated by R. G. Bury, LCL: 234 edited by G. P. Goold (Cambridge, MA: Harvard University Press, 1929), 425.

66 Aristot., *Nic. Eth*. 2.2.1; Aristotle, *The Nicomachean Ethics: Greek Text*, LCL, edited by Jeffrey Henderson (Cambridge, MA: Harvard University Press, 1934), 74.

67 Aristotle, *The Nicomachean Ethics*, translated by H. Rackham, LCL: 29, revised edition, edited by Jeffrey Henderson (Cambridge, MA: Harvard University Press, 1934), 75.

In example 54, in the midst of an argument regarding how one's actions illustrate the motives behind them, Aristotle interjects the reminder that both he and the reader have mentioned this before. The whole first two clauses are what was said before, so the referential use of the Perfect comes after the citation, rather than before. The conjunction καθάπερ is similar to the examples found in the later Pauline epistles. This example is also similar to the category A examples since the Perfect is in a separate clause from the cited material, and it involves a lexeme of communication, εἰρήκαμεν.

> 55.) ὥσπερ γὰρ εἴρηται, ἐλευθέριός ἐστιν ὁ κατὰ τὴν οὐσίαν δαπανῶν καὶ εἰς ἃ δεῖ· ὁ δ᾽ ὑπερβάλλων ἄσωτος. [68]

In fact, <u>as was said</u> before, the liberal man is one who spends in proportion to his means as well as on the right objects; while he that exceeds his means is prodigal.[69]

In example 55, Aristotle uses the Perfect εἴρηται to precede the citation. This is similar again to examples discovered in the Pauline corpus collected in Category A. The Perfect is a lexeme of communication and the citation follows. No ὅτι precedes the citation in this example.

> 56.) <u>οἶδα</u> δὲ καὶ τοῦτο, <u>ὅτι</u> πολλῷ κρεῖττόν ἐστιν ἰδιώτῃ δανείσαντα χρεωκοπεῖσθαι ἢ πόλει· ὑπὸ ἰδιώτου μὲν γὰρ τις ἀποστερόμενος ἐχθρὸν ἕνα προσκέκτηται, καὶ τοῦτον ἀσθενῆ· ὑπὸ δὲ πόλεως ζημιοῦται μὲν οὐδὲν ἧττον, ἐχθροὺς δὲ πολλοὺς ἔχει καὶ οὐχ ἕνα. [70]

I <u>know</u> withal <u>that</u> 'tis much better to lose a Debt by a Private person than by a Community. For he that is Defrauded by a Private person makes himself but One Enemy, and him no very Dreadful one: but he that is Abused by a whole City, as his Loss is not less, so the Damage is far greater, gaining himself, instead of One, a Multitude of Enemies.[71]

Example 56 has the lexeme οἶδα followed shortly by ὅτι, being one of the most common constructions for a category A referential Perfect. The communication lexeme is in the Perfect tense-form and the item known by the writer is in the content

---

68 Aristot., *Nic. Eth.* 4.1.23; Aristotle, *The Nicomachean Ethics: Greek Text*, LCL, edited by Jeffrey Henderson (Cambridge, MA: Harvard University Press, 1934), 194.

69 Aristotle, *The Nicomachean Ethics*, translated by H. Rackham, LCL: 29, revised edition, edited by Jeffrey Henderson (Cambridge, MA: Harvard University Press, 1934), 195.

70 Phalar., *Ep.*, 83.2.8-83.2.10; Hercher, 432.

71 Stephen Whately, *The Epistles of Phalaris Translated into English from the Original Greek* (London: Leach, 1699), 83.

clause headed by ὅτι. This type was observed frequently in both the Pauline corpus and the analysis corpus.

57.) Προήγαγον γὰρ πλέον σταδίων τεσσάρων ἐκ τῆς πόλεως, καὶ πρός τινα τόπον ἐκέλευσαν κατακύψαντα συνακοῦσαι τοῦ γινομένου ψόφου τῆς ἀπαντήσεως τῶν ὑδάτων· ὥστε συμφανές μοι γεγονέναι τὸ μέγεθος τῶν ἀγγείων, <u>καθὼς δεδήλωται</u>. [72]

They led me more than four furlongs outside the city and bade me peer down towards a certain spot and listen to the noise that was made by the meeting of the waters, so that the great size of the reservoirs became manifest to me, <u>as has already been pointed out</u>.[73]

In example 57, Aristeas shows a different communication lexeme found in a similar category A construction. This letter is roughly 200 years before Paul. The Perfect comes after the reference, rather than before, however it is quite similar to the other category A examples in that the Perfect is in a clause separate from the reference. No use of ὅτι is apparent in this example.

58.) Ἤκουόν σε <u>λελυπῆσθαι</u> <u>ὅτι</u> τὰ Ἀθηναίων τέκνα πληγὰς ἡμῖν ἐνέτεινε μεθύοντα, καὶ δεινὰ πάσχειν, εἰ σοφία <u>πεπαρῴνηται</u>. [74]

I heard that <u>you are grieved</u> <u>that</u> the Athenian youths, drunk with wine, laid blows on me, and that you suffer great distress that wisdom <u>should be treated with drunken violence</u>.[75]

Diogenes uses a Perfect to introduce referential material in his letter to Melesippus. The first Perfect in example 58 uses an emotional lexeme λελυπῆσθαι rather than a communication lexeme to introduce the referential material. In all other respects it is configured just like the category A constructions found in the Pauline corpus. The Perfect precedes the ὅτι clause. The second Perfect tense-form in this example is stative in that it functions to describe mistreated wisdom.

---

72 Ariste., *ad Philocr.*, 91; A. Pelletier, *Lettre d'Aristée à Philocrate*, Sources Chrétiennes: 89 (Paris: Éditions du Cerf, 1962), 100-240.

73 Robert Henry Charles, editor, *Pseudepigrapha of the Old Testament*, vol. 2 (Oxford: Clarendon Press, 1913), 103.

74 Diog. Sin., *Ep. ad Meles.*, 20.1.1; Malherbe, 112.

75 Malherbe, 113.

59.) <u>οἶδα</u> δὲ <u>ὅτι</u>, εἰ καὶ οἱ ἄλλοι ἄνθρωποι ὁμοίως διέκειντο, ἥττονα ἂν ἦν κακὰ ἐν τῷ βίῳ.[76]

And <u>I know</u> <u>that</u> if other men, too, felt the same way, there would be less evil in life.[77]

In one of the Socratic epistles another example of οἶδα is used to introduce referential material. Example 59 has the Perfect preceding the ὅτι clause, much like those found in the Pauline corpus. Many of these exist throughout the analysis corpus. The point of showing this example is to show that this construction exists throughout the timespan of the corpus.

60.) καίπερ, ὡς <u>οἶσθα</u>, οὐδαμῇ πιθανὸς ὢν τῷ πρὸς χάριν ὑφίεσθαι τοῦ δοκοῦντος. [78]

as <u>you know</u>, he is by no means the sort of man to surrender his own opinion as a favour to anyone.[79]

Plutarch uses the Perfect in a referential way in example 60. Plutarch is roughly 100 years after Paul. This example is typical of those found in the Pauline corpus. The Perfect precedes the clause referred to.

61.) <u>ὅπερ</u> ἐν ἑτέρῳ Εὐαγγελίῳ <u>γέγραπται</u>, τὸ Εἰ ἐγὼ ἐν Πνεύματι Θεοῦ ἐκβάλλω τὰ δαιμόνια, τῆς αὐτῆς φύσεως τῷ Πατρὶ καὶ Υἱῷ τὸ Πνεῦμα τὸ ἅγιον. [80]

<u>which</u> in another Gospel <u>reads</u>, "If I by the Spirit of God cast out devils," then the Holy Spirit is of the same nature as the Father and Son.[81]

In example 61, Basil of Caesarea uses the Perfect in his letter to the Caesareans to precede a quotation from the Gospels. This example is like those of category A in the Pauline corpus. The Perfect is in a subordinate clause separate from the cited material. The material proves a point where Basil argues for the divinity of the Holy Spirit and the Holy Spirit having equal substance with God. The readers

---

76 Socr. Ep., *de Socr.* 1.10.8-1.10.9; Malherbe, 224.

77 Malherbe, 225.

78 Plut., *De coh. ira*, 1; Plutarch, *Moralia*, ed. W. C. Helmbold, vol. 6 (Medford, MA: Harvard University Press, 1939), 94.

79 Plutarch, *Moralia*, ed. W. C. Helmbold, vol. 6 (Medford, MA: Harvard University Press, 1939), 95.

80 Basil. *L.*, 8.25; Basil of Caesarea, *Saint Basil: The Letters: Greek*, LCL:1, edited by E. Capps et al. (Cambridge, MA: Harvard University Press, 1926–1934), 86–88.

81 Basil of Caesarea, *Saint Basil: The Letters*, translated by Roy J. Deferrari and Martin R. P. McGuire, LCL:1, edited by E. Capps et al. (Cambridge, MA: Harvard University Press, 1926–1934), 87–89.

would be familiar with Gospels, so his citation would evoke that memory in the minds of his readers.

A few category B constructions were observed in the analysis corpus. These were fewer than the category A constructions, and seemingly less frequent in the diachronic corpus than they were in the Pauline corpus. However, the few that exist are quite similar to those found in the Pauline corpus. More of these may yet emerge once the corpus is tagged.

62.) πρὸς δὲ τὴν θηριότητα μάλιστ᾿ ἂν ἁρμόττοι λέγειν τὴν ὑπὲρ ἡμᾶς ἀρετήν, ἡρωϊκήν τινα καὶ θείαν, ὥσπερ Ὅμηρος περὶ <τοῦ> Ἕκτορος πεποίηκε λέγοντα τὸν Πρίαμον, ὅτι σφόδρα ἦν ἀγαθός, οὐδὲ ἐῴκει ἀνδρός γε θνητοῦ πάϊς ἔμμεναι ἀλλὰ θεοῖο. [82]

As the opposite of Bestiality it will be most suitable to speak of Superhuman Virtue, or goodness on a heroic or divine scale; just as Homer has represented Priam as saying of Hector, on account of his surpassing valour—nor seemed to be The son of mortal man, but of a god.[83]

In example 62, Aristotle uses a Perfect in a subordinate clause where he introduces an example of logic similar to his own from Homer. The translator rendered the Perfect, πεποίηκε, "has represented," which seems to be communicative, but the lexeme is more general than that. The lexeme is one of general action, either "do," or "make." Although a citation follows, it is further removed and follows λέγοντα in the next clause, rather than πεποίηκε. This is a category B construction, since the Perfect is inside the clause beginning with ὥσπερ.

63.) ὥσπερ αὖ τοὐναντίον, Ἀρταξέρξης αἰσθόμενος Ὦχον τὸν υἱὸν ἐπιβεβουλευκότα τοῖς ἀδελφοῖς ἀθυμήσας ἀπέθανε. [84]

So again, on the contrary, when Artaxerxes perceived that his son Ochus had plotted against his brothers, he despaired and died.[85]

82 Aristot., *Nic. Eth.* 7.1.1; Aristotle, *The Nicomachean Ethics: Greek Text*, LCL, edited by Jeffrey Henderson (Cambridge, MA: Harvard University Press, 1934), 374.

83 Aristotle, *The Nicomachean Ethics*, translated by H. Rackham, LCL: 29, revised edition, edited by Jeffrey Henderson (Cambridge, MA: Harvard University Press, 1934), 375.

84 Plut., *De frat. amor.*, 5; Plutarch, *Moralia*, Vol. 6, edited by W. C. Helmbold (Medford, MA: Harvard University Press, 1939), 258.

85 Plutarch, *Moralia*, Vol. 6, edited by W. C. Helmbold (Medford, MA: Harvard University Press, 1939), 259.

In example 63, Plutarch uses a Perfect in a supplemental role as the main verb in a clause which explains why the events of the main clause occur. In the main clause Artaxerxes despairs and dies, but the timing of his death is explained in the supplemental clause which involves the participle, αἰσθόμενος, contains a Perfect main verb that provides the content of what Artaxerxes perceived. The supplemental information provides both the timing of Artaxerxes' death and a plausible reason for it.

> 64.) Ἡσυχία οὖν ἀρχὴ καθάρσεως τῇ ψυχῇ, μήτε γλώττης λαλούσης τὰ τῶν ἀνθρώπων, μήτε ὀφθαλμῶν εὐχροίας σωμάτων καὶ συμμετρίας περισκοπούντων, μήτε ἀκοῆς τὸν τόνον τῆς ψυχῆς ἐκλυούσης ἐν ἀκροάμασι μελῶν πρὸς ἡδονὴν πεποιημένων, μήτε ῥήμασιν εὐτραπέλων καὶ γελοιαστῶν ἀνθρώπων, ὃ μάλιστα λύειν τῆς ψυχῆς τὸν τόνον πέφυκε.[86]

The very beginning of the soul's purgation is tranquillity, in which the tongue is not given to discussing the affairs of men, nor the eyes to contemplating rosy cheeks or comely bodies, nor the ears to lowering the tone of the soul by listening to songs whose sole object is to amuse, or to words spoken by wits and buffoons—a practice which above all things tends to relax the tone of the soul.[87]

In example 64, Basil of Caesarea writes to Gregory of Nazianzus and uses a Perfect in a supplemental clause while explaining a meditative practice. The translator chose to render the Perfect with "tends," but might have rendered it "is natural" as well. Either way the clause containing the Perfect adds a note to the overall explanation. The supplemental clause does not begin with ὅτι, but clearly is like those in the Pauline corpus.

All three of these examples use Perfect non-communicative lexemes in a subordinate clause that provide additional information to the mainline. None of these lexemes belong to communication lexemes, and this trend was also observed in the Pauline corpus data where the lexical variety was much greater in the category B constructions. Also, examples both precede and follow the Pauline corpus by several centuries, showing that the Perfect is used in referential ways over time.

---

86 Basil. *L.*, 2.5; Basil of Caesarea, *Saint Basil: The Letters: Greek*, LCL:1, edited by E. Capps et al. (Cambridge, MA: Harvard University Press, 1926–1934), 12.

87 Basil of Caesarea, *Saint Basil: The Letters*, translated by Roy J. Deferrari and Martin R. P. McGuire, LCL:1, edited by E. Capps et al. (Cambridge, MA: Harvard University Press, 1926–1934), 13.

7.3. Significant Differences between the Two Corpora

One of the differences between both corpora is that Paul uses Perfect tenses in supplemental ways more frequently than the other writers observed. Category B constructions were less frequent than category A construction in the analysis corpus. Although the Pauline corpus contains examples, no ἵνα + Perfect constructions were observed in the analysis corpus outside those in the Pauline corpus.[88] Perfects were observed in all the time periods to have perfective eventive readings as well as imperfective stative readings, but only the Pauline corpus showed definite examples of the same lexeme being used both ways. If certain lexemes were always stative, while others were always eventive, one could argue that the lexeme itself predicts eventive vs. stative Perfects and conclude that stativity was a lexical item. This does not seem to be the case, as the data shows that the adverb when present will inform the reader as to whether the author intended an eventive reading or a stative reading. It is expected that more lexemes will be discovered where the same lexeme uses both perfective and imperfective readings outside the Pauline corpus once the entire corpus is tagged.

Once the diachronic epistolary and moral literature corpus can be morphologically tagged and searched electronically, it will be possible to observe statistical changes between the time periods, and thus say more about the differences between Paul and the other letter writers. It is expected that this area can be developed more once refined statistics are available. Since the works of Aristotle and Basil of Caesarea are morphologically tagged,[89] it is possible currently to compare those statistically with the Pauline corpus. Comparing three corpora will be useful to show larger trends, but the results will be tentative, as more data is needed to show fine changes along the grammaticalisation path.

7.4. The Diachronic Trend in the Data

Three changes are observed. The use of the Perfect referring to an event perfectively in some cases, and referring to a state imperfectively in others changes in frequency over time. Perhaps this is due to the wider variety of lexemes used in the later periods, but this analysis is beyond the scope of this research, and this question deserves a fuller and separate study. This study shows that both options are available for the Perfect during all time periods observed, and this choice is available to the speaker or author generally. The Perfect found in later periods

---

88 Some may yet be found once the analysis corpus is tagged.
89 Logos has both of these tagged and searchable.

occurs with more lexical variety than the earlier periods, but this seems unrelated to the complex aspect. Greater variety is relevant to the grammaticalisation of the Perfect tense, where it acquires more uses the longer it exists in a language. The use of the Perfect inside the supplemental clause occurs more frequently during the 1st Century and onward. This also reflects greater grammaticalisation.

7.5. Situating Paul within the Trend

Paul appears to fit into the main stream of Greek letter writers and moralists in his usage of the synthetic Perfect. His frequency of certain category B constructions is perhaps higher than earlier writers, but he does not appear to step outside of the usage observed for his time. He uses more active lexemes and a greater variety of lexemes than do the earlier writers in category B constructions. Paul uses at least one lexeme both perfectively and imperfectively, where the first occurrence is perfective and eventive, and then the following ones are imperfective and stative. Paul also uses the ἵνα + Perfect construction. Both having the same lexeme as either stative or as eventive and use of ἵνα with Perfects embedded within the subordinate clause is unobserved among the other writers. Paul's use of the Perfect shows that it has grammaticalised along expected paths, acquiring a greater variety of lexemes, lexeme types, and linguistic environments, along with being used in more situations than earlier writers.

8. Conclusion

This chapter shows that building a corpus of epistolary literature and moral discourse is a useful tool for analysing the Pauline corpus. Although building a corpus of only epistolary literature faced problems of balance, these were overcome by adding in moral literature, which helped by providing more data for centuries that lacked epistolary documents. The analysis corpus as designed is unable to be morphologically tagged, so this prevents some types of searches within the data. This limitation also prevents a full statistical analysis. In spite of these limitations, the corpus was searched manually for examples of Perfect tenses used both perfectively and imperfectively, and many of these were found. Both prior to Paul and after Paul's time, Greek philosophers and letter writers were using the Perfect tense-form either as a perfective event, or as an imperfective state. The Perfect middle participle was most frequently an imperfective state, and the indicative Perfects were more frequently occurring in perfective eventive roles. This was not a rule, as sometimes the opposite was observed. Overall, the diachronic analysis of Greek epistles and moral discourse shows that the imperfective aspect and the perfective aspect were both used for the Greek synthetic Perfect in all the periods of Greek literature, thus anchoring Paul's usage of both aspects of the Perfect within the normal development pattern for the Greek language.

Conclusion

1. Summary and Restatement of the Thesis

This project has demonstrated that the Greek synthetic Perfect tense-form found prominently in the Pauline corpus contains both the perfective and the imperfective verbal aspects. This understanding is contrary to verbal aspect ideas where a single aspect is understood for the synthetic Perfect tense-form. The morphology of the synthetic Perfect tense-form contains both a lexical core that mirrors the Aorist tense-form and points to perfectivity for the event and a reduplicant that grammaticalises imperfectivity which focuses upon a state relevant to the event. This study developed a complex aspect model defined in the third chapter, that involves both of these aspects mapped onto a specific morpheme within the Perfect tense-form. This model connects imperfectivity and stativity to the reduplicant and perfectivity to the event referenced by the lexical core. These two aspects are in tension with each other in the Perfect tense-form. This noticed tension allows for readings of the synthetic Perfect tense-form in some places similar to Present tense-forms of stative lexemes, and in other places eventive past-like readings similar to the Aorist tense of eventive lexemes. This same tension accounts for the wide range of Perfect tense-form uses, and the changes the Perfect undergoes over time. When viewed over the diachronic spectrum, the instability this tension produces helps account for the demise of the synthetic Perfect tense-form prior to the rise of the periphrastic Perfect of Modern Neohellenic. The fact that the Perfect emphasises either a state or a prior action does not mean one aspect or the other was cancelled. They are both always present, but not always emphasised. They cannot be cancelled by context; thus, they satisfy semantic requirements.

This study connects the wide range of uses for the Perfect tense-form to the complex aspect model developed in this project. This study considers the complex aspect of the Perfect tense-form within its diachronic development in order to explain its change of focus from a present-like state in the Epic Period of Greek literature to a past-like action closer to the Byzantine Period. This shift is parallel to the formation of preterite tenses cross-linguistically and fits the cline noticed in Grammaticalisation Theory where perfect tenses eventually become simple past tenses.

This study concludes that the Pauline corpus primarily uses the Greek synthetic Perfect over the periphrastic Perfect and uses this form as both a present-like state and a past-like action, confirming the complex aspect developed in Chapter 3. One instance of the Perfect in the Pauline corpus uses the same Perfect tense both ways while having contextual support for both of these aspects. Adverb collocation is the primary tool to determine if each Perfect tense verb had a stative or eventive focus. The Pauline usage of the Perfect was analysed against a diachronic epistolary and moral literature corpus, comprised of letters and moral discourses written in Greek over a period of 800 years. This analysis corpus provided a diachronic tool for situating the usage of the Perfect within the Pauline corpus, and anchoring the claims made regarding the Perfect tense-form usage in the Pauline corpus. The complex model for understanding the verbal aspect of the Greek synthetic Perfect tense-form was used to analyse the periphrastic Perfect also. The synthetic form was found to mirror the periphrastic form both in its aspect complexity and in the specific organisation of the components of the verb where perfectivity and imperfectivity reside. The lexical core of the synthetic form contains the perfective aspect and attaches it onto the event, mirroring the main lexical verb of the periphrastic Perfect. Grammaticalisation is seen in the Greek synthetic Perfect tense-form through its extension into more supplementary roles, using more active lexemes. The reduplicant of the synthetic form holds an imperfective aspect on a repeated syllable, yielding a stative sense, thus mirroring the auxiliary verb of the synthetic form both in its stative focus and its imperfective aspect. The reduplicant has desemanticised from a repetition of the verb's original lexical meaning, to a simple state. It also has eroded its morphological bulk arriving at general imperfectivity. The stative and imperfective focus of the reduplicant is near the end of the cline of reduplication.

This study connects insights from Grammaticalisation Theory, Indo-European Linguistics, and reduplication studies to the problem of identifying the verbal aspect of the Greek synthetic Perfect tense-form. Grammaticalisation Theory helped to understand the Perfect as a tense-form in motion as well as identify distinctive uses along its development. Cross-linguistic Indo-European studies found many parallels among languages similar to Greek illustrating the cline of Perfectives and the relationship between the synthetic Perfect tense-form and perfectivity. Reduplication studies helped illustrate the imperfectivity found among reduplicated items. Together these three areas of study uniformly affirmed the proposal for a complex aspect for the Perfect.

2. Contribution to Knowledge

This project contributes to theoretical linguistics by further refining the definition of the linguistic category of verbal aspect as "a manner of viewing a situation" rather than "a viewpoint." This definition serves to restrict the elements belonging to the set of items labelled "verbal aspects." This project defines complex aspect for the Perfect tense-form, establishes the validity of this concept, and analyses instances of the Perfect in Greek literature using this concept. Additionally, the complex aspect of the Perfect better explains the changes in meaning for the Perfect tense over time than do single-aspect approaches.

This project differs in method from other approaches in that it emphasises a diachronic approach more than a synchronic approach when answering questions related to morphology and is careful to connect morphology of the verb form to the verbal aspect properties. Additionally, the approach of this project combines the benefits of Grammaticalisation Theory and a Corpus-based approach to analyse the verbal aspect of the Perfect. Grammaticalisation explains the reduplication, explains the change of the Perfect toward a past-like event, and shows the periphrastic Perfect to be parallel in its development to the synthetic Perfect. The corpus-based approach validated the complex aspect of the Perfect, by demonstrating both perfective events and imperfective states for the Perfect over a diachronic spectrum.

This project contributes to biblical studies by analysing the verbal aspect of the Perfect within the Pauline corpus. It analyses the linguistic issues typically addressed in the Greek text commentaries and applies them to exegesis. This project likewise situates Paul among the other Greek letter writers and moralists. Paul uses the Perfect tense-form inside supplemental clauses more often than other Greek writers and employs more lexical variety, particularly active lexemes, in those clauses. The Perfect is grammaticalising further during the timeframe of the New Testament, as it occurs in more situations than earlier texts. The acquisition of more active lexemes in supplemental clauses establishes that the emphasis has shifted closer to an eventive Perfect than did the Classical Greek examples.

This project critiques the definition of verbal aspect in the literature review, and the individual aspect for the Perfect tense, clarifying the semantics of the Perfect. As a result of this clarity, this study refines statements regarding the Perfect in the various grammars and commentaries throughout this project as they are encountered.

Lastly, the complex aspect of the Perfect provides a rationale for how the synthetic Perfect and periphrastic Perfect are similar in their aspectual composition. Complex aspect also answers why both types have similar usages for both present states and past events. This similarity between both types of Perfects suggests that complex aspect is a better way to understand the Perfect tenses cross-linguistically.

3. Limitations of the Research

Several limitations emerged in this research. First, the diachronic epistolary and moral literature corpus has limitations in its size and its diachronic distribution. This was partly due to restrictions related to accessing digital texts and partly due to some centuries having fewer available texts for analysis. Secondly, the analysis corpus was untagged at the time of sample selection, and this forced the examples to be gleaned manually, and prevented a more thorough statistically based study. In spite of these limitations, the analysis corpus provided samples of verbal usage that diachronically supported the complex aspect developed in this project for the Perfect. Thirdly, this study focused on one tense-form, rather than on the Greek tense system as a whole. This decision allowed for a greater emphasis on the Perfect, but did not discuss how the Perfect related to the other tense-forms in terms of oppositions. Fourthly, this project did not analyse tense, temporal relationships, and *Aktionsarten* of the Perfect in detail.

4. Suggestions for Further Research

Several items are suggested for continuing research on the Greek Perfect and for connecting this research to other matters of Greek grammar. Firstly, morphologically tagging the diachronic epistolary and moral literature corpus will allow using statistical analysis. Additionally, the meaningfulness of any statistical approach will be enhanced with a larger corpus. More genres other than the epistolary corpus will be included alongside the epistolary corpus in order to provide more detail regarding the similarities and differences between letter genre and other genres. Currently only moral discourses are included. Secondly, analysing the Greek tense system as a whole in light of the complex aspect for the Perfect developed in this project will show how the oppositions work between the tenses for various lexemes. For example, noticing when an author chooses a Perfect where an earlier author chose an Aorist, would enhance the overall picture of a Perfect tense undergoing diachronic development. Performing adverb collocation studies on all the tenses is expected to enhance the findings for all the tenses. Thirdly, the various *Aktionsarten* relevant to the Perfect will be analysed to show how the complex aspect of the Perfect relates to its *Aktionsarten*. Another area for further investigation is to analyse the manuscript tradition of the Pauline corpus to see if the complex aspect described in this paper would explain any of the situations where the manuscripts have differences in tense-form, where the Aorist or Present was found instead of a Perfect or other way around where a Perfect was found instead of the Aorist or Present. The places where these forms share an aspect could explain why a scribe might copy a tense-form different than the exemplar.

Bibliography

Primary Sources

Adams, Charles Darwin. *The Speeches of Aeschines: With an English Translation*. London: Heinemann, 1919.

Anatolios, Khaled. *Athanasius*. The Early Church Fathers. Edited by Carol Harrison. London: Routledge, 2004.

Babbitt, Frank Cole, ed. *Plutarch, Moralia*. vol. 1. Medford, MA: Harvard University Press, 1927.

———. *Plutarch, Moralia*. vol. 2. Medford, MA: Harvard University Press, 1928.

Bernardakis, Gregorius N., ed. *Plutarch, Moralia*. vol. 1. Medford, MA: Teubner, 1888.

———. *Plutarch, Moralia*. vol. 3. Medford, MA: Teubner, 1891.

Bing, Peter, and Regina Höschele. *Aristaenetus, Erotic Letters*. Writings from the Greco-Roman World:32. Atlanta: SBL, 2014.

Burnet, John, ed. *Plato: Platonis Opera*. Medford, MA: Oxford University Press, 1903.

Bury, R. G., translator. *Timaeus, Critias, Cleitophon, Menexenus, Epistles*. Vol. 9. Plato in Twelve Volumes. Loeb Classical Library: 234. Edited by G. P. Goold. Cambridge, MA: Harvard University Press, 1929.

Capps E., et al., eds. *Saint Basil: The Letters: Greek*. Vol. 1. Loeb Classical Library. Cambridge, MA: Harvard University Press, 1926–1934.

———. *Saint Basil: The Letters: Greek*. Vol. 4. Loeb Classical Library. Cambridge, MA: Harvard University Press, 1926–1934.

Charles, Robert Henry, editor, *Pseudepigrapha of the Old Testament*. vol. 2. Oxford: Clarendon Press, 1913.

Deferrari, Roy J., and Martin R. P. McGuire, translators. *Saint Basil: The Letters*. Vol. 1. Loeb Classical Library. Edited by G. P. Goold. Cambridge, MA: Harvard University Press, 1926.

———. *Saint Basil: The Letters*. Vol. 4. Loeb Classical Library. Edited by G. P. Goold. Cambridge, MA: Harvard University Press, 1934.

Diels, H. *Philodemos Über die Götter*. Drittes Buch. Vols. 1 & 2. Berlin: Königlich-Preussische Akademie der Wissenschaften, 1917.

Dillon, John M., and Wolfgang Polleichtner. *Iamblichus of Chalcis: The Letters*. Writings from the Greco-Roman World:19. Atlanta: SBL, 2009.

Dindorfii, Guiliemi. *Demosthenis Orationes*. Vol. 3. Orationes XLI-LXI. Prooemia, Epistolae, Index Historicus. Lipsiae: Teubneri, 1857.

Fitzgerald, John T., Dirk Obbink, and Glenn S. Holland, eds. *Philodemus and the New Testament World*. NTSupp:109. Leiden: Brill, 2004.

Goertz, Ioannes. *De Chionis Quae Feruntur Epistulis*. Lipsiae: Bornensis, 1912.

Goold, G. P., ed. *Plato, Timaeus, Critias, Cleitophon, Menexenus, Epistles: Greek Text*. Loeb Classical Library. Cambridge, MA: Harvard University Press, 1929.

Granholm, Patrick. *Alciphron: Letters of the Courtesans, Edited with Introduction, Translation and Commentary*. Uppsala: University of Uppsala, 2012.

Helmbold, W. C., ed. *Plutarch, Moralia*. vol. 6. Medford, MA: Harvard University Press, 1939.

Henderson, Jeffrey, ed. *Aristotle, The Nicomachean Ethics: Greek Text*, Loeb Classical Library. Cambridge, MA: Harvard University Press, 1934.

Hercher, Rudophus. *Epistolographoi Hellenikoi*. Paris: Didot, 1873.

Jensen, Christian Cornelius. *Philodemi Peri Oikonomias*. Lipsiae: Teubneri, 1906.

Kayser, Carl Ludwig. *Flavii Philostrati Opera*. Vol. 2. Philostratus the Athenian. Leipzig: Teubner, 1871.

Klauck, Hans-Josef. *Ancient Letters and the New Testament: A Guide to Context and Exegesis*. Waco, TX: Baylor University Press, 2006.

Konstan, David, Diskin Clay, Clarence E. Glad, Johan C. Thorn, and James Ware. *Philodemus: On Frank Criticism*. SBL Texts and Translations:43 Greco-Roman Series:13. Atlanta: Scholars, 1998.

Long, A. A., and D. N. Sedley. *The Hellenistic Philosophers. Vol. 2. Greek and Latin Texts with Notes and Bibliography*. Cambridge: Cambridge University Press, 1987.

Malherbe, Abraham J. *The Cynic Epistles: A Study Edition*. SBL Sources for Biblical Study:12. Missoula, MT: Scholars, 1977.

Mekler, Segofredus. *Academicorum Philosophorum Index Herculanensis*. Berolini: Apud Weidmannos, 1902.

Meinekio, Augusto. *Alciphronis Rhetoris: Epistolae*. Lipsiae: Teubneri, 1853.

Mendelssohn, Lvdovici. *Aristeae ad Philocratem Epistvla*. Edited by Paulus Wendland. Lipsiae: Teubneri, 1900.

Murray, A. T. *Homer: The Iliad with an English translation*. Vol. 1. Loeb Classical Library. Edited by G. P. Goold. Cambridge, MA: Cambridge University Press, 1978.

Obbink, Dirk, ed. *Philodemus, On Piety: Part 1, Critical Text with Commentary.* Oxford: Clarendon, 1996.

Oldfather, W. A. *Epictetus: The Discourses as Reported by Arrian, The Manual, and Fragments: With an English Translation.* 2 vols. Loeb Classical Library. Cambridge, MA: Harvard University Press, 1925 and 1928.

Pelletier, A. *Lettre d'Aristée à Philocrate.* Sources chrétiennes: 89. Paris: Éditions du Cerf, 1962.

Rackham, H., translator. *Aristotle, The Nicomachean Ethics,* Loeb Classical Library: 29, Revised edition. Edited by Jeffrey Henderson. Cambridge, MA; London: Harvard University Press, 1934.

Rosenmeyer, Patricia A. *Ancient Greek Literary Letters: Selections in Translation.* Routlege Classical Translations. London: Routledge, 2006.

Rouse, W. H. D., ed. *The Moral Discourses of Epictetus.* Everyman's Library:404. London: Dent, 1910.

Schaff, Philip, ed. *Athanasius: Select Works and Letters.* New York: Christian Literature, 1892.

Talbot, Alice-Mary Maffry. *The Correspondence of Athanasius I Patriarch of Constantinople: Letters to the Emperor Andronicus II, Members of the Imperial Family, and Officials.* Dumbarton Oaks Texts:3. Washington, DC: Dumbarton Oaks, 1975.

Thesleff, Holger. *An Introduction to the Pythagorean Writings of the Hellenistic Period.* Acta Academiae Aboensis. Humaniora 24:3. Åbo: Åbo Akademi, 1961.

Trapp, Michael, ed. *Greek and Latin Letters: An Anthology, with Translation.* Cambridge: Cambridge University Press, 2003.

Tsouna, Voula. *The Ethics of Philodemus.* Oxford: Oxford University Press, 2007.

———. *Philodemus, On Property Management.* Writings from the Greco-Roman World:33. Atlanta: SBL, 2012.

Whately, Stephen. *The Epistles of Phalaris Translated into English from the Original Greek.* London: Leach, 1699.

Worthington, Ian, and John Miles Foley. *Epea and Grammata: Oral and Written Communication in Ancient Greece. Orality and Literacy in Ancient Greece, Vol.4.* Mnemosyne Supplements:230. Leiden: Brill, 2001.

Worthington, Ian, translator. *Demosthenes, Speeches 60 and 61, Prologues, Letters.* The Oration of Classical Greece:10, Edited by Michael Gagarin. Austin: University of Austin Press, 2006.

Wright, Benjamin G., III. *The Letter of Aristeas: "Aristeas to Philocrates" or "On the Translation of the Law of the Jews."* CEJL. Berlin: de Gruyter, 2015.

Wyrwa, Dietmar. *Epistulae I-IV Ad Serapionem.* Athanasius Werke: Die Dogmatischen Schriften. Erster Band: Erster Tiel:Lfg 4. Berlin: de Gruyter, 2010.

Secondary Sources

Aarts, Bas. "Corpus Linguistics, Chomsky, and Fuzzy Tree Fragments." 5–13 in *Corpus Linguistics and Linguistic Theory: Papers from the Twentieth International Conference on English Language Research on Computerized Corpora (ICAME 20) Freiburg im Breisgau 1999.* Language and Computers: 33. Edited by Christian Mair, and Marianna Hundt. Leiden: Belgium, 2000.

Abraham, Werner, and Leonid Kulikov, eds. *Tense-Aspect, Transitivity and Causality*. Studies in Language Companion Series:50. Amsterdam: John Benjamins, 1999.

Adrados, Francisco Rodriguez. *A History of the Greek Language: From Its Origins to the Present.* Leiden: Brill, 2005.

Aerts, Willem Johan. *Periphrastica: An Investigation into the Use of εἶναι an ἔχειν as Auxiliaries or Pseudo-auxiliaries in Greek from Homer up to the Present Day*. Amsterdam: Hakkert, 1965.

Alexiadou, Artemis. "On Aspectual and Temporal Adverbs." 145–152 in *Themes in Greek Linguistics*, CILT: 117. Edited by Irene Philippaki-Warburton, Katarina Nicolaidas, and Maria Sifianou. Amsterdam: Benjamins, 1993.

Alexiadou, Artemis, Geoffrey Horrocks, and Melita Stavrou, eds. *Studies in Greek Syntax*. Studies in Natural Language and Linguistics Theory:43. Dordrecht: Kluwer, 1999.

Allen, Rutger J. "Tense and Aspect in Classical Greeek: Two Historical Developments; Augment and Perfect," 81–121 in *The Greek Verb Revisited: A Fresh Approach for Biblical Exegesis*. Edited by Runge and Fresch. Bellingham, WA: Lexham, 2016.

Andersen, Henning, ed. *Language Contacts in Prehistory: Studies in Stratigraphy*. CILT:239. Amsterdam: John Benjamins, 2003.

Anderson, Gregory D. S. *Auxiliary Verb Constructions*. Oxford Studies in Typology and Linguistic Theory. Oxford: Oxford University Press, 2006.

Armstrong, D. "Ancient Greek Aorist as the Aspect of Countable Action." 1–11 in *Syntax and Semantics*: 14. *Tense and Aspect*. Edited by P. Tedeschi and A. Zaenen. New York: Academic, 1981.

Aubrey, Michael G. "The Greek Perfect and the Categorization of Tense and Aspect: Towards a Descriptive Apparatus for Operators in Role and Reference Grammar." MA thesis, Trinity Western University, 2014.

———. "The Value of Linguistically Informed Exegesis," 191–201 in *Linguistics and Biblical Exegesis*. Edited by Douglas Mangum and Josh Westbury. Bellingham, WA: Lexham, 2017.

Bache, Carl. "Aspect and Aktionsart: Towards a Semantic Distinction." *Journal of Linguistics* 18 (1982): 57–72.

———. "The Semantics of Grammatical Categories: A Dialectical Approach." *JL* 21 (1985): 51–77.

———. *The Study of Aspect, Tense and Action: Towards a Theory of the Semantics of Grammatical Categories*. 2nd rev. ed. Frankfurt am Main: Peter Lang, 1997.

———. *Verbal Aspect: A General Theory and Its Application to Present-Day English*. Odense University Studies in English: 8. Odense: Odense University Press, 1985.

———. "Verbal Categories, Form-meaning Relationships and the English Perfect." 43–60 in *Tense, Aspect and Action*. Empirical Approaches to Language Typology, 12. Edited by Carl Bache, Hans Basboll, and Carl-Erik Lindberg. Berlin: Mouton de Gruyter, 1994.

Bache, Carl, Hans Basbøll, and Carl-Erik Lindberg, eds. *Tense, Aspect and Action*. Empirical Approaches to Language Typology:12. Berlin: de Gruyter, 1994.

Bailey, Charles-James N. *Essays on Time-Based Linguistic Analysis*. Oxford: Clarendon, 1996.

Baker, Paul. "Corpus Methods in Linguistics." 93–113 in *Research Methods in Linguistics*. Edited by Lia Litosseliti. London: Continuum, 2010.

Barr, James Albert. *The Semantics of Biblical Language*. Oxford: Oxford University Press, 1961.

Bartolotta, Annamaria. "Root Lexical Features and Inflectional Marking of Tense in Proto-Indo-European." *JL* 45 (2009): 505–532.

———. "IE *weid-* as a Root with Dual Subcategorizationisation Features in the Homeric Poems." 265–291 in Universal Grammar in the Reconstruction of Ancient Languages. *SGG:83*. Edited by Katalin É. Kiss. Berlin: de Gruyter, 2005.

Bary, Corien. "Aspect in Ancient Greek: A Semantic Analysis of the Aorist and Imperfective," PhD diss., Radboud Universiteit Nijmegen, 2009.

———. "Tense in Ancient Greek Reports." *Journal of Greek Linguistics* 12 (2012): 29–50.

Bary, Corien, and Markus Egg. "Variety in Ancient Greek Aspect Interpretation." *Linguist and Philos* 35 (2012): 111–134.

Beekes, Robert S. P. *Comparative Indo-European Linguistics: An Introduction*. Amsterdam: John Benjamins, 1995.

———. *Pre-Greek Phonology, Morphology, Lexicon*. BIIEL:2. Leiden: Brill, 2014.

Beekes, Robert S. P., and Lucian van Beek. *Etymological Dictionary of Greek*. 2 Volumes. Leiden Indo-European Etymological Dictionary Series vol. 10/2. Leiden: Brill, 2010.

Bentein, Klaas. "Have-Perfects in Post-Classical and Early Byzantine Greek." *Emerita: Revista de Lingüística y Filología Clásica* 81, no. 1 (2013): 151–182.

———. "The Periphrastic Perfect in Ancient Greek: A Diachronic Mental Space Analysis." *Transactions of the Philological Society* 110, no. 2 (2012): 171–121.

———. *Verbal Periphrasis in Ancient Greek: Have- and Be- Constructions*. Oxford: Oxford University Press, 2016.

Biber, Douglas, Susan Conrad, and Randi Reppen. *Corpus Linguistics: Investigating Language Structure and Use*. Cambridge Approaches to Linguistics. Cambridge: Cambridge University Press, 1998.

Binnick, Robert I. *Time and the Verb: A Guide to Tense and Aspect*. Oxford: Oxford University Press, 1991.

Bird, Steven, Ewan Klein, and Edward Loper. *Natural Language Processing with Python: Analyzing Text with the Natural Language Toolkit*. Sebastopol, CA: O'Reilly, 2009.

Black, David Alan. *Learn to Read New Testament Greek*. Expanded Edition. Nashville, TN: Broadman & Holman, 1994.

———. *Linguistics for Students of New Testament Greek: A Survey of Basic Concepts and Applications*. 3rd ed. Grand Rapids, MI: Baker, 1995.

Blass, F., A. Debrunner, and Robert Funk. *A Greek Grammar of the New Testament and Other Early Christian Literature*. Chicago, IL: University of Chicago Press, 1961.

Bortone, Peitro. *Greek Prepositions: From Antiquity to the Present*. Oxford: Oxford University Press, 2010.

Brookins, Timothy. "Rethinking the Grammaticalization of Time in Greek Indicative Verbs." *JBL* 137, no. 1 (Spring 2008): 147–168.

Brugmann, K. *Griechische Grammatik. II. i: Lautlehre, Stammbildungs und Flexionslehre, Syntax* (1st edition, 1885) 4th edition edited by A. Thumb. Munich: C. H. Beck, 1913.

Bubenik, Vit, John Hewson, and Sarah Rose, eds. *Grammatical Change in Indo-European Languages: Papers Presented at the Workshop on Indo-European Linguistics at the*

XVIIIth *International Conference on Historical Linguistics, Montreal, 2007.* CILT:305. Amsterdam: John Benjamins, 2009.

Burton, Ernest De Witt. *Syntax of the Moods and Tenses in New Testament Greek*, 3rd ed. Edinburgh: T&T Clark, 1898.

Buth, Randall. "Perfect Greek Morphology and Pedagogy." 416–429 in *The Greek Verb Revisited: A Fresh Approach for Biblical Exegesis.* Edited by Steven R. Runge and Christopher J. Fresch. Bellingham, WA: Lexham, 2016.

———. "Verbs Perception and Aspect: Greek Lexicography and Grammar." 177–198 in *Biblical Greek Language and Lexicography: Essays in Honor of Frederick W. Danker.* Edited by Bernard A. Taylor, John A. L. Lee, Peter R. Burton, and Richard E. Whitaker. Grand Rapids, MI: Eerdmans, 2004.

Buttmann, Alexander. *A Grammar of the New Testament Greek.* Andover: Draper, 1873.

Buttmann, Philip. *Intermediate or Larger Greek Grammar.* London: Black, Young and Young, 1833.

Bybee, Joan. *Morphology: A Study of the Relation Between Meaning and Form.* Amsterdam: John Benjamins, 1985.

Bybee, Joan, Osten Dahl. "The Creation of Tense and Aspect Systems in the Languages of the World." *Studies in Language* 13–1 (1989): 51–103.

Bybee, Joan, Revere Perkins, and William Pagliuca. *Evolution of Grammar: Tense, Aspect, and Modality in the Languages of the World.* Chicago, IL: University of Chicago Press, 1994.

Campbell, Constantine R. *Advances in the Study of the Greek: New Insights for Reading the New Testament.* Grand Rapids, MI: Zondervan, 2015.

———. *Basics of Verbal Aspect in Biblical Greek.* Grand Rapids, MI: Zondervan, 2008.

———. *Verbal Aspect, the Indicative Mood, and Narrative: Soundings in the Greek of the New Testament.* SBG:13. Edited by D. A. Carson. New York: Peter Lang, 2007.

———. *Verbal Aspect and Non-Indicative Verbs: Further Soundings in the Greek of the New Testament.* SBG:15. Edited by D. A. Carson. New York: Peter Lang, 2008.

Caragounis, Chrys C. *The Development of Greek and the New Testament: Morphology, Syntax, Phonology, and Textual Transmission.* Grand Rapids, MI: Baker, 2004, 2006.

———. *New Testament Language and Exegesis.* WUNT: 323. Tubingen: Mohr Siebeck, 2014.

Carson, Donald A. "An Introduction to the Perfect Debate." 18–25 in *Biblical Greek Language and Linguistics: Open Questions in Current Research.* JSNT Supp: 80. Edited by Stanley E. Porter and D. A. Carson. Sheffield: JSOT, 1993.

Ceccarelli, Paola. *Ancient Greek Letter Writing: A Cultural History (600 BC–150 BC).* Oxford: Oxford Univeristy Press, 2013.

Cennamo, Michaela. "The Rise and Development of Analytic Perfects in Italo-Romance." 115–142 in *Grammatical Change and Linguistic Theory: The Rosendal Papers.* LA:113. Edited by Thórhallur Eythórsson. Amsterdam: Benjamins, 2008.

Chantraine, Pierre. *Dictionaire Étymologique de la Langue Grecque: Histoire des Mots.* Sous la direction de Alain Blanc, Charles de Lamberterie, Jean-Louis Perpillon. Paris: Klincksiek, 1999.

———. *Histoire du Parfait Grec.* Paris: Klinkensieck, 1927.

Chomsky, Noam. *Aspects of the Theory of Syntax.* Cambridge, MA: Massachusetts Institute of Technology Press, 1965.

Cinque, Guglielmo. "Issues in Adverbial Syntax." *Lingua* 114 (2004): 683–710.

Clackson, James. *Indo-European Linguistics: An Introduction.* Cambridge Textbooks in Linguistics. Cambridge: Cambridge University Press, 2007.

Comrie, Bernard. *Aspect: An Introduction to the study of Verbal Aspect and Related Problems.* Cambridge Textbooks in Linguistics. Cambridge: Cambridge University Press, 1976.

———. *Language Universals and Linguistic Typology: Syntax and Morphology,* 2nd ed. Chicago, IL: University of Chicago Press, 1989.

Cotterell, Peter and Max Turner. *Linguistics and Biblical Interpretation.* Downers Grove, IL: Intervarsity, 1989.

Crellin, Robert. "The Greek Perfect Active System: 200 BC–AD 150," PhD diss., Pembroke College: University of Cambridge, 2012.

———. "The Greek Perfect through Gothic Eyes: Evidence for the Existence of a Unitary Semantic for the Greek Perfect in New Testament Greek." *JGL* 14 (2014): 5–42.

Crisafulli, Virgil Santi. "Aspect and Tense Distribution in Homeric Greek." PhD Diss., University of North Carolina, 1967.

Curtius, Georg. *The Greek Verb: Its Structure and Development.* Translated by Augustus S. Wilkins and Edwin B. England. London: John Murray, 1880.

Cuzzolin, Pierluigi, Ignazio Putzu, and Paolo Ramat. "The Indo-European Adverb in Diachronic and Typological Perspective." *Indogermanische Forschungen* 111 (2006): 6–38.

Dahl, Eystein. "Tense and Aspect in Indo-Iranian Part 1: Present and Aorist." *Language and Linguistics Compass* 5, no. 5 (2011): 265–281.

———. "Tense and Aspect in Indo-Iranian Part 2: The Perfect, Futurate, Participial and Periphrastic Categories." *Language and Linguistics Compass* 5, no. 5 (2011): 282–296.

———. *Time, Tense and Aspect in Early Vedic Grammar: Exploring Inflectional Semantics in the Rigveda.* Brill's Studies in Indo-European Languages & Linguistics: 5. Leiden: Brill, 2010.

Dahl, Östen. "Aspect: Basic Principals." In *Concise Encyclopedia of Grammatical Categories.* Edited by Keith Brown and Jim Miller. Oxford: Elsevier, 1999.

———. *Tense and Aspect in the Languages of Europe.* Empirical Approaches to Language Typology: 20, EUROTYP: 6. Berlin: Mouton de Gruyter, 2000.

———. *Tense and Aspect Systems.* Oxford: Blackwell, 1985.

Dana, H. E., and Julius R. Mantey. *A Manual Grammar of the Greek New Testament.* New York: Macmillan, 1955.

Decker, Rodney J. *Temporal Deixis of the Greek Verb in the Gospel of Mark with Reference to Verbal Aspect.* SBG:10. New York: Peter Lang, 2001.

Deo, Ashwini. "Tense and Aspect in the Indo-Aryan Languages: Variation and Diachrony." PhD Diss., Stanford University, 2006.

Desagulier, Guillaume. "Noam Chomsky's Colorless Green Idea: « Corpus Linguistics Doesn't Mean Anything »," in *Around the Word,* 05/12/2017, online, available from https://corpling.hypotheses.org/252.

Drinka, Bridget. "The Development of the Perfect in Indo-European: Stratigraphic Evidence of Prehistoric Areal Influence." 77–105 in *Language Contacts in Prehistory: Studies in Stratigraphy.* CILT:239. Edited by Henning Andersen. Amsterdam: John Benjamins, 2003.

———. "The Evolution of Grammar: Evidence from the Indo-European Perfects." 117–133 in *Historical Linguistics 1997: Selected of Papers from the 13th International Conference on*

Historical Linguistics, Dusseldorf, 10–17 August, 1997. CILT:164. Edited by Monika S. Schmid, Jennifer R. Austin, and Dieter Stein. Amsterdam: John Benjamins, 1998.

Ellis, Nicolas J. "Aspect-Prominence, Morpho-Syntax, and a Cognitive Linguistic Framework for the Greek Verb." 122–160 in *The Greek Verb Revisited: A Fresh Approach for Biblical Exegesis.* Edited by Steven R. Runge and Christopher J. Fresch. Bellingham, WA: Lexham, 2016.

van Emde Boas, Evert, Albert Rijksbaron, Luuk Huitink, and Mattheiu de Bakker. *Cambridge Grammar of Classical Greek.* Cambridge: Cambridge University Press, 2019.

Evans, Trevor V. "The Greek Epistolary Perfect." *Glotta* 75, no. 3/4 (1999): 194–221.

———. *Verbal Syntax in the Greek Pentateuch: Natural Greek Usage and Hebrew Interference.* Oxford: Oxford University Press, 2001.

Exler, Rev. Francis Xavier J. *A Study in Greek Epistolography: The Form of the Ancient Greek Letter.* Washington, DC: Catholic University of America, 1923. Reprint, Eugene, OR: Wipf & Stock, 2003.

Eythorsson, Thorhallur, ed. *Grammatical Change and Linguistic Theory: The Rosendal Papers.* Linguistik Aktuell:113. Amsterdam: John Benjamins, 2008.

Fanning, Buist M. *Verbal Aspect in New Testament Greek.* Oxford Theological Monographs. Oxford: Clarendon, 1990.

Fernández, Paula Lorente. *L'aspect Verbal en Grec Ancien: Le Choice des Themes Verbaux chez Isocrate.* BCILL:111. Louvain-La-Neuve: Peeters, 2003.

Fischer, Olga, Anette Rosenbach, and Dieter Stein, eds. *Pathways of Change: Grammaticalization in English.* Studies in Language Companion Series. Amsterdam: John Benjamins, 2000.

Fischer, Olga, Muriel Norde, and Harry Perridon. *Up and Down the Cline—The Nature of Grammaticalization.* Typological Studies in Language:59. Amsterdam: John Benjamins, 2004.

Frampton, John. *Distributed Reduplication.* Linguistic Inquiry Monographs:52. Edited by Samuel Jay Keiser. Cambridge, MA: Massachusetts Institute of Technology Press, 2009.

Friedrich, Paul. "On Aspect Theory and Homeric Aspect." *International Journal of American Linguistics* 40, no. 4, part 2. (October 1974): S 1–S 44.

Gerö, Eva-Carin, and Arnim von Stechow. "Tense in Time: The Greek Perfect." 251–293 in *Words in Time: Diachronic Semantics from Different Points of View.* Edited by Regine Eckardt, Klaus von Heusinger and Christoph Schwarze. Berlin: Mouton de Gruyter, 2002.

Giannakis, Georgios. "Studies in the Syntax and Semantics of the Reduplication Presents in Homeric Greek and Indo-European." PhD diss., University of California, 1992.

Glynn, Dylan and Kerstin Fischer, eds. *Quantitative Methods in Cognitive Semantics: Corpus-Driven Approaches.* Cognitive Linguistics Research:46. Berlin: de Gruyter, 2010.

Guéron, Jacqueline. "On Tense and Aspect." *Lingua* 117 (2007): 367–391.

Hancil, Sylvie, and Ekkehard König. *Grammaticalization—Theory and Data.* SLCS:162. Amsterdam: John Benjamins, 2014.

Harris, Murray J. *Prepositions and Theology in the Greek New Testament: An Essential Reference Resource for Exegesis.* Grand Rapids, MI: Zondervan, 2012.

Harris, Zellig. *The Mathematical Structure of Language.* Interscience Tracts in Pure and Applied Mathematics: 21. London: Wiley, 1968.

Harry, J. E. "The Perfect Forms in Later Greek from Aristotle to Justinian." *Transactions and Proceedings of the American Philological Association* 37 (1906): 53–72.

Haspelmath, Martin. "From Resultative to Perfect in Ancient Greek." 187–224 in *Nuevos estudios sobre construcciones resultativos. Funcion* 11–12. Edited by José Luis Iturrioz Leza. Guadalajara: Universidad de Guadalajara, Centro de Investigación de Lenguas Indígenas, 1992.

———. "The Grammaticalization of Passive Morphology." *Studies in Language* 14–1 (1990): 25–72.

———. *From Space to Time: Temporal Adverbials in the World's Languages.* LINCOM Studies in Theoretical Linguistics:03. Munchen: LINCOM Europa, 1997.

Hatina, Thomas R. "The Perfect Tense-Form in Colossians: Verbal Aspect, Temporality, and the Challenge of Translation." 249–250 in *Translating the Bible: Problems and Prospects*, JSNTSup 173. Edited by Stanley E. Porter and Richard S. Hess. Sheffield: Sheffield Academic Press, 1999.

———. "The Perfect Tense-Form in Recent Debate: Galatians as a Case Study." *Filologia Neotestamentica* 15, no. 8 (1995): 3–22.

Haug, Dag. "Aristotle's Kinesis/Energeia-test and the Semantics of the Greek Perfect." *Linguistics* 42–2 (2004): 387–418.

Heine, Bernd. *Auxiliaries: Cognitive Forces and Grammaticalization.* Oxford: Oxford University Press, 1993.

Heine, Bernd, and Tania Kuteva. *The Changing Languages of Europe.* Oxford: Oxford University Press, 2006.

Herweg, Michael. "A Critical Examination of Two Classical Approaches to Aspect." *Journal of Semantics* 8 (1991): 363–402.

Hewson, John. "Four Kinds of Aspect." *LACUS Forum* 24 (1998): 161–170.

Hewson, John, and Vit Bubenik, eds. *Tense and Aspect in Indo-European Languages: Theory, Typology, and Diachrony.* CILT:145. Amsterdam: John Benjamins, 1997.

Hill, A. A., ed. *The Proceedings of The Third Texas Conference on Problems of Linguistic Analysis in English, May 9–12, 1958.* Austin: University of Texas Press, 1962.

Hogeweg, Lotte, Helen de Hoop, and Andrej Malchukov, eds. *Cross-Linguistic Semantics of Tense, Aspect and Modality.* Linguistik Aktuell:148. Amsterdam: John Benjamins, 2009.

Hollebrandse, Bart, Angeliek van Hout, and Co Vet, eds. *Crosslinguistic Views on Tense, Aspect and Modality.* Cahiers Chronos:13. Amsterdam: Rodopi, 2005.

Holton, David, Peter Mackridge, and Irene Philippaki-Warburton. *Greek: An Essential Grammar of the Modern Language.* London: Routledge, 2004.

———. *Greek: A Comprehensive Grammar.* 2nd ed. London: Routledge, 2012.

Hopper, Paul J., ed. *Tense-Aspect: Between Semantics & Pragmatics.* Typological Studies in Language:1. Amsterdam: John Benjamins, 1982.

Hopper, Paul J., and Elizabeth Closs Traugott. *Grammaticalization.* 2nd ed. Cambridge Textbooks in Linguistics. Cambridge: Cambridge University Press, 2003.

Horrocks, Geoffrey. Greek: *A History of the Language and Its Speakers.* 2nd ed. West Sussex: Wiley-Blackwell, 2010.

Hurch, Bernhard, ed. *Studies on Reduplication.* Berlin: de Gruyter, 2005.

Hwang, Chung Hee, and Lenhart K. Schubert. "Interpreting Tense, Aspect and Time Adverbials: A Compositional, Unified Approach." 238–264 in *Temporal Logic. Lecture Notes in Computer Science*. Lecture Notes in Artificial Intelligence:827. Edited by D. M. Gabbay and H. J. Ohlbach. Berlin: Springer, 1994.

Iatradou, Sabine, Elena Anagnostopoulou, and Roumyana Izvorski. "Observations About the Form and Meaning of the Perfect." 189–238 in *Perfect Explorations*. Interface Explorations, Vol. 2. Edited by Artemis Alexiadou, Monika Rathert and Arnim von Stechow, M. Kenstowicz. Berlin: de Gruyter, 2003, 2012.

Inkelas, Sharon, and Cheryl Zoll. *Reduplication: Doubling in Morphology*. Cambridge Studies in Linguistics. Cambridge: Cambridge University Press, 2005.

Jackendoff, Ray. *Semantic Interpretation in Generative Grammar*. Current Studies in Linguistics. Cambridge, MA: MIT Press, 1972.

Jannaris, Antonius N. *An Historical Greek Grammar*. London: Macmillan, 1897.

Janssen, Marjolijne C. "Perfectly Absent: The Emergence of the Modern Greek Perfect in Early Modern Greek." *Byzantine and Modern Greek Studies* 37, no. 2 (2013): 245–260.

Johanson, Lars. "Viewpoint Operators in European Languages." 26–187 in *Tense and Aspect in the Languages of Europe*. Edited by Östen Dahl. Empirical Approaches to Language Typology: 20, EUROTYP: 6. Berlin: Mouton de Gruyter, 2000.

Johnson, Marion R. "Unified Temporal Theory of Tense and Aspect." 145–175 in *Tense and Aspect*. Syntax and Semantics: 14. Edited by Philip J. Tedeschi and Annie Zaenen. New York: Academic Press, 1981.

de Jonge, Casper C. *Between Grammar and Rhetoric: Dionysius of Halicarnassus on Language, Linguistics and Literuature*. Mnemosyne Supplements:301. Leiden: Brill, 2008.

Kahn, Charles H. *The Verb "Be" in Ancient Greek*. Indianapolis, IN: Hackett, 2003.

Katz, Graham. "Manner Modification of State Verbs." 220–248 in *Adjectives and Adverbs: Syntax, Semantics, and Discourse*. Oxford Studies in Theoretical Linguistics, Edited by Louise McNally and Christopher Kennedy. Oxford: Oxford University Press, 2008.

Kilgariff, Adam, Vit Baisa, Jan Bušta, Miloš Jakubíček, Vojtěch Kovář, Jan Michelfeit, Pavel Rychlý, and Vit Suchomel. "The Sketch Engine: Ten Years On." *Lexicography ASIALEX* 1 (2014): 7–36.

Kiparsky, Paul. "Aspect and Event Structure in Vedic." 29–61 in *The Yearbook of South Asian Languages and Linguistics*. Edited by Rajendra Singh and Tanmoy Bhattacharya. London: Sage, 1998.

Klein, Wolfgang. *Time in Language*. Germanic Linguistics. London: Routledge, 1994.

Klein, Wolfgang and Ping Li. *The Expressions of Time*. The Expressions of Cognitive Semantics:3. Edited by Wolfgang Klein and Stephen Levinsohn. Berlin: de Gruyter 2009.

Koester, Almut. "Building Small Specialised Corpora." 66–79 in *The Routledge Handbook of Corpus Linguistics*. Edited by Anne O'Keeffe and Michael McCarthy. London: Routledge, 2010.

Kulikov, Leonid. "Reduplication in the Vedic Verb: Indo-European Inheritance, Analogy and Iconicity." In *Studies in Reduplication*. Edited by Bernhard Hurch. Berlin: de Gruyter, 2005.

Kulikov, Leonid, and Nikolaos Lavidas, eds. *Proto-Indo-European Syntax and its Development*. Benjamins Current Topics:75. Amsterdam: John Benjamins, 2015.

Kuryłowicz, Jerzy. *The Inflectional Categories of Indo-Eurpoean*. Heidelberg: Winter, 1964.

Kuteva, Tania. "On 'sit'/'stand'/'lie' auxiliation." *Linguistics* 27–2 (1999): 191–213.

Langslow, David, ed. *Jacob Wackernagel "Lectures on Syntax," with Special Reference to Greek, Latin, and Germanic*. Oxford. Oxford University Press, 2009.

Lavidas, Nikolaos, and Gabarell Drachman. "On the Verbal Complements of Aspectual Verbs." *Journal of Greek Linguistics* 12 (2012): 305–333.

Lehmann, Christian. *Thoughts on Grammaticalization*, 3rd ed. Classics in Linguistics:1. Edited by Martin Haspelmath and Stefan Muller. Berlin: Language Science, 2015.

Lehmann, Winfred P. *Proto-Indo European Phonology*. Austin, TX: University of Texas Press, 1952.

———. *Theoretical Bases of Indo-European Linguistics*. London: Routledge, 1993.

Lichtenberk, Frantisek. "On the Gradualness of Grammaticalization." 37–80 in *Approaches to Grammaticalization: Focus on Theoretical and Methodological Issues*, 19:1. Edited by Elizabeth Closs Traugott and Bernd Heine. Amsterdam: John Benjamins, 1991.

Lindstedt, Jouko. "The Perfect—Aspectual, Temporal and Evidential." 365–383 in *Tense and Aspect in the Languages of the World*. Edited by Östen Dahl. Berlin: de Gruyter, 2000.

Lloyd, Albert L. *Anatomy of the Verb: The Gothic Verb as a Model for a Unified Theory of Aspect, Actional Types, and Verbal Velocity*. SLCS:4. Amsterdam: John Benjamins, 1979.

Lotspiech, C. M. "A Theory of Ablaut," *Journal of English and Germanic Philology* 16, no. 2 (1917): 173–186.

Luraghi, Silvia. *On the Meaning of Prepositions and Cases: The Expression of Semantic Roles in Ancient Greek*. SLCS: 67. Amsterdam: John Benjamins, 2003.

Luraghi, Silvia, and Eleonora Sausa. "New Approaches to New Testament Greek Linguistics." *Studi Italiani di Linguistica Teorica e Applicata* 45, no. 1 (2016): 123–144.

Luraghi, Silvia, and Vit Bubenik. *Continuum Companion to Historical Linguistics*. London: Continuum, 2010.

Lyons, John. *Introduction to Theoretical Linguistics*. Cambridge: Cambridge University Press, 1968.

———. *Language and Linguistics: An Introduction*. Cambridge: Cambridge University Press, 1981.

Machen, J. Gresham. *New Testament Greek for Beginners*. New York: Macmillan, 1923.

Mallory, J. P., and D. Q. Adams. *The Oxford Introduction to Proto Indo-European and the Proto Indo-European World*. Oxford: Oxford University Press, 2006, 2007, 2008.

Mandilaras, B. G. *The Verb in the Greek non-literary Papyrii*. Athens: Hellenic Ministry of Culture and Sciences, 1973.

Markey, T. L. "Deixis and Diathesis: The Case of the Greek κ- Perfect." *Indogermanische Forschungen* 85 (1980): 279–297.

Matthiae, Augustus. *A Copius Greek Grammar*. 5th ed. 2 vols. London: Murray, 1832.

McCoard, Robert William. *The English Perfect: Tense-Choice and Pragmatic Inferences*. Amsterdam: North Holland, 1978.

McCray, Stanley. "On the Notion of Morpho-Syntactic Stability: Aspekt vs. Aktionsart in Indo-European." *Indogermanische Forschungen* 87 (1982): 15–21.

McEnery, Tony, and Andrew Hardie. *Corpus Linguistics: Method, Theory, and Practice*. Cambridge Textbooks in Linguistics. Cambridge: Cambridge University Press, 2012.

McEnery, Tony, and Andrew Wilson. *Corpus Linguistics: An Introduction*. Edinburgh Textbooks in Empirical Linguistics. Edinburgh: Edinburgh University Press, 2001.

McEnery, Tony, Richard Xiao, and Yukio Tono. *Corpus-Based Language Studies: An Advanced Resource Book*. Routledge Applied Linguistics. London: Routledge, 2006.

McIntyre, Linda Lee. "Classical Reduplication." PhD Diss., University of North Carolina, 1992.

McKay, Kenneth L. "Aspect in Imperatival Constructions in New Testament Greek." *NovT* 27, no. 3 (1985): 201–226.

———. *Greek Grammar for Students: A Concise Grammar of Classical Attic with Special Reference to Aspect in the Verb.* Canberra: Dept. of Classics, Australian National University, 1974.

———. *A New Syntax of the Verb in New Testament Greek: An Aspectual Approach.* SBG:5. Edited by D. A. Carson. New York: Peter Lang, 1994.

———. "On the Perfect and Other Aspects in New Testament Greek." *NovT* 23, no. 4 (1981): 289–329.

———. "On the Perfect and Other Aspects in the Greek Non-Literary Papyri." *BICS* 27 (1980): 23–49.

———. "Style and Significance in the Language of John 21:15–17." *NovT* 27, no. 3 (1985): 319–333.

———. "Time and Aspect in New Testament Greek." *NovT* 34, no. 3 (July 1992): 209—228.

———. "The Use of the Ancient Greek Perfect Down to the Second Century A.D." *BICS* 12 (1965) 1–21.

McNally, Louise, and Christopher Kennedy. *Adjectives and Adverbs: Syntax, Semantics, and Discourse.* Oxford Studies in Theoretical Linguistics. Oxford: Oxford University Press, 2008.

Meier-Brügger, Michael. *Indo-European Linguistics.* Berlin: De Gruyter, 2003.

Miller, Gary D. *Complex Verb Formation.* CILT:95. Amsterdam: John Benjamins, 1993.

Młynarczyk, A. K. *Aspectual Pairing in Polish.* Utrecht: LOT, 2004.

Moorhouse, A. C. *The Syntax of Sophocles.* Mnemosyne Supp: 75. Leiden: Brill, 1982.

Morwood, James. *Oxford Grammar of Classical Greek.* Oxford: Oxford University Press, 2001.

Moser, Amalia. "Aspect and Aktionsart: A Study on the Nature of Grammatical Categories," 99–120 in *Major Trends in Theoretical and Applied Linguistics*: 1. Edited by Nikolaos Lavidas, Thomai Alexiou and Areti-Maria Sougari. London: Versita, 2014.

———. "The Changing Relationship of Tense and Aspect in the History of Greek." *Sprachtypologie und Universalienforschung* 61, no. 1 (Berlin, 2008): 5–18.

———. "Tense and Aspect after the New Testament." 539–562 in *The Greek Verb Revisited: A Fresh Approach for Biblical Exegesis.* Edited by Steven R. Runge and Christopher J. Fresch. Bellingham, WA: Lexham, 2016.

Moulton, James Hope. *A Grammar of New Testament Greek.* Vol. 1, Prolegomena. 3rd ed. Edinburgh: T & T Clark, 1908.

Mounce, William D. *Basics of Biblical Greek: Grammar.* 3rd ed. Grand Rapids, MI: Zondervan, 2009.

Mourelatos, A. P. D. "Events, Processes, and States." *Linguistics and Philosophy* 2 (1978): 415–434.

Muir, John. *Life and Letters in the Ancient Greek World.* Monographs in Classical Studies. London: Routledge, 2009.

Mumm, Peter Arnold. "Retrospektivität im Rigveda: Aorist und Perfekt." 157–188 in *Indogermanische Syntax: Fragen und Perspektiven.* Edited by Heinrich Hettrich and Jeong-Soo Kim. Weisbaden: Riechart, 2002.

Niepokuj, Mary. *The Development of Verbal Reduplication in Indo-European.* JIES Monograph: 24. Washington, D. C.: Institute for the Study of Man, 1997.

O'Donnell, Matthew Brook. *Corpus Linguistics & the Greek of the New Testament.* New Testament Monographs:6. Sheffield: Sheffield Phoenix, 2005.

Olsen, Mari Jean Broman. "A Semantic and Pragmatic Model of Lexical and Grammatical Aspect." PhD diss., Northwestern University, 1994.

Pang, Francis G. H. *Revisting Aspect and Aktionsart: A Corpus Approach to Koine Greek Event Typology.* LBS:14 Leiden: Brill, 2016.

Pappas, Panayiotis A. *Variation and Morphosyntactic Change in Greek: From Clitics to Affixes.* Palgrave Studies in Language History and Language Change. Hampshire: Palgrave Macmillan, 2004.

Petard, Adeline, and Frank Brisard, eds. *Cognitive Approaches to Tense, Aspect, and Epistemic Modality.* Human Cognitive Processing:29. Amsterdam: John Benjamins, 2011.

Porter, Stanley E. *The Apostle Paul: His Life, Thought, and Letters.* Grand Rapids, MI: Eerdmans, 2016.

———. "Aspect Theory and Lexicography." 207–222 in *Biblical Greek Language and Lexicography: Essays in Honor of Frederick W. Danker.* Edited by Bernard A. Taylor, John A. L. Lee, Peter R. Burton, and Richard E. Whitaker. Grand Rapids, MI: Eerdmans, 2004.

———. *Idioms of the Greek New Testament.* Biblical Languages: Greek:2. 2nd ed. Sheffield: Sheffield, 1999.

———. "Introduction: Diglossia and Other Topics in New Testament Linguistics." 13–16 in *Diglossia and Other Topics in New Testament Linguistics.* JSNT Supp: 193. Studies in New Testament Greek: 6. Sheffield: Sheffield, 2000.

———. "In Defence of Verbal Aspect." 26–45 in *Biblical Greek Language and Linguistics: Open Questions in Current Research.* JSNT Supp: 80. Edited by Stanley E. Porter and D. A. Carson. Sheffield: JSOT, 1993.

———. *Linguistic Analysis of the Greek New Testament: Studies in Tools, Methods, and Practice.* Grand Rapids, MI: Baker, 2015.

———. *The Pauline Canon.* Pauline Studies:1. Dordrecht: Springer, 2004.

———. *Verbal Aspect in the Greek of the New Testament, with Reference to Tense and Mood.* SBG:1. Edited by D. A. Carson. New York: Peter Lang, 1989, 1993.

Porter, Stanley E., and Andrew W. Pitts. "New Testament Greek Language and Linguistics in Recent Research." *CBR* 62 (2008): 214–255.

Porter, Stanley E. and D. A. Carson, eds. *Biblical Greek Language and Linguistics: Open Questions in Current Research.* Journal for the Study of the New Testament Supplement Series: 80. Sheffield: JSOT, 1993.

Porter, Stanley E., Gregory P. Fewster, and Christopher D. Land. *Modeling Biblical Language: Selected Papers from the McMaster Divinity College Linguistics Circle.* LBS:13. Leiden: Brill, 2016.

Porter, Stanley E., Jeffrey T. Reed, and Matthew Brook O'Donnell. *Fundamentals of New Testament Greek.* Grand Rapids, MI: Eerdmans, 2010.

Porter, Stanley E. and Matthew Brook O'Donnell. "Semantics in Romans," 154–204 in *Diglossia and Other Topics in New Testament Linguistics.* JSNT Supp: 193. Studies in New Testament Greek: 6. Sheffield: Sheffield, 2000.

Porter, Stanley E. and Sean A. Adams, eds. *Paul and the Ancient Letter Form.* Leiden: Brill, 2010.

Psaltou-Joycey, Angeliki. "Specification of Temporal Intervals and Situations in the Perfect." 153–160 in *Themes in Greek Linguistics*, CILT: 117. Edited by Irene Philippaki-Warburton, Katarina Nicolaidas, and Maria Sifianou. Amsterdam: Benjamins, 1993.

Ralli, Angela. "Morphology in Greek Linguistics: The State of the Art." *JGL* 4 (2003): 77–129.

Reichenbach, Hans. *The Elements of Symbolic Logic.* London: Collier-MacMillan, 1947.

Ricketts, Ernie Clarence. "Discourse Function of Tense, Aspect, and Mood in Ancient Greek Hortatory Epistles." PhD Diss., University of Texas at Arlington, 1999.

Rijksbaron, Albert. *The Syntax and Semantics of the Verb in Classical Greek: An Introduction.* Amsterdam: Gieben, 1984.

———. *The Syntax and Semantics of the Verb in Classical Greek: 3rd edition.* Amsterdam: Gieben, 2002.

Ringe, Donald A., Jr. "The Perfect Tenses in Greek Inscriptions. Vols.1 and 2." PhD Diss., Yale University, 1964.

Rix, Helmut. *Historische Grammatik des Grieschen: Laut- und Formenlehre.* Darmstadt: Wissenschaftliche Buchgesellschaft, 1992.

Robertson, A. T. *A Grammar of the Greek New Testament in the Light of Historical Research.* New York: Hodder and Stoughton, 1914.

Robertson, Paul M. *Paul's Letters and Contemporary Greco-Roman Literature: Theorizing a New Taxonomy.* NovTSupp:167. Edited by M. M. Mitchell and D. P. Moessner. Leiden: Brill, 2016.

Robins, R. H. "Dionysius Thrax and the Western Grammatical Tradition." *Transactions of the Philological Society* 56 (1957): 67–106.

———. *A Short History of Linguistics.* London: Longmans, 1979.

Rothmayr, Antonia. *The Structure of Stative Verbs.* Lingusitik Aktuell:143. Amsterdam: John Benjamins, 2009.

Rubino, Carl. "Reduplication: Form, Function and Distribution." 11–29 in *Studies on Reduplication*, EALT: 28. Edited by Bernard Hurch. Berlin: Mouton de Gruyter, 2005.

Ruipérez, Martín Sánchez. *Estructura del Sistema de Aspectos y Tiempos del Verbo Griego Antiguo: Analisis Funcional Sincronico.* Salamanca: Colegio Trilingue de la Universidad del Consejo Superior de Investigaciones Cientificas, 1954.

Runge, Steven E. "The Contribution of Verb Forms, Connectives, and Dependency to Grounding Status in Nonnarrative Discourse." 221–272 in *The Greek Verb Revisited: A Fresh Approach for Biblical Exegesis.* Edited by Steven E. Runge and Christopher J. Fresch. Bellingham, WA: Lexham, 2016.

Sandell, Ryan. "The Morphology of Reduplicated Presents in Vedic and Indo-European." 223–254 in *Proceedings of the 22nd Annual UCLA Indo-European Conference*, eds. Stephanie W. Jamison, H. Craig Melchert, and Brent Vine. Bremen: Hempen, 2001.

———. "Reduplication and Grammaticalization in Vedic Sanskrit." Presented at ICHL: 20. Osaka: National Museum of Ethnology, 2011.

Saperstein, Andrew David. "A Word-and-Paradigm Approach to Reduplication." PhD diss., Ohio State University, 1997.

Sasse, Hans-Jürgen. "Aspect and Aktionsart." 535–538 in *Encyclopedia of Language and Linguistics.* Edited by Keith Brown. Amsterdam: Elsevier, 2006.

de Saussure, Louis, Jacques Moeschler, and Genoveva Puskás, eds. *Recent Advances in the Syntax and Semantics of Tense, Aspect and Modality*. Trends in Linguistics: Studies and Monographs:185. Berlin: de Gruyter, 2007.

———. *Tense, Mood and Aspect: Theoretical and Descriptive Issues*. Cahiers Chronos:17. Amsterdam: Rodopi, 2007.

Schmid, Monika S., Jennifer R. Austin, and Dieter Stein. *Historical Linguistics 1997: Selected papers from the 13th International Conference on Historical Linguistics, Dusseldorf, 10–17 August*. CILT:164. Amsterdam: John Benjamins, 1997.

Schmidt, Daryl. "Verbal Aspect in Greek: Two Approaches." 63–73 in *Biblical Greek Language and Linguistics: Open Questions in Current Research*. JSNTS 80. Edited by Donald Carson and Stanley Porter. Sheffield: Sheffield Academic Press, 1993.

Sedlacek, James E. "Corpus Composition and Methods for Diachronic Research of Greek Epistolary Literature: Struggles in Obtaining a Meaningful Balance." Forthcoming.

——— "A Diachronic Analysis of The Form of the Greek Perfect and Its Associated Uses: Arguing for a Complex Verbal Aspect." *Proceedings of the 13th International Conference on Greek Linguistics (7–9/9/2017, London): Selected Papers* (London: University of Westminster, 2019: online at http://icgl13.westminster.ac.uk/) 235–247. Accessed 1 January 2020.

———. "Reimagining Οἶδα, Indo-European Etymology, Morphology, and Semantics Point to Its Aspect." *Conversations with the Biblical World* 36 (2016): 206–220.

Shields, Kenneth. *A History of Indo-European Verb Morphology*. CILT:88. Amsterdam: Benjamins, 1992.

Shyldkrot, Hava Bat-Zeev, and Nicole le Querler, eds. *Les Périphrases Verbales*. Lingvisticae Investigationes Supplementa:25. Amsterdam: John Benjamins, 2005.

Sicking, C. M. J., and P. Stork. *Two Studies in the Semantics of the Verb in Classical Greek*. Memnosyne Supplements:160. Leiden: Brill, 1996.

Silva, Moises. "A Response to Fanning and Porter on Verbal Aspect." *Biblical Greek Language and Linguistics: Open Questions in Current Research*. JSNT Supp: 80. Edited by Stanley E. Porter and D. A. Carson. Sheffield: JSOT, 1993.

Smith, Carlota. *The Parameter of Aspect*. Studies in Linguistics and Philosophy: 43. Dordrecht: Springer, 1997.

Smyth, Herbert Weir. *Greek Grammar for Colleges*. New York: American Book Company, 1920.

von Stechow, Arnim. "Eine erweiterte Extended-Now Theorie für Perfekt und Futur." *LiLi* 113, no. 29:1 (March 1999): 86–118.

von Stechow, Arnim, and Dieter Wunderlich, eds. *Semantik*. HSK:6. Berlin: de Gruyter, 1991.

Szemerenyi, Oswald. *Introduction to Indo-European Linguistics*. Oxford: Clarendon, 1966.

Szemerenyi, Oswald. "The Origin of Aspect in the Indo-European Languages." *Glotta* 65 (1987): 1–18.

Taylor, Bernard A., John A. L. Lee, Peter R. Burton, and Richard E. Whitaker, eds. *Biblical Greek Language and Lexicography: Essays in Honor of Frederick W. Danker*. Grand Rapids, MI: Eerdmans, 2004.

Tedeschi, Philip J., and Annie Zaenen, eds. *Tense and Aspect*. Syntax and Semantics:14. New York: Academic, 1981.

Thelin, Nils B. *Towards a Theory of Aspect, Tense and Actionality in Slavic.* Acta Universitatis Upsaliensis. Studia Slavica Upsaliensa:18. Stockholm: Almqvist & Wiksell, 1978.

Thelin, Nils B, ed. *Verbal Aspect in Discourse: Contributions to the Semantics of Time and Temporal Perspective in Slavic and Non-Slavic Languages.* Pragmatics and Beyond:5. Amsterdam: John Benjamins, 1990.

Traugott, Elizabeth Closs, and Bernd Heine. *Approaches to Grammaticalization.* 2 vols. Typological Studies of Languages 19:1, 2. Amsterdam, John Benjamins, 1991.

Tresham, Aaron Keith. "Tense and Aspect in Paul's Epistle to the Romans." ThD Diss., The Master's Seminary, 2011.

Tucker, Elizabeth Fawcett. *The Creation of Morphological Regularity: Early Greek Verbs in -eo, -ao, -oo, -uo, and -io.* Historische Sprachforshung:35 Gottingen: Vandenhoeck & Ruprecht, 1990.

Turner, Nigel. *Syntax.* Grammar of NT Greek: 3. Edinburgh: T & T Clark, 1963.

Veloudis, Ioannis. "The Pragmatic Category 'Perfect.'" 129–136 in *Themes in Greek Linguistics*, CILT: 117. Edited by Irene Philippaki-Warburton, Katarina Nicolaidas, and Maria Sifianou. Amsterdam: Benjamins, 1993.

Verhoeven, Elisabeth, Stavros Skopeteas, Yong-Min Shin, Yoko Nishina, and Johannes Helmbrecht, eds. *Studies on Grammaticalization.* Trends in Linguistics: Studies and Monographs:205. Berlin: de Gruyter, 2008.

Verkuyl, Henk J. *On the Compositional Nature of the Aspects.* FL supplementary Series, 15: Dordrecht: D. Reidel, 1972.

Versteegh, C. H. M. "The Stoic Verbal System." *Hermes* 108, no. 3 (1980): 338–357.

Wackernagel, Jacob. *Kleine Schriften.* 3 Banden. Göttingen: Vandenhoeck und Ruprecht, 1955, 1979.

———. "Studien zum Griechischen Perfectum." 3–21 in *Programm zur Akademischen Preisverteilung* (Göttingen: Universitatus Georgiae Augustae, 1904), reprinted in *Kleine Schriften*, II (Göttingen: Vandenhoek and Ruprecht, 1953), 1000–1021.

Walde, Alois. *Vergleichendes Worterbuch der Indogermanischen Sprachen.* Herausgegeben und Bearbeitet von Julius Pokorny. 3 Banden. (Originally published in 1930, 1927, and 1932). Berlin und Leipzig: Walter De Gruyter, 1973.

Wallace, Daniel B. *Greek Grammar, Beyond the Basics: An Exegetical Syntax of the New Testament.* Grand Rapids, MI: Zondervan, 1996.

Weima, Jeffery A. D. *Paul the Ancient Letter Writer: An Introduction to Epistolary Analysis.* Grand Rapids, MI: Baker, 2016.

White, John L. "Ancient Greek Letters." 85–105 in *Greco-Roman Literature and the New Testament.* SBL Sources for Biblical Study: 21. Edited by David E. Aune. Atlanta: Scholars, 1988.

Wischer, Ilse, and Gabriele Diewald. *New Reflections on Grammaticalization.* Typological Studies in Language:49. Amsterdam: John Benjamins, 2002.

Xydopoulos, George J. "Tense and Temporal Adverbs in Greek." 263–276 in *Studies in Greek Syntax*, Studies in Natural Language and Linguistic Theory: 43. Edited by Artemis Alexiadou, Geoffrey Horrocks, and Melita Stavrou. New York: Springer, 1999.

Zukoff, Sam. "On the Origins of Attic Reduplication." 257–278 in *Proceedings of the 25th Annual UCLA Indo-European Conference.* Edited by Stephanie W. Jamison, H. Craig Melchert, and Brent Vine. Bremen: Hampen, 2014.

———. "The Phonology of Verbal Reduplication in Ancient Greek: An Optimality Theory Approach." MA diss., The University of Georgia, 2012.

Text Commentaries

Abbott, Thomas Kingsmill. *A Critical and Exegetical Commentary on the Epistles to the Ephesians and the Colossians*. ICC. New York: Scribner's, 1909.

Anders, Max. *Galatians-Colossians*. HNTC: 8. Nashville, TN: Broadman & Holman, 1999.

Arichea, Daniel C., and Eugene Albert Nida. *A Handbook on Paul's Letter to the Galatians*. UBS Handbook Series. New York: United Bible Societies, 1976.

Baker, William R. *2 Corinthians*. The College Press NIV Commentary. Joplin, MO: College Press, 1999.

Barnett, Paul. *The Second Epistle to the Corinthians*. NICNT. Grand Rapids, MI: Eerdmans, 1997.

Barth, Marcus. *Ephesians: Introduction, Translation, and Commentary on Chapters 1–3*. AB:34. New Haven, CT: Yale, 2008.

Barth, Marcus, Helmut Blanke, and Astrid B. Beck. *Colossians: A New Translation with Introduction and Commentary*. AB: 34A. New Haven, CT: Yale University Press, 2005.

Best, Ernest. *A Critical and Exegetical Commentary on Ephesians*. ICC. Edinburgh: T&T Clark, 1998.

Blanke, Helmut, and Astrid B. Beck. *Colossians: A New Translation with Introduction and Commentary*. AB:34A. New Haven, CT: Yale University Press, 2008.

Boles, Kenneth L. *Galatians & Ephesians*. The College Press NIV Commentary. Joplin, MO: College Press, 1993.

Bratcher, Robert G., and Eugene Albert Nida. *A Handbook on Paul's Letter to the Ephesians*. UBS Handbook Series. New York: United Bible Societies, 1993.

Bruce, F. F. *The Epistle to the Galatians: A Commentary on the Greek Text*. NIGTC. Grand Rapids, MI: Eerdmans, 1982.

Burton, Ernest De Witt. *A Critical and Exegetical Commentary on the Epistle to the Galatians*. ICC. New York: Scribner's, 1920.

Conzelmann, Hans. *1 Corinthians: A Commentary on the First Epistle to the Corinthians*. Hermeneia—A Critical and Historical Commentary on the Bible. Philadelphia, PA: Fortress, 1975.

Cottrell, Jack. *Romans*. The College Press NIV Commentary. Joplin, MO: College Press, 1996.

Cranfield, C. E. B. *A Critical and Exegetical Commentary on the Epistle to the Romans*. ICC. London: T&T Clark, 2004.

Dunn, James D. G. *Romans 1–8*. WBC:38a. Dallas: Word, 1998.

Ellicott, Charles J. *St. Paul's First Epistle to the Corinthians: With a Critical and Grammatical Commentary*. London: Longmans, 1887.

Fee, Gordon D. *The First Epistle to the Corinthians*. NICNT. Grand Rapids, MI: Eerdmans, 1987.

Fitzmyer, Joseph A., S. J. *Romans: A New Translation with Introduction and Commentary* AB:33. New Haven, CT: Yale University Press, 2008.

Furnish, Victor Paul. *II Corinthians: Translated with Introduction, Notes, and Commentary.* AB:32A. New Haven, CT: Yale University Press, 2008.

Hansen, G. Walter. *Galatians.* The IVP New Testament Commentary Series. Downers Grove, IL: InterVarsity, 1994.

Harris, Murray J. *The Second Epistle to the Corinthians: A Commentary on the Greek Text.* NIGTC. Grand Rapids, MI: Eerdmans, 2005.

Jewett, Robert, and Roy David Kotansky. *Romans: A Commentary.* Hermeneia—A Critical and Historical Commentary on the Bible. Edited by Eldon Jay Epp. Minneapolis, MN: Fortress, 2006.

Johnson, Alan F. *1 Corinthians.* The IVP New Testament Commentary Series: 7. Downers Grove, IL: InterVarsity, 2004.

Lange, John Peter, et al. *A Commentary on the Holy Scriptures: Romans.* Bellingham, WA: Lexham, 2008.

Lenski, R. C. H. *The Interpretation of St. Paul's Epistle to the Romans.* Columbus, OH: Lutheran Book Concern, 1936.

———. *The Interpretation of St. Paul's Epistles to the Colossians, to the Thessalonians, to Timothy, to Titus and to Philemon.* Columbus, OH: Lutheran Book Concern, 1937.

———. *The Interpretation of St. Paul's First and Second Epistle to the Corinthians.* Minneapolis, MN: Augsburg, 1963.

Lincoln, Andrew T. *Ephesians.* WBC:42. Dallas: Word, 1990.

Lohse, Edward. *Colossians and Philemon A Commentary on the Epistles to the Colossians and to Philemon.* Hermeneia—A Critical and Historical Commentary on the Bible. Philadelphia, PA: Fortress, 1971.

Longenecker, Richard N. *Galatians.* WBC:41. Dallas, TX: Word, 1998.

Martin, Ralph P. *2 Corinthians.* WBC:40. Dallas, TX: Word, 1998.

Melick, Richard R. *Philippians, Colossians, Philemon.* NAC:32. Nashville, TN: Broadman & Holman, 1991.

Moo, Douglas J. *The Epistle to the Romans.* NICNT. Grand Rapids, MI: Eerdmans, 1996.

Morris, Leon. *The Epistle to the Romans.* PNTC. Grand Rapids, MI: Eerdmans, 1988.

Mounce, Robert H. *Romans.* NAC: 27. Nashville, TN: Broadman & Holman, 1995.

O'Brien, Peter Thomas. *The Letter to the Ephesians.* PNTC. Grand Rapids, MI: Eerdmans, 1999.

Orr, William F., and James Arthur Walther. *I Corinthians: A New Translation, Introduction, with a Study of the Life of Paul, Notes, and Commentary.* AB: 32. New Haven, CT: Yale University Press, 2008.

Osborne, Grant R. *Romans.* The IVP New Testament Commentary Series. Downers Grove, IL: InterVarsity, 2004.

Oster, Richard. *1 Corinthians.* The College Press NIV Commentary. Joplin, MO: College Press, 1995.

Plummer, Alfred. *A Critical and Exegetical Commentary on the Second Epistle of St. Paul to the Corinthians.* ICC. New York: T&T Clark, 1915.

Robertson, Archibald, and Alfred Plummer, *A Critical and Exegetical Commentary on the First Epistle of St. Paul to the Corinthians.* ICC. New York: T&T Clark, 1911.

Schreiner, Thomas R. *Romans.* BECNT:6. Grand Rapids, MI: Baker, 1998.

Thiselton, Anthony C. *The First Epistle to the Corinthians: A Commentary on the Greek Text.* NIGTC. Grand Rapids, MI: Eerdmans, 2000.

Thrall, Margaret E. *A Critical and Exegetical Commentary on the Second Epistle of the Corinthians.* ICC. London: T&T Clark, 2004.

Toews, John E. *Romans.* Believers Church Bible Commentary. Scottdale, PA: Herald Press, 2004.

Appendix A

Rationale and Purpose of the Appendices

The first set of appendices include the data used for discovering the core aspectual morphemes of Perfect tenses. Appendix B contains a chart that shows all the morphological components and processes of each Perfect in the Pauline corpus. This data was collected in order to determine what morphemes might be associated with aspect, contrasting the morphemes that have a different purpose. Appendix C contains a chart that shows all of the stems and occurrences of the verbs that use that stem within the Pauline corpus. It contains both ordinal numbers by each instance and cardinal numbers at the end to tally the totals. Appendix D orders that same list of stems by frequency for ease of viewing. These three appendices together inform the morphological analysis of the stem of the Perfect leading to the conclusion that it mirrors the Aorist in its stem vowel. Some of this data was reported in section 3.2.2.1.

This second set of charts include collocate data used to determine which Perfects were eventive and which ones were stative. Appendix E contains a chart that tracks various contextual items collocated with each Perfect in the Pauline corpus. This collection was performed in order to establish which contextual items might be predictors of certain behaviours of the Perfect tense-forms. The adverb and adverbial prepositions appear to be the most important of these. Appendix F contains specific adverb data collocated with Perfect tenses that appear to have a stative force. Appendix G contains specific adverb data collocated with Perfect tenses that appear to have eventive force. Appendix H contains a chart of adverb frequency data, and Appendix I identifies key adverbs for the searches. These 5 appendices together inform section 3.2.5 where adverb data helps to show that some Perfects focus on the event and others on the state. Appendix J contains specific adverb data collocated with Perfects that were used in supplemental clauses of categories A and B described in section 4.1.4.

Appendix K contains a list of the Pauline Perfect tense form examples from which the examples were selected for analysis in Chapter 4. Appendix L contains all the observed examples from the analysis corpus that were consulted to compare and contrast the Pauline corpus. Many of these were used in Chapter 5. Appendix M contains all the available forms for the verbs found as a Perfect tense-form in the Pauline corpus.

Appendix B

Chart of Morphemes

This appendix contains a chart of the morphemes present in each perfect tense-form in the Pauline corpus. They are organised by verse order in the corpus. The Perfect tense-forms are presented first, followed by the Pluperfect. An additional chart at the end will analyze productive morphological patterns observed in the first chart. These patterns are observed repeatedly whenever the same conditions occur.

Perfect tense-forms							
Reference	Pf tense-form	Reduplicant	Present Stem	Pf Affix to the Stem	Middle to Active	Active to Middle	Aorist Affix to the Stem
Rom 1:1	ἀφωρισμένος	ὁ → ὠ	ὁριζ	ζ → σ	σ → κ	---	ζ → σ
Rom 1:17	γέγραπται	+ γε	γραφ	--- (active) φ → π (middle)	π → φ	φ → π	--- (strong) φ → π (weak)
Rom 1:29	πεπληρωμένους	+ πε	πληρο	ο(υ) → ω	+ κ	- κ	ο(υ) → ω
Rom 2:2	οἴδαμεν	+ Ϝε	Ϝιδ	---	---	α → η	unclear
Rom 2:19	πέποιθάς	+ πε	πειθ	ειθ → οιθ	---	θ → σ	ειθ → ιθ
Rom 2:24	γέγραπται	+ γε	γραφ	--- (active) φ → π (middle)	π → φ	φ → π	--- (strong) φ → π (weak)
Rom 2:25	γέγονεν	+ γε	γν from γιγν	γν → γον or γεν (weak Pf)	---	γον → γος	γν → γεν

Perfect tense-forms							
Rom 3:4	γέγραπται	+ γε	γραφ	--- (active) φ → π (middle)	π → φ	φ → π	--- (strong) φ → π (weak)
Rom 3:10	γέγραπται	+ γε	γραφ	--- (active) φ → π (middle)	π → φ	φ → π	--- (strong) φ → π (weak)
Rom 3:13	ἀνεῳγμένος	οι → εφ	οιγ	οιγ → εῳχ	γ → χ	---	οιγ → οιχ or εῳχ
Rom 3:19	οἴδαμεν	+ ϝε	ϝιδ	---	---	α → η	unclear
Rom 3:21	πεφανέρωται	+ πε	φανερο	ο(υ) → ω	+ κ	- κ	ο(υ) → ω
Rom 3:25	προγεγονότων	+ γε	γν from γιγν	γν → γον or γεν (weak Pf)	---	γον → γος	γν → γεν
Rom 4:1	εὑρηκέναι	---	ἑυρι	ι → η	+ κ	- κ	ι → η
Rom 4:14	κεκένωται	+ κε	κενο	ο(υ) → ω	+ κ	- κ	ο(υ) → ω
Rom 4:14	κατήργηται	ε → η	αργε	α → η and ε → η	+ κ	- κ	α → η and ε → η
Rom 4:17	γέγραπται	+ γε	γραφ	--- (active) φ → π (middle)	π → φ	φ → π	--- (strong) φ → π (weak)
Rom 4:17	τέθεικά	+ τε	θη	---	+ κ	- κ	---
Rom 4:18	εἰρημένον	+ ει	ρε	ε → η	+ κ	- κ	ε → η or ο
Rom 4:19	νενεκρωμένον	+ νε	νεκρο	ο(υ) → ω	+ κ	- κ	ο(υ) → ω
Rom 4:21	ἐπήγγελται	α → η	αγγελλ	αγγελλ → ηγγελ	+ κ	- κ	αγγελλ → ηγγελ
Rom 5:2	ἐσχήκαμεν	---	εχ	εχ → εσχη	+ κ	- κ	εχ → εσχο
Rom 5:2	ἐστήκαμεν	+ ἑ	στη	---	--- (strong) + κ (weak)	- κ	---
Rom 5:3	εἰδότες	+ ϝε	ϝιδ	---	---	ο → η	unclear
Rom 5:5	ἐκκέχυται	+ κε	χε	χε → χυ	+ κ	- κ	χε → χυ
Rom 6:5	γεγόναμεν	+ γε	γν from γιγν	γν → γον or γεν (weak Pf)	---	γον → γος	γν → γεν
Rom 6:7	δεδικαίωται	+ δε	δικαιο	ο(υ) → ω	+ κ	- κ	ο(υ) → ω
Rom 6:9	εἰδότες	+ ϝε	ϝιδ	---	---	ο → η	unclear
Rom 6:16	οἴδατε	+ ϝε	ϝιδ	---	---	ο → η	unclear
Rom 7:2	δέδεται	+ δε	δε	δε → δη or no change	+ κ	- κ	δε → δη
Rom 7:2	κατήργηται	ε → η	αργε	α → η and ε → η	+ κ	- κ	α → η and ε → η
Rom 7:14	οἴδαμεν	+ ϝε	ϝιδ	---	---	α → η	unclear
Rom 7:14	πεπραμένος	+ πε	πρα	---	+ κ	- κ	περα
Rom 7:18	οἶδα	+ ϝε	ϝιδ	---	---	α → η	unclear
Rom 8:22	οἴδαμεν	+ ϝε	ϝιδ	---	---	α → η	unclear
Rom 8:26	οἴδαμεν	+ ϝε	ϝιδ	---	---	α → η	unclear

Perfect tense-forms						
Rom 8:27	οἶδεν	+ ϝε	ϝιδ	-·-	---	α → η	unclear
Rom 8:28	οἴδαμεν	+ ϝε	ϝιδ	---	---	α → η	unclear
Rom 8:36	γέγραπται	+ γε	γραφ	--- (active) φ → π (middle)	π → φ	φ → π	--- (strong) φ → π (weak)
Rom 8:38	πέπεισμαι	+ πε	πειθ	θ → σ	+ κ	- κ	θ → σ
Rom 8:38	ἐνεστῶτα	ἑ	στη	στο or στω (strong only)	+ κ (weak only)	- κ	---
Rom 9:6	ἐκπέπτωκεν	+ πε	πτω	---	+ κ	- κ	πτω → πεσ
Rom 9:13	γέγραπται	+ γε	γραφ	--- (active) φ → π (middle)	π → φ	φ → π	--- (strong) φ → π (weak)
Rom 9:19	ἀνθέστηκεν	+ ἑ	στη	---	---(strong) + κ (weak)	- κ	---
Rom 9:22	κατηρτισμένα	α → η	αρτιζ	- ζ	+ κ	- κ	- ζ
Rom 9:25	ἠγαπημένην	α → η	αγαπα	Final α → η	+ κ	- κ	Final α → η
Rom 9:25	ἠγαπημένην	α → η	αγαπα	Final α → η	+ κ	- κ	Final α → η
Rom 9:29	προείρηκεν	+ ει	ρε	ε → η	+ κ	- κ	ε → η or ο
Rom 9:33	γέγραπται	+ γε	γραφ	--- (active) φ → π (middle)	π → φ	φ → π	--- (strong) φ → π (weak)
Rom 10:15	γέγραπται	+ γε	γραφ	--- (active) φ → π (middle)	π → φ	φ → π	--- (strong) φ → π (weak)
Rom 11:2	οἶδατε	+ ϝε	ϝιδ	---	---	ο → η	unclear
Rom 11:5	γέγονεν	+ γε	γν from γιγν	γν → γον or γεν (weak Pf)	---	γον → γος	γν → γεν
Rom 11:8	γέγραπται	+ γε	γραφ	--- (active) φ → π (middle)	π → φ	φ → π	--- (strong) φ → π (weak)
Rom 11:20	ἔστηκας	+ ἑ	στη	---	---(strong) + κ (weak)	- κ	---
Rom 11:25	γέγονεν	+ γε	γν from γιγν	γν → γον or γεν (weak Pf)	---	γον → γος	γν → γεν
Rom 11:26	γέγραπται	+ γε	γραφ	--- (active) φ → π (middle)	π → φ	φ → π	--- (strong) φ → π (weak)
Rom 12:19	γέγραπται	+ γε	γραφ	--- (active) φ → π (middle)	π → φ	φ → π	--- (strong) φ → π (weak)
Rom 13:1	τεταγμέναι	+ τε	τασσ	σσ → γ or χ	γ → χ	χ → γ	σσ → γ or χ
Rom 13:2	ἀνθέστηκεν	+ ἑ	στη	---	---(strong) + κ (weak)	- κ	---
Rom 13:2	ἀνθεστηκότες	+ ἑ	στη	---	---(strong) + κ (weak)	- κ	---
Rom 13:8	πεπλήρωκεν	+ πε	πληρο	ο(υ) → ω	+ κ	- κ	ο(υ) → ω
Rom 13:11	εἰδότες	+ ϝε	ϝιδ	---	---	ο → η	unclear
Rom 13:12	ἤγγικεν	ε → η	εγγιζ	- ζ	+ κ	- κ	- ζ

Perfect tense-forms							
Rom 14:11	γέγραπται	+ γε	γραφ	--- (active) φ → π (middle)	π → φ	φ → π	--- (strong) φ → π (weak)
Rom 14:14	οἶδα	+ ϝε	ϝιδ	---	---	α → η	unclear
Rom 14:14	πέπεισμαι	+ πε	πειθ	θ → σ	+ κ	- κ	θ → σ
Rom 14:23	κατακέκριται	+ κε	κριν	κρι	+ κ	- κ	---
Rom 15:3	γέγραπται	+ γε	γραφ	--- (active) φ → π (middle)	π → φ	φ → π	--- (strong) φ → π (weak)
Rom 15:8	γεγενῆσθαι	+ γε	γν from γιγν	γν → γον or γεν (weak Pf)	---	γον → γος	γν → γεν
Rom 15:9	γέγραπται	+ γε	γραφ	--- (active) φ → π (middle)	π → φ	φ → π	--- (strong) φ → π (weak)
Rom 15:14	πέπεισμαι	+ πε	πειθ	θ → σ	+ κ	- κ	θ → σ
Rom 15:14	πεπληρωμένοι	+ πε	πληρο	ο(υ) → ω	+ κ	- κ	ο(υ) → ω
Rom 15:16	ἡγιασμένη	α → η	ἁγιαζ	- ζ	+ κ	- κ + σ	- ζ
Rom 15:19	πεπληρωκέναι	+ πε	πληρο	ο(υ) → ω	+ κ	- κ	ο(υ) → ω
Rom 15:21	γέγραπται	+ γε	γραφ	--- (active) φ → π (middle)	π → φ	φ → π	--- (strong) φ → π (weak)
Rom 15:21	ἀκηκόασιν	+ ακ	ακου	ακου → ηκο	+ κ	- κ	---
Rom 15:29	οἶδα	+ ϝε	ϝιδ	---	---	α → η	unclear
Rom 16:7	γέγονεν	+ γε	γν from γιγν	γν → γον or γεν (weak Pf)	---	γον → γος	γν → γεν
Rom 16:25	σεσιγημένου	+ σε	σιγα	Final α → η	+ κ	- κ	Final α → η
1 Cor 1:2	ἡγιασμένοις	α → η	ἁγιαζ	- ζ	+ κ	- κ + σ	- ζ
1 Cor 1:10	κατηρτισμένοι	α → η	αρτιζ	- ζ	+ κ	- κ + σ	- ζ
1 Cor 1:13	μεμέρισται	+ με	μεριζ	- ζ	+ κ	- κ + σ	- ζ
1 Cor 1:16	οἶδα	+ ϝε	ϝιδ	---	---	α → η	unclear
1 Cor 1:19	γέγραπται	+ γε	γραφ	--- (active) φ → π (middle)	π → φ	φ → π	--- (strong) φ → π (weak)
1 Cor 1:23	ἐσταυρωμένον	+ ε	σταυρο	ο(υ) → ω	+ κ	- κ	ο(υ) → ω
1 Cor 1:28	ἐξουθενημένα	---	ουθενε	---	+ κ	- κ	---
1 Cor 1:31	γέγραπται	+ γε	γραφ	--- (active) φ → π (middle)	π → φ	φ → π	--- (strong) φ → π (weak)
1 Cor 2:2	εἰδέναι	+ ϝε	ϝιδ	---	---	ο → η	unclear
1 Cor 2:2	ἐσταυρωμένον	+ ε	σταυρο	ο(υ) → ω	+ κ	- κ	ο(υ) → ω
1 Cor 2:7	ἀποκεκρυμμένην	+ κε	κρυπτ	πτ → φ	μ → φ	φ → μ	πτ → φ or ψ
1 Cor 2:8	ἔγνωκεν	+ ε	γνω	---	+ κ	- κ	---
1 Cor 2:9	γέγραπται	+ γε	γραφ	--- (active) φ → π (middle)	π → φ	φ → π	--- (strong) φ → π (weak)
1 Cor 2:11	οἶδεν	+ ϝε	ϝιδ	---	---	α → η	unclear

Perfect tense-forms

1 Cor 2:11	ἔγνωκεν	+ ε	γνω	---	+ κ	- κ	---
1 Cor 2:12	εἰδῶμεν	+ ϝε	ϝιδ	---	---	α → η	unclear
1 Cor 3:16	οἴδατε	+ ϝε	ϝιδ	---	---	α → η	unclear
1 Cor 3:19	γέγραπται	+ γε	γραφ	--- (active) φ → π (middle)	π → φ	φ → π	--- (strong) φ → π (weak)
1 Cor 3:22	ἐνεστῶτα	+ ἑ	στη	στο or στω (strong only)	+ κ (weak only)	- κ	---
1 Cor 4:4	σύνοιδα	+ ϝε	ϝιδ	---	---	α → η	unclear
1 Cor 4:4	δεδικαίωμαι	+ δε	δικαιο	o(υ) → ω	+ κ	- κ	o(υ) → ω
1 Cor 4:6	γέγραπται	+ γε	γραφ	--- (active) φ → π (middle)	π → φ	φ → π	--- (strong) φ → π (weak)
1 Cor 4:8	κεκορεσμένοι	+ κε	κορενν	νν → σ or - νν	σ → κ	κ → σ	νν → σ
1 Cor 4:19	πεφυσιωμένων	+ πε	φυσιο	o(υ) → ω	+ κ	- κ	o(υ) → ω
1 Cor 5:2	πεφυσιωμένοι ἐστὲ	+ πε	φυσιο	o(υ) → ω	+ κ	- κ	o(υ) → ω
1 Cor 5:3	κέκρικα	+ κε	κριν	κρι	+ κ	- κ	---
1 Cor 5:6	οἴδατε	+ ϝε	ϝιδ	---	---	α → η	unclear
1 Cor 6:2	οἴδατε	+ ϝε	ϝιδ	---	---	α → η	unclear
1 Cor 6:3	οἴδατε	+ ϝε	ϝιδ	---	---	α → η	unclear
1 Cor 6:4	ἐξουθενημένους	---	ουθενε	---	+ κ	- κ	---
1 Cor 6:9	οἴδατε	+ ϝε	ϝιδ	---	---	α → η	unclear
1 Cor 6:15	οἴδατε	+ ϝε	ϝιδ	---	---	α → η	unclear
1 Cor 6:16	οἴδατε	+ ϝε	ϝιδ	---	---	α → η	unclear
1 Cor 6:19	οἴδατε	+ ϝε	ϝιδ	---	---	α → η	unclear
1 Cor 7:10	γεγαμηκόσιν	+ γε	γαμε	ε → η	+ κ	- κ	ε → α or η
1 Cor 7:14	ἡγίασται	α → η	ἁγιαζ	- ζ	+ κ	- κ + σ	- ζ
1 Cor 7:14	ἡγίασται	α → η	ἁγιαζ	- ζ	+ κ	- κ + σ	- ζ
1 Cor 7:15	δεδούλωται	+ δε	δουλο	o(υ) → ω	+ κ	- κ	o(υ) → ω
1 Cor 7:15	κέκληκεν	+ κε	καλε	καλε → κλη	+ κ	- κ	--- καλε → κλη only in passive
1 Cor 7:16	οἴδας	+ ϝε	ϝιδ	---	---	α → η	unclear
1 Cor 7:16	οἴδας	+ ϝε	ϝιδ	---	---	α → η	unclear
1 Cor 7:17	κέκληκεν	+ κε	καλε	καλε → κλη	+ κ	- κ	--- καλε → κλη only in passive
1 Cor 7:18	περιτετμημένος	+ τε	τεμν	τεμν → τμη	+ κ	- κ	τεμν → τμη or τεμ

Perfect tense-forms

1 Cor 7:18	κέκληταί	+ κε	καλε	καλε → κλη	+ κ	- κ	--- καλε → κλη only in passive
1 Cor 7:25	ἠλεημένος	ε → η	ελεε	ελεε → ελεη	+ κ	- κ	ελεε → ελεη
1 Cor 7:26	ἐνεστῶσαν	+ έ	στη	στο or στω (strong only)	+ κ (weak only)	- κ	---
1 Cor 7:27	δέδεσαι	+ δε	δε	δε → δη or no change	+ κ	- κ	δε → δη
1 Cor 7:27	λέλυσαι	+ λε	λυ	----	+ κ	- κ	---
1 Cor 7:29	συνεσταλμένος ἐστίν	+ ε	στελλ	στελλ → σταλ	+ κ	- κ	στελλ → σταλ
1 Cor 7:34	μεμέρισται	+ με	μεριζ	- ζ	+ κ	- κ + σ	- ζ
1 Cor 7:37	ἕστηκεν	+ έ	στη	---	---(strong) + κ (weak)	- κ	---
1 Cor 7:37	κέκρικεν	+ κε	κριν	κρι	+ κ	- κ	---
1 Cor 7:39	δέδεται	+ δε	δε	δε → δη or no change	+ κ	- κ	δε → δη
1 Cor 8:1	οἴδαμεν	+ ϝε	ϝιδ	---	---	α → η	unclear
1 Cor 8:2	ἐγνωκέναι	+ ε	γνω	---	+ κ	- κ	---
1 Cor 8:3	ἔγνωσται	+ ε	γνω	---	+ κ	- κ	---
1 Cor 8:4	οἴδαμεν	+ ϝε	ϝιδ	---	---	α → η	unclear
1 Cor 9:1	ἑόρακα	+ έ	ὁρα	---	+ κ	- κ	---
1 Cor 9:9	γέγραπται	+ γε	γραφ	--- (active) φ → π (middle)	π → φ	φ → π	--- (strong) φ → π (weak)
1 Cor 9:13	οἴδατε	+ ϝε	ϝιδ	---	---	α → η	unclear
1 Cor 9:15	κέχρημαι	+ κε	χρα	Final α → η	+ κ	- κ	Final α → η
1 Cor 9:17	πεπίστευμαι	+ πε	πιστευ	---	+ κ	- κ	----
1 Cor 9:22	γέγονα	+ γε	γν from γιγν	γν → γον or γεν (weak Pf)	---	γον → γος	γν → γεν
1 Cor 9:24	οἴδατε	+ ϝε	ϝιδ	---	---	α → η	unclear
1 Cor 10:7	γέγραπται	+ γε	γραφ	--- (active) φ → π (middle)	π → φ	φ → π	--- (strong) φ → π (weak)
1 Cor 10:11	κατήντηκεν	+ ε	αντα	Final α → η	+ κ	- κ	Final α → η
1 Cor 10:12	ἑστάναι	+ έ	στη	---	---(strong) + κ (weak)	- κ	---
1 Cor 10:13	εἴληφεν	+ ει	λαμβαν	λαμβαν → ληφ	Endings only	Endings only	λαμβαν → λαβ or ληφ
1 Cor 11:2	μέμνησθε	+ με	μνη	---	+ κ	- κ	---
1 Cor 11:3	εἰδέναι	+ ϝε	ϝιδ	---	---	α → η	unclear
1 Cor 11:5	ἐξυρημένη	+ ε	ξυρε	ε → η	+ κ	- κ	ε → η or α

Perfect tense-forms							
1 Cor 11:15	δέδοται	+ δε	δω	---	+ κ	- κ	---
1 Cor 12:2	οἶδατε	+ ϝε	ϝιδ	---	---	α → η	unclear
1 Cor 13:1	γέγονα	+ γε	γν from γιγν	γν → γον or γεν (weak Pf)	---	γον → γος	γν → γεν
1 Cor 13:2	εἰδῶ	+ ϝε	ϝιδ	---	---	α → η	unclear
1 Cor 13:11	γέγονα	+ γε	γν from γιγν	γν → γον or γεν (weak Pf)	---	γον → γος	γν → γεν
1 Cor 13:11	κατήργηκα	ε → η	αργε	α → η and ε → η	+ κ	- κ	α → η and ε → η
1 Cor 14:11	εἰδῶ	+ ϝε	ϝιδ	---	---	α → η	unclear
1 Cor 14:16	οἶδεν	+ ϝε	ϝιδ	---	---	α → η	unclear
1 Cor 14:21	γέγραπται	+ γε	γραφ	--- (active) φ → π (middle)	π → φ	φ → π	--- (strong) φ → π (weak)
1 Cor 15:1	ἑστήκατε	+ ἑ	στη	---	--- (strong) + κ (weak)	- κ	---
1 Cor 15:4	ἐγήγερται	+ εγε	εγειρ	εγειρ → εγερ	+ κ	- κ	--- (weak) or εγειρ → γρ (strong)
1 Cor 15:12	ἐγήγερται	+ εγε	εγειρ	εγειρ → εγερ	+ κ	- κ	--- (weak) or εγειρ → γρ (strong)
1 Cor 15:13	ἐγήγερται	+ εγε	εγειρ	εγειρ → εγερ	+ κ	- κ	--- (weak) or εγειρ → γρ (strong)
1 Cor 15:14	ἐγήγερται	+ εγε	εγειρ	εγειρ → εγερ	+ κ	- κ	--- (weak) or εγειρ → γρ (strong)
1 Cor 15:16	ἐγήγερται	+ εγε	εγειρ	εγειρ → εγερ	+ κ	- κ	--- (weak) or εγειρ → γρ (strong)
1 Cor 15:17	ἐγήγερται	+ εγε	εγειρ	εγειρ → εγερ	+ κ	- κ	--- (weak) or εγειρ → γρ (strong)
1 Cor 15:19	ἠλπικότες ἐσμὲν	+ ε	ελπιζ	- ζ	+ κ	- κ + σ	- ζ
1 Cor 15:20	ἐγήγερται	+ εγε	εγειρ	εγειρ → εγερ	+ κ	- κ	--- (weak) or εγειρ → γρ (strong)
1 Cor 15:20	κεκοιμημένων	+ κε	κοιμα	Final α → η	+ κ	- κ	Final α → η
1 Cor 15:27	ὑποτέτακται	+ τε	τασσ	σσ → γ or χ	γ → χ	χ → γ	σσ → γ or χ
1 Cor 15:45	γέγραπται	+ γε	γραφ	--- (active) φ → π (middle)	π → φ	φ → π	--- (strong) φ → π (weak)

Perfect tense-forms							
1 Cor 15:54	γεγραμμένος	+ γε	γραφ	--- (active) φ → π (middle)	π → φ	φ → π π before μ is μμ	--- (strong) φ → π (weak)
1 Cor 15:58	εἰδότες	+ ϝε	ϝιδ	---	---	α → η	unclear
1 Cor 16:9	ἀνέῳγεν	οι → ῳ	οιγ	οιγ → εῳχ	γ → χ	---	οιγ → οιχ or εῳχ
1 Cor 16:15	οἴδατε	+ ϝε	ϝιδ	---	---	α → η	unclear
2 Cor 1:7	εἰδότες	+ ϝε	ϝιδ	---	---	α → η	unclear
2 Cor 1:9	ἐσχήκαμεν	---	εχ	εχ → εσχη	+ κ	- κ	εχ → εσχο
2 Cor 1:9	πεποιθότες ὦμεν	+ πε	πειθ	ειθ → οιθ	---	θ → σ	ειθ → ιθ
2 Cor 1:10	ἠλπίκαμεν	+ ε	ελπιζ	- ζ	+ κ	- κ + σ	- ζ
2 Cor 1:19	γέγονεν	+ γε	γν from γιγν	γν → γον or γεν (weak Pf)	---	γον → γος	γν → γεν
2 Cor 1:24	ἑστήκατε	+ ἑ	στη	---	+ κ	- κ	---
2 Cor 2:3	πεποιθὼς	+ πε	πειθ	ειθ → οιθ	---	θ → σ	ειθ → ιθ
2 Cor 2:5	λελύπηκεν	+ λε	λυπε	ε → η	+ κ	- κ	ε → η
2 Cor 2:5	λελύπηκεν	+ λε	λυπε	ε → η	+ κ	- κ	ε → η
2 Cor 2:10	κεχάρισμαι	+ κε	χαριζ	- ζ	+ κ	- κ + σ	- ζ
2 Cor 2:10	κεχάρισμαι	+ κε	χαριζ	- ζ	+ κ	- κ + σ	- ζ
2 Cor 2:12	ἀνεῳγμένης	οι → ῳ	οιγ	οιγ → εῳχ	γ → χ	---	οιγ → οιχ or εῳχ
2 Cor 2:13	ἔσχηκα	---	εχ	εχ → εσχη	+ κ	- κ	εχ → εσχο
2 Cor 3:2	ἐγγεγραμμένη	+ γε	γραφ	--- (active) φ → π (middle)	π → φ	φ → π π before μ is μμ	--- (strong) φ → π (weak)
2 Cor 3:3	ἐγγεγραμμένη	+ γε	γραφ	--- (active) φ → π (middle)	π → φ	φ → π π before μ is μμ	--- (strong) φ → π (weak)
2 Cor 3:7	ἐντετυπωμένη	+ ε	τυπο	ο → ω	+ κ	- κ	ο → ω
2 Cor 3:10	δεδόξασται	+ δε	δοξαζ	- ζ	+ κ	- κ + σ	- ζ
2 Cor 3:10	δεδοξασμένον	+ δε	δοξαζ	- ζ	+ κ	- κ + σ	- ζ
2 Cor 3:18	ἀνακεκαλυμμένῳ	+ κε	καλυπτ	καλυπτ → καλυφ	Endings only	Endings only π before μ is μμ	καλυπτ → καλυφ
2 Cor 4:3	κεκαλυμμένον	+ κε	καλυπτ	καλυπτ → καλυφ	Endings only	Endings only π before μ is μμ	καλυπτ → καλυφ

Perfect tense-forms							
2 Cor 4:3	κεκαλυμμένον	+ κε	καλυπτ	καλυπτ → καλυφ	Endings only	Endings only π before μ is μμ	καλυπτ → καλυφ
2 Cor 4:13	γεγραμμένον	+ γε	γραφ	--- (active) φ → π (middle)	π → φ	φ → π π before μ is μμ	--- (strong) φ → π (weak)
2 Cor 4:14	εἰδότες	+ ϝε	ϝιδ	---	---	α → η	unclear
2 Cor 5:1	οἴδαμεν	+ ϝε	ϝιδ	---	---	α → η	unclear
2 Cor 5:6	εἰδότες	+ ϝε	ϝιδ	---	---	α → η	unclear
2 Cor 5:11	εἰδότες	+ ϝε	ϝιδ	---	---	α → η	unclear
2 Cor 5:11	πεφανερώμεθα	+ πε	φανερο	ο(υ) → ω	+ κ	- κ	ο(υ) → ω
2 Cor 5:11	πεφανερῶσθαι	+ πε	φανερο	ο(υ) → ω	+ κ	- κ	ο(υ) → ω
2 Cor 5:16	οἴδαμεν	+ ϝε	ϝιδ	---	---	α → η	unclear
2 Cor 5:16	ἐγνώκαμεν	+ ε	γνω	---	+ κ	- κ	---
2 Cor 5:17	γέγονεν	+ γε	γν from γιγν	γν → γον or γεν (weak Pf)	---	γον → γος	γν → γεν
2 Cor 6:11	ἀνέῳγεν	οι → ῳ	οιγ	οιγ → εῳχ	γ → χ	---	οιγ → οιχ or εῳχ
2 Cor 6:11	πεπλάτυνται	+ πε	πλατυν	---	?	?	---
2 Cor 7:3	προείρηκα	+ ει	ρε	ε → η	+ κ	- κ	ε → η or ο
2 Cor 7:4	πεπλήρωμαι	+ πε	πληρο	ο(υ) → ω	+ κ	- κ	ο(υ) → ω
2 Cor 7:5	ἔσχηκεν	---	εχ	εχ → εσχη	+ κ	- κ	εχ → εσχο
2 Cor 7:13	παρακεκλήμεθα	+ κε	καλε	καλε → κλη	+ κ	- κ	καλε → κλη
2 Cor 7:13	ἀναπέπαυται	+ πε	παυ	---	+ κ	- κ	---
2 Cor 7:14	κεκαύχημαι	+ κε	καυχα	Final α → η	Deponent	Deponent	Final α → η
2 Cor 8:1	δεδομένην	+ δε	δω	---	+ κ	- κ	---
2 Cor 8:15	γέγραπται	+ γε	γραφ	--- (active) φ → π (middle)	π → φ	φ → π	--- (strong) φ → π (weak)
2 Cor 9:2	οἶδα	+ ϝε	ϝιδ	---	---	α → η	unclear
2 Cor 9:2	παρεσκεύασται	+ ε	σκευαζ	- ζ	+ κ	- κ + σ	- ζ
2 Cor 9:3	παρεσκευασμένοι ἦτε	+ ε	σκευαζ	- ζ	+ κ	- κ + σ	- ζ
2 Cor 9:5	προεπηγγελμένην	+ ε	αγγελλ	αγγελλ → ηγγελ	+ κ	- κ	αγγελλ → ηγγελ
2 Cor 9:7	προήρηται	+ ε	αιρε	ε → η	+ κ	- κ	ε → η
2 Cor 9:9	γέγραπται	+ γε	γραφ	--- (active) φ → π (middle)	π → φ	φ → π	--- (strong) φ → π (weak)
2 Cor 10:7	πέποιθεν	+ πε	πειθ	θ → σ	+ κ	- κ	θ → σ
2 Cor 10:10	ἐξουθενημένος	---	ουθενε	---	+ κ	- κ	---

Perfect tense-forms							
2 Cor 11:5	ὑστερηκέναι	---	ὑστερε	ε → η	+ κ	- κ	ε → η
2 Cor 11:11	οἶδεν	+ ϝε	ϝιδ	---	---	α → η	unclear
2 Cor 11:21	ἠσθενήκαμεν	+ ε	ασθενε	ε → η	+ κ	- κ	ε → η
2 Cor 11:25	πεποίηκα	+ πε	ποιε	ποιε → ποιη	+ κ	- κ	ποιε → ποιη
2 Cor 11:31	οἶδεν	+ ϝε	ϝιδ	---	---	α → η	unclear
2 Cor 12:2	οἶδα	+ ϝε	ϝιδ	---	---	α → η	unclear
2 Cor 12:2	οἶδα	+ ϝε	ϝιδ	---	---	α → η	unclear
2 Cor 12:2	οἶδα	+ ϝε	ϝιδ	---	---	α → η	unclear
2 Cor 12:2	οἶδεν	+ ϝε	ϝιδ	---	---	α → η	unclear
2 Cor 12:3	οἶδα	+ ϝε	ϝιδ	---	---	α → η	unclear
2 Cor 12:3	οἶδα	+ ϝε	ϝιδ	---	---	α → η	unclear
2 Cor 12:3	οἶδεν	+ ϝε	ϝιδ	---	---	α → η	unclear
2 Cor 12:9	εἴρηκέν	+ ει	ρε	ε → η	+ κ	- κ	ε → η or ο
2 Cor 12:11	γέγονεν	+ γε	γν from γιγν	γν → γον or γεν (weak Pf)	---	γον → γος	γν → γεν
2 Cor 12:17	ἀπέσταλκα	+ ε	στελλ	στελλ → σταλ	+ κ	- κ	στελλ → σταλ
2 Cor 12:21	προημαρτηκότων	+ ε	ἁμαρταν	ἁμαρταν → ἁμαρτη	+ κ	- κ	ἁμαρταν → ἁμαρτη
2 Cor 13:2	προείρηκα	+ ει	ρε	ε → η	+ κ	- κ	ε → η or ο
2 Cor 13:2	προημαρτηκόσιν	+ ε	ἁμαρταν	ἁμαρταν → ἁμαρτη	+ κ	- κ	ἁμαρταν → ἁμαρτη
Gal 1:4	ἐνεστῶτος	+ ἑ	στη	στο or στω (strong only)	+ κ (weak only)	- κ	---
Gal 1:9	προειρήκαμεν	+ ει	ρε	ε → η	+ κ	- κ	ε → η or ο
Gal 2:7	πεπίστευμαι	+ πε	πιστευ	---	+ κ	- κ	---
Gal 2:11	κατεγνωσμένος ἦν	+ ε	γνω	---	+ κ	- κ + σ	---
Gal 2:16	εἰδότες	+ ϝε	ϝιδ	---	---	α → η	unclear
Gal 2:19	συνεσταύρωμαι	+ ε	σταυρο	ο(υ) → ω	+ κ	- κ	ο(υ) → ω
Gal 3:1	ἐσταυρωμένος	+ ε	σταυρο	ο(υ) → ω	+ κ	- κ	ο(υ) → ω
Gal 3:10	γέγραπται	+ γε	γραφ	--- (active) φ → π (middle)	π → φ	φ → π	--- (strong) φ → π (weak)
Gal 3:10	γεγραμμένοις	+ γε	γραφ	--- (active) φ → π (middle)	π → φ	φ → π	--- (strong) φ → π (weak)
Gal 3:13	γέγραπται	+ γε	γραφ	--- (active) φ → π (middle)	π → φ	φ → π	--- (strong) φ → π (weak)
Gal 3:15	κεκυρωμένην	+ κε	κυρο	ο(υ) → ω	+ κ	- κ	ο(υ) → ω
Gal 3:17	προκεκυρωμένην	+ κε	κυρο	ο(υ) → ω	+ κ	- κ	ο(υ) → ω
Gal 3:17	γεγονὼς	+ γε	γν from γιγν	γν → γον or γεν (weak Pf)	---	γον → γος	γν → γεν

Perfect tense-forms							
Gal 3:18	κεχάρισται	+ κε	χαριζ	- ζ	+ κ	- κ + σ	- ζ
Gal 3:19	ἐπήγγελται	α → η	αγγελλ	αγγελλ → ηγγελ	+ κ	- κ	αγγελλ → ηγγελ
Gal 3:24	γέγονεν	+ γε	γν from γιγν	γν → γον or γεν (weak Pf)	---	γον → γος	γν → γεν
Gal 4:3	ἤμεθα δεδουλωμένοι	+ δε	δουλο	ο(υ) → ω	+ κ	- κ	ο(υ) → ω
Gal 4:8	εἰδότες	+ ϝε	ϝιδ	---	---	α → η	unclear
Gal 4:11	κεκοπίακα	+ κε	κοπια	Final α → η	+ κ	- κ	Final α → η
Gal 4:13	οἴδατε	+ ϝε	ϝιδ	---	---	α → η	unclear
Gal 4:16	γέγονα	+ γε	γν from γιγν	γν → γον or γεν (weak Pf)	---	γον → γος	γν → γεν
Gal 4:22	γέγραπται	+ γε	γραφ	--- (active) φ → π (middle)	π → φ	φ → π	--- (strong) φ → π (weak)
Gal 4:23	γεγέννηται	+ γε	γεννα	Final α → η			Final α → η
Gal 4:27	γέγραπται	+ γε	γραφ	--- (active) φ → π (middle)	π → φ	φ → π	--- (strong) φ → π (weak)
Gal 5:10	πέποιθα	+ πε	πειθ	ειθ → οιθ	---	θ → σ	ειθ → ιθ
Gal 5:11	κατήργηται	α → η	αργε	α → η and ε → η	+ κ	- κ	α → η and ε → η
Gal 5:14	πεπλήρωται	+ πε	πληρο	ο(υ) → ω	+ κ	- κ	ο(υ) → ω
Gal 6:14	ἐσταύρωται	+ ε	σταυρο	ο(υ) → ω	+ κ	- κ	ο(υ) → ω
Eph 1:6	ἠγαπημένῳ	+ ε	αγαπα	Final α → η	+ κ	- κ	Final α → η
Eph 1:12	προηλπικότας	+ ε	ελπιζ	- ζ	+ κ	- κ + σ	- ζ
Eph 1:18	πεφωτισμένους	+ πε	φοτιζ	- ζ	+ κ	- κ + σ	- ζ
Eph 1:18	εἰδέναι	+ ϝε	ϝιδ	---	---	ο → η	unclear
Eph 2:5	ἐστε σεσωσμένοι	+ σε	σωζ	- ζ	+ κ	- κ + σ	- ζ
Eph 2:8	ἐστε σεσωσμένοι	+ σε	σωζ	- ζ	+ κ	- κ + σ	- ζ
Eph 2:12	ἀπηλλοτριωμένοι	α → η	αλλοτριο	ο(υ) → ω	+ κ	- κ	ο(υ) → ω
Eph 3:9	ἀποκεκρυμμένου	+ κε	κρυπτ	πτ → φ	μ → φ	φ → μ	πτ → φ or ψ
Eph 3:17	ἐρριζωμένοι	+ ε	ριζο	ο(υ) → ω	+ κ	- κ	ο(υ) → ω
Eph 3:17	τεθεμελιωμένοι	+ τε	θεμελιο	ο(υ) → ω	+ κ	- κ	ο(υ) → ω
Eph 4:18	ἐσκοτωμένοι	+ ε	σκοτο	ο(υ) → ω	+ κ	- κ	ο(υ) → ω
Eph 4:18	ἀπηλλοτριωμένοι	α → η	αλλοτριο	ο(υ) → ω	+ κ	- κ	ο(υ) → ω
Eph 4:19	ἀπηλγηκότες	+ ε	αλγε	ε → η	+ κ	- κ	ε → η
Eph 5:5	ἴστε	+ ϝε	ϝιδ	---	---	ο → η	unclear
Eph 6:8	εἰδότες	+ ϝε	ϝιδ	---	---	ο → η	unclear
Eph 6:9	εἰδότες	+ ϝε	ϝιδ	---	---	ο → η	unclear
Eph 6:16	πεπυρωμένα	+ πε	πυρο	ο(υ) → ω	+ κ	- κ	ο(υ) → ω
Eph 6:21	εἰδῆτε	+ ϝε	ϝιδ	---	---	ο → η	unclear

Perfect tense-forms							
Phil 1:6	πεποιθὼς	+ πε	πειθ	ειθ → οιθ	---	θ → σ	ειθ → ιθ
Phil 1:11	πεπληρωμένοι	+ πε	πληρο	ο(υ) → ω	+ κ	- κ	ο(υ) → ω
Phil 1:12	ἐλήλυθεν	+ ελε	ερχ/ελυ	+ θ	---	- θ + σ	+ θ
Phil 1:14	πεποιθότας	+ πε	πειθ	ειθ → οιθ	---	θ → σ	ειθ → ιθ
Phil 1:16	εἰδότες	+ ϝε	ϝιδ	---	---	ο → η	unclear
Phil 1:19	οἶδα	+ ϝε	ϝιδ	---	---	α → η	unclear
Phil 1:25	πεποιθὼς	+ πε	πειθ	ειθ → οιθ	---	θ → σ	ειθ → ιθ
Phil 1:25	οἶδα	+ ϝε	ϝιδ	---	---	α → η	unclear
Phil 2:15	διεστραμμένης	+ ε	στρεφ	--- (weak) στροφ (strong) [active] _____ ____ στραφ (weak) and στροφ (strong) [middle]			--- (weak) στραφ (strong)
Phil 2:24	πέποιθα	+ πε	πειθ	ειθ → οιθ	---	θ → σ	ειθ → ιθ
Phil 3:3	πεποιθότες	+ πε	πειθ	ειθ → οιθ	---	θ → σ	ειθ → ιθ
Phil 3:4	πεποιθέναι	+ πε	πειθ	ειθ → οιθ	---	θ → σ	ειθ → ιθ
Phil 3:7	ἥγημαι	?	ἥγε	ε → η	Deponent	Deponent	ε → η
Phil 3:12	τετελείωμαι	+ τε	τελειο	ο(υ) → ω	+ κ	- κ	ο(υ) → ω
Phil 3:13	κατειληφέναι	+ ει	λαμβαν	λαμβαν → ληφ	Endings only	Endings only	λαμβαν → λαβ or ληφ
Phil 4:12	οἶδα	+ ϝε	ϝιδ	---	---	α → η	unclear
Phil 4:12	οἶδα	+ ϝε	ϝιδ	---	---	α → η	unclear
Phil 4:12	μεμύημαι	+ με	μυε	ε → η	+ κ	- κ	ε → η
Phil 4:15	οἴδατε	+ ϝε	ϝιδ	---	---	α → η	unclear
Phil 4:18	πεπλήρωμαι	+ πε	πληρο	ο(υ) → ω	+ κ	- κ	ο(υ) → ω
Col 1:16	ἔκτισται	+ ε	κτιζ	- ζ	+ κ	- κ + σ	- ζ
Col 1:17	συνέστηκεν	+ ἑ	στη	---	--- (strong) + κ (weak)	- κ	---
Col 1:17	ὄντας ἀπηλλοτριωμένους	α → η	αλλοτριο	ο(υ) → ω	+ κ	- κ	ο(υ) → ω
Col 1:21	τεθεμελιωμένοι	+ τε	θεμελιο	ο(υ) → ω	+ κ	- κ	ο(υ) → ω
Col 1:23	ἀποκεκρυμμένον	+ κε	καλυπτ	καλυπτ → καλυφ	Endings only	Endings only π before μ is μμ	καλυπτ → καλυφ
Col 1:26	εἰδέναι	+ ϝε	ϝιδ	---	---	α → η	unclear
Col 2:1	ἑόρακαν	+ ἑ	ὁρα	---	+ κ	- κ	---
Col 2:7	ἐρριζωμένοι	+ ε	ριζο	ο(υ) → ω	+ κ	- κ	ο(υ) → ω

Perfect tense-forms

Col 2:10	ἐστὲ ... πεπληρωμένοι	+ πε	πληρο	ο(υ) → ω	+ κ	- κ	ο(υ) → ω
Col 2:14	ἤρκεν	+ ε	αιρε	ε → η	+ κ	- κ	ε → η
Col 2:18	ἑόρακεν	+ ἑ	ὁρα	---	+ κ	- κ	---
Col 3:3	κέκρυπται	+ κε	κρυπτ	κρυπτ	πτ → φ	μ → φ	φ → μ
Col 3:12	ἠγαπημένοι	+ ε	αγαπα	Final α → η	+ κ	- κ	Final α → η
Col 3:24	εἰδότες	+ ϝε	ϝιδ	---	---	α → η	unclear
Col 4:1	εἰδότες	+ ϝε	ϝιδ	---	---	α → η	unclear
Col 4:3	δέδεμαι	+ δε	δε	δε → δη or no change	+ κ	- κ	δε → δη
Col 4:6	ἠρτυμένος	+ ε	αρτυ	---	+ κ	- κ	---
Col 4:6	εἰδέναι	+ ϝε	ϝιδ	---	---	α → η	unclear
Col 4:12	πεπληροφορημένοι	+ πε	πληροφορε	ε → η	+ κ	- κ	ε → η
1 Thess 1:4	εἰδότες	+ ϝε	ϝιδ	---	---	α → η	unclear
1 Thess 1:4	ἠγαπημένοι	+ ε	αγαπα	Final α → η	+ κ	- κ	Final α → η
1 Thess 1:5	οἴδατε	+ ϝε	ϝιδ	---	---	α → η	unclear
1 Thess 1:8	ἐξήχηται	---	εξηχε	ε → η	+ κ	- κ	ε → η
1 Thess 1:8	ἐξελήλυθεν	+ ελε	ερχ/ελυ	+ θ	---	- θ + σ	+ θ
1 Thess 2:1	οἴδατε	+ ϝε	ϝιδ	---	---	α → η	unclear
1 Thess 2:1	γέγονεν	+ γε	γν from γιγν	γν → γον or γεν (weak Pf)	---	γον → γος	γν → γεν
1 Thess 2:2	οἴδατε	+ ϝε	ϝιδ	---	---	α → η	unclear
1 Thess 2:4	δεδοκιμάσμεθα	+ δε	δοκιμαζ	- ζ	+ κ	- κ + σ	- ζ
1 Thess 2:5	οἴδατε	+ ϝε	ϝιδ	---	---	α → η	unclear
1 Thess 2:11	οἴδατε	+ ϝε	ϝιδ	---	---	α → η	unclear
1 Thess 3:3	οἴδατε	+ ϝε	ϝιδ	---	---	α → η	unclear
1 Thess 3:4	οἴδατε	+ ϝε	ϝιδ	---	---	α → η	unclear
1 Thess 4:2	οἴδατε	+ ϝε	ϝιδ	---	---	α → η	unclear
1 Thess 4:4	εἰδέναι	+ ϝε	ϝιδ	---	---	α → η	unclear
1 Thess 4:5	εἰδότα	+ ϝε	ϝιδ	---	---	α → η	unclear
1 Thess 5:2	οἴδατε	+ ϝε	ϝιδ	---	---	α → η	unclear
1 Thess 5:12	εἰδέναι	+ ϝε	ϝιδ	---	---	α → η	unclear
2 Thess 1:8	εἰδόσιν	+ ϝε	ϝιδ	---	---	α → η	unclear
2 Thess 2:2	ἐνέστηκεν	+ ἑ	στη	---	---(strong) + κ (weak)	- κ	---
2 Thess 2:6	οἴδατε	+ ϝε	ϝιδ	---	---	α → η	unclear
2 Thess 2:13	ἠγαπημένοι	+ ε	αγαπα	Final α → η	+ κ	- κ	Final α → η
2 Thess 3:4	πεποίθαμεν	+ πε	πειθ	ειθ → οιθ	---	θ → σ	ειθ → ιθ

Perfect tense-forms							
2 Thess 3:7	οἴδατε	+ ϝε	ϝιδ	---	---	α → η	unclear
1 Tim 1:8	οἴδαμεν	+ ϝε	ϝιδ	---	---	α → η	unclear
1 Tim 1:9	εἰδὼς	+ ϝε	ϝιδ	---	---	α → η	unclear
1 Tim 2:14	γέγονεν	+ γε	γν from γιγν	γν → γον or γεν (weak Pf)	---	γον → γος	γν → γεν
1 Tim 3:5	οἶδεν	+ ϝε	ϝιδ	---	---	α → η	unclear
1 Tim 3:15	εἰδῇς	+ ϝε	ϝιδ	---	---	α → η	unclear
1 Tim 4:2	κεκαυστηριασμένων	+ κε	καυστηριαζ	- ζ	+ κ	- κ + σ	- ζ
1 Tim 4:3	ἐπεγνωκόσι	+ ε	γνω	---	+ κ	- κ	---
1 Tim 4:6	παρηκολούθηκας	+ ε	ακολουθε	---	+ κ	- κ	---
1 Tim 4:10	ἠλπίκαμεν	+ ε	ελπιζ	- ζ	+ κ	- κ + σ	- ζ
1 Tim 5:5	μεμονωμένη	+ με	μονο	ο(υ) → ω	+ κ	- κ	ο(υ) → ω
1 Tim 5:5	ἤλπικεν	+ ε	ελπιζ	- ζ	+ κ	- κ + σ	- ζ
1 Tim 5:6	τέθνηκεν	+ τε	θνη	--- (weak) θνα (strong)	+ κ	- κ	θαν (strong)
1 Tim 5:8	ἤρνηται	+ ε	αρνε	ε → η	Deponent	Deponent	ε → η
1 Tim 5:9	γεγονυῖα	+ γε	γν from γιγν	γν → γον or γεν (weak Pf)	---	γον → γος	γν → γεν
1 Tim 5:17	προεστῶτες	ἑ	στη	στο or στω (strong only)	+ κ (weak only)	- κ	---
1 Tim 6:4	τετύφωται	+ τε	τυφο	ο(υ) → ω	+ κ	- κ	ο(υ) → ω
1 Tim 6:5	διεφθαρμένων	+ ε	φθειρ	ει → α (weak) ει → ο (strong)	+ κ	- κ	--- (weak) ει → α (strong)
1 Tim 6:5	ἀπεστερημένων	+ ε	στερε	ε → η	+ κ	- κ	ε → η
1 Tim 6:17	ἠλπικέναι	+ ε	ελπιζ	- ζ	+ κ	- κ + σ	- ζ
2 Tim 1:4	μεμνημένος	+ με	μνη	---	+ κ	- κ	---
2 Tim 1:5	πέπεισμαι	+ πε	πειθ	θ → σ	+ κ	- κ	θ → σ
2 Tim 1:12	οἶδα	+ ϝε	ϝιδ	---	---	α → η	unclear
2 Tim 1:12	πεπίστευκα	+ πε	πιστευ	---	+ κ	- κ	---
2 Tim 1:12	πέπεισμαι	+ πε	πειθ	θ → σ	+ κ	- κ	θ → σ
2 Tim 1:15	οἶδας	+ ϝε	ϝιδ	---	---	α → η	unclear
2 Tim 2:8	ἐγήγερμένον	+ εγε	εγειρ	εγειρ → εγερ	+ κ	- κ	--- (weak) or εγειρ → γρ (strong)
2 Tim 2:9	δέδεται	+ δε	δε	δε → δη or no change	+ κ	- κ	δε → δη
2 Tim 2:18	γεγονέναι	+ γε	γν from γιγν	γν → γον or γεν (weak Pf)	---	γον → γος	γν → γεν

Perfect tense-forms							
2 Tim 2:19	ἕστηκεν	+ ἑ	στη	---	---(strong) +κ (weak)	-κ	---
2 Tim 2:21	ἡγιασμένον	α → η	ἁγιαζ	-ζ	+κ	-κ+σ	-ζ
2 Tim 2:21	ἡτοιμασμένον	+ ε or ἑ	ἑτοιμαζ	-ζ	+κ	-κ+σ	-ζ
2 Tim 2:23	εἰδώς	+ Ϝε	Ϝιδ	---	---	α → η	unclear
2 Tim 2:26	ἐζωγρημένοι	+ ε	ζωγρε	ε → η	+κ	-κ	ε → η
2 Tim 3:4	τετυφωμένοι	+ τε	τυφο	ο(υ) → ω	+κ	-κ	ο(υ) → ω
2 Tim 3:5	ἠρνημένοι	+ ε	αρνε	ε → η	Deponent	Deponent	ε → η
2 Tim 3:6	σεσωρευμένα	+ σε	σωρευ	---	+κ	-κ	---
2 Tim 3:8	κατεφθαρμένοι	+ ε	φθειρ	ει → α (weak) ει → ο (strong)	+κ	-κ	--- (weak) ει → α (strong)
2 Tim 3:14	εἰδώς	+ Ϝε	Ϝιδ	---	---	α → η	unclear
2 Tim 3:15	οἶδας	+ Ϝε	Ϝιδ	---	---	α → η	unclear
2 Tim 3:17	ἐξηρτισμένος	α → η	αρτιζ	-ζ	+κ	-κ	-ζ
2 Tim 4:6	ἐφέστηκεν	+ ἑ	στη	---	---(strong) +κ (weak)	-κ	---
2 Tim 4:7	ἠγώνισμαι	α → η	αγωνιζ	-ζ	Deponent	Deponent	-ζ
2 Tim 4:7	τετέλεκα	+ τε	τελε	---	+κ	-κ	---
2 Tim 4:7	τετήρηκα	+ τε	τηρε	ε → η	+κ	-κ	ε → η
2 Tim 4:8	ἠγαπηκόσι	+ ε	αγαπα	Final α → η	+κ	-κ	Final α → η
Tit 1:15	μεμιαμμένοις	+ με	μιαιν	αι → α	+κ	-κ	αι → η
Tit 1:15	μεμίανται	+ με	μιαιν	αι → α	+κ	-κ	αι → η
Tit 1:16	εἰδέναι	+ Ϝε	Ϝιδ	---	---	α → η	unclear
Tit 2:3	δεδουλωμένας	+ δε	δουλο	ο(υ) → ω	+κ	-κ	ο(υ) → ω
Tit 3:8	πεπιστευκότες	+ πε	πιστευ	---	+κ	-κ	---
Tit 3:11	εἰδώς	+ Ϝε	Ϝιδ	---	---	α → η	unclear
Tit 3:11	ἐξέστραπται	+ ε	στρεφ	--- (weak) ε → ο (strong)	α → ε (weak) ---(strong)	ε → α (weak) ---(strong)	--- (weak) ε → α (strong)
Tit 3:12	κέκρικα	+ κε	κριν	κρι	+κ	-κ	---
Phlm 1:7	ἀναπέπαυται	+ πε	παυ	---	+κ	-κ	---
Phlm 1:21	πεποιθώς	+ πε	πειθ	ειθ → οιθ	---	θ → σ	ειθ → ιθ
Phlm 1:21	εἰδώς	+ Ϝε	Ϝιδ	---	---	α → η	unclear
Pluperfect tense-forms							
Rom 7:7	ᾔδειν	+ Ϝε	Ϝιδ	---	---	α → η	unclear

Perfect tense-forms

Productive Morphological Patterns Observed in the Chart Above

type	Present Stem	Pf Affix to the Stem	Middle to Active	Active to Middle	Aorist Affix to the Stem
Kappatic ζ	Stem with final ζ	Drop ζ	+ κ	κ goes to σ	Drop ζ
Strong aspirated stem	Stem with final aspirant	No change (active voice) Loss of aspiration (middle voice)	Aspiration of the stem final	Loss of aspiration	No change (strong stem) Loss of aspiration (weak stem)
Contract vowel kappatic	Stem with final vowel	Final vowel lengthening	+ κ	- κ	Final vowel lengthening
Indo-European Ablaut	Stem with ει vowel inside	ει → οι	No change	No change	ει → ι
Reduplicated Present	Present tense-form had a reduplicated stem	No stem change; reduplication vowel changes	+ κ or ablaut	- κ or ablaut	No stem change; Often a loss of reduplication

Appendix C

Chart of Stem Count

This appendix contains a chart counting the stems and verbs represented among the Perfect tense-forms in the Pauline corpus. They are organised alphabetically by the Present stem. The number in the left two columns is not a tally, but contains ordinal numbers. An additional chart at the end will tally the data in the first chart counting total stems and total verbs. The numbers reported at the end are cardinal numbers and report a tally.

Perfect tense-forms					
Count of stem occurrence	Count of verb occurrence	Reference	Perfect tense-form	Reduplicant	Present Stem
1	1	Rom 9:25	ἠγαπημένην	α → η	αγαπα
2	2	Rom 9:25	ἠγαπημένην	α → η	αγαπα
3	3	Eph 1:6	ἠγαπημένῳ	+ ε	αγαπα
4	4	Col 3:12	ἠγαπημένοι	+ ε	αγαπα
5	5	1 Thess 1:4	ἠγαπημένοι	+ ε	αγαπα
6	6	2 Thess 2:13	ἠγαπημένοι	+ ε	αγαπα
7	7	2 Tim 4:8	ἠγαπηκόσι	+ ε	αγαπα
1	1	Rom 4:21	ἐπήγγελται	α → η	αγγελλ
2	2	Gal 3:19	ἐπήγγελται	α → η	αγγελλ

Perfect tense-forms					
3	1	2 Cor 9:5	προεπηγγελμένην	+ ε	αγγελλ
1	1	Rom 15:16	ἡγιασμένη	α → η	ἁγιαζ
2	2	1 Cor 1:2	ἡγιασμένοις	α → η	ἁγιαζ
3	3	1 Cor 7:14	ἡγίασται	α → η	ἁγιαζ
4	4	1 Cor 7:14	ἡγίασται	α → η	ἁγιαζ
5	5	2 Tim 2:21	ἡγιασμένον	α → η	ἁγιαζ
1	1	2 Tim 4:7	ἠγώνισμαι	α → η	αγωνιζ
1	1	Col 2:14	ἦρκεν	+ ε	αιρε
2	1	2 Cor 9:7	προῄρηται	+ ε	αιρε
1	1	1 Tim 4:6	παρηκολούθηκας	+ ε	ακολουθε
1	1	Rom 15:21	ἀκηκόασιν	+ ακ	ακου
1	1	Eph 4:19	ἀπηλγηκότες	+ ε	αλγε
1	1	Eph 2:12	ἀπηλλοτριωμένοι	α → η	αλλοτριο
2	2	Eph 4:18	ἀπηλλοτριωμένοι	α → η	αλλοτριο
3	3	Col 1:17	ὄντας ἀπηλλοτριωμένους	α → η	αλλοτριο
1	1	2 Cor 12:21	προημαρτηκότων	+ ε	ἁμαρταν
2	2	2 Cor 13:2	προημαρτηκόσιν	+ ε	ἁμαρταν
1	1	1 Cor 10:11	κατήντηκεν	+ ε	αντα
1	1	Rom 4:14	κατήργηται	ε → η	αργε
2	2	Rom 7:2	κατήργηται	ε → η	αργε
3	3	1 Cor 13:11	κατήργηκα	ε → η	αργε
4	4	Gal 5:11	κατήργηται	α → η	αργε
1	1	1 Tim 5:8	ἤρνηται	+ ε	αρνε
2	2	2 Tim 3:5	ἠρνημένοι	+ ε	αρνε
1	1	Rom 9:22	κατηρτισμένα	α → η	αρτιζ
2	2	1 Cor 1:10	κατηρτισμένοι	α → η	αρτιζ
3	1	2 Tim 3:17	ἐξηρτισμένος	α → η	αρτιζ
1	1	Col 4:6	ἠρτυμένος	+ ε	ἀρτυ
1	1	2 Cor 11:21	ἠσθενήκαμεν	+ ε	ασθενε
1	1	1 Cor 7:10	γεγαμηκόσιν	+ γε	γαμε
1	1	Rom 15:8	γεγενῆσθαι	+ γε	γεννα
2	2	Gal 4:23	γεγέννηται	+ γε	γεννα
1	1	Rom 2:25	γέγονεν	+ γε	γν from γιγν
2	2	Rom 6:5	γεγόναμεν	+ γε	γν from γιγν
3	3	Rom 11:5	γέγονεν	+ γε	γν from γιγν
4	4	Rom 11:25	γέγονεν	+ γε	γν from γιγν
5	5	Rom 16:7	γέγονεν	+ γε	γν from γιγν

Perfect tense-forms					
6	6	1 Cor 9:22	γέγονα	+ γε	γν from γιγν
7	7	1 Cor 13:1	γέγονα	+ γε	γν from γιγν
8	8	1 Cor 13:11	γέγονα	+ γε	γν from γιγν
9	9	2 Cor 1:19	γέγονεν	+ γε	γν from γιγν
10	10	2 Cor 5:17	γέγονεν	+ γε	γν from γιγν
11	11	2 Cor 12:11	γέγονεν	+ γε	γν from γιγν
12	12	Gal 3:17	γεγονὼς	+ γε	γν from γιγν
13	13	Gal 3:24	γέγονεν	+ γε	γν from γιγν
14	14	Gal 4:16	γέγονα	+ γε	γν from γιγν
15	15	1 Thess 2:1	γέγονεν	+ γε	γν from γιγν
16	16	1 Tim 2:14	γέγονεν	+ γε	γν from γιγν
17	17	1 Tim 5:9	γεγονυῖα	+ γε	γν from γιγν
18	18	2 Tim 2:18	γεγονέναι	+ γε	γν from γιγν
19	1	Rom 3:25	προγεγονότων	+ γε	γν from γιγν
1	1	1 Cor 2:8	ἔγνωκεν	+ ε	γνω
2	2	1 Cor 2:11	ἔγνωκεν	+ ε	γνω
3	3	1 Cor 8:2	ἐγνωκέναι	+ ε	γνω
4	4	1 Cor 8:3	ἔγνωσται	+ ε	γνω
5	5	2 Cor 5:16	ἐγνώκαμεν	+ ε	γνω
6	1	Gal 2:11	κατεγνωσμένος ἦν	+ ε	γνω
7	1	1 Tim 4:3	ἐπεγνωκόσι	+ ε	γνω
1	1	Rom 1:17	γέγραπται	+ γε	γραφ
2	2	Rom 2:24	γέγραπται	+ γε	γραφ
3	3	Rom 3:4	γέγραπται	+ γε	γραφ
4	4	Rom 3:10	γέγραπται	+ γε	γραφ
5	5	Rom 4:17	γέγραπται	+ γε	γραφ
6	6	Rom 8:36	γέγραπται	+ γε	γραφ
7	7	Rom 9:13	γέγραπται	+ γε	γραφ
8	8	Rom 9:33	γέγραπται	+ γε	γραφ
9	9	Rom 10:15	γέγραπται	+ γε	γραφ
10	10	Rom 11:8	γέγραπται	+ γε	γραφ
11	11	Rom 11:26	γέγραπται	+ γε	γραφ
12	12	Rom 12:19	γέγραπται	+ γε	γραφ
13	13	Rom 14:11	γέγραπται	+ γε	γραφ
14	14	Rom 15:3	γέγραπται	+ γε	γραφ
15	15	Rom 15:9	γέγραπται	+ γε	γραφ
16	16	Rom 15:21	γέγραπται	+ γε	γραφ

Perfect tense-forms						
17	17	1 Cor 1:19	γέγραπται	+ γε	γραφ
18	18	1 Cor 1:31	γέγραπται	+ γε	γραφ
19	19	1 Cor 2:9	γέγραπται	+ γε	γραφ
20	20	1 Cor 3:19	γέγραπται	+ γε	γραφ
21	21	1 Cor 4:6	γέγραπται	+ γε	γραφ
22	22	1 Cor 9:9	γέγραπται	+ γε	γραφ
23	23	1 Cor 10:7	γέγραπται	+ γε	γραφ
24	24	1 Cor 14:21	γέγραπται	+ γε	γραφ
25	25	1 Cor 15:45	γέγραπται	+ γε	γραφ
26	26	1 Cor 15:54	γεγραμμένος	+ γε	γραφ
27	27	2 Cor 3:2	ἐγγεγραμμένη	+ γε	γραφ
28	28	2 Cor 3:3	ἐγγεγραμμένη	+ γε	γραφ
29	29	2 Cor 4:13	γεγραμμένον	+ γε	γραφ
30	30	2 Cor 8:15	γέγραπται	+ γε	γραφ
31	31	2 Cor 9:9	γέγραπται	+ γε	γραφ
32	32	Gal 3:10	γέγραπται	+ γε	γραφ
33	33	Gal 3:10	γεγραμμένοις	+ γε	γραφ
34	34	Gal 3:13	γέγραπται	+ γε	γραφ
35	35	Gal 4:22	γέγραπται	+ γε	γραφ
36	36	Gal 4:27	γέγραπται	+ γε	γραφ
1	1	Rom 7:2	δέδεται	+ δε	δε
2	2	1 Cor 7:27	δέδεσαι	+ δε	δε
3	3	1 Cor 7:39	δέδεται	+ δε	δε
4	4	Col 4:3	δέδεμαι	+ δε	δε
5	5	2 Tim 2:9	δέδεται	+ δε	δε
1	1	Rom 6:7	δεδικαίωται	+ δε	δικαιο
2	2	1 Cor 4:4	δεδικαίωμαι	+ δε	δικαιο
1	1	1 Thess 2:4	δεδοκιμάσμεθα	+ δε	δοκιμαζ
1	1	2 Cor 3:10	δεδόξασται	+ δε	δοξαζ
2	2	2 Cor 3:10	δεδοξασμένον	+ δε	δοξαζ
1	1	1 Cor 7:15	δεδούλωται	+ δε	δουλο
2	2	Gal 4:3	ἤμεθα δεδουλωμένοι	+ δε	δουλο
3	3	Tit 2:3	δεδουλωμένας	+ δε	δουλο
1	1	1 Cor 11:15	δέδοται	+ δε	δω
2	2	2 Cor 8:1	δεδομένην	+ δε	δω
1	1	Rom 13:12	ἤγγικεν	ε → η	εγγιζ
1	1	1 Cor 15:4	ἐγήγερται	+ εγε	εγειρ

Perfect tense-forms					
2	2	1 Cor 15:12	ἐγήγερται	+ εγε	εγειρ
3	3	1 Cor 15:13	ἐγήγερται	+ εγε	εγειρ
4	4	1 Cor 15:14	ἐγήγερται	+ εγε	εγειρ
5	5	1 Cor 15:16	ἐγήγερται	+ εγε	εγειρ
6	6	1 Cor 15:17	ἐγήγερται	+ εγε	εγειρ
7	7	1 Cor 15:20	ἐγήγερται	+ εγε	εγειρ
8	8	2 Tim 2:8	ἐγηγερμένον	+ εγε	εγειρ
1	1	1 Cor 7:25	ἠλεημένος	ε → η	ελεε
1	1	1 Cor 15:19	ἠλπικότες ἐσμὲν	+ ε	ελπιζ
2	2	2 Cor 1:10	ἠλπίκαμεν	+ ε	ελπιζ
3	3	1 Tim 4:10	ἠλπίκαμεν	+ ε	ελπιζ
4	4	1 Tim 5:5	ἤλπικεν	+ ε	ελπιζ
5	5	1 Tim 6:17	ἠλπικέναι	+ ε	ελπιζ
6	1	Eph 1:12	προηλπικότας	+ ε	ελπιζ
1	1	1 Thess 1:8	ἐξήχηται	----	εξηχε
1	1	Phil 1:12	ἐλήλυθεν	+ ελε	ερχ/ελυ
2	1	1 Thess 1:8	ἐξελήλυθεν	+ ελε	ερχ/ελυ
1	1	2 Tim 2:21	ἡτοιμασμένον	+ ε or ἑ	ἑτοιμαζ
1	1	Rom 4:1	εὑρηκέναι	----	ἑυρι
1	1	Rom 5:2	ἐσχήκαμεν	----	εχ
2	2	2 Cor 1:9	ἐσχήκαμεν	----	εχ
3	3	2 Cor 2:13	ἔσχηκα	----	εχ
4	4	2 Cor 7:5	ἔσχηκεν	----	εχ
1	1	2 Tim 2:26	ἐζωγρημένοι	+ ε	ζωγρε
1	1	Phil 3:7	ἥγημαι	?	ἡγε
1	1	Eph 3:17	τεθεμελιωμένοι	+ τε	θεμελιο
2	2	Col 1:21	τεθεμελιωμένοι	+ τε	θεμελιο
1	1	Rom 4:17	τέθεικά	+ τε	θη
1	1	1 Tim 5:6	τέθνηκεν	+ τε	θνη
1	1	1 Cor 7:15	κέκληκεν	+ κε	καλε
2	2	1 Cor 7:17	κέκληκεν	+ κε	καλε
3	3	1 Cor 7:18	κέκληταί	+ κε	καλε
4	1	2 Cor 7:13	παρακεκλήμεθα	+ κε	καλε
1	1	2 Cor 4:3	κεκαλυμμένον	+ κε	καλυπτ
2	2	2 Cor 4:3	κεκαλυμμένον	+ κε	καλυπτ
3	3	Col 3:3	κέκρυπται	+ κε	καλυπτ
4	1	2 Cor 3:18	ἀνακεκαλυμμένῳ	+ κε	καλυπτ

Perfect tense-forms					
5	1	Col 1:23	ἀποκεκρυμμένον	+ κε	καλυπτ
1	1	1 Tim 4:2	κεκαυστηριασμένων	+ κε	καυστηριαζ
1	1	2 Cor 7:14	κεκαύχημαι	+ κε	καυχα
1	1	Rom 4:14	κεκένωται	+ κε	κενο
1	1	1 Cor 15:20	κεκοιμημένων	+ κε	κοιμα
1	1	Gal 4:11	κεκοπίακα	+ κε	κοπια
1	1	1 Cor 4:8	κεκορεσμένοι	+ κε	κορενν
1	1	1 Cor 5:3	κέκρικα	+ κε	κριν
2	2	1 Cor 7:37	κέκρικεν	+ κε	κριν
3	3	Tit 3:12	κέκρικα	+ κε	κριν
4	1	Rom 14:23	κατακέκριται	+ κε	κριν
1	1	1 Cor 2:7	ἀποκεκρυμμένην	+ κε	κρυπτ
2	2	Eph 3:9	ἀποκεκρυμμένου	+ κε	κρυπτ
1	1	Col 1:16	ἔκτισται	+ ε	κτιζ
1	1	Gal 3:15	κεκυρωμένην	+ κε	κυρο
2	2	Gal 3:17	προκεκυρωμένην	+ κε	κυρο
1	1	1 Cor 10:13	εἴληφεν	+ ει	λαμβαν
2	1	Phil 3:13	κατειληφέναι	+ ει	λαμβαν
1	1	1 Cor 7:27	λέλυσαι	+ λε	λυ
1	1	2 Cor 2:5	λελύπηκεν	+ λε	λυπε
2	2	2 Cor 2:5	λελύπηκεν	+ λε	λυπε
1	1	1 Cor 1:13	μεμέρισται	+ με	μεριζ
2	2	1 Cor 7:34	μεμέρισται	+ με	μεριζ
1	1	Tit 1:15	μεμιαμμένοις	+ με	μιαιν
2	2	Tit 1:15	μεμίανται	+ με	μιαιν
1	1	1 Cor 11:2	μέμνησθε	+ με	μνη
2	2	2 Tim 1:4	μεμνημένος	+ με	μνη
1	1	1 Tim 5:5	μεμονωμένη	+ με	μονο
1	1	Phil 4:12	μεμύημαι	+ με	μυε
1	1	Rom 4:19	νενεκρωμένον	+ νε	νεκρο
1	1	1 Cor 11:5	ἐξυρημένη	+ ε	ξυρε
1	1	Rom 3:13	ἀνεῳγμένος	οι → εω	οιξ
2	2	1 Cor 16:9	ἀνέῳγεν	οι → ω	οιξ
3	3	2 Cor 2:12	ἀνεῳγμένης	οι → ω	οιξ
4	4	2 Cor 6:11	ἀνέῳγεν	οι → ω	οιξ
1	1	1 Cor 9:1	ἑόρακα	+ ἑ	ὁρα
2	2	Col 2:1	ἑόρακαν	+ ἑ	ὁρα

Perfect tense-forms					
3	3	Col 2:18	ἑόρακεν	+ ἑ	ὁρα
1	1	Rom 1:1	ἀφωρισμένος	ὁ → ὡ	ὁριζ
1	1	1 Cor 1:28	ἐξουθενημένα	---	ουθενε
2	2	1 Cor 6:4	ἐξουθενημένους	---	ουθενε
3	3	2 Cor 10:10	ἐξουθενημένος	---	ουθενε
1	1	2 Cor 7:13	ἀναπέπαυται	+ πε	παυ
2	2	Phlm 1:7	ἀναπέπαυται	+ πε	παυ
1	1	Rom 2:19	πέποιθάς	+ πε	πειθ
2	2	Rom 8:38	πέπεισμαι	+ πε	πειθ
3	3	Rom 14:14	πέπεισμαι	+ πε	πειθ
4	4	Rom 15:14	πέπεισμαι	+ πε	πειθ
5	5	2 Cor 1:9	πεποιθότες ὦμεν	+ πε	πειθ
6	6	2 Cor 2:3	πεποιθὼς	+ πε	πειθ
7	7	2 Cor 10:7	πέποιθεν	+ πε	πειθ
8	8	Gal 5:10	πέποιθα	+ πε	πειθ
9	9	Phil 1:6	πεποιθὼς	+ πε	πειθ
10	10	Phil 1:14	πεποιθότας	+ πε	πειθ
11	11	Phil 1:25	πεποιθὼς	+ πε	πειθ
12	12	Phil 2:24	πέποιθα	+ πε	πειθ
13	13	Phil 3:3	πεποιθότες	+ πε	πειθ
14	14	Phil 3:4	πεποιθέναι	+ πε	πειθ
15	15	2 Thess 3:4	πεποίθαμεν	+ πε	πειθ
16	16	2 Tim 1:5	πέπεισμαι	+ πε	πειθ
17	17	2 Tim 1:12	πέπεισμαι	+ πε	πειθ
18	18	Phlm 1:21	πεποιθὼς	+ πε	πειθ
1	1	1 Cor 9:17	πεπίστευμαι	+ πε	πιστευ
2	2	Gal 2:7	πεπίστευμαι	+ πε	πιστευ
3	3	2 Tim 1:12	πεπίστευκα	+ πε	πιστευ
4	4	Tit 3:8	πεπιστευκότες	+ πε	πιστευ
1	1	2 Cor 6:11	πεπλάτυνται	+ πε	πλατυν
1	1	Rom 1:29	πεπληρωμένους	+ πε	πληρο
2	2	Rom 13:8	πεπλήρωκεν	+ πε	πληρο
3	3	Rom 15:14	πεπληρωμένοι	+ πε	πληρο
4	4	Rom 15:19	πεπληρωκέναι	+ πε	πληρο
5	5	2 Cor 7:4	πεπλήρωμαι	+ πε	πληρο
6	6	Gal 5:14	πεπλήρωται	+ πε	πληρο
7	7	Phil 1:11	πεπληρωμένοι	+ πε	πληρο

Perfect tense-forms

8	8	Phil 4:18	πεπλήρωμαι	+ πε	πληρο
9	9	Col 2:10	ἐστὲ ... πεπληρωμένοι	+ πε	πληρο
1	1	Col 4:12	πεπληροφορημένοι	+ πε	πληροφορε
1	1	2 Cor 11:25	πεποίηκα	+ πε	ποιε
1	1	Rom 7:14	πεπραμένος	+ πε	πρα
1	1	Rom 9:6	ἐκπέπτωκεν	+ πε	πτω
1	1	Eph 6:16	πεπυρωμένα	+ πε	πυρο
1	1	Rom 4:18	εἰρημένον	+ ει	ρε
2	2	2 Cor 12:9	εἴρηκέν	+ ει	ρε
3	1	Rom 9:29	προείρηκεν	+ ει	ρε
4	2	2 Cor 7:3	προείρηκα	+ ει	ρε
5	3	2 Cor 13:2	προείρηκα	+ ει	ρε
6	4	Gal 1:9	προειρήκαμεν	+ ει	ρε
1	1	Eph 3:17	ἐρριζωμένοι	+ ε	ριζο
2	2	Col 2:7	ἐρριζωμένοι	+ ε	ριζο
1	1	Rom 16:25	σεσιγημένου	+ σε	σιγα
1	1	2 Cor 9:2	παρεσκεύασται	+ ε	σκευαζ
2	2	2 Cor 9:3	παρεσκευασμένοι ἦτε	+ ε	σκευαζ
1	1	Eph 4:18	ἐσκοτωμένοι	+ ε	σκοτο
1	1	1 Cor 1:23	ἐσταυρωμένον	+ ε	σταυρο
2	2	1 Cor 2:2	ἐσταυρωμένον	+ ε	σταυρο
3	3	Gal 2:19	συνεσταύρωμαι	+ ε	σταυρο
4	4	Gal 3:1	ἐσταυρωμένος	+ ε	σταυρο
5	5	Gal 6:14	ἐσταύρωται	+ ε	σταυρο
1	1	1 Cor 7:29	συνεσταλμένος ἐστίν	+ ε	στελλ
2	2	2 Cor 12:17	ἀπέσταλκα	+ ε	στελλ
1	1	1 Tim 6:5	ἀπεστερημένων	+ ε	στερε
1	1	Rom 5:2	ἑστήκαμεν	+ ἑ	στη
2	2	Rom 11:20	ἕστηκας	+ ἑ	στη
3	3	1 Cor 7:37	ἕστηκεν	+ ἑ	στη
4	4	1 Cor 10:12	ἑστάναι	+ ἑ	στη
5	5	1 Cor 15:1	ἑστήκατε	+ ἑ	στη
6	6	2 Cor 1:24	ἑστήκατε	+ ἑ	στη
7	7	2 Tim 2:19	ἕστηκεν	+ ἑ	στη
8	1	Rom 9:19	ἀνθέστηκεν	+ ἑ	στη
9	2	Rom 13:2	ἀνθέστηκεν	+ ἑ	στη
10	3	Rom 13:2	ἀνθεστηκότες	+ ἑ	στη

Perfect tense-forms					
11	1	Rom 8:38	ἐνεστῶτα	ἐ	στη
12	2	1 Cor 3:22	ἐνεστῶτα	+ ἐ	στη
13	3	1 Cor 7:26	ἐνεστῶσαν	+ ἐ	στη
14	4	Gal 1:4	ἐνεστῶτος	+ ἐ	στη
15	5	2 Thess 2:2	ἐνέστηκεν	+ ἐ	στη
16	1	2 Tim 4:6	ἐφέστηκεν	+ ἐ	στη
17	1	1 Tim 5:17	προεστῶτες	ἐ	στη
18	1	Col 1:17	συνέστηκεν	+ ἐ	στη
1	1	Phil 2:15	διεστραμμένης	+ ε	στρεφ
2	1	Tit 3:11	ἐξέστραπται	+ ε	στρεφ
1	1	Eph 2:5	ἐστε σεσωσμένοι	+ σε	σωζ
2	2	Eph 2:8	ἐστε σεσωσμένοι	+ σε	σωζ
1	1	2 Tim 3:6	σεσωρευμένα	+ σε	σωρευ
1	1	Rom 13:1	τεταγμέναι	+ τε	τασσ
2	1	1 Cor 15:27	ὑποτέτακται	+ τε	τασσ
1	1	2 Tim 4:7	τετέλεκα	+ τε	τελε
1	1	Phil 3:12	τετελείωμαι	+ τε	τελειο
1	1	1 Cor 7:18	περιτετμημένος	+ τε	τεμν
1	1	2 Tim 4:7	τετήρηκα	+ τε	τηρε
1	1	2 Cor 3:7	ἐντετυπωμένη	+ ε	τυπο
1	1	1 Tim 6:4	τετύφωται	+ τε	τυφο
2	2	2 Tim 3:4	τετυφωμένοι	+ τε	τυφο
1	1	2 Cor 11:5	ὑστερηκέναι	---	ὑστερε
1	1	Rom 3:21	πεφανέρωται	+ πε	φανερο
2	2	2 Cor 5:11	πεφανερώμεθα	+ πε	φανερο
3	2	2 Cor 5:11	πεφανερῶσθαι	+ πε	φανερο
1	1	1 Tim 6:5	διεφθαρμένων	+ ε	φθειρ
2	1	2 Tim 3:8	κατεφθαρμένοι	+ ε	φθειρ
1	1	Eph 1:18	πεφωτισμένους	+ πε	φοτιζ
1	1	1 Cor 4:19	πεφυσιωμένων	+ πε	φυσιο
2	2	1 Cor 5:2	πεφυσιωμένοι	+ πε	φυσιο
1	1	2 Cor 2:10	κεχάρισμαι	+ κε	χαριζ
2	2	2 Cor 2:10	κεχάρισμαι	+ κε	χαριζ
3	3	Gal 3:18	κεχάρισται	+ κε	χαριζ
1	1	Rom 5:5	ἐκκέχυται	+ κε	χε
1	1	1 Cor 9:15	κέχρημαι	+ κε	χρα
1	1	Rom 2:2	οἴδαμεν	+ ϝε	ϝιδ

Perfect tense-forms					
2	2	Rom 3:19	οἴδαμεν	+ ϝε	ϝιδ
3	3	Rom 5:3	εἰδότες	+ ϝε	ϝιδ
4	4	Rom 6:9	εἰδότες	+ ϝε	ϝιδ
5	5	Rom 6:16	οἴδατε	+ ϝε	ϝιδ
6	6	Rom 7:14	οἴδαμεν	+ ϝε	ϝιδ
7	7	Rom 7:18	οἶδα	+ ϝε	ϝιδ
8	8	Rom 8:22	οἴδαμεν	+ ϝε	ϝιδ
9	9	Rom 8:26	οἴδαμεν	+ ϝε	ϝιδ
10	10	Rom 8:27	οἶδεν	+ ϝε	ϝιδ
11	11	Rom 8:28	οἴδαμεν	+ ϝε	ϝιδ
12	12	Rom 11:2	οἴδατε	+ ϝε	ϝιδ
13	13	Rom 13:11	εἰδότες	+ ϝε	ϝιδ
14	14	Rom 14:14	οἶδα	+ ϝε	ϝιδ
15	15	Rom 15:29	οἶδα	+ ϝε	ϝιδ
16	16	1 Cor 1:16	οἶδα	+ ϝε	ϝιδ
17	17	1 Cor 2:2	εἰδέναι	+ ϝε	ϝιδ
18	18	1 Cor 2:11	οἶδεν	+ ϝε	ϝιδ
19	19	1 Cor 2:12	εἰδῶμεν	+ ϝε	ϝιδ
20	20	1 Cor 3:16	οἴδατε	+ ϝε	ϝιδ
21	21	1 Cor 4:4	σύνοιδα	+ ϝε	ϝιδ
22	22	1 Cor 5:6	οἴδατε	+ ϝε	ϝιδ
23	23	1 Cor 6:2	οἴδατε	+ ϝε	ϝιδ
24	24	1 Cor 6:3	οἴδατε	+ ϝε	ϝιδ
25	25	1 Cor 6:9	οἴδατε	+ ϝε	ϝιδ
26	26	1 Cor 6:15	οἴδατε	+ ϝε	ϝιδ
27	27	1 Cor 6:16	οἴδατε	+ ϝε	ϝιδ
28	28	1 Cor 6:19	οἴδατε	+ ϝε	ϝιδ
29	29	1 Cor 7:16	οἶδας	+ ϝε	ϝιδ
30	30	1 Cor 7:16	οἶδας	+ ϝε	ϝιδ
31	31	1 Cor 8:1	οἴδαμεν	+ ϝε	ϝιδ
32	32	1 Cor 8:4	οἴδαμεν	+ ϝε	ϝιδ
33	33	1 Cor 9:13	οἴδατε	+ ϝε	ϝιδ
34	34	1 Cor 9:24	οἴδατε	+ ϝε	ϝιδ
35	35	1 Cor 11:3	εἰδέναι	+ ϝε	ϝιδ
36	36	1 Cor 12:2	οἴδατε	+ ϝε	ϝιδ
37	37	1 Cor 13:2	εἰδῶ	+ ϝε	ϝιδ
38	38	1 Cor 14:11	εἰδῶ	+ ϝε	ϝιδ

Perfect tense-forms					
39	39	1 Cor 14:16	οἶδεν	+ ϝε	ϝιδ
40	40	1 Cor 15:58	εἰδότες	+ ϝε	ϝιδ
41	41	1 Cor 16:15	οἴδατε	+ ϝε	ϝιδ
42	42	2 Cor 1:7	εἰδότες	+ ϝε	ϝιδ
43	43	2 Cor 4:14	εἰδότες	+ ϝε	ϝιδ
44	44	2 Cor 5:1	οἴδαμεν	+ ϝε	ϝιδ
45	45	2 Cor 5:6	εἰδότες	+ ϝε	ϝιδ
46	46	2 Cor 5:11	εἰδότες	+ ϝε	ϝιδ
47	47	2 Cor 5:16	οἴδαμεν	+ ϝε	ϝιδ
48	48	2 Cor 9:2	οἶδα	+ ϝε	ϝιδ
49	49	2 Cor 11:11	οἶδεν	+ ϝε	ϝιδ
50	50	2 Cor 11:31	οἶδεν	+ ϝε	ϝιδ
51	51	2 Cor 12:2	οἶδα	+ ϝε	ϝιδ
52	52	2 Cor 12:2	οἶδα	+ ϝε	ϝιδ
53	53	2 Cor 12:2	οἶδα	+ ϝε	ϝιδ
54	54	2 Cor 12:2	οἶδεν	+ ϝε	ϝιδ
55	55	2 Cor 12:3	οἶδα	+ ϝε	ϝιδ
56	56	2 Cor 12:3	οἶδα	+ ϝε	ϝιδ
57	57	2 Cor 12:3	οἶδεν	+ ϝε	ϝιδ
58	58	Gal 2:16	εἰδότες	+ ϝε	ϝιδ
59	59	Gal 4:8	εἰδότες	+ ϝε	ϝιδ
60	60	Gal 4:13	οἴδατε	+ ϝε	ϝιδ
61	61	Eph 1:18	εἰδέναι	+ ϝε	ϝιδ
62	62	Eph 5:5	ἴστε	+ ϝε	ϝιδ
63	63	Eph 6:8	εἰδότες	+ ϝε	ϝιδ
64	64	Eph 6:9	εἰδότες	+ ϝε	ϝιδ
65	65	Eph 6:21	εἰδῆτε	+ ϝε	ϝιδ
66	66	Phil 1:16	εἰδότες	+ ϝε	ϝιδ
67	67	Phil 1:19	οἶδα	+ ϝε	ϝιδ
68	68	Phil 1:25	οἶδα	+ ϝε	ϝιδ
69	69	Phil 4:12	οἶδα	+ ϝε	ϝιδ
70	70	Phil 4:12	οἶδα	+ ϝε	ϝιδ
71	71	Phil 4:15	οἴδατε	+ ϝε	ϝιδ
72	72	Col 1:26	εἰδέναι	+ ϝε	ϝιδ
73	73	Col 3:24	εἰδότες	+ ϝε	ϝιδ
74	74	Col 4:1	εἰδότες	+ ϝε	ϝιδ
75	75	Col 4:6	εἰδέναι	+ ϝε	ϝιδ

Perfect tense-forms					
76	76	1 Thess 1:4	εἰδότες	+ ϝε	ϝιδ
77	77	1 Thess 1:5	οἴδατε	+ ϝε	ϝιδ
78	78	1 Thess 2:1	οἴδατε	+ ϝε	ϝιδ
79	79	1 Thess 2:2	οἴδατε	+ ϝε	ϝιδ
80	80	1 Thess 2:5	οἴδατε	+ ϝε	ϝιδ
81	81	1 Thess 2:11	οἴδατε	+ ϝε	ϝιδ
82	82	1 Thess 3:3	οἴδατε	+ ϝε	ϝιδ
83	83	1 Thess 3:4	οἴδατε	+ ϝε	ϝιδ
84	84	1 Thess 4:2	οἴδατε	+ ϝε	ϝιδ
85	85	1 Thess 4:4	εἰδέναι	+ ϝε	ϝιδ
86	86	1 Thess 4:5	εἰδότα	+ ϝε	ϝιδ
87	87	1 Thess 5:2	οἴδατε	+ ϝε	ϝιδ
88	88	1 Thess 5:12	εἰδέναι	+ ϝε	ϝιδ
89	89	2 Thess 1:8	εἰδόσιν	+ ϝε	ϝιδ
90	90	2 Thess 2:6	οἴδατε	+ ϝε	ϝιδ
91	91	2 Thess 3:7	οἴδατε	+ ϝε	ϝιδ
92	92	1 Tim 1:8	οἴδαμεν	+ ϝε	ϝιδ
93	93	1 Tim 1:9	εἰδώς	+ ϝε	ϝιδ
94	94	1 Tim 3:5	οἶδεν	+ ϝε	ϝιδ
95	95	1 Tim 3:15	εἰδῇς	+ ϝε	ϝιδ
96	96	2 Tim 1:12	οἶδα	+ ϝε	ϝιδ
97	97	2 Tim 1:15	οἶδας	+ ϝε	ϝιδ
98	98	2 Tim 2:23	εἰδώς	+ ϝε	ϝιδ
99	99	2 Tim 3:14	εἰδώς	+ ϝε	ϝιδ
100	100	2 Tim 3:15	οἶδας	+ ϝε	ϝιδ
101	101	Tit 1:16	εἰδέναι	+ ϝε	ϝιδ
102	102	Tit 3:11	εἰδώς	+ ϝε	ϝιδ
103	103	Phlm 1:21	εἰδώς	+ ϝε	ϝιδ
Pluperfect tense-forms					
104	104	Rom 7:7	ᾔδειν	+ ϝε	ϝιδ
Tally					
103		Count of total stems			
	128	Count of total verbs			

Appendix D

Chart of Stems by Frequency

This appendix contains a chart of the verbal stems in order of frequency represented by the Perfect tense-forms in the Pauline corpus. They are organised from most frequent to least frequent. Where several stems share the same frequency, they are ordered alphabetically.

Perfect tense-forms	
Tally of stem occurrence	Present Stem
104	ϝιδ
36	γραφ
19	γν from γιγν
18	πειθ
18	στη
9	πληρο
8	εγειρ
7	αγαπα
7	γνω
6	ελπιζ
6	ρε
5	ἁγιαζ

Perfect tense-forms	
5	δε
5	καλυπτ
5	σταυρο
4	αργε
4	εχ
4	καλε
4	κριν
4	οιξ
4	πιστευ
3	αγγελλ
3	αλλοτριο
3	αρτιζ
3	δουλο
3	ὁρα
3	ουθενε
3	φανερο
3	χαριζ
2	αιρε
2	ἁμαρταν
2	αρνε
2	γεννα
2	δικαιο
2	δοξαζ
2	δω
2	ερχ/ελυ
2	θεμελιο
2	κρυπτ
2	κυρο
2	λαμβαν
2	λυπε
2	μεριζ
2	μιαιν
2	μνη
2	παυ
2	ριζο
2	σκευαζ
2	στελλ

Perfect tense-forms	
2	στρεφ
2	σωζ
2	τασσ
2	τυφο
2	φθειρ
2	φυσιο
1	αγωνιζ
1	ακολουθε
1	ακου
1	αλγε
1	αντα
1	αρτυ
1	ασθενε
1	γαμε
1	δοκιμαζ
1	εγγιζ
1	ελεε
1	εξηχε
1	ἑτοιμαζ
1	ἑυρι
1	ζωγρε
1	ἡγε
1	θη
1	θνη
1	καυστηριαζ
1	καυχα
1	κενο
1	κοιμα
1	κοπια
1	κορεννꞔ
1	κτιζ
1	λυ
1	μονο
1	μυε
1	νεκρο
1	ξυρε
1	ὁριζ

Perfect tense-forms	
1	πλατυν
1	πληροφορε
1	ποιε
1	πρα
1	πτω
1	πυρο
1	σιγα
1	σκοτο
1	στερε
1	σωρευ
1	τελε
1	τελειο
1	τεμν
1	τηρε
1	τυπο
1	ὑστερε
1	φοτιζ
1	χε
1	χρα

Appendix E
Chart of Context

This appendix contains a chart of the Perfect tense-forms in the order they occur in the Pauline Corpus. This chart tracks several elements in close context to the Perfect tense-form that provide clues as to its verbal aspect.

Pauline	Perfect tense-forms						
Reference	Pf tense-form	Modifiers	Modifier function	Direct Object	Verbal parallel	Agent	Stative, Actional, or Both
Rom 1:1	ἀφωρισμένος	Preposition	Direction or purpose	---	---	None	Stative
Rom 1:17	γέγραπται	---	---	---	---	None	Stative
Rom 1:29	πεπληρωμένους	Dative	Content	---	---	None	Stative
Rom 2:2	οἴδαμεν	---	---	ὅτι clause	---	We	Stative
Rom 2:19	πέποιθάς	---	---	σεαυτὸν	2:17 – 2:23 a long string of Present tense-forms	You	Stative
Rom 2:24	γέγραπται	---	---	---	---	None	Stative
Rom 2:25	γέγονεν	---	---	---	2 Present tense-forms in the verse	None	Stative
Rom 3:4	γέγραπται	---	---	---	---	None	Stative
Rom 3:10	γέγραπται	---	---	ὅτι clause	---	None	Stative

Pauline	Perfect tense-forms						
Rom 3:13	ἀνεῳγμένος	---	---	---	3:12b – 3:14 several Present tense-forms	None	Stative
Rom 3:19	οἴδαμεν	---	---	ὅτι clause	---	We	Stative
Rom 3:21	πεφανέρωται	Preposition	Separation	---	---	None	Stative
Rom 3:25	προγεγονότων	Prefix	Temporal past	---	Aorist in the preceding main clause	None	Stative
Rom 4:1	εὑρηκέναι	---	---	Τί	---	Abraham	Actional
Rom 4:14	κεκένωται	---	---	---	Both Perfect tense-forms are in parallel	None	Stative
Rom 4:14	κατήργηται	---	---	---	Both Perfect tense-forms are in parallel	None	Stative
Rom 4:17	γέγραπται	---	---	ὅτι clause	---	None	Stative
Rom 4:17	τέθεικά	---	---	σε	---	God	Actional
Rom 4:18	εἰρημένον	---	---	---	---	None	Stative
Rom 4:19	νενεκρωμένον	Adverb	Temporal anterior	---	Aorist in preceding main clause and Aorist preceding this verb in the same clause	None	Stative
Rom 4:21	ἐπήγγελται				Aorists preceding and following in the main clause	God	Stative
Rom 5:2	ἐσχήκαμεν	Dative; Preposition	Instrument; direction	τὴν προσαγωγὴν	Aorist + Present in Preceding verse, now Pf + Present	We	Actional
Rom 5:2	ἑστήκαμεν	Preposition	location		Aorist + Present in Preceding verse, now Pf + Present	We	Actional
Rom 5:3	εἰδότες	---	---	ὅτι clause	Present tense-form preceding in the main clause	We	Stative
Rom 5:5	ἐκκέχυται	Preposition; Prefix; Preposition	Location; Direction; Agent	---	No strong parallel	Holy Spirit	Stative
Rom 6:5	γεγόναμεν	Dative	Realm	σύμφυτοι	Contrasted with a Future	We	Stative
Rom 6:7	δεδικαίωται	Preposition	Separation		An Aorist in the clause	The one	Stative

Pauline	Perfect tense-forms						
Rom 6:9	εἰδότες	---	---	ὅτι clause	---	We	Stative
Rom 6:16	οἴδατε	---	---	ὅτι clause	---	You	Stative
Rom 7:2	δέδεται	Dative; Dative	Locative; Instrument	---	---	---	Stative
Rom 7:2	κατήργηται	Preposition	Separation	---	---	---	Stative
Rom 7:14	οἴδαμεν	---	---	ὅτι clause	---	We	Stative
Rom 7:14	πεπραμένος	Preposition	Locative	---	Present tense-forms in the clause	None	Stative
Rom 7:18	οἶδα	---	---	ὅτι clause	---	I	Stative
Rom 8:22	οἴδαμεν	---	---	ὅτι clause	---	We	Stative
Rom 8:26	οἴδαμεν	---	---	τὸ	Present tense-forms in the clause	We	Stative
Rom 8:27	οἶδεν	---	---	τί	Present tense-forms in the clause	The one	Stative
Rom 8:28	οἴδαμεν	---	---	ὅτι clause	---	We	Stative
Rom 8:36	γέγραπται	---	---	ὅτι clause	---	---	Stative
Rom 8:38	πέπεισμαι	---	---	ὅτι clause	---	I	Stative
Rom 8:38	ἐνεστῶτα	---	---	---	---	---	Stative
Rom 9:6	ἐκπέπτωκεν	---	---	---	---	The Word	Unclear
Rom 9:13	γέγραπται	---	---	---	---	---	Stative
Rom 9:19	ἀνθέστηκεν	Preposition	Direct object	τῷ ... βουλήματι	---	Who	Actional
Rom 9:22	κατηρτισμένα	Preposition	Purpose	---	---	---	Stative
Rom 9:25	ἠγαπημένην	---	---	----	---	---	Stative
Rom 9:25	ἠγαπημένην	---	---	----	---	---	Stative
Rom 9:29	προείρηκεν	Prefix	Temporal anterior	Citation	---	Isaiah	Actional
Rom 9:33	γέγραπται	---	---	---	---	---	Stative
Rom 10:15	γέγραπται	---	---	---	---	---	Stative
Rom 11:2	οἴδατε	---	---	τί	---	You	Stative
Rom 11:5	γέγονεν	Preposition; Adverb; Preposition	Locative; temporal; the standard	---	Aorists in 11:4	---	stative
Rom 11:8	γέγραπται	---	---	---	---	---	Stative
Rom 11:20	ἕστηκας	Dative	Instrument	---	Aorist in preceding parallel clause	You	Actional

Pauline	Perfect tense-forms						
Rom 11:25	γέγονεν	Dative; Preposition	Indirect object; Temporal	---	---	---	Stative
Rom 11:26	γέγραπται	---	---	---	---	---	Stative
Rom 12:19	γέγραπται	---	---	---	---	---	Stative
Rom 13:1	τεταγμέναι	Preposition	Agent	---	Present tense-forms in clause	God	Stative
Rom 13:2	ἀνθέστηκεν	Dative	Direct object	τῇ ... διαταγῇ	Unclear	The one	Actional
Rom 13:2	ἀνθεστηκότες	---	---		Unclear	The one	Actional
Rom 13:8	πεπλήρωκεν	---	---	νόμον	Present tense-forms	The one	Actional
Rom 13:11	εἰδότες	---	---	τὸν καιρόν	---	We	Stative
Rom 13:12	ἤγγικεν	---	---	---	Aorist	The day	Unclear
Rom 14:11	γέγραπται	---	---	---	---	---	Stative
Rom 14:14	οἶδα	Preposition	Realm	ὅτι clause	---	I	Stative
Rom 14:14	πέπεισμαι	Preposition	Realm	ὅτι clause	---	I	Stative
Rom 14:23	κατακέκριται	---	---	---	Aorist		Stative
Rom 15:3	γέγραπται	---	---	---	---	---	Stative
Rom 15:8	γεγενῆσθαι	Preposition	representation	διάκονον	Present tense-form preceding	Unclear	Stative
Rom 15:9	γέγραπται	---	---	---	---	---	Stative
Rom 15:14	πέπεισμαι	Preposition	Reference	ὅτι clause	---	I	Stative
Rom 15:14	πεπληρωμένοι	Dative	Content	---	Present tense-forms before and after in parallel	Ones	Stative
Rom 15:16	ἡγιασμένη	Preposition	Instrument	---	Aorist in clause	The nations	Stative
Rom 15:19	πεπληρωκέναι	Preposition; Preposition	Location; location	τὸ εὐαγγέλιον	Aorist in preceding clause, where this one is subordinate to	I	Actional
Rom 15:21	γέγραπται	---	---	---	---	---	Stative
Rom 15:21	ἀκηκόασιν	---	---	---	---	Those	Stative

Pauline	Perfect tense-forms						
Rom 15:29	οἶδα	---	---	ὅτι clause	---	I	Stative
Rom 16:7	γέγονεν	Preposition; Preposition	Temporal anterior; realm	---	Unclear	The ones	Stative
Rom 16:25	σεσιγημένου	Dative	Temporal	---	---	Mystery	Stative
1 Cor 1:2	ἡγιασμένοις	Preposition	Realm	---	---	The ones	Stative
1 Cor 1:10	κατηρτισμένοι	Preposition	Realm	---	---	You	Stative
1 Cor 1:13	μεμέρισται	---	---	---	Aorists	---	Stative
1 Cor 1:16	οἶδα	---	---	εἰ	Aorists	I	Stative
1 Cor 1:19	γέγραπται	---	---	---	---	---	Stative
1 Cor 1:23	ἐσταυρωμένον	---	---	---	---	---	Stative
1 Cor 1:28	ἐξουθενημένα	---	---	---	---	---	Stative
1 Cor 1:31	γέγραπται	---	---	---	---	---	Stative
1 Cor 2:2	εἰδέναι	Preposition	Location	τι	Aorist and Perfect	I	Unclear
1 Cor 2:2	ἐσταυρωμένον	---	---	---	---	---	Stative
1 Cor 2:7	ἀποκεκρυμμένην	Preposition	Realm or instrument	---	---	The one	Stative
1 Cor 2:8	ἔγνωκεν	---	---	σοφίαν (v. 7)	Aorists	The rulers	Unclear
1 Cor 2:9	γέγραπται	---	---	---	---	---	Stative
1 Cor 2:11	οἶδεν	---	---	τὰ	---	Who	Stative
1 Cor 2:11	ἔγνωκεν	---	---	τὰ	---	One	Stative
1 Cor 2:12	εἰδῶμεν	---	---	τὰ	---	We	Stative
1 Cor 3:16	οἴδατε	---	---	ὅτι	---	You	Stative
1 Cor 3:19	γέγραπται	---	---	---	---	---	Stative
1 Cor 3:22	ἐνεστῶτα	---	---	---	---	---	Stative
1 Cor 4:4	σύνοιδα	Dative	Realm	οὐδὲν	---	I	Stative
1 Cor 4:4	δεδικαίωμαι	Preposition	Realm	---	---	---	Stative
1 Cor 4:6	γέγραπται	---	---	---	---	---	Stative
1 Cor 4:8	κεκορεσμένοι	Adverb	Temporal	---	Several Aorists	---	Stative
1 Cor 4:19	πεφυσιωμένων	---	---	---	---	The people	Stative
1 Cor 5:2	πεφυσιωμένοι ἐστὲ	---	---	---	Aorist	Ones	stative
1 Cor 5:3	κέκρικα	Adverb	Temporal	τὸν	Aorist	I	Actional
1 Cor 5:6	οἴδατε	---	---	ὅτι	---	You	Stative
1 Cor 6:2	οἴδατε	---	---	ὅτι	---	You	Stative
1 Cor 6:3	οἴδατε	---	---	ὅτι	---	You	Stative

Pauline	Perfect tense-forms						
1 Cor 6:4	ἐξουθενημένους	Preposition	Realm	---	---	---	Stative
1 Cor 6:9	οἴδατε	---	---	ὅτι	---	You	Stative
1 Cor 6:15	οἴδατε	---	---	ὅτι	---	You	Stative
1 Cor 6:16	οἴδατε	---	---	ὅτι	---	You	Stative
1 Cor 6:19	οἴδατε	---	---	ὅτι	---	You	Stative
1 Cor 7:10	γεγαμηκόσιν	---	--	---	---	Ones	Stative
1 Cor 7:14	ἡγίασται	Preposition	Realm	---	Present tense-forms	---	Stative
1 Cor 7:14	ἡγίασται	Preposition	Realm	---	Present tense-forms	---	Stative
1 Cor 7:15	δεδούλωται	Preposition	Realm	---	Present and Perfects	---	Stative
1 Cor 7:15	κέκληκεν	Preposition	Realm	ὑμᾶς	Present and Perfects	God	Actional
1 Cor 7:16	οἶδας	---	---	εἰ	Aorists	You	Stative
1 Cor 7:16	οἶδας	---	---	εἰ	Aorists	You	Stative
1 Cor 7:17	κέκληκεν	---	---	ἕκαστον	---	God	Actional
1 Cor 7:18	περιτετμημένος	---	---	---	Aorist and Present	---	Stative
1 Cor 7:18	κέκληταί	Preposition	Manner	---	Aorist and Present	---	Stative
1 Cor 7:25	ἠλεημένος	Preposition	Agency	---	Presents	The Lord	Stative
1 Cor 7:26	ἐνεστῶσαν	---	---	---	Presents	---	Stative
1 Cor 7:27	δέδεσαι	Dative	Personal interest	---	Presents	---	Stative
1 Cor 7:27	λέλυσαι	Preposition	Separation	---	Presents	---	Stative
1 Cor 7:29	συνεσταλμένος ἐστίν	---	---	---	Presents, also one is in periphrasis	---	Stative
1 Cor 7:34	μεμέρισται	---	---	---	---	---	Stative
1 Cor 7:37	ἕστηκεν	Preposition	Realm	---	Presents	The one	Stative
1 Cor 7:37	κέκρικεν	Preposition	Realm	τοῦτο	Presents	The one	Actional
1 Cor 7:39	δέδεται	Preposition	Temporal duration	---	---	The wife	Stative
1 Cor 8:1	οἴδαμεν	---	---	ὅτι	---	We	Stative
1 Cor 8:2	ἐγνωκέναι	---	---	τι	It precedes the presents in context	The one	Actional
1 Cor 8:3	ἔγνωσται	Preposition	Agency	---	Presents	God	Stative
1 Cor 8:4	οἴδαμεν	---	---	ὅτι	---	We	Stative
1 Cor 9:1	ἑόρακα	---	---	Ἰησοῦν	Presents	I	Stative
1 Cor 9:9	γέγραπται	Preposition	Location	ὅτι	---	We	Stative

Pauline	Perfect tense-forms						
1 Cor 9:13	οἴδατε	---	---	ὅτι	---	You	Stative
1 Cor 9:15	κέχρημαι	---	---	οὐδενὶ	---	I	Stative
1 Cor 9:17	πεπίστευμαι	---	---	οἰκονομίαν	Presents	---	Stative
1 Cor 9:22	γέγονα	Dative	Indirect object	πάντα	Aorist	I	Stative
1 Cor 9:24	οἴδατε	---	---	ὅτι	---	You	Stative
1 Cor 10:7	γέγραπται	---	---	---	---	---	Stative
1 Cor 10:11	κατήντηκεν	Preposition	Identification	---	Aorists	Ends	Stative
1 Cor 10:12	ἑστάναι	---	---	---	---	The one	Stative
1 Cor 10:13	εἴληφεν	---	---	ὑμᾶς	---	Temptation	Actional
1 Cor 11:2	μέμνησθε	---	---	πάντα	Aorist	You	Actional
1 Cor 11:3	εἰδέναι	---	---	ὅτι	Presents	You	Stative
1 Cor 11:5	ἐξυρημένη	---	---	---	Presents	---	Stative
1 Cor 11:15	δέδοται	Preposition	Replacement	---	Present	---	Stative
1 Cor 12:2	οἴδατε	---	---	ὅτι	Presents	You	Stative
1 Cor 13:1	γέγονα	---	---	χαλκὸς; κύμβαλον	Present	---	Stative
1 Cor 13:2	εἰδῶ	---	---	μυστήρια; γνῶσιν	Presents	I	Stative
1 Cor 13:11	γέγονα	---	---	ἀνήρ	Imperfects are temporally prior in context	---	Stative
1 Cor 13:11	κατήργηκα	---	---	τὰ	Imperfects are temporally prior in context	I	Actional
1 Cor 14:11	εἰδῶ	---	---	τὴν δύναμιν	Future consequent upon this clause	I	Stative
1 Cor 14:16	οἶδεν	---	---	τί	Presents	He	Stative
1 Cor 14:21	γέγραπται	Preposition	Location	---	---	---	Stative
1 Cor 15:1	ἑστήκατε	Preposition	Location	---	---	you	Stative
1 Cor 15:4	ἐγήγερται	Preposition	Temporal	---	Embedded among Aorists	He	Actional

Pauline	Perfect tense-forms						
1 Cor 15:12	ἐγήγερται	Preposition	Source	---	---	He	Stative
1 Cor 15:13	ἐγήγερται	---	---	---	---	Christ	Stative
1 Cor 15:14	ἐγήγερται	---	---	---	In a conditional clause, protasis	Christ	Stative
1 Cor 15:16	ἐγήγερται	---	---	---	In a conditional clause, apodosis	Christ	Stative
1 Cor 15:17	ἐγήγερται	---	---	---	In a conditional clause, protasis	Christ	Stative
1 Cor 15:19	ἠλπικότες ἐσμὲν	Preposition	Location	ἐν τῇ ζωῇ ταύτῃ	In a conditional clause, protasis	we	Stative
1 Cor 15:20	ἐγήγερται	Preposition Adverb	Source Temporal	---	---	Christ	Stative
1 Cor 15:20	κεκοιμημένων	---	---	---	Substantive participle	Those	Stative
1 Cor 15:27	ὑποτέτακται	Preposition	Subordination	πάντα	In a relative clause	He	Actional
1 Cor 15:45	γέγραπται	---	---	Citation	citational	It	Stative
1 Cor 15:54	γεγραμμένος	---	---	---	Adjectival	The word	Stative
1 Cor 15:58	εἰδότες	---	---	Content clause	referential	---	Stative
1 Cor 16:9	ἀνέῳγεν	Dative	Reference	---	---	A door	Actional
1 Cor 16:15	οἴδατε	---	---	Content clause	referential	---	Stative
2 Cor 1:7	εἰδότες	---	---	Content clause	referential	---	Stative
2 Cor 1:9	ἐσχήκαμεν	Preposition	Locational	τὸ ἀπόκριμα	---	We	Actional
2 Cor 1:9	πεποιθότες ὦμεν	Preposition	Locational	---	---	We	Stative
2 Cor 1:10	ἠλπίκαμεν	Preposition	Direction	Content clause	---	We	Actional
2 Cor 1:19	γέγονεν	Preposition	Location	ναὶ	---	It	Stative
2 Cor 1:24	ἑστήκατε	Dative	Means or instrument	---	---	You	Actional
2 Cor 2:3	πεποιθὼς	Preposition	Location	Content clause	Referential	I	Actional
2 Cor 2:5	λελύπηκεν	---	---	---	Conditional clause, protasis	Anyone	Actional
2 Cor 2:5	λελύπηκεν	---	---	πάντας ὑμᾶς	Conditional clause, apodosis	Anyone	Actional

Pauline	Perfect tense-forms						
2 Cor 2:10	κεχάρισμαι	---	---	ὃ	---	I	Actional
2 Cor 2:10	κεχάρισμαι	Preposition Preposition	Person of interest, Witnesss	τι	Conditional clause, protasis	I	Actional
2 Cor 2:12	ἀνεῳγμένης	Dative, Dative	Interest Location	---	Adjectival	Door	Stative
2 Cor 2:13	ἔσχηκα	Preposition	Location	ἄνεσιν	---	I	Actional
2 Cor 3:2	ἐγγεγραμμένη	Preposition	Location	---	Adjectival	A letter	Stative
2 Cor 3:3	ἐγγεγραμμένη	Dative Dative Preposition preposition	Means Means Location Location	---	Adjectival	A letter	Stative
2 Cor 3:7	ἐντετυπωμένη	Dative Preposition	Means Location		Adjectival	The ministry	Actional
2 Cor 3:10	δεδόξασται	Preposition	Cause	---	---	It	---
2 Cor 3:10	δεδοξασμένον	Preposition	Manner	---	---	It	---
2 Cor 3:18	ἀνακεκαλυμμένῳ	---	---	---	Adjectival	We	Stative
2 Cor 4:3	κεκαλυμμένον	---	---	---	Periphrastic Adjectival	Gospel	Stative
2 Cor 4:3	κεκαλυμμένον	Preposition	Location	---	Periphrastic Adjectival	It	Stative
2 Cor 4:13	γεγραμμένον	---	---	---	---	Thing or what	Stative
2 Cor 4:14	εἰδότες	---	---	Content clause	Citational	We	Actional
2 Cor 5:1	οἴδαμεν	---	---	Content clause	Citational	We	Actional
2 Cor 5:6	εἰδότες	---	---	Content clause	Citational	We	Actional
2 Cor 5:11	εἰδότες	---	---	Content clause	Citational	We	Actional
2 Cor 5:11	πεφανερώμεθα	Dative	Indirect object	---	---	We	---
2 Cor 5:11	πεφανερῶσθαι	Preposition	Location	---	---	We	---
2 Cor 5:16	οἴδαμεν	Preposition	Manner	οὐδένα	---	We	Actional
2 Cor 5:16	ἐγνώκαμεν	Preposition	Manner	Χριστόν	---	We	Actional
2 Cor 5:17	γέγονεν	---	---	---	---	The new thing	Stative
2 Cor 6:11	ἀνέῳγεν	Preposition	Indirect object/ reference	---		The mouth	Actional
2 Cor 6:11	πεπλάτυνται	---	---	---	---	Our heart	Stative
2 Cor 7:3	προείρηκα	Attached preposition	Temporal	Content clause	---	I	Actional

Pauline	Perfect tense-forms						
2 Cor 7:4	πεπλήρωμαι	Dative	Substance	---	---	I	Stative
2 Cor 7:5	ἔσχηκεν	---	---	ἄνεσιν	---	Our flesh	Actional
2 Cor 7:13	παρακεκλήμεθα	---	---	---	Resulting state	we	Stative
2 Cor 7:13	ἀναπέπαυται	Preposition	Agent	---	---	His spirit	Actional
2 Cor 7:14	κεκαύχημαι	Dative Preposition	Indirect object Person referenced	---	---	I	Actional
2 Cor 8:1	δεδομένην	Preposition	Location	---	---	Grace	Actional
2 Cor 8:15	γέγραπται	---	---	Content clause	Citational	It	Stative
2 Cor 9:2	οἶδα	---	---	προθυμίαν	Referential	I	Actional
2 Cor 9:2	παρεσκεύασται	Prepositional	Temporal	---	---	You	Actional
2 Cor 9:3	παρεσκευασμένοι ἦτε	---	---	---	Periphrastic	You	Stative
2 Cor 9:5	προεπηγγελμένην	Attached preposition	Temporal	---	Adjectival	The one	Stative
2 Cor 9:7	προῄρηται	Dative Preposition Attached	Location Temporal	---	---	Each	---
2 Cor 9:9	γέγραπται	---	---	---	Citational	It	Stative
2 Cor 10:7	πέποιθεν	Dative	Location	Content clause	Conditional clause, protasis	Anyone	Actional
2 Cor 10:10	ἐξουθενημένος	---	---	---	Adjectival	---	Stative
2 Cor 11:5	ὑστερηκέναι	Genitive	Comparative	---	Infinitive	I	Stative
2 Cor 11:11	οἶδεν	---	---	---	---	God	Stative
2 Cor 11:21	ἠσθενήκαμεν	---	---	---	Subordinate clause	We	Stative
2 Cor 11:25	πεποίηκα	Preposition	Location	νυχθήμερον	Series of Aorists, narrative summary	I	Actional
2 Cor 11:31	οἶδεν	---	---	Content clause	Referential	God	Actional
2 Cor 12:2	οἶδα	Preposition	Location	ἄνθρωπον	Referential	I	---
2 Cor 12:2	οἶδα	---	---	Content clause	Referential	I	---
2 Cor 12:2	οἶδα	---	---	Content clause	Referential	I	---
2 Cor 12:2	οἶδεν	---	---	---	---	God	Stative

Pauline	Perfect tense-forms						
2 Cor 12:3	οἶδα	Preposition	Location	ἄνθρωπον	Referential	I	---
2 Cor 12:3	οἶδα	---	---	Content clause	Referential	I	---
2 Cor 12:3	οἶδεν	---	---	---	---	God	Stative
2 Cor 12:9	εἴρηκέν	Dative	Indirect object	Content clause	Citational	He	Actional
2 Cor 12:11	γέγονεν	---	---	ἄφρων as a PN	Copulua-like	I	Stative
2 Cor 12:17	ἀπέσταλκα	Dative	Indirect object	---	Supplemental clause	I	Actional
2 Cor 12:21	προημαρτηκότων	Attached preposition	Temporal	---	Substantival	---	---
2 Cor 13:2	προείρηκα	---	---	Content clause	Contrasted with the Present tense here	I	Actional
2 Cor 13:2	προημαρτηκόσιν	Attached preposition	Temporal	---	Substantival	---	Stative
Gal 1:4	ἐνεστῶτος	---	---	---	Adjectival	---	Stative
Gal 1:9	προειρήκαμεν	Attached preposition	Temporal	Content clause	---	We	Stative
Gal 2:7	πεπίστευμαι	---	---	τὸ εὐαγγέλιον	Subordinate clause	I	Stative
Gal 2:11	κατεγνωσμένος ἦν	---	---	---	Periphrastic Adjectival	He	Stative
Gal 2:16	εἰδότες	---	---	Content clause	Referential	We	Stative
Gal 2:19	συνεσταύρωμαι	Dative and attached preposition	Association	---	---	We	Stative
Gal 3:1	ἐσταυρωμένος	---	---	---	Substantive	Christ	Stative
Gal 3:10	γέγραπται	---	---	Content clause	Citational	It	Stative
Gal 3:10	γεγραμμένοις	Preposition	Location	---	Substantive	Things	Stative
Gal 3:13	γενόμενος	Preposition	Representation	κατάρα as a PN	Copula-like	Law	Stative
Gal 3:13	γέγραπται	---	---	Content clause	Citational	It	Stative
Gal 3:15	κεκυρωμένην	---	---	διαθήκην	---	---	Stative
Gal 3:17	προκεκυρωμένην	Preposition Attached preposition	Agent Temporal	διαθήκην	---	---	Stative

Pauline	Perfect tense-forms						
Gal 3:17	γεγονὼς	Preposition	Temporal	---	---	Law	Actional
Gal 3:18	κεχάρισται	Dative Preposition	Indirect object Instrument	Inheritance is implied	---	God	Actional
Gal 3:19	ἐπήγγελται	---	---	---	Adjectival	The one who	Stative
Gal 3:24	γέγονεν	Preposition	Directional	παιδαγωγὸς as a PN	Copula-like	The law	Stative
Gal 4:3	ἤμεθα δεδουλωμένοι	Preposition	Subordinating	---	Periphrastic	We	Stative
Gal 4:8	εἰδότες	Adverb	Temporal	θεὸν	Subordinate clause	You	Stative
Gal 4:11	κεκοπίακα	Adverb Preposition	Manner Directional	---	---	I	Actional
Gal 4:13	οἴδατε	---	---	Content clause	Referential	You	Stative
Gal 4:16	γέγονα	Dative	Indirect object	ἐχθρὸς as a PN	Copula-like	I	Stative
Gal 4:22	γέγραπται	---	---	Content clause	Citational	It	Stative
Gal 4:23	γεγέννηται	Preposition Preposition	Manner Source	---	---	One	Actional
Gal 4:27	γέγραπται	---	---	Content clause	Citational	It	Stative
Gal 5:10	πέποιθα	Preposition Preposition	Reference Location	Content clause	Referential	I	Actional
Gal 5:11	κατήργηται	---	---	---	Conditional clause, apodosis	The offense	Stative
Gal 5:14	πεπλήρωται	Preposition	Location	---	---	The law	Stative
Gal 6:14	ἐσταύρωται	Dative Dative Genitive	Reference Reference Means	---	---	The world ... I	Actional
Eph 1:6	ἠγαπημένῳ	---	---	---	Prepositional phrase, Adjectival	He	Stative
Eph 1:12	προηλπικότας	Attached preposition Preposition	Temporal Standard	---	---	We	Stative
Eph 1:18	πεφωτισμένους	---	---	---	Adjectival	Eyes	Stative
Eph 1:18	εἰδέναι	---	---	Content clause	Purpose/ result infinitive referential	You	Stative
Eph 2:5	ἐστε σεσῳσμένοι	Dative	Instrumental	---	Periphrastic	You	Stative
Eph 2:8	ἐστε σεσῳσμένοι	Dative Genitive	Instrumental means	---	Periphrastic	You	Stative
Eph 2:12	ἀπηλλοτριωμένοι	Genitive	Separation	---	---	You	Stative

Pauline	Perfect tense-forms						
Eph 3:9	ἀποκεκρυμμένου	Preposition Preposition	Temporal Location	---	Adjectival		Stative
Eph 3:17	ἐρριζωμένοι	Preposition	Location	---	Substantival	We	Stative
Eph 3:17	τεθεμελιωμένοι	Preposition	Location	---	Substantival	We	Stative
Eph 4:18	ἐσκοτωμένοι ... ὄντες	Dative	Location	---	Periphrastic	We	Stative
Eph 4:18	ἀπηλλοτριωμένοι	Genitive	Separation	---	---	We	Stative
Eph 4:19	ἀπηλγηκότες	---	---	---	Substantival	They	Stative
Eph 5:5	ἴστε γινώσκοντες	---	---	Content clause	Periphrastic, referential	You	Stative
Eph 6:8	εἰδότες	---	---	Content clause	Referential	You	Stative
Eph 6:9	εἰδότες	---	---	Content clause	Referential	You	Stative
Eph 6:16	πεπυρωμένα	---	---	---	Adjectival	---	Stative
Eph 6:21	εἰδῆτε	---	---	Content clause	Referential	You	Stative
Phil 1:6	πεποιθὼς	---	---	Content clause	Referential	You	Stative
Phil 1:11	πεπληρωμένοι	Preposition Preposition	Source Direction	καρπὸν	Substantive	---	Stative
Phil 1:12	ἐλήλυθεν	Preposition Preposition	Reference Goal	---	Subordinate clause	The things	Stative
Phil 1:14	πεποιθότας	Dative Dative	Location Instrument	---	Explanatory clause	Brothers	Stative
Phil 1:16	εἰδότες	---	---	Content clause	Referential	You	Stative
Phil 1:19	οἶδα	---	---	Content clause	Referential	I	Stative
Phil 1:25	πεποιθὼς	---	---	τοῦτο	Referential	I	Stative
Phil 1:25	οἶδα	---	---	Content clause	Referential	I	Stative
Phil 2:15	διεστραμμένης	---	---	---	Adjectival	---	Stative
Phil 2:24	πέποιθα	Preposition	Location	---	Referential	I	Stative
Phil 3:3	πεποιθότες	Preposition	Location	---	---	We	Stative
Phil 3:4	πεποιθέναι	Preposition	Location	---	Conditional clause, protasis	Anyone	Stative
Phil 3:7	ἥγημαι	Preposition	Reference	ταῦτα	---	I	Stative
Phil 3:12	τετελείωμαι	Adverb	Temporal	ἐξανάστασιν	Explanatory clause	I	Stative
Phil 3:13	κατειληφέναι	---	---	---	Infinitive	I	Stative

Pauline	Perfect tense-forms						
Phil 4:12	οἶδα	---	---	Infinitive	---	I	Stative
Phil 4:12	οἶδα	---	---	Infinitive	---	I	Stative
Phil 4:12	μεμύημαι	Preposition Preposition	Reference Reference	4 infinitives	---	I	Stative
Phil 4:15	οἴδατε	---	---	Content clause	Referential	You	Stative
Phil 4:18	πεπλήρωμαι	---	---	---	---	I	Stative
Col 1:16	ἔκτισται	Preposition Preposition	Agent Purpose	---	---	All things	Stative
Col 1:17	συνέστηκεν	Attached preposition	Association	---	---	All things	
Col 1:21	ὄντας ἀπηλλοτριωμένους	Adverb Preposition Preposition	Temporal Location Instrument	---	Periphrastic	You	Stative
Col 1:23	τεθεμελιωμένοι	---	---	---	Substantive	---	Stative
Col 1:26	ἀποκεκρυμμένον	Preposition Preposition	Temporal Separation	---	Adjectival	---	Stative
Col 2:1	εἰδέναι	---	---	ἡλίκον ἀγῶνα	Infinitive	You	---
Col 2:1	ἑόρακαν	Preposition	Manner	τὸ πρόσωπόν	Relative clause	who	Actional
Col 2:7	ἐρριζωμένοι	Preposition	Location	---	Substantival	---	Stative
Col 2:10	ἐστὲ ... πεπληρωμένοι	Preposition	Location	---	Periphrastic	---	Stative
Col 2:14	ἦρκεν	Preposition	Separation	αὐτὸ	---	God	Actional
Col 2:18	ἑόρακεν	---	---	ἃ	---	He	Actional
Col 3:3	κέκρυπται	Preposition Preposition	Association Location	---	---	Life	Stative
Col 3:12	ἠγαπημένοι	---	---	---	Substantive	---	Stative
Col 3:24	εἰδότες	---	---	Content clause	Referential	You	Stative
Col 4:1	εἰδότες	---	---	Content clause	Referential	You	Stative
Col 4:3	δέδεμαι	Preposition	Reference	---	Explanatory clause	I	Stative
Col 4:6	ἠρτυμένος	Dative	Instrument	---	---	You	Stative
Col 4:6	εἰδέναι	---	---	Content clause	Referential	You	Stative
Col 4:12	πεπληροφορημένοι	Preposition	Reference	---	Substantive	---	Stative
1 Thess 1:4	εἰδότες	---	---	Content clause	Referential	You	Stative
1 Thess 1:4	ἠγαπημένοι	---	---	---	Adjectival	---	Stative

Pauline	Perfect tense-forms						
1 Thess 1:5	οἴδατε	---	---	Content clause	Referential	You	Stative
1 Thess 1:8	ἐξήχηται	Preposition Preposition	Source Location	---	---	Word	Actional
1 Thess 1:8	ἐξελήλυθεν	Preposition Preposition Preposition	Location Location Location	---	---	Faith	Actional
1 Thess 2:1	οἴδατε	---	---	Content clause	Referential	You	Stative
1 Thess 2:1	γέγονεν	---	---	κενὴ as a PN	Copula-like	It	Stative
1 Thess 2:4	δεδοκιμάσμεθα	Preposition	Agent	---	Subordinate clause	We	Actional
1 Thess 2:5	οἴδατε	---	---	Content clause	Subordinate clause, referential	You	Stative
1 Thess 2:11	οἴδατε	---	---	Content clause	Subordinate clause, referential	You	Stative
1 Thess 3:3	οἴδατε	---	---	Content clause	Referential	You	Stative
1 Thess 3:4	οἴδατε	---	---	Content clause	Subordinate clause, referential	You	Stative
1 Thess 4:2	οἴδατε	---	---	Content clause	Referential	You	Stative
1 Thess 4:4	εἰδέναι	---	---	Content clause	Referential	You	Stative
1 Thess 4:5	εἰδότα	---	---	Content clause	Referential	Who	Stative
1 Thess 5:2	οἴδατε	Adverb	Manner	Content clause	Referential	Who	---
1 Thess 5:12	εἰδέναι	---	---	Content clause	Referential	Who	Stative
2 Thess 1:8	εἰδόσιν	---	---	θεὸν	Referential	They	Stative
2 Thess 2:2	ἐνέστηκεν	---	---	---	Subordinate clause	He	Actional
2 Thess 2:6	οἴδατε	Adverb	Temporal	τὸ κατέχον	Referential	You	Stative
2 Thess 2:13	ἠγαπημένοι	Preposition	Agent	---	---	Brothers	Actional
2 Thess 3:4	πεποίθαμεν	Preposition Preposition	Location Reference	Content clause	Referential	We	Actional
2 Thess 3:7	οἴδατε	---	---	Content clause	Referential	You	Stative

Pauline	Perfect tense-forms						
1 Tim 1:8	οἴδαμεν	---	---	Content clause	Referential	We	Stative
1 Tim 1:9	εἰδώς	---	---	τοῦτο	Referential	We	Stative
1 Tim 2:14	γέγονεν	Preposition	Location/ status	---	Copula-like	She	Stative
1 Tim 3:5	οἶδεν	---	---	Content clause	Conditional clause, apodosis, referential	someone	Stative
1 Tim 3:15	εἰδῇς	---	---	Content clause	Subordinate clause, Referential	You	Stative
1 Tim 4:2	κεκαυστηριασμένων	---	---	τὴν ἰδίαν συνείδησιν	Adjectival	Whose	Stative
1 Tim 4:3	ἐπεγνωκόσι	---	---	τὴν ἀλήθειαν	Substantival	They	Stative
1 Tim 4:6	παρηκολούθηκας	Dative	Location	---	---	You	Stative
1 Tim 4:10	ἠλπίκαμεν	Preposition	Location	---	Subordinate clause	We	Actional
1 Tim 5:5	μεμονωμένη	---	---	---	Substantive	---	Stative
1 Tim 5:5	ἤλπικεν	Preposition	Location	---	---	She	Actional
1 Tim 5:6	τέθνηκεν	---	---	---	---	She	Stative
1 Tim 5:8	ἤρνηται	---	---	τὴν πίστιν	Conditional clause, apodosis	He	Stative
1 Tim 5:9	γεγονυῖα	---	---	γυνή as a PN	Copula-like	She	Stative
1 Tim 5:17	προεστῶτες	Adverb Attached preposition	Manner Temporal	---	Adjectival	Elders	Stative
1 Tim 6:4	τετύφωται	---	---	---	Conditional clause, apodosis	He	Stative
1 Tim 6:5	διεφθαρμένων	---	---	τὸν νοῦν	Adjectival	People	Stative
1 Tim 6:5	ἀπεστερημένων	Attached preposition	Separation	τῆς ἀληθείας	Substantive	People	Stative
1 Tim 6:17	ἠλπικέναι	Preposition	Location	---	---	The rich	Stative
2 Tim 1:4	μεμνημένος	Genitive	Reference	---	---	I	Stative
2 Tim 1:5	πέπεισμαι	---	---	Content clause	Referential	I	Stative
2 Tim 1:12	οἶδα	---	---	ᾧ	Referential	I	Stative
2 Tim 1:12	πεπίστευκα	Dative	Location	---	Referential	I	Stative
2 Tim 1:12	πέπεισμαι	Dative	Location	Content clause	Referential	I	Stative

Pauline	Perfect tense-forms						
2 Tim 1:15	οἶδας	---	---	Content clause	Referential	You	Stative
2 Tim 2:8	ἐγηγερμένον	Preposition	Separation	---	Substantival	He	Stative
2 Tim 2:9	δέδεται	---	---	---	---	Word	Stative
2 Tim 2:18	γεγονέναι	Adverb	Temporal	---	Indirect speech	Resurrection	Stative
2 Tim 2:19	ἕστηκεν	---	---	---	---	Foundation	Stative
2 Tim 2:21	ἡγιασμένον	---	---	---	Conditional clause, apodosis	Anyone	Stative
2 Tim 2:21	ἡτοιμασμένον	Preposition	Purpose/ direction	---	Supplemental clause	Anyone	Stative
2 Tim 2:23	εἰδὼς	---	---	Content clause	Referential	You	Stative
2 Tim 2:26	ἐζωγρημένοι	Preposition Preposition	Agent Direction/ purpose	---	Explanatory clause	Those	Actional
2 Tim 3:4	τετυφωμένοι	---	---	---	Substantive	---	Stative
2 Tim 3:5	ἠρνημένοι	---	---	τὴν ... δύναμιν	---	People	Stative
2 Tim 3:6	σεσωρευμένα	Dative	Instrument	---	---	They	Stative
2 Tim 3:8	κατεφθαρμένοι	Attached preposition	Standard	τὸν νοῦν	Adjectival	Men	Stative
2 Tim 3:14	εἰδὼς	---	---	Content clause	Supplemental clause	You	Stative
2 Tim 3:15	οἶδας	Preposition	Temporal	ἱερὰ γράμματα	---	You	Stative
2 Tim 3:17	ἐξηρτισμένος	Preposition	Goal	---	Supplemental clause	Man	Actional
2 Tim 4:6	ἐφέστηκεν	Attached preposition	Temporal point	---	---	Time	Actional
2 Tim 4:7	ἠγώνισμαι	---	---	τὸν καλὸν ἀγῶνα	----	I	Stative
2 Tim 4:7	τετέλεκα	---	---	τὸν δρόμον	---	I	Stative
2 Tim 4:7	τετήρηκα	---	---	τὴν πίστιν	---	I	Stative
2 Tim 4:8	ἠγαπηκόσι	---	---	τὴν ἐπιφάνειαν	Substantival	Them	Stative
Tit 1:15	μεμιαμμένοις	---	---	---	---	Those	Stative
Tit 1:15	μεμίανται	---	---	---	---	Mind	Stative
Tit 1:16	εἰδέναι	---	---	θεὸν	Referential	They	Stative
Tit 2:3	δεδουλωμένας	Dative	Instrument	---	---	Women	Stative

Pauline	Perfect tense-forms						
Tit 3:8	πεπιστευκότες	Dative	Location	---	---	Those	Stative
Tit 3:11	εἰδώς	---	---	Content clause	Supplemental clause	You	Stative
Tit 3:11	ἐξέστραπται	---	---	---	Adjectival	Person	Stative
Tit 3:12	κέκρικα	---	---	παραχειμάσαι	Explanatory clause	I	Actional
Phlm 1:7	ἀναπέπαυται	Preposition	Agent	---	Explanatory clause	Hearts	Actional
Phlm 1:21	πεποιθώς	Dative	Referent	---	---	I	Actional
Phlm 1:21	εἰδώς	---	---	Content clause	Supplemental clause	I	Actional

Pluperfect tense-forms							
Rom 7:7	ἤδειν	---	---	ἐπιθυμίαν	Example clause	I	Stative

Appendix F

Chart of Adverbial Modification of Stative Perfects

Reference	Stative	Durative time	Unmodified	Adjectival	Copula-like	Substantive	Present Time Adv	Reflexive	Opposition	Subordinating	Specification
Rom 1:1	1										
Rom 1:17			1								
Rom 1:28						1					
Rom 2:2			1								
Rom 2:18			1								
Rom 2:24			1								
Rom 2:25	1		1		1						
Rom 3:4			1								
Rom 3:10			1								
Rom 3:13	1		1	1							
Rom 3:19			1								
Rom 3:21											
Rom 3:25				1							
Rom 4:1											

Reference	Stative	Durative time	Unmodified	Adjectival	Copula-like	Substantive	Present Time Adv	Reflexive	Opposition	Subordinating	Specification
Rom 4:14a			1	1							
Rom 4:14b			1	1							
Rom 4:17			1								
Rom 4:18	?		1			1					
Rom 4:19	1			1			1				
Rom 4:21			1								
Rom 5:2a											
Rom 5:2b											
Rom 5:3			1								
Rom 5:5											
Rom 6:5	1				1						
Rom 6:7											
Rom 6:9			1								
Rom 6:16			1								
Rom 7:2a											
Rom 7:2b											
Rom 7:14a			1								
Rom 7:14b										?	
Rom 7:18			1								
Rom 8:22			1								
Rom 8:26			1								
Rom 8:27			1								
Rom 8:28			1								
Rom 8:36			1								
Rom 8:38a			1								
Rom 8:38b	1		1			1					
Rom 9:6			1								
Rom 9:13			1								
Rom 9:19									1		
Rom 9:22				1							
Rom 9:25a	1		1			1					
Rom 9:25b	1		1			1					
Rom 9:29											

Reference	Stative	Durative time	Unmodified	Adjectival	Copula-like	Substantive	Present Time Adv	Reflexive	Opposition	Subordinating	Specification
Rom 9:33			1								
Rom 10:15			1								
Rom 11:2			1								
Rom 11:5	1				1						
Rom 11:8			1								
Rom 11:20											
Rom 11:25					1						
Rom 11:26			1								
Rom 12:19			1								
Rom 13:1											
Rom 13:2a									1		
Rom 13:2b			1						1		
Rom 13:8			1								
Rom 13:11			1								
Rom 13:12			1								
Rom 14:11			1								
Rom 14:14a			1								
Rom 14:14b											
Rom 14:23			1								
Rom 15:3			1								
Rom 15:8	1		1		1						
Rom 15:9			1								
Rom 15:14a											
Rom 15:14b											
Rom 15:16											
Rom 15:19											
Rom 15:21			1								
Rom 15:29			1								
Rom 16:7											
Rom 16:25	1	1									
1 Cor 1:2	1										
1 Cor 1:10						1					
1 Cor 1:13			1								

Reference	Stative	Durative time	Unmodified	Adjectival	Copula-like	Substantive	Present Time Adv	Reflexive	Opposition	Subordinating	Specification
1 Cor 1:16			1								
1 Cor 1:19			1								
1 Cor 1:23	1		1	?		?					
1 Cor 1:28			1			1					
1 Cor 1:31			1								
1 Cor 2:2	1		1	1							
1 Cor 2:7	1		1	1							
1 Cor 2:8			1								
1 Cor 2:9			1								
1 Cor 2:11			1								
1 Cor 2:12			1								
1 Cor 3:16			1								
1 Cor 3:19			1								
1 Cor 3:22						1					
1 Cor 4:4a											
1 Cor 4:4b											
1 Cor 4:6			1								
1 Cor 4:8											
1 Cor 4:19	1		1			1					
1 Cor 5:2			1			1					
1 Cor 5:3											
1 Cor 5:6			1								
1 Cor 6:2			1								
1 Cor 6:3			1								
1 Cor 6:4	1					1					
1 Cor 6:9			1								
1 Cor 6:15			1								
1 Cor 6:16			1								
1 Cor 6:19			1								
1 Cor 7:10	1		1			1					
1 Cor 7:14a											
1 Cor 7:14b											
1 Cor 7:15	1										

Reference	Stative	Durative time	Unmodified	Adjectival	Copula-like	Substantive	Present Time Adv	Reflexive	Opposition	Subordinating	Specification
1 Cor 7:16a			1								
1 Cor 7:16b			1								
1 Cor 7:17			1								
1 Cor 7:18a	1		1			1					
1 Cor 7:18b											
1 Cor 7:25						1					
1 Cor 7:26	1		1	1							
1 Cor 7:27											
1 Cor 7:29						1					
1 Cor 7:34	1		1								
1 Cor 7:37a											
1 Cor 7:37b											
1 Cor 7:39	1	1									
1 Cor 8:1			1								
1 Cor 8:2			1								
1 Cor 8:3											
1 Cor 8:4			1								
1 Cor 9:1											
1 Cor 9:9											
1 Cor 9:13			1								
1 Cor 9:15											
1 Cor 9:17			1								
1 Cor 9:22	1				1						
1 Cor 9:24			1								
1 Cor 10:7			1								
1 Cor 10:11											
1 Cor 10:12			1								
1 Cor 10:13			1								
1 Cor 11:2			1								
1 Cor 11:3			1								
1 Cor 11:5	1		1			1					
1 Cor 11:15									1		
1 Cor 12:2			1								

Reference	Starive	Durative time	Unmodified	Adjectival	Copula-like	Substantive	Present Time Adv	Reflexive	Opposition	Subordinating	Specification
1 Cor 13:1	1		1		1						
1 Cor 13:2			1								
1 Cor 13:11	1		1		1						
1 Cor 14:11			1								
1 Cor 14:16			1								
1 Cor 14:21											
1 Cor 15:1											
1 Cor 15:4											
1 Cor 15:12											
1 Cor 15:13			1								
1 Cor 15:14			1								
1 Cor 15:16			1								
1 Cor 15:17			1								
1 Cor 15:19		1				1					
1 Cor 15:20a	1	1									
1 Cor 15:20b	1		1			1					
1 Cor 15:27										1	
1 Cor 15:45			1								
1 Cor 15:54			1								
1 Cor 15:58			1								
1 Cor 16:9											
1 Cor 16:15			1								
2 Cor 1:7			1								
2 Cor 1:9a											
2 Cor 1:9b						1					
2 Cor 1:10											
2 Cor 1:19											
2 Cor 1:24											
2 Cor 2:3											
2 Cor 2:5a			1								
2 Cor 2:5b											
2 Cor 2:10a			1								
2 Cor 2:10b											

Reference	Stative	Durative time	Unmodified	Adjectival	Copula-like	Substantive	Present Time Adv	Reflexive	Opposition	Subordinating	Specification
2 Cor 2:12				1							
2 Cor 2:13											
2 Cor 3:2				1							
2 Cor 3:3				1							
2 Cor 3:7											
2 Cor 3:10a											
2 Cor 3:10b			1	1							
2 Cor 3:18	1		1	1							
2 Cor 4:3a			1			1					
2 Cor 4:3b						1					
2 Cor 4:13	1		1			1					
2 Cor 4:14			1								
2 Cor 5:1			1								
2 Cor 5:6			1								
2 Cor 5:11a			1								
2 Cor 5:11b											
2 Cor 5:11c											
2 Cor 5:16a											
2 Cor 5:16b											
2 Cor 5:17	1		1								
2 Cor 6:11a											
2 Cor 6:11b	1		1								
2 Cor 7:3											
2 Cor 7:4	1										
2 Cor 7:5			1								
2 Cor 7:13a	1		1								
2 Cor 7:13b											
2 Cor 7:14											
2 Cor 8:1	1			1							
2 Cor 8:15			1								
2 Cor 9:2a			1								
2 Cor 9:2b											
2 Cor 9:3	1		1			1					

Reference	Stative	Durative time	Unmodified	Adjectival	Copula-like	Substantive	Present Time Adv	Reflexive	Opposition	Subordinating	Specification
2 Cor 9:5	1			1							
2 Cor 9:7											
2 Cor 9:9			1								
2 Cor 10:7											
2 Cor 10:10	1		1	1							
2 Cor 11:5											
2 Cor 11:11			1								
2 Cor 11:21	1		1								
2 Cor 11:24											
2 Cor 11:31			1								
2 Cor 12:2a											
2 Cor 12:2b			1								
2 Cor 12:2c			1								
2 Cor 12:2d			1								
2 Cor 12:3a			1								
2 Cor 12:3b			1								
2 Cor 12:3c			1								
2 Cor 12:9											
2 Cor 12:11	1		1		1						
2 Cor 12:17											
2 Cor 12:21						1					
2 Cor 13:2a			1								
2 Cor 13:2b						1					
Gal 1:4	1		1	1							
Gal 1:9											
Gal 2:7			1								
Gal 2:11			1			1					
Gal 2:16			1			1					
Gal 2:19											
Gal 3:1			1			1					
Gal 3:10a			1								
Gal 3:10b						1					
Gal 3:13a					1						

Reference	Stative	Durative time	Unmodified	Adjectival	Copula-like	Substantive	Present Time Adv	Reflexive	Opposition	Subordinating	Specification
Gal 3:13b			1								
Gal 3:15			1								
Gal 3:17a											
Gal 3:17b											
Gal 3:18											
Gal 3:19			1	1							
Gal 3:24	1				1						
Gal 4:3						1				1	
Gal 4:8			1								
Gal 4:11											
Gal 4:13			1								
Gal 4:16	1		1		1						
Gal 4:22			1								
Gal 4:23											
Gal 4:27			1								
Gal 5:10											
Gal 5:11	1		1								
Gal 5:14											
Gal 6:14											
Eph 1:6	1		1	1							
Eph 1:11			1								
Eph 1:17	1		1	1							
Eph 2:5						1					
Eph 2:8						1					
Eph 2:12						1					
Eph 3:9	1	1		1							
Eph 3:17						1					
Eph 4:18a											
Eph 4:18b											
Eph 4:19			1			1					
Eph 5:5			1			1					
Eph 6:8			1								
Eph 6:9			1								

Reference	Stative	Durative time	Unmodified	Adjectival	Copula-like	Substantive	Present Time Adv	Reflexive	Opposition	Subordinating	Specification
Eph 6:16			1	1							
Eph 6:21			1								
Phil 1:5			1								
Phil 1:10						1					
Phil 1:12											
Phil 1:14				1							
Phil 1:16			1								
Phil 1:19			1								
Phil 1:25a			1								
Phil 1:25b			1								
Phil 2:15			1	1							
Phil 2:24				1							
Phil 3:3											
Phil 3:4											
Phil 3:7											
Phil 3:12											
Phil 3:13			1								
Phil 4:12a			1								
Phil 4:12b			1								
Phil 4:12c											
Phil 4:15			1								
Phil 4:18	1		1								
Col 1:16											
Col 1:17											
Col 1:21											
Col 1:23			1			1					
Col 1:26		1		1							
Col 2:1			1								
Col 2:7						1					
Col 2:10						1					
Col 2:14											
Col 2:18			1								
Col 3:3											

Reference	Stative	Durative time	Unmodified	Adjectival	Copula-like	Substantive	Present Time Adv	Reflexive	Opposition	Subordinating	Specification
Col 3:12			1			1					
Col 3:24			1								
Col 4:1			1								
Col 4:3											
Col 4:6a											
Col 4:6b			1								
Col 4:12						1					
1 Thess 1:4			1								
1 Thess 1:5			1								
1 Thess 1:8a											
1 Thess 1:8b											
1 Thess 2:1a			1								
1 Thess 2:1b	1		1		1						
1 Thess 2:2			1								
1 Thess 2:4											
1 Thess 2:5			1								
1 Thess 2:11			1								
1 Thess 3:3			1								
1 Thess 3:4			1								
1 Thess 4:2			1								
1 Thess 4:4			1								
1 Thess 4:5			1								
1 Thess 5:2											
1 Thess 5:12			1								
2 Thess 1:8			1	1							
2 Thess 2:2			1								
2 Thess 2:6											
2 Thess 2:13				1							
2 Thess 3:4											
2 Thess 3:7			1	1							
1 Tim 1:8			1								
1 Tim 1:8			1								
1 Tim 2:14											

Reference	Stative	Durative time	Unmodified	Adjectival	Copula-like	Substantive	Present Time Adv	Reflexive	Opposition	Subordinating	Specification
1 Tim 3:5			1								
1 Tim 3:15			1								
1 Tim 4:2	1		1	1							
1 Tim 4:3			1			1					
1 Tim 4:6											
1 Tim 4:10											
1 Tim 5:5a			1			1					
1 Tim 5:5b											
1 Tim 5:6	1		1								
1 Tim 5:8			1								
1 Tim 5:9	1		1		1						
1 Tim 5:17				1							
1 Tim 6:4	1		1								
1 Tim 6:5a	1		1	1							
1 Tim 6:5b						1					
1 Tim 6:17											
2 Tim 1:4											
2 Tim 1:5			1								
2 Tim 1:12a			1								
2 Tim 1:12b											
2 Tim 1:12c											
2 Tim 1:15			1								
2 Tim 2:8						1					
2 Tim 2:9	1		1								
2 Tim 2:18											
2 Tim 2:19	1		1								
2 Tim 2:21a	1		1	1							
2 Tim 2:21b				1							
2 Tim 2:23			1								
2 Tim 2:26											
2 Tim 3:4	1		1			1					
2 Tim 3:5			1								
2 Tim 3:6											

Reference	Stative	Durative time	Unmodified	Adjectival	Copula-like	Substantive	Present Time Adv	Reflexive	Opposition	Subordinating	Specification
2 Tim 3:8											
2 Tim 3:14			1								
2 Tim 3:17											
2 Tim 4:6											
2 Tim 4:7a			1								
2 Tim 4:7b			1								
2 Tim 4:7c			1								
2 Tim 4:8			1			1					
Titus 1:15a	1		1								
Titus 1:15b	1		1								
Titus 1:16			1								
Titus 2:3											
Titus 3:8						1					
Titus 3:11a			1								
Titus 3:11b	1		1								
Titus 3:12			1								
Phlm 1:7											
Phlm 1:21a											
Phlm 1:21b			1								
Rom 7:7			1								
Totals:	62	6	228	36	14	49	1	0	4	2	0

Appendix G

Chart of Adverbial Modification of Eventive Perfects

Reference	Eventive	Manner	Prior time	Specific time	Unmodified	Source	Referent	Purpose	Content	Separation	Means / Instrument	Agency	Interest	Directional / Goal
Rom 1:1								1						
Rom 1:17					1									
Rom 1:28		?							?					
Rom 2:2					1									
Rom 2:18					1									
Rom 2:24					1									
Rom 2:25					1									
Rom 3:4					1									
Rom 3:10					1									
Rom 3:13					1									
Rom 3:19					1									
Rom 3:21	1		1							1				
Rom 3:25			1											

Reference	Eventive	Manner	Prior time	Specific time	Unmodified	Source	Referent	Purpose	Content	Separation	Means / Instrument	Agency	Interest	Directional / Goal
Rom 4:1		?												
Rom 4:14a					1									
Rom 4:14b					1									
Rom 4:17					1									
Rom 4:18					1									
Rom 4:19														
Rom 4:21					1									
Rom 5:2a	1							1			1	1		
Rom 5:2b														
Rom 5:3					1									
Rom 5:5	1											1		
Rom 6:5														
Rom 6:7	1									1				
Rom 6:9					1									
Rom 6:16					1									
Rom 7:2a	1										1			
Rom 7:2b	1									1				
Rom 7:14a					1									
Rom 7:14b		?												
Rom 7:18					1									
Rom 8:22					1									
Rom 8:26					1									
Rom 8:27					1									
Rom 8:28					1									
Rom 8:36					1									
Rom 8:38a					1									
Rom 8:38b					1									
Rom 9:6					1									
Rom 9:13					1									
Rom 9:19														
Rom 9:22								1						
Rom 9:25a					1									

Reference	Eventive	Manner	Prior time	Specific time	Unmodified	Source	Referent	Purpose	Content	Separation	Means / Instrument	Agency	Interest	Directional / Goal
Rom 9:25b					1									
Rom 9:29			1											
Rom 9:33					1									
Rom 10:15					1									
Rom 11:2					1									
Rom 11:5														
Rom 11:8					1									
Rom 11:20											?			
Rom 11:25						?	?			?				
Rom 11:26					1									
Rom 12:19					1									
Rom 13:1	1											1		
Rom 13:2a														
Rom 13:2b					1									
Rom 13:8					1									
Rom 13:11					1									
Rom 13:12					1									
Rom 14:11					1									
Rom 14:14a					1									
Rom 14:14b														
Rom 14:23					1									
Rom 15:3					1									
Rom 15:8					1									
Rom 15:9					1									
Rom 15:14a							1							
Rom 15:14b									1					
Rom 15:16	1										1			
Rom 15:19														
Rom 15:21					1									
Rom 15:29					1									
Rom 16:7			1											
Rom 16:25														

Reference	Eventive	Manner	Prior time	Specific time	Unmodified	Source	Referent	Purpose	Content	Separation	Means / Instrument	Agency	Interest	Directional / Goal
1 Cor 1:2														
1 Cor 1:10		2												
1 Cor 1:13					1									
1 Cor 1:16					1									
1 Cor 1:19					1									
1 Cor 1:23					1									
1 Cor 1:28					1									
1 Cor 1:31					1									
1 Cor 2:2					1									
1 Cor 2:7					1									
1 Cor 2:8					1									
1 Cor 2:9					1									
1 Cor 2:11					1									
1 Cor 2:12					1									
1 Cor 3:16					1									
1 Cor 3:19					1									
1 Cor 3:22														
1 Cor 4:4a														
1 Cor 4:4b											1			
1 Cor 4:6					1									
1 Cor 4:8			1											
1 Cor 4:19					1									
1 Cor 5:2					1									
1 Cor 5:3			1											
1 Cor 5:6					1									
1 Cor 6:2					1									
1 Cor 6:3					1									
1 Cor 6:4														
1 Cor 6:9					1									
1 Cor 6:15					1									
1 Cor 6:16					1									
1 Cor 6:19					1									

Reference	Eventive	Manner	Prior time	Specific time	Unmodified	Source	Referent	Purpose	Content	Separation	Means / Instrument	Agency	Interest	Directional / Goal
1 Cor 7:10					1									
1 Cor 7:14a														
1 Cor 7:14b														
1 Cor 7:15														
1 Cor 7:16a					1									
1 Cor 7:16b					1									
1 Cor 7:17					1									
1 Cor 7:18a					1									
1 Cor 7:18b	1	1												
1 Cor 7:25	1					1					?			
1 Cor 7:26					1									
1 Cor 7:27	1									1				
1 Cor 7:29														
1 Cor 7:34					1									
1 Cor 7:37a	1													
1 Cor 7:37b	1													
1 Cor 7:39														
1 Cor 8:1					1									
1 Cor 8:2					1									
1 Cor 8:3	1											1		
1 Cor 8:4					1									
1 Cor 9:1	1													
1 Cor 9:9														
1 Cor 9:13	1				1									
1 Cor 9:15	1													
1 Cor 9:17					1									
1 Cor 9:22							1							
1 Cor 9:24					1									
1 Cor 10:7					1									
1 Cor 10:11	1												1	
1 Cor 10:12	1				1									
1 Cor 10:13	1				1									

Reference	Eventive	Manner	Prior time	Specific time	Unmodified	Source	Referent	Purpose	Content	Separation	Means / Instrument	Agency	Interest	Directional / Goal
1 Cor 11:2					1									
1 Cor 11:3					1									
1 Cor 11:5					1									
1 Cor 11:15														
1 Cor 12:2					1									
1 Cor 13:1					1									
1 Cor 13:2					1									
1 Cor 13:11					1									
1 Cor 14:11					1									
1 Cor 14:16					1									
1 Cor 14:21														
1 Cor 15:1														
1 Cor 15:4	1			1										
1 Cor 15:12	1									1				
1 Cor 15:13					1									
1 Cor 15:14					1									
1 Cor 15:16					1									
1 Cor 15:17					1									
1 Cor 15:19														
1 Cor 15:20a	1									1				
1 Cor 15:20b					1									
1 Cor 15:27														
1 Cor 15:45					1									
1 Cor 15:54					1									
1 Cor 15:58					1									
1 Cor 16:9	1												1	
1 Cor 16:15					1									
2 Cor 1:7					1									
2 Cor 1:9a	1													
2 Cor 1:9b														
2 Cor 1:10	1													
2 Cor 1:19														

Reference	Eventive	Manner	Prior time	Specific time	Unmodified	Source	Referent	Purpose	Content	Separation	Means / Instrument	Agency	Interest	Directional / Goal
2 Cor 1:24	1										?			
2 Cor 2:3														
2 Cor 2:5a	1				1									
2 Cor 2:5b	1	1												
2 Cor 2:10a					1									
2 Cor 2:10b	1	1												
2 Cor 2:12														
2 Cor 2:13	1													
2 Cor 3:2														
2 Cor 3:3											1			
2 Cor 3:7	1	1												
2 Cor 3:10a	1	1												
2 Cor 3:10b					1									
2 Cor 3:18					1									
2 Cor 4:3a					1									
2 Cor 4:3b														
2 Cor 4:13					1									
2 Cor 4:14					1									
2 Cor 5:1					1									
2 Cor 5:6					1									
2 Cor 5:11a					1									
2 Cor 5:11b														
2 Cor 5:11c														
2 Cor 5:16a	1	1												
2 Cor 5:16b	1	1												
2 Cor 5:17					1									
2 Cor 6:11a	1												1	
2 Cor 6:11b					1									
2 Cor 7:3			1											
2 Cor 7:4									1					
2 Cor 7:5	1				1									
2 Cor 7:13a					1									

Reference	Eventive	Manner	Prior time	Specific time	Unmodified	Source	Referent	Purpose	Content	Separation	Means / Instrument	Agency	Interest	Directional / Goal
2 Cor 7:13b	1											1		
2 Cor 7:14	1						1							
2 Cor 8:1														
2 Cor 8:15					1									
2 Cor 9:2a					1									
2 Cor 9:2b				1										
2 Cor 9:3					1									
2 Cor 9:5	1		1											
2 Cor 9:7			1											
2 Cor 9:9					1									
2 Cor 10:7									1					
2 Cor 10:10					1									
2 Cor 11:5														
2 Cor 11:11					1									
2 Cor 11:21					1									
2 Cor 11:24														
2 Cor 11:31					1									
2 Cor 12:2a														
2 Cor 12:2b					1									
2 Cor 12:2c					1									
2 Cor 12:2d					1									
2 Cor 12:3a					1									
2 Cor 12:3b					1									
2 Cor 12:3c					1									
2 Cor 12:9													1	
2 Cor 12:11					1									
2 Cor 12:17														1
2 Cor 12:21			1											
2 Cor 13:2a					1									
2 Cor 13:2b			1											
Gal 1:4					1									
Gal 1:9	1		1											

Reference	Eventive	Manner	Prior time	Specific time	Unmodified	Source	Referent	Purpose	Content	Separation	Means / Instrument	Agency	Interest	Directional / Goal
Gal 2:7					1									
Gal 2:11					1									
Gal 2:16					1									
Gal 2:19														
Gal 3:1					1									
Gal 3:10a					1									
Gal 3:10b														
Gal 3:13a														
Gal 3:13b					1									
Gal 3:15					1									
Gal 3:17a	1		1									1		
Gal 3:17b	1			1										
Gal 3:18											1			
Gal 3:19					1									
Gal 3:24														1
Gal 4:3														
Gal 4:8					1									
Gal 4:11	1	1												1
Gal 4:13					1									
Gal 4:16					1									
Gal 4:22					1									
Gal 4:23	1	1												
Gal 4:27					1									
Gal 5:10	1						1							
Gal 5:11					1									
Gal 5:14														
Gal 6:14	1						2				1			
Eph 1:6					1									
Eph 1:11			1											
Eph 1:17					1									
Eph 2:5											1			
Eph 2:8											2			

Reference	Eventive	Manner	Prior time	Specific time	Unmodified	Source	Referent	Purpose	Content	Separation	Means / Instrument	Agency	Interest	Directional / Goal
Eph 2:12										1				
Eph 3:9														
Eph 3:17														
Eph 4:18a														
Eph 4:18b										1				
Eph 4:19					1									
Eph 5:5					1									
Eph 6:8					1									
Eph 6:9					1									
Eph 6:16					1									
Eph 6:21					1									
Phil 1:5					1									
Phil 1:10	1					1								1
Phil 1:12	1						1							1
Phil 1:14	1										1			
Phil 1:16					1									
Phil 1:19					1									
Phil 1:25a					1									
Phil 1:25b					1									
Phil 2:15					1									
Phil 2:24														
Phil 3:3														
Phil 3:4														
Phil 3:7							1							
Phil 3:12			1											
Phil 3:13					1									
Phil 4:12a					1									
Phil 4:12b					1									
Phil 4:12c							2							
Phil 4:15					1									
Phil 4:18					1									
Col 1:16	1							1				1		

Reference	Eventive	Manner	Prior time	Specific time	Unmodified	Source	Referent	Purpose	Content	Separation	Means / Instrument	Agency	Interest	Directional / Goal
Col 1:17														
Col 1:21			1								1			
Col 1:23					1									
Col 1:26										1				
Col 2:1					1									
Col 2:7														
Col 2:10														
Col 2:14										1				
Col 2:18					1									
Col 3:3														
Col 3:12					1									
Col 3:24					1									
Col 4:1					1									
Col 4:3							1							
Col 4:6a											1			
Col 4:6b					1									
Col 4:12							1							
1 Thess 1:4					1									
1 Thess 1:5					1									
1 Thess 1:8a						1								
1 Thess 1:8b														
1 Thess 2:1a					1									
1 Thess 2:1b					1									
1 Thess 2:2					1									
1 Thess 2:4	1											1		
1 Thess 2:5					1									
1 Thess 2:11					1									
1 Thess 3:3					1									
1 Thess 3:4					1									
1 Thess 4:2					1									
1 Thess 4:4					1									
1 Thess 4:5					1									

Reference	Eventive	Manner	Prior time	Specific time	Unmodified	Source	Referent	Purpose	Content	Separation	Means / Instrument	Agency	Interest	Directional / Goal
1 Thess 5:2														
1 Thess 5:12					1									
2 Thess 1:8					1									
2 Thess 2:2					1									
2 Thess 2:6			?	?										
2 Thess 2:13												1		
2 Thess 3:4							1							
2 Thess 3:7					1									
1 Tim 1:8					1									
1 Tim 1:8					1									
1 Tim 2:14														1
1 Tim 3:5					1									
1 Tim 3:15					1									
1 Tim 4:2					1									
1 Tim 4:3					1									
1 Tim 4:6														
1 Tim 4:10														
1 Tim 5:5a					1									
1 Tim 5:5b														
1 Tim 5:6					1									
1 Tim 5:8					1									
1 Tim 5:9					1									
1 Tim 5:17	1	1	1											
1 Tim 6:4					1									
1 Tim 6:5a					1									
1 Tim 6:5b										1				
1 Tim 6:17														
2 Tim 1:4							1							
2 Tim 1:5					1									
2 Tim 1:12a					1									
2 Tim 1:12b														
2 Tim 1:12c														

Reference	Eventive	Manner	Prior time	Specific time	Unmodified	Source	Referent	Purpose	Content	Separation	Means / Instrument	Agency	Interest	Directional / Goal
2 Tim 1:15					1									
2 Tim 2:8										1				
2 Tim 2:9					1									
2 Tim 2:18			1											
2 Tim 2:19					1									
2 Tim 2:21a					1									
2 Tim 2:21b								?						?
2 Tim 2:23					1									
2 Tim 2:26	1							?				1		?
2 Tim 3:4					1									
2 Tim 3:5					1									
2 Tim 3:6											1			
2 Tim 3:8														
2 Tim 3:14					1									
2 Tim 3:17														1
2 Tim 4:6				1										
2 Tim 4:7a					1									
2 Tim 4:7b					1									
2 Tim 4:7c					1									
2 Tim 4:8					1									
Titus 1:15a					1									
Titus 1:15b					1									
Titus 1:16					1									
Titus 2:3													1	
Titus 3:8														
Titus 3:11a					1									
Titus 3:11b					1									
Titus 3:12					1									
Phlm 1:7												1		
Phlm 1:21a							1							
Phlm 1:21b					1									
Rom 7:7					1									
Totals:	54	12	18	4	228	3	15	4	3	12	14	11	5	7

Appendix H

Adverb Frequency Data

Adverbial collocate type or function	Stative	Strong Correlation?	Eventive	Strong Correlation?	Indefinite
Durative time	66.67%	Yes	0.00%	No	33.33%
Unmodified	---	---	---	---	---
Adjectival	44.44%	No	0.06%	No	50.00%
Substantive	26.53%	No	0.04%*	No	65.31%
Copula-like	85.71%	Yes	0.00%	No	14.28%
Present time	100.00%	Yes	0.00%	No	0.00%
Opposition	0.00%	No	0.00%	No	100.00%
Subordination	0.00%	No	0.00%	No	100.00%
Manner	0.00%	No	84.62%	Yes	15.38%
Prior Time	5.55%*	No	27.78%	No	72.22%
Specific Time	0.00%	No	100.00%	Yes	0.00%
Source	0.00%	No	50.00%	No	50.00%
Referent	6.67%	No	31.25%	No	56.25%
Purpose	25.00%	No	25.00%	No	50.00%
Content	33.33%	No	0.00%	No	66.67%
Separation	8.33%*	No	50.00%	No	50.00%
Means or Instrument	0.00%	No	35.71%	No	64.29%

Adverbial collocate type or function	Stative	Strong Correlation?	Eventive	Strong Correlation?	Indefinite
Agent	0.00%	No	81.82%	Yes	18.18%
Interest	0.00%	No	40.00%	No	60.00%
Direction or Goal	28.57%	No	42.86%	No	28.57%
Citational	0.00%	No	0.00%	No	100.00%
Locative	8.77%	No	12.28%	No	78.95%
Direct or indirect Object	4.11%	No	20.55%	No	75.34%
Association	20.00%	No	0.00%	No	80.00%x
Postural	0.00%	No	0.00%	No	100.00%
Periphrastic	28.57%	No	0.00%	No	88.24%
Comparative	0.00%	No	0.00%	No	100.00%
Standard or Basis	16.67%	No	33.33%	No	50.00%
Extent	0.00%	No	100.00%	Yes	0.00%
Focus	0.00%	No	0.00%	No	100.00%
Representation	0.00%	No	0.00%	No	100.00%

Appendix I

Key Adverbs

A list of the more significant adverbs of manner, expressions of agency, and expressions of durative time found within the Pauline corpus. These are more significant than other modifiers in that they definitely predict eventive or stative Perfects, where other modifiers are less predictable.

References	Adverb Word String	POS	Eventive	Stative	Function
1 Cor 1:10	ἐν τῷ αὐτῷ νοῒ	εν + dat	Y		Manner
1 Cor 1:10	ἐν τῇ αὐτῇ γνώμῃ	εν + dat	y		Manner
1 Cor 7:18b	ἐν ἀκροβυστίᾳ	εν + dat	Y		Manner
2 Cor 2:5b	ἀπὸ μέρους	από + gen	Y		Manner
2 Cor 3:7	ἐν γράμμασιν	εν + dat	Y		Manner
2 Cor 3:10a	ἐν τούτῳ τῷ μέρει	εν + dat	Y		Manner
2 Cor 5:16a	κατὰ σάρκα	κατά + acc	Y		Manner
2 Cor 5:16b	κατὰ σάρκα	κατά + acc	Y		Manner
Gal 4:11	εἰκῇ	Bare adv	Y		Manner
Gal 4:23	κατὰ σάρκα	κατά + acc	Y		Manner
1 Tim 5:17	καλῶς	Bare adv	Y		Manner
Rom 5:2	δι' οὗ	διὰ + gen	Y		Agency
Rom 5:5	διὰ πνεύματος ἁγίου	διὰ + gen	Y		Agency

References	Adverb Word String	POS	Eventive	Stative	Function
Rom 13:1	ὑπὸ θεοῦ	υπό + gen	Y		Agency
1 Cor 7:25	ὑπὸ κυρίου	υπό + gen	Y		Agency
1 Cor 8:3	ὑπ' αὐτοῦ	υπό + gen	Y		Agency
2 Cor 7:13b	ἀπὸ πάντων ὑμῶν	από + gen	Y		Agency
Gal 3:17a	ὑπὸ τοῦ θεοῦ	υπό + gen	Y		Agency
Col 1:16	δι' αὐτοῦ	διά + gen	Y		Agency
1 Thess 2:4	ὑπὸ τοῦ θεοῦ	υπό + gen	Y		Agency
2 Thess 2:13	ὑπὸ κυρίου	υπό + gen	Y		Agency
2 Tim 2:26	ὑπ' αὐτοῦ	υπό + gen	Y		Agency
Phlm 1:7	διὰ σοῦ	διά + gen	Y		Agency
Rom 16:25	χρόνοις αἰωνίοις	Bare dat		Y	Durative Time
1 Cor 7:39	ἐφ' ὅσον χρόνον	επι + acc		Y	Durative Time
1 Cor 15:19	ἐν τῇ ζωῇ ταύτῃ	εν + dat		Y	Durative Time
1 Cor 15:20a	Νυνὶ	Adv + dat		Y	Durative Time
Eph 3:9	ἀπὸ τῶν αἰώνων	από + gen		Y	Durative Time
Col 1:26	ἀπὸ τῶν αἰώνων	από + gen		Y	Durative Time

Chart of Adverbial Modification of Perfects Used in Citational or Referential Ways

Reference	Citational	Locative	Direct Object or Indirect Object	Association	Postural	Periphrastic	Unmodified	Comparative	Standard or Basis	Extent	Focus	Representation
Rom 1:1												
Rom 1:17	1						1					
Rom 1:28												
Rom 2:2	1						1					
Rom 2:18	1						1					
Rom 2:24	1						1					
Rom 2:25							1					
Rom 3:4	1						1					
Rom 3:10	1						1					
Rom 3:13							1					
Rom 3:19	1						1					
Rom 3:21												
Rom 3:25												
Rom 4:1												

Reference	Citational	Locative	Direct Object or Indirect Object	Association	Postural	Periphrastic	Unmodified	Comparative	Standard or Basis	Extent	Focus	Representation
Rom 4:14a							1					
Rom 4:14b							1					
Rom 4:17	1						1					
Rom 4:18							1					
Rom 4:19												
Rom 4:21			1				1					
Rom 5:2a												
Rom 5:2b		1			1							
Rom 5:3	1						1					
Rom 5:5		1										
Rom 6:5				1								
Rom 6:7												
Rom 6:9	1						1					
Rom 6:16	1						1					
Rom 7:2a			1									
Rom 7:2b												
Rom 7:14a	1						1					
Rom 7:14b						1						
Rom 7:18	1						1					
Rom 8:22	1						1					
Rom 8:26	1						1					
Rom 8:27	1						1					
Rom 8:28	1						1					
Rom 8:36	1						1					
Rom 8:38a	1						1					
Rom 8:38b							1					
Rom 9:6							1					
Rom 9:13	1						1					
Rom 9:19					1							
Rom 9:22												
Rom 9:25a							1					
Rom 9:25b							1					
Rom 9:29	1											

Reference	Citational	Locative	Direct Object or Indirect Object	Association	Postural	Periphrastic	Unmodified	Comparative	Standard or Basis	Extent	Focus	Representation
Rom 9:33	1						1					
Rom 10:15	1						1					
Rom 11:2	1						1					
Rom 11:5									1			
Rom 11:8	1						1					
Rom 11:20		?			1							
Rom 11:25		?										
Rom 11:26	1						1					
Rom 12:19	1						1					
Rom 13:1												
Rom 13:2a					1							
Rom 13:2b					1		1					
Rom 13:8							1					
Rom 13:11	1						1					
Rom 13:12							1					
Rom 14:11	1						1					
Rom 14:14a	1	1					1					
Rom 14:14b	1											
Rom 14:23							1					
Rom 15:3	1						1					
Rom 15:8							1					
Rom 15:9	1						1					
Rom 15:14a	1											
Rom 15:14b												
Rom 15:16												
Rom 15:19		1	1									
Rom 15:21	1						1					
Rom 15:29	1						1					
Rom 16:7		1										
Rom 16:25												
1 Cor 1:2		1										
1 Cor 1:10						1						
1 Cor 1:13							1					

Reference	Citational	Locative	Direct Object or Indirect Object	Association	Postural	Periphrastic	Unmodified	Comparative	Standard or Basis	Extent	Focus	Representation
1 Cor 1:16	1						1					
1 Cor 1:19	1						1					
1 Cor 1:23							1					
1 Cor 1:28							1					
1 Cor 1:31	1						1					
1 Cor 2:2							1					
1 Cor 2:7							1					
1 Cor 2:8			1				1					
1 Cor 2:9	1						1					
1 Cor 2:11			1				1					
1 Cor 2:12			1				1					
1 Cor 3:16	1						1					
1 Cor 3:19	1						1					
1 Cor 3:22		?			1							
1 Cor 4:4a			1	1								
1 Cor 4:4b												
1 Cor 4:6							1					
1 Cor 4:8						1						
1 Cor 4:19							1					
1 Cor 5:2						1	1					
1 Cor 5:3			1									
1 Cor 5:6	1						1					
1 Cor 6:2	1						1					
1 Cor 6:3	1						1					
1 Cor 6:4		1										
1 Cor 6:9	1						1					
1 Cor 6:15	1						1					
1 Cor 6:16	1						1					
1 Cor 6:19	1						1					
1 Cor 7:10							1					
1 Cor 7:14a		1										
1 Cor 7:14b		1										
1 Cor 7:15		1										

Reference	Citational	Locative	Direct Object or Indirect Object	Association	Postural	Periphrastic	Unmodified	Comparative	Standard or Basis	Extent	Focus	Representation
1 Cor 7:16a	1						1					
1 Cor 7:16b	1						1					
1 Cor 7:17			1				1					
1 Cor 7:18a							1					
1 Cor 7:18b												
1 Cor 7:25												
1 Cor 7:26							1					
1 Cor 7:27												
1 Cor 7:29						1						
1 Cor 7:34							1					
1 Cor 7:37a		1			1							
1 Cor 7:37b		1	1									
1 Cor 7:39												
1 Cor 8:1	1						1					
1 Cor 8:2	1						1					
1 Cor 8:3												
1 Cor 8:4	1						1					
1 Cor 9:1			1									
1 Cor 9:9	1	1										
1 Cor 9:13	1						1					
1 Cor 9:15			1							1		
1 Cor 9:17			1				1					
1 Cor 9:22												
1 Cor 9:24	1						1					
1 Cor 10:7	1						1					
1 Cor 10:11												
1 Cor 10:12							1					
1 Cor 10:13			1				1					
1 Cor 11:2			1				1					
1 Cor 11:3	1						1					
1 Cor 11:5							1					
1 Cor 11:15												
1 Cor 12:2	1						1					

Reference	Citational	Locative	Direct Object or Indirect Object	Association	Postural	Periphrastic	Unmodified	Comparative	Standard or Basis	Extent	Focus	Representation
1 Cor 13:1							1					
1 Cor 13:2	1						1					
1 Cor 13:11							1					
1 Cor 14:11	1						1					
1 Cor 14:16	1						1					
1 Cor 14:21	1	1										
1 Cor 15:1		1			1							
1 Cor 15:4									1			
1 Cor 15:12												
1 Cor 15:13							1					
1 Cor 15:14							1					
1 Cor 15:16							1					
1 Cor 15:17							1					
1 Cor 15:19		1				1						
1 Cor 15:20a												
1 Cor 15:20b							1					
1 Cor 15:27			1									
1 Cor 15:45	1						1					
1 Cor 15:54	1						1					
1 Cor 15:58	1						1					
1 Cor 16:9												
1 Cor 16:15	1						1					
2 Cor 1:7	1						1					
2 Cor 1:9a		1	1									
2 Cor 1:9b						1			1			
2 Cor 1:10			1						1			
2 Cor 1:19		1	1									
2 Cor 1:24			?									
2 Cor 2:3	1										1	
2 Cor 2:5a							1					
2 Cor 2:5b			1									
2 Cor 2:10a			1				1					
2 Cor 2:10b			1									

Reference	Citational	Locative	Direct Object or Indirect Object	Association	Postural	Periphrastic	Unmodified	Comparative	Standard or Basis	Extent	Focus	Representation
2 Cor 2:12		1										
2 Cor 2:13		1										
2 Cor 3:2		1										
2 Cor 3:3		1										
2 Cor 3:7		1										
2 Cor 3:10a												
2 Cor 3:10b			1				1					
2 Cor 3:18							1					
2 Cor 4:3a						1	1					
2 Cor 4:3b		1				1						
2 Cor 4:13							1					
2 Cor 4:14	1						1					
2 Cor 5:1	1						1					
2 Cor 5:6	1						1					
2 Cor 5:11a	1						1					
2 Cor 5:11b			1									
2 Cor 5:11c		1										
2 Cor 5:16a			1									
2 Cor 5:16b			1									
2 Cor 5:17							1					
2 Cor 6:11a												
2 Cor 6:11b							1					
2 Cor 7:3	1											
2 Cor 7:4												
2 Cor 7:5			1				1					
2 Cor 7:13a			1				1					
2 Cor 7:13b												
2 Cor 7:14			1									
2 Cor 8:1		1										
2 Cor 8:15	1						1					
2 Cor 9:2a	1						1					
2 Cor 9:2b												
2 Cor 9:3							1					

Reference	Citational	Locative	Direct Object or Indirect Object	Association	Postural	Periphrastic	Unmodified	Comparative	Standard or Basis	Extent	Focus	Representation
2 Cor 9:5												
2 Cor 9:7		1										
2 Cor 9:9	1						1					
2 Cor 10:7		1										
2 Cor 10:10							1					
2 Cor 11:5								1				
2 Cor 11:11							1					
2 Cor 11:21							1					
2 Cor 11:24		1	1									
2 Cor 11:31	1						1					
2 Cor 12:2a		1	1									
2 Cor 12:2b			1				1					
2 Cor 12:2c			1				1					
2 Cor 12:2d							1					
2 Cor 12:3a			1				1					
2 Cor 12:3b			1				1					
2 Cor 12:3c							1					
2 Cor 12:9			1									
2 Cor 12:11							1					
2 Cor 12:17			1									
2 Cor 12:21												
2 Cor 13:2a			1				1					
2 Cor 13:2b												
Gal 1:4							1					
Gal 1:9			1									
Gal 2:7			1				1					
Gal 2:11						1	1					
Gal 2:16	1						1					
Gal 2:19				1								
Gal 3:1							1					
Gal 3:10a	1						1					
Gal 3:10b		1										
Gal 3:13a												1

Reference	Citational	Locative	Direct Object or Indirect Object	Association	Postural	Periphrastic	Unmodified	Comparative	Standard or Basis	Extent	Focus	Representation
Gal 3:13b	1						1					
Gal 3:15			1				1					
Gal 3:17a			1									
Gal 3:17b												
Gal 3:18			1									
Gal 3:19							1					
Gal 3:24						1						
Gal 4:3												
Gal 4:8	1						1					
Gal 4:11												
Gal 4:13	1						1					
Gal 4:16							1					
Gal 4:22	1						1					
Gal 4:23												
Gal 4:27	1						1					
Gal 5:10		1	1									
Gal 5:11							1					
Gal 5:14		1										
Gal 6:14												
Eph 1:6		1					1					
Eph 1:11									1			
Eph 1:17			1				1					
Eph 2:5						1						
Eph 2:8						1						
Eph 2:12												
Eph 3:9		1										
Eph 3:17		1										
Eph 4:18a		1				1						
Eph 4:18b												
Eph 4:19							1					
Eph 5:5			1			1	1					
Eph 6:8	1						1					
Eph 6:9	1						1					

Reference	Citational	Locative	Direct Object or Indirect Object	Association	Postural	Periphrastic	Unmodified	Comparative	Standard or Basis	Extent	Focus	Representation
Eph 6:16							1					
Eph 6:21	1						1					
Phil 1:5	1						1					
Phil 1:10			1									
Phil 1:12												
Phil 1:14		1										
Phil 1:16	1						1					
Phil 1:19	1						1					
Phil 1:25a	1						1					
Phil 1:25b	1						1					
Phil 2:15							1					
Phil 2:24		1	1									
Phil 3:3		1										
Phil 3:4		1										
Phil 3:7			1									
Phil 3:12			1									
Phil 3:13							1					
Phil 4:12a			1				1					
Phil 4:12b			1				1					
Phil 4:12c			4									
Phil 4:15	1						1					
Phil 4:18							1					
Col 1:16												
Col 1:17		1		1	1							
Col 1:21		1				1						
Col 1:23							1					
Col 1:26												
Col 2:1			1				1					
Col 2:7		1										
Col 2:10		1				1						
Col 2:14			1									
Col 2:18			1				1					
Col 3:3		1		1								

Reference	Citational	Locative	Direct Object or Indirect Object	Association	Postural	Periphrastic	Unmodified	Comparative	Standard or Basis	Extent	Focus	Representation
Col 3:12							1					
Col 3:24	1						1					
Col 4:1	1						1					
Col 4:3												
Col 4:6a												
Col 4:6b	1						1					
Col 4:12												
1 Thess 1:4	1						1					
1 Thess 1:5	1						1					
1 Thess 1:8a		1										
1 Thess 1:8b		1										
1 Thess 2:1a			1				1					
1 Thess 2:1b							1					
1 Thess 2:2	1						1					
1 Thess 2:4												
1 Thess 2:5	1						1					
1 Thess 2:11	1						1					
1 Thess 3:3	1						1					
1 Thess 3:4	1						1					
1 Thess 4:2	1						1					
1 Thess 4:4	1						1					
1 Thess 4:5	1						1					
1 Thess 5:2	1											
1 Thess 5:12	1						1					
2 Thess 1:8	1						1					
2 Thess 2:2							1					
2 Thess 2:6	1											
2 Thess 2:13												
2 Thess 3:4		1	1									
2 Thess 3:7	1						1					
1 Tim 1:8	1						1					
1 Tim 1:8	1						1					
1 Tim 2:14												

Reference	Citational	Locative	Direct Object or Indirect Object	Association	Postural	Periphrastic	Unmodified	Comparative	Standard or Basis	Extent	Focus	Representation
1 Tim 3:5	1						1					
1 Tim 3:15	1						1					
1 Tim 4:2			1				1					
1 Tim 4:3			1				1					
1 Tim 4:6		1										
1 Tim 4:10		1										
1 Tim 5:5a							1					
1 Tim 5:5b		1										
1 Tim 5:6							1					
1 Tim 5:8			1				1					
1 Tim 5:9							1					
1 Tim 5:17					1							
1 Tim 6:4							1					
1 Tim 6:5a							1					
1 Tim 6:5b												
1 Tim 6:17		1										
2 Tim 1:4												
2 Tim 1:5	1						1					
2 Tim 1:12a	1						1					
2 Tim 1:12b		1										
2 Tim 1:12c		1										
2 Tim 1:15	1						1					
2 Tim 2:8												
2 Tim 2:9							1					
2 Tim 2:18												
2 Tim 2:19							1					
2 Tim 2:21a							1					
2 Tim 2:21b												
2 Tim 2:23	1						1					
2 Tim 2:26												
2 Tim 3:4							1					
2 Tim 3:5			1				1					
2 Tim 3:6												

Reference	Citational	Locative	Direct Object or Indirect Object	Association	Postural	Periphrastic	Unmodified	Comparative	Standard or Basis	Extent	Focus	Representation
2 Tim 3:8			1						1			
2 Tim 3:14	1						1					
2 Tim 3:17												
2 Tim 4:6		1			1							
2 Tim 4:7a			1				1					
2 Tim 4:7b			1				1					
2 Tim 4:7c			1				1					
2 Tim 4:8			1				1					
Titus 1:15a							1					
Titus 1:15b							1					
Titus 1:16			1				1					
Titus 2:3												
Titus 3:8		1										
Titus 3:11a	1						1					
Titus 3:11b							1					
Titus 3:12			1				1					
Phlm 1:7												
Phlm 1:21a	1											
Phlm 1:21b	1						1					
Rom 7:7			1				1					
Totals:	125	57	73	5	11	17	228	1	6	1	1	1

Appendix K

Chart of Pauline Corpus Examples with Perfects

Romans 1

¹ Παῦλος δοῦλος Χριστοῦ Ἰησοῦ, κλητὸς ἀπόστολος ἀφωρισμένος <u>εἰς εὐαγγέλιον θεοῦ</u>,
Stative, passive, modified by purpose phrase in accusative

¹⁷ δικαιοσύνη γὰρ θεοῦ ἐν αὐτῷ ἀποκαλύπτεται ἐκ πίστεως εἰς πίστιν, καθὼς γέγραπται· <u>ὁ δὲ δίκαιος ἐκ πίστεως ζήσεται.</u>
Citational, active, unmodified, has a reference content of citation.

²⁸ Καὶ καθὼς οὐκ ἐδοκίμασαν τὸν θεὸν ἔχειν ἐν ἐπιγνώσει, παρέδωκεν αὐτοὺς ὁ θεὸς εἰς ἀδόκιμον νοῦν, ποιεῖν τὰ μὴ καθήκοντα, ²⁹ πεπληρωμένους <u>πάσῃ ἀδικίᾳ πονηρίᾳ πλεονεξίᾳ κακίᾳ</u>, μεστοὺς φθόνου φόνου ἔριδος δόλου κακοηθείας, ψιθυριστάς
Substantival, passive, modified by 4 datives of manner or perhaps content

Romans 2

¹ . . . τὰ γὰρ αὐτὰ πράσσεις ὁ κρίνων. ² οἴδαμεν δὲ <u>ὅτι τὸ κρίμα τοῦ θεοῦ ἐστιν κατὰ ἀλήθειαν ἐπὶ τοὺς τὰ τοιαῦτα πράσσοντας.</u>
Citational, Active, unmodified, has a DO of content

¹⁸ καὶ γινώσκεις τὸ θέλημα καὶ δοκιμάζεις τὰ διαφέροντα κατηχούμενος ἐκ τοῦ νόμου,
¹⁹ πέποιθάς τε <u>σεαυτὸν ὁδηγὸν εἶναι τυφλῶν</u>, φῶς τῶν ἐν σκότει,
Citational, active, unmodified, has a direct object, the content of citation.
²⁴ <u>τὸ γὰρ ὄνομα τοῦ θεοῦ δι’ ὑμᾶς βλασφημεῖται ἐν τοῖς ἔθνεσιν</u>, καθὼς γέγραπται.
Citational, passive, unmodified, has a direct object, the content of citation.
²⁵ Περιτομὴ μὲν γὰρ ὠφελεῖ ἐὰν νόμον πράσσῃς· ἐὰν δὲ παραβάτης νόμου ᾖς, ἡ περιτομή σου <u>ἀκροβυστία</u> γέγονεν.
Copula use, stative, unmodified. Has a PN.

Romans 3

⁴ μὴ γένοιτο· γινέσθω δὲ ὁ θεὸς ἀληθής, πᾶς δὲ ἄνθρωπος ψεύστης, καθὼς γέγραπται· <u>ὅπως ἂν δικαιωθῇς ἐν τοῖς λόγοις σου καὶ νικήσεις ἐν τῷ κρίνεσθαί σε</u>.
Citational, passive, unmodified, has a direct object, the content of citation.
¹⁰ καθὼς γέγραπται <u>ὅτι οὐκ ἔστιν δίκαιος οὐδὲ εἷς</u>,
Citational, passive, unmodified, has a direct object, the content of citation.
¹³ τάφος ἀνεῳγμένος ὁ λάρυγξ αὐτῶν, ταῖς γλώσσαις αὐτῶν ἐδολιοῦσαν, ἰὸς ἀσπίδων ὑπὸ τὰ χείλη αὐτῶν·
Stative, Passive, adjectival, unmodified. (same phrase found in Ep. ad Theophilum Imperatorem de Imaginibus 10.62)
¹⁹ οἴδαμεν δὲ <u>ὅτι ὅσα ὁ νόμος λέγει τοῖς ἐν τῷ νόμῳ λαλεῖ</u>, ἵνα πᾶν στόμα φραγῇ καὶ ὑπόδικος γένηται πᾶς ὁ κόσμος τῷ θεῷ·
Citational, active, unmodified, has a direct object, the content of citation.
²¹ <u>Νυνὶ</u> δὲ <u>χωρὶς νόμου</u> δικαιοσύνη θεοῦ πεφανέρωται μαρτυρουμένη ὑπὸ τοῦ νόμου καὶ τῶν προφητῶν,
Passive, separation genitive modifies an action. Action is in the past, adv is "by now."
²⁵ ὃν προέθετο ὁ θεὸς ἱλαστήριον διὰ [τῆς] πίστεως ἐν τῷ αὐτοῦ αἵματι εἰς ἔνδειξιν τῆς δικαιοσύνης αὐτοῦ διὰ τὴν πάρεσιν τῶν <u>προ</u>γεγονότων ἁμαρτημάτων
Adjectival, marked with deixis for prior time, unmodified other than the preposition

Romans 4

¹ Τί οὖν ἐροῦμεν εὑρηκέναι Ἀβραὰμ τὸν προπάτορα ἡμῶν <u>κατὰ σάρκα</u>;
Active, Possibly modified by "according the flesh." As an adv of manner.

¹⁴ εἰ γὰρ οἱ ἐκ νόμου κληρονόμοι, κεκένωται ἡ πίστις καὶ κατήργηται ἡ ἐπαγγελία·

First, Middle, unmodified, adjectival

Second, middle, unmodified, adjectival

¹⁷ καθὼς γέγραπται <u>ὅτι πατέρα πολλῶν ἐθνῶν τέθεικά σε</u>, κατέναντι οὗ ἐπίστευσεν θεοῦ τοῦ ζῳοποιοῦντος τοὺς νεκροὺς καὶ καλοῦντος τὰ μὴ ὄντα ὡς ὄντα.

Citational, passive, unmodified, has a direct object, the content of citation.

¹⁸Ὃς παρ᾽ ἐλπίδα ἐπ᾽ ἐλπίδι ἐπίστευσεν εἰς τὸ γενέσθαι αὐτὸν πατέρα πολλῶν ἐθνῶν κατὰ τὸ εἰρημένον· οὕτως ἔσται τὸ σπέρμα σου,

Passive, unmodified, substantival, part of a PP.

¹⁹ καὶ μὴ ἀσθενήσας τῇ πίστει κατενόησεν τὸ ἑαυτοῦ σῶμα [ἤδη] νενεκρωμένον, ἑκατονταετής που ὑπάρχων, καὶ τὴν νέκρωσιν τῆς μήτρας Σάρρας·

Adjectival, passive, stative, modified by adverb "already."

²¹ καὶ πληροφορηθεὶς ὅτι <u>ὃ ἐπήγγελται</u> δυνατός ἐστιν καὶ ποιῆσαι.

Middle, unmodified, has relative pronoun DO, preposition changes the lexical class.

Romans 5

² δι᾽ <u>οὗ</u> καὶ τὴν προσαγωγὴν ἐσχήκαμεν [<u>τῇ πίστει</u>] <u>εἰς τὴν χάριν ταύτην ἐν ᾗ</u> ἐστήκαμεν καὶ καυχώμεθα ἐπ᾽ ἐλπίδι τῆς δόξης τοῦ θεοῦ.

First, active, modified by genitive PP of agency, dative means, and accusative PP of purpose.

Second, modified by locative PP.

³ οὐ μόνον δέ, ἀλλὰ καὶ καυχώμεθα ἐν ταῖς θλίψεσιν, εἰδότες <u>ὅτι ἡ θλῖψις ὑπομονὴν</u> <u>κατεργάζεται,</u>

Citational, active, unmodified, has a direct object, the content of citation.

⁵ ἡ δὲ ἐλπὶς οὐ καταισχύνει, ὅτι ἡ ἀγάπη τοῦ θεοῦ ἐκκέχυται <u>ἐν ταῖς καρδίαις</u> ἡμῶν <u>διὰ πνεύματος ἁγίου τοῦ</u> δοθέντος ἡμῖν.

Active, modified by locative dative PP and genitive PP of agent.

Romans 6

⁵ εἰ γὰρ <u>σύμφυτοι</u> γεγόναμεν <u>τῷ ὁμοιώματι</u> τοῦ θανάτου αὐτοῦ, ἀλλὰ καὶ τῆς ἀναστάσεως ἐσόμεθα·

Active modified by dative phrase dependent on the "with" preposition.

⁷ ὁ γὰρ ἀποθανὼν δεδικαίωται <u>ἀπὸ τῆς ἁμαρτίας.</u>

passive, modified by a genitive PP of separation.

⁹ εἰδότες <u>ὅτι Χριστὸς ἐγερθεὶς ἐκ νεκρῶν</u> οὐκέτι ἀποθνῄσκει, θάνατος αὐτοῦ οὐκέτι κυριεύει.

Citational, active, unmodified, has a direct object, the content of citation.

¹⁶ οὐκ οἴδατε <u>ὅτι ᾧ παριστάνετε ἑαυτοὺς δούλους εἰς ὑπακοήν, δοῦλοί ἐστε ᾧ ὑπακούετε</u>, ἤτοι ἁμαρτίας εἰς θάνατον ἢ ὑπακοῆς εἰς δικαιοσύνην;

Citational, active, unmodified, has a direct object, the content of citation.

Romans 7

² ἡ γὰρ ὕπανδρος γυνὴ <u>τῷ ζῶντι ἀνδρὶ</u> δέδεται <u>νόμῳ</u>· ἐὰν δὲ ἀποθάνῃ ὁ ἀνήρ, κατήργηται <u>ἀπὸ τοῦ νόμου τοῦ ἀνδρός.</u>

First, middle, modified by dative IO and dative means.

Second, middle, modified by separation genitive PP.

¹⁴ Οἴδαμεν γὰρ <u>ὅτι ὁ νόμος πνευματικός ἐστιν</u>, ἐγὼ δὲ σάρκινός εἰμι πεπραμένος <u>ὑπὸ τὴν ἁμαρτίαν.</u>

First, Citational, active, unmodified, has a direct object, the content of citation.

Second, passive, periphrastic, modified by "under sin," which is either subordination, agency or basis.

¹⁸ Οἶδα γὰρ <u>ὅτι οὐκ οἰκεῖ ἐν ἐμοί</u>, τοῦτ᾽ ἔστιν ἐν τῇ σαρκί μου, ἀγαθόν· τὸ γὰρ θέλειν παράκειταί μοι, τὸ δὲ κατεργάζεσθαι τὸ καλὸν οὔ·

Citational, active, unmodified, has a direct object, the content of citation.

Romans 8

²² οἴδαμεν γὰρ <u>ὅτι πᾶσα ἡ κτίσις συστενάζει καὶ συνωδίνει ἄχρι τοῦ νῦν·</u>

Citational, active, unmodified, has a direct object, the content of citation.

²⁶ Ὡσαύτως δὲ καὶ τὸ πνεῦμα συναντιλαμβάνεται τῇ ἀσθενείᾳ ἡμῶν· <u>τὸ γὰρ τί προσευξώμεθα καθὸ</u> δεῖ οὐκ οἴδαμεν, ἀλλὰ αὐτὸ τὸ πνεῦμα ὑπερεντυγχάνει στεναγμοῖς ἀλαλήτοις·

Citational, active, unmodified, has a direct object, the content of citation.

²⁷ ὁ δὲ ἐραυνῶν τὰς καρδίας οἶδεν <u>τί τὸ φρόνημα τοῦ πνεύματος</u>, ὅτι κατὰ θεὸν ἐντυγχάνει ὑπὲρ ἁγίων.

Citational, active, unmodified, has a direct object, the content of citation.

²⁸ Οἴδαμεν δὲ <u>ὅτι τοῖς ἀγαπῶσιν τὸν θεὸν πάντα συνεργεῖ εἰς ἀγαθόν, τοῖς κατὰ πρόθεσιν κλητοῖς οὖσιν.</u>

Citational, active, unmodified, has a direct object, the content of citation.

³⁶ καθὼς γέγραπται <u>ὅτι ἕνεκεν σοῦ θανατούμεθα ὅλην τὴν ἡμέραν, ἐλογίσθημεν ὡς</u> <u>πρόβατα σφαγῆς.</u>

Citational, passive, unmodified, has a direct object, the content of citation.

³⁸ πέπεισμαι γὰρ <u>ὅτι οὔτε θάνατος οὔτε ζωὴ οὔτε ἄγγελοι οὔτε ἀρχαὶ οὔτε ἐνεστῶτα</u> <u>οὔτε μέλλοντα οὔτε δυνάμεις</u>

First Citational, passive, unmodified, has a direct object, the content of citation.

Second is substantival "things that have been placed," unmodified and stative.

Romans 9

⁶ Οὐχ οἷον δὲ ὅτι ἐκπέπτωκεν ὁ λόγος τοῦ θεοῦ. οὐ γὰρ πάντες οἱ ἐξ Ἰσραὴλ οὗτοι Ἰσραήλ·

Active, intransitive. Unmodified.

¹³ καθὼς γέγραπται· <u>τὸν Ἰακὼβ ἠγάπησα, τὸν δὲ Ἡσαῦ ἐμίσησα.</u>

Citational, passive, unmodified, has a direct object, the content of citation.

¹⁹ Ἐρεῖς μοι οὖν· τί [οὖν] ἔτι μέμφεται; <u>τῷ</u> γὰρ <u>βουλήματι αὐτοῦ</u> τίς ἀνθέστηκεν;

Active, Takes a dative object, also has preposition of opposition, posture verb.

²² εἰ δὲ θέλων ὁ θεὸς ἐνδείξασθαι τὴν ὀργὴν καὶ γνωρίσαι τὸ δυνατὸν αὐτοῦ ἤνεγκεν ἐν πολλῇ μακροθυμίᾳ σκεύη ὀργῆς κατηρτισμένα <u>εἰς ἀπώλειαν,</u>

Adjectival, Passive, modified by accusative purpose or goal.

²⁵ ὡς καὶ ἐν τῷ Ὡσηὲ λέγει· καλέσω τὸν οὐ λαόν μου λαόν μου καὶ τὴν οὐκ ἠγαπημένην ἠγαπημένην·

First, Passive, substantival, unmodified.

Second, Passive, substantival, unmodified.

²⁹ καὶ καθὼς <u>προείρηκεν</u> Ἡσαΐας· <u>εἰ μὴ κύριος σαβαὼθ ἐγκατέλιπεν ἡμῖν σπέρμα, ὡς</u> <u>Σόδομα ἂν ἐγενήθημεν καὶ ὡς Γόμορρα ἂν ὡμοιώθημεν.</u>

Citational, active, modified by its prefix, a deictic past marker, has a direct object, the content of citation.

³³ καθὼς γέγραπται· <u>ἰδοὺ τίθημι ἐν Σιὼν λίθον προσκόμματος καὶ πέτραν σκανδάλου,</u> <u>καὶ ὁ πιστεύων ἐπ᾽ αὐτῷ οὐ καταισχυνθήσεται.</u>

Citational, passive, unmodified, has a direct object, the content of citation.

Romans 10

[15] πῶς δὲ κηρύξωσιν ἐὰν μὴ ἀποσταλῶσιν; καθὼς γέγραπται· <u>ὡς ὡραῖοι οἱ πόδες τῶν</u> <u>εὐαγγελιζομένων [τὰ] ἀγαθά.</u>
Citational, passive, unmodified, has a direct object, the content of citation.

Romans 11

[2] οὐκ ἀπώσατο ὁ θεὸς τὸν λαὸν αὐτοῦ ὃν προέγνω. ἢ οὐκ οἴδατε ἐν Ἠλίᾳ τί λέγει ἡ γραφή, <u>ὡς ἐντυγχάνει τῷ θεῷ κατὰ τοῦ Ἰσραήλ;</u>
Citational, active, unmodified, has a direct object, the content of citation.
[5] οὕτως οὖν καὶ ἐν τῷ νῦν καιρῷ λεῖμμα <u>κατ᾽ ἐκλογὴν</u> χάριτος γέγονεν·
Active, change-of-state, modified by the standard that dictates the becoming, copula-like.
[8] καθὼς γέγραπται· <u>ἔδωκεν αὐτοῖς ὁ θεὸς πνεῦμα κατανύξεως, ὀφθαλμοὺς τοῦ μὴ</u> <u>βλέπειν καὶ ὦτα τοῦ μὴ ἀκούειν, ἕως τῆς σήμερον ἡμέρας.</u>
Citational, passive, unmodified, has a direct object, the content of citation.
[20] καλῶς· τῇ ἀπιστίᾳ ἐξεκλάσθησαν, σὺ δὲ <u>τῇ πίστει</u> ἕστηκας. μὴ ὑψηλὰ φρόνει ἀλλὰ φοβοῦ·
Active, postural, modified by location (realm), or means.
[25] Οὐ γὰρ θέλω ὑμᾶς ἀγνοεῖν, ἀδελφοί, τὸ μυστήριον τοῦτο, ἵνα μὴ ἦτε [παρ᾽] ἑαυτοῖς φρόνιμοι, ὅτι πώρωσις <u>ἀπὸ μέρους τῷ Ἰσραὴλ</u> γέγονεν ἄχρι οὗ τὸ πλήρωμα τῶν ἐθνῶν εἰσέλθῃ
Active, change of state, modified by dative location or an IO, and possibly genitive of separation or source, although the genitive might be best modifying the verbal noun, "hardening."
[26] καὶ οὕτως πᾶς Ἰσραὴλ σωθήσεται, καθὼς γέγραπται· <u>ἥξει ἐκ Σιὼν ὁ ῥυόμενος,</u> <u>ἀποστρέψει ἀσεβείας ἀπὸ Ἰακώβ.</u>
Citational, passive, unmodified, has a direct object, the content of citation.

Romans 12

[19] μὴ ἑαυτοὺς ἐκδικοῦντες, ἀγαπητοί, ἀλλὰ δότε τόπον τῇ ὀργῇ, γέγραπται γάρ· <u>ἐμοὶ</u> <u>ἐκδίκησις, ἐγὼ ἀνταποδώσω, λέγει κύριος.</u>
Citational, passive, unmodified, has a direct object, the content of citation.

Romans 13

[1] Πᾶσα ψυχὴ ἐξουσίαις ὑπερεχούσαις ὑποτασσέσθω. οὐ γὰρ ἔστιν ἐξουσία εἰ μὴ ὑπὸ θεοῦ, αἱ δὲ οὖσαι <u>ὑπὸ θεοῦ</u> τεταγμέναι εἰσίν.
Passive, actional, modified by agent.

[2] ὥστε ὁ ἀντιτασσόμενος τῇ ἐξουσίᾳ <u>τῇ</u> τοῦ θεοῦ <u>διαταγῇ</u> ἀνθέστηκεν, οἱ δὲ ἀνθεστηκότες ἑαυτοῖς κρίμα λήμψονται.
First, Active, actional, modified by dative object.
Second, active, actional and unmodified.

[8] Μηδενὶ μηδὲν ὀφείλετε εἰ μὴ τὸ ἀλλήλους ἀγαπᾶν· ὁ γὰρ ἀγαπῶν τὸν ἕτερον <u>νόμον</u> πεπλήρωκεν.
Active, actional, direct object, unmodified.

[11] Καὶ τοῦτο εἰδότες τὸν καιρόν, <u>ὅτι ὥρα ἤδη ὑμᾶς ἐξ ὕπνου ἐγερθῆναι, νῦν γὰρ ἐγγύτερον ἡμῶν ἡ σωτηρία ἢ ὅτε ἐπιστεύσαμεν.</u>
Citational, active, unmodified, has a direct object, the content of citation.

[12] ἡ νὺξ προέκοψεν, ἡ δὲ ἡμέρα ἤγγικεν. ἀποθώμεθα οὖν τὰ ἔργα τοῦ σκότους, ἐνδυσώμεθα [δὲ] τὰ ὅπλα τοῦ φωτός.
Active, change of proximity, unmodified.

Romans 14

[11] γέγραπται γάρ· <u>ζῶ ἐγώ, λέγει κύριος, ὅτι ἐμοὶ κάμψει πᾶν γόνυ καὶ πᾶσα γλῶσσα ἐξομολογήσεται τῷ θεῷ.</u>
Citational, passive, unmodified, has a direct object, the content of citation.

[14] οἶδα καὶ πέπεισμαι <u>ἐν κυρίῳ Ἰησοῦ ὅτι οὐδὲν κοινὸν δι' ἑαυτοῦ</u>, εἰ μὴ τῷ λογιζομένῳ τι κοινὸν εἶναι, ἐκείνῳ κοινόν.
First active, Citational, unmodified, has a direct object, the content of citation.
Second passive, Citational, modified by locative realm, has a direct object, the content of citation.

[23] ὁ δὲ διακρινόμενος ἐὰν φάγῃ κατακέκριται, ὅτι οὐκ ἐκ πίστεως· πᾶν δὲ ὃ οὐκ ἐκ πίστεως ἁμαρτία ἐστίν.
Middle, actional, unmodified.

Romans 15

³ καὶ γὰρ ὁ Χριστὸς οὐχ ἑαυτῷ ἤρεσεν, ἀλλὰ καθὼς γέγραπται· <u>οἱ ὀνειδισμοὶ τῶν ὀνειδιζόντων σε ἐπέπεσαν ἐπ᾽ ἐμέ</u>.

Citational, passive, unmodified, has a direct object, the content of citation.

⁸ λέγω γὰρ Χριστὸν <u>διάκονον</u> γεγενῆσθαι περιτομῆς ὑπὲρ ἀληθείας θεοῦ, εἰς τὸ βεβαιῶσαι τὰς ἐπαγγελίας τῶν πατέρων,

Copula use A = B. stative, unmodified. Has a PN.

⁹ τὰ δὲ ἔθνη ὑπὲρ ἐλέους δοξάσαι τὸν θεόν, καθὼς γέγραπται· <u>διὰ τοῦτο ἐξομολογήσομαί σοι ἐν ἔθνεσιν καὶ τῷ ὀνόματί σου ψαλῶ</u>.

Citational, passive, unmodified, has a direct object, the content of citation.

¹⁴ Πέπεισμαι δέ, ἀδελφοί μου, καὶ αὐτὸς ἐγὼ <u>περὶ ὑμῶν ὅτι καὶ αὐτοὶ μεστοί ἐστε ἀγαθωσύνης</u>, πεπληρωμένοι <u>πάσης [τῆς] γνώσεως</u>, δυνάμενοι καὶ ἀλλήλους νουθετεῖν.

First, Middle, Citational, modified by referent topic, has a direct object, the content of citation.

Second, passive, modified by genitive of content.

¹⁶ εἰς τὸ εἶναί με λειτουργὸν Χριστοῦ Ἰησοῦ εἰς τὰ ἔθνη, ἱερουργοῦντα τὸ εὐαγγέλιον τοῦ θεοῦ, ἵνα γένηται ἡ προσφορὰ τῶν ἐθνῶν εὐπρόσδεκτος, ἡγιασμένη <u>ἐν πνεύματι ἁγίῳ</u>.

Passive, modified my adverb of means or instrument.

¹⁹ ἐν δυνάμει σημείων καὶ τεράτων, ἐν δυνάμει πνεύματος [θεοῦ]. ὥστε με <u>ἀπὸ Ἰερουσαλὴμ καὶ κύκλῳ μέχρι τοῦ Ἰλλυρικοῦ</u> πεπληρωκέναι τὸ εὐαγγέλιον τοῦ Χριστοῦ,

Active, has direct object, modified by geophraphy–From X until Y spatially.

²¹ ἀλλὰ καθὼς γέγραπται· <u>οἷς οὐκ ἀνηγγέλη περὶ αὐτοῦ ὄψονται, καὶ οἳ οὐκ ἀκηκόασιν συνήσουσιν</u>.

Citational, passive, unmodified, has a direct object, the content of citation.

²⁹ οἶδα δὲ <u>ὅτι ἐρχόμενος πρὸς ὑμᾶς ἐν πληρώματι εὐλογίας Χριστοῦ ἐλεύσομαι</u>.

Citational, active, unmodified, has a direct object, the content of citation.

Romans 16

⁷ ἀσπάσασθε Ἀνδρόνικον καὶ Ἰουνιᾶν τοὺς συγγενεῖς μου καὶ συναιχμαλώτους μου, οἵτινές εἰσιν ἐπίσημοι ἐν τοῖς ἀποστόλοις, οἳ καὶ <u>πρὸ ἐμοῦ</u> γέγοναν <u>ἐν Χριστῷ</u>.

Middle, modified my temporal adverb "before" and realm of becoming, "in Christ."

²⁵ [Τῷ δὲ δυναμένῳ ὑμᾶς στηρίξαι κατὰ τὸ εὐαγγέλιόν μου καὶ τὸ κήρυγμα Ἰησοῦ Χριστοῦ, κατὰ ἀποκάλυψιν μυστηρίου <u>χρόνοις αἰωνίοις</u> σεσιγημένου, ²⁶ φανερωθέντος δὲ νῦν διά τε γραφῶν προφητικῶν κατ᾽ ἐπιταγὴν τοῦ αἰωνίου θεοῦ εἰς ὑπακοὴν

πίστεως εἰς πάντα τὰ ἔθνη γνωρισθέντος, ²⁷ μόνῳ σοφῷ θεῷ, διὰ Ἰησοῦ Χριστοῦ, ᾧ ἡ δόξα εἰς τοὺς αἰῶνας, ἀμήν.]

Passive, stative, modified by temporal dative of duration.

1 Corinthians 1

² τῇ ἐκκλησίᾳ τοῦ θεοῦ τῇ οὔσῃ ἐν Κορίνθῳ, ἡγιασμένοις <u>ἐν Χριστῷ Ἰησοῦ</u>, κλητοῖς ἁγίοις, σὺν πᾶσιν τοῖς ἐπικαλουμένοις τὸ ὄνομα τοῦ κυρίου ἡμῶν Ἰησοῦ Χριστοῦ ἐν παντὶ τόπῳ, αὐτῶν καὶ ἡμῶν·

passive, modified by realm locative.

¹⁰ Παρακαλῶ δὲ ὑμᾶς, ἀδελφοί, διὰ τοῦ ὀνόματος τοῦ κυρίου ἡμῶν Ἰησοῦ Χριστοῦ, ἵνα τὸ αὐτὸ λέγητε πάντες καὶ μὴ ᾖ ἐν ὑμῖν σχίσματα, ἦτε δὲ κατηρτισμένοι <u>ἐν τῷ αὐτῷ νοῒ</u> καὶ <u>ἐν τῇ αὐτῇ γνώμῃ</u>.

Periphrastic, substantive, passive, modified by two datives of manner.

¹³ μεμέρισται ὁ Χριστός; μὴ Παῦλος ἐσταυρώθη ὑπὲρ ὑμῶν, ἢ εἰς τὸ ὄνομα Παύλου ἐβαπτίσθητε;

Middle, unmodified.

¹⁶ ἐβάπτισα δὲ καὶ τὸν Στεφανᾶ οἶκον, λοιπὸν οὐκ οἶδα <u>εἴ τινα ἄλλον ἐβάπτισα</u>.

Citational, object of content for "know," Unmodified.

¹⁹ γέγραπται γάρ· <u>ἀπολῶ τὴν σοφίαν τῶν σοφῶν καὶ τὴν σύνεσιν τῶν συνετῶν ἀθετήσω.</u>

Citational, passive, unmodified, has a direct object, the content of citation.

²³ ἡμεῖς δὲ κηρύσσομεν Χριστὸν ἐσταυρωμένον, Ἰουδαίοις μὲν σκάνδαλον, ἔθνεσιν δὲ μωρίαν,

Stative, adjectival or PN, passive, unmodified.

²⁸ καὶ τὰ ἀγενῆ τοῦ κόσμου καὶ τὰ ἐξουθενημένα ἐξελέξατο ὁ θεός, τὰ μὴ ὄντα, ἵνα τὰ ὄντα καταργήσῃ,

Passive, substantive, unmodified.

³¹ ἵνα καθὼς γέγραπται· <u>ὁ καυχώμενος ἐν κυρίῳ καυχάσθω</u>.

Citational, passive, unmodified, has a direct object, the content of citation.

1 Corinthians 2

² οὐ γὰρ ἔκρινά τι εἰδέναι ἐν ὑμῖν εἰ μὴ Ἰησοῦν Χριστὸν καὶ τοῦτον ἐσταυρωμένον.

Adjectival, stative, unmodified.

[7] ἀλλὰ λαλοῦμεν θεοῦ σοφίαν ἐν μυστηρίῳ τὴν ἀποκεκρυμμένην, ἣν προώρισεν ὁ θεὸς πρὸ τῶν αἰώνων εἰς δόξαν ἡμῶν,

Adjectival, stative, unmodified.

[8] ἣν οὐδεὶς τῶν ἀρχόντων τοῦ αἰῶνος τούτου ἔγνωκεν· εἰ γὰρ ἔγνωσαν, οὐκ ἂν τὸν κύριον τῆς δόξης ἐσταύρωσαν.

Active, cognitive, has a direct object in the form of a relative pronoun, unmodified.

[9] ἀλλὰ καθὼς γέγραπται· <u>ἃ ὀφθαλμὸς οὐκ εἶδεν καὶ οὖς οὐκ ἤκουσεν καὶ ἐπὶ καρδίαν ἀνθρώπου οὐκ ἀνέβη, ἃ ἡτοίμασεν ὁ θεὸς τοῖς ἀγαπῶσιν αὐτόν.</u>

Citational, passive, has a direct object, the content of citation, unmodified.

[11] τίς γὰρ οἶδεν ἀνθρώπων τὰ τοῦ ἀνθρώπου εἰ μὴ τὸ πνεῦμα τοῦ ἀνθρώπου τὸ ἐν αὐτῷ; οὕτως καὶ <u>τὰ</u> τοῦ θεοῦ οὐδεὶς ἔγνωκεν εἰ μὴ τὸ πνεῦμα τοῦ θεοῦ.

Active, cognitive, unmodified, has a direct object in the form of a plural article.

[12] ἡμεῖς δὲ οὐ τὸ πνεῦμα τοῦ κόσμου ἐλάβομεν ἀλλὰ τὸ πνεῦμα τὸ ἐκ τοῦ θεοῦ, ἵνα εἰδῶμεν <u>τὰ</u> ὑπὸ τοῦ θεοῦ χαρισθέντα ἡμῖν·

Active, cognitive, unmodified, has a direct object in the form of a plural article.

1 Corinthians 3

[16] Οὐκ οἴδατε <u>ὅτι ναὸς θεοῦ ἐστε καὶ τὸ πνεῦμα τοῦ θεοῦ οἰκεῖ ἐν ὑμῖν;</u>

Citational, active, unmodified, has a direct object, the content of citation.

[19] ἡ γὰρ σοφία τοῦ κόσμου τούτου μωρία παρὰ τῷ θεῷ ἐστιν. γέγραπται γάρ· <u>ὁ δρασσόμενος τοὺς σοφοὺς ἐν τῇ πανουργίᾳ αὐτῶν·</u>

Citational, passive, unmodified, has a direct object, the content of citation.

[22] εἴτε Παῦλος εἴτε Ἀπολλῶς εἴτε Κηφᾶς, εἴτε κόσμος εἴτε ζωὴ εἴτε θάνατος, εἴτε <u>ἐνεστῶτα</u> εἴτε μέλλοντα· πάντα ὑμῶν,

Active substantival, modified by its internal preposition. "stand in place" a causative.

1 Corinthians 4

[4] <u>οὐδὲν</u> γὰρ <u>ἐμαυτῷ σύν</u>οιδα, ἀλλ᾽ οὐκ <u>ἐν τούτῳ</u> δεδικαίωμαι, ὁ δὲ ἀνακρίνων με κύριός ἐστιν.

First, Active, has direct object, content of the knowing, and modified by dative of association.

Second, middle, modified by dative of manner, or instrument.

⁶ Ταῦτα δέ, ἀδελφοί, μετεσχημάτισα εἰς ἐμαυτὸν καὶ Ἀπολλῶν δι' ὑμᾶς, ἵνα ἐν ἡμῖν μάθητε τὸ μὴ ὑπὲρ ἃ γέγραπται, ἵνα μὴ εἷς ὑπὲρ τοῦ ἑνὸς φυσιοῦσθε κατὰ τοῦ ἑτέρου. Passive, unmodified.

⁸ ἤδη κεκορεσμένοι ἐστέ, ἤδη ἐπλουτήσατε, χωρὶς ἡμῶν ἐβασιλεύσατε· καὶ ὄφελόν γε ἐβασιλεύσατε, ἵνα καὶ ἡμεῖς ὑμῖν συμβασιλεύσωμεν. Periphrastic. You are already ones having been satiated/filled. If "already" modifies only the auxiliary, then the Pf is unmodified. If "already" modifies both, then the action of satiating is what is modified in the Pf as being complete.

¹⁹ ἐλεύσομαι δὲ ταχέως πρὸς ὑμᾶς ἐὰν ὁ κύριος θελήσῃ, καὶ γνώσομαι οὐ τὸν λόγον τῶν πεφυσιωμένων ἀλλὰ τὴν δύναμιν· Substantive unmodified stative.

1 Corinthians 5

² καὶ ὑμεῖς πεφυσιωμένοι ἐστὲ καὶ οὐχὶ μᾶλλον ἐπενθήσατε, ἵνα ἀρθῇ ἐκ μέσου ὑμῶν ὁ τὸ ἔργον τοῦτο πράξας; Periphrastic, substantival, unmodified

³ ἐγὼ μὲν γάρ, ἀπὼν τῷ σώματι παρὼν δὲ τῷ πνεύματι, ἤδη κέκρικα ὡς παρὼν τὸν οὕτως τοῦτο κατεργασάμενον· Active, has a direct object, modified by "already" indicating that the act of judging is complete.

⁶ Οὐ καλὸν τὸ καύχημα ὑμῶν. οὐκ οἴδατε ὅτι μικρὰ ζύμη ὅλον τὸ φύραμα ζυμοῖ; Citational, active, unmodified, has a direct object, the content of citation.

1 Corinthians 6

² ἢ οὐκ οἴδατε ὅτι οἱ ἅγιοι τὸν κόσμον κρινοῦσιν; καὶ εἰ ἐν ὑμῖν κρίνεται ὁ κόσμος, ἀνάξιοί ἐστε κριτηρίων ἐλαχίστων; Citational, active, unmodified, has a direct object, the content of citation.

³ οὐκ οἴδατε ὅτι ἀγγέλους κρινοῦμεν, μήτι γε βιωτικά; Citational, active, unmodified, has a direct object, the content of citation.

⁴ βιωτικὰ μὲν οὖν κριτήρια ἐὰν ἔχητε, τοὺς ἐξουθενημένους ἐν τῇ ἐκκλησίᾳ, τούτους καθίζετε; Substantival, stative, modified by realm.

⁹ Ἢ οὐκ οἴδατε ὅτι ἄδικοι θεοῦ βασιλείαν οὐ κληρονομήσουσιν; μὴ πλανᾶσθε· οὔτε πόρνοι οὔτε εἰδωλολάτραι οὔτε μοιχοὶ οὔτε μαλακοὶ οὔτε ἀρσενοκοῖται ¹⁰ οὔτε

κλέπται οὔτε πλεονέκται, οὐ μέθυσοι, οὐ λοίδοροι, οὐχ ἅρπαγες βασιλείαν θεοῦ κληρονομήσουσιν.

Citational, active, unmodified, has a direct object, the content of citation.

¹⁵ οὐκ οἴδατε <u>ὅτι τὰ σώματα ὑμῶν μέλη Χριστοῦ ἐστιν</u>; ἄρας οὖν τὰ μέλη τοῦ Χριστοῦ ποιήσω πόρνης μέλη; μὴ γένοιτο.

Citational, active, unmodified, has a direct object, the content of citation.

¹⁶ [ἢ] οὐκ οἴδατε <u>ὅτι ὁ κολλώμενος τῇ πόρνῃ ἓν σῶμά ἐστιν</u>; ἔσονται γάρ, φησίν, οἱ δύο εἰς σάρκα μίαν.

Citational, active, unmodified, has a direct object, the content of citation.

¹⁹ ἢ οὐκ οἴδατε <u>ὅτι τὸ σῶμα ὑμῶν ναὸς τοῦ ἐν ὑμῖν ἁγίου πνεύματός ἐστιν οὗ ἔχετε ἀπὸ θεοῦ, καὶ οὐκ ἐστὲ ἑαυτῶν;</u>

Citational, active, unmodified, has a direct object, the content of citation.

1 Corinthians 7

¹⁰ Τοῖς δὲ γεγαμηκόσιν παραγγέλλω, οὐκ ἐγὼ ἀλλὰ ὁ κύριος, γυναῖκα ἀπὸ ἀνδρὸς μὴ χωρισθῆναι, ¹¹ -ἐὰν δὲ καὶ χωρισθῇ, μενέτω ἄγαμος ἢ τῷ ἀνδρὶ καταλλαγήτω,- καὶ ἄνδρα γυναῖκα μὴ ἀφιέναι.

Substantive, stative, unmodified.

¹⁴ ἡγίασται γὰρ ὁ ἀνὴρ ὁ ἄπιστος <u>ἐν τῇ γυναικὶ</u> καὶ ἡγίασται ἡ γυνὴ ἡ ἄπιστος <u>ἐν τῷ ἀδελφῷ</u>· ἐπεὶ ἄρα τὰ τέκνα ὑμῶν ἀκάθαρτά ἐστιν, νῦν δὲ ἄγιά ἐστιν.

First, Passive, modified by PP where the object is the locus for sanctification.

Second, Passive, modified by PP where the object is the locus for sanctification.

¹⁵ εἰ δὲ ὁ ἄπιστος χωρίζεται, χωριζέσθω· οὐ δεδούλωται ὁ ἀδελφὸς ἢ ἡ ἀδελφὴ ἐν τοῖς τοιούτοις· <u>ἐν</u> δὲ <u>εἰρήνῃ</u> κέκληκεν ὑμᾶς ὁ θεός.

Middle, stative, modified by dative PP of realm.

¹⁶ τί γὰρ οἶδας, γύναι, <u>εἰ τὸν ἄνδρα σώσεις</u>; ἢ τί οἶδας, ἄνερ, <u>εἰ τὴν γυναῖκα σώσεις</u>;

Citational, active, unmodified, has a direct object, the content of citation.

Citational, active, unmodified, has a direct object, the content of citation.

¹⁷ Εἰ μὴ ἑκάστῳ ὡς ἐμέρισεν ὁ κύριος, <u>ἕκαστον</u> ὡς κέκληκεν ὁ θεός, οὕτως περιπατείτω. καὶ οὕτως ἐν ταῖς ἐκκλησίαις πάσαις διατάσσομαι.

Active, direct obj "each", unmodified.

¹⁸ περιτετμημένος τις ἐκλήθη, μὴ ἐπισπάσθω· <u>ἐν ἀκροβυστίᾳ</u> κέκληταί τις, μὴ περιτεμνέσθω.

First, substantive, unmodified, stative

Second, active, modified by manner PP, actional.

²⁵ Περὶ δὲ τῶν παρθένων ἐπιταγὴν κυρίου οὐκ ἔχω, γνώμην δὲ δίδωμι ὡς ἠλεημένος <u>ὑπὸ κυρίου</u> πιστὸς εἶναι.

Substantive, eventive, modified by agent of the action.

²⁶ Νομίζω οὖν τοῦτο καλὸν ὑπάρχειν διὰ τὴν ἐνεστῶσαν ἀνάγκην, ὅτι καλὸν ἀνθρώπῳ τὸ οὕτως εἶναι.

Adjectival, stative, unmodified.

²⁷ δέδεσαι γυναικί, μὴ ζήτει λύσιν· λέλυσαι <u>ἀπὸ γυναικός</u>, μὴ ζήτει γυναῖκα.

Passive, modified by genitive PP of separation containing the item loosed from.

²⁹ Τοῦτο δέ φημι, ἀδελφοί, ὁ καιρὸς <u>συνεσταλμένος</u> ἐστίν· τὸ λοιπόν, ἵνα καὶ οἱ ἔχοντες γυναῖκας ὡς μὴ ἔχοντες ὦσιν

Periphrastic, Predicate nominative, substantive, modified only by attached preposition of association.

³⁴ καὶ μεμέρισται. καὶ ἡ γυνὴ ἡ ἄγαμος καὶ ἡ παρθένος μεριμνᾷ τὰ τοῦ κυρίου, ἵνα ᾖ ἁγία καὶ τῷ σώματι καὶ τῷ πνεύματι· ἡ δὲ γαμήσασα μεριμνᾷ τὰ τοῦ κόσμου, πῶς ἀρέσῃ τῷ ἀνδρί.

Middle, unmodified, stative.

³⁷ ὃς δὲ ἕστηκεν <u>ἐν τῇ καρδίᾳ</u> αὐτοῦ ἑδραῖος μὴ ἔχων ἀνάγκην, ἐξουσίαν δὲ ἔχει περὶ τοῦ ἰδίου θελήματος καὶ <u>τοῦτο</u> κέκρικεν <u>ἐν τῇ ἰδίᾳ καρδίᾳ</u>, τηρεῖν τὴν ἑαυτοῦ παρθένον, καλῶς ποιήσει.

First, Active, locative realm of activity.

Second, active, has a direct object, and modified by locative realm of activity.

³⁹ Γυνὴ δέδεται <u>ἐφ' ὅσον χρόνον</u> ζῇ ὁ ἀνὴρ αὐτῆς· ἐὰν δὲ κοιμηθῇ ὁ ἀνήρ, ἐλευθέρα ἐστὶν ᾧ θέλει γαμηθῆναι, μόνον ἐν κυρίῳ.

Intransitive middle. Modified by duration of time. Stative. "upon as much time as . . . " = "over"

1 Corinthians 8

¹ Περὶ δὲ τῶν εἰδωλοθύτων, οἴδαμεν ὅτι <u>πάντες γνῶσιν ἔχομεν</u>. ἡ γνῶσις φυσιοῖ, ἡ δὲ ἀγάπη οἰκοδομεῖ·

Citational, active, unmodified, has a direct object, the content of citation.

² εἴ τις δοκεῖ ἐγνωκέναι <u>τι</u>, οὔπω ἔγνω καθὼς δεῖ γνῶναι·

Citational, active, unmodified, has a direct object, the content of citation.

³ εἰ δέ τις ἀγαπᾷ τὸν θεόν, οὗτος ἔγνωσται <u>ὑπ' αὐτοῦ</u>.

Passive, active, modified by the agent of the mental action.

⁴ Περὶ τῆς βρώσεως οὖν τῶν εἰδωλοθύτων, οἴδαμεν ὅτι <u>οὐδὲν εἴδωλον ἐν κόσμῳ καὶ ὅτι οὐδεὶς θεὸς εἰ μὴ εἷς</u>.

Citational, active, unmodified, has a direct object, the content of citation.

1 Corinthians 9

[1] Οὐκ εἰμὶ ἐλεύθερος; οὐκ εἰμὶ ἀπόστολος; οὐχὶ Ἰησοῦν τὸν κύριον ἡμῶν ἑόρακα; οὐ τὸ ἔργον μου ὑμεῖς ἐστε ἐν κυρίῳ;
Active, has direct object, the item seen or perceived.

[9] ἐν γὰρ τῷ Μωϋσέως νόμῳ γέγραπται· οὐ κημώσεις βοῦν ἀλοῶντα. μὴ τῶν βοῶν μέλει τῷ θεῷ
Citational, middle, modified by dative location of the source, has a direct object, the content of citation.

[13] Οὐκ οἴδατε ὅτι οἱ τὰ ἱερὰ ἐργαζόμενοι [τὰ] ἐκ τοῦ ἱεροῦ ἐσθίουσιν, οἱ τῷ θυσιαστηρίῳ παρεδρεύοντες τῷ θυσιαστηρίῳ συμμερίζονται;
Citational, active, unmodified, has a direct object, the content of citation.

[15] Ἐγὼ δὲ οὐ κέχρημαι οὐδενὶ τούτων. Οὐκ ἔγραψα δὲ ταῦτα, ἵνα οὕτως γένηται ἐν ἐμοί· καλὸν γάρ μοι μᾶλλον ἀποθανεῖν ἤ- τὸ καύχημά μου οὐδεὶς κενώσει.
"I have used to/for nothing of these things" middle, actional, modified by extent, and has a direct object in Genitive.

[17] εἰ γὰρ ἑκὼν τοῦτο πράσσω, μισθὸν ἔχω· εἰ δὲ ἄκων, οἰκονομίαν πεπίστευμαι·
Passive, unmodified, direct object.

[22] ἐγενόμην τοῖς ἀσθενέσιν ἀσθενής, ἵνα τοὺς ἀσθενεῖς κερδήσω· τοῖς πᾶσιν γέγονα πάντα, ἵνα πάντως τινὰς σώσω.
Passive, and modified with dative of referent, copula-like.

[24] Οὐκ οἴδατε ὅτι οἱ ἐν σταδίῳ τρέχοντες πάντες μὲν τρέχουσιν, εἷς δὲ λαμβάνει τὸ βραβεῖον; οὕτως τρέχετε ἵνα καταλάβητε.
Citational, active, unmodified, has a direct object, the content of citation.

1 Corinthians 10

[7] μηδὲ εἰδωλολάτραι γίνεσθε καθώς τινες αὐτῶν, ὥσπερ γέγραπται· ἐκάθισεν ὁ λαὸς φαγεῖν καὶ πεῖν καὶ ἀνέστησαν παίζειν.
Citational, passive, unmodified, has a direct object, the content of citation.

[11] ταῦτα δὲ τυπικῶς συνέβαινεν ἐκείνοις, ἐγράφη δὲ πρὸς νουθεσίαν ἡμῶν, εἰς οὓς τὰ τέλη τῶν αἰώνων κατήντηκεν.
Intransitive, active, modified by accusative PP of interest.

[12] Ὥστε ὁ δοκῶν ἑστάναι βλεπέτω μὴ πέσῃ.

Active, actional, unmodified. An infinitive in a subordinate clause.

¹³ πειρασμὸς <u>ὑμᾶς</u> οὐκ εἴληφεν εἰ μὴ ἀνθρώπινος· πιστὸς δὲ ὁ θεός, ὃς οὐκ ἐάσει ὑμᾶς πειρασθῆναι ὑπὲρ ὃ δύνασθε ἀλλὰ ποιήσει σὺν τῷ πειρασμῷ καὶ τὴν ἔκβασιν τοῦ δύνασθαι ὑπενεγκεῖν.

Active, actional, direct object in pronoun, unmodified

1 Corinthians 11

² Ἐπαινῶ δὲ ὑμᾶς ὅτι <u>πάντα</u> μου μέμνησθε καί, καθὼς παρέδωκα ὑμῖν, τὰς παραδόσεις κατέχετε.

Passive, has direct object "all things," unmodified

³ Θέλω δὲ ὑμᾶς εἰδέναι ὅτι <u>παντὸς ἀνδρὸς ἡ κεφαλὴ ὁ Χριστός ἐστιν, κεφαλὴ δὲ γυναικὸς ὁ ἀνήρ, κεφαλὴ δὲ τοῦ Χριστοῦ ὁ θεός</u>.

Citational, active, unmodified, has a direct object, the content of citation.

⁵ πᾶσα δὲ γυνὴ προσευχομένη ἢ προφητεύουσα ἀκατακαλύπτῳ τῇ κεφαλῇ καταισχύνει τὴν κεφαλὴν αὐτῆς· ἓν γάρ ἐστιν καὶ τὸ αὐτὸ τῇ ἐξυρημένῃ.

Substantive, unmodified, stative

¹⁵ γυνὴ δὲ ἐὰν κομᾷ δόξα αὐτῇ ἐστιν; ὅτι ἡ κόμη <u>ἀντὶ περιβολαίου</u> δέδοται [αὐτῇ].

Passive, modified by preposition of opposition.

1 Corinthians 12

² Οἴδατε <u>ὅτι ὅτε ἔθνη ἦτε πρὸς τὰ εἴδωλα τὰ ἄφωνα ὡς ἂν ἤγεσθε ἀπαγόμενοι</u>.

Citational, active, unmodified, has a direct object, the content of citation.

1 Corinthians 13

¹ Ἐὰν ταῖς γλώσσαις τῶν ἀνθρώπων λαλῶ καὶ τῶν ἀγγέλων, ἀγάπην δὲ μὴ ἔχω, γέγονα <u>χαλκὸς</u> ἠχῶν <u>ἢ κύμβαλον</u> ἀλαλάζον.

Active, unmodified, has PN, copula-like.

² καὶ ἐὰν ἔχω προφητείαν καὶ εἰδῶ <u>τὰ μυστήρια πάντα</u> καὶ <u>πᾶσαν τὴν γνῶσιν</u> καὶ ἐὰν ἔχω πᾶσαν τὴν πίστιν ὥστε ὄρη μεθιστάναι, ἀγάπην δὲ μὴ ἔχω, οὐθέν εἰμι.

Citational, active, unmodified, has a direct object, the content of citation.

¹¹ ὅτε ἤμην νήπιος, ἐλάλουν ὡς νήπιος, ἐφρόνουν ὡς νήπιος, ἐλογιζόμην ὡς νήπιος· ὅτε γέγονα <u>ἀνήρ</u>, κατήργηκα τὰ τοῦ νηπίου.

Active, unmodified, has PN, copula-like.

1 Corinthians 14

[11] ἐὰν οὖν μὴ εἰδῶ <u>τὴν δύναμιν τῆς φωνῆς</u>, ἔσομαι τῷ λαλοῦντι βάρβαρος καὶ ὁ λαλῶν ἐν ἐμοὶ βάρβαρος.

Citational, active, unmodified, has a direct object, the content of citation.

[16] ἐπεὶ ἐὰν εὐλογῇς [ἐν] πνεύματι, ὁ ἀναπληρῶν τὸν τόπον τοῦ ἰδιώτου πῶς ἐρεῖ τὸ ἀμὴν ἐπὶ τῇ σῇ εὐχαριστίᾳ; ἐπειδὴ <u>τί λέγεις</u> οὐκ οἶδεν·

Citational, active, unmodified, has a direct object, the content of citation.

[21] <u>ἐν τῷ νόμῳ</u> γέγραπται <u>ὅτι ἐν ἑτερογλώσσοις καὶ ἐν χείλεσιν ἑτέρων λαλήσω τῷ λαῷ τούτῳ καὶ οὐδ᾽ οὕτως εἰσακούσονταί μου, λέγει κύριος.</u>

Citational, passive, modified by dative PP containing the location of the source, has a direct object, the content of citation.

1 Corinthians 15

[1] Γνωρίζω δὲ ὑμῖν, ἀδελφοί, τὸ εὐαγγέλιον ὃ εὐηγγελισάμην ὑμῖν, ὃ καὶ παρελάβετε, <u>ἐν ᾧ</u> καὶ ἑστήκατε, [2] δι᾽ οὗ καὶ σῴζεσθε, τίνι λόγῳ εὐηγγελισάμην ὑμῖν εἰ κατέχετε, ἐκτὸς εἰ μὴ εἰκῇ ἐπιστεύσατε.

Active, actional, location of realm of standing.

[4] καὶ ὅτι ἐτάφη καὶ ὅτι ἐγήγερται <u>τῇ ἡμέρᾳ τῇ τρίτῃ κατὰ τὰς γραφὰς</u>

Passive, modified by dative location of time for the action, modified by accusative PP of standard. Actional.

[12] Εἰ δὲ Χριστὸς κηρύσσεται ὅτι <u>ἐκ νεκρῶν</u> ἐγήγερται, πῶς λέγουσιν ἐν ὑμῖν τινες ὅτι ἀνάστασις νεκρῶν οὐκ ἔστιν;

Passive, modified by item separated from, actional

[13] εἰ δὲ ἀνάστασις νεκρῶν οὐκ ἔστιν, οὐδὲ Χριστὸς ἐγήγερται·

Passive, unmodified, stative.

[14] εἰ δὲ Χριστὸς οὐκ ἐγήγερται, κενὸν ἄρα [καὶ] τὸ κήρυγμα ἡμῶν, κενὴ καὶ ἡ πίστις ὑμῶν·

Passive, unmodified, stative.

[16] εἰ γὰρ νεκροὶ οὐκ ἐγείρονται, οὐδὲ Χριστὸς ἐγήγερται·

Passive, unmodified, stative.

[17] εἰ δὲ Χριστὸς οὐκ ἐγήγερται, ματαία ἡ πίστις ὑμῶν, ἔτι ἐστὲ ἐν ταῖς ἁμαρτίαις ὑμῶν,

Passive, unmodified, stative.

[19] εἰ <u>ἐν τῇ ζωῇ ταύτῃ ἐν Χριστῷ</u> ἠλπικότες ἐσμὲν μόνον, ἐλεεινότεροι πάντων ἀνθρώπων ἐσμέν.

Periphrastic, substantive, modified by object of placing our hope, and location of time in this life.

²⁰ <u>Νυνὶ</u> δὲ Χριστὸς ἐγήγερται <u>ἐκ νεκρῶν</u> ἀπαρχὴ τῶν κεκοιμημένων.

First, Passive, modified by item separated from, actional. temporally modified by "by now" referring to a state.

Second, substantival, stative, unmodified

²⁷ πάντα γὰρ ὑπέταξεν <u>ὑπὸ τοὺς πόδας αὐτοῦ</u>. ὅταν δὲ εἴπῃ ὅτι <u>πάντα ὑποτέτακται</u>, δῆλον ὅτι ἐκτὸς τοῦ ὑποτάξαντος αὐτῷ τὰ πάντα.

Middle, actional, modified by attached preposition of subordination, which links back to the elided "his feet," also has direct object "all things."

⁴⁵ οὕτως καὶ γέγραπται· <u>ἐγένετο ὁ πρῶτος ἄνθρωπος Ἀδὰμ εἰς ψυχὴν ζῶσαν, ὁ ἔσχατος Ἀδὰμ εἰς πνεῦμα ζῳοποιοῦν.</u>

Citational, passive, unmodified, has a direct object, the content of citation.

⁵⁴ ὅταν δὲ τὸ φθαρτὸν τοῦτο ἐνδύσηται ἀφθαρσίαν καὶ τὸ θνητὸν τοῦτο ἐνδύσηται ἀθανασίαν, τότε γενήσεται ὁ λόγος ὁ γεγραμμένος· κατεπόθη ὁ θάνατος εἰς νῖκος.

Citational, passive, unmodified, substantival.

⁵⁸ Ὥστε, ἀδελφοί μου ἀγαπητοί, ἑδραῖοι γίνεσθε, ἀμετακίνητοι, περισσεύοντες ἐν τῷ ἔργῳ τοῦ κυρίου πάντοτε, εἰδότες <u>ὅτι ὁ κόπος ὑμῶν οὐκ ἔστιν κενὸς ἐν κυρίῳ</u>.

Citational, active, unmodified, has a direct object, the content of citation.

1 Corinthians 16

⁹ θύρα γάρ <u>μοι</u> ἀνέῳγεν μεγάλη καὶ ἐνεργής, καὶ ἀντικείμενοι πολλοί.

Active, actional, modified by dative of interest.

¹⁵ Παρακαλῶ δὲ ὑμᾶς, ἀδελφοί· οἴδατε <u>τὴν οἰκίαν Στεφανᾶ, ὅτι ἐστὶν ἀπαρχὴ τῆς Ἀχαΐας καὶ εἰς διακονίαν τοῖς ἁγίοις ἔταξαν ἑαυτούς·</u>

Citational, active, has a direct object, unmodified, the content of citation.

2 Corinthians 1

⁷ καὶ ἡ ἐλπὶς ἡμῶν βεβαία ὑπὲρ ὑμῶν εἰδότες <u>ὅτι ὡς κοινωνοί ἐστε τῶν παθημάτων, οὕτως καὶ τῆς παρακλήσεως.</u>

Citational, active, has a direct object, unmodified, the content of citation.

⁹ ἀλλὰ αὐτοὶ <u>ἐν ἑαυτοῖς τὸ ἀπόκριμα</u> τοῦ θανάτου ἐσχήκαμεν, ἵνα μὴ πεποιθότες ὦμεν <u>ἐφ᾽ ἑαυτοῖς</u> ἀλλ᾽ <u>ἐπὶ τῷ θεῷ</u> τῷ ἐγείροντι τοὺς νεκρούς·

First, active, actional, modified by locus for item possessed, has direct object.

Second, periphrastic, substantival, modified by negative basis, followed by positive basis.

¹⁰ ὃς ἐκ τηλικούτου θανάτου ἐρρύσατο ἡμᾶς καὶ ῥύσεται, <u>εἰς ὃν</u> ἠλπίκαμεν [<u>ὅτι</u>] <u>καὶ ἔτι ῥύσεται,</u>

Active, actional coginitive, modified by direction PP indicating basis, and has a DO.

¹⁹ ὁ τοῦ θεοῦ γὰρ υἱὸς Ἰησοῦς Χριστὸς ὁ ἐν ὑμῖν δι' ἡμῶν κηρυχθείς, δι' ἐμοῦ καὶ Σιλουανοῦ καὶ Τιμοθέου, οὐκ ἐγένετο ναὶ καὶ οὒ ἀλλὰ <u>ναὶ ἐν αὐτῷ</u> γέγονεν.

Active, has direct object, modified by dative PP indicating realm or locus.

²⁴ οὐχ ὅτι κυριεύομεν ὑμῶν τῆς πίστεως ἀλλὰ συνεργοί ἐσμεν τῆς χαρᾶς ὑμῶν· <u>τῇ</u> γὰρ <u>πίστει</u> ἑστήκατε.

Active, intransitive, modified by dative of locative realm or instrumental dative.

2 Corinthians 2

³ καὶ ἔγραψα τοῦτο αὐτό, ἵνα μὴ ἐλθὼν λύπην σχῶ ἀφ' ὧν ἔδει με χαίρειν, πεποιθὼς <u>ἐπὶ πάντας ὑμᾶς ὅτι ἡ ἐμὴ χαρὰ πάντων ὑμῶν ἐστιν.</u>

Citational, active, modified by accusative PP of focus of trust, has a direct object, the content of citation.

⁵ Εἰ δέ τις λελύπηκεν, οὐκ <u>ἐμὲ</u> λελύπηκεν, ἀλλὰ <u>ἀπὸ μέρους</u>, ἵνα μὴ ἐπιβαρῶ, <u>πάντας ὑμᾶς.</u>

First, active, actional, unmodified, no DO.

Second, active, actional, has a DO pronoun, and a following collective pronoun, modified by genitive PP of manner.

¹⁰ ᾧ δέ τι χαρίζεσθε, κἀγώ· καὶ γὰρ ἐγὼ <u>ὃ</u> κεχάρισμαι, εἴ <u>τι</u> κεχάρισμαι, <u>δι' ὑμᾶς ἐν προσώπῳ Χριστοῦ,</u>

First, Middle, mental activity, has DO, unmodified.

Second, middle, mental activity, has DO, modified by person of focus, and witness.

¹² Ἐλθὼν δὲ εἰς τὴν Τρῳάδα εἰς τὸ εὐαγγέλιον τοῦ Χριστοῦ καὶ θύρας <u>μοι</u> ἀνεῳγμένης <u>ἐν κυρίῳ,</u>

Adjectival, middle, has a dative of interest, modified by dative PP of locus.

¹³ οὐκ ἔσχηκα <u>ἄνεσιν τῷ πνεύματί</u> μου τῷ μὴ εὑρεῖν με Τίτον τὸν ἀδελφόν μου, ἀλλὰ ἀποταξάμενος αὐτοῖς ἐξῆλθον εἰς Μακεδονίαν.

Active, has DO, modified by Dative of locus.

2 Corinthians 3

² ἡ ἐπιστολὴ ἡμῶν ὑμεῖς ἐστε, ἐγγεγραμμένη <u>ἐν ταῖς καρδίαις</u> ἡμῶν, γινωσκομένη καὶ ἀναγινωσκομένη ὑπὸ πάντων ἀνθρώπων,
adjectival, middle, modified by dative of locus.

³ φανερούμενοι ὅτι ἐστὲ ἐπιστολὴ Χριστοῦ διακονηθεῖσα ὑφ' ἡμῶν, ἐγγεγραμμένη οὐ <u>μέλανι</u> ἀλλὰ <u>πνεύματι</u> θεοῦ ζῶντος, οὐκ ἐν <u>πλαξὶν λιθίναις</u> ἀλλ' ἐν <u>πλαξὶν καρδίαις σαρκίναις.</u>
adjectival, middle, modified negatively by dative of instrument followed by positive dative of instrument, and both for dative of substance.

⁷ Εἰ δὲ ἡ διακονία τοῦ θανάτου <u>ἐν γράμμασιν</u> ἐντετυπωμένη <u>λίθοις</u> ἐγενήθη ἐν δόξῃ, ὥστε μὴ δύνασθαι ἀτενίσαι τοὺς υἱοὺς Ἰσραὴλ εἰς τὸ πρόσωπον Μωϋσέως διὰ τὴν δόξαν τοῦ προσώπου αὐτοῦ τὴν καταργουμένην,
Middle, actional, modified by dative of substance, and dative PP of manner.

¹⁰ καὶ γὰρ οὐ δεδόξασται τὸ δεδοξασμένον <u>ἐν τούτῳ τῷ μέρει εἵνεκεν τῆς ὑπερβαλλούσης δόξης.</u>
First, Middle, modified by dative PP of manner, and modified by genitive PP of reason.
Second, Middle, adjectival, unmodified.

¹⁸ ἡμεῖς δὲ πάντες ἀνακεκαλυμμένῳ προσώπῳ τὴν δόξαν κυρίου κατοπτριζόμενοι τὴν αὐτὴν εἰκόνα μεταμορφούμεθα ἀπὸ δόξης εἰς δόξαν καθάπερ ἀπὸ κυρίου πνεύματος.
Adjectival, unmodified, stative.

2 Corinthians 4

³ εἰ δὲ καὶ ἔστιν κεκαλυμμένον τὸ εὐαγγέλιον ἡμῶν, <u>ἐν τοῖς ἀπολλυμένοις</u> ἐστὶν κεκαλυμμένον,
First, substantival, periphrastic, unmodified
Second, Substantival, periphrastic, modified by dative PP indicative locus

¹³ Ἔχοντες δὲ τὸ αὐτὸ πνεῦμα τῆς πίστεως κατὰ τὸ γεγραμμένον· ἐπίστευσα, διὸ ἐλάλησα, καὶ ἡμεῖς πιστεύομεν, διὸ καὶ λαλοῦμεν,
Middle, substantival, unmodified, stative.

¹⁴ εἰδότες <u>ὅτι ὁ ἐγείρας τὸν κύριον Ἰησοῦν καὶ ἡμᾶς σὺν Ἰησοῦ ἐγερεῖ καὶ παραστήσει σὺν ὑμῖν.</u>
Citational, active, has a direct object, unmodified, the content of citation.

2 Corinthians 5

[1] Οἴδαμεν γὰρ <u>ὅτι ἐὰν ἡ ἐπίγειος ἡμῶν οἰκία τοῦ σκήνους καταλυθῇ, οἰκοδομὴν ἐκ θεοῦ ἔχομεν, οἰκίαν ἀχειροποίητον αἰώνιον ἐν τοῖς οὐρανοῖς.</u>
Citational, active, unmodified, has a direct object, the content of citation.

[6] Θαρροῦντες οὖν πάντοτε καὶ εἰδότες <u>ὅτι ἐνδημοῦντες ἐν τῷ σώματι ἐκδημοῦμεν ἀπὸ τοῦ κυρίου·</u>
Citational, active, unmodified, has a direct object, the content of citation.

[11] Εἰδότες οὖν <u>τὸν φόβον τοῦ κυρίου ἀνθρώπους πείθομεν</u>, <u>θεῷ</u> δὲ πεφανερώμεθα· ἐλπίζω δὲ καὶ <u>ἐν ταῖς συνειδήσεσιν ὑμῶν</u> πεφανερῶσθαι.
First, Citational, active, unmodified, has a direct object, the content of citation.
Second, causative-passive, modified by dative IO, agent missing.
Third, Causative-passive, modified by dative PP of locus or realm.

[16] Ὥστε ἡμεῖς ἀπὸ τοῦ νῦν <u>οὐδένα</u> οἴδαμεν <u>κατὰ σάρκα</u>· εἰ καὶ ἐγνώκαμεν <u>κατὰ σάρκα Χριστόν</u>, ἀλλὰ νῦν οὐκέτι γινώσκομεν.
First, Active, mental action, has direct object, modified by PP of manner.
Second, active mental action, has direct object, modified by PP of manner.

[17] ὥστε εἴ τις ἐν Χριστῷ, καινὴ κτίσις· τὰ ἀρχαῖα παρῆλθεν, ἰδοὺ γέγονεν καινά·
Active, intransitive, unmodified, stative.

2 Corinthians 6

[11] Τὸ στόμα ἡμῶν ἀνέῳγεν <u>πρὸς ὑμᾶς</u>, Κορίνθιοι, ἡ καρδία ἡμῶν πεπλάτυνται·
First, active, modified by accusative PP of interest
Second, middle, unmodified, stative.

2 Corinthians 7

[3] πρὸς κατάκρισιν οὐ λέγω· <u>προείρηκα</u> γὰρ <u>ὅτι ἐν ταῖς καρδίαις ἡμῶν ἐστε εἰς τὸ συναποθανεῖν καὶ συζῆν.</u>
Citational, active, has a direct object, the content of citation, modified by internal temporal preposition

[4] πολλή μοι παρρησία πρὸς ὑμᾶς, πολλή μοι καύχησις ὑπὲρ ὑμῶν· πεπλήρωμαι <u>τῇ παρακλήσει</u>, ὑπερπερισσεύομαι τῇ χαρᾷ ἐπὶ πάσῃ τῇ θλίψει ἡμῶν.
Middle, stative, modified by dative content.

⁵ Καὶ γὰρ ἐλθόντων ἡμῶν εἰς Μακεδονίαν οὐδεμίαν ἔσχηκεν <u>ἄνεσιν</u> ἡ σὰρξ ἡμῶν ἀλλ᾽ ἐν παντὶ θλιβόμενοι· ἔξωθεν μάχαι, ἔσωθεν φόβοι.

Active, unmodified, has DO,

¹³ διὰ τοῦτο παρακεκλήμεθα. Ἐπὶ δὲ τῇ παρακλήσει ἡμῶν περισσοτέρως μᾶλλον ἐχάρημεν ἐπὶ τῇ χαρᾷ Τίτου, ὅτι ἀναπέπαυται τὸ πνεῦμα αὐτοῦ <u>ἀπὸ πάντων ὑμῶν</u>·

First, middle, unmodified, stative.

Second, middle, modified by agent, actional.

¹⁴ ὅτι εἴ τι <u>αὐτῷ ὑπὲρ ὑμῶν</u> κεκαύχημαι, οὐ κατησχύνθην, ἀλλ᾽ ὡς πάντα ἐν ἀληθείᾳ ἐλαλήσαμεν ὑμῖν, οὕτως καὶ ἡ καύχησις ἡμῶν ἡ ἐπὶ Τίτου ἀλήθεια ἐγενήθη.

Middle, actional, modified by person spoken to, and PP of person spoken about.

2 Corinthians 8

¹ Γνωρίζομεν δὲ ὑμῖν, ἀδελφοί, τὴν χάριν τοῦ θεοῦ τὴν δεδομένην <u>ἐν ταῖς ἐκκλησίαις</u> τῆς Μακεδονίας,

Middle, Adjectival, modified by dative PP of locus

¹⁵ καθὼς γέγραπται· <u>ὁ τὸ πολὺ οὐκ ἐπλεόνασεν, καὶ ὁ τὸ ὀλίγον οὐκ ἠλαττόνησεν.</u>

Citational, middle, unmodified, has a direct object, the content of citation,

2 Corinthians 9

² οἶδα γὰρ τὴν <u>προθυμίαν</u> ὑμῶν ἣν ὑπὲρ ὑμῶν καυχῶμαι Μακεδόσιν, ὅτι Ἀχαΐα <u>παρεσκεύασται ἀπὸ πέρυσι</u>, καὶ τὸ ὑμῶν ζῆλος ἠρέθισεν τοὺς πλείονας.

First, citational, active, unmodified, has DO content of citation.

Second, middle, modified by PP of deictic time.

³ ἔπεμψα δὲ τοὺς ἀδελφούς, ἵνα μὴ τὸ καύχημα ἡμῶν τὸ ὑπὲρ ὑμῶν κενωθῇ ἐν τῷ μέρει τούτῳ, ἵνα καθὼς ἔλεγον παρεσκευασμένοι ἦτε,

Predicate nominative, substantive, periphrastic, middle, unmodified, stative

⁵ ἀναγκαῖον οὖν ἡγησάμην παρακαλέσαι τοὺς ἀδελφούς, ἵνα προέλθωσιν εἰς ὑμᾶς καὶ προκαταρτίσωσιν τὴν <u>προ</u>επηγγελμένην εὐλογίαν ὑμῶν, ταύτην ἑτοίμην εἶναι οὕτως ὡς εὐλογίαν καὶ μὴ ὡς πλεονεξίαν.

Adjectival, middle, modified only by the temporal attached preposition, stative in relation to the gift, actional in relation to the temporal preposition.

⁷ ἕκαστος καθὼς <u>προῄρηται τῇ καρδίᾳ</u>, μὴ ἐκ λύπης ἢ ἐξ ἀνάγκης· ἱλαρὸν γὰρ δότην ἀγαπᾷ ὁ θεός.

Middle, modified by dative of locus or realm, modified by past time preposition.

⁹ καθὼς γέγραπται· <u>ἐσκόρπισεν, ἔδωκεν τοῖς πένησιν, ἡ δικαιοσύνη αὐτοῦ μένει εἰς</u> <u>τὸν αἰῶνα</u>.

Citational, middle, unmodified, has DO of content.

2 Corinthians 10

⁷ Τὰ κατὰ πρόσωπον βλέπετε. εἴ τις πέποιθεν <u>ἑαυτῷ Χριστοῦ</u> εἶναι, τοῦτο λογιζέσθω πάλιν ἐφ᾽ ἑαυτοῦ, ὅτι καθὼς αὐτὸς Χριστοῦ, οὕτως καὶ ἡμεῖς.

In a protasis clause, active, modified by dative locus, followed by DO of content.

¹⁰ ὅτι αἱ ἐπιστολαὶ μέν, φησίν, βαρεῖαι καὶ ἰσχυραί, ἡ δὲ παρουσία τοῦ σώματος ἀσθενὴς καὶ ὁ λόγος ἐξουθενημένος.

Adjectival, unmodified, passive, stative.

2 Corinthians 11

⁵ Λογίζομαι γὰρ μηδὲν ὑστερηκέναι <u>τῶν ὑπερλίαν ἀποστόλων</u>.

Infinitive, "has been lacking", modified by genitive of comparison.

¹¹ διὰ τί; ὅτι οὐκ ἀγαπῶ ὑμᾶς; ὁ θεὸς οἶδεν.

Active, unmodified, mental action.

²¹ κατὰ ἀτιμίαν λέγω, ὡς ὅτι ἡμεῖς ἠσθενήκαμεν. Ἐν ᾧ δ᾽ ἄν τις τολμᾷ, ἐν ἀφροσύνῃ λέγω, τολμῶ κἀγώ.

In a subordinate clause, active, unmodified, stative.

²⁴ Ὑπὸ Ἰουδαίων πεντάκις τεσσεράκοντα παρὰ μίαν ἔλαβον, ²⁵ τρὶς ἐρραβδίσθην, ἅπαξ ἐλιθάσθην, τρὶς ἐναυάγησα, <u>νυχθήμερον ἐν τῷ βυθῷ</u> πεποίηκα·

Generic verb, has DO, modified by locative PP.

³¹ ὁ θεὸς καὶ πατὴρ τοῦ κυρίου Ἰησοῦ οἶδεν, ὁ ὢν εὐλογητὸς εἰς τοὺς αἰῶνας, <u>ὅτι οὐ</u> <u>ψεύδομαι</u>.

Citational, active, unmodified, has DO of content.

2 Corinthians 12

² οἶδα <u>ἄνθρωπον ἐν Χριστῷ</u> πρὸ ἐτῶν δεκατεσσάρων, <u>εἴτε ἐν σώματι</u> οὐκ οἶδα, <u>εἴτε</u> <u>ἐκτὸς τοῦ σώματος</u> οὐκ οἶδα, ὁ θεὸς οἶδεν, ἁρπαγέντα τὸν τοιοῦτον ἕως τρίτου οὐρανοῦ.

First, has DO of content, modified by locative realm

Second, has DO of content, unmodified

Third, has DO of content, unmodified

Fourth, unmodified.

³ καὶ οἶδα <u>τὸν τοιοῦτον ἄνθρωπον</u>, <u>εἴτε ἐν σώματι εἴτε χωρὶς τοῦ σώματος</u> οὐκ οἶδα, ὁ θεὸς οἶδεν,

First, has DO of content,

Second, has DO of content,

Third, unmodified.

⁹ καὶ εἴρηκέν <u>μοι</u>· <u>ἀρκεῖ σοι ἡ χάρις μου, ἡ γὰρ δύναμις ἐν ἀσθενείᾳ τελεῖται</u>. ἥδιστα οὖν μᾶλλον καυχήσομαι ἐν ταῖς ἀσθενείαις μου, ἵνα ἐπισκηνώσῃ ἐπ᾽ ἐμὲ ἡ δύναμις τοῦ Χριστοῦ.

Active, modified by dative of interest, has DO of content.

¹¹ Γέγονα <u>ἄφρων</u>, ὑμεῖς με ἠναγκάσατε. ἐγὼ γὰρ ὤφειλον ὑφ᾽ ὑμῶν συνίστασθαι· οὐδὲν γὰρ ὑστέρησα τῶν ὑπερλίαν ἀποστόλων εἰ καὶ οὐδέν εἰμι.

Stative, has a PN, unmodified, copula-like.

¹⁷ μή τινα <u>ὧν</u> ἀπέσταλκα <u>πρὸς ὑμᾶς</u>, δι᾽ αὐτοῦ ἐπλεονέκτησα ὑμᾶς;

Active, has DO of relative pronoun, modified by direction PP.

²¹ μὴ πάλιν ἐλθόντος μου ταπεινώσῃ με ὁ θεός μου πρὸς ὑμᾶς καὶ πενθήσω πολλοὺς τῶν <u>προημαρτηκότων</u> καὶ μὴ μετανοησάντων ἐπὶ τῇ ἀκαθαρσίᾳ καὶ πορνείᾳ καὶ ἀσελγείᾳ ᾗ ἔπραξαν.

Substantival, modified only by its internal preposition of time.

2 Corinthians 13

² προείρηκα καὶ προλέγω, ὡς παρὼν τὸ δεύτερον καὶ ἀπὼν νῦν, τοῖς <u>προημαρτηκόσιν</u> καὶ τοῖς λοιποῖς πᾶσιν, <u>ὅτι ἐὰν ἔλθω εἰς τὸ πάλιν οὐ φείσομαι</u>,

First, Active, has DO of content, unmodified.

Second, substantival, modified by internal preposition.

Galatians 1

⁴ τοῦ δόντος ἑαυτὸν ὑπὲρ τῶν ἁμαρτιῶν ἡμῶν, ὅπως ἐξέληται ἡμᾶς ἐκ τοῦ αἰῶνος τοῦ ἐνεστῶτος πονηροῦ κατὰ τὸ θέλημα τοῦ θεοῦ καὶ πατρὸς ἡμῶν, ⁵ ᾧ ἡ δόξα εἰς τοὺς αἰῶνας τῶν αἰώνων, ἀμήν.

Adjectival, unmodified, stative.

⁹ ὡς <u>προειρήκαμεν</u> καὶ ἄρτι πάλιν λέγω· <u>εἴ τις ὑμᾶς εὐαγγελίζεται παρ᾽ ὃ παρελάβετε, ἀνάθεμα ἔστω</u>.

Active, modified by only the internal preposition, has DO of content.

Galatians 2

⁷ ἀλλὰ τοὐναντίον ἰδόντες ὅτι πεπίστευμαι <u>τὸ εὐαγγέλιον</u> τῆς ἀκροβυστίας καθὼς Πέτρος τῆς περιτομῆς,
Part of a subordinate clause, has DO of content, unmodified.

¹¹ Ὅτε δὲ ἦλθεν Κηφᾶς εἰς Ἀντιόχειαν, κατὰ πρόσωπον αὐτῷ ἀντέστην, ὅτι κατεγνωσμένος ἦν.
Periphrastic, substantival, passive, unmodified.

¹⁶ εἰδότες [δὲ] <u>ὅτι οὐ δικαιοῦται ἄνθρωπος ἐξ ἔργων νόμου ἐὰν μὴ διὰ πίστεως Ἰησοῦ Χριστοῦ</u>, καὶ ἡμεῖς εἰς Χριστὸν Ἰησοῦν ἐπιστεύσαμεν, ἵνα δικαιωθῶμεν ἐκ πίστεως Χριστοῦ καὶ οὐκ ἐξ ἔργων νόμου, ὅτι ἐξ ἔργων νόμου οὐ δικαιωθήσεται πᾶσα σάρξ.
Active, citational, unmodified, has DO of content.

¹⁹ ἐγὼ γὰρ διὰ νόμου νόμῳ ἀπέθανον, ἵνα θεῷ ζήσω. <u>Χριστῷ</u> συνεσταύρωμαι·
Middle, modified by dative of association.

Galatians 3

¹ Ὦ ἀνόητοι Γαλάται, τίς ὑμᾶς ἐβάσκανεν, οἷς κατ' ὀφθαλμοὺς Ἰησοῦς Χριστὸς προεγράφη ἐσταυρωμένος;
Substantive, unmodified.

¹⁰ Ὅσοι γὰρ ἐξ ἔργων νόμου εἰσίν, ὑπὸ κατάραν εἰσίν· γέγραπται γὰρ <u>ὅτι ἐπικατάρατος</u> <u>πᾶς ὃς οὐκ ἐμμένει πᾶσιν τοῖς γεγραμμένοις ἐν</u> <u>τῷ βιβλίῳ</u> <u>τοῦ νόμου τοῦ ποιῆσαι αὐτά</u>.
First, citational, has DO of content, unmodified.
Second, substantival, middle, modified by location PP.

¹³ Χριστὸς ἡμᾶς ἐξηγόρασεν ἐκ τῆς κατάρας τοῦ νόμου γενόμενος <u>ὑπὲρ ἡμῶν κατάρα</u>, ὅτι γέγραπται· <u>ἐπικατάρατος πᾶς ὁ κρεμάμενος ἐπὶ ξύλου</u>,
First, middle, has PN, copula-like, modified by genitive PP of representation.
Second, citational, unmodified, has DO of content.

¹⁵ Ἀδελφοί, κατὰ ἄνθρωπον λέγω· ὅμως ἀνθρώπου κεκυρωμένην <u>διαθήκην</u> οὐδεὶς ἀθετεῖ ἢ ἐπιδιατάσσεται.
Middle, has DO, unmodified.

¹⁷ τοῦτο δὲ λέγω· <u>διαθήκην προκεκυρωμένην</u> <u>ὑπὸ τοῦ θεοῦ</u> ὁ <u>μετὰ τετρακόσια καὶ</u> <u>τριάκοντα ἔτη</u> γεγονὼς νόμος οὐκ ἀκυροῖ εἰς τὸ καταργῆσαι τὴν ἐπαγγελίαν.
First, Middle, has DO, modified by preposition of prior time, and by genitive agent PP.
Second, active, modified by temporal phrase "after 400 years."

[18] εἰ γὰρ ἐκ νόμου ἡ κληρονομία, οὐκέτι ἐξ ἐπαγγελίας· <u>τῷ</u> δὲ <u>Ἀβραὰμ δι᾽ ἐπαγγελίας</u> κεχάρισται ὁ θεός.
Middle, has IO, modified by instrumental PP.

[19] Τί οὖν ὁ νόμος; τῶν παραβάσεων χάριν προσετέθη, ἄχρις οὗ ἔλθῃ τὸ σπέρμα ᾧ ἐπήγγελται, διαταγεὶς δι᾽ ἀγγέλων ἐν χειρὶ μεσίτου.
Adjectival, unmodified,

[24] ὥστε ὁ νόμος <u>παιδαγωγὸς</u> ἡμῶν γέγονεν <u>εἰς Χριστόν</u>, ἵνα ἐκ πίστεως δικαιωθῶμεν·
Stative, has PN, modified by direction PP.

Galatians 4

[3] οὕτως καὶ ἡμεῖς, ὅτε ἦμεν νήπιοι, <u>ὑπὸ τὰ στοιχεῖα</u> τοῦ κόσμου ἤμεθα δεδουλωμένοι·
Periphrastic, substantive, modified by subordinating accusative PP.

[8] Ἀλλὰ τότε μὲν οὐκ εἰδότες <u>θεὸν ἐδουλεύσατε τοῖς φύσει μὴ οὖσιν θεοῖς·</u>
Citational, active, has DO of content, unmodified.

[11] φοβοῦμαι ὑμᾶς μή πως <u>εἰκῇ</u> κεκοπίακα <u>εἰς ὑμᾶς</u>.
Active, modified by accusative directional PP, modified by adverb of manner.

[13] οἴδατε δὲ <u>ὅτι δι᾽ ἀσθένειαν τῆς σαρκὸς εὐηγγελισάμην ὑμῖν τὸ πρότερον,</u>
Citational, active, has DO of content, unmodified.

[16] ὥστε <u>ἐχθρὸς</u> ὑμῶν γέγονα ἀληθεύων ὑμῖν;
Stative, active, unmodified, has PN, copula-like.

[22] γέγραπται γὰρ ὅτι <u>Ἀβραὰμ δύο υἱοὺς ἔσχεν, ἕνα ἐκ τῆς παιδίσκης καὶ ἕνα ἐκ τῆς ἐλευθέρας.</u>
Citational, middle, has DO of content, unmodified.

[23] ἀλλ᾽ ὁ μὲν ἐκ τῆς παιδίσκης <u>κατὰ σάρκα</u> γεγέννηται, ὁ δὲ ἐκ τῆς ἐλευθέρας δι᾽ ἐπαγγελίας.
Middle, actional, modified by accusative PP of manner.

[27] γέγραπται γάρ· <u>εὐφράνθητι, στεῖρα ἡ οὐ τίκτουσα, ῥῆξον καὶ βόησον, ἡ οὐκ ὠδίνουσα· ὅτι πολλὰ τὰ τέκνα τῆς ἐρήμου μᾶλλον ἢ τῆς ἐχούσης τὸν ἄνδρα.</u>
Citational, middle, unmodified, has DO of content.

Galatians 5

[10] ἐγὼ πέποιθα <u>εἰς ὑμᾶς ἐν κυρίῳ ὅτι οὐδὲν ἄλλο φρονήσετε</u>· ὁ δὲ ταράσσων ὑμᾶς βαστάσει τὸ κρίμα, ὅστις ἐὰν ᾖ.

Active, has DO of content, modified by accusative PP of reference, and dative PP of realm.

¹¹ Ἐγὼ δέ, ἀδελφοί, εἰ περιτομὴν ἔτι κηρύσσω, τί ἔτι διώκομαι; ἄρα κατήργηται τὸ σκάνδαλον τοῦ σταυροῦ.

Middle, stative, unmodified.

¹⁴ ὁ γὰρ πᾶς νόμος <u>ἐν ἑνὶ λόγῳ</u> πεπλήρωται, ἐν τῷ· ἀγαπήσεις τὸν πλησίον σου ὡς σεαυτόν.

Middle, modified by Dative PP of specification (locus)

Galatians 6

¹⁴ Ἐμοὶ δὲ μὴ γένοιτο καυχᾶσθαι εἰ μὴ ἐν τῷ σταυρῷ τοῦ κυρίου ἡμῶν Ἰησοῦ Χριστοῦ, <u>δι' οὗ ἐμοὶ</u> κόσμος ἐσταύρωται κἀγὼ <u>κόσμῳ</u>.

Middle, actional, modified by two datives of reference, modified by genitive of means.

Ephesians 1

⁶ εἰς ἔπαινον δόξης τῆς χάριτος αὐτοῦ ἧς ἐχαρίτωσεν ἡμᾶς ἐν τῷ ἠγαπημένῳ.

Adjectival, stative, unmodified.

¹¹ Ἐν ᾧ καὶ ἐκληρώθημεν <u>προορισθέντες</u> <u>κατὰ πρόθεσιν</u> τοῦ τὰ πάντα ἐνεργοῦντος κατὰ τὴν βουλὴν τοῦ θελήματος αὐτοῦ ¹² εἰς τὸ εἶναι ἡμᾶς εἰς ἔπαινον δόξης αὐτοῦ τοὺς προηλπικότας ἐν τῷ Χριστῷ.

Adjectival, modified by accusative PP of standard, and by internal temporal preposition.

¹⁷ ἵνα ὁ θεὸς τοῦ κυρίου ἡμῶν Ἰησοῦ Χριστοῦ, ὁ πατὴρ τῆς δόξης, δώῃ ὑμῖν πνεῦμα σοφίας καὶ ἀποκαλύψεως ἐν ἐπιγνώσει αὐτοῦ, ¹⁸ πεφωτισμένους <u>τοὺς ὀφθαλμοὺς</u> τῆς καρδίας [ὑμῶν] εἰς τὸ εἰδέναι ὑμᾶς τίς ἐστιν ἡ ἐλπὶς τῆς κλήσεως αὐτοῦ, τίς ὁ πλοῦτος τῆς δόξης τῆς κληρονομίας αὐτοῦ ἐν τοῖς ἁγίοις,

Adjectival, has DO, unmodified, stative.

Ephesians 2

⁵ καὶ ὄντας ἡμᾶς νεκροὺς τοῖς παραπτώμασιν συνεζωοποίησεν τῷ Χριστῷ,- <u>χάριτί</u> ἐστε σεσῳσμένοι-

Substantive, periphrastic, modified by instrumental dative.

⁸ Τῇ γὰρ χάριτί ἐστε σεσῳσμένοι διὰ πίστεως· καὶ τοῦτο οὐκ ἐξ ὑμῶν, θεοῦ τὸ δῶρον·
Substantive, periphrastic, modified by instrumental dative, and genitive PP of means.

¹² ὅτι ἦτε τῷ καιρῷ ἐκείνῳ χωρὶς Χριστοῦ, ἀπηλλοτριωμένοι τῆς πολιτείας τοῦ Ἰσραὴλ καὶ ξένοι τῶν διαθηκῶν τῆς ἐπαγγελίας, ἐλπίδα μὴ ἔχοντες καὶ ἄθεοι ἐν τῷ κόσμῳ.
Substantive, modified by genitive of separation.

Ephesians 3

⁹ καὶ φωτίσαι [πάντας] τίς ἡ οἰκονομία τοῦ μυστηρίου τοῦ ἀποκεκρυμμένου ἀπὸ τῶν αἰώνων ἐν τῷ θεῷ τῷ τὰ πάντα κτίσαντι,
Adjectival, modified by temporal PP of duration, and dative PP of location.

¹⁷ κατοικῆσαι τὸν Χριστὸν διὰ τῆς πίστεως ἐν ταῖς καρδίαις ὑμῶν, ἐν ἀγάπῃ ἐρριζωμένοι καὶ τεθεμελιωμένοι,
Substantival, modified by dative PP of realm.

Ephesians 4

¹⁸ ἐσκοτωμένοι τῇ διανοίᾳ ὄντες, ἀπηλλοτριωμένοι τῆς ζωῆς τοῦ θεοῦ διὰ τὴν ἄγνοιαν τὴν οὖσαν ἐν αὐτοῖς, διὰ τὴν πώρωσιν τῆς καρδίας αὐτῶν,
First, periphrastic, modified by dative of locus,
Second, modified by genitive of separation,

¹⁹ οἵτινες ἀπηλγηκότες ἑαυτοὺς παρέδωκαν τῇ ἀσελγείᾳ εἰς ἐργασίαν ἀκαθαρσίας πάσης ἐν πλεονεξίᾳ.
Substantive, unmodified.

Ephesians 5

⁵ τοῦτο γὰρ ἴστε γινώσκοντες, ὅτι πᾶς πόρνος ἢ ἀκάθαρτος ἢ πλεονέκτης, ὅ ἐστιν εἰδωλολάτρης, οὐκ ἔχει κληρονομίαν ἐν τῇ βασιλείᾳ τοῦ Χριστοῦ καὶ θεοῦ.
Periphrastic, substantive, unmodified, has DO of content

Ephesians 6

[8] εἰδότες <u>ὅτι ἕκαστος ἐάν τι ποιήσῃ ἀγαθόν, τοῦτο κομίσεται παρὰ κυρίου εἴτε δοῦλος</u> <u>εἴτε ἐλεύθερος.</u>
Citational, active, unmodified, has DO of content,

[9] Καὶ οἱ κύριοι, τὰ αὐτὰ ποιεῖτε πρὸς αὐτούς, ἀνιέντες τὴν ἀπειλήν, εἰδότες <u>ὅτι καὶ</u> <u>αὐτῶν καὶ ὑμῶν ὁ κύριός ἐστιν ἐν οὐρανοῖς καὶ προσωπολημψία οὐκ ἔστιν παρ' αὐτῷ.</u>
Citational, active, unmodified, has DO of content,

[16] ἐν πᾶσιν ἀναλαβόντες τὸν θυρεὸν τῆς πίστεως, ἐν ᾧ δυνήσεσθε πάντα τὰ βέλη τοῦ πονηροῦ [τὰ] πεπυρωμένα σβέσαι·
Adjectival, middle, unmodified.

[21] Ἵνα δὲ εἰδῆτε καὶ ὑμεῖς <u>τὰ κατ' ἐμέ, τί πράσσω</u>, πάντα γνωρίσει ὑμῖν Τύχικος ὁ ἀγαπητὸς ἀδελφὸς καὶ πιστὸς διάκονος ἐν κυρίῳ,
Citational, active, unmodified, has DO of content,

Philippians 1

[5] ἐπὶ τῇ κοινωνίᾳ ὑμῶν εἰς τὸ εὐαγγέλιον ἀπὸ τῆς πρώτης ἡμέρας ἄχρι τοῦ νῦν, [6] πεποιθὼς αὐτὸ τοῦτο, <u>ὅτι ὁ ἐναρξάμενος ἐν ὑμῖν ἔργον ἀγαθὸν ἐπιτελέσει ἄχρι ἡμέρας</u> <u>Χριστοῦ Ἰησοῦ.</u>
Citational, active, has DO of content, unmodified.

[10] εἰς τὸ δοκιμάζειν ὑμᾶς τὰ διαφέροντα, ἵνα ἦτε εἰλικρινεῖς καὶ ἀπρόσκοποι εἰς ἡμέραν Χριστοῦ, [11] πεπληρωμένοι <u>καρπὸν</u> δικαιοσύνης τὸν <u>διὰ Ἰησοῦ Χριστοῦ εἰς δόξαν καὶ</u> <u>ἔπαινον</u> θεοῦ.
Substantive, middle, has DO of content, modified by genitive PP of source, and accusative PP of direction.

[12] Γινώσκειν δὲ ὑμᾶς βούλομαι, ἀδελφοί, ὅτι τὰ <u>κατ' ἐμὲ</u> μᾶλλον <u>εἰς προκοπὴν</u> τοῦ εὐαγγελίου ἐλήλυθεν,
Active, modified by accusative of reference, and accusative of goal.

[14] καὶ τοὺς πλείονας τῶν ἀδελφῶν <u>ἐν κυρίῳ</u> πεποιθότας <u>τοῖς δεσμοῖς</u> μου περισσοτέρως τολμᾶν ἀφόβως τὸν λόγον λαλεῖν.
Active, Adjectival, modified by dative of locus, and dative of instrument.

[16] οἱ μὲν ἐξ ἀγάπης, εἰδότες <u>ὅτι εἰς ἀπολογίαν τοῦ εὐαγγελίου κεῖμαι,</u>
Citational, active, has DO of content, unmodified.

[19] οἶδα γὰρ <u>ὅτι τοῦτό μοι ἀποβήσεται εἰς σωτηρίαν διὰ τῆς ὑμῶν δεήσεως καὶ</u> <u>ἐπιχορηγίας τοῦ πνεύματος Ἰησοῦ Χριστοῦ</u>
Citational, active, has DO of content, unmodified.

²⁵ καὶ <u>τοῦτο</u> πεποιθὼς οἶδα <u>ὅτι μενῶ καὶ παραμενῶ πᾶσιν ὑμῖν εἰς τὴν ὑμῶν προκοπὴν</u> <u>καὶ χαρὰν τῆς πίστεως,</u>

First, Citational, active, has DO of content, unmodified.

Second, Citational, active, has DO of content, unmodified.

Philippians 2

¹⁵ ἵνα γένησθε ἄμεμπτοι καὶ ἀκέραιοι, τέκνα θεοῦ ἄμωμα μέσον γενεᾶς σκολιᾶς καὶ διεστραμμένης, ἐν οἷς φαίνεσθε ὡς φωστῆρες ἐν κόσμῳ,

Adjectival, middle, unmodified.

²⁴ πέποιθα δὲ <u>ἐν κυρίῳ ὅτι καὶ αὐτὸς ταχέως ἐλεύσομαι.</u>

Active, has DO of content, modified by dative of realm.

Philippians 3

³ ἡμεῖς γάρ ἐσμεν ἡ περιτομή, οἱ πνεύματι θεοῦ λατρεύοντες καὶ καυχώμενοι ἐν Χριστῷ Ἰησοῦ καὶ οὐκ <u>ἐν σαρκὶ</u> πεποιθότες,

Active, modified by dative PP of locus.

⁴ καίπερ ἐγὼ ἔχων πεποίθησιν καὶ ἐν σαρκί. Εἴ τις δοκεῖ ἄλλος πεποιθέναι <u>ἐν σαρκί,</u> ἐγὼ μᾶλλον·

Active, modified by dative PP of locus.

⁷ [Ἀλλὰ] ἅτινα ἦν μοι κέρδη, ταῦτα ἥγημαι <u>διὰ τὸν Χριστὸν</u> ζημίαν.

Middle, has DO relative pronoun, modified by accusative PP of reference.

¹² Οὐχ ὅτι ἤδη ἔλαβον ἢ <u>ἤδη</u> τετελείωμαι, διώκω δὲ εἰ καὶ καταλάβω, ἐφ᾽ ᾧ καὶ κατελήμφθην ὑπὸ Χριστοῦ [Ἰησοῦ].

Middle, has DO in previous verse, implied here, is modified by adverb of prior time just like the Aorist before it.

¹³ ἀδελφοί, ἐγὼ ἐμαυτὸν οὐ λογίζομαι κατειληφέναι· ἓν δέ, τὰ μὲν ὀπίσω ἐπιλανθανόμενος τοῖς δὲ ἔμπροσθεν ἐπεκτεινόμενος,

Infinitive, active, unmodified.

Philippians 4

¹² οἶδα καὶ <u>ταπεινοῦσθαι</u>, οἶδα καὶ <u>περισσεύειν</u>· ἐν παντὶ καὶ <u>ἐν πᾶσιν</u> μεμύημαι, καὶ <u>χορτάζεσθαι</u> καὶ <u>πεινᾶν</u> καὶ <u>περισσεύειν</u> καὶ <u>ὑστερεῖσθαι</u>·

First, active, DO infinitive, unmodified

Second, active, DO infinitive, unmodified

Third, middle, 4 DO infinitives, modified by 2 dative PPs of reference

[15] οἴδατε δὲ καὶ ὑμεῖς, Φιλιππήσιοι, <u>ὅτι ἐν ἀρχῇ τοῦ εὐαγγελίου, ὅτε ἐξῆλθον ἀπὸ</u> <u>Μακεδονίας, οὐδεμία μοι ἐκκλησία ἐκοινώνησεν εἰς λόγον δόσεως καὶ λήμψεως εἰ μὴ</u> <u>ὑμεῖς μόνοι,</u>

Citational, active, has DO of content, unmodified.

[18] ἀπέχω δὲ πάντα καὶ περισσεύω· πεπλήρωμαι δεξάμενος παρὰ Ἐπαφροδίτου τὰ παρ' ὑμῶν, ὀσμὴν εὐωδίας, θυσίαν δεκτήν, εὐάρεστον τῷ θεῷ.

Middle, unmodified, stative.

Colossians 1

[16] ὅτι ἐν αὐτῷ ἐκτίσθη τὰ πάντα ἐν τοῖς οὐρανοῖς καὶ ἐπὶ τῆς γῆς, τὰ ὁρατὰ καὶ τὰ ἀόρατα, εἴτε θρόνοι εἴτε κυριότητες εἴτε ἀρχαὶ εἴτε ἐξουσίαι· τὰ πάντα <u>δι' αὐτοῦ</u> καὶ <u>εἰς αὐτὸν</u> ἔκτισται·

Middle, modified by genitive PP of agent, and accusative PP of purpose.

[17] καὶ αὐτός ἐστιν πρὸ πάντων καὶ τὰ πάντα <u>ἐν αὐτῷ συνέστηκεν,</u>

Active, modified by dative PP of locus, and internal preposition of association.

[21] Καὶ ὑμᾶς <u>ποτε</u> ὄντας ἀπηλλοτριωμένους καὶ ἐχθροὺς <u>τῇ διανοίᾳ ἐν τοῖς ἔργοις τοῖς</u> <u>πονηροῖς</u>, [22] νυνὶ δὲ ἀποκατήλλαξεν ἐν τῷ σώματι τῆς σαρκὸς αὐτοῦ διὰ τοῦ θανάτου παραστῆσαι ὑμᾶς ἁγίους καὶ ἀμώμους καὶ ἀνεγκλήτους κατενώπιον αὐτοῦ,

Periphrastic, middle, modified by dative of realm, and dative PP of instrument or means, modified by prior temporal adverb. A temporal shift is observed since the next phrase has a present or recentness deixis adverb contrasting with the prior nature of this one.

[23] εἴ γε ἐπιμένετε τῇ πίστει τεθεμελιωμένοι καὶ ἑδραῖοι καὶ μὴ μετακινούμενοι ἀπὸ τῆς ἐλπίδος τοῦ εὐαγγελίου οὗ ἠκούσατε, τοῦ κηρυχθέντος ἐν πάσῃ κτίσει τῇ ὑπὸ τὸν οὐρανόν, οὗ ἐγενόμην ἐγὼ Παῦλος διάκονος.

Substantival, unmodified, middle.

[26] τὸ μυστήριον τὸ ἀποκεκρυμμένον <u>ἀπὸ τῶν αἰώνων</u> καὶ <u>ἀπὸ τῶν γενεῶν</u>- νῦν δὲ ἐφανερώθη τοῖς ἁγίοις αὐτοῦ,

Adjectival, middle, modified by temporal PP of duration, and genitive PP of separation.

Colossians 2

¹ Θέλω γὰρ ὑμᾶς εἰδέναι <u>ἡλίκον ἀγῶνα</u> ἔχω ὑπὲρ ὑμῶν καὶ τῶν ἐν Λαοδικείᾳ καὶ ὅσοι οὐχ ἑόρακαν τὸ πρόσωπόν μου ἐν σαρκί,
Active, Infinitive, has DO of content, unmodified.

⁷ ἐρριζωμένοι καὶ ἐποικοδομούμενοι <u>ἐν αὐτῷ</u> καὶ βεβαιούμενοι τῇ πίστει καθὼς ἐδιδάχθητε, περισσεύοντες ἐν εὐχαριστίᾳ.
Substantival, middle, modified by dative PP of locus.

¹⁰ καὶ ἐστὲ <u>ἐν αὐτῷ</u> πεπληρωμένοι, ὅς ἐστιν ἡ κεφαλὴ πάσης ἀρχῆς καὶ ἐξουσίας.
Substantival, middle, modified by dative PP of locus. Periphrastic.

¹⁴ ἐξαλείψας τὸ καθ' ἡμῶν χειρόγραφον τοῖς δόγμασιν ὃ ἦν ὑπεναντίον ἡμῖν, καὶ <u>αὐτὸ</u> ἦρκεν <u>ἐκ τοῦ μέσου</u> προσηλώσας αὐτὸ τῷ σταυρῷ·
Active, has DO of prounoun, modified by Genitive of separation.

¹⁸ μηδεὶς ὑμᾶς καταβραβευέτω θέλων ἐν ταπεινοφροσύνῃ καὶ θρησκείᾳ τῶν ἀγγέλων, <u>ἃ</u> ἑόρακεν ἐμβατεύων, εἰκῇ φυσιούμενος ὑπὸ τοῦ νοὸς τῆς σαρκὸς αὐτοῦ,
Active, had DO of relative pronoun, unmodified.

Colossians 3

³ ἀπεθάνετε γὰρ καὶ ἡ ζωὴ ὑμῶν κέκρυπται <u>σὺν τῷ Χριστῷ ἐν τῷ θεῷ</u>.
Middle, is modified by dative PP of association, and dative PP of locus.

¹² Ἐνδύσασθε οὖν, ὡς ἐκλεκτοὶ τοῦ θεοῦ ἅγιοι καὶ ἠγαπημένοι, σπλάγχνα οἰκτιρμοῦ χρηστότητα ταπεινοφροσύνην πραΰτητα μακροθυμίαν,
Middle, substantival, unmodified.

²⁴ εἰδότες ὅτι <u>ἀπὸ κυρίου ἀπολήμψεσθε τὴν ἀνταπόδοσιν τῆς κληρονομίας. τῷ κυρίῳ Χριστῷ δουλεύετε·</u>
Citational, active, unmodified, has DO of content.

Colossians 4

¹ Οἱ κύριοι, τὸ δίκαιον καὶ τὴν ἰσότητα τοῖς δούλοις παρέχεσθε, εἰδότες ὅτι <u>καὶ ὑμεῖς ἔχετε κύριον ἐν οὐρανῷ</u>.
Citational, active, unmodified, has DO of content.

³ προσευχόμενοι ἅμα καὶ περὶ ἡμῶν, ἵνα ὁ θεὸς ἀνοίξῃ ἡμῖν θύραν τοῦ λόγου λαλῆσαι τὸ μυστήριον τοῦ Χριστοῦ, <u>δι' ὃ</u> καὶ δέδεμαι,
Middle, modified by accusative PP of reference.

⁶ ὁ λόγος ὑμῶν πάντοτε ἐν χάριτι, <u>ἅλατι</u> ἠρτυμένος, εἰδέναι <u>πῶς δεῖ ὑμᾶς ἑνὶ ἑκάστῳ</u> <u>ἀποκρίνεσθαι</u>.

First, Middle, modified by dative of instrument.

Second, infinitive, citational, DO of content. unmodified

¹² ἀσπάζεται ὑμᾶς Ἐπαφρᾶς ὁ ἐξ ὑμῶν, δοῦλος Χριστοῦ [Ἰησοῦ], πάντοτε ἀγωνιζόμενος ὑπὲρ ὑμῶν ἐν ταῖς προσευχαῖς, ἵνα σταθῆτε τέλειοι καὶ πεπληροφορημένοι <u>ἐν παντὶ</u> <u>θελήματι</u> τοῦ θεοῦ.

Substantive, modified by dative PP of reference.

1 Thessalonians 1

⁴ εἰδότες, ἀδελφοὶ ἠγαπημένοι ὑπὸ [τοῦ] θεοῦ, <u>τὴν ἐκλογὴν ὑμῶν</u>,

Citational, active, unmodified, has DO of content.

⁵ ὅτι τὸ εὐαγγέλιον ἡμῶν οὐκ ἐγενήθη εἰς ὑμᾶς ἐν λόγῳ μόνον ἀλλὰ καὶ ἐν δυνάμει καὶ ἐν πνεύματι ἁγίῳ καὶ [ἐν] πληροφορίᾳ πολλῇ, καθὼς οἴδατε <u>οἷοι ἐγενήθημεν [ἐν]</u> <u>ὑμῖν δι' ὑμᾶς</u>.

Citational, active, unmodified, has DO of content.

⁸ <u>ἀφ' ὑμῶν</u> γὰρ ἐξήχηται ὁ λόγος τοῦ κυρίου οὐ μόνον <u>ἐν τῇ Μακεδονίᾳ</u> καὶ [ἐν τῇ] Ἀχαΐᾳ, ἀλλ' <u>ἐν παντὶ τόπῳ</u> ἡ πίστις ὑμῶν ἡ πρὸς τὸν θεὸν ἐξελήλυθεν, ὥστε μὴ χρείαν ἔχειν ἡμᾶς λαλεῖν τι.

First, Middle, modified by genitive PP of source, dative PP of location.

Second, active, modified by dative PP of location.

1 Thessalonians 2

¹ Αὐτοὶ γὰρ οἴδατε, ἀδελφοί, <u>τὴν εἴσοδον ἡμῶν τὴν πρὸς ὑμᾶς ὅτι οὐ</u> <u>κενὴ γέγονεν</u>,

First, Active, unmodified, has DO of content,

Second, active, unmodified, has PN, copula-like, stative,

² ἀλλὰ προπαθόντες καὶ ὑβρισθέντες, καθὼς οἴδατε, <u>ἐν Φιλίπποις ἐπαρρησιασάμεθα</u> <u>ἐν τῷ θεῷ ἡμῶν λαλῆσαι πρὸς ὑμᾶς τὸ εὐαγγέλιον τοῦ θεοῦ ἐν πολλῷ ἀγῶνι</u>.

Citational, unmodified, has object of content, active.

⁴ ἀλλὰ καθὼς δεδοκιμάσμεθα <u>ὑπὸ τοῦ θεοῦ</u> πιστευθῆναι τὸ εὐαγγέλιον, οὕτως λαλοῦμεν, οὐχ ὡς ἀνθρώποις ἀρέσκοντες ἀλλὰ θεῷ τῷ δοκιμάζοντι τὰς καρδίας ἡμῶν.

Middle, modified by agent.

⁵ <u>Οὔτε γὰρ ποτε ἐν λόγῳ κολακείας ἐγενήθημεν</u>, καθὼς οἴδατε, οὔτε ἐν προφάσει πλεονεξίας, θεὸς μάρτυς,

Citational, unmodified, has object of content, active.

[11] καθάπερ οἴδατε, <u>ὡς ἕνα ἕκαστον ὑμῶν ὡς πατὴρ τέκνα ἑαυτοῦ</u>

Citational, unmodified, has object of content, active.

1 Thessalonians 3

[3] τὸ μηδένα σαίνεσθαι ἐν ταῖς θλίψεσιν ταύταις. αὐτοὶ γὰρ οἴδατε <u>ὅτι εἰς τοῦτο κείμεθα</u>·

Citational, unmodified, has object of content, active.

[4] καὶ γὰρ ὅτε πρὸς ὑμᾶς ἦμεν, προελέγομεν ὑμῖν <u>ὅτι μέλλομεν θλίβεσθαι</u>, καθὼς καὶ ἐγένετο καὶ οἴδατε.

Citational, unmodified, has object of content, active.

1 Thessalonians 4

[2] οἴδατε γὰρ <u>τίνας παραγγελίας ἐδώκαμεν ὑμῖν διὰ τοῦ κυρίου Ἰησοῦ</u>.

Citational, unmodified, has object of content, active.

[4] εἰδέναι ἕκαστον ὑμῶν <u>τὸ ἑαυτοῦ σκεῦος κτᾶσθαι ἐν ἁγιασμῷ καὶ τιμῇ</u>,

Citational, unmodified, has object of content, active.

[5] μὴ ἐν πάθει ἐπιθυμίας καθάπερ καὶ τὰ ἔθνη τὰ μὴ εἰδότα <u>τὸν θεόν,</u>

Citational, unmodified, has object of content, active.

1 Thessalonians 5

[2] αὐτοὶ γὰρ <u>ἀκριβῶς</u> οἴδατε <u>ὅτι ἡμέρα κυρίου ὡς κλέπτης ἐν νυκτὶ οὕτως ἔρχεται.</u>

Citational, modified by adverb of manner, has object of content, active.

[12] Ἐρωτῶμεν δὲ ὑμᾶς, ἀδελφοί, εἰδέναι <u>τοὺς κοπιῶντας ἐν ὑμῖν</u> καὶ προϊσταμένους ὑμῶν ἐν κυρίῳ καὶ νουθετοῦντας ὑμᾶς [13] καὶ ἡγεῖσθαι αὐτοὺς ὑπερεκπερισσοῦ ἐν ἀγάπῃ διὰ τὸ ἔργον αὐτῶν. εἰρηνεύετε ἐν ἑαυτοῖς.

Infinitive, Citational, unmodified, has object of content, active.

2 Thessalonians 1

[8] ἐν πυρὶ φλογός, διδόντος ἐκδίκησιν τοῖς μὴ εἰδόσιν <u>θεὸν</u> καὶ τοῖς μὴ ὑπακούουσιν τῷ εὐαγγελίῳ τοῦ κυρίου ἡμῶν Ἰησοῦ,

Adjectival, Citational, unmodified, has object of content, active.

2 Thessalonians 2

² εἰς τὸ μὴ ταχέως σαλευθῆναι ὑμᾶς ἀπὸ τοῦ νοὸς μηδὲ θροεῖσθαι, μήτε διὰ πνεύματος μήτε διὰ λόγου μήτε δι' ἐπιστολῆς ὡς δι' ἡμῶν, ὡς ὅτι ἐνέστηκεν ἡ ἡμέρα τοῦ κυρίου·
Active, in subordinate clause, Unmodified,

⁶ καὶ <u>νῦν τὸ κατέχον</u> οἴδατε εἰς τὸ ἀποκαλυφθῆναι αὐτὸν ἐν τῷ ἑαυτοῦ καιρῷ.
Citational, modified by adverb of present time or recent past, has object of content, active.

¹³ ἡμεῖς δὲ ὀφείλομεν εὐχαριστεῖν τῷ θεῷ πάντοτε περὶ ὑμῶν, ἀδελφοὶ ἠγαπημένοι <u>ὑπὸ κυρίου</u>, ὅτι εἴλατο ὑμᾶς ὁ θεὸς ἀπαρχὴν εἰς σωτηρίαν ἐν ἁγιασμῷ πνεύματος καὶ πίστει ἀληθείας,
Adjectival, modified by agent, middle.

2 Thessalonians 3

⁴ πεποίθαμεν δὲ <u>ἐν κυρίῳ ἐφ' ὑμᾶς</u>, <u>ὅτι ἃ παραγγέλλομεν [καὶ] ποιεῖτε καὶ ποιήσετε.</u>
Active, modified by dative PP of realm, and accusative PP of reference, has DO of content.

⁷ Αὐτοὶ γὰρ οἴδατε <u>πῶς δεῖ μιμεῖσθαι ἡμᾶς</u>, ὅτι οὐκ ἠτακτήσαμεν ἐν ὑμῖν
Citational, unmodified, has object of content, active.

1 Timothy 1

⁸ Οἴδαμεν δὲ <u>ὅτι καλὸς ὁ νόμος, ἐάν τις αὐτῷ νομίμως χρῆται,</u>
Citational, unmodified, has object of content, active.

⁹ εἰδὼς <u>τοῦτο</u>, ὅτι δικαίῳ νόμος οὐ κεῖται, ἀνόμοις δὲ καὶ ἀνυποτάκτοις, ἀσεβέσι καὶ ἁμαρτωλοῖς, ἀνοσίοις καὶ βεβήλοις, πατρολῴαις καὶ μητρολῴαις, ἀνδροφόνοις
Citational, unmodified, has object of content, active.

1 Timothy 2

¹⁴ καὶ Ἀδὰμ οὐκ ἠπατήθη, ἡ δὲ γυνὴ ἐξαπατηθεῖσα <u>ἐν παραβάσει</u> γέγονεν·
Active, modified by dative PP of destination

1 Timothy 3

⁵ (εἰ δέ τις <u>τοῦ ἰδίου οἴκου προστῆναι</u> οὐκ οἶδεν, πῶς ἐκκλησίας θεοῦ ἐπιμελήσεται;),
Citational, unmodified, has object of content, active.
¹⁵ ἐὰν δὲ βραδύνω, ἵνα εἰδῇς <u>πῶς δεῖ ἐν οἴκῳ θεοῦ ἀναστρέφεσθαι,</u> ἥτις ἐστὶν ἐκκλησία
θεοῦ ζῶντος, στῦλος καὶ ἑδραίωμα τῆς ἀληθείας.
Citational, unmodified, has object of content, active.

1 Timothy 4

² ἐν ὑποκρίσει ψευδολόγων, κεκαυστηριασμένων <u>τὴν ἰδίαν συνείδησιν,</u>
Adjectival, middle, stative, has accusative DO, unmodified.
³ κωλυόντων γαμεῖν, ἀπέχεσθαι βρωμάτων, ἃ ὁ θεὸς ἔκτισεν εἰς μετάλημψιν μετὰ
εὐχαριστίας τοῖς πιστοῖς καὶ <u>ἐπεγνωκόσι</u> <u>τὴν ἀλήθειαν.</u>
Active, Substantival, has DO in accusative, unmodified.
⁶ Ταῦτα ὑποτιθέμενος τοῖς ἀδελφοῖς καλὸς ἔσῃ διάκονος Χριστοῦ Ἰησοῦ, ἐντρεφόμενος
τοῖς λόγοις τῆς πίστεως καὶ τῆς καλῆς διδασκαλίας ᾗ παρηκολούθηκας·
Active, modified by dative relative pronoun of locus.
¹⁰ εἰς τοῦτο γὰρ κοπιῶμεν καὶ ἀγωνιζόμεθα, ὅτι ἠλπίκαμεν <u>ἐπὶ θεῷ</u> ζῶντι, ὅς ἐστιν
σωτὴρ πάντων ἀνθρώπων μάλιστα πιστῶν.
Active, modified by dative PP of locus, in a subordinated clause.

1 Timothy 5

⁵ ἡ δὲ ὄντως χήρα καὶ μεμονωμένη ἤλπικεν <u>ἐπὶ θεὸν</u> καὶ προσμένει ταῖς δεήσεσιν καὶ
ταῖς προσευχαῖς νυκτὸς καὶ ἡμέρας,
First, middle, Substantive, unmodified.
Second, active, modified by accusative PP of locus,
⁶ ἡ δὲ σπαταλῶσα ζῶσα τέθνηκεν.
Active, unmodified, stative.
⁸ εἰ δέ τις τῶν ἰδίων καὶ μάλιστα οἰκείων οὐ προνοεῖ, <u>τὴν πίστιν</u> ἤρνηται καὶ ἔστιν
ἀπίστου χείρων.
Middle, has accusative DO, unmodified.
⁹ Χήρα καταλεγέσθω μὴ <u>ἔλαττον ἐτῶν ἑξήκοντα</u> γεγονυῖα, ἑνὸς ἀνδρὸς γυνή,
Active, stative, unmodified, has ADJ in PN position, copula-like.

¹⁷ Οἱ <u>καλῶς</u> <u>προεστῶτες</u> πρεσβύτεροι διπλῆς τιμῆς ἀξιούσθωσαν, μάλιστα οἱ κοπιῶντες ἐν λόγῳ καὶ διδασκαλίᾳ.

Adjectival, active, modified by adverb of manner and by internal preposition of prior time.

1 Timothy 6

⁴ τετύφωται, μηδὲν ἐπιστάμενος, ἀλλὰ νοσῶν περὶ ζητήσεις καὶ λογομαχίας, ἐξ ὧν γίνεται φθόνος ἔρις βλασφημίαι, ὑπόνοιαι πονηραί,

Middle, unmodified, stative. Apodosis.

⁵ διαπαρατριβαὶ <u>διε</u>φθαρμένων ἀνθρώπων <u>τὸν νοῦν</u> καὶ <u>ἀπε</u>στερημένων <u>τῆς ἀληθείας</u>, νομιζόντων πορισμὸν εἶναι τὴν εὐσέβειαν.

First, Adjectival, middle, unmodified, DO, stative.

Second, Substantival, middle, has genitive DO with separation idea from the internal preposition,

¹⁷ Τοῖς πλουσίοις ἐν τῷ νῦν αἰῶνι παράγγελλε μὴ ὑψηλοφρονεῖν μηδὲ ἠλπικέναι <u>ἐπὶ</u> <u>πλούτου ἀδηλότητι</u> ἀλλ᾽ ἐπὶ θεῷ τῷ παρέχοντι ἡμῖν πάντα πλουσίως εἰς ἀπόλαυσιν,

Infinitive, active, modified by dative PP of locus.

2 Timothy 1

⁴ ἐπιποθῶν σε ἰδεῖν, μεμνημένος <u>σου</u> τῶν δακρύων, ἵνα χαρᾶς πληρωθῶ,

Middle, modified by a genitive OBJ of reference.

⁵ ὑπόμνησιν λαβὼν τῆς ἐν σοὶ ἀνυποκρίτου πίστεως, ἥτις ἐνῴκησεν πρῶτον ἐν τῇ μάμμῃ σου Λωΐδι καὶ τῇ μητρί σου Εὐνίκῃ, πέπεισμαι δὲ <u>ὅτι καὶ ἐν σοί</u>.

Citational, unmodified, has object of content, middle.

¹² δι᾽ ἣν αἰτίαν καὶ ταῦτα πάσχω· ἀλλ᾽ οὐκ ἐπαισχύνομαι, οἶδα γὰρ ᾧ πεπίστευκα καὶ πέπεισμαι <u>ὅτι δυνατός ἐστιν τὴν παραθήκην μου φυλάξαι εἰς ἐκείνην τὴν ἡμέραν</u>.

First, Citational, unmodified, has object of content, active.

Second, active, modified by dative pronoun of locus

Third, middle, modified by the same dative of locus.

¹⁵ Οἶδας <u>τοῦτο</u>, ὅτι ἀπεστράφησάν με πάντες οἱ ἐν τῇ Ἀσίᾳ, ὧν ἐστιν Φύγελος καὶ Ἑρμογένης.

Citational, unmodified, has object of content, active.

2 Timothy 2

[8] Μνημόνευε Ἰησοῦν Χριστὸν ἐγηγερμένον <u>ἐκ νεκρῶν</u>, ἐκ σπέρματος Δαυίδ, κατὰ τὸ εὐαγγέλιόν μου,
Substantival, middle, modified by genitive PP of separation,
[9] ἐν ᾧ κακοπαθῶ μέχρι δεσμῶν ὡς κακοῦργος, ἀλλὰ ὁ λόγος τοῦ θεοῦ οὐ δέδεται·
Middle, unmodified, stative.
[18] οἵτινες περὶ τὴν ἀλήθειαν ἠστόχησαν, λέγοντες [τὴν] ἀνάστασιν <u>ἤδη</u> γεγονέναι, καὶ ἀνατρέπουσιν τὴν τινων πίστιν.
Active, modified by adverb of prior time.
[19] ὁ μέντοι στερεὸς θεμέλιος τοῦ θεοῦ ἕστηκεν, ἔχων τὴν σφραγῖδα ταύτην· ἔγνω κύριος τοὺς ὄντας αὐτοῦ, καί· ἀποστήτω ἀπὸ ἀδικίας πᾶς ὁ ὀνομάζων τὸ ὄνομα κυρίου.
Active, unmodified, stative.
[21] ἐὰν οὖν τις ἐκκαθάρῃ ἑαυτὸν ἀπὸ τούτων, ἔσται σκεῦος εἰς τιμήν, ἡγιασμένον, εὔχρηστον τῷ δεσπότῃ, <u>εἰς πᾶν ἔργον ἀγαθὸν</u> ἡτοιμασμένον.
First, adjectival, middle, unmodified, stative,
Second, adjectival, middle, modified by Accusative PP of direction/purpose,
[23] τὰς δὲ μωρὰς καὶ ἀπαιδεύτους ζητήσεις παραιτοῦ, εἰδὼς <u>ὅτι γεννῶσιν μάχας</u>·
Citational, unmodified, has object of content, active.
[26] καὶ ἀνανήψωσιν ἐκ τῆς τοῦ διαβόλου παγίδος, ἐζωγρημένοι <u>ὑπ' αὐτοῦ εἰς τὸ ἐκείνου θέλημα</u>.
Middle, modified by genitive PP of agent, and dative PP of direction/purpose.

2 Timothy 3

[4] προδόται προπετεῖς τετυφωμένοι, φιλήδονοι μᾶλλον ἢ φιλόθεοι,
Middle, substantive, unmodified, stative.
[5] ἔχοντες μόρφωσιν εὐσεβείας <u>τὴν</u> δὲ <u>δύναμιν</u> αὐτῆς ἠρνημένοι· καὶ τούτους ἀποτρέπου.
Middle, has DO of content, unmodified.
[6] ἐκ τούτων γάρ εἰσιν οἱ ἐνδύνοντες εἰς τὰς οἰκίας καὶ αἰχμαλωτίζοντες γυναικάρια σεσωρευμένα <u>ἁμαρτίαις</u>, ἀγόμενα ἐπιθυμίαις ποικίλαις,
Middle, modified by dative of instrument.
[8] ὃν τρόπον δὲ Ἰάννης καὶ Ἰαμβρῆς ἀντέστησαν Μωϋσεῖ, οὕτως καὶ οὗτοι ἀνθίστανται τῇ ἀληθείᾳ, ἄνθρωποι <u>κατ</u>εφθαρμένοι <u>τὸν νοῦν</u>, ἀδόκιμοι περὶ τὴν πίστιν.
Middle, has accusative DO, modified by internal preposition indicating a standard.
[14] Σὺ δὲ μένε ἐν οἷς ἔμαθες καὶ ἐπιστώθης, εἰδὼς <u>παρὰ τίνων ἔμαθες</u>,

Citational, unmodified, has object of content, active.

¹⁷ ἵνα ἄρτιος ᾖ ὁ τοῦ θεοῦ ἄνθρωπος, <u>πρὸς πᾶν ἔργον ἀγαθὸν</u> ἐξηρτισμένος.

Middle, modified by accusative PP of goal.

2 Timothy 4

⁶Ἐγὼ γὰρ ἤδη σπένδομαι, καὶ ὁ καιρὸς <u>τῆς ἀναλύσεώς μου</u> ἐφέστηκεν.

Active, modified by genitive of locus (temporal), headed by the internal preposition for spatial location.

⁷ <u>τὸν καλὸν ἀγῶνα</u> ἠγώνισμαι, <u>τὸν δρόμον</u> τετέλεκα, <u>τὴν πίστιν</u> τετήρηκα·

First, middle, has accusative DO, unmodified.

Second, active, has accusative DO, unmodified.

Third, active, has accusative DO, unmodified.

⁸ λοιπὸν ἀπόκειταί μοι ὁ τῆς δικαιοσύνης στέφανος, ὃν ἀποδώσει μοι ὁ κύριος ἐν ἐκείνῃ τῇ ἡμέρᾳ, ὁ δίκαιος κριτής, οὐ μόνον δὲ ἐμοὶ ἀλλὰ καὶ πᾶσι τοῖς ἠγαπηκόσι <u>τὴν ἐπιφάνειαν</u> αὐτοῦ.

Substantival, active, has DO accusative, unmodified.

Titus 1

¹⁵ πάντα καθαρὰ τοῖς καθαροῖς· τοῖς δὲ μεμιαμμένοις καὶ ἀπίστοις οὐδὲν καθαρόν, ἀλλὰ μεμίανται αὐτῶν καὶ ὁ νοῦς καὶ ἡ συνείδησις.

First, middle, unmodified, stative

Second, middle, unmodified, stative.

¹⁶ <u>θεὸν</u> ὁμολογοῦσιν εἰδέναι, τοῖς δὲ ἔργοις ἀρνοῦνται, βδελυκτοὶ ὄντες καὶ ἀπειθεῖς καὶ πρὸς πᾶν ἔργον ἀγαθὸν ἀδόκιμοι.

Infinitive, active, has accusative DO, unmodified.

Titus 2

³ Πρεσβύτιδας ὡσαύτως ἐν καταστήματι ἱεροπρεπεῖς, μὴ διαβόλους μὴ <u>οἴνῳ πολλῷ</u> δεδουλωμένας, καλοδιδασκάλους,

Middle, modified by dative of instrument.

Titus 3

[8] Πιστὸς ὁ λόγος· καὶ περὶ τούτων βούλομαί σε διαβεβαιοῦσθαι, ἵνα φροντίζωσιν καλῶν ἔργων προΐστασθαι οἱ πεπιστευκότες <u>θεῷ</u>· ταῦτά ἐστιν καλὰ καὶ ὠφέλιμα τοῖς ἀνθρώποις.

Substantival, active, modified by dative of locus.

[11] εἰδὼς <u>ὅτι ἐξέστραπται ὁ τοιοῦτος καὶ ἁμαρτάνει ὢν αὐτοκατάκριτος</u>.

First, Citational, unmodified, has object of content, active.

Second, middle, unmodified, stative.

[12] Ὅταν πέμψω Ἀρτεμᾶν πρὸς σὲ ἢ Τύχικον, σπούδασον ἐλθεῖν πρός με εἰς Νικόπολιν, ἐκεῖ γὰρ κέκρικα <u>παραχειμάσαι</u>.

Active, mental activity, unmodified, has infinitive DO of decision.

Philemon 1

[7] χαρὰν γὰρ πολλὴν ἔσχον καὶ παράκλησιν ἐπὶ τῇ ἀγάπῃ σου, ὅτι τὰ σπλάγχνα τῶν ἁγίων ἀναπέπαυται <u>διὰ σοῦ</u>, ἀδελφέ.

Middle, modified by genitive PP of agency.

[21] Πεποιθὼς <u>τῇ ὑπακοῇ σου</u> ἔγραψά σοι, εἰδὼς <u>ὅτι καὶ ὑπὲρ ἃ λέγω ποιήσεις</u>.

First Citational, modified by dative of reference, active.

Second, Citational, unmodified, has object of content, active.

Pluperfect

Romans 7

[7] Τί οὖν ἐροῦμεν; ὁ νόμος ἁμαρτία; μὴ γένοιτο· ἀλλὰ τὴν ἁμαρτίαν οὐκ ἔγνων εἰ μὴ διὰ νόμου· τήν τε γὰρ <u>ἐπιθυμίαν</u> οὐκ ᾔδειν εἰ μὴ ὁ νόμος ἔλεγεν· οὐκ ἐπιθυμήσεις.

Active, mental activity, has accusative DO of content, unmodified.

Appendix L

Chart of Analysis Corpus Examples with Perfects

This chart contains examples drawn from the diachronic corpus. The time span of this corpus includes roughly 800 years, from 400 years before Paul's time until 400 years after his time. The corpus is comprised of moral letters, personal letters, and moral discourse to represent as close of a genre to that of Paul as is possible for the range of time. Examples are arranged in roughly chronological order, beginning with Plato's epistles and ending with those of the Church Father, Basil of Caearea.

Diachronic   Examples of Perfect tense-forms in context

Reference	Pf tense-form	Modifiers	Modifier function	Direct Object	Agent	Stative, Eventive, or Both	Specialised Function
Plato to Dionysius, Letter 2:310 C	εἰρηκότων	πρὸς σέ	Indirect object	τι	The subjects	Both	Historical event
	καὶ ταῦτα λέγω ὡς οὐχ ὑγιές τι Κρατιστόλου καὶ Πολυξένου πρὸς σὲ εἰρηκότων,						
Plato to Dionysius, Letter 2:311 D	πέπρακται	κατὰ τὴν ἔμπροσθεν συνουσίαν / μὴ καλῶς	Durative temporal / Manner	τι	---	Eventive	Historical
	τοῦτο οὖν ἡμῖν ἔτι, σὺν θεῷ εἰπεῖν, ἔξεστιν, εἴ τι ἄρα μὴ καλῶς πέπρακται κατὰ τὴν ἔμπροσθεν συνουσίαν, ἐπανορθώσασθαι καὶ ἔργῳ καὶ λόγῳ·						
Plato to Dionysius, Letter 2:312 D	πέπομφας	---	---	him (implied)	you	Eventive	Historical event
	ὑπὲρ οὗ σὺ πέπομφας ἀπορούμενος.						
Plato to Dionysius, Letter 2:313 C	γεγονότων	---	---	---	These things	Stative	Descriptive
	εὑρήκαμεν	κατὰ τὴν ἐμὴν δόξαν	Qualifies the verb	---	we	Both	Logical conclusion
	Τούτων δὴ γεγονότων καὶ ἐχόντων οὕτω, σχεδὸν κατὰ τὴν ἐμὴν δόξαν εὑρήκαμεν ὃ σὺ ἐπέστειλας, ὅπως δεῖ πρὸς ἀλλήλους ἡμᾶς ἔχειν.						
Plato to Dionysius, Letter 3:315 B	γέγραφας	---	---	citation	You	Both	Citational, Historical event
	καὶ γέγραφας, ὡς φασί, χαῖρε καὶ ἡδόμενον βίοτον διάσωζε τυράννου·						
Plato to Dionysius, Letter 3:317 E	οἶσθα	---	---	πάντα	You	Stative	Referential
	—οἶσθα γὰρ δὴ σὺ πάντα τἀντεῦθεν ἤδη γενόμενα—						
Plato to Dion of Syracuse, Letter 4:321 B	πέπρακται	---	---	τι	you	Eventive	Contrastive
	ἐπιστέλλετε δὲ καὶ ὅ τι πέπρακται ὑμῖν ἢ πράττοντες τυγχάνετε, ὡς ἡμεῖς πολλὰ ἀκούοντες οὐδὲν ἴσμεν.						

Diachronic   Examples of Perfect tense-forms in context

					I	Both	Supplemental
Plato to Dion of Syracuse, Letter 4:321 B	εἴρηται	---	---	---	---	---	Supplemental
	ἴσμεν	---	---	οὐδέν	We	Stative	Referential
ἡμεῖς δέ, καθάπερ εἴρηται, πολλὰ ἀκούοντες περὶ τῶν τῇδε οὐδὲν ἴσμεν.							

Diachronic Examples of Perfect tense-forms in context

Reference	Pf tense-form	Modifiers	Modifier function	Direct Object	Agent	Stative, Eventive, or Both	Specialised Function
Plato to Perdiccas, Letter 5:322 A	ἔοικεν	---	---	---	It	Stative	Supplemental
	εἰδέναι	---	---	τὰ δημοκρατίᾳ	Πλάτων	Stative	Referential
Πλάτων, ὡς ἔοικεν, προσποιεῖται μὲν τὰ δημοκρατίᾳ συμφέροντα εἰδέναι,							
Plato to Hermeias, Erastus and Corsicas, Letter 6:322 E	διατετρίφθαι	διὰ + τοῦ βίου	Durative adv	---	---	Stative	Descriptive
ἄπειροι γάρ εἰσι διὰ τὸ μεθ᾽ ἡμῶν μετρίων ὄντων καὶ οὐ᾽ κακῶν συχνὸν διατετρίφθαι τοῦ βίου·							
Plato to Hermeias, Erastus and Corsicas, Letter 6:323 A	συγγεγονότι	---	---	---	I		Supplemental
	εἰληφέναι	---	---	ἐμπειρίας	Ἑρμείας		
ταύτην δ᾽ αὖ τὴν δύναμιν Ἑρμείας μοι φαίνεται φύσει τε, ὅσα [323a] μήπω συγγεγονότι, καὶ τέχνῃ δι᾽ ἐμπειρίας εἰληφέναι.							
Plato to Dion, Letter 7:332 B-C	ἐμβεβλημένας	ὑπὸ βαρβάρων	agent	---	ὑπὸ βαρβάρων	Eventive	Supplemental Sequential action
	κεκτημένοι	---	---	φίλους	they	Stative	Describes Athenians
ἔτι δὲ Ἀθηναῖοι πρὸς τούτους, οὐκ αὐτοὶ κατοικίσαντες, οὐκ ἄκοντας τῶν Ἑλλήνων πόλεις ὑπὸ βαρβάρων ἐμβεβλημένας πολλὰς τῶν βαρβάρων ἐμβεβλημένας ἀλλ᾽ οἰκουμένας παραλαβόντες, ὅμως ἑβδομήκοντα ἔτη διεφύλαξαν τὴν ἀρχὴν φίλους ἄνδρας φίλους ἐν ταῖς πόλεσιν ἑκάστας κεκτημένοι.							

Diachronic   Examples of Perfect tense-forms in context

Reference	Perfect form	Complement	Category	Other	Subject	Aspect	Function
Plato to Diom. Letter 7:334 D-E	τέθνηκεν	καλῶς	manner	---	Διωνα	Eventive	Historical Example
Plato to Diom. Letter 7:336 C	ἀκηκόατε	παρ' ἐμοῦ / σαφῶς	Source / manner	---	you	Both	Supplemental
Plato to Archytas, Letter 12:359 D	παραδεδομένος	---	---	---	---	Stative	Supplemental
Aristotle. Nicomachean Ethics, 2.2 1103 B	εἰρήκαμεν	---	---	---	we	Eventive	Supplemental Historical Citational
Aristotle. Nicomachean Ethics, 2.2 1105 A	ἐγκεχρωσμένον	τῷ βίῳ	locative	---	---	Stative	Descriptive
Aristotle. Nicomachean Ethics, 3.1 1111 B	Διωρισμένων	---	---	ἑκουσίου and ἀκουσίου	we	Eventive	Sequential past actions
Aristotle. Nicomachean Ethics, 3.5 1113 B	εἰρημένος	νῦν	Temporal	---	we	Eventive	Referential
Aristotle. Nicomachean Ethics, 3.7 1116 A	εἴρηται	---	---	---	---	Eventive	Referential Historical
Ethics, 3.7 1116 A	εἴρηται	---	---	---	---	Undecided	Referential

Context:

Plato to Diom. Letter 7:334 D-E — καὶ ἐμοὶ πείθεσθε Διὸς τρίτου σωτῆρος χάριν, εἶτα εἰς Διονύσιον βλέψαντες καὶ Δίωνα, ὃν ἐὰν μὲν μὴ πειθόμενος ζῇ τὰ νῦν οὐ καλῶς, ὁ δὲ πειθόμενος τέθνηκεν καλῶς·

Plato to Diom. Letter 7:336 C — ἐπὶ Δ... δὲ ὀργίθων τὰς ἐκείνου βουλήσεις πειρᾶσθαι ἀποτελεῖν—αἱ δὲ ἦσαν, ἀκηκόατε παρ' ἐμοῦ σαφῶς.

Plato to Archytas, Letter 12:359 D — ἄνδρες ἀγαθοί, ὡς ὁ παραδεδομένος μῦθος δηλοῖ.

Aristotle. Nicomachean Ethics, 2.2 1103 B — πῶς πρακτέον αὐτάς; αὗται γὰρ εἰσι κύριαι καὶ τοῦ ποιὰς γενέσθαι τὰς ἕξεις, καθάπερ εἰρήκαμεν.

Aristotle. Nicomachean Ethics, 2.2 1105 A — διὸ χαλεπὸν ἀποτρίψασθαι τοῦτο τὸ πάθος ἐγκεχρωσμένον τῷ βίῳ.

Aristotle. Nicomachean Ethics, 3.1 1111 B — Διωρισμένων δὲ τοῦ τε ἑκουσίου καὶ τοῦ ἀκουσίου, περὶ προαιρέσεως ἕπεται διελθεῖν.

Aristotle. Nicomachean Ethics, 3.5 1113 B — ἢ τοῖς γε νῦν εἰρημένοις ἀμφισβητητέον, καὶ τὸν ἄνθρωπον οὐ φατέον ἀρχὴν εἶναι οὐδὲ γεννητὴν τῶν πράξεων ὥσπερ καὶ τέκνων.

Aristotle. Nicomachean Ethics, 3.7 1116 A — Καθάπερ οὖν εἴρηται, ἡ ἀνδρεία μεσότης ἐστὶ περὶ θαρραλέα καὶ φοβερά ἐν οἷς εἴρηται, καὶ ὅτι καλὸν θαρρεῖ τε καὶ ὑπομένει, ἢ ὅτι αἰσχρὸν τὸ μή.

Reference	Pf tense-form	Modifiers	Modifier function	Direct Object	Agent	Stative	Specialised Function
Aristotle. Nicomachean Ethics, 3.7 1116 B	ὡπλισμένοι	---	---	---	---	Stative	descriptive
ὥσπερ οὖν ἀνόπλοις ὡπλισμένοι μάχονται καὶ ἀθληταὶ ἰδιώταις·							

Diachronic Examples of Perfect tense-forms in context

Reference	Pf tense-form	Modifiers	Modifier function	Direct Object	Agent	Stative, Eventive, or Both	Specialised Function
Aristotle. Nicomachean Ethics, 4.1 1120 B	εἴρηται	---	---	---	it	Eventive	Referential Historical
ὥσπερ γὰρ εἴρηται, ἐλευθέριός ἐστιν ὁ κατὰ τὴν οὐσίαν δαπανῶν καὶ εἰς ἃ δεῖ· ὁ δ᾿ ὑπερβάλλων ἄσωτος.							
Aristotle. Nicomachean Ethics, 4.2 1123 A	εἴρηται	---	---	---	it	Eventive	Referential Historical
ὁ δ᾿ ὑπερβάλλων καὶ βάναυσος τῷ παρὰ τὸ δέον ἀναλίσκειν ὑπερβάλλει, ὥσπερ εἴρηται.							
Aristotle. Nicomachean Ethics, 4.5 1126 A	εἴρηται	πρότερον	Temporal	---	it	Eventive	Historical Referential
Ὃ δὲ καὶ ἐν τοῖς πρότερον εἴρηται, καὶ ἐκ τῶν λεγομένων δῆλον.							
Aristotle. Nicomachean Ethics, 5.1 1129 B	ὡρισμένα	ὑπὸ τῆς νομοθετικῆς	Agent	---	νομοθετικῆς	Eventive	Explanatory
ἐπεὶ δ᾿ ὁ παράνομος ἄδικος ἦν ὁ δὲ νόμιμος δίκαιος, δῆλον ὅτι πάντα τὰ νόμιμά ἐστί πως δίκαια· τά τε γὰρ ὁρισμένα ὑπὸ τῆς νομοθετικῆς νόμιμά ἐστι, καὶ ἕκαστον τούτων δίκαιον εἶναι φαμέν.							
Aristotle. Nicomachean Ethics, 6.4 1140 B	διεφθαρμένω	---	---	---	---	Stative	Descriptive
τῷ δὲ διεφθαρμένῳ δι᾿ ἡδονὴν ἢ λύπην εὐθὺς οὐ φαίνεται ἀρχή, οὐδὲ δεῖν τούτου ἕνεκεν οὐδὲ διὰ τοῦθ᾿ αἱρεῖσθαι πάντα καὶ πράττειν·							
Aristotle. Nicomachean Ethics, 7.1 1145 A	πεποίηκε	περὶ <τοῦ> Ἕκτορος	reference	---	Ὅμηρος	Eventive	Referential Historical
ὥσπερ Ὅμηρος περὶ <τοῦ> Ἕκτορα πεποίηκε λέγοντα τὸν Πρίαμον, ὅτι σφόδρα ἦν ἀγαθός, οὐδὲ ἐῴκει ἀνδρός γε θνητοῦ πάις ἔμμεναι ἀλλὰ θεοῖο.							

Diachronic	Examples of Perfect tense-forms in context							
Aristotle. Nicomachean Ethics, 7.7 1150 B	πεπληγμένος	ὥσπερ ὁ Θεοδέκτου Φιλοκτήτης ὑπὸ τοῦ ἔχεος πεπληγμένος ἢ ὁ Καρκίνου ἐν τῇ Ἀλόπῃ Κερκύων,	ὑπὸ τοῦ ἔχεος	Agent		---	Eventive	Historical Referential
Aristotle. Nicomachean Ethics, 8.3 1157 A	δεδοκιμασμένος	οὐ γὰρ ῥᾴδιον οὐδενὶ πιστεῦσαι περὶ τοῦ ἐν πολλῷ χρόνῳ ὑφ' αὑτοῦ δεδοκιμασμένου·	ὑφ' αὑτοῦ; ἐν πολλῷ χρόνῳ	Agent; Durative temporal		himself	Both	Example Historical / Repeated action
Aristotle. Nicomachean Ethics, 9.8 1169 B	εἴρηται	οὕτω μὲν οὖν φίλαυτον εἶναι δεῖ, καθάπερ εἴρηται· ὡς δ' οἱ πολλοί, οὐ χρή.	---			we	Eventive	Referential / Historical
Aristotle. Nicomachean Ethics, 10.8 1179 B	τετάχθαι	διὸ νόμοις δεῖ τετάχθαι τὴν τροφὴν καὶ τὰ ἐπιτηδεύματα.	νόμοις	Means		---	Event	Conclusion
Aristotle. Nicomachean Ethics, 10.9 1180 B	γεγραμμένον	γεγραμμένον δ' ἢ ἀγράφων, οὐδὲν ἂν δόξειε διαφέρειν, οὐδὲ δι' ὧν εἰς ἢ πολλοὶ παιδευθήσονται, ὥσπερ οὐδ' ἐπὶ μουσικῆς καὶ γυμναστικῆς καὶ τῶν ἄλλων ἐπιτηδευμάτων.	---			---	Stative	Descriptive
Alciphron's Epistles Glykera to Bakchis, 4:2, line 1	βεβούληται	Ὁ Μένανδρος ἡμῶν ἐπὶ τὴν τῶν Ἰσθμίων θέαν εἰς τὴν Κόρινθον ἐλθεῖν βεβούληται.	---			Μένανδρος	Eventive	Historical
Speusippus to Philip, section 14 line 9–11	πεποίηκεν	Ἀλλὰ γὰρ τὰς λοιπὰς σκηνψεις γράφειν ἐπιλείπει μοι τὸ βιβλίον· τοσαύτην ἡμῖν σπάνιν βιβλίων βασιλεὺς Αἴγυπτον λαβὼν πεποίηκεν.	ἡμῖν; σπάνιν	Indirect object		βασιλεύς	Eventive	Historical
Phalaris Epistles 83:2 lines 8–10	οἶδα	οἶδα δὲ καὶ τοῦτο, ὅτι πολλῷ κρεῖττόν ἐστιν ἰδιώτῃ δανείσαντα χρεωκοπεῖσθαι ἢ πόλει-	ὅτι clause			I	Stative	Referential

	Pf tense-form	Modifiers	Modifier function	Direct Object	Agent	Stative	Referential
Phalaris Epistles 124:1 line 13	οἶδα	--	--	--	I	Stative	Referential

εἰ δὲ αἰσχύνεσθε γυμνῶσαι τὰς αἰτίας, ἐφ' αἷς καταγορεῖτε, τὴν δικαίῳ πολεμήσετε ἐπ' αὐταῖς μὰ τοὺς θεοὺς οὐκ οἶδα.

Diachronic Examples of Perfect tense-forms in context

Reference	Pf tense-form	Modifiers	Modifier function	Direct Object	Agent	Stative, Eventive, or Both	Specialised Function
Phalaris Epistles 95:1 line 6	οἶδαμεν	πείρᾳ	manner	--	I	Eventive	Referential

πείρᾳ γὰρ οἶδαμεν τὴν τοῦ φεύγειν ἀτυχίαν ὅσον ἐστὶ κακόν.

| Phalaris Epistles 21:1 line 12 | οἶδα | -- | -- | ὅτι clause | I | Stative | Referential |

οἶδα γοῦν, ὅτι διὰ τὴν δόσιν τῶν χαριστηρίων πάντες εὔχεσθε προδόται μᾶλλον Ἀκραγαντίνων ἢ τυραννοκτόνοι Φαλάριδος ἀκουσθῆναι.

| *Aristeas to Philocrates*, 91 | δεδήλωται | -- | -- | -- | It | | Supplemental |

ὥστε συμφανές μοι γεγονέναι τὸ μέγεθος τῶν ἀγγείων, καθὼς δεδήλωται.

| *Aristeas to Philocrates*, 307 | προειρήκαμεν | προ- | temporal | -- | I | | Citational/Supplemental |

Καθὼς δὲ προειρήκαμεν, οὕτως καθ' ἑκάστην εἰς τὸν τόπον, ἔχοντα τερπνότητα διὰ τὴν ἡσυχίαν καὶ καταύγειαν, συναγόμενοι τὸ προκείμενον ἐπετέλουν.

| Epistles of Diogenes, *To Eugnesius*, 8:2, Line 6 | ἀφῄρησαι | τῆς τυραννίδος | Item deprived of | -- | You | Eventive | Historical |

ἀλλ' ἐγὼ μὲν οὐχ ὅτι τῆς τυραννίδος ἀφῄρησαι ἄχθομαι, ὦ Διονύσιε, ἀλλ' ὅτι ἐλευθεριάζεις ἐν τῇ Ἑλλάδι τὰ νῦν,

| Epistles of Diogenes, *To Melesippus*, 20:1, Line 1 | λελυπῆσθαι | -- | -- | ὅτι clause | σε | Stative | Referential |

Ἥκουσόν σε λελυπῆσθαι ὅτι τὰ Ἀθηναίων τέκνα πληγὰς ἡμῖν ἐνέτεινε μεθύοντα, καὶ δεινὰ πάσχειν, εἰ σοφία πεπαρῴνηται.

Diachronic	Examples of Perfect tense-forms in context							
Epistles of Diogenes, *To Perdiccas*, 45:1, Line 6	οἶσθα	---	καὶ οὐκ οἶσθα ὅτι δράσας τοῦτο ἀντιπείσῃ.	---	ὅτι clause	You	Stative	Referential
Socratic Epistles, *Of Socrates*, 1:10, line 8	οἶδα	---	οἶδα δὲ ὅτι, εἰ καὶ οἱ ἄλλοι ἄνθρωποι ὁμοίως διέκειντο, ἥττονα ἂν ἦν κακὰ ἐν τῷ βίῳ.	---	ὅτι clause	I	Stative	Referential
Letters of Philostratus, Epistle 1:7	περιβεβλημένον	περι-	ὁρῶ δὲ ἐγὼ τὸν Ἡρακλέα ἐν ταῖς γραφαῖς δορὰν θηρίου περιβεβλημένον καὶ τὰ πολλὰ χαμαὶ καθεύδοντα,	direction	δορὰν	Ἡρακλέα	Eventive	Sequential past action
Letters of Philostratus, Epistle 2:2	κεχληρῶσθω	---	νόμος τε γὰρ παριγητέος ἐς φύσιν καὶ φύσις ἐς νόμον καὶ καλοίμεν αὐτοῖν τὸ μὲν ἀρχήν, τὸ δ᾽ ἑπόμενον, κεχληρῶσθω δὲ ἀρχὴν μὲν φύσις, νόμος δὲ τὸ ἑπέσθαι, οὔτε γὰρ ἂν νόμος ἐτειχοποίησεν ἢ ὑπὲρ τείχους ὁπλίσεν,	---	φύσις	We	Stative	
Letters of Anacharsis, To Solon, Letter 2, Line 16	κεκοσμήκασι	ἄλλος	ἄλλοι γὰρ ἄλλως κατὰ νόμους πατέρων κεκοσμήκασι τὰ σώματα.	manner	τὰ σώματα	Others	Eventive	Supplemental
Plutarch, *Advice to the Bride and Groom*, 1.43	ἡρμοσμένον	εὖ	εὖ τοίνυν ἡρμοσμένον τὸν οἶκον εἶναι δεῖ τῷ μέλλοντι ἁρμόζεσθαι πόλιν καὶ ἀγορὰν καὶ φίλους·	manner	---	The one who	Both	Descriptive of house and still focusing on act
Plutarch, *Advice to the Bride and Groom*, 1.48	γεγραμμένα	πρὸς Ἀριστύλλαν ὑπὸ Τιμοξένας	περὶ δὲ φιλοκοσμίας σὺ μέν, ὦ Εὐρυδίκη, τὰ πρὸς Ἀριστύλλαν ὑπὸ Τιμοξένας γεγραμμένα ἀναγνοῦσα πειρῶ διαμνημονεύειν	Indirect obj agent	τά	Τιμοξένας	Both	Historical event Citational

Reference	Pf tense-form	Modifiers	Modifier function	Direct Object	Agent	ὁ	Stative	Descriptive
Plutarch, *How a Man become Aware of His Progress in Virtue*, 1.8	πεπληγώς	---	---	---	---	---	Stative	Descriptive

Αἰσχύλος μὲν γὰρ Ἰσθμοῖ θεώμενος ἀγῶνα πυκτῶν, ἐπεὶ πληγέντος τοῦ ἑτέρου τὸ θέατρον ἐξέκραγε, νύξας Ἴωνα τὸν Χῖον ᾽ὁρᾷς᾽ ἔφη ᾽οἷον ἡ ἄσκησίς ἐστιν; ὁ πεπληγὼς σιωπᾷ, οἱ δὲ θεώμενοι βοῶσιν᾽

Diachronic Examples of Perfect tense-forms in context

Reference	Pf tense-form	Modifiers	Modifier function	Direct Object	Agent	Stative, Eventive, or Both	Specialised Function
Plutarch, *How a Man become Aware of His Progress in Virtue*, 1.12	διακεχυμένον	ὑπὸ τοῦ λόγου	means	---	---	Eventive	Referential
Plutarch, *On Being a Busybody*, 1.3	συγκεκαλυμμένον	---		---	---	Stative	Descriptive
Plutarch, *On Being a Busybody*, 1.6	εἰρημένον	ἀληθῶς	Manner	---	---	Both	Referential
Plutarch, *On Being a Busybody*, 1.7	κεκρυμμένα	---		---	---	Stative	Descriptive of goods
Plutarch, *On Being a Busybody*, 1.11	γέγραπται	---		---	---	Stative	Referential

ὅρα δὴ καὶ τὸ τοῦ Ζήνωνος ὁποῖόν ἐστιν. ἠξίου γὰρ ἀπὸ τῶν ὀνείρων ἕκαστον αὑτοῦ συναισθάνεσθαι προκόπτοντος, εἰ μήθ᾽ ἡδόμενον αἰσχρῷ τινι ἑαυτὸν μήτε τι προσιέμενον ἢ πράττοντα τῶν δεινῶν καὶ ἀτόπων ὁρᾷ κατὰ τοὺς ὕπνους, ἀλλ᾽ οἷον ἐν βυθῷ γαλήνης ἀκλύστου καταφανεῖ διαλάμπει τῆς ψυχῆς τὸ φανταστικὸν καὶ παθητικὸν διακεχυμένον ὑπὸ τοῦ λόγου.

καίτοι γε τὸ τοῦ Αἰγυπτίου χάριεν πρὸς τὸν ἐρωτῶντα τί φέρει συγκεκαλυμμένον,

καὶ τὸ οἴμοι, τὸ κακὸν τῆς εὐτυχίας ὡς μᾶλλον ἐς οὓς φέρεται θνητῶν ἐπὶ τῶν πολυπραγμόνων ἐστὶν ἀληθῶς εἰρημένον.

ἀλλ᾽ ὅταν τὰ κεκρυμμένα ζητοῦντες ἐν ἀλλοτρίοις σκεύεσι καὶ φορτίοις ἀναστρέφωνται·

ὑποβάλλοντας αὐτοῖς ὅτι χρήσιμον οὐδὲν οὐδ᾽ ἐπιτερπὲς ἐν τούτοις γέγραπται·

Diachronic   Examples of Perfect tense-forms in context

Diachronic	Form	Examples of Perfect tense-forms in context	Phrase	Means	Oedipus	Eventive	Historical
Plutarch, *On Being a Busybody*, 1.14	ἐξημμένος	οἶμαι πρὸς αὐτῷ γ᾽ εἰμὶ τῷ δεινῷ λέγειν, ὅμως ἐξημμένος ὑπὸ τοῦ πάθους καὶ σφαδάζων ἀποκρίνεται κἄγωγ᾽ ἀκούειν· ἀλλ᾽ ὅμως ἀκουστέον.	ὑπὸ τοῦ πάθους	Means	---	Eventive	Historical
Plutarch, *On Being a Busybody*, 1.15	κεκώλυται	ὅταν δὲ τις οἷς ἔξεστι τρέφων τὸ πολύπραγμον, ἰσχυρὸν ἀπεργάσηται καὶ βίαιον, οὐκέτι ῥᾳδίως, πρὸς ἃ κεκώλυται φερόμενα διὰ συνήθειαν, κρατεῖν δυνατός ἐστιν.	---	---	---	Stative	Descriptive of things
Plutarch, *On Being a Busybody*, 1.16	βεβούλευται		κακὸν	---	τις	Uncertain	Irrealis
Plutarch, *On Being a Busybody*, 1.16	πεποίηκεν	ἀλλ᾽ οἱ μὲν συκοφάντας ζητοῦσιν, εἴ τις ἢ βεβούλευται κακὸν ἢ πεποίηκεν· οἱ δὲ πολυπράγμονες καὶ τὰς ἀβουλήτους ἀτυχίας τῶν πέλας ἐλέγχοντες εἰς μέσον ἐκφέρουσι.	κακὸν	---	τις	Uncertain	Irrealis
Plutarch, *On Brotherly Love*, 1.5	ἐπιβεβούλευκότα	ὥσπερ αὖ τοὐναντίον, Ἀρταξέρξης αἰσθόμενος Ὦχον τὸν υἱὸν ἐπιβεβουλευκότα τοῖς ἀδελφοῖς ἀθυμήσας ἀπέθανε.	τοῖς ἀδελφοῖς	Dative of object	Ὦχον	Eventive	Historical
Plutarch, *On Brotherly Love*, 1.5	εἴρηκεν	χαλεποὶ πόλεμοι γὰρ ἀδελφῶν, ὡς Εὐριπίδης εἴρηκεν,	---	---	Εὐριπίδης	Eventive	Historical Referential
Plutarch, *On Brotherly Love*, 1.8	εἰρηκώς	εἶ γοῦν ὁ Θηβαῖος Ἐτεοκλῆς πρὸς τὸν ἀδελφὸν εἰρηκώς,	πρὸς τὸν ἀδελφὸν	Reference	Ἐτεοκλῆς	Eventive	Historical Referential
Plutarch, *On Brotherly Love*, 1.11	ἀπολωλεκότες	τὸ δὲ μέγιστον καὶ τιμιώτατον τῶν πατρῴων, φιλίαν ἀδελφοῦ καὶ πίστιν, ἀπολωλεκότες.	τὸ μέγιστον	---	They	Stative	
Plutarch, *On Brotherly Love*, 1.12	τεθνηκότος	εἶπεν, ᾗ ἐβουλόμην, τἀδελφοῦ τεθνηκότος.	---	---	---	Stative	Descriptive of brother
Plutarch, *On Brotherly Love*, 1.20	εἴρηται	ὁ μὲν γὰρ εὐγνώμων καὶ κοινός, ὥσπερ εἴρηται, μᾶλλον ἐγκραθεὶς δι᾽ ἀμφοτέραν σύνδεσμος ἔσται τῆς φιλαδελφίας	---	---	We	Eventive	Historical Referential

Reference	Pf tense-form	Modifiers	Modifier function	Direct Object	Agent	Stative, Eventive, or Both	Specialised Function
Plutarch, On Brotherly Love, 1.20	γέγραπται	διὰ πλειόνων	manner	---		It	Eventive	Referential / Historical
	ἀλλὰ περὶ ταύτης μὲν ἑτέρωθι τῆς γνώμης γέγραπται τὰ δοκοῦντα διὰ πλειόνων						
Plutarch, On Control of Anger, 1.1	προστέθεικεν	---	---	τῶν φαύλων	ὁ χρόνος	Undecided	Irrealis
	ἀφῄρηκεν	---	---	τῶν φαύλων	ὁ χρόνος	Undecided	Irrealis
	εἴ τι χρηστὸν ὁ χρόνος προστέθεικεν ἢ τῶν φαύλων ἀφῄρηκεν.						
Plutarch, On Control of Anger, 1.1	οἶσθα				You	Stative	Referential
	καίπερ, ὡς οἶσθα, οὐδαμῇ πιθανὸς ὢν τῷ πρὸς χάριν ὑφίεσθαι τοῦ δοκοῦντος.						

Diachronic Examples of Perfect tense-forms in context

Reference	Pf tense-form	Modifiers	Modifier function	Direct Object	Agent	Stative, Eventive, or Both	Specialised Function
Plutarch, On Control of Anger, 1.6	οἶδα	---		---	I	Stative	Referential
	ἐγὼ γοῦν, εἰ̓ μὲν ὀρθῶς οὐκ οἶδα, ταύτην δὲ τῆς ἰατρείας ἀρχὴν ποιησάμενος,						
Plutarch, On the Delays of Divine Vengeance, 1.12	πέπαυνται	οὐ πολὺς χρόνος	Temporal	πέμποντες	Λοκροί	Eventive	Historical
	καὶ μὴν οὐ πολὺς χρόνος, ἀφ᾽ οὗ Λοκροὶ πέμποντες εἰς Τροίαν πέπαυνται τὰς παρθένους,						
Plutarch, On the Delays of Divine Vengeance, 1.13	κεχάλκευται	ψυχρᾷ φλογί	Means		---	Both	Descriptive of heart
	εἰ̓ μὴ μέλαιναν καρδίαν κεχάλκευται ψυχρᾷ φλογὶ κατ᾽ αὐτὸν τὸν Πίνδαρον᾽						
Plutarch, On Moral Virtue, 1.3	διημαρτημένης				---	Stative	Descriptive
	καὶ γὰρ τὸ πάθος εἶναι λόγου πονηρὸν καὶ ἀκόλαστον ἐκ φαύλης καὶ διημαρτημένης κρίσεως σφοδρότητα καὶ ῥώμην προσλαβούσης.						
Plutarch, On the Love of Wealth, 1.6	πεπαῦσθαι	---			Δημάδην	Stative	Descriptive of Subject
	ὥσπερ ὁ Δημοσθένης· ἔλεγε πρὸς τοὺς νομίζοντας τῆς πονηρίας τὸν Δημάδην πεπαῦσθαι,						

Diachronic Examples of Perfect tense-forms in context

Diachronic	Perfect form	Context (Greek)	Modifier	Type	Object	Subject	Aspect	Function
Plutarch, *On Tranquillity of the Mind*, 1.1	δεδεγμένον	παρὰ Φουνδάνου τοῦ κρατίστου γράμματα δεδεγμένον,	παρὰ Φουνδάνου	Identifying sender	γράμματα	he	Eventive	Historical
Plutarch, *On Tranquillity of the Mind*, 1.2	εἴρηται	τὸν γὰρ καλῶν ἢ παραλειφθείς οὐχ ἧττον ἢ τῶν φαύλων ἢ πρᾶξις ἀναρὸν ἐστι καὶ ταραχῶδες, ὡς εἴρηται.	---	---	---	it	Eventive	Referential Historical
Plutarch, *On Tranquillity of the Mind*, 1.11	περικεχυμένης	ὅπλων καὶ ἵππων καὶ στρατιᾶς περικεχυμένης·	---	---	---	they	Stative	Descriptive of all three nouns
Basil to Gregory of Nazianzus, Letter 2:5	πέφυκε	ὁ μάλιστα λύειν τῆς ψυχῆς τὸν τόνον πέφυκε.	---	---	---	It	Stative	Supplemental
Basil to Gregory of Nazianzus, Letter 2:6	ἐσπουδακότα	οὕτω δεῖ καὶ τὸν ἐσπουδακότα ἑαυτὸν πᾶσι τοῖς μέρεσι τῆς ἀρετῆς ἀπεργάσασθαι τέλειον	---	---	---	The one	Stative	Descriptive
Basil to the Caesareans, Letter 8:2	τετυχήκαμεν	ἀλλ' ἐπειδή, σὺν Θεῷ, τοῦ σκοποῦ κατὰ δύναμιν τετυχήκαμεν εὑρόντες σκεῦος ἐκλογῆς καὶ φρέαρ βαθύ,	κατὰ δύναμιν	standard	τοῦ σκοποῦ	We	Undecided	Reason
Basil to the Caesareans, Letter 8:9	οἶδα	τὰς γὰρ συγκρίσεις οἶδα κυρίως ἐπὶ τῶν τῆς αὐτῆς φύσεως γινομένας.	---	---	---	I	Stative	Referential
Basil to the Caesareans, Letter 8:15	ἡτοίμασται	καὶ τὸ Οὐκ ἔστιν ἐμὸν δοῦναι, ἀλλ' οἷς ἡτοίμασται ὑπὸ τοῦ Πατρός.	ὑπὸ τοῦ Πατρός	agent	---	Πατρός	Eventive	Explanatory
Basil to the Caesareans, Letter 8:19	γέγραπται	γέγραπται γάρ, Ὅταν ὑποταγῇ αὐτῷ τὰ πάντα, τότε καὶ αὐτὸς ὁ Υἱὸς ὑποταγήσεται τῷ ὑποτάξαντι αὐτῷ τὰ πάντα. οὐ φοβῇ, ἄνθρωπε, τὸν Θεὸν ἀνυπότακτον ὀνομαζόμενον;	---	---	The citation	it	Both	Citational

	πέπτωκεν	ὡς ἀστραπὴ	manner	---	δυνάμεως	Eventive	Historical
Basil to the Caesareans, Letter 8:21	πέπτωκεν	ὡς ἀστραπὴ	manner	---	δυνάμεως	Eventive	Historical
Basil to the Caesareans, Letter 8:25	γέγραπται	ἐν ἑτέρῳ Εὐαγγελίῳ	Source	The citation	It	Both	Citational
Basil to the Caesareans, Letter 8:27	πεποίηκεν	---	---	τὰ φυσικὰ κριτήρια	Θεός	Eventive	Restates another Aorist

ἀφορῶν εἰς τὴν φύσιν τῆς ἀντικειμένης δυνάμεως, ἥτις ὡς ἀστραπὴ πέπτωκεν ἀπὸ τοῦ οὐρανοῦ, καὶ ἐξέπεσε τῆς ὄντως ζωῆς διὰ τὸ ἐπίκτητον ἐσχηκέναι τὴν ἁγιότητα καὶ ἐπηκολουθηκέναι τῇ κακῇ βουλῇ τὴν ἀλλοίωσιν.

ὅπερ ἐν ἑτέρῳ Εὐαγγελίῳ γέγραπται, τὸ Εἰ ἐγὼ ἐν Πνεύματι Θεοῦ ἐκβάλλω τὰ δαιμόνια, τῆς αὐτῆς φύσεως τῷ Πατρὶ καὶ Υἱῷ τὸ Πνεῦμα τὸ ἅγιον.

Ἅμα δὲ καὶ τοῦτο λεκτέον, ὅτι τὰ φυσικὰ κριτήρια ἀδίδακτα πεποίηκεν ὁ κτίσας ἡμᾶς Θεός.

Appendix M

Chart of Selected Verbs Found in the Perfect Tense-Form within the Pauline Corpus Fully Conjugated

This appendix contains charts of a vast number of verbal forms, including indicative, modal, participial, and infinitival forms, for four of the verbs that Paul uses with a Perfect tense-form. It is as extensive as was possible, taking advantage of diachrony where able to do so. The purpose of this appendix was to create a tool so that a search for commonalities between the Perfects and other tense-forms could be conducted. This appendix is heavily reduced from a much larger database of verbal forms for all of the verbs that Paul uses with a Perfect tense. The data from the larger database was used to analyse the examples in Appendix B, which in turn was narrowed down to report a few examples in this appendix. Of the verbs in this appendix, nine individual forms are selected from each of the four verbs and reported in section 3.2.2.1.1., with an analysis. This report in section 3.2.2.1.1. was a small sample of what was analysed. This report in section 3.2.2.1.1. illustrates in a small way what was seen over the examples in this appendix and in the database. The database is much too large to be included in hard copy version as it is over 2500 pages, so an online version is made available in pdf format at <https://sedlacekj6.wixsite.com/mysite/research-projects-1>.

φανερόω

Active Voice					
Indicative					
	Present	Imperfect	Aorist	Perfect	Future	Pluperfect
1s	φανερῶ	ἐφανέρουν	ἐφανέρωσα	πεφανέρωκα	φανερώσω	ἐπεφανερώκη
2s	φανεροῖς	ἐφανέρους	ἐφανέρωσας	πεφανέρωκας	φανερώσεις	ἐπεφανερώκης
3s	φανεροῖ	ἐφανέρου	ἐφανέρωσε	πεφανέρωκε	φανερώσει	ἐπεφανερώκει
1p	φανεροῦμεν	ἐφανερoῦμεν	ἐφανερώσαμεν	πεφανερώκαμεν	φανερώσομεν	ἐπεφανερώκεμεν
2p	φανεροῦτε	ἐφανεροῦτε	ἐφανερώσατε	πεφανερώκατε	φανερώσετε	ἐπεφανερώκετε
3p	φανεροῦσι	ἐφανέρουν	ἐφανέρωσαν	πεφανερώκασι	φανερώσουσι	ἐπεφανερώκεσαν
2d	φανεροῦτον	ἐφανεροῦτον	ἐφανερώσατον	πεφανερώκατον	φανερώσετον	ἐπεφανερώκειτον
3d	φανεροῦτον	ἐφανερούτην	ἐφανερωσάτην	πεφανερώκατον	φανερώσετον	ἐπεφανερωκείτην
Subjunctive					
1s	φανερῶ	---	φανερώσω	πεφανερώκω	---	---
2s	φανεροῖς	---	φανερώσῃς	πεφανερώκῃς	---	---
3s	φανεροῖ	---	φανερώσῃ	πεφανερώκῃ	---	---
1p	φανερῶμεν	---	φανερώσωμεν	πεφανερώκωμεν	---	---
2p	φανερῶτε	---	φανερώσητε	πεφανερώκητε	---	---
3p	φανερῶσι	---	φανερώσωσι	πεφανερώκωσι	---	---
2d	φανερῶτον	---	φανερώσητον	πεφανερώκητον	---	---
3d	φανερῶτον	---	φανερώσητον	πεφανερώκητον	---	---
Optative					
1s	φανεροῖμι	---	φανερώσαιμι	πεφανερώκοιμι	φανερώσοιμι	---
2s	φανεροῖς	---	φανερώσειας	πεφανερώκοις	φανερώσοις	---
3s	φανεροῖ	---	φανερώσειε	πεφανερώκοι	φανερώσοι	---
1p	φανεροῖμεν	---	φανερώσαιμεν	πεφανερώκοιμεν	φανερώσοιμεν	---
2p	φανεροῖτε	---	φανερώσαιτε	πεφανερώκοιτε	φανερώσοιτε	---
3p	φανεροῖεν	---	φανερώσειαν	πεφανερώκοιεν	φανερώσοιεν	---
2d	φανεροῖτον	---	φανερώσαιτον	πεφανερώκοιτον	φανερώσοιτον	---
3d	φανεροίτην	---	φανερωσαίτην	πεφανερωκοίτην	φανερωσοίτην	---
Imperative					
1s	---	---	---	---	---	---
2s	φανέρου	---	φανέρωσον	πεφανέρωκε	---	---
3s	φανερούτω	---	φανερωσάτω	πεφανερωκέτω	---	---
1p	---	---	---	---	---	---
2p	φανεροῦτε	---	φανερώσατε	πεφανερώκετε	---	---

Active Voice

3p	φανερούτωσαν	---	φανερωσάτωσαν	πεφανερωκέτωσ	---	---
2d	φανερούτον	---	φανερώσατον	πεφανερώκετον	---	---
3d	φανερούτων	---	φανερωσάτων	πεφανερωκέτων	---	---

Middle Voice

Indicative

	Present	Imperfect	Aorist	Perfect	Future	Pluperfect
1s	φανεροῦμαι	ἐφανερούμην	ἐφανερωσάμην	πεφανέρωμαι	φανερώσομαι	ἐπεφανερώμην
2s	φανεροῖ	ἐφανεροῦ	ἐφανερώσω	πεφανέρωσαι	φανερώσει	ἐπεφανέρωσο
3s	φανεροῦται	ἐφανεροῦτο	ἐφανερώσατο	πεφανέρωται	φανερώσεται	ἐπεφανέρωτο
1p	φανερούμεθα	ἐφανερούμεθα	ἐφανερωσάμεθα	πεφανερώμεθα	φανερωσόμεθα	ἐπεφανερώμεθα
2p	φανεροῦσθε	ἐφανεροῦσθε	ἐφανερώσασθε	πεφανέρωσθε	φανερώσεσθε	ἐπεφανέρωσθε
3p	φανεροῦνται	ἐφανεροῦντο	ἐφανερώσαντο	πεφανέρωνται	φανερώσονται	ἐπεφανέρωντο
2d	φανεροῦσθον	ἐφανεροῦσθον	ἐφανερώσασθον	πεφανέρωσθον	φανερώσεσθον	ἐπεφανέρωσθον
3d	φανεροῦσθον	ἐφανερούσθην	ἐφανερωσάσθην	πεφανέρωσθον	φανερώσεσθον	ἐπεφανερώσθην

Subjunctive

1s	φανερῶμαι	---	φανερώσωμαι	---	---	---
2s	φανεροῖ	---	φανερώσῃ	---	---	---
3s	φανερῶται	---	φανερώσηται	---	---	---
1p	φανερώμεθα	---	φανερωσώμεθα	---	---	---
2p	φανερῶσθε	---	φανερώσησθε	---	---	---
3p	φανερῶνται	---	φανερώσαῖντο	---	---	---
2d	φανερῶσθον	---	φανερώσαῖσθον	---	---	---
3d	φανερῶσθον	---	φανερωσαῖσθην	---	---	---

Optative

1s	φανεροίμην	---	φανερωσαίμην	---	φανερωσοίμην	---
2s	φανεροῖο	---	φανερώσαῖο	---	φανερώσοῖο	---
3s	φανεροῖτο	---	φανερώσαῖτο	---	φανερώσοῖτο	---
1p	φανεροίμεθα	---	φανερωσαίμεθα	---	φανερωσοίμεθα	---
2p	φανεροῖσθε	---	φανερώσαῖσθε	---	φανερώσοῖσθε	---
3p	φανεροῖντο	---	φανερώσαῖντο	---	φανερώσοῖντο	---
2d	φανεροῖσθον	---	φανερώσαῖσθον	---	φανερώσοῖσθον	---
3d	φανεροῖσθην	---	φανερωσαῖσθην	---	φανερωσοῖσθην	---

Imperative

1s	---	---	---	---	---	---
2s	φανεροῦ	---	φανέρωσαι	πεφανέρωσο	---	---

Middle Voice						
3s	φανερούσθω	---	φανερωσάσθω	πεφανερώσθω	---	---
1p	---	---	---	---	---	---
2p	φανεροῦσθε	---	φανερώσασθε	πεφανέρωσθε	---	---
3p	φανερούσθωσαν	---	φανερωσάσθωσα	πεφανερώσθωσα	---	---
2d	φανεροῦσθον	---	φανερώσασθον	πεφανέρωσθον	---	---
3d	φανεροῦσθων	---	φανερωσάσθων	πεφανερώσθων	---	---

Passive Voice		
Indicative		
	Aorist	Future
1s	ἐφανερώθην	φανερωθήσομαι
2s	ἐφανερώθης	φανερωθήσει
3s	ἐφανερώθη	φανερωθήσεται
1p	ἐφανερώθημεν	φανερωθησόμεθ
2p	ἐφανερώθητε	φανερωθήσεσθε
3p	ἐφανερώθησαν	φανερωθήσονται
2d	ἐφανερώθητον	φανερωθήσεσθο
3d	ἐφανερωθήτην	φανερωθήσεσθο
Subjunctive		
1s	φανερωθῶ	---
2s	φανερωθῇς	---
3s	φανερωθῇ	---
1p	φανερωθῶμεν	---
2p	φανερωθῆτε	---
3p	φανερωθῶσι	---
2d	φανερωθῆτον	---
3d	φανερωθῆτον	---
Optative		
1s	φανερωθείην	φανερωθησοίμην
2s	φανερωθείης	φανερωθήσοιο
3s	φανερωθείη	φανερωθήσοιτο
1p	φανερωθεῖμεν	φανερωθησοίμεθ
2p	φανερωθεῖτε	φανερωθήσοισθε
3p	φανερωθεῖεν	φανερωθήσοιντο
2d	φανερωθεῖτον	φανερωθήσοισθο
3d	φανερωθείτην	φανερωθησοίσθη

Passive Voice		
Imperative		
1s	---	---
2s	φανερώθητι	---
3s	φανερωθήτω	---
1p	---	---
2p	φανερώθητε	---
3p	φανερωθήτωσαν	---
2d	φανερώθητον	---
3d	φανερωθήτων	---

Infinitive	Present	Aorist	Perfect	Future
Active	φανεροῦν	φανερῶσαι	πεφανερωκέναι	φανερώσειν
Middle	φανεροῦσθαι	φανερώσασθαι	πεφανερῶσθαι	φανερώσεσθαι
Passive	---	φανερωθῆναι	---	φανερωθήσεσθαι

Active Voice Participles				
Masculine				
	Present	Aorist	Perfect	Future
Nom ms	φανερῶν	φανερώσας	πεφανερωκώς	φανερώσων
Voc ms	φανερῶν	φανερῶσαν	πεφανερωκώς	φανερῶσον
Acc ms	φανεροῦντα	φανερώσαντα	πεφανερωκότα	φανερώσοντα
Gen ms	φανεροῦντος	φανερώσαντος	πεφανερωκότος	φανερώσοντος
Dat ms	φανεροῦντι	φανερώσαντι	πεφανερωκότι	φανερώσοντι
Nom mp	φανεροῦντες	φανερώσαντες	πεφανερωκότες	φανερώσοντες
Voc mp	φανεροῦντες	φανερώσαντες	πεφανερωκότες	φανερώσοντες
Acc mp	φανεροῦντας	φανερώσαντας	πεφανερωκότας	φανερώσοντας
Gen mp	φανερούντων	φανερωσάντων	πεφανερωκότων	φανερωσόντων
Dat mp	φανεροῦσι	φανερώσασι	πεφανερωκῶσι	φανερώσουσι
Nom md	φανεροῦντε	φανερώσαντε	πεφανερωκότε	φανερώσοντε
Voc md	φανεροῦντε	φανερώσαντε	πεφανερωκότε	φανερώσοντε
Acc md	φανεροῦντε	φανερώσαντε	πεφανερωκότε	φανερώσοντε
Gen md	φανερούντοῖν	φανερωσάντοῖν	πεφανερωκότοῖν	φανερωσόντοῖν
Dat md	φανερούντοῖν	φανερωσάντοῖν	πεφανερωκότοῖν	φανερωσόντοῖν

Active Voice Participles				
Feminine				
	Present	Aorist	Perfect	Future
Nom fs	φανεροῦσα	φανερώσᾱσα	πεφανερωκυῖα	φανερώσουσα
Voc fs	φανεροῦσα	φανερώσᾱσα	πεφανερωκυῖα	φανερώσουσα
Acc fs	φανεροῦσαν	φανερώσᾱσαν	πεφανερωκυῖαν	φανερώσουσαν
Gen fs	φανερούσης	φανερωσᾱ́σης	πεφανερωκυίᾱς	φανερωσούσης
Dat fs	φανερούσῃ	φανερωσᾱ́σῃ	πεφανερωκυίᾳ	φανερωσούσῃ
Nom fp	φανεροῦσαι	φανερώσᾱσαι	πεφανερωκυῖαι	φανερώσουσαι
Voc fp	φανεροῦσαι	φανερώσᾱσαι	πεφανερωκυῖαι	φανερώσουσαι
Acc fp	φανερούσᾱς	φανερωσᾱ́σᾱς	πεφανερωκυίᾱς	φανερωσούσᾱς
Gen fp	φανερουσῶν	φανερωσᾱσῶν	πεφανερωκυιῶν	φανερωσουσῶν
Dat fp	φανερούσαις	φανερωσᾱ́σαις	πεφανερωκυίαις	φανερωσούσαις
Nom fd	φανερούσᾱ	φανερωσᾱ́σᾱ	πεφανερωκυίᾱ	φανερωσούσᾱ
Voc fd	φανερούσᾱ	φανερωσᾱ́σᾱ	πεφανερωκυίᾱ	φανερωσούσᾱ
Acc fd	φανερούσᾱ	φανερωσᾱ́σᾱ	πεφανερωκυίᾱ	φανερωσούσᾱ
Gen fd	φανερούσαιν	φανερωσᾱ́σαιν	πεφανερωκυίαιν	φανερωσούσαιν
Dat fd	φανερούσαιν	φανερωσᾱ́σαιν	πεφανερωκυίαιν	φανερωσούσαιν
Neuter				
	Present	Aorist	Perfect	Future
Nom ns	φανεροῦν	φανερῶσαν	πεφανερωκόν	φανερῶσον
Voc ns	φανεροῦν	φανερῶσαν	πεφανερωκός	φανερῶσον
Acc ns	φανεροῦν	φανερῶσαν	πεφανερωκότα	φανερῶσον
Gen ns	φανεροῦντος	φανερώσαντος	πεφανερωκότος	φανερώσοντος
Dat ns	φανεροῦντι	φανερώσαντι	πεφανερωκότι	φανερώσοντι
Nom np	φανεροῦντα	φανερώσαντα	πεφανερωκότες	φανερώσοντα
Voc np	φανεροῦντα	φανερώσαντα	πεφανερωκότες	φανερώσοντα
Acc np	φανεροῦντα	φανερώσαντα	πεφανερωκότας	φανερώσοντα
Gen np	φανερούντων	φανερωσάντων	πεφανερωκότων	φανερωσόντων
Dat np	φανεροῦσι	φανερώσᾱσι	πεφανερωκῶσι	φανερώσουσι
Nom nd	φανεροῦντε	φανερώσαντε	πεφανερωκότε	φανερώσοντε
Voc nd	φανεροῦντε	φανερώσαντε	πεφανερωκότε	φανερώσοντε
Acc nd	φανεροῦντε	φανερώσαντε	πεφανερωκότε	φανερώσοντε
Gen nd	φανερούντοιν	φανερωσάντοιν	πεφανερωκότοιν	φανερωσόντοιν
Dat nd	φανερούντοιν	φανερωσάντοιν	πεφανερωκότοιν	φανερωσόντοιν

Middle Voice Participles

Masculine

	Present	Aorist	Perfect	Future
Nom ms	φανερούμενος	φανερωσάμενος	πεφανερωμένος	φανερωσόμενος
Voc ms	φανερούμενε	φανερωσάμενε	πεφανερωμένε	φανερωσόμενε
Acc ms	φανερούμενον	φανερωσάμενον	πεφανερωμένον	φανερωσόμενον
Gen ms	φανερουμένου	φανερωσαμένου	πεφανερωμένου	φανερωσομένου
Dat ms	φανερουμένῳ	φανερωσαμένῳ	πεφανερωμένῳ	φανερωσομένῳ
Nom mp	φανερούμενοι	φανερωσάμενοι	πεφανερωμένοι	φανερωσόμενοι
Voc mp	φανερούμενοι	φανερωσάμενοι	πεφανερωμένοι	φανερωσόμενοι
Acc mp	φανερουμένους	φανερωσαμένους	πεφανερωμένους	φανερωσομένους
Gen mp	φανερουμένων	φανερωσαμένων	πεφανερωμένων	φανερωσομένων
Dat mp	φανερουμένοις	φανερωσαμένοις	πεφανερωμένοις	φανερωσομένοις
Nom md	φανερουμένω	φανερωσαμένω	πεφανερωμένω	φανερωσομένω
Voc md	φανερουμένω	φανερωσαμένω	πεφανερωμένω	φανερωσομένω
Acc md	φανερουμένω	φανερωσαμένω	πεφανερωμένω	φανερωσομένω
Gen md	φανερουμένοῖν	φανερωσαμένοῖν	πεφανερωμένοῖν	φανερωσομένοῖν
Dat md	φανερουμένοῖν	φανερωσαμένοῖν	πεφανερωμένοῖν	φανερωσομένοῖν

Feminine

	Present	Aorist	Perfect	Future
Nom fs	φανερουμένη	φανερωσαμένη	πεφανερωμένη	φανερωσομένη
Voc fs	φανερουμένη	φανερωσαμένη	πεφανερωμένη	φανερωσομένη
Acc fs	φανερουμένην	φανερωσαμένην	πεφανερωμένην	φανερωσομένην
Gen fs	φανερουμένης	φανερωσαμένης	πεφανερωμένης	φανερωσομένης
Dat fs	φανερουμένῃ	φανερωσαμένῃ	πεφανερωμένῃ	φανερωσομένῃ
Nom fp	φανερουμέναι	φανερωσαμέναι	πεφανερωμέναι	φανερωσομέναι
Voc fp	φανερουμέναι	φανερωσαμέναι	πεφανερωμέναι	φανερωσομέναι
Acc fp	φανερουμένᾱς	φανερωσαμένᾱς	πεφανερωμένᾱς	φανερωσομένᾱς
Gen fp	φανερουμενῶν	φανερωσαμενῶν	πεφανερωμενῶν	φανερωσομενῶν
Dat fp	φανερουμέναις	φανερωσαμέναις	πεφανερωμέναις	φανερωσομέναις
Nom fd	φανερουμένᾱ	φανερωσαμένᾱ	πεφανερωμένᾱ	φανερωσομένᾱ
Voc fd	φανερουμένᾱ	φανερωσαμένᾱ	πεφανερωμένᾱ	φανερωσομένᾱ
Acc fd	φανερουμένᾱ	φανερωσαμένᾱ	πεφανερωμένᾱ	φανερωσομένᾱ
Gen fd	φανερουμέναῖν	φανερωσαμέναῖν	πεφανερωμέναῖν	φανερωσομέναῖν
Dat fd	φανερουμέναῖν	φανερωσαμέναῖν	πεφανερωμέναῖν	φανερωσομέναῖν

Middle Voice Participles

Neuter

	Present	Aorist	Perfect	Future
Nom ns	φανερούμενον	φανερωσάμενον	πεφανερωμένον	φανερωσόμενον
Voc ns	φανερούμενον	φανερωσάμενον	πεφανερωμένον	φανερωσόμενον
Acc ns	φανερούμενον	φανερωσάμενον	πεφανερωμένον	φανερωσόμενον
Gen ns	φανερουμένου	φανερωσαμένου	πεφανερωμένου	φανερωσομένου
Dat ns	φανερουμένῳ	φανερωσαμένῳ	πεφανερωμένῳ	φανερωσομένῳ
Nom np	φανερούμενα	φανερωσάμενα	πεφανερωμένα	φανερωσόμενα
Voc np	φανερούμενα	φανερωσάμενα	πεφανερωμένα	φανερωσόμενα
Acc np	φανερούμενα	φανερωσάμενα	πεφανερωμένα	φανερωσόμενα
Gen np	φανερουμένων	φανερωσαμένων	πεφανερωμένων	φανερωσομένων
Dat np	φανερουμένοῖς	φανερωσαμένοῖς	πεφανερωμένοῖς	φανερωσομένοῖς
Nom nd	φανερουμένω	φανερωσαμένω	πεφανερωμένω	φανερωσομένω
Voc nd	φανερουμένω	φανερωσαμένω	πεφανερωμένω	φανερωσομένω
Acc nd	φανερουμένω	φανερωσαμένω	πεφανερωμένω	φανερωσομένω
Gen nd	φανερουμένοῖν	φανερωσαμένοῖν	πεφανερωμένοῖν	φανερωσομένοῖν
Dat nd	φανερουμένοῖν	φανερωσαμένοῖν	πεφανερωμένοῖν	φανερωσομένοῖν

Passive Voice Participles

Masculine

	Aorist	Future
Nom ms	φανερωθείς	φανερωθησόμενος
Voc ms	φανερωθείς	φανερωθησόμενε
Acc ms	φανερωθέντα	φανερωθησόμενον
Gen ms	φανερωθέντος	φανερωθησομένου
Dat ms	φανερωθέντι	φανερωθησομένῳ
Nom mp	φανερωθέντες	φανερωθησόμενοι
Voc mp	φανερωθέντες	φανερωθησόμενοι
Acc mp	φανερωθέντας	φανερωθησομένους
Gen mp	φανερωθέντων	φανερωθησομένων
Dat mp	φανερωθεῖσι	φανερωθησομένοῖς
Nom md	φανερωθέντε	φανερωθησομένω
Voc md	φανερωθέντε	φανερωθησομένω
Acc md	φανερωθέντε	φανερωθησομένω
Gen md	φανερωθέντοῖν	φανερωθησομένοῖν
Dat md	φανερωθέντοῖν	φανερωθησομένοῖν

Passive Voice Participles		
Feminine		
	Aorist	Future
Nom fs	φανερωθεῖσα	φανερωθησομένη
Voc fs	φανερωθεῖσα	φανερωθησομένη
Acc fs	φανερωθεῖσαν	φανερωθησομένην
Gen fs	φανερωθείσης	φανερωθησομένης
Dat fs	φανερωθείσῃ	φανερωθησομένῃ
Nom fp	φανερωθεῖσαι	φανερωθησομέναι
Voc fp	φανερωθεῖσαι	φανερωθησομέναι
Acc fp	φανερωθείσᾱς	φανερωθησομένᾱς
Gen fp	φανερωθεισῶν	φανερωθησομενῶν
Dat fp	φανερωθείσαις	φανερωθησομέναις
Nom fd	φανερωθείσᾱ	φανερωθησομένᾱ
Voc fd	φανερωθείσᾱ	φανερωθησομένᾱ
Acc fd	φανερωθείσᾱ	φανερωθησομένᾱ
Gen fd	φανερωθείσαιν	φανερωθησομέναιν
Dat fd	φανερωθείσαιν	φανερωθησομέναιν
Neuter		
	Aorist	Future
Nom ns	φανερωθέν	φανερωθησόμενον
Voc ns	φανερωθέν	φανερωθησόμενον
Acc ns	φανερωθέν	φανερωθησόμενον
Gen ns	φανερωθέντος	φανερωθησομένου
Dat ns	φανερωθέντι	φανερωθησομένῳ
Nom np	φανερωθέντα	φανερωθησόμενα
Voc np	φανερωθέντα	φανερωθησόμενα
Acc np	φανερωθέντα	φανερωθησόμενα
Gen np	φανερωθέντων	φανερωθησομένων
Dat np	φανερωθεῖσι	φανερωθησομένοις
Nom nd	φανερωθέντε	φανερωθησομένω
Voc nd	φανερωθέντε	φανερωθησομένω
Acc nd	φανερωθέντε	φανερωθησομένω
Gen nd	φανερωθέντοιν	φανερωθησομένοιν
Dat nd	φανερωθέντοιν	φανερωθησομένοιν

εὑρίσκω

Active Voice					
Indicative					
	Present	Imperfect	Aorist	Perfect	Future	Pluperfect
1s	εὑρίσκω	ηὕρισκον	εὗρησα	ηὕρηκα	εὑρήσω	ηὑρήκη
2s	εὑρίσκεις	ηὕρισκες	εὗρησας	ηὕρηκας	εὑρήσεις	ηὑρήκης
3s	εὑρίσκει	ηὕρισκε	εὗρησε	ηὕρηκε	εὑρήσει	ηὑρήκει
1p	εὑρίσκομεν	ηὑρίσκομεν	εὑρήσαμεν	ηὑρήκαμεν	εὑρήσομεν	ηὑρήκεμεν
2p	εὑρίσκετε	ηὑρίσκετε	εὑρήσατε	ηὑρήκατε	εὑρήσετε	ηὑρήκετε
3p	εὑρίσκουσι	ηὕρισκον	εὗρησαν	ηὑρήκασι	εὑρήσουσι	ηὑρήκεσαν
2d	εὑρίσκετον	ηὑρίσκετον	εὑρήσατον	ηὑρήκατον	εὑρήσετον	ηὑρήκειτον
3d	εὑρίσκετον	ηὑρισκέτην	εὑρησάτην	ηὑρήκατον	εὑρήσετον	ηὑρηκείτην
Subjunctive					
1s	εὑρίσκω	---	εὑρήσω	ηὑρήκω	---	---
2s	εὑρίσκῃς	---	εὑρήσῃς	ηὑρήκῃς	---	---
3s	εὑρίσκῃ	---	εὑρήσῃ	ηὑρήκῃ	---	---
1p	εὑρίσκωμεν	---	εὑρήσωμεν	ηὑρήκωμεν	---	---
2p	εὑρίσκητε	---	εὑρήσητε	ηὑρήκητε	---	---
3p	εὑρίσκωσι	---	εὑρήσωσι	ηὑρήκωσι	---	---
2d	εὑρίσκητον	---	εὑρήσητον	ηὑρήκητον	---	---
3d	εὑρίσκητον	---	εὑρήσητον	ηὑρήκητον	---	---
Optative					
1s	εὑρίσκοιμι	---	εὑρήσαιμι	ηὑρήκοιμι	εὑρήσοιμι	---
2s	εὑρίσκοις	---	εὑρήσειας	ηὑρήκοις	εὑρήσοις	---
3s	εὑρίσκοι	---	εὑρήσειε	ηὑρήκοι	εὑρήσοι	---
1p	εὑρίσκοιμεν	---	εὑρήσαιμεν	ηὑρήκοιμεν	εὑρήσοιμεν	---
2p	εὑρίσκοιτε	---	εὑρήσαιτε	ηὑρήκοιτε	εὑρήσοιτε	---
3p	εὑρίσκοιεν	---	εὑρήσειαν	ηὑρήκοιεν	εὑρήσοιεν	---
2d	εὑρίσκοιτον	---	εὑρήσαιτον	ηὑρήκοιτον	εὑρήσοιτον	---
3d	εὑρισκοίτην	---	εὑρησαίτην	ηὑρηκοίτην	εὑρησοίτην	---
Imperative					
1s	---	---	---	---	---	---
2s	εὕρισκε	---	εὗρησον	ηὕρηκε	---	---
3s	εὑρισκέτω	---	εὑρησάτω	ηὑρηκέτω	---	---
1p	---	---	---	---	---	---
2p	εὑρίσκετε	---	εὑρήσατε	ηὑρήκετε	---	---
3p	εὑρισκέτωσαν	---	εὑρησάτωσαν	ηὑρηκέτωσαν	---	---

Active Voice						
2d	εὑρίσκετον	---	εὑρήσατον	ηὑρήκετον	---	---
3d	εὑρισκέτων	---	εὑρησάτων	ηὑρηκέτων	---	---

Additional Active Aorists and Perfects			
Indicative			
	Strong Aorist	Late Imperfect	Late Aorist	Late Strong Aorist
1s	εὗρον	εὕρισκον	εὗρα	ηὗρον
2s	εὗρες	εὕρισκες	εὗρας	ηὗρες
3s	εὗρε	εὕρισκε	εὗρε	ηὗρε
1p	εὕρομεν	εὑρίσκομεν	εὕραμεν	ηὕρομεν
2p	εὕρετε	εὑρίσκετε	εὕρατε	ηὕρετε
3p	εὗρον	εὕρισκον	εὗραν	ηὗρον
2d	εὕρετον	εὑρίσκετον	εὕρατον	ηὕρετον
3d	εὑρέτην	εὑρισκέτην	εὑράτην	ηὑρέτην
Subjunctive			
1s	εὕρω	---	εὕρω	---
2s	εὕρῃς	---	εὕρῃς	---
3s	εὕρῃ	---	εὕρῃ	---
1p	εὕρωμεν	---	εὕρωμεν	---
2p	εὕρητε	---	εὕρητε	---
3p	εὕρωσι	---	εὕρωσι	---
2d	εὕρητον	---	εὕρητον	---
3d	εὕρητον	---	εὕρητον	---
Optative			
1s	εὕροιμι	---	εὕραιμι	---
2s	εὕροις	---	εὕρειας	---
3s	εὕροι	---	εὕρειε	---
1p	εὕροιμεν	---	εὕραιμεν	---
2p	εὕροιτε	---	εὕραιτε	---
3p	εὕροιεν	---	εὕρειαν	---
2d	εὕροιτον	---	εὕραιτον	---
3d	εὑροίτην	---	εὑραίτην	---
Imperative			
1s	---	---	---	---
2s	εὗρε	---	εὗρον	---
3s	εὑρέτω	---	εὑράτω	---

Additional Active Aorists and Perfects			
1p	---	---	---	---
2p	εὕρετε	---	εὕρατε	---
3p	εὑρέτωσαν	---	εὑράτωσαν	---
2d	εὕρετον	---	εὕρατον	---
3d	εὑρέτων	---	εὑράτων	---

Middle Voice

Indicative

	Present	Imperfect	Aorist	Perfect	Future	Pluperfect
1s	ηὑρίσκομαι	ηὑρισκόμην	εὑρησάμην	ηὕρημαι	εὑρήσομαι	ηὑρήμην
2s	ηὑρίσκει	ηὑρίσκου	εὑρήσω	ηὕρησαι	εὑρήσει	ηὕρησο
3s	ηὑρίσκεται	ηὑρίσκετο	εὑρήσατο	ηὕρηται	εὑρήσεται	ηὕρητο
1p	ηὑρισκόμεθα	ηὑρισκόμεθα	εὑρησάμεθα	ηὑρήμεθα	εὑρησόμεθα	ηὑρήμεθα
2p	ηὑρίσκεσθε	ηὑρίσκεσθε	εὑρήσασθε	ηὕρησθε	εὑρήσεσθε	ηὕρησθε
3p	ηὑρίσκονται	ηὑρίσκοντο	εὑρήσαντο	ηὕρηνται	εὑρήσονται	ηὕρηντο
2d	ηὑρίσκεσθον	ηὑρίσκεσθον	εὑρήσασθον	ηὕρησθον	εὑρήσεσθον	ηὕρησθον
3d	ηὑρίσκεσθον	ηὑρισκέσθην	εὑρησάσθην	ηὕρησθον	εὑρήσεσθον	ηὑρήσθην

Subjunctive

1s	εὑρίσκωμαι	---	εὑρήσωμαι	---	---	---
2s	εὑρίσκῃ	---	εὑρήσῃ	---	---	---
3s	εὑρίσκηται	---	εὑρήσηται	---	---	---
1p	εὑρισκώμεθα	---	εὑρησώμεθα	---	---	---
2p	εὑρίσκησθε	---	εὑρήσησθε	---	---	---
3p	εὑρίσκωνται	---	εὑρήσωνται	---	---	---
2d	εὑρίσκησθον	---	εὑρήσησθον	---	---	---
3d	εὑρίσκησθον	---	εὑρήσησθον	---	---	---

Optative

1s	εὑρισκοίμην	---	εὑρησαίμην	---	εὑρησοίμην	---
2s	εὑρίσκοιο	---	εὑρήσαιο	---	εὑρήσοιο	---
3s	εὑρίσκοιτο	---	εὑρήσαιτο	---	εὑρήσοιτο	---
1p	εὑρισκοίμεθα	---	εὑρησαίμεθα	---	εὑρησοίμεθα	---
2p	εὑρίσκοισθε	---	εὑρήσαισθε	---	εὑρήσοισθε	---
3p	εὑρίσκοιντο	---	εὑρήσαιντο	---	εὑρήσοιντο	---
2d	εὑρίσκοισθον	---	εὑρήσαισθον	---	εὑρήσοισθον	---
3d	εὑρισκοίσθην	---	εὑρησαίσθην	---	εὑρησοίσθην	---

Imperative

Middle Voice					
1s	---	---	---	---	---	---
2s	εὑρίσκου	---	εὕρησαι	ηὕρησο	---	---
3s	εὑρισκέσθω	---	εὑρησάσθω	ηὑρήσθω	---	---
1p	---	---	---	---	---	---
2p	εὑρίσκεσθε	---	εὑρήσασθε	ηὕρησθε	---	---
3p	εὑρισκέσθωσαν	---	εὑρησάσθωσαν	ηὑρήσθωσαν	---	---
2d	εὑρίσκεσθον	---	εὑρήσασθον	ηὕρησθον	---	---
3d	εὑρισκέσθων	---	εὑρησάσθων	ηὑρήσθων	---	---

Additional Middle Aorists and Perfects				
Indicative				
	Strong Aorist	Later Imperfect	Later Aorist	Later Strong Aorist
1s	εὑρόμην	εὑρισκόμην	εὑράμην	ηὑρόμην
2s	εὕρου	εὑρίσκου	εὕρω	ηὕρου
3s	εὕρετο	εὑρίσκετο	εὕρατο	ηὕρετο
1p	εὑρόμεθα	εὑρισκόμεθα	εὑράμεθα	ηὑρόμεθα
2p	εὕρεσθε	εὑρίσκεσθε	εὕρασθε	ηὕρεσθε
3p	εὕροντο	εὑρίσκοντο	εὕραντο	ηὕροντο
2d	εὕρεσθον	εὑρίσκεσθον	εὕρασθον	ηὕρεσθον
3d	εὑρέσθην	εὑρισκέσθην	εὑράσθην	ηὑρέσθην
Subjunctive				
1s	εὕρωμαι	---	εὕρωμαι	---
2s	εὕρῃ	---	εὕρῃ	---
3s	εὕρηται	---	εὕρηται	---
1p	εὑρώμεθα	---	εὑρώμεθα	---
2p	εὕρησθε	---	εὕρησθε	---
3p	εὕρωνται	---	εὕρωνται	---
2d	εὕρησθον	---	εὕρησθον	---
3d	εὕρησθον	---	εὕρησθον	---
Optative				
1s	εὑροίμην	---	εὑραίμην	---
2s	εὕροιο	---	εὕραιο	---
3s	εὕροιτο	---	εὕραιτο	---
1p	εὑροίμεθα	---	εὑραίμεθα	---
2p	εὕροισθε	---	εὕραισθε	---
3p	εὕροιντο	---	εὕραιντο	---

Additional Middle Aorists and Perfects						
2d	εὑροῖσθον	---	εὑραῖσθον	---
3d	εὑροίσθην	---	εὑραίσθην	---
Imperative				
1s	---	---	---	---
2s	εὑροῦ	---	εὕραι	---
3s	εὑρέσθω	---	εὑράσθω	---
1p	---	---	---	---
2p	εὕρεσθε	---	εὕρασθε	---
3p	εὑρέσθωσαν	---	εὑράσθωσαν	---
2d	εὕρεσθον	---	εὕρασθον	---
3d	εὑρέσθων	---	εὑράσθων	---

Passive Voice			
Indicative			
	Aorist	Future	Strong Aorist
1s	ηὑρέθην	εὑρεθήσομαι	εὑρέθην
2s	ηὑρέθης	εὑρεθήσει	εὑρέθης
3s	ηὑρέθη	εὑρεθήσεται	εὑρέθη
1p	ηὑρέθημεν	εὑρεθησόμεθα	εὑρέθημεν
2p	ηὑρέθητε	εὑρεθήσεσθε	εὑρέθητε
3p	ηὑρέθησαν	εὑρεθήσονται	εὑρέθησαν
2d	ηὑρέθητον	εὑρεθήσεσθον	εὑρέθητον
3d	ηὑρεθήτην	εὑρεθήσεσθον	εὑρεθήτην

Infinitive					
	Present	Imperfect	Aorist	Perfect	Future
Active	εὑρίσκειν	---	εὑρῆσαι	ηὑρηκέναι	εὑρήσειν
Middle	εὑρίσκεσθαι	---	εὑρήσασθαι	ηὑρῆσθαι	εὑρήσεσθαι
Passive	---	---	εὑρεθῆναι	---	εὑρεθήσεσθαι

Alternate Infinitive forms				
	Present	Imperfect	Aorist	Later Aorist
Active	---	---	εὑρεῖν	εὗραι
Middle	---	---	εὑρέσθαι	εὕρασθαι
Passive	---	---	---	---

Active Voice Participles

Masculine

	Present	Aorist	Perfect	Future	Strong Aorist	Later Aorist
Nom ms	εὑρίσκων	εὑρήσᾱς	ηὑρηκώς	εὑρήσων	εὑρών	εὕρᾱς
Voc ms	εὑρίσκον	εὑρήσαν	ηὑρηκώς	εὑρήσον	εὑρών	εὗραν
Acc ms	εὑρίσκοντα	εὑρήσαντα	ηὑρηκότα	εὑρήσοντα	εὑρόντα	εὕραντα
Gen ms	εὑρίσκοντος	εὑρήσαντος	ηὑρηκότος	εὑρήσοντος	εὑρόντος	εὕραντος
Dat ms	εὑρίσκοντι	εὑρήσαντι	ηὑρηκότι	εὑρήσοντι	εὑρόντι	εὕραντι
Nom mp	εὑρίσκοντες	εὑρήσαντες	ηὑρηκότες	εὑρήσοντες	εὑρόντες	εὕραντες
Voc mp	εὑρίσκοντες	εὑρήσαντες	ηὑρηκότες	εὑρήσοντες	εὑρόντες	εὕραντες
Acc mp	εὑρίσκοντας	εὑρήσαντας	ηὑρηκότας	εὑρήσοντας	εὑρόντας	εὕραντας
Gen mp	εὑρισκόντων	εὑρησάντων	ηὑρηκότων	εὑρησόντων	εὑρόντων	εὑράντων
Dat mp	εὑρίσκουσι	εὑρήσᾱσι	ηὑρηκῶσι	εὑρήσουσι	εὑροῦσι	εὕρᾱσι
Nom md	εὑρίσκοντε	εὑρήσαντε	ηὑρηκότε	εὑρήσοντε	εὑρόντε	εὕραντε
Voc md	εὑρίσκοντε	εὑρήσαντε	ηὑρηκότε	εὑρήσοντε	εὑρόντε	εὕραντε
Acc md	εὑρίσκοντε	εὑρήσαντε	ηὑρηκότε	εὑρήσοντε	εὑρόντε	εὕραντε
Gen md	εὑρισκόντοῖν	εὑρησάντοῖν	ηὑρηκότοῖν	εὑρησόντοῖν	εὑρόντοῖν	εὑράντοῖν
Dat md	εὑρισκόντοῖν	εὑρησάντοῖν	ηὑρηκότοῖν	εὑρησόντοῖν	εὑρόντοῖν	εὑράντοῖν

Feminine

	Present	Aorist	Perfect	Future	Strong Aorist	Later Aorist
Nom fs	εὑρίσκουσα	εὑρήσᾱσα	ηὑρηκυῖα	εὑρήσουσα	εὑροῦσα	εὕρᾱσα
Voc fs	εὑρίσκουσα	εὑρήσᾱσα	ηὑρηκυῖα	εὑρήσουσα	εὑροῦσα	εὕρᾱσα
Acc fs	εὑρίσκουσαν	εὑρήσᾱσαν	ηὑρηκυῖαν	εὑρήσουσαν	εὑροῦσαν	εὕρᾱσαν
Gen fs	εὑρισκούσης	εὑρησᾱσης	ηὑρηκυίᾱς	εὑρησούσης	εὑρούσης	εὑρᾱσης
Dat fs	εὑρισκούσῃ	εὑρησᾱσῃ	ηὑρηκυίᾳ	εὑρησούσῃ	εὑρούσῃ	εὑρᾱσῃ
Nom fp	εὑρίσκουσαι	εὑρήσᾱσαι	ηὑρηκυῖαι	εὑρήσουσαι	εὑροῦσαι	εὕρᾱσαι
Voc fp	εὑρίσκουσαι	εὑρήσᾱσαι	ηὑρηκυῖαι	εὑρήσουσαι	εὑροῦσαι	εὕρᾱσαι
Acc fp	εὑρισκούσᾱς	εὑρησᾱσᾱς	ηὑρηκυίᾱς	εὑρησούσᾱς	εὑρούσᾱς	εὑρᾱσᾱς
Gen fp	εὑρισκουσῶν	εὑρησᾱσῶν	ηὑρηκυιῶν	εὑρησουσῶν	εὑρουσῶν	εὑρᾱσῶν

Active Voice Participles

Dat fp	εὑρισκούσαις	εὑρησάσαις	ηὑρηκυίαις	εὑρησούσαις	εὑρούσαις	εὑράσαις
Nom fd	εὑρισκούσᾱ	εὑρησάσᾱ	ηὑρηκυίᾱ	εὑρησούσᾱ	εὑρούσᾱ	εὑράσᾱ
Voc fd	εὑρισκούσᾱ	εὑρησάσᾱ	ηὑρηκυίᾱ	εὑρησούσᾱ	εὑρούσᾱ	εὑράσᾱ
Acc fd	εὑρισκούσᾱ	εὑρησάσᾱ	ηὑρηκυίᾱ	εὑρησούσᾱ	εὑρούσᾱ	εὑράσᾱ
Gen fd	εὑρισκούσαῖν	εὑρησάσαῖν	ηὑρηκυίαῖν	εὑρησούσαῖν	εὑρούσαῖν	εὑράσαῖν
Dat fd	εὑρισκούσαῖν	εὑρησάσαῖν	ηὑρηκυίαῖν	εὑρησούσαῖν	εὑρούσαῖν	εὑράσαῖν

Neuter

	Present	Aorist	Perfect	Future	Strong Aorist	Later Aorist
Nom ns	εὑρίσκον	εὕρησαν	ηὕρηκός	εὑρῆσον	εὑρόν	εὗραν
Voc ns	εὑρίσκον	εὕρησαν	ηὕρηκός	εὑρῆσον	εὑρόν	εὗραν
Acc ns	εὑρίσκον	εὕρησαν	ηὕρηκός	εὑρῆσον	εὑρόν	εὗραν
Gen ns	εὑρίσκοντος	εὑρήσαντος	ηὑρηκότος	εὑρήσοντος	εὑρόντος	εὗραντος
Dat ns	εὑρίσκοντι	εὑρήσαντι	ηὑρηκότι	εὑρήσοντι	εὑρόντι	εὗραντι
Nom np	εὑρίσκοντα	εὑρήσαντα	ηὑρηκότα	εὑρήσοντα	εὑρόντα	εὗραντα
Voc np	εὑρίσκοντα	εὑρήσαντα	ηὑρηκότα	εὑρήσοντα	εὑρόντα	εὗραντα
Acc np	εὑρίσκοντα	εὑρήσαντα	ηὑρηκότα	εὑρήσοντα	εὑρόντα	εὗραντα
Gen np	εὑρισκόντων	εὑρησάντων	ηὑρηκότων	εὑρησόντων	εὑρόντων	εὑράντων
Dat np	εὑρίσκουσι	εὑρήσᾱσι	ηὑρηκῶσι	εὑρήσουσι	εὑροῦσι	εὑρᾱσι
Nom nd	εὑρίσκοντε	εὑρήσαντε	ηὑρηκότε	εὑρήσοντε	εὑρόντε	εὗραντε
Voc nd	εὑρίσκοντε	εὑρήσαντε	ηὑρηκότε	εὑρήσοντε	εὑρόντε	εὗραντε
Acc nd	εὑρίσκοντε	εὑρήσαντε	ηὑρηκότε	εὑρήσοντε	εὑρόντε	εὗραντε
Gen nd	εὑρισκόντοῖν	εὑρησάντοῖν	ηὑρηκότοῖν	εὑρησόντοῖν	εὑρόντοῖν	εὑράντοῖν
Dat nd	εὑρισκόντοῖν	εὑρησάντοῖν	ηὑρηκότοῖν	εὑρησόντοῖν	εὑρόντοῖν	εὑράντοῖν

Middle Voice Participles

Masculine

	Present	Aorist	Perfect	Future	Strong Aorist	Later Aorist
Nom ms	εὑρισκόμενος	εὑρησάμενος	ηὑρημένος	εὑρησόμενος	εὑρόμενος	εὑράμενος
Voc ms	εὑρισκόμενε	εὑρησάμενε	ηὑρημένε	εὑρησόμενε	εὑρόμενε	εὑράμενε
Acc ms	εὑρισκόμενον	εὑρησάμενον	ηὑρημένον	εὑρησόμενον	εὑρόμενον	εὑράμενον
Gen ms	εὑρισκομένου	εὑρησαμένου	ηὑρημένου	εὑρησομένου	εὑρομένου	εὑραμένου
Dat ms	εὑρισκομένῳ	εὑρησαμένῳ	ηὑρημένῳ	εὑρησομένῳ	εὑρομένῳ	εὑραμένῳ
Nom mp	εὑρισκόμενοι	εὑρησάμενοι	ηὑρημένοι	εὑρησόμενοι	εὑρόμενοι	εὑράμενοι
Voc mp	εὑρισκόμενοι	εὑρησάμενοι	ηὑρημένοι	εὑρησόμενοι	εὑρόμενοι	εὑράμενοι

Middle Voice Participles

Acc mp	εὑρισκομένους	εὑρησαμένους	ᾑρημένους	εὑρησομένους	εὑρομένους	εὑραμένους
Gen mp	εὑρισκομένων	εὑρησαμένων	ᾑρημένων	εὑρησομένων	εὑρομένων	εὑραμένων
Dat mp	εὑρισκομένοις	εὑρησαμένοις	ᾑρημένοις	εὑρησομένοις	εὑρομένοις	εὑραμένοις
Nom md	εὑρισκομένω	εὑρησαμένω	ᾑρημένω	εὑρησομένω	εὑρομένω	εὑραμένω
Voc md	εὑρισκομένω	εὑρησαμένω	ᾑρημένω	εὑρησομένω	εὑρομένω	εὑραμένω
Acc md	εὑρισκομένω	εὑρησαμένω	ᾑρημένω	εὑρησομένω	εὑρομένω	εὑραμένω
Gen md	εὑρισκομένοῖν	εὑρησαμένοῖν	ᾑρημένοῖν	εὑρησομένοῖν	εὑρομένοῖν	εὑραμένοῖν
Dat md	εὑρισκομένοῖν	εὑρησαμένοῖν	ᾑρημένοῖν	εὑρησομένοῖν	εὑρομένοῖν	εὑραμένοῖν

Feminine

	Present	Aorist	Perfect	Future	Strong Aorist	Later Aorist
Nom fs	εὑρισκομένη	εὑρησαμένη	ᾑρημένη	εὑρησομένη	εὑρομένη	εὑραμένη
Voc fs	εὑρισκομένη	εὑρησαμένη	ᾑρημένη	εὑρησομένη	εὑρομένη	εὑραμένη
Acc fs	εὑρισκομένην	εὑρησαμένην	ᾑρημένην	εὑρησομένην	εὑρομένην	εὑραμένην
Gen fs	εὑρισκομένης	εὑρησαμένης	ᾑρημένης	εὑρησομένης	εὑρομένης	εὑραμένης
Dat fs	εὑρισκομένη	εὑρησαμένη	ᾑρημένη	εὑρησομένη	εὑρομένη	εὑραμένη
Nom fp	εὑρισκομέναι	εὑρησαμέναι	ᾑρημέναι	εὑρησομέναι	εὑρομέναι	εὑραμέναι
Voc fp	εὑρισκομέναι	εὑρησαμέναι	ᾑρημέναι	εὑρησομέναι	εὑρομέναι	εὑραμέναι
Acc fp	εὑρισκομένᾱς	εὑρησαμένᾱς	ᾑρημένᾱς	εὑρησομένᾱς	εὑρομένᾱς	εὑραμένᾱς
Gen fp	εὑρισκομενῶν	εὑρησαμενῶν	ᾑρημενῶν	εὑρησομενῶν	εὑρομενῶν	εὑραμενῶν
Dat fp	εὑρισκομέναις	εὑρησαμέναις	ᾑρημέναις	εὑρησομέναις	εὑρομέναις	εὑραμέναις
Nom fd	εὑρισκομένᾱ	εὑρησαμένᾱ	ᾑρημένᾱ	εὑρησομένᾱ	εὑρομένᾱ	εὑραμένᾱ
Voc fd	εὑρισκομένᾱ	εὑρησαμένᾱ	ᾑρημένᾱ	εὑρησομένᾱ	εὑρομένᾱ	εὑραμένᾱ
Acc fd	εὑρισκομένᾱ	εὑρησαμένᾱ	ᾑρημένᾱ	εὑρησομένᾱ	εὑρομένᾱ	εὑραμένᾱ
Gen fd	εὑρισκομέναῖν	εὑρησαμέναῖν	ᾑρημέναῖν	εὑρησομέναῖν	εὑρομέναῖν	εὑραμέναῖν
Dat fd	εὑρισκομέναῖν	εὑρησαμέναῖν	ᾑρημέναῖν	εὑρησομέναῖν	εὑρομέναῖν	εὑραμέναῖν

Neuter

	Present	Aorist	Perfect	Future	Strong Aorist	Later Aorist
Nom ns	εὑρισκόμενον	εὑρησάμενον	ᾑρημένον	εὑρησόμενον	εὑρόμενον	εὑράμενον
Voc ns	εὑρισκόμενον	εὑρησάμενον	ᾑρημένον	εὑρησόμενον	εὑρόμενον	εὑράμενον
Acc ns	εὑρισκόμενον	εὑρησάμενον	ᾑρημένον	εὑρησόμενον	εὑρόμενον	εὑράμενον
Gen ns	εὑρισκομένου	εὑρησαμένου	ᾑρημένου	εὑρησομένου	εὑρομένου	εὑραμένου
Dat ns	εὑρισκομένῳ	εὑρησαμένῳ	ᾑρημένῳ	εὑρησομένῳ	εὑρομένῳ	εὑραμένῳ
Nom np	εὑρισκόμενα	εὑρησάμενα	ᾑρημένα	εὑρησόμενα	εὑρόμενα	εὑράμενα
Voc np	εὑρισκόμενα	εὑρησάμενα	ᾑρημένα	εὑρησόμενα	εὑρόμενα	εὑράμενα
Acc np	εὑρισκόμενα	εὑρησάμενα	ᾑρημένα	εὑρησόμενα	εὑρόμενα	εὑράμενα

Middle Voice Participles						
Gen np	εὑρισκομένων	εὑρησαμένων	ηὑρημένων	εὑρησομένων	εὑρομένων	εὑραμένων
Dat np	εὑρισκομένοις	εὑρησαμένοις	ηὑρημένοις	εὑρησομένοις	εὑρομένοις	εὑραμένοις
Nom nd	εὑρισκομένω	εὑρησαμένω	ηὑρημένω	εὑρησομένω	εὑρομένω	εὑραμένω
Voc nd	εὑρισκομένω	εὑρησαμένω	ηὑρημένω	εὑρησομένω	εὑρομένω	εὑραμένω
Acc nd	εὑρισκομένω	εὑρησαμένω	ηὑρημένω	εὑρησομένω	εὑρομένω	εὑραμένω
Gen nd	εὑρισκομένοιν	εὑρησαμένοιν	ηὑρημένοιν	εὑρησομένοιν	εὑρομένοιν	εὑραμένοιν
Dat nd	εὑρισκομένοιν	εὑρησαμένοιν	ηὑρημένοιν	εὑρησομένοιν	εὑρομένοιν	εὑραμένοιν

Passive Voice Participles		
Masculine		
	Aorist	Future
Nom ms	εὑρεθείς	εὑρεθησόμενος
Voc ms	εὑρεθείς	εὑρεθησόμενε
Acc ms	εὑρεθέντα	εὑρεθησόμενον
Gen ms	εὑρεθέντος	εὑρεθησομένου
Dat ms	εὑρεθέντι	εὑρεθησομένῳ
Nom mp	εὑρεθέντες	εὑρεθησόμενοι
Voc mp	εὑρεθέντες	εὑρεθησόμενοι
Acc mp	εὑρεθέντας	εὑρεθησομένους
Gen mp	εὑρεθέντων	εὑρεθησομένοις
Dat mp	εὑρεθεῖσι	εὑρεθησομένοις
Nom md	εὑρεθέντε	εὑρεθησομένω
Voc md	εὑρεθέντε	εὑρεθησομένω
Acc md	εὑρεθέντε	εὑρεθησομένω
Gen md	εὑρεθέντοιν	εὑρεθησομένοιν
Dat md	εὑρεθέντοιν	εὑρεθησομένοιν
Feminine		
	Aorist	Future
Nom fs	εὑρεθεῖσα	εὑρεθησομένη
Voc fs	εὑρεθεῖσα	εὑρεθησομένη
Acc fs	εὑρεθεῖσαν	εὑρεθησομένην
Gen fs	εὑρεθείσης	εὑρεθησομένης
Dat fs	εὑρεθείσῃ	εὑρεθησομένη
Nom fp	εὑρεθεῖσαι	εὑρεθησομέναι
Voc fp	εὑρεθεῖσαι	εὑρεθησομέναι
Acc fp	εὑρεθείσᾱς	εὑρεθησομένᾱς

Passive Voice Participles		
Gen fp	εὑρεθεισῶν	εὑρεθησομενῶν
Dat fp	εὑρεθείσαις	εὑρεθησομέναις
Nom fd	εὑρεθείσᾱ	εὑρεθησομένᾱ
Voc fd	εὑρεθείσᾱ	εὑρεθησομένᾱ
Acc fd	εὑρεθείσᾱ	εὑρεθησομένᾱ
Gen fd	εὑρεθείσαῖν	εὑρεθησομέναῖν
Dat fd	εὑρεθείσαῖν	εὑρεθησομέναῖν
Neuter		
	Aorist	Future
Nom ns	εὑρεθέν	εὑρεθησόμενον
Voc ns	εὑρεθέν	εὑρεθησόμενον
Acc ns	εὑρεθέν	εὑρεθησόμενον
Gen ns	εὑρεθέντος	εὑρεθησομένου
Dat ns	εὑρεθέντι	εὑρεθησομένῳ
Nom np	εὑρεθέντα	εὑρεθησόμενα
Voc np	εὑρεθέντα	εὑρεθησόμενα
Acc np	εὑρεθέντα	εὑρεθησόμενα
Gen np	εὑρεθέντων	εὑρεθησομένων
Dat np	εὑρεθεῖσι	εὑρεθησομένοις
Nom nd	εὑρεθέντε	εὑρεθησομένω
Voc nd	εὑρεθέντε	εὑρεθησομένω
Acc nd	εὑρεθέντε	εὑρεθησομένω
Gen nd	εὑρεθέντοῖν	εὑρεθησομένοῖν
Dat nd	εὑρεθέντοῖν	εὑρεθησομένοῖν

ἵστημι

Active Voice						
Indicative						
	Present	Imperfect	Aorist	Perfect	Future	Pluperfect
1s	ἵστημι	ἵστην	ἔστησα	ἕστηκα	στήσω	ἑστήκη
2s	ἵστης	ἵστης	ἔστησας	ἕστηκας	στήσεις	ἑστήκης
3s	ἵστησι	ἵστη	ἔστησε	ἕστηκε	στήσει	ἑστήκει
1p	ἵσταμεν	ἵσταμεν	ἐστήσαμεν	ἑστήκαμεν	στήσομεν	ἑστήκεμεν
2p	ἵστατε	ἵστατε	ἐστήσατε	ἑστήκατε	στήσετε	ἑστήκετε
3p	ἱστᾶσι	ἵστασαν	ἔστησαν	ἑστήκασι	στήσουσι	ἑστήκεσαν

Active Voice					
2d	ἵστατον	ἵστατον	ἐστήσατον	ἐστήκατον	στήσετον	ἐστήκειτον
3d	ἵστατον	ἱστάτην	ἐστησάτην	ἐστήκατον	στήσετον	ἐστηκείτην

Subjunctive					
1s	ἱστάω	---	στήσω	ἐστήκω	---	---
2s	ἱστάῃς	---	στήσῃς	ἐστήκῃς	---	---
3s	ἱστάῃ	---	στήσῃ	ἐστήκῃ	---	---
1p	ἱστάωμεν	---	στήσωμεν	ἐστήκωμεν	---	---
2p	ἱστάητε	---	στήσητε	ἐστήκητε	---	---
3p	ἱστάωσι	---	στήσωσι	ἐστήκωσι	---	---
2d	ἵστατον	---	στήσητον	ἐστήκητον	---	---
3d	ἵστατον	---	στήσητον	ἐστήκητον	---	---

Optative					
1s	ἱστάοιμι	---	στήσαιμι	ἐστήκοιμι	στήσοιμι	---
2s	ἱστάοις	---	στήσειας	ἐστήκοις	στήσοις	---
3s	ἱστάοι	---	στήσειε	ἐστήκοι	στήσοι	---
1p	ἱστάοιμεν	---	στήσαιμεν	ἐστήκοιμεν	στήσοιμεν	---
2p	ἱστάοιτε	---	στήσαιτε	ἐστήκοιτε	στήσοιτε	---
3p	ἱστάοιεν	---	στήσειαν	ἐστήκοιεν	στήσοιεν	---
2d	ἱστάοιθον	---	στήσαιτον	ἐστήκοιτον	στήσοιτον	---
3d	ἱσταοίθην	---	στησαίτην	ἐστηκοίτην	στησοίτην	---

Imperative					
1s	---	---	---	---	---	---
2s	ἵστη	---	στῆσον	ἔστηκε	---	---
3s	ἱστάτω	---	στησάτω	ἐστηκέτω	---	---
1p	---	---	---	---	---	---
2p	ἵστατε	---	στήσατε	ἐστήκετε	---	---
3p	ἱστάτωσαν	---	στησάτωσαν	ἐστηκέτωσαν	---	---
2d	ἵστατον	---	στήσατον	ἐστήκετον	---	---
3d	ἱστάτων	---	στησάτων	ἐστηκέτων	---	---

Additional Active Aorists and Perfects		
Indicative		
	Strong Aorist	Alternate Perfect	Strong Perfect
1s	ἔστην	---	---
2s	ἔστης	---	---
3s	ἔστη	---	---

Additional Active Aorists and Perfects		
1p	ἔστημεν	---	ἕσταμεν
2p	ἔστητε	---	ἕστατε
3p	ἔστησαν	---	ἑστᾶσι
2d	ἔστητον	---	ἕστατον
3d	ἐστήτην	---	ἕστατον
Subjunctive		
1s	στῶ	---	---
2s	στῇς	---	---
3s	στῇ	---	---
1p	στῶμεν	---	ἑστῶμεν
2p	στῆτε	---	---
3p	στῶσι	---	ἑστῶσι
2d	στῆτον	---	---
3d	στῆτον	---	---
Optative		
1s	σταίημι	---	ἑσταίην
2s	σταίης	---	---
3s	σταίη	---	---
1p	σταίημεν	---	---
2p	σταίητε	---	---
3p	σταίην	---	---
2d	σταίηθον	---	---
3d	σταιήθην	---	---
Imperative		
1s	---	---	
2s	στη	ἕστασο	ἕσταθι
3s	στήτω	ἑστάσθω	ἑστάτω
1p	---	---	
2p	στῆτε	ἕστασθε	
3p	στήτωσαν	ἑστάσθωσαν	
2d	στῆτον	ἕστασθον	
3d	στήτων	ἑστάσθων	

Middle Voice

Indicative

	Present	Imperfect	Aorist	Perfect	Future	Pluperfect
1s	ἵσταμαι	ἱστάμην	ἐστησάμην	ἕστημαι	στήσομαι	ἑστήμην
2s	ἵστασαι	ἵστασο	ἐστήσω	ἕστησαι	στήσει	ἕστησο
3s	ἵσταται	ἵστατο	ἐστήσατο	ἕστηται	στήσεται	ἕστητο
1p	ἱστάμεθα	ἱστάμεθα	ἐστησάμεθα	ἑστήμεθα	στησόμεθα	ἑστήμεθα
2p	ἵστασθε	ἵστασθε	ἐστήσασθε	ἕστησθε	στήσεσθε	ἕστησθε
3p	ἵστανται	ἵσταντο	ἐστήσαντο	ἕστηνται	στήσονται	ἕστηντο
2d	ἵστασθον	ἵστασθον	ἐστήσασθον	ἕστησθον	στήσεσθον	ἕστησθον
3d	ἵστασθον	ἱστάσθην	ἐστησάσθην	ἕστησθον	στήσεσθον	ἑστήσθην

Subjunctive

1s	ἱστάωμαι	---	στήσωμαι	---	---	---
2s	ἱστάῃ	---	στήσῃ	---	---	---
3s	ἱστάηται	---	στήσηται	---	---	---
1p	ἱσταώμεθα	---	στησώμεθα	---	---	---
2p	ἱστάησθε	---	στήσησθε	---	---	---
3p	ἱστάωνται	---	στήσωνται	---	---	---
2d	ἵστασθον	---	στήσησθον	---	---	---
3d	ἵστασθον	---	στήσησθον	---	---	---

Optative

1s	ἱσταοίμην	---	στησαίμην	---	στησοίμην	---
2s	ἱστάοιο	---	στήσαιο	---	στήσοιο	---
3s	ἱστάοιτο	---	στήσαιτο	---	στήσοιτο	---
1p	ἱσταοίμεθα	---	στησαίμεθα	---	στησοίμεθα	---
2p	ἱστάοισθε	---	στήσαισθε	---	στήσοισθε	---
3p	ἱστάοιντο	---	στήσαιντο	---	στήσοιντο	---
2d	ἱστάοισθον	---	στήσαισθον	---	στήσοισθον	---
3d	ἱσταοίσθην	---	στησαίσθην	---	στησοίσθην	---

Imperative

1s	---	---	---	---	---	---
2s	ἵστασο	---	στῆσαι	ἕστησο	---	---
3s	ἱστάσθω	---	στησάσθω	ἑστήσθω	---	---
1p	---	---	---	---	---	---
2p	ἵστασθε	---	στήσασθε	ἕστησθε	---	---
3p	ἱστάσθωσαν	---	στησάσθωσαν	ἑστήσθωσαν	---	---
2d	ἵστασθον	---	στήσασθον	ἕστησθον	---	---
3d	ἱστάσθων	---	στησάσθων	ἑστήσθων	---	---

Additional Middle Aorists and Perfects		
Indicative		
	Strong Aorist	Alternate Perfect	Alternate Pluperfect
1s	στήμην	ἕσταμαι	ἑστάμην
2s	στῆσο	ἕστασαι	ἕστασο
3s	στῆτο	ἕσταται	ἕστατο
1p	στήμεθα	ἑστάμεθα	ἑστάμεθα
2p	στῆσθε	ἕστασθε	ἕστασθε
3p	στῆντο	ἕστανται	ἕσταντο
2d	στῆσθον	ἕστασθον	ἕστασθον
3d	στήσθην	ἕστασθον	ἑστάσθην
Subjunctive		
1s	στήωμαι	---	---
2s	στήῃ	---	---
3s	στήηται	---	---
1p	στηώμεθα	---	---
2p	στήησθε	---	---
3p	στήωνται	---	---
2d	στήσθον	---	---
3d	στήσθον	---	---
Optative		
1s	στηοίμην	---	---
2s	στήοῖο	---	---
3s	στήοῖτο	---	---
1p	στηοίμεθα	---	---
2p	στήοῖσθε	---	---
3p	στήοῖντο	---	---
2d	στήοῖσθον	---	---
3d	στηοίσθην	---	---
Imperative		
1s	---	---	---
2s	στῆσο	ἕστησο	---
3s	στήσθω	ἑστήσθω	---
1p	---	---	---
2p	στῆσθε	ἕστησθε	---
3p	στήσθωσαν	ἑστήσθωσαν	---
2d	στῆσθον	ἕστασθον	---
3d	στήσθων	ἑστάσθων	---

Passive Voice

Indicative

	Aorist	Future	Strong Aorist
1s	ἐστάθην	σταθήσομαι	ἔστην
2s	ἐστάθης	σταθήσει	ἔστης
3s	ἐστάθη	σταθήσεται	ἔστη
1p	ἐστάθημεν	σταθησόμεθα	ἔστημεν
2p	ἐστάθητε	σταθήσεσθε	ἔστητε
3p	ἐστάθησαν	σταθήσονται	ἔστησαν
2d	ἐστάθητον	σταθήσεσθον	ἔστητον
3d	ἐσταθήτην	σταθήσεσθον	ἐστήτην

Infinitive	Present	Imperfect	Aorist	Perfect	Future
Active	ἱστάναι	---	στῆσαι	ἑστηκέναι	στήσειν
Middle	ἵστασθαι	---	στήσασθαι	ἑστῆσθαι	στήσεσθαι
Passive	---	---	σταθῆναι	---	σταθήσεσθαι

Alternate Infinitive forms	Present	Imperfect	Aorist	Perfect	Another Perfect
Active	---	---	στῆναι	ἑστάσθαι	ἑστάναι
Middle	---	---	---	ἑστάσθαι	---
Passive	---	---	στῆναι	---	---

Active Voice Participles Masculine	Present	Aorist	Perfect	Future	Strong Aorist	Strong Perfect
Nom ms	ἱστάς	στήσᾱς	ἑστηκώς	στήσων	στάς	ἑστώς
Voc ms	ἱστάς	στήσαν	ἑστηκώς	στήσον	στάς	ἑστώς
Acc ms	ἱστάντα	στήσαντα	ἑστηκότα	στήσοντα	στάντα	ἑστότα
Gen ms	ἱστάντος	στήσαντος	ἑστηκότος	στήσοντος	στάντος	ἑστότος
Dat ms	ἱστάντι	στήσαντι	ἑστηκότι	στήσοντι	στάντι	ἑστότι
Nom mp	ἱστάντες	στήσαντες	ἑστηκότες	στήσοντες	στάντες	ἑστότες
Voc mp	ἱστάντες	στήσαντες	ἑστηκότες	στήσοντες	στάντες	ἑστότες

Active Voice Participles						
Acc mp	ἱστάντας	στήσαντας	ἑστηκότας	στήσοντας	στάντας	ἑστότας
Gen mp	ἱστάντων	στησάντων	ἑστηκότων	στησόντων	στάντων	ἑστότων
Dat mp	ἱστᾶσι	στήσᾶσι	ἑστηκῶσι	στήσουσι	στᾶσι	ἑστῶσι
Nom md	ἱστάντε	στήσαντε	ἑστηκότε	στήσοντε	στάντε	ἑστότε
Voc md	ἱστάντε	στήσαντε	ἑστηκότε	στήσοντε	στάντε	ἑστότε
Acc md	ἱστάντε	στήσαντε	ἑστηκότε	στήσοντε	στάντε	ἑστότε
Gen md	ἱστάντοῖν	στησάντοῖν	ἑστηκότοῖν	στησόντοῖν	στάντοῖν	ἑστότοῖν
Dat md	ἱστάντοῖν	στησάντοῖν	ἑστηκότοῖν	στησόντοῖν	στάντοῖν	ἑστότοῖν

Feminine	Present	Aorist	Perfect	Future	Strong Aorist	Strong Perfect
Nom fs	ἱστᾶσα	στήσᾶσα	ἑστηκυῖα	στήσουσα	στᾶσα	ἑστῶσα
Voc fs	ἱστᾶσα	στήσᾶσα	ἑστηκυῖα	στήσουσα	στᾶσα	ἑστῶσα
Acc fs	ἱστᾶσαν	στήσᾶσαν	ἑστηκυῖαν	στήσουσαν	στᾶσαν	ἑστῶσαν
Gen fs	ἱστάσης	στησάσης	ἑστηκυίᾱς	στησούσης	στάσης	ἑστώσης
Dat fs	ἱστάσῃ	στησάσῃ	ἑστηκυίᾳ	στησούσῃ	στάσῃ	ἑστώσῃ
Nom fp	ἱστᾶσαι	στήσᾶσαι	ἑστηκυῖαι	στήσουσαι	στᾶσαι	ἑστῶσαι
Voc fp	ἱστᾶσαι	στήσᾶσαι	ἑστηκυῖαι	στήσουσαι	στᾶσαι	ἑστῶσαι
Acc fp	ἱστᾶσᾱς	στησᾶσᾱς	ἑστηκυίᾱς	στησούσᾱς	στᾶσᾱς	ἑστώσᾱς
Gen fp	ἱστᾶσῶν	στησᾶσῶν	ἑστηκυιῶν	στησουσῶν	στασῶν	ἑστωσῶν
Dat fp	ἱστᾶσαῖς	στησᾶσαῖς	ἑστηκυίαῖς	στησούσαῖς	στάσαῖς	ἑστώσαῖς
Nom fd	ἱστᾶσᾱ	στησᾶσᾱ	ἑστηκυίᾱ	στησούσᾱ	στᾶσᾱ	ἑστώσᾱ
Voc fd	ἱστᾶσᾱ	στησᾶσᾱ	ἑστηκυίᾱ	στησούσᾱ	στᾶσᾱ	ἑστώσᾱ
Acc fd	ἱστᾶσᾱ	στησᾶσᾱ	ἑστηκυίᾱ	στησούσᾱ	στᾶσᾱ	ἑστώσᾱ
Gen fd	ἱστᾶσαῖν	στησᾶσαῖν	ἑστηκυίαῖν	στησούσαῖν	στάσαῖν	ἑστώσαῖν
Dat fd	ἱστᾶσαῖν	στησᾶσαῖν	ἑστηκυίαῖν	στησούσαῖν	στάσαῖν	ἑστώσαῖν

Neuter	Present	Aorist	Perfect	Future	Strong Aorist	Strong Perfect
Nom ns	ἱστάν	στῆσαν	ἑστηκός	στῆσον	στάν	ἑστός
Voc ns	ἱστάν	στῆσαν	ἑστηκός	στῆσον	στάν	ἑστός
Acc ns	ἱστάν	στῆσαν	ἑστηκός	στῆσον	στάν	ἑστός
Gen ns	ἱστάντος	στήσαντος	ἑστηκότος	στήσοντος	στάντος	ἑστότος
Dat ns	ἱστάντι	στήσαντι	ἑστηκότι	στήσοντι	στάντι	ἑστότι
Nom np	ἱστάντα	στήσαντα	ἑστηκότα	στήσοντα	στάντα	ἑστότα
Voc np	ἱστάντα	στήσαντα	ἑστηκότα	στήσοντα	στάντα	ἑστότα
Acc np	ἱστάντα	στήσαντα	ἑστηκότα	στήσοντα	στάντα	ἑστότα

Active Voice Participles						
Gen np	ἱστάντων	στησάντων	ἑστηκότων	στησόντων	στάντων	ἑστότων
Dat np	ἱστᾶσι	στήσᾱσι	ἑστηκῶσι	στήσουσι	στᾶσι	ἑστῶσι
Nom nd	ἱστάντε	στήσαντε	ἑστηκότε	στήσοντε	στάντε	ἑστότε
Voc nd	ἱστάντε	στήσαντε	ἑστηκότε	στήσοντε	στάντε	ἑστότε
Acc nd	ἱστάντε	στήσαντε	ἑστηκότε	στήσοντε	στάντε	ἑστότε
Gen nd	ἱστάντοῖν	στησάντοῖν	ἑστηκότοῖν	στησόντοῖν	στάντοῖν	ἑστότοῖν
Dat nd	ἱστάντοῖν	στησάντοῖν	ἑστηκότοῖν	στησόντοῖν	στάντοῖν	ἑστότοῖν

Middle Voice Participles				
Masculine				
	Perfect	Aorist	Alternative Perfect	Future
Nom ms	ἑστημένος	στησάμενος	ἑσταμένος	στησόμενος
Voc ms	ἑστημένε	στησάμενε	ἑσταμένε	στησόμενε
Acc ms	ἑστημένον	στησάμενον	ἑσταμένον	στησόμενον
Gen ms	ἑστημένου	στησαμένου	ἑσταμένου	στησομένου
Dat ms	ἑστημένῳ	στησαμένῳ	ἑσταμένῳ	στησομένῳ
Nom mp	ἑστημένοι	στησάμενοι	ἑσταμένοι	στησόμενοι
Voc mp	ἑστημένοι	στησάμενοι	ἑσταμένοι	στησόμενοι
Acc mp	ἑστημένους	στησαμένους	ἑσταμένους	στησομένους
Gen mp	ἑστημένων	στησαμένων	ἑσταμένων	στησομένων
Dat mp	ἑστημένοῖς	στησαμένοῖς	ἑσταμένοῖς	στησομένοῖς
Nom md	ἑστημένω	στησαμένω	ἑσταμένω	στησομένω
Voc md	ἑστημένω	στησαμένω	ἑσταμένω	στησομένω
Acc md	ἑστημένω	στησαμένω	ἑσταμένω	στησομένω
Gen md	ἑστημένοῖν	στησαμένοῖν	ἑσταμένοῖν	στησομένοῖν
Dat md	ἑστημένοῖν	στησαμένοῖν	ἑσταμένοῖν	στησομένοῖν
Feminine				
	Perfect	Aorist	Alternative Perfect	Future
Nom fs	ἑστημένη	στησαμένη	ἑσταμένη	στησομένη
Voc fs	ἑστημένη	στησαμένη	ἑσταμένη	στησομένη
Acc fs	ἑστημένην	στησαμένην	ἑσταμένην	στησομένην
Gen fs	ἑστημένης	στησαμένης	ἑσταμένης	στησομένης
Dat fs	ἑστημένη	στησαμένη	ἑσταμένη	στησομένη
Nom fp	ἑστημέναι	στησαμέναι	ἑσταμέναι	στησομέναι
Voc fp	ἑστημέναι	στησαμέναι	ἑσταμέναι	στησομέναι
Acc fp	ἑστημένᾱς	στησαμένᾱς	ἑσταμένᾱς	στησομένᾱς

Middle Voice Participles				
Gen fp	ἑστημενῶν	στησαμενῶν	ἑσταμενῶν	στησομενῶν
Dat fp	ἑστημέναις	στησαμέναις	ἑσταμέναις	στησομέναις
Nom fd	ἑστημένᾱ	στησαμένᾱ	ἑσταμένᾱ	στησομένᾱ
Voc fd	ἑστημένᾱ	στησαμένᾱ	ἑσταμένᾱ	στησομένᾱ
Acc fd	ἑστημένᾱ	στησαμένᾱ	ἑσταμένᾱ	στησομένᾱ
Gen fd	ἑστημέναῖν	στησαμέναῖν	ἑσταμέναῖν	στησομέναῖν
Dat fd	ἑστημέναῖν	στησαμέναῖν	ἑσταμέναῖν	στησομέναῖν

Neuter				
	Present	Aorist	Perfect	Future
Nom ns	ἑστημένον	στησάμενον	ἑσταμένον	στησόμενον
Voc ns	ἑστημένον	στησάμενον	ἑσταμένον	στησόμενον
Acc ns	ἑστημένον	στησάμενον	ἑσταμένον	στησόμενον
Gen ns	ἑστημένου	στησαμένου	ἑσταμένου	στησομένου
Dat ns	ἑστημένῳ	στησαμένῳ	ἑσταμένῳ	στησομένῳ
Nom np	ἑστημένα	στησάμενα	ἑσταμένα	στησόμενα
Voc np	ἑστημένα	στησάμενα	ἑσταμένα	στησόμενα
Acc np	ἑστημένα	στησάμενα	ἑσταμένα	στησόμενα
Gen np	ἑστημένων	στησαμένων	ἑσταμένων	στησομένων
Dat np	ἑστημένοῖς	στησαμένοῖς	ἑσταμένοῖς	στησομένοῖς
Nom nd	ἑστημένω	στησαμένω	ἑσταμένω	στησομένω
Voc nd	ἑστημένω	στησαμένω	ἑσταμένω	στησομένω
Acc nd	ἑστημένω	στησαμένω	ἑσταμένω	στησομένω
Gen nd	ἑστημένοῖν	στησαμένοῖν	ἑσταμένοῖν	στησομένοῖν
Dat nd	ἑστημένοῖν	στησαμένοῖν	ἑσταμένοῖν	στησομένοῖν

Passive Voice Participles			
Masculine			
	Aorist	Future	Strong Aorist
Nom ms	σταθείς	σταθησόμενος	στείς
Voc ms	σταθείς	σταθησόμενε	στείς
Acc ms	σταθέντα	σταθησόμενον	στέντα
Gen ms	σταθέντος	σταθησομένου	στέντος
Dat ms	σταθέντι	σταθησομένῳ	στέντι
Nom mp	σταθέντες	σταθησόμενοι	στέντες
Voc mp	σταθέντες	σταθησόμενοι	στέντες
Acc mp	σταθέντας	σταθησομένους	στέντας

Passive Voice Participles			
Gen mp	σταθέντων	σταθησομένων	στέντων
Dat mp	σταθεῖσι	σταθησομένοις	στεῖσι
Nom md	σταθέντε	σταθησομένω	στέντε
Voc md	σταθέντε	σταθησομένω	στέντε
Acc md	σταθέντε	σταθησομένω	στέντε
Gen md	σταθέντοῖν	σταθησομένοῖν	στέντοῖν
Dat md	σταθέντοῖν	σταθησομένοῖν	στέντοῖν
Feminine			
	Aorist	Future	Strong Aorist
Nom fs	σταθεῖσα	σταθησομένη	στεῖσα
Voc fs	σταθεῖσα	σταθησομένη	στεῖσα
Acc fs	σταθεῖσαν	σταθησομένην	στεῖσαν
Gen fs	σταθείσης	σταθησομένης	στείσης
Dat fs	σταθείσῃ	σταθησομένῃ	στείσῃ
Nom fp	σταθεῖσαι	σταθησομέναι	στεῖσαι
Voc fp	σταθεῖσαι	σταθησομέναι	στεῖσαι
Acc fp	σταθείσᾱς	σταθησομένᾱς	στείσᾱς
Gen fp	σταθεισῶν	σταθησομενῶν	στεισῶν
Dat fp	σταθείσαις	σταθησομέναις	στείσαις
Nom fd	σταθείσᾱ	σταθησομένᾱ	στείσᾱ
Voc fd	σταθείσᾱ	σταθησομένᾱ	στείσᾱ
Acc fd	σταθείσᾱ	σταθησομένᾱ	στείσᾱ
Gen fd	σταθείσαῖν	σταθησομέναῖν	στείσαῖν
Dat fd	σταθείσαῖν	σταθησομέναῖν	στείσαῖν
Neuter			
	Aorist	Future	
Nom ns	σταθέν	σταθησόμενον	στέν
Voc ns	σταθέν	σταθησόμενον	στέν
Acc ns	σταθέν	σταθησόμενον	στέν
Gen ns	σταθέντος	σταθησομένου	στέντος
Dat ns	σταθέντι	σταθησομένῳ	στέντι
Nom np	σταθέντα	σταθησόμενα	στέντα
Voc np	σταθέντα	σταθησόμενα	στέντα
Acc np	σταθέντα	σταθησόμενα	στέντα
Gen np	σταθέντων	σταθησομένων	στέντων
Dat np	σταθεῖσι	σταθησομένοις	στεῖσι
Nom nd	σταθέντε	σταθησομένω	στέντε

Passive Voice Participles			
Voc nd	σταθέντε	σταθησομένω	στέντε
Acc nd	σταθέντε	σταθησομένω	στέντε
Gen nd	σταθέντοῖν	σταθησομένοῖν	στέντοῖν
Dat nd	σταθέντοῖν	σταθησομένοῖν	στέντοῖν

τάσσω

Active Voice						
Indicative						
	Present	Imperfect	Aorist	Perfect	Future	Pluperfect
1s	τάσσω	ἔτασσον	ἔταξα	τέταχα	τάξω	ἐτετάχη
2s	τάσσεις	ἔτασσες	ἔταξας	τέταχας	τάξεις	ἐτετάχης
3s	τάσσει	ἔτασσε	ἔταξε	τέταχε	τάξει	ἐτετάχει
1p	τάσσομεν	ἐτάσσομεν	ἐτάξαμεν	τετάχαμεν	τάξομεν	ἐτετάχεμεν
2p	τάσσετε	ἐτάσσετε	ἐτάξατε	τετάχατε	τάξετε	ἐτετάχετε
3p	τάσσουσι	ἔτασσον	ἔταξαν	τετάχασι	τάξουσι	ἐτετάχεσαν
2d	τάσσετον	ἐτάσσετον	ἐτάξατον	τετάχατον	τάξετον	ἐτετάχειτον
3d	τάσσετον	ἐτασσέτην	ἐταξάτην	τετάχατον	τάξετον	ἐτεταχείτην
Subjunctive						
1s	τάσσω	---	τάξω	τετάχω	---	---
2s	τάσσῃς	---	τάξῃς	τετάχῃς	---	---
3s	τάσσῃ	---	τάξῃ	τετάχῃ	---	---
1p	τάσσωμεν	---	τάξωμεν	τετάχωμεν	---	---
2p	τάσσητε	---	τάξητε	τετάχητε	---	---
3p	τάσσωσι	---	τάξωσι	τετάχωσι	---	---
2d	τάσσητον	---	τάξητον	τετάχητον	---	---
3d	τάσσητον	---	τάξητον	τετάχητον	---	---
Optative						
1s	τάσσοιμι	---	τάξαιμι	τετάχοιμι	τάξοιμι	---
2s	τάσσοις	---	τάξειας	τετάχοις	τάξοις	---
3s	τάσσοι	---	τάξειε	τετάχοι	τάξοι	---
1p	τάσσοιμεν	---	τάξαιμεν	τετάχοιμεν	τάξοιμεν	---
2p	τάσσοιτε	---	τάξαιτε	τετάχοιτε	τάξοιτε	---
3p	τάσσοιεν	---	τάξειαν	τετάχοιεν	τάξοιεν	---
2d	τάσσοιτον	---	τάξαιτον	τετάχοιτον	τάξοιτον	---
3d	τασσοίτην	---	ταξαίτην	τεταχοίτην	ταξοίτην	---

Active Voice					
Imperative					
1s	---	---	---	---	---	---
2s	τάσσε	---	τάξον	τέταχε	---	---
3s	τασσέτω	---	ταξάτω	τεταχέτω	---	---
1p	---	---	---	---	---	---
2p	τάσσετε	---	τάξατε	τετάχετε	---	---
3p	τασσέτωσαν	---	ταξάτωσαν	τεταχέτωσαν	---	---
2d	τάσσετον	---	τάξατον	τετάχετον	---	---
3d	τασσέτων	---	ταξάτων	τεταχέτων	---	---

Additional Active Aorists and Perfects		
Indicative		
	Strong Aorist	Strong Future
1s	---	---
2s	---	---
3s	---	---
1p	---	---
2p	---	---
3p	---	---
2d	---	---
3d	---	---
Subjunctive		
1s	ταγῶ	---
2s	ταγῇς	---
3s	ταγῇ	---
1p	ταγῶμεν	---
2p	ταγῆτε	---
3p	ταγῶσι	---
2d	ταγῆτον	---
3d	ταγῆτον	---
Optative		
1s	ταγείην	ταγησοίμην
2s	ταγείης	ταγήσοιο
3s	ταγείη	ταγήσοιτο
1p	ταγεῖμεν	ταγησοίμεθα
2p	ταγεῖτε	ταγήσοισθε

Additional Active Aorists and Perfects		
3p	ταγεῖεν	ταγήσοῖντο
2d	ταγεῖτον	ταγήσοῖσθον
3d	ταγείτην	ταγησοῖσθην

Imperative		
1s	---	---
2s	τάγητι	---
3s	ταγήτω	---
1p	---	---
2p	τάγητε	---
3p	ταγήτωσαν	---
2d	τάγητον	---
3d	ταγήτων	---

Middle Voice						
Indicative						
	Present	Imperfect	Aorist	Perfect	Future	Pluperfect
1s	τάσσομαι	ἐτασσόμην	ἐταξάμην	ἐτέταγμαι	τάξομαι	ἐτετάγμην
2s	τάσσει	ἐτάσσου	ἐτάξω	ἐτέταξαι	τάξει	ἐτέταξο
3s	τάσσεται	ἐτάσσετο	ἐτάξατο	ἐτέτακται	τάξεται	ἐτέτακτο
1p	τασσόμεθα	ἐτασσόμεθα	ἐταξάμεθα	ἐτετάγμεθα	ταξόμεθα	ἐτετάγμεθα
2p	τάσσεσθε	ἐτάσσεσθε	ἐτάξασθε	ἐτέταχθε	τάξεσθε	ἐτέταχθε
3p	τάσσονται	ἐτάσσοντο	ἐτάξαντο	---	τάξονται	---
2d	τάσσεσθον	ἐτάσσεσθον	ἐτάξασθον	ἐτέταχθον	τάξεσθον	ἐτέταχθον
3d	τάσσεσθον	ἐτασσέσθην	ἐταξάσθην	ἐτέταχθον	τάξεσθον	ἐτετάχθην
Subjunctive						
1s	τάσσωμαι	---	τάξωμαι	---	---	---
2s	τάσσῃ	---	τάξῃ	---	---	---
3s	τάσσηται	---	τάξηται	---	---	---
1p	τασσώμεθα	---	ταξώμεθα	---	---	---
2p	τάσσησθε	---	τάξησθε	---	---	---
3p	τάσσωνται	---	τάξωνται	---	---	---
2d	τάσσησθον	---	τάξησθον	---	---	---
3d	τάσσησθον	---	τάξησθον	---	---	---
Optative						
1s	τασσοίμην	---	ταξαίμην	---	ταξοίμην	---
2s	τάσσοιο	---	τάξαιο	---	τάξοιο	---

Middle Voice					
3s	τάσσοιτο	---	τάξαιτο	---	τάξοιτο	---
1p	τασσοίμεθα	---	ταξαίμεθα	---	ταξοίμεθα	---
2p	τάσσοισθε	---	τάξαισθε	---	τάξοισθε	---
3p	τάσσοιντο	---	τάξαιντο	---	τάξοιντο	---
2d	τάσσοισθον	---	τάξαισθον	---	τάξοισθον	---
3d	τασσοίσθην	---	ταξαίσθην	---	ταξοίσθην	---

Imperative					
1s	---	---	---	---	---	---
2s	τάσσου	---	τάξαι	τέταξο	---	---
3s	τασσέσθω	---	ταξάσθω	τετάχθω	---	---
1p	---	---	---	---	---	---
2p	τάσσεσθε	---	τάξασθε	τέταχθε	---	---
3p	τασσέσθωσαν	---	ταξάσθωσαν	τετάχθωσαν	---	---
2d	τάσσεσθον	---	τάξασθον	τέταχθον	---	---
3d	τασσέσθων	---	ταξάσθων	τετάχθων	---	---

Passive Voice			
Indicative			
	Strong Aorist	Future	Strong Aorist	Strong Future
1s	ἐτάχθην	ταχθήσομαι	ἐτάγην	ταγήσομαι
2s	ἐτάχθης	ταχθήσει	ἐτάγης	ταγήσει
3s	ἐτάχθη	ταχθήσεται	ἐτάγη	ταγήσεται
1p	ἐτάχθημεν	ταχθησόμεθα	ἐτάγημεν	ταγησόμεθα
2p	ἐτάχθητε	ταχθήσεσθε	ἐτάγητε	ταγήσεσθε
3p	ἐτάχθησαν	ταχθήσονται	ἐτάγησαν	ταγήσονται
2d	ἐτάχθητον	ταχθήσεσθον	ἐτάγητον	ταγήσεσθον
3d	ἐταχθήτην	ταχθήσεσθον	ἐταγήτην	ταγήσεσθον

Subjunctive			
1s	ταχθῶ	---	---	---
2s	ταχθῆς	---	---	---
3s	ταχθῇ	---	---	---
1p	ταχθῶμεν	---	---	---
2p	ταχθῆτε	---	---	---
3p	ταχθῶσι	---	---	---
2d	ταχθῆτον	---	---	---
3d	ταχθῆτον	---	---	---

Passive Voice				
Optative				
1s	ταχθείην	ταχθησοίμην	---	---
2s	ταχθείης	ταχθήσοιο	---	---
3s	ταχθείη	ταχθήσοιτο	---	---
1p	ταχθεῖμεν	ταχθησοίμεθα	---	---
2p	ταχθεῖτε	ταχθήσοισθε	---	---
3p	ταχθεῖεν	ταχθήσοιντο	---	---
2d	ταχθεῖτον	ταχθήσοισθον	---	---
3d	ταχθείτην	ταχθησοίσθην	---	---
Imperative				
1s	---	---	---	---
2s	τάχθητι	---	---	---
3s	ταχθήτω	---	---	---
1p	---	---	---	---
2p	τάχθητε	---	---	---
3p	ταχθήτωσαν	---	---	---
2d	τάχθητον	---	---	---
3d	ταχθήτων	---	---	---

Infinitive	Present	Imperfect	Aorist	Perfect	Future
Active	τάσσειν	---	τάξαι	τεταχέναι	τάξειν
Middle	τάσσεσθαι	---	τάξασθαι	τετάχθαι	τάξεσθαι
Passive	---	---	ταχθῆναι	---	ταχθήσεσθαι

Alternate	Infinitive forms	
	Perfect	Aorist
Active	---	---
Middle	---	---
Passive	ταγήσεσθαι	ταγῆναι

Active Voice Participles				
Masculine				
	Present	Aorist	Perfect	Future
Nom ms	τάσσων	τάξᾱς	τεταχώς	τάξων
Voc ms	τάσσον	τάξαν	τεταχώς	τάξον
Acc ms	τάσσοντα	τάξαντα	τεταχότα	τάξοντα
Gen ms	τάσσοντος	τάξαντος	τεταχότος	τάξοντος
Dat ms	τάσσοντι	τάξαντι	τεταχότι	τάξοντι
Nom mp	τάσσοντες	τάξαντες	τεταχότες	τάξοντες
Voc mp	τάσσοντες	τάξαντες	τεταχότες	τάξοντες
Acc mp	τάσσοντας	τάξαντας	τεταχότας	τάξοντας
Gen mp	τασσόντων	ταξάντων	τεταχότων	ταξόντων
Dat mp	τάσσουσι	τάξᾱσι	τεταχῶσι	τάξουσι
Nom md	τάσσοντε	τάξαντε	τεταχότε	τάξοντε
Voc md	τάσσοντε	τάξαντε	τεταχότε	τάξοντε
Acc md	τάσσοντε	τάξαντε	τεταχότε	τάξοντε
Gen md	τασσόντοῖν	ταξάντοῖν	τεταχότοῖν	ταξόντοῖν
Dat md	τασσόντοῖν	ταξάντοῖν	τεταχότοῖν	ταξόντοῖν
Feminine				
	Present	Aorist	Perfect	Future
Nom fs	τάσσουσα	τάξᾱσα	τεταχυῖα	τάξουσα
Voc fs	τάσσουσα	τάξᾱσα	τεταχυῖα	τάξουσα
Acc fs	τάσσουσαν	τάξᾱσαν	τεταχυῖαν	τάξουσαν
Gen fs	τασσούσης	ταξᾱσης	τεταχυίᾱς	ταξούσης
Dat fs	τασσούσῃ	ταξᾱσῃ	τεταχυίᾳ	ταξούσῃ
Nom fp	τάσσουσαι	τάξᾱσαι	τεταχυῖαι	τάξουσαι
Voc fp	τάσσουσαι	τάξᾱσαι	τεταχυῖαι	τάξουσαι
Acc fp	τασσούσᾱς	ταξᾱσᾱς	τεταχυίᾱς	ταξούσᾱς
Gen fp	τασσουσῶν	ταξᾱσῶν	τεταχυιῶν	ταξουσῶν
Dat fp	τασσούσαῖς	ταξᾱσαῖς	τεταχυίαῖς	ταξούσαῖς
Nom fd	τασσούσᾱ	ταξᾱσᾱ	τεταχυίᾱ	ταξούσᾱ
Voc fd	τασσούσᾱ	ταξᾱσᾱ	τεταχυίᾱ	ταξούσᾱ
Acc fd	τασσούσᾱ	ταξᾱσᾱ	τεταχυίᾱ	ταξούσᾱ
Gen fd	τασσούσαῖν	ταξᾱσαῖν	τεταχυίαῖν	ταξούσαῖν
Dat fd	τασσούσαῖν	ταξᾱσαῖν	τεταχυίαῖν	ταξούσαῖν

Active Voice Participles				
Neuter				
	Present	Aorist	Perfect	Future
Nom ns	τάσσον	τάξαν	τεταχός	τάξον
Voc ns	τάσσον	τάξαν	τεταχός	τάξον
Acc ns	τάσσον	τάξαν	τεταχός	τάξον
Gen ns	τάσσοντος	τάξαντος	τεταχότος	τάξοντος
Dat ns	τάσσοντι	τάξαντι	τεταχότι	τάξοντι
Nom np	τάσσοντα	τάξαντα	τεταχότα	τάξοντα
Voc np	τάσσοντα	τάξαντα	τεταχότα	τάξοντα
Acc np	τάσσοντα	τάξαντα	τεταχότα	τάξοντα
Gen np	τασσόντων	ταξάντων	τεταχότων	ταξόντων
Dat np	τάσσουσι	τάξᾱσι	τεταχῶσι	τάξουσι
Nom nd	τάσσοντε	τάξαντε	τεταχότε	τάξοντε
Voc nd	τάσσοντε	τάξαντε	τεταχότε	τάξοντε
Acc nd	τάσσοντε	τάξαντε	τεταχότε	τάξοντε
Gen nd	τασσόντοῖν	ταξάντοῖν	τεταχότοῖν	ταξόντοῖν
Dat nd	τασσόντοῖν	ταξάντοῖν	τεταχότοῖν	ταξόντοῖν

Middle Voice Participles				
Masculine				
	Present	Aorist	Perfect	Future
Nom ms	τασσόμενος	ταξάμενος	τεταγμένος	ταξόμενος
Voc ms	τασσόμενε	ταξάμενε	τεταγμένε	ταξόμενε
Acc ms	τασσόμενον	ταξάμενον	τεταγμένον	ταξόμενον
Gen ms	τασσομένου	ταξαμένου	τεταγμένου	ταξομένου
Dat ms	τασσομένῳ	ταξαμένῳ	τεταγμένῳ	ταξομένῳ
Nom mp	τασσόμενοι	ταξάμενοι	τεταγμένοι	ταξόμενοι
Voc mp	τασσόμενοι	ταξάμενοι	τεταγμένοι	ταξόμενοι
Acc mp	τασσομένους	ταξαμένους	τεταγμένους	ταξομένους
Gen mp	τασσομένων	ταξαμένων	τεταγμένων	ταξομένων
Dat mp	τασσομένοῖς	ταξαμένοῖς	τεταγμένοῖς	ταξομένοῖς
Nom md	τασσομένω	ταξαμένω	τεταγμένω	ταξομένω
Voc md	τασσομένω	ταξαμένω	τεταγμένω	ταξομένω
Acc md	τασσομένω	ταξαμένω	τεταγμένω	ταξομένω
Gen md	τασσομένοῖν	ταξαμένοῖν	τεταγμένοῖν	ταξομένοῖν
Dat md	τασσομένοῖν	ταξαμένοῖν	τεταγμένοῖν	ταξομένοῖν

Middle Voice Participles			
Feminine			
	Present	Aorist	Perfect	Future
Nom fs	τασσομένη	ταξαμένη	τεταγμένη	ταξομένη
Voc fs	τασσομένη	ταξαμένη	τεταγμένη	ταξομένη
Acc fs	τασσομένην	ταξαμένην	τεταγμένην	ταξομένην
Gen fs	τασσομένης	ταξαμένης	τεταγμένης	ταξομένης
Dat fs	τασσομένῃ	ταξαμένῃ	τεταγμένῃ	ταξομένῃ
Nom fp	τασσομέναι	ταξαμέναι	τεταγμέναι	ταξομέναι
Voc fp	τασσομέναι	ταξαμέναι	τεταγμέναι	ταξομέναι
Acc fp	τασσομένᾱς	ταξαμένᾱς	τεταγμένᾱς	ταξομένᾱς
Gen fp	τασσομενῶν	ταξαμενῶν	τεταγμενῶν	ταξομενῶν
Dat fp	τασσομέναις	ταξαμέναις	τεταγμέναις	ταξομέναις
Nom fd	τασσομένᾱ	ταξαμένᾱ	τεταγμένᾱ	ταξομένᾱ
Voc fd	τασσομένᾱ	ταξαμένᾱ	τεταγμένᾱ	ταξομένᾱ
Acc fd	τασσομένᾱ	ταξαμένᾱ	τεταγμένᾱ	ταξομένᾱ
Gen fd	τασσομέναιν	ταξαμέναιν	τεταγμέναιν	ταξομέναιν
Dat fd	τασσομέναιν	ταξαμέναιν	τεταγμέναιν	ταξομέναιν
Neuter			
	Present	Aorist	Perfect	Future
Nom ns	τασσόμενον	ταξάμενον	τεταγμένον	ταξόμενον
Voc ns	τασσόμενον	ταξάμενον	τεταγμένον	ταξόμενον
Acc ns	τασσόμενον	ταξάμενον	τεταγμένον	ταξόμενον
Gen ns	τασσομένου	ταξαμένου	τεταγμένου	ταξομένου
Dat ns	τασσομένῳ	ταξαμένῳ	τεταγμένῳ	ταξομένῳ
Nom np	τασσόμενα	ταξάμενα	τεταγμένα	ταξόμενα
Voc np	τασσόμενα	ταξάμενα	τεταγμένα	ταξόμενα
Acc np	τασσόμενα	ταξάμενα	τεταγμένα	ταξόμενα
Gen np	τασσομένων	ταξαμένων	τεταγμένων	ταξομένων
Dat np	τασσομένοις	ταξαμένοις	τεταγμένοις	ταξομένοις
Nom nd	τασσομένω	ταξαμένω	τεταγμένω	ταξομένω
Voc nd	τασσομένω	ταξαμένω	τεταγμένω	ταξομένω
Acc nd	τασσομένω	ταξαμένω	τεταγμένω	ταξομένω
Gen nd	τασσομένοιν	ταξαμένοιν	τεταγμένοιν	ταξομένοιν
Dat nd	τασσομένοιν	ταξαμένοιν	τεταγμένοιν	ταξομένοιν

Passive Voice Participles				
Masculine				
	Aorist	Future	Strong Aorist	Strong Future
Nom ms	ταχθείς	ταχθησόμενος	ταγείς	ταγθησόμενος
Voc ms	ταχθείς	ταχθησόμενε	ταγείς	ταγθησόμενε
Acc ms	ταχθέντα	ταχθησόμενον	ταγέντα	ταγθησόμενον
Gen ms	ταχθέντος	ταχθησομένου	ταγέντος	ταγθησομένου
Dat ms	ταχθέντι	ταχθησομένῳ	ταγέντι	ταγθησομένῳ
Nom mp	ταχθέντες	ταχθησόμενοι	ταγέντες	ταγθησόμενοι
Voc mp	ταχθέντες	ταχθησόμενοι	ταγέντες	ταγθησόμενοι
Acc mp	ταχθέντας	ταχθησομένους	ταγέντας	ταγθησομένους
Gen mp	ταχθέντων	ταχθησομένων	ταγέντων	ταγθησομένων
Dat mp	ταχθεῖσι	ταχθησομένοῖς	ταγεῖσι	ταγθησομένοῖς
Nom md	ταχθέντε	ταχθησομένω	ταγέντε	ταγθησομένω
Voc md	ταχθέντε	ταχθησομένω	ταγέντε	ταγθησομένω
Acc md	ταχθέντε	ταχθησομένω	ταγέντε	ταγθησομένω
Gen md	ταχθέντοῖν	ταχθησομένοῖν	ταγέντοῖν	ταγθησομένοῖν
Dat md	ταχθέντοῖν	ταχθησομένοῖν	ταγέντοῖν	ταγθησομένοῖν
Feminine				
	Aorist	Future	Strong Aorist	Strong Future
Nom fs	ταχθεῖσα	ταχθησομένη	ταγεῖσα	ταγθησομένη
Voc fs	ταχθεῖσα	ταχθησομένη	ταγεῖσα	ταγθησομένη
Acc fs	ταχθεῖσαν	ταχθησομένην	ταγεῖσαν	ταγθησομένην
Gen fs	ταχθείσης	ταχθησομένης	ταγείσης	ταγθησομένης
Dat fs	ταχθείσῃ	ταχθησομένῃ	ταγείσῃ	ταγθησομένῃ
Nom fp	ταχθεῖσαι	ταχθησομέναι	ταγεῖσαι	ταγθησομέναι
Voc fp	ταχθεῖσαι	ταχθησομέναι	ταγεῖσαι	ταγθησομέναι
Acc fp	ταχθείσᾱς	ταχθησομένᾱς	ταγείσᾱς	ταγθησομένᾱς
Gen fp	ταχθεισῶν	ταχθησομενῶν	ταγεισῶν	ταγθησομενῶν
Dat fp	ταχθείσαῖς	ταχθησομέναῖς	ταγείσαῖς	ταγθησομέναῖς
Nom fd	ταχθείσᾱ	ταχθησομένᾱ	ταγείσᾱ	ταγθησομένᾱ
Voc fd	ταχθείσᾱ	ταχθησομένᾱ	ταγείσᾱ	ταγθησομένᾱ
Acc fd	ταχθείσᾱ	ταχθησομένᾱ	ταγείσᾱ	ταγθησομένᾱ
Gen fd	ταχθείσαῖν	ταχθησομέναῖν	ταγείσαῖν	ταγθησομέναῖν
Dat fd	ταχθείσαῖν	ταχθησομέναῖν	ταγείσαῖν	ταγθησομέναῖν

Passive Voice Participles				
Neuter				
	Aorist	Future	Strong Aorist	Strong Future
Nom ns	ταχθέν	ταχθησόμενον	ταγέν	ταγθησόμενον
Voc ns	ταχθέν	ταχθησόμενον	ταγέν	ταγθησόμενον
Acc ns	ταχθέν	ταχθησόμενον	ταγέν	ταγθησόμενον
Gen ns	ταχθέντος	ταχθησομένου	ταγέντος	ταγθησομένου
Dat ns	ταχθέντι	ταχθησομένῳ	ταγέντι	ταγθησομένῳ
Nom np	ταχθέντα	ταχθησόμενα	ταγέντα	ταγθησόμενα
Voc np	ταχθέντα	ταχθησόμενα	ταγέντα	ταγθησόμενα
Acc np	ταχθέντα	ταχθησόμενα	ταγέντα	ταγθησόμενα
Gen np	ταχθέντων	ταχθησομένων	ταγέντων	ταγθησομένων
Dat np	ταχθεῖσι	ταχθησομένοῖς	ταγεῖσι	ταγθησομένοῖς
Nom nd	ταχθέντε	ταχθησομένω	ταγέντε	ταγθησομένω
Voc nd	ταχθέντε	ταχθησομένω	ταγέντε	ταγθησομένω
Acc nd	ταχθέντε	ταχθησομένω	ταγέντε	ταγθησομένω
Gen nd	ταχθέντοῖν	ταχθησομένοῖν	ταγέντοῖν	ταγθησομένοῖν
Dat nd	ταχθέντοῖν	ταχθησομένοῖν	ταγέντοῖν	ταγθησομένοῖν

Author Index

Aarts, Bas. 169
Abbott, Thomas Kingsmill. 129, 132
Adams, D. Q.. 160
Alexiadou, Artemis. 101
Allen, Rutger J.. 2, 84
Anders, Max. 118
Arichea, Daniel C.. 116
Aubrey, Michael. 3

Babbitt, Frank Cole. 186, 191
Bache, Carl. 21–23, 49, 55
Baker, Paul. 169, 171–172
Baker, William R.. 125
Bakker, Matthieu, de. 98
Barnett, Paul. 124
Barr, James Albert. 167
Barth, Markus. 119, 128, 130, 132
Bary, Corien. 17, 49
Beck, Astrid T.. 132
Beekes, Robert S. P.. 75, 107, 159–160

Bernardakis, Gregorius N.. 186, 191
Best, Ernest. 119, 129–130, 132
Biber, Douglas. 171
Binnick, Robert I.. 32
Black, David Alan. 3–4, 155–156
Blanke, Helmut. 132
Blass, Friedrich. 97, 149, 156
Boles, Kenneth L.. 129–130
Bortone, Pietro. 91
Bratcher, Robert G.. 119
Brookins, Timothy. 10
Bruce, F. F.. 117, 125, 134
Burnet, John. 184
Burton, Ernest DeWitt. 96, 117, 124–125
Bury, R. G.. 184, 188–189, 193
Buth, Randall. 72
Buttmann, Alexander. 95
Buttmann, Philip. 95
Bybee, Joan. 2, 10, 79, 81, 82, 168

Campbell, Constantine R.. 2–4, 10, 12, 14–15, 19–20, 23, 35–38, 40–42, 46, 48, 52, 54, 59–60, 65, 139, 155, 158

Capps, E.. 187, 192, 196, 198

Caragounis, Chrys C.. 3, 33–34, 37, 44, 61, 85–86, 88, 170

Carson, Donald A.. 30, 39

Ceccarelli, Paola. 173

Cennamo, Michaela. 87

Chantraine, Pierre. 37, 39, 159, 188, 190

Charles, Robert Henry. 195

Chomsky, Noam. 169–170

Clackson, James. 75

Comrie, Bernard S.. 9, 14, 16, 18, 20–21, 24, 42, 49, 55

Conrad, Susan. 171

Conzelmann, Hans. 112, 138

Cotterell, Peter. 3–4

Cottrell, Jack. 108, 122

Cranfield, C. E. B.. 106, 110, 146

Crellin, Robert. 10, 44–46, 51–52, 72, 82

Curtius, Georg. 82, 96

Dahl, Eystein. 18, 26, 48–51, 60–61, 72

Dahl, Östen. 2, 19, 168

Dana, H. E.. 156

Debrunner, Albert. 97, 149, 156

Deferrari, Roy J.. 187, 192, 196, 198

Desagulier, Guillaume. 170

Dowty, David. 21

Drinka, Bridget. 77, 80

Dunn, James D. G.. 105–106, 122, 132, 145, 147

Ellicott, Charles J.. 112, 130

Ellis, Nicholas J.. 72

Emde Boas, Evert, van. 98

Evans, Trevor V.. 23, 31, 34, 38, 41–42, 158–159

Fanning, Buist M.. 2–3, 10–11, 14–16, 18–19, 21–25, 28–32, 40–44, 46, 50–52, 54, 65, 72, 76–77

Fee, Gordon D.. 138

Fitzmyer, Joseph A., S. J.. 106, 122, 146

Frampton, John. 79–80

Freed, Alice. 21

Friedrich, Paul. 84

Furnish, Victor Paul. 115, 124, 134

Granholm, Patrick. 190

Halliday, Michael A. K.. 39

Hansen, G. Walter. 117

Hardie, Andrew. 169

Harris, Murray J.. 91, 114–115, 117, 121, 124, 127, 134

Harris, Zellig. 90

Haspelmath, Martin. 59, 77, 84

Hatcher, Anna Granville. 170

Heine, Bernd. 62, 168

Helmbold, W. C.. 186, 197

Henderson, Jeffrey. 184, 189, 193–194, 197

Hercher, Rudolph. 194

Hill, A. A.. 170

Holton, David. 89

Hopper, Paul J.. 62

Horrocks, Geoffrey. 2

Huitink, Luuk. 98

Inkelas, Sharon. 78

Jackendoff, Ray. 90

Jannaris, Antonius N.. 96

Jewett, Robert. 106, 122, 145, 147

Johanson, Lars. 73

Johnson, Alan F.. 138

Johnson, Marion R.. 48

Kahn, Charles H.. 160

Katz, Graham. 90

Kayser, Carl Ludwig. 185
Klein, Wolfgang. 17, 48
Koester, Almut. 171
Kotansky, Roy David. 106, 122, 145, 147
Kuteva, Tania. 62, 90, 168

Lange, John Peter. 108, 122, 129
Langslow, David. 159
Lehmann, Christian. 62
Lehmann, Winfred P.. 76, 160
Lenski, R. C. H.. 106, 116, 127, 132, 134
Levinsohn, Stephen H.. 167
Lichtenberk, Frantisek. 179
Lincoln, Andrew T.. 119, 129, 132
Lohse, Edward. 132
Longenecker, Richard N.. 125
Luraghi, Silvia. 91
Lyons, John. 59

Machen, J. Gresham. 155–156
Mackridge, Peter. 89
Malherbe, Abraham. 190, 195–196
Mallory, J. P.. 160
Mantey, Julius R.. 156
Martin, Ralph P.. 115, 125, 127
Matthiae, Augustus. 95
McCoard, William. 41, 44, 48
McEnery, Tony. 169–170, 172
McGuire, Martin R. P.. 187, 192, 196, 198
McKay, Kenneth L.. 10, 24, 26–27, 38–39, 41, 43, 47, 84, 155, 188, 190
Meier-Brügger, Michael. 76
Mellick, Richard R.. 134
Moo, Douglas J.. 106, 122
Moorhouse, A. C.. 24
Morris, Leon. 109, 122, 146
Morwood, James. 156
Moser, Amalia. 84

Moulton, James Hope. 97
Mounce, Robert H.. 107
Mounce, William D.. 155–156
Mourelatos, A. P. D.. 44
Murray, A. T.. 156

Nida, Eugene Albert. 116, 119
Niepokuj, Mary. 72

O'Brien, Peter Thomas. 129, 132
O'Donnell, Matthew Brook. 3, 156, 168, 171
Olsen, Mary Jean Broman. 12–13, 17–18, 24, 26–27, 31–32, 42, 44
Orr, William F.. 139
Osborne, Grant R.. 122
Oster, Richard. 112

Pagliuca, William. 2, 79, 81–82
Pelletier, A.. 195
Perkins, Revere. 2, 79, 81–82
Philippaki-Warburton, Irene. 89
Plummer, Alfred. 112, 126, 137
Porter, Stanley E.. 2–3, 10, 12, 14–16, 20–21, 24, 30–31, 39–40, 42–43, 46–47, 52, 55, 59–60, 65, 82, 91, 139, 153, 155–156, 158, 167, 173
Psaltou-Joycey, Angeliki. 101

Rackham, H.. 185, 189, 193–194
Reed, Jeffrey T.. 156, 167
Reichenbach, Hans. 48
Reppen, Randi. 171
Ricketts, Ernie Clarence. 10
Rijksbaron, Albert. 69, 98
Rix, Helmut. 107
Robertson, Archibald T.. 97, 112, 137
Robins, R. H.. 43
Rothmayr, Antonia. 90
Rubino, Carl. 88
Runge, Steven E.. 153, 167

Sandell, Ryan. 79
Schmidt, Daryl. 21, 31, 42
Schreiner, Thomas R.. 106, 122
Sedlacek, James E.. 154
Shields, Kenneth. 75
Sicking, C. M. J.. 10, 69
Silva, Moisés. 39
Smith, Carlota. 17, 20, 22, 31
Smyth, Herbert Weir. 156
Stork, P.. 10
Szemerényi, Oswald J. L.. 75–76

Thiselton, Anthony C.. 112
Thrall, Margaret E.. 125, 127
Toews, John E.. 123
Tono, Yukio. 172
Traugott, Elizabeth Closs. 62
Turner, Max. 3–4
Turner, Nigel. 22, 24, 97

van Beek, Lucian. 107, 160
Veloudis, Ioannis. 10
Versteegh, C. H. M.. 2
von Stechow, Arnim. 48

Wackernagel, Jacob. 37, 78, 159
Walde, Aloise. 161
Wallace, Daniel. 91, 98, 108, 117, 142, 156
Walther, James Arthur. 139
Whately, Stephen. 194
White, John L.. 173
Wilson, Andrew. 170

Xiao, Richard. 172
Xydopoulos, George J.. 179

Zoll, Cheryl. 78
Zukoff, Sam. 10, 79, 81

Text Reference Index

1 Cor 10
  7. 148
1 Cor 15
  12-29. 137, 139
  16. 110
  4. 70, 135, 139
1 Cor 16
  3. 66
  9. 111
1 Cor 2
  7. 118
  9. 162, 164
1 Thess 2
  11. 149
1 Thess 4
  5. 150
2 Cor 2
  10. 123–125
  12. 111–112
  3. 68
2 Cor 3

18. 113
  4. 113
2 Cor 6
  11. 111, 114
  17. 105
2 Cor 7
  13. 133
  14. 126–127

Alciphron, *Ep. Glykera ad Bakchis,* 4
  2.1. 190
Aristeas, *Ep. ad Philocrates,* 91. 195
Aristotle, *Eth. nic.,* 2.2 1105 A. 184
Aristotle, *Eth. nic.,* 5.1 1129 B. 189
Aristotle, *Eth.nic.,* 2.2 1103 B. 193
Aristotle, *Eth.nic.,* 4.1 1120 B. 194
Aristotle, *Eth.nic.,* 7.1 1145 A. 197

Basil of Caesarea, *Ep. ad Caesareans,* 8
  21. 192
  25. 196

Basil of Caesarea, *Ep. ad Gregory of Nazianzus*, 2
6. 187
Basil of Caesarea, *Ep. ad Gregory of Nazianzus*, 2.5. 198

Col 1
12. 130–132
26. 118
Col 3
3 \f. 180
Col 4
3. 111
Cor 16
18. 134

de Socrates, 1
10, 8. 196
Diogenes, *Ep. ad Eugnesius.*, 8
2.6. 190
Diogenes, *Ep. ad Melesippus*, 20.1, 1. 195

Eph 2
12. 130–131
4. 129
5. 127, 129
7. 129
8. 128–129
Eph 3
9. 70, 93, 118
Eph 4
18. 130–132

Gal 1
15. 105
Gal 2
12. 67, 105
Gal 3
18. 123, 125–126
Gal 4
11. 92
23. 116

Hab 2
4. 146
Homer, *Il.*, 1.365. 156
Homer, *Il.*, 11.408. 158
Homer, *Il.*, 13.674-675. 158
Homer, *Il.*, 20.433-434. 158
Hos 6
1-3. 138

Luke 6
22. 105

Phalaris, *Ep.*, 124.1, 13. 194
Philostratus, *Ep.*, 2.2. 185
Phlm 1
7. 133–134
Plato, *Ep. ad Dionysius*, 2
213 C. 184
310 C. 188
311 D. 188
Plato, *Ep. ad Dionysius*, 3
315 B. 193
Plutarch, *Cohib. ira*, 1.1. 196
Plutarch, *Conj. praec.*, 1.48. 191
Plutarch, *Curios.*, 1.7. 186
Plutarch, *Frat. amor.*, 1.5. 197
Plutarch, *Virt. prof.*, 1.8. 186

Rom 1
1. 104
17. 146
Rom 11
2. 148
25. 151
Rom 13
1. 93, 109
Rom 15
16. 151
Rom 2
17. 125
2. 145, 158, 164
24. 149

Rom 3
  10. 147
  25. 107
  4. 147
Rom 4
  2. 125

Rom 5
  11. 125
  5. 121
Rom 8
  21. 125

Subject Index

ablaut. 75, 108, 162

adverb. 6, 39, 45–46, 49, 69–70, 90–94, 101, 104, 106, 114, 116–117, 119–121, 133, 137, 140, 142, 173, 184, 188–189, 192, 199
  role of. 58, 70, 94, 135, 179, 204, 207
  types of. 91, 101, 103

Aktionsart. 11–12, 14–16, 19–22, 28–31, 36, 40, 42–43, 52–55, 57, 97–99, 206–207

Aorist tense-form. 10, 19, 26, 29–30, 33–35, 37, 39, 41–44, 46, 49–50, 53–56, 58, 64, 67–68, 72–73, 75–77, 83, 89, 95, 97–98, 100, 105, 108, 110–111, 113, 115–118, 121, 123–128, 130–131, 133–134, 136–137, 139, 153, 156, 161–162, 164, 188, 192, 203, 207

augment. 19, 38, 73, 162

auxiliation. 63, 77, 87–89, 204

awkward construction. 92–93

bias. 4, 56, 59–60

biblical studies. 3, 7, 167–168, 205

choice. 14–15, 18, 23, 25, 64, 155

collocation. 6, 45, 58, 89–93, 125, 129, 140, 179, 204, 207

complex aspect. xiv, xv, 4–7, 58, 71, 78, 83, 88, 94–97, 99–100, 103, 120, 135, 140, 150, 152–154, 165, 167–168, 200, 203–207

deductive approaches. 60–61

diachronic analysis. xiv, 5–6, 53, 55–56, 58, 61, 72, 77–78, 83, 85, 97, 168, 171–172, 175, 178–179, 187, 201, 203–207
  shift. 57, 72, 78, 96

eclectic approaches. 59–61

epistle genre. 167, 174, 176, 179, 196, 201

exegesis. xiii, xv, 3–4, 205
Extended-Now Theory. 48

Future tense-form. 35, 67, 124, 126, 128, 130
grammaticalisation. xiv, 5–6, 24, 35, 42, 55, 61–63, 79, 81–82, 89, 96, 100, 167, 169–170, 178–179, 183, 200, 203–206
  cline. xiv, 5, 62, 79–80, 94, 100, 167, 179, 204
  clitic. 62–63
  decategoricalisation. 62, 79
  desemanticisation. 62–63, 79, 100, 204
  erosion. 62–63, 79, 100, 204
  extension. 62–63, 100, 204
  pathway. 199–200
  stages of. 179
Greek grammars. 2–4, 19, 50, 94–99, 117, 155–156, 158, 206

Imperfect tense-form. 27–28, 35, 37, 45, 54, 64, 68, 73, 95
implicature. 12–13, 35, 41, 47, 65
inductive approaches. 36, 60–61

linguistic fossil. 75, 82, 104, 159
linguistics. xiii, xv–4, 6–7, 11–12, 16, 19, 27, 38–39, 51, 62, 167
  ancient. 2
  cognitive. 22, 40, 60–61
  comparative. 61
  corpus linguistics. xiv, 2, 5, 7, 52, 58, 61, 168–169, 171, 178
    corpus design. 170–171, 200
    corpus-based approaches. 168–171, 179, 205
    corpus-driven approaches. 168–169, 171
    critiques. 169
    morphological tagging. 156, 179, 184, 187, 192, 197, 199–200, 207

cross-linguistic. 2, 5, 37, 61, 72, 78–79, 81–82, 87, 100, 168, 204–206
  formal. 12, 17, 21, 28, 48, 59–61
  functional. 2, 15, 21, 26, 28, 35–36, 39–40, 48, 50, 57, 59–61, 95–96, 104, 141, 164
  generative. 36, 60
  historical. 61, 169–170
  Indo-European. 1, 4, 48, 51, 61, 75–78, 87, 107–108, 159, 161–162, 205
  lexical semantics. 12
  pragmatics. 5, 12–13, 15, 23, 31, 35–36, 48, 96, 104, 106, 122, 134, 145–147, 153, 165
  semantics. 9–14, 19, 30–31, 35, 46, 48, 50, 52, 90, 103, 136, 206
    lexical. 34
  structural. 6
  theoretical. 169
  theoretical linguistics. 205
  typology. 48, 60–61

morpheme. 14, 19, 40, 43, 52, 56–57, 72–73, 75–76, 100, 104–105, 108, 110, 113, 118, 120–121, 126, 128, 131, 183, 203
morphology. xiv, 5–6, 11, 14, 18, 27, 29–30, 35, 40, 47–48, 52, 57–58, 61, 63–64, 72–73, 77, 82, 100, 103–105, 107–108, 110–111, 113–116, 118, 120–124, 127–128, 131, 133, 155–156, 184, 187, 199–200, 203, 205, 207

objectivity. 14–16, 18, 20–22, 25, 27, 36, 43, 54, 56, 59–60, 64–66, 71
Pauline Corpus. xiv, xv–1, 4, 6–7, 56, 58, 65, 70, 73, 91–92, 94, 99, 103–104, 120, 126, 135, 140, 146, 153–156, 158, 161, 168, 170–172, 174, 179, 183–185, 187, 192, 194–200, 203–205, 207

Perfect tense-form. xiv–2, 4–7, 9–13, 18–19, 21, 25–26, 28–58, 63–66, 68–78, 81–101, 103–105, 107–128, 130–131, 133–142, 144–156, 158–162, 164–165, 167–168, 172, 174, 179–201, 203–207

Pluperfect tense-form. 1, 10, 28–29, 32, 34–35, 38, 40, 42–44

Present tense-form. 10, 19, 26–29, 33, 35–37, 41, 43–45, 48, 50, 52–57, 64–65, 72–73, 75–76, 83, 89, 97, 108, 115, 124, 126, 128, 136, 162, 186, 203, 207

proximity. 23, 35–37, 47, 54

reduplication. xiv, 5–6, 38, 48, 58, 63, 72–73, 75–76, 78–83, 87–89, 96, 99–100, 104–105, 107–108, 110–116, 118, 120–124, 127–128, 131, 133–134, 153–155, 160, 162, 203–205

remoteness. 23, 25, 35, 37, 40, 46, 48, 54–55

subjectivity. 6, 11, 14–16, 18, 20–21, 23, 25, 27, 43, 48, 53–54, 60–61, 64–66, 71
    criterion of. 14, 20–21, 25, 27
synchronic analysis. 55, 205

temporal reference. 9, 16, 24, 43–44, 46
    absolute. 16, 54
    relative. 16, 54
tense. 11, 16–17, 21, 24–25, 28, 31–32, 34, 40, 43, 46–47, 52, 54, 57, 98–99
    future. 17, 67, 108, 120

non-past. 30
past. 17, 27, 29–30, 32–34, 39, 43–45, 48–49, 53–54, 84, 89, 95–96, 98, 147, 204
present. 17, 33, 43–44, 46–47, 49, 53–54, 95–96, 115, 139
system. 206–207
timeless. 47, 97
time
    event. 17, 24, 26–27, 32, 44, 49, 51, 69
    internal. 18, 24
    reference. 17, 26–27, 32, 44, 46, 49–51, 71, 95–96, 109, 114, 116, 120, 139
    speech. 44, 49–50, 96, 139
    topic. 17

verbal aspect. xiv–2, 4–7, 9–32, 34–40, 42–43, 52–58, 64–66, 71–73, 76, 78, 82, 87–88, 91, 94, 99–100, 103–104, 120, 136, 139, 153, 155, 168, 203–205
verbal moods
    Imperative. 115, 185
    Indicative. 37, 47, 50, 67–68, 70, 75, 111–116, 120–121, 123, 126, 133, 135, 155, 158, 162, 187, 189–190, 192, 200
    Infinitive. 75, 77, 87, 89, 160, 190
    Injunctive. 47
    Participle. 68, 70, 75, 77, 86, 89, 104–111, 113–114, 118–121, 124, 128–132, 135, 150, 152, 183–189, 191, 200
    Subjunctive. 67, 111, 128, 161
verbal stem. xiv, xv, 5, 18–19, 38, 45, 51–52, 54, 57, 72–74, 76–77, 79, 81–83, 88, 99–100, 104–105, 108, 110–111, 113–116, 118, 120–121, 123–124, 126, 128, 131, 134, 151, 153–154, 162, 203–204, 229

Studies in Biblical Greek

D. A. Carson
General Editor

This series of monographs is designed to promote and publish the latest research into biblical Greek (Old and New Testaments). The series does not assume that biblical Greek is a distinct dialect within the larger world of *koine*, but focuses on these corpora because it recognizes the particular interest they generate. Research into the broader evidence of the period, including epigraphical and inscriptional materials, is welcome in the series, provided the results are cast in terms of their bearing on biblical Greek. Primarily, however, the series is devoted to fresh philological, syntactical, text-critical, and linguistic study of the Greek of the biblical books, with the subsidiary aim of displaying the contribution of such study to accurate exegesis.

For additional information about this series or for the submission of manuscripts, please contact:

editorial@peterlang.com

To order books, please contact our Customer Service Department at:

peterlang@presswarehouse.com (within the U.S.)
orders@peterlang.com (outside the U.S.)

Or browse online at WWW.PETERLANG.COM